OPERATIONS MANAGEMENT

Operations Management

Second edition

Terry Hill

First edition 2000
Reprinted three times
This edition published 2005 by
PALGRAVE MACMILLAN
Houndmills, Basingstoke, Hampshire RG21 6XS and
175 Fifth Avenue, New York, N.Y. 10010
Companies and representatives throughout the world

PALGRAVE MACMILLAN is the global academic imprint of the Palgrave Macmillan division of St. Martin's Press, LLC and of Palgrave Macmillan Ltd. Macmillan® is a registered trademark in the United States, United Kingdom and other countries. Palgrave is a registered trademark in the European Union and other countries.

ISBN 1–4039–3466–5 paperback
ISBN 1–4039–9112–X hardback

This book is printed on paper suitable for recycling and made from fully managed and sustained forest sources.

A catalogue record for this book is available from the British Library.

A catalog record for this book is available from the Library of Congress.

10 9 8 7 6 5 4 3 2 1
14 13 12 11 10 09 08 07 06 05

Printed in China

About the Author

Terry Hill, BA, MSc, MA, PhD

Emeritus Fellow, University of Oxford

Terry Hill is an internationally acclaimed thinker and writer on operations strategy and operations management. He was previously at London Business School and the University of Bath where he held Chairs in Operations Management. He has also held faculty positions at the Universities of Warwick in the UK and Ohio State and North Carolina (Chapel Hill) in the USA. Currently he is an Emeritus Fellow at the University of Oxford, Adjunct Professor at The Ohio State University and Visiting Professor at the University of Pretoria.

Terry Hill regularly teaches at the London Business School, University of Oxford, Politecnico di Milano, Stockholm School of Economics, the Technical University of Denmark and University of Pretoria. His research areas are principally in the field of operations strategy and supply chain management and include major government-funded research contracts in the manufacturing sector and, more recently, business-funded research contracts in the service sector.

Prior to his academic career, Terry Hill worked in the manufacturing sector for over ten years including plant management positions. He has developed a consultancy practice in the fields of operations management and operations strategy. His client base includes Johnson & Johnson, GlaxoSmithKline, Abbott Laboratories, Standard Life Assurance Company, RPC Containers, LINPAC, AMCOR, Celerant Consulting and Rolls-Royce.

Terry Hill has published a number of books and articles during his long and distinguished career, including *Small Business: Production/Operations Management,* Macmillan – now Palgrave Macmillan (1987), *The Strategy Quest,* AMD Publishing (1998), *Manufacturing Strategy: Text and Cases*, 2nd edn, Palgrave – now Palgrave Macmillan (2000) and *Manufacturing Strategy: Text and Cases*, 3rd edn, McGraw-Hill/Irwin (2000).

To PM, AJ, JB, SA and HH

Short Contents

Long Contents

List of Case Examples

Plots and Characters

The plot

Managing operations typically involves plenty of hard work. To get through this, most operations managers use a combination of determination, grit and, most importantly, a sense of humour. To illustrate some of the ideas and concepts discussed in the book, a number of points in each chapter are reflected in the life of a small computer games design company. The company itself consists of seven key members who have an intrinsic role in the business, people who you may well have met at work, through friends or simply encountered in your everyday lives. A detailed description of each person is given in the cast list, and his or her position is now briefly summarized:

- **The boss** – Mr James is responsible for running the business
- **Operations executive** – Wiggins coordinates the people and activities necessary to deliver projects on time and in line with design specifications
- **Personal assistant** – Liz endeavours to manage Mr James's diary and provide moral support to the rest of the people in the business in times of need
- **Marketing and sales executive** – Gianni is the smooth-talking member of the group, responsible for developing the appropriate business image both with clients and in the media
- **Artist** – Dave is the artistic force within the company, creating the characters within each computer game
- **IT technician** – Neil maintains and runs all the computer equipment within the company, providing help desk support to everyone's IT needs
- **Slacker** – nobody really knows what Lloyd does, but he seems to keep turning up every morning and seems to do as little as possible

Together these seven people strive to develop and deliver computer games to an expectant market. However, in doing so, they must also be sure to meet the demands of head office. Three people play key roles to ensure this happens:

- **Publisher** – Anna works with Mr James and his team to ensure the plans and strategies are in line with the those of head office
- **Consultant** – Mr Ayres is employed by head office to work with each of its companies, to look at how they work and identify potential areas for improvement
- **Media and press** – Travis coordinates all the press activity for head office,

letting them know about the different products in the pipeline and when they will be released into the market

As well as these, there are two other main characters that Wiggins comes into contact with while escaping from the office for a brief period of relaxation, reflection and nourishment at lunchtime:

■ Hot dog vendor – Ralph runs Wiggins's favourite hot dog stand, which provides a brief period of solace at lunch time during an often hectic day

■ Restaurant manager – Sophie is the manager at the self-service restaurant around the corner from the office

The cast

Mr James The boss

With his head buried in the latest management book, Mr James is convinced that there is an easy solution to all his problems and that it's just simply a question of finding it. For him, providing leadership equates to setting demands and demanding that everyone meets the targets without assessing how relevant or realistic they are.

Everyone gets apprehensive when he goes on a training programme as they know the outcome will be yet another panacea drive. This is just one example of his style – he's not really sure what he is doing, but hopes that if he does enough some will work. He thinks that change is the most important thing in the business (an end in itself) and that everyone in the office respects him, even if they don't like him.

Likes: management gurus, cutting corners and his own image
Dislikes: difficult decisions, last month's management fad

Wiggins Operations executive

The hero of the company, Wiggins is the glue that binds the organization together. He has the ability to see the good in everyone, but at the same time never ceases to be astonished by Mr James's view of the world and his inability to understand the impact of his actions on the people around him.

Wiggins is responsible for the on-time delivery of products and handling the problems that arise. He constantly juggles the different aspects and characters around him, keeping a balance in line with the overall needs of the business.

Likes: hard work, his job and people
Dislikes: unrealistic expectations, management fads and cutting corners

Liz Personal assistant

Cheerful and friendly, Liz is the consummate professional. No task is beyond her keen intellect and honed business sense, yet her presence is taken for granted, especially by Mr James who would be lost without her.

It is not uncommon for her to spark an idea, have it totally ignored and then for Gianni to repeat it only moments later and gain the kudos. Nevertheless, Liz soldiers on, refreshed by good books, gossip and the occasional hot chocolate.

Likes: being organized, Marmite, books and doing a good job
Dislikes: messiness, laziness and having her ideas stolen

Gianni Marketing and sales executive

Smart, slick and cool, Gianni sees himself as the force that drives the company forward. He desperately tries to project the image of being a creative genius and would probably love to steal Dave's job if only he had the creative spark. Reality is far from the truth as his creativity is sorely limited. To his credit, though, he never panics and never loses his cool. His real talent is in dealing with top executives from other organizations.

Likes: fast cars, beautiful women and shooting people with his fingers
Dislikes: cheap coffee

Dave Artist

Young, talented and volatile, Dave is a stereotype artist. Computer programmers and finance executives are his enemy, for they constantly restrict his creative impulses and wrongly interpret his ideas.
He spends his days fixated by the belief that artists are the only real talent and the most valuable people in the business. He is normally personable and polite, but quickly becomes ill-tempered if he feels that his intellectual property is being tampered with or questioned.

Likes: music festivals, reggae and comic books
Dislikes: programmers, figures of authority and having his creativity restricted

Neil IT technician

Serious to a fault and massively pedantic, Neil is the ultimate in computer geek technology. His technical competence is matched only by his utter contempt for anyone stupid enough to require his help. He cannot comprehend how people exist in the world without the capability to maintain their own computers and effectively use and update relevant software.

He is loved when his skills are needed and mocked when they are not, except by Dave who mocks him regardless. Dave and Neil both know that they must work together to make the company function, yet always seem to be in conflict with each other.

Likes: *Star Trek*, *Lord of the Rings* and computer games
Dislikes: people who don't understand computers

Lloyd Slacker

The word 'slacker' is a good description of Lloyd. For him, it is always someone else's problem, someone else's responsibility or someone else's fault. His track record in the company includes several years' worth of drinkable, yet instantly forgettable cups of tea. How he stays on the payroll is a wonder.

Likes: sitting doing nothing while pretending to be busy
Dislikes: being asked to do something

Anna Publisher

Always immaculately presented and dressed from head to toe in Prada, Anna is the archetypal young professional. Her education, determination and ambition have made her successful in a man's world. She is intelligent, outgoing and doesn't suffer fools lightly.

Her role is to manage and work with Mr James and his team to ensure that the products they design and produce will meet the exacting standards and financial expectations of head office. A task not always as simple as it appears.

Likes: shoes, clothes, restaurants and travel
Dislikes: sexist remarks, being late and being talked to

Mr Ayres Consultant

The Darth Vader of business consultancy, Mr Ayres has the ability to make even the most capable of people apprehensive. Mr James sees him as the archetypal head office investigator and Mr Ayres is not diverted by Mr James's excuses, nor is he charmed by Gianni's smooth appearance, words and style. It is almost impossible to shake him off the scent when he feels that he is onto something, and beware those who do not live up to his exacting standards.

Likes: flawlessly run operations and smart attire
Dislikes: stupidity, ignorance and excuses

Travis Media and press

Wearing the latest trainers and ironic T-shirt, Travis has all the markings of someone obsessed by the glitzy world of media. He coordinates all the press activity for head office, letting them know which products are in the pipeline and when they are due in the shops.

Likes: a free lunch and a large expense account
Dislikes: being tied down to deadlines or commitments

Ralph Hot dog vendor

A longtime friend and associate of Wiggins, Ralph provides solace from the many irrational and incomprehensible day-to-day happenings within the office. The 30 minutes of respite helps Wiggins through the day.

Likes: freedom and being his own boss
Dislikes: unnecessary stress

Sophie Restaurant manager

When Ralph is away, or Wiggins simply fancies a change, the alternative place for a break is the self-service restaurant around the corner from the office. Sophie is very particular about how the place is run.

Likes: everything spick and span
Dislikes: not getting her own way

Preface

Approach

The increasingly competitive nature of markets over the past 20 years has re-emphasized the key role of operations in bringing about the growth and profitability of organizations. Fast, on-time delivery, providing services and products right first time and the need to cut costs are increasingly important factors in most markets. How well operations is managed to bring these about is a key corporate issue. As a function responsible for 60–70 per cent of costs, assets and people (while also contributing much to the way organizations compete), the emphasis has swung in terms of what is key in operations. From a historical bias towards techniques, the approach has moved to one that stresses and highlights the effective management of this large business function. This book is designed to contribute to this ongoing focus and perspective. It is oriented towards a managerial perspective of operations and is set within the context of its significant contribution to the overall success of an organization.

Despite its importance, the area of operations management is often misunderstood by both business students and managers within firms. This misunderstanding is generated partly by the way the subject is presented and taught, and partly by the way the function is perceived and explained by operations managers to their fellow executives.

However, part of the problem also lies in the changing field of study. Originally, the conceptual orientation and emphasis within operations was towards the management of the area. Later, specialist developments introduced techniques that made useful, sometimes fundamental, contributions to help manage operations. From this developed a strong, often overriding, impetus to teach and develop operations management as a body of techniques involving detailed analysis and tactical considerations, but often not discriminating between the usefulness or relevance of one approach or technique to another. Furthermore, this emphasis towards the quantitative perspective as a way to resolve and present operations management issues also increasingly included explanations and mathematical derivations of the formulae and solutions proposed.

The outcomes were significant. In the academic world, operations management became uninteresting and apparently lacked business relevance. Demand fell and growth in faculty resources, research and teaching did not match the general expansion experienced in business education at the undergraduate, postgraduate and post-experience levels. Within the service and manufacturing sectors of the economy, the role became devalued. Consequently, the critical perspectives of this large and substantial function were not clearly recognized and were often inadequately presented. Typical results were unbalanced corporate argument, inappropriate allocation of key management resources to operations and a failure to attract the necessary management talent into the area by matching task, responsibilities and contribution with appropriate status, influence and reward.

Operations has rightly returned to the top of the corporate agenda and this text has been designed to serve the needs of those who intend to take on the operations management role and those whose roles will relate to this function in a range of businesses. In particular it can be used by:

- students as part of an undergraduate or MBA-level course of study, with explanations and further application through class discussion and the use of appropriate case studies

- managers who can apply the knowledge, concepts and ideas to their own situation to increase their understanding of how to improve their contribution to the overall business performance.

Structure and content

The text is structured in five parts as illustrated by the book plan reproduced at the start of each chapter.

Part 1 introduces the three key themes which underpin the rest of the book; the overall operations management task, market issues and the development of business and operations strategies and the management of people.

Part 2 concerns the design and development of services and products and the delivery systems by which they are produced and delivered.

Part 3 covers the central management tasks within operations and deals with capacity, technology, scheduling and execution, quality, inventory, the significant role of managing the supply chain and process and delivery system reliability and maintenance.

Part 4 addresses the essential task of improving the operations function. It discusses time and productivity and the ways to improve operations performance.

Part 5 illustrates operations management in practice with the inclusion of more than 30 long case studies covering the range of topics presented in the preceding text.

Learning aids

The text is complemented by a number of features to help student learning. These include:

- Opening statements at the start of each chapter place each topic in the context of the business and highlight the key role in managing each aspect of operations.

- Executive overviews at the start of each chapter provide an outline of the topics to be covered and highlight the key issues to be addressed.

- Case examples illustrate current developments and practices in operations management and support the concepts and detail within the text. These are taken from a variety of companies and organizations to reflect the breadth of operations activities and range from the secret recipe of a Scottish fish and chip takeaway to turnaround times at the world's largest port in Singapore. Each case example includes questions to encourage critical reflection on the key issues and weblinks (if appropriate) to enable further investigation.

- **Exhibits** present concepts in tabular or graphic form to provide deeper illustration of the issues under discussion. They include a number of cartoons intended to bring a smile but also to reinforce the points in question.

- **Reflections** at the end of each chapter discuss the key issues for debate in the topic and encourage readers to evaluate critically current and future trends.

- **Key elements** summarize and recap the key concepts of each topic and provide a useful checklist for revision purposes.

- **Self-check multiple-choice questions** at the end of each chapter enable readers to quickly check their understanding (as answers are provided at the back of the book) of the key concepts before moving on.

- **Study activities** at the end of each chapter provide suggested topics for classroom discussion and assignments to help develop practical skills.

- **Exploring further** references additional reading and provides pointers to help extend understanding of the key issues and concepts of each chapter topic.

- **Long case studies** in the final part of the book provide a basis for class discussion and illustrate the range of topics covered within the narrative. The breadth and range of the topics featured is summarized in the Case matrix on the next page.

New to this edition

This edition has been substantially revised with four key aims:

- **To update content to reflect recent research and current practice**

  There are two new chapters – Chapter 5 Designing Service Delivery Systems and Chapter 7 Location and Layout – and over 30 new case examples throughout the text and six new long case studies have been added to Part 5. In addition there is new material on e-procurement, outsourcing and co-sourcing (in Chapter 13) and expanded discussion of operations strategy and market linkage (in Chapter 2) and enterprise resource planning (in Chapter 10). As highlighted below, there is also additional material on people management issues (in Chapter 3).

- **To increase the coverage of service operations throughout**

  A new dedicated chapter on service delivery system design covers the influences on system design and the need for alignment of delivery systems to market needs. There is new material on service inventory issues (in Chapter 12) and new case examples and long case studies feature service organizations and issues.

- **To stress the importance of the contribution of people to the success of operations management**

  The topic is now introduced in the first part of the text (Chapter 3) and there is new material on recruitment, appraisals, outsourcing and temporary staff and appropriate legislation.

CASE MATRIX

Case title	1 Managing Operations	2 Operations Strategy	3 Managing People	4 Designing and Developing Services and Products	5 Designing Service Delivery Systems	6 Designing Manufacturing Processes	7 Location and Layout	8 Managing Capacity	9 Technology Developments	10 Operations Scheduling and Execution	11 Managing Quality	12 Managing Inventory	13 Managing the Supply Chain	14 Process and Delivery System Reliability and Maintenance	15 Time and Productivity	16 Improving Operations
Ash Electrics										●						○
Berwick Carpets															◑	○
British Airways		◑	○		●		○	●			○					
Caltrex Engineering (A)						○		○		○		●			◑	
Caltrex Engineering (B)						○				○		●				
Fabritex		●				○					○					
Future Investments Group				●		○			●		○	◑				◑
Georgian Frames						○										○
Ghent Fireworks								●		◑				○		●
Holmgren Engineering			◑			●						●			○	●
Hunting Swift										●						
The Ipswich Hospital NHS Trust			●												◑	●
Lloyds TSB	○	●			◑					●						
McDonald's Corporation		◑			◑					●						
Northmore Finance Direct			◑	○		●		◑		●						
Platt Green Electronics			○		●		◑		●				◑			
Pret A Manger									○	●						
Redman Company			◑							● ●						
Richmond Plastics		○	◑			○				●						
Riviona Bank			●		●				○	●						◑
Selfridges					●					◑						
Southwest Airlines		◑	○		○				○	●						◑
Spencer Thomson		◑	○		◑		◑			○						◑
Tile Products			◑			●				●	◑	◑			●	●
Too Short the Day	●												◑			
The Turn of the Unfriendly Card	◑	●	●		●		◑			○		●				◑
Weavers Homeopathic Products		◑				●	◑	●								◑
What They Teach You at Disney U	●			●						●						●
Wilson Pharmaceuticals																●
Yuppie Products		◑								●		○				
Zara						●				●		◑	●			

Notes 1 ● ◑ ○ Indicates the relevance to that particular chapter, the darkest being most relevant.

2 ░ Indicates case studies from the service sector.

● To enhance the ease of use of the book as a learning tool for students

New self-check questions, long case discussion questions, weblinks and additional cartoons help to enhance the learning experience.

Users of the previous edition will note some changes in chapter titles and numbers. These are summarized in the table below for clarity.

Topic	This edition	Previous edition
Managing operations	Chapter 1	Chapter 1
Operations strategy	Chapter 2	Chapter 2
Managing people	Chapter 3	Chapter 15
Designing and developing services and products	Chapter 4	Chapter 3
Designing service delivery systems	Chapter 5	None
Designing manufacturing processes	Chapter 6	within Chapters 4 & 5
Location and layout	Chapter 7	within Chapter 5
Managing capacity	Chapter 8	Chapter 6
Technology developments	Chapter 9	Chapter 7
Operations scheduling and execution	Chapter 10	Chapter 8
Managing quality	Chapter 11	Chapter 9
Managing inventory	Chapter 12	Chapter 10
Managing the supply chain	Chapter 13	Chapter 11
Process and delivery system reliability and maintenance	Chapter 14	Chapter 12
Time and productivity	Chapter 15	Chapter 13
Improving operations	Chapter 16	Chapter 14

Companion resources

Lecturers who adopt this text for class use can obtain the following resources to support their teaching:

● printed and bound teaching manual containing detailed case notes for all the long case studies in the text

● access to the companion website (http://www.palgrave.com/business/hill) containing PowerPoint slide lecture presentations and additional long case studies.

If you are interested in attending one of Terry Hill's well-established Faculty Programmes for lecturers, please contact the publishers or your local sales representative.

Students can access Excel files containing manipulable data from the long case studies, and relevant weblinks, at:

http://www.palgrave.com/business/hill.

To all those who use this book, I trust you find it helpful. It is vital that operations takes its full part in the running of companies and that the concepts and issues involved form part of a more complete understanding of the business.

Good luck!

Terry Hill

Managing Operations and People for Business and Markets

You will see from the contents that the book is divided into five parts. Part 1 describes the operations management role and comprises three chapters that cover the content of the job (the tasks involved) and the style of management (the managing people dimension) as follows:

Chapter	Dimension	Detail
1	Content	The day-to-day or operational tasks
2		The strategic task
3	Style	Managing people

A glance at the book map shows that these three chapters sit above the 'inputs – operations process – outputs' sequence that precedes each chapter. This reflects the overarching nature of these fundamental aspects of the operations management task in the following ways:

- the topics covered in the rest of the book comprise the detail that makes up the day-to-day or operational element of the job
- the day-to-day tasks need to be managed partly within the context of the strategic role of operations
- managing people, the key resource of an organization, underpins all aspects of the operational task.

Dealing with these three topics at the start is most appropriate, as it highlights their importance, reflects the core nature of these tasks and also introduces perspectives that permeate the rest of the book.

book map

Part

1
- 1 Managing Operations
- 2 Operations Strategy
- 3 Managing People

2

PROCESSES

- 4 Designing and Developing Services & Products
- 5 Designing Service Delivery Systems
- 6 Designing Manufacturing Processes
- 7 Location and Layout
- 8 Managing Capacity
- 9 Technology Developments
- 10 Operations Scheduling and Execution
- 11 Managing Quality

3
- 12 Managing Inventory
- 13 Managing the Supply Chain

4
- 14 Process and Delivery System Reliability and Maintenance
- 15 Time and Productivity
- 16 Improving Operations

5
- Managing Operations in Practice: Long Case Studies

SUPPLIERS

INPUTS

OUTPUTS

CUSTOMERS

Managing Operations

Why is managing
operations
important?

*Effectively managing operations is a key factor in
maintaining and improving an organization's
growth and prosperity. The high proportion of an
organization's staff, costs and investments that
reside within this function and its role in supporting
the needs of customers highlight the central nature
of the operations task.*

Executive overview

The book map opposite the beginning of this chapter highlights the position of this chapter within the whole of the book. As you would anticipate, it is shown as having an overarching dimension to depict the all-embracing nature of this topic. In particular, the aspects covered here relate to the role of operations management within organizations and review the following:

- **Defining operations management** – the opening section of the chapter explains what the operations management task comprises, giving illustrations from organizations in different sectors.

- **An overview of the operations management role** – introduces the day-to-day (or operational) and strategic roles of operations, together with the key task of managing people.

- **The nature of organizations** – with the growth of businesses, groups of tasks are completed by a number of departments or functions and one of these is operations.

- **The task of managing operations** – transforming inputs into saleable outputs is at the core of day-to-day operations management. What this involves is discussed and illustrated.

- **Operations management in a developing economy** – the varying nature of the operations task in the primary, secondary and tertiary sectors is discussed and the mix between these within nations is examined.

- **The purchase** – customers purchase a mix of services and products. How these differ and the operations management response are examined.

- **Size of the operations task** – the fact that operations typically comprises 60–70 per cent of people, assets and costs is discussed.

- **The role of the operations manager** – the variety and nature of the tasks of the operations manager are outlined.

- **Services versus manufacturing** – the similarities and differences between these two sectors are reviewed and examples given to illustrate the issues involved.

Introduction

Let's first of all summarize what the operations management task comprises as this will give you an overall view of what is involved and what is covered by this book:

1 Companies sell services and goods to customers. To do this they purchase the inputs they need such as materials, services and energy. They then process these inputs through the skills of the people, the equipment or processes and systems or procedures into the

required outputs (services and products) to be sold in their markets. How complicated the 'processing' phase is will vary. For example:

- a retailer purchases products, unpacks and displays them and processes their subsequent resale.
- a hospital processes patients (its customers). The range of healthcare provided can involve complicated procedures over a long period.
- a restaurant buys in food and prepares this into a range of menus. On the other hand, it buys in soft drinks, bottled water and wine, stores them and then serves them with relatively little additional processing.
- a garment manufacturer buys in a range of materials in terms of material types and colours, cotton threads, trims, buttons, zips and other accessories. The materials are then cut to meet different styles and sizes and sewn together, with relevant trim, buttons, zips and other accessories added during the operations process. After pressing and final inspection the finished garments are packed and despatched to different retail outlets.

2 The operations function concerns managing the inputs into the system (often referred to as the 'external phase of the supply chain') and also the processes used for converting these into the outputs sold to customers.

3 Operations is responsible for efficiently managing these tasks and seeking ways to make improvements throughout, in order to better meet the objectives and targets set by the business itself and the needs of its customers.

4 Underpinning these activities is the key task of managing the people within the operations function in such a way that meets agreed schedules, productivity levels and other business targets, while helping develop them in terms of broadening their skills base and facilitating personal development opportunities.

5 This book addresses the various aspects of these tasks and discusses and reviews the range of topics involved and the alternative approaches that may be followed under each heading.

The content and planning of the book

The book map provided at the beginning of this and every subsequent chapter represents the overview described above and also details the topics addressed in each of the chapters. It shows how the book is planned and put together, which is now explained below:

1 The blocks in the centre of the diagram show the core sets of tasks managed by operations. These comprise taking the inputs and converting them within the operations process into the outputs sold to customers.

2 Within these three stages, the specific issues, approaches and controls addressed or used by operations managers to undertake these tasks are highlighted. These, in turn, constitute the title and content of the individual chapters throughout the book.

3 You will note that three chapter headings are shown as being of an overarching nature with regard to the 'inputs', 'operations process' and 'outputs' stages. This will become clearer when the topics are discussed. Consequently, these three topics, Managing Operations, Operations Strategy and Managing People, are dealt with at the beginning of the book and, as you would expect, reappear in order to reinforce their role as providing essential context and linkage throughout.

4   Finally, the circles in which the topic titles appear are colour coded to help you see where you are (in black), what has been covered (in white) and what is to come (in grey). The key to this colour coding is in the top left-hand corner of the diagram at the start of each chapter.

Managing operations: an overview of the role

The contribution and value-adding role of operations management is at the heart of most organizations. Whether it is a pair of jeans, midday snack, live concert, haircut, PC or hospital check-up, operations is central to its provision. To successfully manage operations within a business concerns two distinct but complimentary aspects which, in turn, comprise two dimensions:

1   Content – what an operations manager does in terms of the tasks and responsibilities involved:
    ● **the internal day-to-day or operational role** that involves managing the set of tasks and responsibilities within operations necessary to provide the services or products to be sold, for example managing capacity and controlling costs.
    ● **the external or strategic role** that concerns meeting the competitive drivers within a company's markets for which operations is responsible, for example providing a service right first time and delivering a service on time.

2   Style – how an operations manager handles the people management task:
    ● **the internal role** concerns managing the people within the operations function itself and also the people interface between operations and other functions within an organization, so as to meet people's own personal needs, the needs of the operations functions and also those of the overall business.
    ● **the external role** involves managing the people interface outside the organization at both the supplier and customer end of the supply chain.

To illustrate these characteristics of the operations management role, Portioli, a sandwich and coffee bar within London's finance centre, is used in Case example 1.1

Case example 1   OPERATIONS MANAGEMENT TASKS AT PORTIOLI SANDWICH AND COFFEE BAR

Opening at 7am to catch the early breakfast and coffee demands of nearby office staff, Portioli remains open throughout the day until 5.30pm when customer demand falls away.

Capacity management – one of the core operations tasks is to meet the demands of customers in terms of, for example, providing the full range of products on offer, meeting the product specifications (for example the taste and freshness of the sandwiches and coffee) and matching customer lead time expectations. Using past experience to forecast demand in terms of the hour of the day, the day of the week and the week of the year will provide data in terms of the number of customers and the types and quantities of food and beverages involved. With these insights, operations can determine staff levels at different times of the day and week to ensure that queue lengths are in line with waiting time targets while staff costs are kept to a minimum.

Supply chain and inventory management – demand forecasts would also be used to manage the supply of beverages and food while taking into account existing inventory. This role would include ensuring that product specifications (for example taste, freshness and look of the different foods) were met by suppliers and maintained within the operations function by appropriate storage and refrigeration provision. To this end daily deliveries of a range of breads, pastries, food ingredients and salads are scheduled before 7am while other food and beverages (such as butter, coffee, tea and some sandwich fillings) are held in stock, with deliveries arranged once, twice or sometimes three times a week. Working with suppliers to guarantee that ingredients meet agreed specifications and that deliveries are on time are key features of all outlets in the Portioli Group.

Scheduling, delivery systems and managing quality – other aspects that directly affect the smooth running of the delivery system include layout, procedures and the movement of staff from the part of the service delivery system in which customers are served (known as the 'front office') to those parts of the delivery system that do not interface with the customer (known as the 'back office'), where activities such as the advance preparation of sandwich fillings take place.

As food preparation starts at 6am and staff typically work an eight-hour day, scheduling appropriate levels of staff in terms of the mix of skills needed is a key operations task, especially given the need for occasional overtime working to cover for holidays and absence. Scheduling staff to ensure that the necessary skills are available is an integral part of managing food and service quality levels at all times.

The market – demand has increased year on year over the last decade. The competitive criteria that are considered as key features in Portioli's sales growth include the quality and freshness of the food and beverages sold, the range of products on sale, short waiting times, prices that are in line with nearby competitors and a no-quibble refund should customers feel dissatisfied. The outlet itself is well positioned in relation to underground and bus services and while some seating is available, most customers prefer the takeaway service on offer.

Case question	Review Portioli's sandwich and coffee bar and identify, using the book map at the beginning of this chapter:

- how the operations process works
- which chapter topics in the book are reflected in the details provided.

As you will see from the above case, the breadth of the tasks and range of management skills involved make the operations management area a demanding and, at the same time, fascinating role. It links strategy to action, requires coordination across functions and involves managing the largest part of an organization. To accomplish this, operations manages most of the assets, costs and resources necessary to produce the services and goods sold to consumers or other organizations. On the strategy dimension, the operations role is especially fulfilling as it supports many of the attributes that help sell the services and products involved, for example being on time, meeting the service or product specification, fast delivery and low price.

The operations role is best described as exciting, rich in issues, full of challenges, central to the process of a business and about managing through and with people. The day-to-day role is full of interest and variety, while its strategic contribution is central to maintaining and growing sales and profits.

Origins of the name 'operations management'

The term 'production management' was predominantly used in the past with the early emergence of the manufacturing sector. Indeed, in many companies this title is still appropriately in use. However, the enlargement of the role to include responsibility for other tasks in the supply chain, such as purchasing and despatch, led to a change in title to that of 'operations management'. Furthermore, the growth of the service sector in industrially developed countries has reinforced this change to 'operations management' as a more appropriate, general title. The title of this book, therefore, reflects both this shift and the dual emphasis of the operations task in the service and manufacturing sectors.

The nature of organizations

To provide a service or product requires certain tasks to be completed. Essentially, they include design, buying materials and/or services from others, creating the services and products to meet the needs of customers (for example by adding to them in some way, changing the shape of materials, assembling parts, giving advice, processing information or requests, arranging services or selling a product to customers), selling them and accounting for the cash or credit transactions involved. When an organization is small, several of these tasks are typically completed by one person. As a business grows, sets of tasks are separated off into departments or functions and managed by different people. While the tasks remain the same (albeit larger and more complex), the organizational structure to manage and provide them has altered.

To cope with the complexity that comes with size, organizations separate the tasks involved in managing the business into functions and these 'parts' of a business are then responsible for managing a range of tasks. Operations is one such function and, as explained earlier, its prime role is to provide the services or produce the products that are then sold to customers. Similarly, a sales and marketing function would be responsible for selling to and working with customers, while the accounting and finance function sends out the invoices for goods sold and collects payment. In addition, these executive or 'line functions', as they are called, will be supported by specialist departments (for example IT) that provide advice and expertise within a given field to help better manage these executive functions and the organization overall. As the function responsible for providing the services and products sold to customers, operations plays a key role in any organization, no matter what its size.

The operations manager's task

The operations function is that part of an organization responsible for providing the services or producing the goods that a company sells in its markets. Some organizations provide services such as medical care, banking facilities, the processing of information and requests and retail sales, while others produce physical items such as furniture, building materials and stationery.

Exhibit 1.1 Overview of the operations process – transforming inputs into outputs

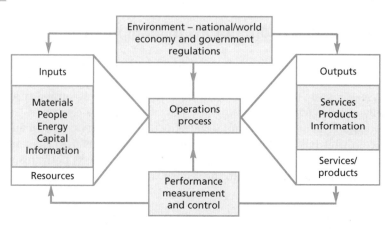

| Exhibit 1.2 | An overview of the service and manufacturing sectors |

Sector	Organization	Inputs	Operations process	Outputs
Services	Air passenger transport	Airports Booking systems Aircraft Aircrews Ground staff Fuel Food	Passenger reservations Flight schedules Check-in Aircraft and equipment maintenance Aircraft cleaning and provisioning Meals and crew scheduling Boarding procedures In-flight procedures Baggage claim	Customers booked on appropriate flights in terms of timing and convenience Customers progressed through the pre-boarding phase of the service delivery system Customers transported safely and on time to chosen destinations
	Computing centre	Buildings Computing equipment Stationery Toner Energy People	Updating records Printing Enveloping Distribution	Information to internal and/or external customers using agreed distribution alternatives and in line with agreed schedules
	Restaurant	Buildings Equipment – kitchen and restaurant Food Energy People	Table setting Order taking Food preparation and cooking Table waiting Drinks provision Dishwashing General cleaning	Food, wine and other drinks provided in line with customers' selection and preferred timings Aim is repeat visits from satisfied customers
Manufacturing	Bakery	Buildings Equipment Food ingredients Packaging Energy People	Mixing Baking Packaging Equipment maintenance Distribution	Range of packed bakery items delivered to warehouses and retail outlets that are fresh and in line with consumer shopping patterns
	Garments	Range of cloths and threads Accessories (for example buttons and ribbons) Buildings Equipment Energy People	Cutting Garment making Packaging Equipment maintenance Warehousing Distribution	Range of garments Distribution to warehouses and retail outlets to meet seasonal demand patterns
	Packaging	Buildings Equipment Paper and film Inks Energy People	Cylinder and plate preparation Equipment maintenance Printing Slitting Packing Distribution	Packaging to meet customer specifications Distribution to customers' manufacturing plants in line with agreed schedules

Notes 1 In services, customers (or their requests/enquiries), customer surrogates (a car being serviced in a garage is a customer surrogate) and/or information are processed.
2 In manufacturing, products are processed.
3 As you will see later, customers may provide capacity as part of the 'inputs', for example in fast-food restaurants.

The operations task, however, is common to all the diverse range of services and goods that make up a national economy. It concerns the transformation process that involves taking inputs and converting them into outputs, together with the various support functions closely associated with this basic task. Exhibit 1.1 provides a simplified overview of what is involved while Exhibit 1.2 gives examples from both the service and manufacturing sectors. The level of complexity within the operations function will vary depending upon several factors, including:

● The size of an organization and associated service/product volumes

● The nature of the services and products provided

● The technology levels embodied in both the services/products involved and the processes used within the operations function

● The extent to which the services and products are made in-house.

A final factor that impacts the design and management of the operations process or delivery system is the nature of what is processed. As Exhibit 1.3 illustrates, the presence of the customer in the system will impact its design and the operations management task involved, as explained more fully in Chapter 5. The examples given in Exhibit 1.3 have been chosen to illustrate these differences whereas often what constitutes the offering is a mix of these. For example, car servicing will comprise interfacing with the customer as well as processing the automobile (the customer surrogate) and invoice preparation and payment. Purchasing furniture will involve customer advice and the paperwork involved in the invoicing and guarantee phases of the purchase as well as the product itself.

To sustain or improve corporate prosperity it is essential to achieve the level of effectiveness required to compete successfully in chosen markets. To do this, it is necessary for those activities responsible for the provision of services or goods to be well managed. These tasks are, therefore, critical to the success of an organization. Operations managers oversee these tasks. They control the inputs and processes that together provide the services or produce the goods that a business sells. But, as with other functional executives, operations managers have a strategic, as well as operational, dimension to their responsibilities. They

Exhibit 1.3 Examples of service and product processing

Sector	What is processed	Examples	Customer involvement in the process or delivery system
Service	Customers	Beauty salons, hospitals, health farms, physiotherapists and restaurants	In the process or delivery system
	Customer surrogates	Garages, repair shops and dry cleaning outlets	Detached from the process or delivery system
	Information	Tax accountants, passport offices, lawyers, computing centres and insurance	
Manufacturing	Products	Chemicals, furniture, motor vehicles, personal computers, food and pharmaceuticals	

have to develop a functional strategy as part of the corporate debate that identifies and agrees the strategic direction an organization needs to follow.

It is, therefore, the development and control in both these activities that constitute the role of the operations manager.

The operations manager within the organization

The operations manager is usually responsible for a whole range of functions within an organization. These functions will differ depending upon whether it is a service or manufacturing business, and the nature of the items provided. Exhibit 1.4 shows a typical organizational set-up for an operations manager within a large manufacturing company.

Exhibit 1.4 Operations management functions in a large manufacturing company

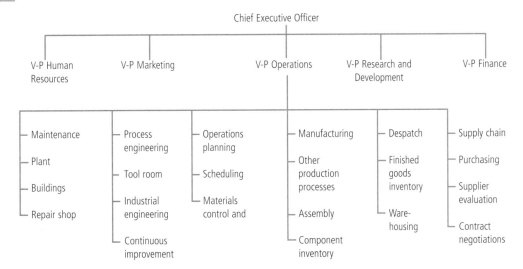

Notes 1 The descriptions 'director' and 'vice-president (V-P)' are used in organizations to denote similar roles.
2 Quality assurance (see later in Chapter 11) here reports to the V-P Research and Development.
3 Inspection is undertaken by the operator responsible for completing the task.
4 Many of the activities within industrial engineering (for example continuous improvement – see Chapter 16) are undertaken by the staff who have the prime responsibility for completing the task. Here the industrial engineering staff train and advise throughout.

Exhibit 1.5 provides examples of typical core tasks within operations, which are central to the provision of the service or product involved. In addition, and reporting into the operations function, there will be a number of support departments, as shown for each example. Finally, there will also be a number of specialist functions that provide advice and expertise but report elsewhere in the organization.

Exhibit 1.5   Operations jobs and specialist functions in three organizations

Type of business	Some typical jobs in operations		Typical specialist functions that report elsewhere in an organization
	Core tasks	Support departments	
Hospital	Hospital director Medical staff: – Doctors – Ward sisters – Nurses	Reception Maintenance Cleaning Porters	Microbiology Pathology Pharmacy Physiotherapy
Print company	V-P operations Print manager Finishing manager Supervisors Team leaders Operators	Ink manager Plate production Scheduling	Design Pay office Accounts Quality assurance
Transport company	V-P operations Depot managers Drivers	Vehicle maintenance Scheduling	Building and equipment maintenance Pay office Accounting

Operations management in a developing economy

National economies comprise a mix of primary (for example agriculture), secondary (for example manufacturing) and tertiary (for example services) sectors. As economies develop, the balance between these different sectors changes, as illustrated in Exhibit 1.6. The differences under the three headings reflect the general activities associated with the individual countries involved. For example, the relatively high percentage of gross domestic product (GDP) created by the primary sector in Norway and South Africa reflects respectively the North Sea oil and gas exploration and mining activities within these countries. Similarly, the high percentage of GDP created by the secondary sector of Japan signals its role as a major manufacturing nation.

However, looking at the overall mix change from 1980 to 2002 shows a similar pattern. The service sector continues to grow in itself and as a percentage of each country's GDP.

The operations management role, no matter what sector, is similar in terms of task and significance. Growing foodstuffs, extracting minerals, making products or providing services are parts of the basic task of any business and central to its continued success. Therefore, whether or not you are or intend to be in operations, it is essential that you understand the concepts and approaches involved, the interfaces this function has within a business and its key role in helping to grow sales and meet an organization's short- and long-term financial goals.

Finally, although it is useful to separate activities into primary, secondary and tertiary sectors in order to help identify, understand and discuss the whole, in reality they form part of a total economy. The mutual interdependence between the sectors is acknowledged and addressed within developed countries at both the national and corporate levels. Arguments suggesting that developed nations can rely on the tertiary sector as a way of sustaining stan-

Exhibit 1.6 Percentage of GDP by sector group for selected countries, 1980 and 2002

Country	Percentage of gross domestic product by sector					
	1980			2002		
	Primary	Secondary	Tertiary	Primary	Secondary	Tertiary
Australia	12	28	60	9	18	73
Belgium	3	39	58	2	26	72
Canada	12	33	55	8	25	67
France	6	40	54	4	25	71
Germany	4	47	49	2	26	72
Italy	7	40	53	3	24	73
Japan	5	41	54	2	30	68
Norway	24	28	48	19	15	76
Singapore	2	36	62	1	31	68
South Africa	31	29	40	12	20	68
Spain	8	40	52	4	27	69
Sweden	5	41	54	3	23	74
UK	7	38	55	3	21	76
USA	8	29	63	4	20	76

Notes   These sectors include the following activities:
   Primary   – agriculture, mining and quarrying.
   Secondary – manufacturing and construction.
   Tertiary   – utilities, wholesale/retail trade, transport, services and others. ('Others' are unclassified activities that constitute in all instances
                 a relatively high percentage of the total GDP. This category is included in 'tertiary' since the activities are neither 'primary' nor
                 'secondary'.)

Source UN Bulletin of Statistics.

dards of living or improving below-average trade performance are without foundation. Each sector is not only an integral part of one economy but performance in one sector will often have an impact on another. For example, a large part of many service sales comprises a product provided by activities in the primary and/or secondary sectors (for example foodstuffs and equipment).

The purchase – a mix of services and products

Goods are tangible items purchased by individuals or organizations for subsequent use. Services are intangible items that are consumed at the time of provision, with a customer taking away or retaining the benefits of that service. However, in many situations, what is provided or produced by an organization can be a mixture of both services and goods. In some instances there will be a heavy accent on service, and in others, the reverse. Exhibit 1.7 shows a range of items sold and the mix between the service and product content provided. The purchase mix represented here is intuitively derived, and others may consider the balance to differ from that shown. The purpose, however, is to illustrate that what we buy is a mix of both a service and a product and the mix will differ depending upon the offering. Take, for example, the difference between the purchase of 'regular maintenance' and 'breakdown maintenance' shown in Exhibit 1.7. Invariably, the technical job content in a breakdown is less than for regular maintenance, whereas the service content is the reverse – if you break down a skilled mechanic comes to you and your car thus constituting more service content in the offering mix than in regular service maintenance when you take your car to a garage. It is important, therefore, when considering Exhibit 1.7, to bear in

| Exhibit 1.7 | Service/product mixes in a range of purchases |

The purchase	Mix	
	100% service	100% product
Health farm		
Management consultancy		
Computer bureau		
Breakdown maintenance		
Regular maintenance		
High-quality restaurant meal		
Meal in a fast-food restaurant		
Make-to-order, high-cost goods		
Low-cost consumable goods		
Vending machines		

mind that its purpose is to draw attention to the service/product mix that constitutes a business. Hence, the question to be answered is 'Are we a manufacturing organization with an auxiliary service, or a service organization with a facilitating good?[1]

Thus, services and products are packages of explicit and implicit benefits provided or made by a supporting set of processes often using services and/or goods respectively as part of the package provision. For example, compare a cup of coffee provided by a vending machine and the same item provided in the lounge of a good hotel. The former service offers convenient, 24-hour, fast delivery of a product. The product specification is controlled by the service delivery system and hence the product range offered is limited, both in terms of width and specification: coffee is provided in a number of combinations (for example regular or decaffeinated, with or without milk and sugar) and in a disposable cup. On the other hand, coffee provided in the lounge of a good hotel comprises significantly different service factors – choice, presentation, comfort and normally a slower, 'more leisurely' service at a higher price. In the former coffee provision, the ratio of goods to service in the total package mix would be considerably higher than in the latter.

Size of the operations task

Operations management is concerned with handling the physical resources necessary to provide a service or make a product. To accomplish this, the available facilities need to be managed to meet the cost budgets laid down, while also readapting the resources as and when new services and products are introduced. In addition, this task is complicated by two factors. First, the dynamic nature of today's business environment requires the effective management of these resources in times of economic uncertainty and social change.

Second, the size of the task compounds the problems associated with managing operations, as this function is unique in terms of its overall size. As explained below, in a typical organization the operations function employs most of the people, uses and manages most of the organization's assets and spends most of the money:

1 People – the operations task concerns the management of a large number of people.

Most employees are usually involved in the mainline activities of a business (that is, those providing services or making products). A high percentage of the support staff will also come under an operations manager's control, as illustrated earlier in Exhibits 1.4 and 1.5. The result is that the total number of staff in this function usually accounts for 60–70 per cent of all those employed by an organization.

2   Assets – operations is responsible for the effective use of some 60–70 per cent of an organization's total assets. On the fixed assets side, it is usually accountable for land and buildings, together with plant and equipment, which make up a large percentage of the total fixed asset investment list. On the current assets side, it is responsible for the inventory holding, which, as shown in Chapter 12, is a high percentage of the current assets investment. Since these together constitute a large part of the total investment made, the operations function takes on the responsibility for effectively managing the most significant proportion of an organization's use of funds.

3   Costs – the operations function accounts for the major portion of an organization's expenditure. As the majority of the direct costs, such as staff and materials, are incurred in this area, together with much of the overhead costs involved, it is by far the largest budget area within a business.

These features mean that the sound management of the operations process is critical to an organization's short- and long-term success. The efficient use and control of the assets and costs involved are core to the cost structure and budgets of a business. Similarly, as markets are changing quickly, understanding the business capability of operations is a key factor in successfully delivering corporate strategy. However, translating these tasks into the right combination of equipment, people, procedures and processes to meet the needs of customers and markets is a demanding and time-consuming job. These areas of activity are not only large in themselves but they are all interrelated parts of the whole task. Furthermore, decisions made in this area are difficult to change because of their complex nature and the high investment cost usually associated with past actions and future proposals.

The role of the operations manager

The last section highlighted the size of the operations management task. This section describes the key features that make up the role. Some of these features relate to successfully managing the internal or day-to-day tasks, some the external or strategic tasks while others highlight the need to manage people. The features of the operations task, and their size and importance, create a demanding and absorbing management role. It is concerned with detail yet must address corporate issues of significant size and importance. The key aspects of the job are outlined below.

Managing a large cost centre

As explained in the previous section, operations accounts for a large part of the asset investment and typically has the largest budget within an organization. One consequence is that operations managers are responsible for a large cost centre. If operations budgets and output levels are met, then the cost structure of a business will be sustained.

Managing the short and long term

It is necessary that operations is managed efficiently in the short term. The task of providing services or producing goods is a short-term function. A day's lost output will never be recovered without additional costs being incurred. Customers who go elsewhere are lost business, sometimes for ever. That is the nature of the short-term operations task. It is thus essential that the day-to-day activities are well controlled and coordinated, and meet budgeted outputs. To meet monthly targets requires that each day's target is met. Other departments, such as sales, work on a different time basis, with no one expecting the period sales target to be met pro rata each day. As a consequence, substantial pressure is, and has to be, exerted to meet short-term operations targets.

So, what are some of the consequences of needing to meet these short-term goals? They include:

- the job is problem-oriented and solution-driven. Operations managers need to react quickly to resolve problems at source. Handling the symptoms as they appear will only bring temporary respite. The causes need to be identified and handled.
- it is a job that requires practical outcomes, 'indeed in this sense its practicability is overwhelming'.[2]
- 'pressure is also a distinctive feature'[3] of the job due to the tasks involved, the time constraints imposed and the dependency upon a whole range of activities, some of which are outside the direct control of the operations function either because of the organization's reporting system or because they are externally sourced.

The time pressures on operations managers often result in them having to make as good a decision as possible in any given situation. To think of a better decision at a later date is usually of little value. It would be too late and the consequences of the delay would normally outweigh the gains involved. It is essential, therefore, that operations managers use their experience to good effect.

But it is equally important that the longer term requirements do not take a secondary role. In a function controlling such a large portion of revenue expenditure, the longer term developments of the operations function need to be given the necessary time and attention, because, here, small percentage improvements invariably lead to large actual savings.

Managing technology

The operations manager is a manager of technology, both product, service and process. However, the degree of technology will differ from sector to sector and one organization to the next. And, in many situations, the level of technology involved is quite low. In most instances, the operations manager needs not so much to understand the technology itself but more importantly the business trade-offs that can be delivered by the technology in place or being proposed. In this way, operations uses technology to provide services or make products for a company's markets, with technical expertise provided by support staff.

Coordinating the whole

Like managers of other departments, the operations manager breaks down the total task into subsystems as a way to control the whole. This is essential in order to cope. However, the operations manager's role is to control these subsystems while also controlling the total system. But, as the operations task is large, the subsystems will usually be numerous and interrelated, making this coordinating role all the more difficult.

Exhibit 1.8   Managing the subsystems and specialist support can have its off day!

© AMD Publishing

In addition, the activities of many of the support and specialist functions that form part of an organization will be to help operations complete its tasks, as illustrated earlier in Exhibit 1.5. Therefore, it is equally important for operations managers to be involved with and contribute to the specialist's tasks and activities as far as they relate to their own area of responsibility. They need to set the agenda for these support activities and be proactive in establishing directives, agreeing the tasks and specification for the work on hand, and facilitate the essential relationship between and with them (see Exhibit 1.8).

Managing the flow of work and money

Operations is responsible for the flow of work through a business and the flow of money. The role of controlling work is an integral part of operations. As Exhibit 1.1 illustrates, the fundamental tasks involved in providing services and producing products concern managing the flow of work from inputs to outputs. The flow of money involves managing costs in the form of purchases and processing costs, that is, money flowing out of the organization. When services are provided or products are made and then sold, customers pay for these at the time or at a later date and money flows back into the organization (see Exhibit 1.9). Meeting customer lead times while keeping costs and other expenditures, such as inventory, under control is a core task within any business. Operations is responsible for managing both these flows, as the one is tied to the other.

To help establish the link between the flow of work and the flow of money, have a go at reproducing Exhibit 1.9 for a garage that sells new and used cars and also provides a vehicle maintenance service. It will be easier to keep the vehicle selling and vehicle maintenance activities separate for the purposes of this exercise, by completing a work and money flow diagram for the two parts of the business.

Exhibit 1.9   Work and money flows

Money flow Out	Money flow In	Current assets		Work and materials flow	Activity description
✓		Inventory	Raw materials and components	Materials/components	The necessary materials/components are bought from outside
✓			Work-in-progress (WIP)	Staff and other materials/components added	The necessary tasks to provide the service or produce the product are completed
✓			Finished goods	More staff and materials/components added	Service/product now complete and is or can be sold
	✓	Cash sales		Finished services/goods are sold	Cash sales
		Debtors		Finished services/goods are sold	Credit sales
	✓	Cash			Payment made for credit sales

Note   In some cases, payments are made when certain stages have been completed (for example stage payments may be made in the building/construction industry) or at the end of a time period (for example management consultations usually invoice on a weekly basis).

Uses the common denominators of time and money

To help manage a business, the activities involved are expressed using the same common denominator. Many activities use money as the base as this is the most appropriate way to ensure that 'like is compared with like'. Thus, sales are expressed in terms of monetary value (£, € or $) and not in terms of the number of services or products sold. The reason is that for a restaurant to measure its level of activity by the number of meals provided would take no account of the number or type of course selected and served.

Operations, on the other hand, uses time as a more appropriate common denominator by which to express its activities. The reason is that the monetary value of the services and products provided does not adequately relate to the operations task involved. For example, it takes longer to produce a lasagne than prepare a fillet steak but the menu price for each would be the reverse. And as operations needs to assess, for example, the level of capacity it needs at different times of the day and week, it has to work out the number of hours involved to meet forecast sales and what this means in terms of different types of staff.

The use of time as a common denominator for the activities involved serves well the needs of operations. But these activities will also be translated into monetary terms to meet the needs of corporate reporting systems. How the one translates into the other has, therefore, to be well understood and managed by operations, although it will be the accounting and finance function in a business that will undertake the translation task. A distinctive part of the operations management role, therefore, concerns being able to work knowledgeably on both time and money fronts.

Managing the process through people

At the core of this role is the task of managing the operations process through people. The number of people within the operations function and the range of skills and responsibilities involved was highlighted earlier. Managing this key resource in order to meet both the short- and long-term dimensions of the task, while also addressing the wide range of development needs and career expectations of those involved, is central to the role of operations management. While the people issues are picked up throughout the book, they are dealt with in detail in Chapter 3.

Linking the thinking and doing ends of a business

The operations function forms the interface between the thinking end (strategic direction) and the doing end (meeting the needs of customers) of a business. It provides the essential link between the corporate view and the operational task. On the strategy dimension, it links direction to action. Without action, strategic discussion and debate has little value. Thus, translating strategy into action is fundamental to the ongoing success of a business and operations has a key role in getting this done. In the same way, operations links corporate philosophies and values with the views of work held by those who complete the task. It is essential to link the top and bottom of businesses as this helps to forge the coherence and cooperation essential for the success of the enterprise (see Exhibit 1.10).

Exhibit 1.10 Strategic vision normally offers more direction than provided by Mr James

© AMD Publishing

Managing complexity

The perspective that best captures the essence of the tasks outlined here is that operations concerns the management of complexity. The size and diversity of the tasks involved and the implications of decisions in terms of investment, costs and people are significant in size and fundamental in nature. The challenge of the job comes not from the nature of the individual tasks and decisions for which the operations manager is responsible – in themselves they are often quite simple – but from the number of these that have to be completed or made at the same time and the complex interrelationships that exist. Also, as operations is part of the core activities of most organizations, the work of specialists will be largely concerned with giving support and advice to the operations function. They will be involved not only with improving this function per se but also with developing the interrelated activities of operations and other departments.

Taking this mix together results in a demanding and complex job that requires, on the one hand, the fast, day-to-day pace of the short term to be underpinned and delivered while, on the other hand, the long-term direction is secured, and all this within the context of providing appropriate interface and cooperation within the overall business. Add to this the essential need to manage the processes and interfaces through the key resource of people and the outcome is a job that is fascinating in its challenge and complex in its execution. Case examples 1.2 and 1.3 illustrate this complexity.

Case example 2   THE ROYAL MAIL GROUP

The Royal Mail Group is one of the UK's largest companies, with annual sales revenues in 2003 of £8.3 billion. It comprises the letters business (Royal Mail), Parcelforce Worldwide, the UK's leading carrier business, and the retailing network (Post Office Ltd). From the mid-1970s until the end of the last century, the Royal Mail Group operated profitably and contributed over £2.5 billion to UK government funds in that period. However, it incurred pre-tax losses in the last two years, as the figures below show.

Year	Pre-tax profit/(loss) £m
2003	(678)
2002	(1113)
2001	81
1999	608

Delivering mail quickly and keeping costs down are at the heart of the Royal Mail. To handle increasing volumes (on average 82 million letters, cards and packages every day, rising to 135 million on peak days), in 1999 the company invested £200 million in a high-tech sorting process (an integrated mail processor) that now enables 90 per cent of all mail to be handled automatically. This helps increase the Royal Mail's next-day delivery targets for first- and second-class mail and handle volumes at peak times such as Christmas. In 2002 the next-day delivery for first-class mail was 92.8 per cent while second-class mail targets were achieved 98.3 per cent of the time.

To do this the Royal Mail employs over 130,000 staff (and typically a further 30,000 temporaries in the Christmas period) and has a transport fleet of 29,000 vehicles. It maintains and collects from 112,000 post boxes and delivers to 27 million addresses.

www.royalmail.com

Case question   Relate the sections on 'Size of the operations task' and 'The role of the operations manager' to this example. What features in this illustration best reflect the operations management task?

Case example 3   KEY LINK IN THE RETAIL CHAIN

Store managers within large retail companies are crucial appointments. When handed the keys to their own store, managers take on a task that is characterized by big numbers. Typically up to 700 staff are employed, with weekly sales revenues of more than £1 million and as many as 200,000 customers entering the door in an average week. While often unrecognized by the outside world, store managers hold a pivotal role in the retail sector. While buyers can source good products at competitive prices and distribution can be fine-tuned to efficiently meet the varying patterns of demand, the key to customer retention is what happens inside the store. It is customers' experience while shopping that affects whether or not they come back. Layout, presentation, queue lengths, availability and, above all, the service received throughout the delivery system are the factors that most influence a customer's decision on where to shop.

The critical nature of getting these operations management appointments right was highlighted recently when the chief executive of Sainsbury's (a leading UK supermarket group, with sales revenue in 2003 of more than £18 billion, 173,000 staff, 6000 items in its product range and more than 500 stores throughout the UK) stated that the performance of some 20 per cent of its store managers was under review and that this decision was part of an overall drive to improve the group's performance. According to many retailing experts, a 'good' store manager can increase the sales revenue of self-service outlets (such as supermarkets) by up to 5 per cent, while in stores heavily dependent on service (such as the electrical sector) the improvement can be as high as 15 per cent, and the best managers can carry these increases down to the bottom line and vice versa. With stores' weekly sales into hundreds of thousands of pounds (and the biggest stores in large national chains averaging over £1 million sales each week), the essential contribution made by a store manager in driving improvements through frontline operations and into higher retail performance is fundamental.

Retailers agree that managing the operations units (the stores themselves) has all the ingredients of what makes a complex job. Staff management is fundamental, especially given the fast-moving environment, changing demand levels and long opening hours that characterize a supermarket store. Tied to this is the management of a sizeable budget that reflects the costs of running a large store. Not only does the job concern managing a large investment, in the form of the buildings, car parks and delivery areas, but also the storing of goods and their management in terms of waste and obsolescence. The

store manager's knowledge of what goes on both in the store and the back office (including supply chain, logistics and stock management) is essential to the running of the operation and this knowledge needs to be matched by being good with customers and alert to actual and potential service issues.

While overall the skill range may be similar, the type of store and its location will add further dimensions to the skill base required to be a successful manager. Hypermarkets vs convenience stores, general retailing vs out-of-town shopping centres, self-service outlets vs those requiring a high level of personal service place a different emphasis on the skills needed. Similarly, running a big store in a rural location is different from managing one in an inner-city environment.

Attracting the right calibre of people is often difficult, given that the long, unsocial hours and weekend working are unattractive dimensions of the job. But on the plus side, the job is people-centric, rich in content, full of energy and buzz and addresses real problems, the solutions to which are fast and rewarding.

www.j-sainsbury.co.uk

| **Case questions** | 1 | What makes up the service/product offering in a supermarket? Take two product and two service elements in an offering and explain what a customer would look for and what would need to be provided to meet these expectations. |
| | 2 | How is the store manager a key link in the supply chain? |

Services versus manufacturing

This first chapter introduces the role of operations management and provides an introduction to some of the factors that impact the nature and characteristics of the operations task. As shown in Exhibit 1.7, organizations provide customers with a mixed offering of a service and product. In turn, this requires the provider to make a product, process information on behalf of a customer, provide a service for a customer, or some combination of these, as illustrated in Exhibit 1.3.

Embodied in these alternatives are different characteristics that either facilitate or restrict what operations can or can't do in the processing task. These differences are fundamental and, as such, are dealt with in more detail in subsequent chapters. What this section does is alert you to these differences so that you get a better feel for the types of issues that operations has to manage in one type of business compared to another. As you go through the different chapters these issues will be revisited and reaffirmed as part of learning about this subject area within the field of business studies.

Exhibit 1.11 summarizes some of those aspects that will be reviewed throughout the book and are now briefly explained.

Nature of the service/product

The characteristics of product, information and customer processing vary in several ways.

Exhibit 1.11   Aspects of product, information and customer processing

Aspects	Processing		
	Product	Information	Customer
Nature of the service/product	Tangible	⟶	Intangible
	Durable	⟶	Perishable
	Highly specified	⟶	Server discretion
Organizational arrangements	Back office	⟶	Front office
Level of customer involvement in the operations process	Low	⟶	High
Typical competitive environment	Traded	⟶	Sheltered

Note   The aspects when processing a customer surrogate (for example the maintenance of your car or suit/dress to be dry-cleaned) are similar to those for processing information.

For example, services are consumed by the customer at the point of provision. This means that the capacity in the process (for example an empty seat on a passenger airline, or an unbooked slot in a hairdressing salon) cannot be held over to another time. This inability to store capacity in the form of inventory results from the perishable nature of capacity in some service delivery systems. This contrasts sharply with a typical manufacturing company. Here, products can be made ahead of demand (for example ice cream is made and stored in times of lower demand as a way of using operations ice cream-making capacity productively as well as helping to meet the higher demand levels of another period). For this reason, a manufacturing company typically finds it easier to handle the imbalances that occur between the levels of demand and capacity.

Information-processing and customer surrogate businesses also have some opportunity to control when tasks are completed. For example, information-processing tasks can be cumulated and then scheduled until the most suitable time for completion, thus enabling demand to be spread in line with available capacity or to cumulate volumes to help lower processing costs. Similarly, the timing of a vehicle or other repair can, to some extent, be managed to better meet the scheduling needs of a business. Even so, the length of time over which scheduling alterations can be made will normally be limited in scale compared to the manufacturer of products. With products, inventory can be made, if required, ahead of time and independent of demand profiles, whereas information processing will invariably be an integral part of a customer's own overall service or procedure. The processing task can only commence on receipt of relevant data and needs to be completed to fit in with a customer's own requirements. Take, for example, a data processing unit that updates the transactions of the customers of its own client, a large high street bank. The necessary data will be delivered at a given day each month, with agreed lead times for completing the updates and sending out the individual statements. Within this time frame the unit is able to schedule the job to best fit its own total workload. Similarly, a garage can schedule the work within its repair shop on a given day around factors such as the skills available, spare part deliveries and the efficient use of staff.

The presence of customers in the system also brings the aspect of server interpretation into the delivery of a service – known as 'server discretion'. In turn, this makes it more difficult to control quality conformance in terms of establishing service levels and measuring performance against these. In the provision of goods, the issues of quality control and measuring performance against specification are more easily managed, given the separation of the making and purchasing events and the control over what and how a product is made.

Organizational arrangements

At the product end, the operations process is largely, and often totally, separated from the customer, whereas in the service sector customers are often involved in the provision. In a service company the delivery system, where possible, is split between the front office and back office. In the former the system interfaces with customers and, for example, handles requests or provides a given service. However, systems and procedures are designed so that certain tasks are undertaken in the back office and, in that way, processing can be delayed until a more convenient time and activities cumulated in order to gain economies of scale and so justify investments as part of the way to reducing costs. Being separated from the customers in the back office also allows procedures and tasks to be undertaken without making essential responses to customers' immediate requirements.

Competitive environment

The tangible nature of products enables the work and supporting technologies that go into making them to be easily transferred, in product form, from the place of manufacture to markets throughout the world. In this way, products are referred to as being 'traded'. As a result, the manufacturing sector has been increasingly competitive from the latter half of the last century, highlighting the truly global nature of these markets. Many services, on the other hand, are classed as being 'sheltered', highlighting the fact that the extent of competition is restricted by the geographical boundaries of such markets – the 'you-do-not-go-to-Hong-Kong-for-a-Chinese-takeaway' syndrome. For example, retailers only compete with the high street outlets within their own town or city. In recent years, however, the format of competition for many service firms has changed. One source of this change has been the increasing use of technology. Online services for the purchase of items such as books, clothes, banking and airline tickets has increasingly moved many service sectors into the traded category. The role of operations in such instances has needed to reflect these new dynamics and business conditions, reinforcing its core contribution to the continued success of a business.

Reflections

Few operations managers would consider their role to be other than demanding, challenging, absorbing and satisfying. They would also tell of its frustrations and complexity: this is bound to be so where a function is required to handle a large number of variables and achieve many diverse and complicated short- and longer term objectives.

To manage such a task effectively requires a range of executive qualities as indicated earlier. To this list need to be added hard work, intellect and experience. To complete the day-to-day tasks requires much physical effort. However, to perceive the whole and instigate through others appropriate initiatives and developments also requires both intellect and experience; the former to appreciate the issues and perspectives involved and the latter to be alert to potential problem areas.

High levels of complexity involve the key role of efficiently managing most of an organization's assets and costs while providing support for the many different needs of customers. To do this is intellectually demanding. Unless operations managers are able to understand the

Exhibit 1.12   The levels of learning

	Levels of learning	Description
Increasingly higher levels of learning	Evaluation	Appraise, compare, conclude, contrast, interpret and explain
	Synthesis	Classify, compile, design, modify, reorganize, formulate, reconstruct and substitute
	Analysis	Select, discriminate, illustrate, separate and distinguish
	Application	Demonstrate, relate, use, compete and prepare
The task of management	Understanding	Explain, extend, generalize, infer, summarize and estimate
	Knowledge	Know, identify, list, name, outline and state

Source From Benjamin S Bloom et al. *Taxonomy of Educational Objectives*, Allyn & Bacon, Boston, MA. Copyright © 1984 by Pearson Education. Adapted by permission of the publisher.

whole, take it apart, fix the parts required and put it back together, they will not be able to efficiently and effectively manage the tasks involved. Exhibit 1.12 underlines this point. As you will see, management concerns the higher levels of learning, from application through to evaluation. The operations task is classic of these demands, a fact gaining increasing recognition not least because of the success of developing nations and the emphasis placed by the more successful upon the management of the operations function. By the early 1980s it was becoming clear that Japanese success was not based upon greater investment in processes but in management, particularly operations. Similarly, the successful growth of international retailers such as Wal-Mart and IKEA has been built on world-class operations capability. Some believe that the managers needed to convert operations into 'a competitive resource may have to be the best rounded and most intellectually able of all corporate managers'.[4] The competences identified included: 'a knowledge of technology… as well as every business function… a thinking style that includes the ability to conceptualize as well as analyse complex trade-offs… [and] managers who are architects of change not house-keepers'.[5]

Recognition of these operations management qualities is a prerequisite for both the service and manufacturing sectors. Those nations that have been unsuccessful in carrying out the operations tasks in manufacturing industries have stood by and watched this sector diminish dramatically in a few years. Next on the list are parts of the service sector. Passenger airlines, data processing, call centre provision, banking and other parts of the financial services sector have already experienced the full weight of global competition. This will not abate in these sectors and is already surfacing elsewhere. The sound management of operations in terms of its internal and external roles has a key contribution to make in the success of companies, sectors and hence nations.

The rest of this book reviews the essential tasks involved and some of the important perspectives that need to be understood by an operations manager. The book attempts to present the concepts underlying this function and show which approaches are the most useful to adopt in order to analyse and evaluate each major part of the whole operations task. The emphasis, therefore, is not on covering all existing techniques or mathematical approaches and explanations. As shown in Exhibit 1.12, the higher levels of learning are those concerned with application, analysis, synthesis and evaluation. Knowledge and understanding are the easier, lower levels of learning; the most difficult task is to do the job effectively. It is not an issue of knowing things but of knowing what to do. This requires the application of relevant knowledge, the analysis of the results of that application, the building back together of the results into an improved form (synthesis) and the evaluation of this in terms of what has to be done. Effective managers are those who are able to do this as a way of continuously developing their own set of responsibilities. Thus, as well as describing the relevant concepts, approaches, tools and techniques within operations, the book also emphasizes the managerial dimension of the task. The book concerns operations management and the text, chapter questions, assignments and case studies provide the opportunity to introduce materials to meet the requirements of all six learning levels.

Key Elements of Managing Operations

- The operations process transforms inputs into outputs that the organization then sells in its chosen markets. Exhibit 1.1 overviews this core task while Exhibit 1.2 provides examples from both the service and manufacturing sectors.

- As operations typically accounts for 60–70 per cent of the people, assets and costs within an organization, its sheer size makes it a demanding management task. In addition, to undertake these activities, operations comprises a wide range of functions and support roles, examples of which are given in Exhibits 1.4 and 1.5.

- Most companies deliver a mix of both services and product as illustrated in Exhibit 1.7 and where an organization chooses to be on this service/product mix continuum will influence its competitive position and the operations task involved.

- While most offerings are a combination of services and products, there are important distinctions in managing operations in the service and manufacturing sectors. These are outlined and overviewed in Exhibit 1.11.

- Most of the people within a typical organization are within the operations function and reflect a wide range of jobs, skills and personal needs. A critical part of the operations role is to manage the operations process through people in such a way as to meet the short- and long-term needs of the business and also the development needs and personal expectations of those involved.

- The intention of this chapter is to set the scene for the rest of the book. The next chapter on operations strategy completes this overview and together they provide the appropriate context for the issues that follow.

Self-check

1   Which of the following is typically **not** the responsibility of the operations function:
    a   Managing the inputs into the system ☐
    b   Selling products to customers ☐
    c   Managing the processes used for converting inputs into outputs that are then sold to customers ☐

2   To cope with the complexity that comes with size, organizations tend to:
    a   Continually develop new services and products ☐
    b   Try to relocate certain activities to areas with low staff costs ☐
    c   Separate the tasks involved in managing the business into functions ☐

3   Typical inputs into an operations process are:
    a   Materials, people, energy, capital and information ☐
    b   Services, products and information ☐
    c   Performance measurement and control ☐

4   Which is an example of a specialist department in a hospital:
    a   Nurses ☐
    b   Doctors ☐
    c   Maintenance ☐

5   Services are:
    a   Tangible items purchased by individuals or organizations for subsequent use ☐
    b   Intangible items that are consumed at the time of provision ☐

Self-check cont'd

c   Both a and b ▢

6   Which of the following affects the size of the operations task:
   a   The number of people involved in the operations process ▢
   b   The number of assets involved in the operations process ▢
   c   Both a and b ▢

7   Managing a cost centre in a business involves:
   a   Understanding the business trade-offs that can be delivered by the technology involved ▢
   b   Addressing the development needs and career expectations of the people involved ▢
   c   Ensuring that budgets and output levels are met ▢

8   An example of information processing is:
   a   Insurance company ▢
   b   Pharmaceutical company ▢
   c   Beauty salon ▢

9   Which of the following is **not** a key difference that affects the operations process within a business:
   a   The nature of the service or product ▢
   b   The level of customer involvement in the operations process ▢
   c   The geographical location of customers ▢

10 The nature of the service or product when processing a customer is:
   a   Durable ▢
   b   Perishable ▢
   c   Both a and b ▢

Study activities

Discussion questions

1   Select two service and two manufacturing businesses of your own choice. From an operations perspective, what are the similarities and differences that exist?

2   What is operations management? What are the key elements of the operations task? Illustrate your answer with examples.

3   Based on Exhibits 1.1 and 1.2, select one manufacturing and one service business other than those used in Exhibit 1.2 itself. Then, complete a similar analysis to that given in Exhibit 1.2.

4   Select two other functions within a service or manufacturing business. For each, identify three links to operations and explain the key dimensions of the activities involved and how they would assist operations to complete its tasks and responsibilities.

5   Analyse the operations function in the university or college department in which you are registered or

in the company in which you work in terms of:
   ● the key operations responsibilities
   ● the size of the operations task
   ● the operations function in the context of the rest of the university/college department or organization
   ● four factors that illustrate the complexity of the operations task. Give reasons for your choice.

6   Identify an operations system in your own life. What are the inputs, operations process activities and outputs involved?

7   Consider the following processes that you frequently encounter:
   ● enrolling on a course
   ● taking lunch
   ● buying a ticket for a concert.

Identify the inputs, operations process and outputs involved.

Assignments

1   Look through McDonald's website (www.mcdonalds.com) and list the dimensions that concern

operations. How many outlets are there throughout the world and how do you think the company ensures effective control over the operations task in order to maintain its desired standards within the service delivery system?

2 Make a list of the top ten companies in the Fortune 500 (www.fortune.com/fortune/fortune500) from 1965, 1985, 1995, 2000 and the current day. Compare these to the current list. Identify the fundamental differences and give reasons for these changes.

Exploring further

Albrecht, K and Bradford, LJ *The Service Advantage*, Dow Jones Irwin, Homewood, IL (1990).

Caltanach, RE, Holdreith, JM, Reinke, DP and Sibik, LK *The Handbook of Environmentally Conscious Manufacturing*, Irwin Professional Publishing, Chicago (1995).

Chase, RB, Aquilano, NJ and Jacobs, PR *Operations Management for Competitive Advantage*, 9th edn, McGraw-Hill/Irwin, Boston (2001).

Collier, DA *Service Management: Operating Decisions,* Prentice Hall, Englewood Cliffs, NJ (1987).

Economist, The 'The size of services', 29 May 1999.

Etienne-Hamilton, EC *Managing World Class Service Business,* South Western College Publishing, Cincinnati (1998).

Flaherty, MT *Global Operations Management*, McGraw-Hill, New York (1996).

Hammer, M and Stanton, S 'How process enterprises really work', *Harvard Business Review*, November–December (1999).

Heizer, J and Render, B *Operations Management*, 7th edn, Pearson/Prentice Hall, Upper Saddle River, NJ (2004).

Heskett, JL *Managing in the Service Economy*, Harvard Business School Press, Boston, MA (1986).

Johnson, R and Clark, E *Service Operations Management,* Financial Times/Prentice Hall, Harlow (2001).

Loog BV, Van Dierdonck, R and Gemmel, P *Services Management: An Integrated Approach*, Financial Times/Pitman Publishing, London (1998).

Lowson, RH *Strategic Operations Management: The New Competitive Advantage,* Routledge, London (2002).

Melnyk, SA and Denzler, DR *Operations Management: a Value-driven Approach,* McGraw-Hill/Irwin, Chicago (1995).

Meredith, JR and Shafer, SM *Operations Management for MBAs*, 2nd edn, John Wiley & Sons, Hoboken, NJ (2002).

Ould, MA *Business Processes,* John Wiley & Sons, New York (1995).

Reid, DR and Sanders, NR *Operations Management,* John Wiley & Sons, New York (2002).

Schmenner, RW *Service Operations Management*, Prentice Hall, Englewood Cliffs, NJ (1995).

Schneider, B and Bowen DE *Winning the Service Game,* Harvard Business School Press, Boston (1995).

Schonberger, R *Building a Chain of Customers,* Hutchinson Business Books, New York (1990).

Slack, N, Chambers, S and Johnson, R *Operations Management,* 4th edn, Financial Times/Prentice Hall, Harlow (2004).

Wild, R *Operations Management,* 6th edn, Continuum, London (2004).

Notes and references

1   Sasser, WE, Olsen, PR and Wyekoff, DD *Management of Service Operations*, Allyn & Bacon, Boston (1978), p. 10.

2   Lawrence, PA *Operations Management: Research and Priorities*, Report to the Social Services Research Council (April 1983), p. 2.

3   Ibid., p. 14.

4   Meyer, R 'Wanted: a new breed of manufacturing manager', in *Manufacturing Issues 1987,* Booz Allen, New York (1987), pp. 26–9.

5   Ibid., p. 28.

book map

Part

1

- 1 Managing Operations
- 2 Operations Strategy
- 3 Managing People

INPUTS **PROCESSES** **OUTPUTS**

SUPPLIERS **CUSTOMERS**

2

- 4 Designing and Developing Services & Products
- 5 Designing Service Delivery Systems
- 6 Designing Manufacturing Processes
- 7 Location and Layout

3

- 8 Managing Capacity
- 9 Technology Developments
- 10 Operations Scheduling and Execution
- 11 Managing Quality
- 12 Managing Inventory
- 13 Managing the Supply Chain

4

- 14 Process and Delivery System Reliability and Maintenance
- 15 Time and Productivity
- 16 Improving Operations

5

- Managing Operations in Practice: Long Case Studies

Operations Strategy

Outline of chapter

Operations provides many factors that influence the repeat purchase of a company's services and products. Consequently, the strategic alignment of operations to the needs of markets is central to the long-term success of organizations.

Why is operations strategy important?

Executive overview

Faced with the pressures of increasing competition, businesses need to coordinate the activities of their principal functions within a coherent strategy. The reality is that companies typically don't do this. When developing their corporate strategies, they fail to embrace all the functional contributions and insights essential to understanding, resolving and agreeing strategic direction. One common and glaring omission in this process is the views and involvement of the operations function.

To explain this phenomenon, outline an approach by which operations can proactively engage in and contribute to the successful development of a corporate strategy and introduce the key concepts and ideas that comprise and underpin an operations strategy, this chapter addresses the following:

- **What is strategy?** – this clarifies the content and role of strategy within a business.

- **Evolution of strategy** – explains how, as companies grow, strategy evolves into three separate but interlinked levels.

- **Levels of strategy** – introduces the different levels of strategy from corporate through business unit to functional, together with a review of business unit strategy formulation.

- **Being market-driven and market-driving** – highlights the strategic mix within most companies that distinguishes between being market-driven, thereby developing the capabilities to meet the demands of a market, to being market-driving, requiring a proactive approach to identify how the competitive dimensions in a market may be changed.

- **Executive roles** – a review of the operational and strategic dimensions of an executive's task.

- **Operations strategy in action** – having set the scene, an example of Wal-Mart's use of operations to help it grow within the highly competitive retail market.

- **Executives roles** – a reminder of the section in Chapter 1 highlighting the operational and strategic roles of executives.

- **Business unit strategy** – looks at the requirement and reality of how strategy at the business unit level is developed and the reasons why this approach tends to be adopted.

- **Reactive role of operations in strategy development** – provides an in-depth explanation of why operations continues to play a reactive role in strategy development.

- **Recognizing difference within strategy formulation** – as today's markets are increasingly different, understanding difference is a central feature of strategy development.

- **Linking marketing and operations** – introduces the need for and approach to linking markets and operations and how this is achieved through markets.

- **Understanding markets** – two sections here look at the reality compared to the approach to be followed in completing the essential task of market reviews.

- **Developing and implementing an operations strategy** – explains one approach to developing an operations strategy and looks in detail at how this is implemented.

- **Operations strategy** – an illustration of operations strategy is provided that links market tasks to operations actions.

Finally, the book map opposite the first page of the chapter shows the position of this topic within the book and illustrates its overarching nature within the operations management field.

What is strategy?

Strategy embodies the aspects of both direction (what to do) and implementation (how to do it). The element of direction concerns the approaches a company can use to help it choose the markets (today and in the future) in which to compete, understand the competitive drivers in these markets while also assessing how it can influence its market position vis-à-vis its competitors. Implementation concerns how it can match or better meet the competitive drivers involved by prioritizing where and how to spend its time and money.

To help appreciate what this means it is useful to reflect on the meaning of the word itself. Derived from the Greek word 'strategos' a general, from 'stratos', army and 'aegin' to lead, the origin of strategy concerned the art of planning and directing large military movements and operations of a campaign or war. The transfer of the word to business activities is understandable and appropriate, where the market becomes the theatre of competition.

The parallels don't stop there. The Greek general would also have divided his army into different units, for example archers, chariots and foot soldiers. As with functions in a business, this leads to specialist skills and capabilities being enhanced. But, the general also quickly found out that to win a battle it was much better if the different parts of his army faced the same direction and their roles and activities in battle were agreed and coordinated. The same parallels also transfer to business and the same need to interface the different aspects of strategy and ensure cooperation and coordination between the parts is one key to success. Perhaps Mr James needs a crash course in the classics (see Exhibit 2.1).

Exhibit 2.1 The purpose of strategy – the James approach!

Evolution of strategy within a business

As companies grow, they cope with the greater level of complexity that results by splitting the total business activity into parts that are called 'functions'. Similarly, further growth leads to companies separating the total, and increasingly diverse, activities that result into two or more business units, divisions or similar organizational arrangements to facilitate managing the increased diversity that comes with size. One outcome of these changes is that strategy development now takes place at three levels – corporate, business unit and functional (see Exhibit 2.2). The substance of this chapter concerns the development and implementation phases of one of the key functional strategies, that of operations. But first, let's look at the three levels of strategy.

Levels of strategy

For most businesses, strategy needs to be developed at three levels (see Exhibit 2.2):

● Corporate – concerns decisions by the business as a whole in terms of the sectors in which it wishes to compete. At this level, companies decide where to invest or divest in terms of the overall business mix they wish to develop today and in the future.

● Business unit – within each chosen sector, an organization will usually have, depending on the terminology used, one or more firms, companies or business units. Each will serve different segments within a sector, although there may be some overlap. Such overlaps could be for reasons of history, convenience, preference, to reflect customer wishes or failure to reach agreement within the overall business.

Each business unit will need to develop a strategy in terms of its markets. Agreement on the current and future markets in which to compete is an essential strategic task and one in which all relevant functions must be involved. It is in these debates that functional differences need to be recognized and where resolution of strategic direction is taken. In that way, appropriate decisions on the markets in which to compete are taken at the business rather than functional level.

Exhibit 2.2 Levels of strategy and their distinctive tasks

Level of strategy	Distinctive tasks
Corporate	Strategic activity at the corporate level concerns the direction of the total business and addresses issues such as where to invest and/or divest, and priorities in terms of sales revenue growth. Implementation concerns the allocation of investment funds in line with these priorities.
Business unit	Business units comprise different parts of a total business. For example, corporate banking, retail banking, financial markets, mortgages, pensions and insurance would be separated into different business units within a bank. For each business unit, strategic direction concerns identifying the markets in which it competes, agreeing where it intends to grow (including new markets), the nature of competition and the relevant competitive criteria in its current and future markets, in terms of maintaining and growing share. Implementation concerns discussing and agreeing how and where to invest, in terms of functional tasks and alternative approaches.
Functional	Each business unit will comprise a number of functions such as sales and marketing, operations and IT that make up the total activities within a business unit. The strategic role of each function is to support those competitive dimensions within a market for which it is wholly or partly responsible. In this way, the market comprises the agenda for functional strategies and becomes the mechanism for determining development and investment priorities. Implementation concerns consistently meeting the competitive norms involved and selecting from alternative approaches to attain the improvement goals laid down.

● Functional – functional strategies prioritize developments and investments in line with the needs of agreed current and future markets. Examples of those criteria relating to different functions are provided in Exhibit 2.3. The strategic task for a function is consistently to meet or improve its level of support for relevant performance criteria. These can either be the sole responsibility of a function (for example meeting the delivery speed requirements of customers is solely an operations management responsibility) or the joint responsibility of two or more functions (for example shortening service/product development lead times would be the joint responsibility of several functions such as design, marketing, engineering, IT and operations).

At this early stage in our discussion on operations strategy, it is useful also to distinguish between market-driven or market-driving strategies.

Exhibit 2.3 Examples of functional strategic responsbilities

Function	Examples of criteria for which it is solely responsible
Design	Product and service design[1]
IT	System developments
Marketing	Brand name and customer relationships
Operations	Delivery reliability and quality conformance

Note   1   In a service company the design function is part of marketing's strategic responsibility.

Market-driven

Being market-driven concerns providing the competitive criteria in a market to the required levels, for example meeting the delivery lead times that customers require or expect, such as keeping queue lengths in a bank to (say) three minutes or less.

Market-driving

On the other hand, market-driving concerns proactively seeking ways to change the competitive norms and hence create a situation where a company can influence its market position vis-à-vis its competitors. In this way, an organization can improve on current, required levels of a given driver to gain a competitive edge. The ways to do this can be either a market-based or a resource-based approach[1] as explained below and summarized in Exhibit 2.4:

● Market-based – here companies proactively identify where market advantage could be gained by outperforming the current norms on one or more relevant market drivers and then allocating resources to this end.

● Resource-based – continuing the theme of being more proactive in arriving at appropriate strategies has seen the emergence of resource-based competition. Again the emphasis is to be knowingly proactive in seeking ways to change the competitive norms for market advantage. The orientation here is to exploit the potential of existing resources and capabilities in order to outperform current norms on one or more competitive drivers. However, it is also essential to ensure that the competitive advantages that result by consciously looking to exploit existing resources or create synergies within the organization are, in fact, what customers need and are willing to pay for should additional costs be involved.

Exhibit 2.4	Market-driven and market-driving strategies		
The strategic mix	Market-driven		Strategy based on understanding current and future markets and recognizing how the competitive drivers are time- and market-specific. Will differ depending on whether it concerns maintaining share, growing share or entering new markets
	Market-driving	market-based	Proactive approach to identify where advantage can be gained by outperforming current norms in one or more drivers and then investing in appropriate resources and capabilities
		resource-based	Exploit the potential of existing resources and capabilities to outperform current norms on one or more competitive drivers

The market-driven and market-driving strategic mix

For most companies their current and future markets will comprise a mix of both market-driven and market-driving strategies. Much of what a company sells, the customers it sells to, the markets in which it competes and how it competes within these today will be similar to yesterday and the same for tomorrow. But, being aware of the need proactively to seek ways to drive markets and exploit resource-based opportunities is an essential element of the strategic task in times when markets are increasingly different and competitive. For this reason, most companies will need to have a strategy that is a mix of the market-driven and market-driving approaches, as illustrated in Exhibit 2.4.

A recap on functional strategy development

At this point, let's pause and reflect. This chapter principally concerns the development of an operations strategy. As a key function within a business, one role of operations (as with other functions) is to contribute to meeting the corporate objectives set by a business and, in so doing, needs to be party to their agreement in order to exploit available opportunities while recognizing the timescales and constraints involved. As Exhibit 2.5 shows, strategy development is an interactive process linking all parts of a business with one another and with the objectives set within a given period. And, the core to this is the markets (recognizing the drivers and driving dimensions referred to earlier) in which a company competes. Note that the separation of the operations strategy in Exhibit 2.5 from the other functional strategy elements is merely to reflect the orientation of this book. It is important to remember that what needs to dominate strategy development is the business itself and not one functional view. Similarly, the Wal-Mart and Kmart illustrations in the next section are not intended to imply that emphasizing one functional strategy is better than emphasizing another but are provided to show the key roles of market understanding in giving direction and the implementation of functional strategies in bringing this about.

Exhibit 2.5 Markets at the centre of strategy development

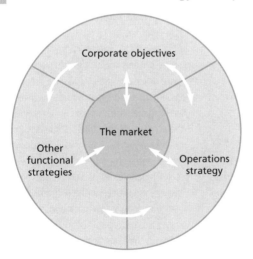

Operations strategy in action

To maintain profitable growth over time requires sound direction and relevant functions providing support for the needs of agreed markets. Operations is being recognized as a major, often dominant, player in determining and securing competitive advantage.

By comparing Wal-Mart with its close rival Kmart in Case example 2.1, we can show how a strategy may or may not work in practice.

Case example 1   COMPARING SUCCESS AT KMART AND WAL-MART

The year 1962 saw the birth of two retailers in the highly competitive retail market in the USA. Both were discount stores that looked alike, sold the same products, sought the same customers and bore similar names – Kmart and Wal-Mart. By the mid-1980s, Kmart was better positioned, with twice the stores, three times the sales revenue and greater visibility through its advertising and large urban presence. In 1987, Joseph Antonini was brought in to head up Kmart and was heralded as having 'get up and go', and a sound plan for growth and profit improvement. Sam Walton, co-founder of Wal-Mart and its CEO until his death in 1992, commented in his autobiography that in the mid-1980s so much about Kmart's stores was superior that at times it looked difficult to compete.

From 1962 to the late 1980s, Wal-Mart had principally located outside small towns and was taking market share from ageing Mom & Pop outlets. Kmart, on the other hand, had competed against other large discount retailers in competitive and expensive urban locations. When Wal-Mart decided to enter this arena, it did so on the back of its strategy to develop operations including extensive investments in sophisticated computer systems to help track and replenish its merchandise quickly and efficiently. To prepare for the encounter, Antonini's strategic focus was on his own strengths: marketing and merchandising. He invested heavily in nationwide television campaigns featuring glamorous television stars as presenters. Kmart's renewed emphasis on advertising and brand served to widen the gap between the two approaches. Kmart continued to be widely known through television, general advertising and its prime store locations. On the other hand, Sam Walton continued to concentrate investments and developments in operations. He invested tens of millions of dollars in a company-wide computer system linking cash registers to head office so enabling stores to quickly restock goods as they were sold. This, together with investments in trucks and distribution centres, not only increased control but also led to significant cost reduction. By the time Wal-Mart's sales matched those of Kmart in 1991, its earnings before tax were more than double and since then the gap has widened (see Exhibits 2.6 and 2.7).

So, Kmart relied heavily on a marketing-based strategy to improve its corporate image, reinforce the Kmart brand name and cultivate brand loyalty, while Wal-Mart's strategy was oriented to operations as its source of advantage – cost reduction to effectively support a wide product range and an operations inventory, allocation and distribution system that kept the shelves filled with the right products. Before Wal-Mart's 'invasion' of Kmart's urban-based territories, Kmart launched a five-year store refurbishment and development initiative, with a budget of $3.5 billion – all part of a strategy to smarten the company's outward appearance. Although relatively few people had seen a Wal-Mart advert let alone a store, the least visible parts of its operations-based strategy were, by the early 1990s, beginning to tell. Wal-Mart's sophisticated scanner, distribution and inventory systems meant that shelves had the right stock and the price discount strategy could be supported by low-cost operations. Internal store procedures such as accurate price labelling meant that delays and customer concerns over the accuracy of the store systems and procedures were rare. Meanwhile, Kmart was filled with distribution horror stories. An internal company report highlighted major loopholes in its service delivery system; empty shelves, employees without the skills and training to plan and control inventory and an in-place replenishment system incapable of ensuring that the price on the shelf was the same as that stored in the cash registers – a problem which led to an out-of-court settlement of some $1 million relating to 72 instances of overcharging. Exhibits 2.6 and 2.7 show the results of the two strategies. Probably the most telling statistic is that whereas Kmart's share of the total market from 1982 to the mid-1990s fell from 34.5 to 22.7 per cent, Wal-Mart's grew from 20.1 to 41.6 per cent in the same period. The ultimate statement of decline came in May 2003 when Kmart went into bankruptcy. Since then

Exhibit 2.6   Sales revenue: Kmart and Wal-Mart

| Year | Sales revenue ($bn) | | | |
| | Kmart | | Wal-Mart | |
	$bn	Index	$bn	Index
1985	22.0	100	6.4	100
1988	27.3	124	16.0	250
1991	34.6	157	32.6	509
1992	37.7	171	43.9	686
1993	36.7	167	55.5	867
1995	32.5	148	82.5	1289
1996	34.4	156	93.6	1463
1998	33.7	153	118.0	1843
1999	35.9	163	137.6	2150
2000	37.0	168	165.0	2578
2001	36.2	165	191.3	2989
2002	30.3	137	217.8	3403

		Earnings before tax		
	Kmart		Wal-Mart	
Year	$m	Index	$m	Index
1985	757	100	502	100
1988	1244	164	1069	213
1991	1301	172	2043	407
1992	1426	188	2554	509
1993	(306)	(40)	3166	631
1995	(313)	(41)	4262	849
1996	330	44	4346	866
1998	755	100	5641	1124
1999	959	127	7170	1428
2000	(370)	(49)	8715	1736
2001	(2725)	(460)	9957	1989
2002	(2900)	(483)	10568	2105

Exhibit 2.7 Earnings before tax: Kmart and Wal-Mart

Wal-Mart's sales now exceed the combined revenues of McDonald's, Coca-Cola and Walt Disney and it is the world's largest company by sales revenue. In the process, it has changed the face of global retailing. Sam Walton never claimed to be an original thinker but is quoted as saying:

> People think we got big by putting big stores in small towns. Really we got big by replacing inventory with information.

By this he meant the retailing technology that Wal-Mart pioneered; for example the company was first to share electronic point-of-sale (EPOS) information with its suppliers, thereby helping reduce inventory and cost.

In the early 1990s it began its international expansion and by the new millennium was already the biggest retailer in Canada and Mexico and had entered Brazil, Argentina, China, South Korea, Germany and the UK. By putting the customer as number 1 (for example the company's 'ten foot attitude' requires all employees coming within 10 feet of customers to look them in the eye, greet them and ask them if they need help), it has transformed the shopping experience for most customers. Couple this with its low-cost strategy based on highly efficient operations and distribution systems and it has the capability to dominate the retail market in several other parts of the world besides North America.

Julian Day (Kmart's new president) has turned things around. Having led the company out of Chapter 11 bankruptcy protection, he announced the first quarterly net profits in a long time – $276 million in the last quarter of 2003.

> By giving careful thought to the processes of sourcing, logistics, pricing, inventory management and in-store presentation, we have significantly improved the profitability of our market basket. Furthermore Mr Day has slashed inventory by 25 per cent in 2003 to $3.3 billion resulting in over $2 billion in cash and cash equivalents.[2]

www.kmart.com; www.walmart.com

Case questions

1 What is the key to Wal-Mart's success to date?
2 Highlight the strategic role of operations in this success story.
3 What strategic changes has Julian Day (the new president of Kmart) introduced as part of the company's recovery plan?

Executive roles – day-to-day and strategic dimensions

As businesses grow, activities are separated out into clusters of similar tasks. These are then managed as functions, which provide a structure to handle the growing complexity that comes with larger organizations, including the opportunity for relevant staff to specialize in one part of the business.

Within each of these functions executives have two sets of tasks:

● Day-to-day – to manage and control the range of activities that fall within their area of responsibility as well as the crossovers between functions. Also known as the 'operational' task.

● Strategic – to develop a functional strategy in line with the needs of agreed markets.

The operational tasks that make up the day-to-day role within operations management are covered by the contents of the book. A glance at the chart at the front of this chapter will give you an overview of what is involved. In simple terms it concerns managing and controlling those tasks necessary to provide services or make products and deliver them to customers. However, there is an equally essential role that concerns developing an operations strategy to support the needs of agreed markets, and although parts of the same executive task, they are different in orientation. For operations management:

- **The operational role** is to manage and control the various, wide-ranging tasks involved in providing services and making products and to do this efficiently by bringing about developments and improvements.

- **The strategic role** is to contribute to the debate about and agreement on the markets in which to compete in terms of retaining customers, growing market share and entering new markets. This could involve a market-driven and market-driving perspective (see Exhibit 2.4). Operations then needs to develop and invest in the delivery systems and infrastructure to provide those competitive dimensions for which it is responsible, for example price and delivery speed. In this way, operational capabilities are guided by strategic requirements (the needs of agreed current and future markets) and so help provide competitive advantage.

Thus, while operational tasks are built on internal efficiency, strategic tasks need to be oriented to external effectiveness; or, put another way, the operational role is to do things right and the strategic role is to do the right things.

Business unit strategy

Functional strategies interface with the business units of which they are part and, in that way, these two levels of strategy need to interface. While this chapter concerns developing an operations strategy, before addressing this let us first look at how a business unit strategy should be developed compared to how it often is.

As discussed earlier, organizations use functions in order to facilitate the management task involved. However, businesses are not a number of different parts or functions, but are wholes. An essential task, therefore, is to rebuild the parts back into a whole and nowhere is this more critical than at the strategic level within a firm. Also, as Exhibit 2.8 illustrates, the heads of functions will appropriately form part of the strategy development group as these parts form the whole business.

Exhibit 2.8 Strategic group composition

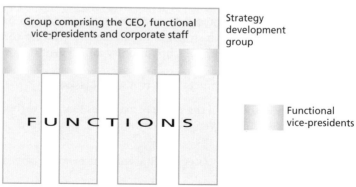

Group comprising the CEO, functional vice-presidents and corporate staff

Strategy development group

FUNCTIONS

Functional vice-presidents

Exhibit 2.9 Ideal business unit strategy-making process

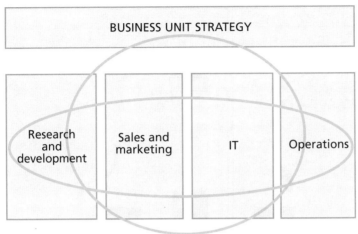

Discussion and agreement about current and future markets have already been high-lighted as an integral part of strategy development. This step requires functions to discuss their views on markets, address and resolve differences and agree on what is best for the business overall. Similarly, the outcomes of this debate would be major inputs into developing a strategy at the business unit level, with the desired process being in line with that outlined in Exhibit 2.9. Functions would debate current and future markets, and highlight constraints and opportunities as part of their input into developing a strategy for the firm, thus again providing both a market-driven and market-driving orientation. Similarly, opportunities and strategic initiatives would be signalled at the business unit level and form part of the essential debate and strategic outcome.

Reality is far from this. 'In many firms, business unit strategy is developed as a series of independent statements. Lacking essential integration, the result is a compilation of distinct, functional strategies that sit side by side, layer on layer in the same corporate binder. Integration is not provided if, in fact, it was ever intended.'[3] The outcome, rather than being similar to that represented by Exhibit 2.9, is more like that shown in Exhibit 2.10, with the dialogue in Exhibit 2.11 reinforcing the point.

Exhibit 2.10 Real-life business unit strategy-making process

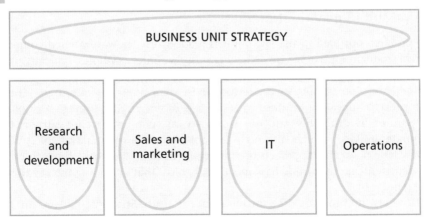

Mr James's view of strategy – the big picture, not whether functions can make it happen

© AMD Publishing

Reasons for current approaches to developing strategy

If the reality of strategy development is so divorced from the essential integrated nature of the task, the question which at once comes to mind is, why? There are several reasons and the key ones are summarized below.

Statements on strategy developments stop at the interface

Statements put forward by academics, consultants and other strategy specialists on how companies should go about developing a strategy allude to integration but in reality ignore this essential step. They stop at the interface. For example, a review of major textbooks and articles on both corporate strategy and marketing strategy would show that they fail to embrace the dimension of operations. Whether it would inhibit the approaches and arguments put forward, make it too complex to describe and explain or signal an implicit belief that delivering strategy is not an integral part of its development, the reality is that the essential interfacing central to Exhibit 2.9 is never aspired to, let alone delivered, in most approaches to corporate and marketing strategy development.

The pursuit of generic strategies

The problem outlined in the last point is made worse, however, when companies seek to resolve strategic approaches by reviewing business units as wholes, typically undertaken by overlaying corporate diversity with generic, strategic solutions. Niche, low-cost, core competence-type arguments are seductive in their apparent offerings.[4] The promise of uniformity is appealing to those with the task of developing strategies for businesses that are typified by difference and not similarity, as such approaches purport to identify a corporate similarity which, although desirable, is inherently not available.[5] What seems to drive the logic of this approach to strategy is, in part, similar to that which sparked the alchemist's dream of turning base metal into gold – that of finding the key that will unlock the strategic maze.

However, nothing could be further from the truth. Strategy problems are complex and the process of resolution is not one that leads to generalizations. Strategy development needs to be a process of distillation, with the task of identifying the very essence of what comprises a business. As competitive pressures grow, markets become increasingly different, not increasingly similar. Without adequate insight companies will be unable to decide the appropriate strategic direction. The overarching view of markets provided by generic strategies is typically reinforced by subsequent actions such as measuring actual sales in total and not by market and segment type. Such reaggregations reinforce the classic view of similarity that characterizes strategy by implying that one dollar of sales is the same as any other dollar of sales.

Strategy outcomes assume a similarity that does not exist

Markets are increasingly different not increasingly similar. However, when companies debate markets the outcomes assume a similarity that does not exist. The aim of the first phase in strategy is to reach agreement about the markets in which a business unit competes or wishes to compete. The key to this is to identify, test and reach agreement on the several markets in which business units typically operate.

The drift to generic strategies was highlighted in the last point. Side by side with this is the tendency for companies to assume a level of similarity within their business that, in fact, is not present. Business units are typically in more markets than they assume. This lack of insight exists because of an inadequate debate about markets, and a failure to seek to identify potential differences. In part this is due to executives allocating too little time to what should be an ongoing, in-depth, corporate-wide discussion. Furthermore, the role model set by strategy discussion has been outputs that have not sought to clarify difference. The outcome is that this critical first step results in a lack of essential insights into the differences that increasingly make up a company's markets.

The extent of this corporate confusion was clearly illustrated by the outcomes of an extensive case-based research programme that comprised in-depth reviews and analyses within 54 of the 160 participating companies. These businesses were all part of a UK government initiative called the Manufacturing Planning and Implementation Scheme. The essence of the scheme was to help companies understand and apply the different phases in developing an operations strategy and then to use these outputs to set and implement priorities in terms of development and investment. To help provide resources to undertake this work, companies were given government grants of 50 per cent of the consultancy fees involved, up to a given maximum. To provide clarity on the context and purpose of the approach embodied in the scheme, guidelines on the intent and an in-depth statement on what to do was also given and further supplemented by forums, individual guidance and feedback on the initial results part way through the scheme.

To evaluate what happened in practice a team of researchers, led by the author, had access to all details within any application. Of the 54 in-depth reviews completed, in only one project was the market review sufficiently adequate to provide the insights necessary to develop an operations strategy. Typical of the outcomes was the following example.[6] The market review undertaken on a medium-sized food company failed to identify any differences within its markets and reported them to be homogeneous. Work by the research team with company executives and using customer data identified and agreed four segments with differing levels of price sensitivity and different delivery lead time requirements, as shown in Exhibit 2.12. Research in the service sector has resulted in similar findings. The Cool2Serve programme also found that most companies do not reach agreement on the segments they serve and the competitive drivers involved.[7]

Exhibit 2.12 Result of researchers' market review

Aspect	Relative position of the four segments
Price sensitivity	most 1 3 least 2 4
Length of delivery lead time	short 4 1 3 long 2

History of functional dominance

Approaches to developing corporate strategy have a history of being dominated by single functions. In many manufacturing companies, for example, the operations function dominated the corporate strategy process until about the mid-1960s. In a world where, up to that time, there was an undercapacity in relation to demand, selling what you could make was typically the dominant thrust of strategy. As the capacity/demand imbalance redressed itself, selling into markets became more difficult and heralded the birth of marketing's key role in the success of companies. This strategic role has, in many companies, been strengthened with the continued growth in competition, especially where markets are increasingly characterized by overcapacity as emerging nations develop or companies enter existing markets in which they currently do not compete. As with operations before, marketing has acquired the mantle of providing strategic direction not only in its own eyes but typically in the eyes of others and the firm as a whole. The outcome is that much of the time marketing's view goes undiscussed and unchallenged.

Markets versus marketing

Coupled with the last point is the fact that many firms fail to make the critical distinction between markets and marketing. Whereas markets comprise the business itself, marketing is a function. Thus, while marketing will play a necessary role in the debate and agreement about markets, it is critical that its views of market needs are countered, challenged and enlarged. For, while its insights are essential to the understanding of markets, they are limited in the perspective they offer on two counts:

- The reality of delivering the needs of markets is only fully understood by those functions charged with undertaking those tasks. While marketing has the responsibility for meeting several of these criteria, there are many that are in the domain of others. In fact in some, if not several, instances, marketing's strategic role is limited, in that other functions are responsible for supporting most, if not all, of the needs of a company's chosen markets.

- The constraints, timescales and investment implications involved in maintaining or improving support for those performance criteria that relate to market success can only be gauged and assessed by the function involved.

Not recognizing these essential differences and not incorporating all relevant perspectives within the strategy debate will only lead to inadequate and superficial outcomes. However, even Gianni's approach in Exhibit 2.13 is a somewhat exaggerated outcome of strategic events.

Exhibit 2.13 Gianni proposes the marketing strategy to take the firm from good to great

The proactive role of marketing in strategy development

One consequence of the last two points is that marketing expects to, is expected to and does take a proactive role in strategy development. While this is the desired stance to be adopted by all relevant functions, many organizations, in acknowledging and supporting marketing's proactive role, fail to recognize the need to incorporate other perspectives essential to the discussion and agreement on markets and strategic direction. The proactive stance adopted by marketing is seen as an implicit (if not explicit) statement that markets and marketing are one and the same and that marketing has a singular role in these essential strategy decisions that are central to the business as a whole.

The reactive role of operations in strategy development

The fact that the operations function has an exacting and critical corporate role to play is never in dispute. Couple this with the high cost and fixed nature (changes take a long time to bring about) of its investments, then it is paramount for a company to understand the business trade-offs involved in operations decisions. As operations is a principal player in providing those criteria that maintain and improve market share and successfully entering new markets, then not knowing how operations will ensure the provision of that support is risk taking of the highest order, especially given the highly competitive and fast-changing nature of today's markets and the fixed and high-cost dimensions involved in development and investment.

Reasons for reactive role of operations in strategy development

Given this scenario, why is it that operations executives adopt their current reactive role and why does the situation appear not to improve? There are several reasons, including those listed below.

Operations managers' view of themselves

A major contribution to this current position is that operations managers also see themselves holding a reactive corporate brief. They believe that their role concerns a requirement to react as well as possible to all that is asked of the operations delivery system. They see their role as the exercise of skill and experience in effectively coping with the exacting and varying demands placed on the system and to reconcile the trade-offs as best they can. But rarely do they explain or provide data to illustrate these trade-offs as part of the corporate strategy debate and so they allow these decisions to be made at the level of the business rather than the level of the operations function.

The company's view of the operations manager's role

The view of operations of its own role is reinforced by the company's view of its strategic contribution. Although chief executive officers (CEOs), managing directors or their equivalents are actively (and appropriately) engaged in discussions with marketing about decisions on markets and customers, the same level of time investment is typically not given to understanding key operations decisions and their impact on market support. A lack of recognition is thereby reflected in the typically low level of involvement that results.

Too late in the corporate debate

Very often operations executives are not involved in business unit strategy discussions until the decisions have started to take shape. The result is that they have less opportunity to contribute to decisions on strategy alternatives and, consequently, always appear to be complaining about the unrealistic demands made of them and the problems that invariably ensue.

Lack of language

Underpinning these organizational barriers is the added difficulty that, on the whole, operations managers do not have a history of explaining their function clearly and effectively to others within the company. This is particularly so for strategy issues that need to be considered and the operations consequences that will arise from the corporate decisions under discussion. Reasons for this failure, however, cannot wholly be placed at the operations manager's door. The knowledge base, concepts and language so essential to providing explanations and insights have not been developed in the same way. Surrogates for strategy in the form of panaceas have more often than not taken the place of strategic inputs, and the support given to these approaches by academics and consultants has reinforced this stance. The regular heralding of just-in-time (JIT) and total quality management (TQM)-type initiatives (explained more fully in Chapters 10 and 11 respectively) have been seen, in part at least, as the strategic contribution of operations. In a similar way, calls to become flexible, for instance, point to an apparent state in operations that offers a capability to do most (if not all) things. Purposefully general, such overtures are without essential definition and direction and, more importantly, purport to offer the rest of the business an ability to support any strategic alternative equally well and without making any trade-offs. Furthermore, when the superficiality of this state is exposed, the pundits for such strategic alternatives merely switch the phrase (to become versatile and agile are two more recent proposals), arguing that the subtle differences in definition remedy the serious misgivings inherent in the discarded phrase. The cycle then restarts.

For many businesses, strategy comprises the independent inputs of different functions. However, this invariably leads to functional conflicts that, without a way of being resolved, will result in inappropriate corporate decisions being taken. Where this concerns process and/or infrastructure investments, it involves two important characteristics. These investments are large in size and fixed in nature. Consequently, they typically take a long time to determine and install, and a long time to change. Thus, it is essential that companies understand the relevance of proposed investments in terms of their current and future markets.

The need to recognize difference at the level of strategy formulation

Any executive being asked 'Are all your businesses the same?' or 'Are all parts of one business the same?' would answer 'no' to both questions. Strategy formulation must acknowledge that reality. To describe a company's strategy as having a uniform approach ignores the essential difference that characterizes today's markets.

In the same way, as markets are different, the strategic response by functions needs to recognize and reflect those differences, and none more so than in operations, with its large and fixed investments.

Developing a functional strategy involves deciding on development and investment priorities that are, in turn, determined by those market needs for which the function is solely or jointly responsible. The book addresses two sets of different but related issues:

1   How does operations management contribute to the corporate strategy debate in such a way that
    - its perspectives are understood

● the needs of the different markets in which a company competes are exposed and agreed

● the investments to develop and the performance criteria to measure those operations capabilities necessary to support the needs of current and future markets are clearly identified?

2 To illustrate the different implementation approaches at the operational level within operations so that appropriate consideration can be given to alternatives, both in terms of market support (doing the right things) and internal efficiency (doing things right).

This chapter outlines the approach to developing strategic direction within operations.[8] The rest of the book details the alternative implementation approaches that may be used at the operational level. Which ones are best for a company will depend upon the nature of the business itself, factors such as size and service/product complexity and the requirements of the markets in which a firm competes. It is necessary, therefore, to review the options detailed in each of the following chapters, both in terms of themselves and also within the context of the strategic trade-offs that have to be made.

Finally, most parts of a business have an impact on one another. Operations investments are substantial (typically 60–70 per cent of the corporate total) and embody a set of fixed trade-offs that will remain constant unless deliberately changed. The competitive dimensions that operations can support will be reflected in the trade-offs embodied in its investments. What operations can do well and less well needs to be clearly recognized as it will impair its level of support in different markets and will signal the desired changes in trade-offs that future investments must provide. Similarly, in its market-driving role, operations needs to clearly explain and communicate ways in which its resources and capabilities (either within the operations function or in conjunction with other functions) can provide competitive advantage and the investment and timescales involved to bring this about.

Similarly, marketing has an impact upon operations. Its decisions make demands upon delivery systems, processes and infrastructure provision. Incremental change, so often the way in which a company's markets move, usually results in a gradual and increasing mismatch between the demands on the operations function and its ability to respond. While operations managers intuitively recognize the consequences of these changes, they typically do not have, as highlighted earlier, the concepts and language to argue their case and alert the company to such issues of strategic importance. The result is frustration and an ever-widening gap between the marketing and operations functions even though they are both essential contributors to the business, its strategy formulation and overall success.

This chapter addresses the need to close the gap by providing approaches to strategy building that bring together marketing and operations, facilitate open discussion about the business and enable sensible resolution of functional differences at the corporate level.

Linking marketing and operations

The importance of linking marketing and operations is as paramount as it is logical. They are, after all, two sides of the same coin. Together, they constitute the basic task in any business – the sale and delivery of services and products. On the surface it would seem simple to unite their efforts to meet the needs and expectations of customers. The reality is often far removed from what should be the desired goal of those involved.

Many current strategy approaches reinforce corporate misunderstanding and promote

Exhibit 2.14 Operations and marketing perspectives on key issues

Issues		Perspectives and goals	
		Operations	Marketing
Services/ products	range	Restricting range enhances volumes, helps reduce cost and simplifies control	Customers typically seek variety. Restricting range reduces segment coverage
	standardization vs customization	Lack of change reduces uncertainty and room for error. Limiting server discretion maintains cost and throughput profiles	Customization often important, particularly in mature markets. Server discretion personalizes service, often at little cost, and enhances customer retention
Costs and profit		Measured on meeting cost budgets. Resists orders that increase costs. Has no control over pricing	Sales revenue is the key performance measure. Profit implications are not part of the decision or evaluation. Higher costs are not part of its budget considerations
Productivity improvements		Reduce unit costs	May cause a decline in quality conformance provision
Location of facilities		Considerations concern costs and the convenience for suppliers and staff	Customers may find it unattractive, undesirable and, for a service business, inaccessible
Managing capacity		High utilization of capacity has an effect on costs and assets. Pressure to manage capacity and thereby keep investment as low as possible	Service/product may be unavailable when needed. Quality compromised in high demand periods
Job design		Oriented to minimizing errors and waste. Simplify tasks and use technology where possible	Employees oriented to operations task and not customer need. Restricts ability to meet changing requirements as they occur
Queues		Optimize use of available capacity by planning for average throughput	Increases lead times. Customers facing long lead times or queues may go elsewhere

interfunctional differences and rivalry. Functional dominance in corporate strategy development is a typical source of such problems. The result is that key functions tend 'to treat one another as competitors for resources rather than coming together to serve the external customers'.[9] This is well illustrated by Exhibit 2.14 that lists the different, often opposing, views held by operations and marketing on a range of issues. In markets that are increasingly competitive, there is an urgent need to close the gap, increase corporate awareness of the differences and difficulties involved in the status quo and facilitate discussion based on an improved understanding of functional perspectives, business options and overall consequences. The way forward is to resolve interfunctional differences not at the level of the function, as is often the case now, but at the level of the business. These genuine conflicts need to be addressed and resolved in terms of what is best for the business as a whole. In that way the tensions, concerns and rivalries that typically characterize the marketing/operations relationship can be set to one side. The focus can then shift from competing functional views about what is best overall, to each function doing its part to implement the chosen strategy.

The question is how? Before addressing this issue, however, Case examples 2.2–2.5 illustrate how the link has been established and the successful outcomes that result.

Case example 2   PRICE LEADERSHIP STRATEGIES AT SAM'S, ALDI AND IKEA

The advent of the warehouse model for distributing food and dry goods provides a good example of companies competing on a price leadership strategy.

Sam's, the US-based chain of outlets, and **Aldi**, the German-based food chain, provide examples of how this has been successful because both companies have supported their chosen price leadership strategy with a clear integration of marketing and operations that cooperate rather than compete in providing this strategy. The basis of these retail offerings is a no-fuss concept. The design is simple, making it easy to shop. Wide gangways, bare floors, inexpensive lighting (basic, bright and abundant), basic displays (often with the manufacturer's original packaging), comprising warehouse-style racking and sturdy wire mesh cages, and limited support staff keep costs down. Of the product range on offer, Aldi keeps a limited (typically about 25 per cent of the range offered by traditional supermarket competitors), mainly own-label range of goods.

Sam's, on the other hand, matches its own market requirements for a one-stop shopping experience, which constitutes customer expectations in the free-spending, low-price, no-hassle US consumer market.

IKEA, the Swedish firm that specializes in complete furnishings for the home from floor coverings and curtains to tables, chairs, bookcases and bedroom suites, provides a further example. In essence, IKEA is a chain of self-service warehouses with current annual revenues of about $16 billion. Operations is clearly linked to the price leadership strategy of the business and delivers a no-fuss, broad and easy-to-take-away range of products. The provision of play areas and restaurant facilities as part of the service delivery system reflects and encourages the concept of the family-based shopping expedition that characterizes these outlets.

www.walmart.com; www.aldi.com; www.ikea.com

Case example 3   OPERATIONS DEVELOPMENTS AT BENETTON

In the mid-1960s Luciano Benetton and his sister Giuliana started designing and making brightly coloured clothes. With cutting-edge designs, the company grew sales and profits year on year. An integral part of this success story has been the company's operations developments to support the whole supply chain.

Information system and manufacturing process investments – in fashion markets, forecasting which styles and colours would sell best is difficult. An integrated information system to provide feedback on current actual sales at each retail outlet, coupled with a manufacturing process that makes woollen garments and then dyes them in line with actual sales, led to major gains for Benetton. Inventory and consequently the size of retail outlets was cut and the products that sold well were the ones that manufacturing made. This fast feedback, short manufacturing lead times and quick deliveries better meet market needs while cutting inventory and asset investments.

Modern manufacturing facilities – the late 1990s saw the opening of Benetton's state-of-the-art manufacturing plants in Castrette, north of Venice. The latest developments are part of a $350 million investment to make tailored apparel, skirts,

jeans and cotton garments. These plants have been integrated with the woollen plant built in 1986 and the automated warehouse handles all the storage, invoicing, pick-up and shipment of garments to the 7000 points of sale around the world. The aim of the latest investments was to reduce staff in the existing cutting and packing operations as a way of matching unit costs from alternative suppliers in the Asia Pacific and other low-cost areas of the world, while maintaining Benetton's local subcontractors' base comprising 200 companies and their 30,000 employees. While many competitors now outsource from countries such as Indonesia and Turkey, Benetton has continued to develop its local supply base while achieving its essential cost reductions through combined investments in operations. In this way it is able to reflect the short lead time requirement of its markets with its in-house and outsourcing policies. High investment in the front and back end of garment making, with local subcontractors providing a short response service – a manufacturing sandwich with advanced technology encasing a more labour-intensive filling – provides low costs and fast response advantages in a competitive, fashion-led market.

www.benetton.com

Case example 4   AMERICAN EXPRESS'S DIFFERENTIATION STRATEGY

American Express is able to charge a price premium for its card, both to its customers and the businesses that accept it for payment, by differentiating itself from other credit cards. Support for this differentiation strategy has, in part, been provided by operations – replacing lost cheques anywhere in the world, immediate use if cards have been lost, mislaid or stolen (with 24-hour replacement to follow) and year-end summaries of card use.

www.americanexpress.com

Case example 5   RESTRUCTURING WITHIN THE HEALTHCARE INDUSTRY

Restructuring within the healthcare industry grew apace in the 1990s, with worldwide annual mergers and acquisitions into four figures and over $60 billion. Delivering the potential is proving harder to bring about. Those that have are looking to changes in delivering care and the operations support involved.

Quantum Health Resources, an Indianapolis-based firm specializing in the treatment of haemophiliacs, reduced by over 20 per cent the typical annual patient bill of $100,000 by assigning 'personal care managers'. In this way drugs are managed, hospitalization due to lack of personal care is cut and drug regimes are under constant review, improving fit and eliminating waste.

ParadigmHealth is a California-based company specializ-

ing in caring for people with catastrophic injuries such as brain damage and serious burns. Annual patient care costs can run as high as $2 million but this has been cut by half through specializing support for patients, treating more people at home and assigning support teams to sets of patients, thereby improving operational support and lowering costs.

The growing need to control and reduce the operational costs of delivering healthcare has led, in the USA, to a spurt of vertical integration by insurance companies moving into the management of hospitals and health clinics. In that way, they recognize that the essential need to link sales and operations can be made, enabling business to grow, deliver a better service and become more profitable.

www.gentiva.com; www.paradigmhealth.com

Case questions	Review the four examples and consider the following questions:
	1 Identify the key way in which operations supports each company's markets.
	2 Now compare each review with one another and table the similarities and differences involved.

Linking corporate objectives and functional strategies through markets

Functional strategies concern investing and developing in ways that support the needs of markets in terms of being both market-driven and market-driving. As Exhibit 2.5 showed earlier, the role of functional strategies is to contribute to meeting agreed business objectives. The form and size of contribution will vary from market to market but the strategic development process for all functions is similar:

- **Phase 1 – understand markets**, ensuring both a market-driven and market-driving approach while maintaining an ongoing, rigorous review throughout this first critical step.

- **Phase 2 – translate** these reviews into strategic tasks. For example, if price is a competitive driver, then the task is to reduce costs; similarly if on-time delivery is a competitive factor, then improving the reliability of meeting customer due dates is the task.

- **Phase 3 – check** that what is currently provided matches what is required in a market-driven scenario or the new level in a market-driving scenario.

- **Phase 4 – develop a strategy** (the prioritizing of investments and developments) to close the gap where the level of provision falls short of the requirement or achieve the new level of performance in a market-driving scenario.

- **Phase 5 – implement** the necessary investment and development priorities.

In this way, companies are better able to coordinate functional contributions, with markets appropriately providing the common agenda for all. Invariably, two functions that are central to this task are operations and marketing, as the next section reflects.

The framework given in Exhibit 2.15 is intended to help explain what currently happens as well as what needs to take place so that the link between corporate marketing decisions and operations can be made. The exhibit shows that the framework has five columns, each representing a step.

Exhibit 2.15 Framework for reflecting operations strategy issues in corporate decisions

Corporate objectives	Marketing strategy	How do you qualify and win orders in the marketplace?	Operations strategy	
			Delivery system choice	Infrastructure choice

• Sales revenue growth
• Survival
• Profit
• Return on investment
• Other financial measures
• Environmental targets
	• Product/service markets and segments
	• Range
	• Mix
	• Volumes
	• Standardization versus customization
	• Level of innovation
	• Leader versus follower alternatives
		• Price
		• Quality conformance
		• Delivery:
		  speed
		  reliability
		• Demand increases
		• Colour range
		• Product/service range
		• Design leadership
		• Technical support supplied
		• Brand name
		• New products and services – time to market
			• Choice of various delivery systems
			• Trade-offs embodied in these choices
			• Make-or-buy decisions
			• Capacity:
			  size
			  timing
			  location
			• Role of inventory in the delivery system
				• Function support
				• Operations planning and control systems
				• Quality assurance and control
				• Systems engineering
				• Clerical procedures
				• Payment systems
				• Work structuring
				• Organizational structure

Notes 1 Although the steps to be followed are given as finite points in a stated procedure, in reality the process will involve statement and restatement, for several of these aspects will impinge on each other.
      2 Column 3 concerns identifying both the relevant order-winners and qualifiers.

Column 3 concerns analysing and understanding the market and is at the centre of the framework. The arrow going from left to right represents the need to link corporate objectives and marketing strategy to the market, while the one going from right to left represents the need to link operations strategy to the market. In this way, how a company competes in its markets and how it may wish to drive the market is at the centre of the debate. This allows functions to discuss current and future markets, how competitors behave and their potential responses in the future, alternative ways of competing in these, the constraints, developments, investments and timescales involved and how they can coordinate their strategic efforts to meet the agreed objectives for the business as a whole. As Exhibit 2.16 illustrates, this is an interactive approach and needs to be an ongoing process forming an integral part of the senior executives' role.

The interactive, ongoing nature of the strategy debate

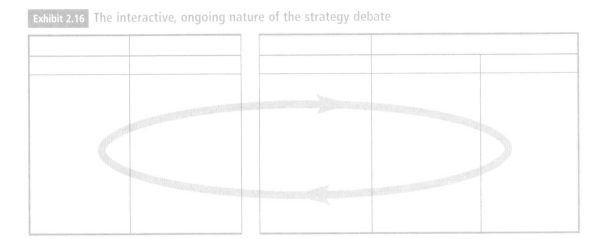

How the framework operates

The objective of using the framework in Exhibit 2.16 is to develop an operations strategy for a business. The steps involved are outlined below. Although presented here in a sequential form they will, in fact, constitute an ongoing set of discussions, with statements and restatements of corporate objectives and functional strategies comprising the outcome of the process.

1 Corporate objectives – these are set by the business as a whole and typically take the form of targets for sales revenue growth, profit, return on investment and other financial measures. They may well include non-financial objectives such as environmental targets.

2 Marketing strategy – developed by the marketing function to meet relevant corporate objectives. It would typically be concerned with approaches to growing sales in existing markets and strategies to enter new markets.

3 How do services and products qualify and win orders in the marketplace? Addressing this question constitutes the core step in the development of functional strategies, where the executive group (see Exhibit 2.8) debates and agrees markets (to include both the market-driven and market-driving dimensions) and the qualifiers and order-winners involved. This step will be expanded on in the next sections.

4 Operations strategy: choice of delivery system – part of the strategic task of operations is to develop a delivery system to provide the services and products involved, as well as underpinning the qualifiers and order-winners (for example price, quality conformance and on-time delivery) that form part of the sale.

5 Operations strategy: choice of infrastructure – operations other strategic task is to develop the relevant aspect of infrastructure (for example organizational structure, procedures and controls) that form part of the way it meets the qualifiers and order-winners for which it is responsible.

Understanding markets – the reality

Let us start by restating the important distinction made earlier in the chapter. Markets and marketing are not the same thing. Whereas markets constitute the business itself, marketing is a function. As there will typically be several markets served by a business, the relevant criteria to keep and grow existing market share, change the rules (become market-driving) and enter new markets will differ from market to market as well as from each other. The strategic role of functions (including marketing and operations) is to debate and agree the markets in which to compete and support those criteria for which they are solely or jointly responsible. In that way, the company becomes market- (as opposed to marketing-) driven.

The cornerstone in all of this is understanding markets. Markets are the essence of a business, the very reason for its existence and, consequently, you can never know too much about them. Identifying differences, supporting these insights with clear explanations and descriptions and verifying them with supporting data would, therefore, be reasonable to expect. The reality is, however, that the necessary clarity is usually not provided. The case examples given earlier are the exception rather than the rule. Instead, current approaches to corporate strategy development typically fail to provide sufficiently adequate insights on which to build functional strategies. One outcome of this is that without adequate clarity, each function's investment and development priorities are in line with what they think are the best aspects to improve. The essential link between market needs and functional strategies is not provided.

Current approaches to market reviews usually embody a number of characteristics that contribute to the general nature of the outcomes and the provision of statements that lack essential meaning. The result is descriptions of markets that imply a similarity that does not exist. For example:

- Markets are usually only looked at and described from a marketing point of view. Segment descriptions are typically based on factors such as geographical regions (for example Europe and North America) and sectors in which customers operate (for example food and financial services) or service/product clusters. While this has a sound rationale from a sales and marketing viewpoint in terms, for instance, of arranging promotional and sales activities and the orientation of technical literature and support, the assumption is carried forward (as it is implied) that such segments are each coherent in terms of the way a company needs to compete. A pause for reflection will lead to a recognition that this is both an unreal and inaccurate inference to draw. Although from the viewpoint of marketing, Europe/North America or food/financial services, for example, are coherent segments, from an operations point of view there will be different sets of demands from groups of customers within these marketing segments and hence these will constitute different markets. Case examples 2.6 and 2.7 illustrate this point.

Case example 6   MARKET POSITIONING OF BOTTLED WATER

Look at a bottle of mineral water and consider that your company provides the label on the outside of the bottle. Now, in which segment would your sales and marketing department place this customer – the one who produces and sells the bottles of mineral water?

The likelihood is that this customer would be placed in the 'beverage' or 'soft drinks' segment (that is, the sector in which your customer operates). From an operations point of view, however, on which product a customer attaches the label it provides is of little consequence. The key issues for operations concern factors such as level of price sensitivity, the length of delivery lead times and the size of demand peaks throughout the year. By segmenting markets, in this instance, by the sector in which a company's customers operate, the implication is that all customers in this beverage segment (our example here) are equally price-sensitive, require similar delivery lead times and have similar demand profiles throughout the year. As you can see, taking only one function's view gives insufficient insight and leads to unfounded assumptions that would result in inappropriate strategic decisions.

Case questions	1 Why would marketing place this customer in a 'beverage' or 'soft drinks' market segment?
	2 Why is operations view of customers to do with criteria such as price sensitivity, length of delivery lead times and the size of demand peaks?
	3 How would you use both perspectives to arrive at an overall strategy?

Case example 7 CUSTOMER SEGMENTATION IN THE ELECTRICITY INDUSTRY

A major UK electricity distributor segmented its customers into large businesses, small and medium-sized enterprises (SMEs) and residential customers. The basis for the segmentation was the relative size of sales revenue per customer account. The initial marketing strategy was to grow sales revenue and, as a consequence, its efforts were directed towards increasing its large business customer portfolio as the best way of meeting this objective. However, a noticeable decline in profits as a percentage of sales led to a review. Operations data revealed that profit margins in the large business segment were, on average, more than 40 per cent lower than for SME customers. Marketing's successful drive to increase sales revenue had also led to a lack of effort to retain, let alone grow, SME customers. The outcome was an increase in overall sales revenue but a decrease in profit percentages.

Case questions	1 List side by side the market dimensions used by marketing and operations above.
	2 How would you use both perspectives to arrive at an operations strategy?

- Views of markets are positioned at too high a level in the strategy process. As emphasized throughout, with growing competition markets are becoming increasingly different rather than increasingly similar as competitors seek to gain customers by changing the offering. The only way to uncover this essential difference is to dig deep. Current approaches fail to do this and result in statements about markets that are broadbrush in nature and inadequate in terms of the insights they provide.

- The inadequacy of the outputs that result is further compounded by a use of general phrases to provide market descriptions. Words and phrases such as 'customer service' and 'delivery' are examples of this. Each can be defined in more than one way, and once there is more than one meaning, misunderstanding and a failure to clarify will follow. The result is that general descriptions are used in analysing markets that in themselves embody more than one segment. One dimension compounds the other, with the result that generalities mask critical and essential insights and necessary clarity is replaced by unhelpful ambiguity (see Case examples 2.6 and 2.7 above).

The result is that the key, first step of clarifying and agreeing markets, the basis on which to link corporate direction and relevant functional support, is not provided. As a consequence, the failure to coordinate strategic direction continues, interfunctional rivalries are reinforced and the approaches used to develop corporate strategy do not deliver the very essence of what is required or intended.

Given the increasingly dynamic, competitive and fast-changing nature of markets, it is of paramount importance that companies improve the way they develop corporate strategy and particularly the need to forge the link between marketing and operations.

In summary, what typically happens now is that:

- Market descriptions are limited to the views of marketing. While these views give essential insights from a marketing perspective, they fail to yield the key differences and provide essential insights into markets from the view of other functions, particularly that of operations.

- The words and phrases used to describe markets are not sufficiently precise to provide the clarity needed to yield essential insights.

- The procedures used are not sufficiently exacting to expose and challenge these critical deficiencies, and inadequate outcomes result.

Given the pivotal role of market understanding to strategy development, how does a company improve its approach in this key phase of the process? This question is answered in the following section.

Understanding markets – the approach to follow

Clarity about markets is essential. Companies are in multiple markets and the outcome of the debate on markets should identify, and provide a clear understanding of, the differences that exist.

The steps to secure these insights are as follows:

1 Avoid general words and phrases – as markets are at the core of a business, using general words and phrases needs to be consciously and rigorously avoided. Each dimension should be expressed on its own and a single definition needs to be associated with each word or phrase used. In this way, each competitive dimension put forward as being relevant can be discussed separately and its relevance assessed. One classic example of this is the phrase 'customer service'. While a desirable objective, the answer to the question 'what does it mean' is not self-evident as it embodies a number of potential meanings. Using 'customer service' to describe the competitive nature of a market thus confuses rather than clarifies.

2 Long lists denote poor strategy process – the outcome of the discussion on how a company competes in its markets is typically a long list. The intention seems to be to leave nothing off the list, thereby covering all aspects. Nothing could be further from the truth. This phase of the strategy process concerns distilling the very essence of how a company has to compete. In this way essential clarity is provided.

3 Separate out order-winners and qualifiers – a further step to improve a company's understanding of its markets is to separate relevant competitive criteria into:

- **Qualifiers** – these criteria get a service or product into a marketplace or onto a customer's shortlist and keep it there. They do not in themselves win orders but provide the opportunity to compete. Conversely, the failure to provide qualifiers at appropriate levels will lead to a loss of orders. In this way, qualifiers are order-losing in nature, as a failure to provide a qualifier results in not being on the list – the opportunity to compete is not in place. In such situations, competitors do not win orders from a rival, rather the rival loses orders to its competitors.

- **Order-winners** – however, having gained entry to a market is only the first step. The task then is to know how to win orders against competitors who have also qualified to be in the same market. With qualifiers, you need to match customers' requirements (as do competitors), whereas with order-winners you need to provide them at a level better than your competitors.

Finally, when applying this concept there are some key points to remember:

- Qualifiers are not less important than order-winners, they are different. Both are essential. With qualifiers, a company needs to qualify and requalify at all times to stay on a customer's shortlist. If you are not on the list, you cannot compete.
- Order-winners and qualifiers are time- and market-specific – they will be different from market to market and will change over time within a market.
- The relevance and importance of order-winners and qualifiers will typically be different to retain market share, grow share in existing markets and enter new markets.
- The relative importance of qualifiers and order-winners will change when moving from being market-driven to being market-driving.
- As highlighted earlier, not all criteria will be either a qualifier or an order-winner. Some criteria do not relate to some markets.

4   Weight qualifiers and order-winners – to improve clarity still further, it is essential to weight qualifiers and order-winners in the following way:

- **Qualifiers** – it is adequate and appropriate to limit the classification of qualifiers into two categories – qualifiers (denoted by a Q) and order-losing sensitive qualifiers (denoted by a QQ). The latter is intended to alert a company to the fact that failure to provide criteria which are considered to be 'order-losing sensitive' will lead to a rapid loss of business.
- **Order-winners** – the appropriate step here is to allocate 100 points across all the order-winners within a market. This forces the different levels of relevance to be exposed and provides an essential step in distilling out importance. It is essential, therefore, to avoid procedures where stars (for example) are allocated as a way of indicating importance, as this approach avoids confronting and resolving the key step of determining the relative importance of one criteria with another. Such approaches bypass the need to discriminate between the relative importance of one criterion vis-à-vis another – as any level of importance can be attributed to any criteria.

Implementing an operations strategy

The reality of implementing a functional strategy is to translate the order-winners and qualifiers for which that function is solely or jointly responsible into relevant actions. The rest of this book addresses the key areas in operations and the detailed approaches to both managing the wide range of tasks that comprise the operations function and the approaches to improving operations, whether in terms of doing things right (the efficiency dimension integral to any management role) and doing the right things (the strategic role concerning support for those criteria in a market for which operations is solely or jointly responsible). Thus, support for markets is a mechanism for identifying those areas that need to be prioritized in terms of investments and developments.

As you will see from Exhibit 2.17, the translation from order-winners and qualifiers into actions is a straightforward step. Implementation, on the other hand, is typically far from easy. Knowing which approach to follow for the best results and then making the developments happen is the underlying management capability. What to do and how best to do it are addressed throughout the different topics covered by this book. The place to start in terms of operations strategy is linking the strategic tasks (that is, the relevant order-winners and qualifiers) to courses of action. Exhibit 2.17 gives an overview of what needs to be completed.

| Exhibit 2.17 | Translating order-winners and qualifiers into actions |

Relevant order-winners and qualifiers	Typical areas for review and improvement
Price	Reduce costs in all areas particularly regarding materials and overheads which typically make up some 70–90 per cent of total costs
Quality conformance	Provide services or make products to specification. Build quality into the process and delivery system rather than checking conformance after the event. Also, improvements here impact costs
Delivery reliability	Assess on-time delivery performance by service/product and customer. Review current approaches to meeting orders – involves discussions on the extent to which services and products can be or are made to order and the role of activities and investments such as scheduling and inventory in meeting these requirements
Delivery speed	Review the elements of the operations process with the purpose of reducing the lead time in the various steps comprising the service delivery system or manufacturing process
Service/product range	Review the process capability and skill base in relation to current and future service/product range requirements. Identify and supplement capabilities in line with proposed needs
Demand spikes	Assess current capacity provision in terms of the ability to rapidly increase in line with known or anticipated changes in demand. Approaches include short-term capacity and inventory-holding alternatives
New services/products – time to market	Identify the elements of lead time within the new service/product development process for which operations is responsible. Assess the work involved and opportunity to reduce the task content, current start times in relation to the overall procedures and opportunities to complete part or all of the task in parallel (rather than in sequence) with other elements of the process
Meeting specific customer needs	Assess current approaches to identify how standard services and products can be modified in line with specific customer requirements and the impact on costs, lead times, quality conformance and the overall schedule

Operations strategy – an illustration

With an understanding of the approach to and outcomes of operations strategy developments, it is opportune to provide a short illustration of what is involved.

Exhibit 2.18 is the outcome of a company's full and extensive debate about its markets. The firm is a contract hire car company. Although it supplies cars to individual customers, the majority of its business is supplying fleets of cars to the public and private sectors. The review provided in Exhibit 2.18 covers the three segments that make up the majority of the company's sales. There are other smaller segments but these have been omitted here. The review has been further simplified by not including the forward look required to highlight any anticipated changes in the relevance of the order-winners and qualifiers and corresponding weightings.

Some key points highlighted by this review, and how they translate into an operations strategy, are now provided:

1 **Markets** – the review illustrates, from an operations strategy point of view, the multi-

Exhibit 2.18 Order-winners and qualifiers in three markets of a contract hire car company

Criteria	Market segment		
	Public sector	Private sector	
		Large fleet user	Small fleet user
Price	60[2]	40	Q[3]
Quality conformance[1]	40	40	50
Financial stability of supplier	QQ	Q	–
ISO 9000 registration	Q	Q	–
Proximity of vehicle supplier	Q	–	–
Existing customer list	–	Q	–
Simplicity of documents and procedures	–	–	Q
One-stop-shop provision	–	–	20
Service specification[4]	–	20	30

Notes 1 Quality conformance concerns fulfilling the service specification within a contract. For new customers, access to existing customer's experience to verify the level of conformance quality achievement would be provided by the company.
2 Order winners have a weighting, the total of which is 100.
3 Q = a qualifier and QQ = an order-losing sensitive qualifier.
4 For large fleet users this includes the ability to meet a customer's specific needs as well as the range of added-value products (for example fuel card provision) on offer.

segmented nature of a company's markets. That the three segments highlighted are different is eminently clear.

2 **Functional strategies** – the criteria listed in Exhibit 2.18 are the sole or joint responsibilities of several functions. When developing each functional strategy, these qualifiers and order-winners would need to be reflected in each function's development and investment priorities.

Exhibit 2.19 highlights those criteria that operations have to support. The remainder would form the strategic task of other functions. For example, service specifications would be a marketing task. Hence, marketing would need to review the current service specifications on offer and propose ways (if need be) to improve the overall specification. This would

Exhibit 2.19 Operations actions arising from Exhibit 2.18

Criteria	Some operations initiatives (that is, strategy) that may result
Price	Develop supplier relations and negotiate contracts for products (for example cars) and services (for example maintenance programmes and insurance) to reduce costs while meeting specifications. Streamline internal processes and procedures to reduce costs
Quality conformance	Meet the agreed service specification and improve its provision
ISO 9000 registration	Continue to meet the ISO provisions and requirements
Simplicity of documents and procedures	Continuously simplify documents and procedures to make them increasingly user-friendly
One-stop-shop provision	Develop the internal capability within operations to provide all aspects of the service offering

typically include the range of services provided and the extent to which the specific needs of large and small fleet users are being met and how any proposed changes would improve that provision. In turn, these marketing proposals would form part of a corporate strategy debate that would include an operations review of any proposals and highlighting any investment and development (together with timescales) that would need to be made to meet any proposed changes.

Exhibit 2.19 lists the criteria for which operations is partly or solely responsible and identifies some of the initiatives that operations may undertake to maintain or improve its provision of these – in other words, the operations strategy.

Reflections

Developing an operations strategy involves a number of phases and the first of these is the most critical but typically the one in which operations does not adequately partake. Being proactively part of and contributing to the ongoing debate about markets, agreeing the order-winners and qualifiers involved in current and future markets and being party to market-driving opportunities comprise the first critical step.

Market- or marketing-led?

Markets are the common denominator of functional strategies. With markets analysed in depth and agreement reached on the current and future directions to follow, the strategic task in operations is to develop the capabilities to support relevant order-winners and qualifiers. However, as highlighted earlier, companies do not always keep in sharp focus the critical difference between being market-led and being marketing-led. To substitute the business (market) perspective by a functional (marketing) perspective will invariably lead to distorted strategies and eventually to corporate disadvantage. Unfortunately, in many businesses, marketing is increasingly characterized as having the perceived role of creating ideas, with the rigour of testing business fit left to others. This trend not only trivializes the important functional perspective of marketing, but detracts from its fundamental strategic contribution.

Moving to a business-level strategic debate

Markets are a business not a functional decision. Whatever the strategic mix between being market-driven and market-driving, they lie at the very centre of strategy development, interconnecting corporate objectives with their delivery and interfacing between functional strategies, as illustrated in Exhibit 2.20. In this way they form the agenda for the development of all functional strategies and help ensure that differences and alternatives are resolved at the level of the business and not the level of the function.

Companies need to seek continuously to line up their functional strategies to the needs of markets. One of the major players in delivering strategy is operations. The critical nature of its role reflects the increasing importance of those order-winners and qualifiers for which it is jointly or solely responsible. As shown in the case examples given throughout the chapter, getting it right in operations results in sizeable and sustainable advantage. Although not the only strategic player, in most organizations its role will be important while in many it will be central to the continued success of the overall business.

Exhibit 2.20 The market interface

Note   Although the marketing and operations functions are illustrated here, all functions with a strategic role would need to be involved in this interfacing procedure.

Key Elements of Operations Strategy

- As companies grow, clusters of activities are separated out and managed as functions. Typical of these are accounting and finance, sales and marketing, human resources, IT, operations and research and development. The reason for this is to facilitate the management of the corporate complexity that follows growth.

- Functions have a dual role to provide the day-to-day management of the areas for which they are responsible and developing strategies to support agreed markets. The latter role is the subject of this chapter, the former is addressed in the rest of the book.

- Functional strategies are one of the three levels at which strategy needs to be formulated.

- As with other functions, operations strategy concerns investments and developments to support the order-winners and qualifiers for which it has sole or joint responsibility.

- Operations needs to be proactive in forging these market discussions, as changing operations is typi-

cally expensive and involves long lead times. In reality, however, operations tends to wait for service, product and market-related discussions to happen and then responds to any outcomes after the event. This reactive style is typical of many operations executives due in part to their own and others' perceptions of what the strategic role of operations should comprise. One additional reason concerns the lack of concepts and language to help explain and deliver operations perspectives within the corporate strategy debate.

- As marketing and operations fulfil the basic activity within an organization (that is, the sale and provision of services and products), linking these together when formulating strategy is a key requirement. The way to achieve this is through identifying and agreeing in which markets a company wishes to compete and grow, and then establishing the current and future order-winners and qualifiers that relate to these. Exhibit 2.15 summarizes this link while Exhibit 2.17 provides examples of how relevant order-winners and qualifiers translate into aspects of operations that need to be reviewed, developed and improved.

● Throughout the chapter, examples of how organizations have successfully developed operations strategies in support of chosen markets are provided. These examples illustrate how an operations strategy works, while the end-of-chapter questions cover issues raised throughout this section. Have a go at answering some of these as a way of checking your understanding.

Self-check

1 Strategy embodies the aspect(s) of:
  a Direction (what to do) ☐
  b Implementation (how to do it) ☐
  c Both a and b ☐

2 Business unit-level strategy within an organization concerns:
  a Identifying the markets in which it competes, agreeing where it intends to grow, the nature of the competition and the relevant competitive criteria ☐
  b How to support the competitive criteria in the market and determining development and investment policies ☐
  c The direction of the total business and issues such as investment and divestment priorities ☐

3 The strategic role of executives concerns:
  a Managing and controlling the range of activities that fall within their area of responsibility ☐
  b How to support the competitive criteria in agreed markets and determining development and investment priorities ☐
  c Both a and b ☐

4 The marketing function typically has sole responsibility for:
  a Service and product design ☐
  b Brand name and customer relationships ☐
  c Systems developments ☐

5 A market-driven strategy is based on:

  a Exploiting the potential of existing resources and capabilities within a business ☐
  b Identifying where advantage can be gained by outperforming current market norms on one or more competitive driver ☐
  c Understanding current and future markets and their competitive drivers ☐

6 Discussion and agreement about current and future markets:
  a Is the sole responsibility of the marketing function in a business ☐
  b Is the responsibility of all the functions within a business ☐
  c Is a corporate, not a functional responsibility ☐

7 When developing strategy, it is important to realize that:
  a Markets are increasingly different ☐
  b Markets are increasingly similar ☐
  c Generic strategies can be applied to all markets ☐

8 An operations perspective on restricting the range of services and products offered by a business is that:
  a Customers typically seek variety and thus restricting range reduces segment coverage ☐
  b Restricting range enhances volumes, helps provide the opportunity to reduce costs and simplifies control ☐

c Restricting range means that technical developments cannot be incorporated into new services or products ▪

9 A typical area for review and improvement if delivery speed is a market order-winner is:

a Reducing costs in all areas particularly regarding materials and overheads ▪

b Reviewing the elements of the operations process ▪

c Reviewing current scheduling methods ▪

10 Market order-winners and qualifiers are:

a Time-specific ▪

b Market-specific ▪

c Both a and b ▪

Study activities

Discussion questions

1 Why would delivery reliability typically be designated an order-losing sensitive qualifier (QQ) for a carton company supplying packaging to a food company?

2 In the early 1970s, when the Japanese entered the European colour television market, they took market share partly on the basis of providing higher levels of conformance quality. Explain how the improvement of this factor worked in terms of gaining sales. In the period of the early 1970s was quality conformance an order-winner or qualifier in the European colour television market? What is this criterion in today's market – an order-winner or qualifier? Explain your reasoning.

3 Why should all functions within a company, including operations, participate in business-level strategic planning?

4 Why are operations-related considerations becoming more important in formulating business strategy? Describe one example from both the manufacturing and service sectors (other than those given in this chapter) that illustrate how they have gained competitive advantage from operations.

5 Many companies fail to appreciate the fact that the most critical orders are the ones to which a company says 'no'. Explain.

Assignments

1 Identify the order-winners and qualifiers for the following enterprises:
● a private medical company
● a company hiring cars for business or leisure
● a pharmaceutical company
● a furniture removal company.

2 What would constitute the operations strategy for the four organizations reviewed in Assignment 1?

3 Search the internet to find a European company with operations in China. What is the stated rationale for this decision? Do you think any other factors are involved?

Exploring further

Baden-Fuller, C and Pitt M *Strategic Innovation*, Thomson, London (1996).

Fine, CH *Clockspeed*, Perseus Books, Reading, MA (1998).

Fitzsimmons, JA and Fitzsimmons, MJ *Service Management: Operations, Strategy and Information Technology*, McGraw-Hill, New York (2000).

Ford, H *Today and Tomorrow*, Productivity Press, Cambridge, MA (1926).

Gibson, R (ed.) *Rethinking the Future*, Nicholas Brealey, London (1997).

Hayes, FH, Pisano, GP and Upton, DM *Competing Through Capabilities*, Free Press, New York (1996).

Hayes, FH, Pisano, GP, Upton, DM and Wheelwright, SC *Operations, Strategy and Technology: pursuing the competitive edge*, John Wiley, New York (2004).

Lovelock, CH and Yip, GS 'Developing global strategies for service business', *California Management Review*, **38**(2) (1996), pp. 64–86.

Lowson, RH *Strategic Operations Management: The New Competitive Advantage*, Routledge, London (2002).

Mintzberg, H, Ahlstrand, B and Lampel, J *Strategy Safari*, Prentice Hall, Hemel Hempstead (1998).

Normann, R *Service Management: Strategy and Leadership in Service Business*, 2nd edn, John Wiley & Sons, Chichester (1991).

Ortega, B *In Sam we Trust: The Untold Story of Sam Walton and How Wal-Mart is Devouring America*, Times Business/Random House, New York (1998).

Porter, ME 'What is strategy?', *Harvard Business Review*, November–December (1996), pp. 61–78.

Porter, ME 'Strategy and the internet', *Harvard Business Review*, March–April (2001), pp. 63–78.

Schonberger, RJ *World Class Manufacturing: The Next Decade*, Free Press, New York (1996).

Sigafoos, RA and Easson, RR *Absolutely, Positively Overnight: The Unofficial Corporate History of Federal Express,* St Lukes Press, Memphis (1988).

Slack, N and Lewis, M *Operations Strategy*, Financial Times/Prentice Hall, Harlow (2002).

Notes and references

1 See, for example, Gagnon, S 'Resource-based competition and the new operations strategy', *International Journal of Operations and Production Management*, **19**(2) (1999) pp. 135–8; Grant, R 'The resource-based theory of competitive advantage: implications for strategy formulation', *California Management Review*, **33** (1991) pp. 114–22.

2 Foster, L 'Kmart records a landmark profit', *Financial Times* (London) 19 March 2004, p. 20.

3 Terry Hill, *The Strategy Quest*, AMD Publishing (1998) p. vii. Copies are available from the publisher whose address is 'Albedo', Dousland, Devon PL20 6NE, UK, or email amd@jm-abode.freeserve.co uk or fax 0044(0)1822 882863.

4 Illustrations of the generic approach to strategy formulation are found in the articles and books of several writers in the field of corporate strategy, of which two classic examples are provided by ME Porter and CK Prahalad and G Hamel. Porter's early contributions include 'How competitive forces shape strategy', *Harvard Business Review*, March–April 1979: 86–93, *Competitive Strategy: Techniques for Analysing Industries and Competitors*, Free Press, New York (1980) and *Competitive Advantage: Creating and Sustaining Superior Performance*, Free Press, New York (1985). Prahalad and Hamel's contributions include 'The core competency of the corporation', *Harvard Business Review*, **68** (1990), pp. 79–91. Both approaches proposed overarching solutions to competitive strategy insights and resolutions – in this way they propose to resolve the increasing diversity that typifies today's corporations by overlaying it with generic solutions.

5 *The Strategy Quest*, op. cit., p. vii.

6 Manufacturing, Planning and Implementation Scheme – Analytical Coordination, Final Report (unpublished).

7 Hill, A and Hill, T 'Customer Service: Aligning Business to Markets', Executive briefing, Templeton College, University of Oxford (2003).

8 These approaches and the issues involved are dealt with in greater depth in the following books by Terry Hill; *Manufacturing Strategy: Text and Cases*, 3rd edn, McGraw-Hill/Irwin, Burr Ridge, IL (2000); *Manufacturing Strategy: Text and Cases*, 2nd edn, Macmillan – now Palgrave Macmillan (2000) and *The Strategy Quest*, op. cit.

9 Schneider, B and Bowen, DE *Winning the Service Game* Harvard Business School Press, Boston, MA (1995), p. 200.

book map

Part

1

- 1 Managing Operations
- 2 Operations Strategy
- 3 Managing People

2

PROCESSES

- 4 Designing and Developing Services & Products
- 5 Designing Service Delivery Systems
- 6 Designing Manufacturing Processes
- 7 Location and Layout
- 8 Managing Capacity
- 9 Technology Developments
- 10 Operations Scheduling and Execution
- 11 Managing Quality

3

- 12 Managing Inventory
- 13 Managing the Supply Chain
- 14 Process and Delivery System Reliability and Maintenance

4

- 15 Time and Productivity
- 16 Improving Operations

5

- Managing Operations in Practice: Long Case Studies

SUPPLIERS

INPUTS

OUTPUTS

CUSTOMERS

Managing People

Outline of chapter

People are central to service and product provision. The operations role of effectively managing this resource together with the other people relationships within and outside a business combine to highlight the key nature of this part of the operations task.

Why is managing people important?

Executive overview

With the content elements now in place, we turn our attention to the important aspect of managing people, the style dimension of the job. As with the first two chapters you will see from the book overview the overriding nature of this aspect of the task. Increasingly companies are recognizing the key task of managing people and are placing appropriate emphasis on this element of the job, particularly in operations. This chapter highlights many important features in this task and the following aspects are covered in detail:

- The opening section highlights the size and nature of changes in the workplace and illustrates these by dimensions such as the increasingly competitive nature of markets, the growing use of temporary staff, employee attitudes to work and their commitment to organizational goals, the higher technical content of jobs, the pace of change, particularly regarding shorter service or product life cycles, the growing dimension of government employment legislation and the relative insecurity of employment.

- General definitions used in describing the job of work are then provided. These include job content that establishes the scope and depth of work, job satisfaction and motivation and how these differ, and job performance and the role of management in creating an environment where the ingredients of skill and attitude can coexist to enhance performance.

- The next section outlines *traditional* approaches to work design. This, in turn, is split into three sections – first, organizational design which includes the use of specialists, hierarchical structures, and the tendency to control from a distance. The second section looks at role design including work patterns and the specialization and contribution of staff. The final section looks at job design including enlargement, rotation, enrichment and work schedules. Each dimension is discussed and how it impacts the current work structures is explained.

- The chapter then moves on to *new* approaches to work design and covers the sectional breakdown used earlier – organizational, role and job redesign. The detailed aspects covered here include the learning organization, what it involves and what it can deliver; developing a change-oriented organization and the cultural and behavioural shifts involved; the changing role of managers in terms of creating conditions where people want responsibility, will learn and hence manage themselves such that they maximize their contribution to an organization as well as their own learning; and the trend towards flatter organizations is introduced and the changes it brings to organizational design are discussed.

- The aspect of role redesign covers the dimensions of employee involvement and empowerment and the different forms it can take. Job redesign is discussed in terms of current job profile and the move towards increasing the scope of work to include elements of planning, doing and evaluating.

- The role of training and development in bringing about these changes is then highlighted.

- The move towards flexitime and job-sharing arrangements is introduced and examples of the schemes used in organizations are explained.

- Other people-related issues including recruitment, staff retention, the growing use of temporary staff, staff appraisals and managing operations overseas are then discussed.

- The final area is that of ergonomics, and the workplace, environmental and behavioural factors are introduced.

Introduction

You will recall from the notes introducing Part 1 of the book that style (how a manager manages people and relationships) is one of the central tasks in managing operations, as it is with other functions. People are a key resource in a business and central to meeting both the operational (day-to-day) and strategic tasks and objectives. It is, therefore, appropriate that this chapter is positioned in Part 1 as it signals the importance and universality of this dimension throughout the book. Furthermore, as you proceed through the rest of the book, you will note frequent references to and detailed discussion about people and their role within the successful undertaking of the tasks that make up the operations function. Operations managers have to meet the challenge of creating an environment that helps people develop their full potential, where people care sufficiently to want to do a good job and the needs of both the people and the business are met within the workplace. Progressive companies have long since recognized the key role of people in the continued success of a business and, therefore, the need to safeguard and nurture their human capital.

Managing 60–70 per cent of those employed and the relationship building that comes with cross-functional activities and outsourcing work constitutes a significant task. While this challenging task competes for attention with all the other operations priorities, the sound and responsive management of human resources in an organization is essential for long-term success. Whereas companies are able to control materials, design business processes and develop procedures to a level that will almost guarantee that the service or product specification is met, the role and contribution of people in the delivery system are essential to ensure this provision. To develop and maintain delivery systems that consistently meet customers' requirements and expectations, companies have to recognize the need for and embody the dimension of employee commitment into their design and delivery. Only in this way can processes be consistently maintained and developed to meet the increasingly competitive nature of today's markets.

Until the last two decades many organizations took the narrow view of the nature and extent of people's contribution in the delivery system – that of completing the physical tasks involved in service and product provision. The role of people in the planning, improvement and evaluation of processes was neither recognized nor required. Why this was so, the change in managing people that is being adopted and the nature of their contribution in today's organizations are discussed in the rest of the chapter.

Changes in the workplace

As economies, societies and technologies develop, so attitudes, expectations and other dimensions that concern the workplace will also change. Businesses need to recognize and anticipate how these developments will affect the nature of work, the changing roles of those involved and how best to manage the people within organizations as they evolve. This section sets out the principal changes that have and are taking place in the workplace so as to set the scene and provide context for the later sections that address approaches and developments to the ways of managing people.

Increasingly competitive nature of markets

The increasingly competitive nature of markets has been already highlighted and, as explained in the last chapter, the strategic role of operations concerns supporting the market-related order-winners and qualifiers for which it is solely or jointly responsible. In many markets, the order-winning and qualifying criteria that relate to operations are becoming more important in terms of both retaining and growing market share. In such circumstances the ability of managers to organize resources to meet these needs is paramount. Central to this provision are the people that work in operations, and how they are managed and motivated is increasingly important to the eventual outputs. Managing an organization's human resources to meet the needs of a business while allowing and encouraging the people involved to attain their full potential is a critical operations management role. As markets become increasingly competitive the contribution of everyone to help an organization meet these new challenges is essential. Part of the way to bring this about lies in the structure of organizations, work design, how well people are motivated to do a good job and the involvement of people in the continuous improvement of all aspects of the operations task and work environment.

Outsourcing aspects of human resource management and growing use of temporary staff

Two significant changes have entered the general style of running organizations in the last five years:

- many people who work for organizations are no longer traditional employees of those organizations
- more and more businesses have outsourced many of the tasks traditionally undertaken by the human resources (HR) function.

The outcome is that businesses no longer have the traditional relationship with their staff and no longer manage major aspects of this relationship with the people who are, in reality, their staff – trends which are likely to grow in the future. While it's one thing to take advantage of the flexibility that comes with using temporary staff or to outsource the more tedious aspects of HR management, it's quite another for companies to take their eye off developing their staff as an essential part of staying competitive and deriving strategic advantage.

If, by outsourcing parts of the HR function, organizations damp down the importance of or even lose their capability to develop and retain key people, they will become seriously disadvantaged. While there is some rationale for outsourcing the more mundane aspects of people management to a third-party provider, organizations need to take great care that they don't damage or destroy their essential relationship with people.[1]

Employee commitment

As economies develop, people's attitude to work and the inherent commitment they have to an organization's goals typically change. While organizations retain many people who are self-motivated, find their work challenging and wish to complete tasks as well as possible, there are many who need to be encouraged to work well. This is not really surprising. Many people go to work for reasons based on custom and necessity. Also, the job opportunities open to many rarely afford a wide choice and are, by and large, prescribed by education, experience, physical and mental abilities, personality and chance. Consequently, many take on jobs that, after a time, tend to become repetitious and dull, a situation that has been increased by the growing number of low prestige jobs (often referred to as 'McJobs', for obvious reasons) in the retail and service sectors.

The ability to inspire the emotional and intellectual commitment of people needs to be high on the corporate agenda and a critical skill that operations executives have to develop and apply. Although the operations task is seen as being inextricably bound up with technology, processes, materials and other tangible dimensions of the job, managing people is not only sizeable (operations executives manage those directly involved in the delivery system as well as a range of support staff) but critical to the operations task and overall success of a business. Consequently, improving people's jobs, creating opportunities for them to influence and improve their working environment and linking their contributions to business outcomes must be provided and sustained.

Technical content of jobs

While the increasing use of technology developments in the workplace has increased the technical dimensions of some roles, for many jobs the technical content has declined. This trend will continue as it forms the basis of the productivity improvement so essential to becoming and remaining competitive in current and future markets. Where the technical content has grown, the higher levels of technology lead to improved processes, with fewer but better educated people for whom the motivational needs must be recognized and met. On the other hand, for those people where the technical content of work has declined, the downside is that the inherent interest that this provides is lost. To compensate for this loss, other ways to motivate people need to be sought and introduced.

Pace of change

Organizations also have to deal with the issues discussed so far in an environment where the rate of change is higher both in terms of frequency and extent. In addition, reducing life cycles, the global nature of markets, the relative insecurity of employment and the worldwide sourcing of services and products add to the dynamics of the business environment in the twenty-first century.

Information-related technologies have changed work roles and organizational relationships. Beepers and mobile telephone systems empower people to interact with others, including customers, outside the formal reporting structures of organizations. Teleworking requires different management skills and staff responses to work. Technology-based provision of services such as call centre arrangements is changing the roles of functions as well as individuals.

Innovations such as these need to be accommodated within revised organizational structures and are challenging operations managers in the new millennium. The pace of change is not easy to live with, but those companies that develop organizations that accept change as a way of life and progressively involve people in better serving their customers and developing and improving their delivery systems will succeed in the future, as the San Diego Zoo development outlined in Case example 3.1 illustrates.

Case example 1 **INTRODUCING WORK TEAMS AT SAN DIEGO ZOO**

Until recently, the wild animals were not the only ones plotting their escape from the San Diego Zoo. Many employees felt as if they were in cages, too. Although their cages were figurative, not literal, the effect was the same: the employees felt as if they were trapped in rigid, dead-end jobs, without the power to make a difference.

In an effort to raise the quality of life for both animals and employees, zoo management decided to restructure radically the way the zoo saw itself. Instead of a place that merely displayed wild animals, the San Diego Zoo transformed itself into an organization that could delight its customers by creatively educating visitors about the animals and their habitats.

Zoo officials got rid of traditional cages and spent millions of dollars to create 'bioclimatic zones' where the animals could feel at home. The employees of each zone were organized into work teams to brainstorm ideas for making the zoo a better place to work as well as for entertaining and educating visitors.

At two of these zones, Gorilla Tropics and Tiger River, the work teams began to function as separate organizations, with team members or immediate supervisors making almost all the decisions on hiring, vacations and budgets. 'It is like managing your own business here', one team member explained.

Not all employees were immediately enamoured with the new arrangement, however. Some cynically saw the work teams as a way for management to squeeze more work out of them. But even the sceptics came round eventually, and now almost everybody agrees that the zoo is a better place to work.

Employees were not the only ones to benefit from the restructuring. Many senior managers at the zoo are also top-notch curators, but the pressure of day-to-day decision making had kept them too preoccupied to pursue their true vocations. With the work teams now handling most of these operating details, the curators can focus on their areas of expertise.[2]

www.sandiegozoo.org

Case questions 1 What aspects of the 'Changes in the workplace' section are illustrated here?
2 What were the key features that brought about these changes?

Legislation

In more developed economies, legislation relating to the workplace has been on the increase over the last decade which, together with other government regulations, government-required paperwork and tax compliance, has added to the burden of employing people both in terms of time and cost. In fact, between 1980 and 2000 the number of US laws and regulations regarding employment policies and practices increased by 60 per cent from 38 to 60. In Europe, the European Union is following a similar path.

However, it is not just the increased paperwork and procedures that managers need to understand, handle and follow but also the need to adhere to these in the context of the threat of legal action. Adding to the number of lawsuits are the growing incidents of sexual harassment cases. Between 1991 and 2000 the number of these cases filed with the Equal Employment Opportunity Commission in the US more than doubled from some 6900 a year to almost 16,000. And for every case filed, ten or more were being settled in-house, each requiring many hours of investigation and hearings. Operations managers are typically in the thick of this. One outcome is the time it takes away from the core tasks of meeting customer needs, improving performance and developing people. They no longer see people as the company's greatest asset but as its greatest liability![3]

General definitions

It will be helpful at this stage to check the definition of some general terms used when discussing work and jobs, such as job content, satisfaction and performance.

Job content

Job content establishes the scope and depth of work. Scope is the range of tasks that make up a job. Thus, a job with narrow scope means that it contains few tasks and will tend to be highly repetitive. A widening of job scope implies that the range of tasks involved is increased horizontally. This increases the variety of the work performed and reduces monotony, but does not increase the responsibilities within a job, or the depth of the work involved. Exhibit 3.1 illustrates how the content of job B is greater than job A on both the dimensions of scope and depth.

Job depth refers to the degree of authority people have to plan and organize the work for which they are responsible. It concerns the level of control that they have over their own working environment. Thus if people have no influence over the planning of their work and have to carry out the plans of others, the job depth is low. Therefore the assembly line worker whose rate of working is controlled by the pace of the line and who carries out the tasks planned by others has a low job content (both low scope and low depth). Similarly, an audio/copy typist who is required to prepare a narrow range of work to an agreed layout and format has a low job content.

Exhibit 3.1 Depth and scope of two jobs

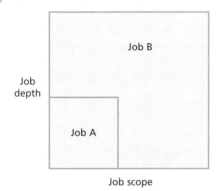

Job satisfaction and motivation

Job satisfaction and motivation are not synonymous. Job satisfaction reflects a person's attitude to the job and the level of interest it holds, and increases organizational loyalty and commitment rather than performance. Motivation, on the other hand, concerns the desire to perform well which could lead to increased effort and a higher performance. The distinction between aspects of work that lead to satisfaction or dissatisfaction and those that motivate people was well drawn by Hertzberg.[4] He emphasized the difference between those factors that led to dissatisfaction if not maintained (referred to as 'hygiene factors') and those that prompted motivation (referred to as 'motivators'). Factors such as physical conditions, security, pay and relationships were put forward as hygiene factors, while aspects of work such as personal growth, responsibility and achievement were classed as motivators. Motivation, therefore, plays an intermediate role between satisfaction and performance, for even a satisfied person will only tend to meet performance standards when adequately motivated.

Job performance

Job performance is dependent not only upon the level of motivation that exists but also upon a person's ability. For good job performance standards to be achieved and sustained, it is essential that both skill and attitude form the ingredients of the work situation. Unless both these aspects are reviewed, therefore, results will be less than adequate.

Traditional approaches to work design

Some of the principal philosophies of organizational, role and job design that have influenced business cultures in the past are now reviewed. It is not intended that this should be an exhaustive list but it aims to provide a basis for later discussion on some key features in work design that organizations are revisiting as a way to better harness the experience and capabilities of staff. As the three topics are part of the same whole, you will note that there is some overlap between them.

Organizational design

As explained in Chapter 2, as organizations grow they cope with the resulting complexity by breaking the business into parts that we call 'functions'. For most companies functions are used as the building blocks by which organizations are structured. While based initially on pragmatism, this brings with it a mix of advantages and disadvantages, some of which the next sections highlight.

Control through specialists

Functions become responsible for parts of the total task which not only makes it more manageable but also enables the staff to become proficient regarding the skills and capabilities that reflect the technical and behavioural dimensions of the job. In addition, organizations also introduce specialists with a brief to improve relevant functions by developing and improving procedures, systems and activities within the broad area of their specialism. The result is that activities that were once completed in one part of an organization are now housed under the control and auspices of the specialist function. This has taken place for several reasons:

- the traditional view often held by organizations was that all activities of a similar nature should be under one function
- an executive function (one responsible for part of the principal activity of an organization such as operations and sales) was willing to shed some of its total task
- a specialist function's inclination to grow the size of its area of responsibility.

These developments have, in turn, led to a number of problems:

- Developments in specialist fields have often outpaced the understanding of those managers responsible for the executive functions in which the specialist advice and developments will be applied. Hence, the eventual users and custodians of technology have difficulty in participating in discussions on the technology developments in question, both in terms of technical fit and appropriateness of application.

- Some tasks best performed by an executive function such as operations are now performed elsewhere.

- Ownership of the development and maintenance of the systems and procedures is typically seen by an organization to be part of a specialist and not a user function's responsibilities. This view is compounded by the fact that the staff necessary to complete the development and maintenance tasks are available only in specialist departments. As a result, control over priorities and work orientation tends to reside outside the direct influence of user functions.

Hierarchical structures

The breaking down of work was mirrored in the hierarchical structure that typified most organizations. Staff groups were responsible to supervisors or team leaders and so on up the organization through different managerial reporting systems. The resulting structures reinforced a command and control style and led to reduced authority at different levels of an organization. Such developments were seen as consistent with the functional/specialist structures and also served to confirm this approach and style as being the best way to manage organizations.

Control from a distance

One further outcome was that the controls and procedures were too often designed and installed from a distance. The approach was one of analytical detachment from the reality of the function or business concerned, with the solution based upon some theoretical view of what should take place rather than developing the controls and procedures around what really happens. Classically these organizational developments reinforced the separation of the key functions from essential aspects of the executive task. The outcome was an increased lack of ownership by those parts of a business that were responsible for meeting the needs of customers and markets.

Role design

The drive towards specialization and the hierarchical nature of organizations also impacted the roles within the different parts of a business as explained in the following sections.

Work patterns

The pattern of work that followed the functional/specialist elements of organizational design helped separate work into its constituent parts, so that the planning, doing and evaluating elements that make up work were undertaken by different groups of staff reporting in different functional structures. The resulting roles suffered from the inherent difficulty of splitting tasks into parts and then trying to put them back together.

Specialization of staff

As volumes increased, the move towards higher volume systems and processes brought with it the design of jobs based on specialization. Higher investment in the delivery system, underpinned by higher volumes, often further reduced the technical content of a job and presented a simple, repetitive task at each step in the process. These developments merely served to reinforce the trend in work patterns.

This basic concept of specialization has been central to increasing the effectiveness of delivery systems and has, without doubt, made a significant contribution to the growing prosperity of nations and the high standard of living now available to most industrialized communities. However, these potential gains in productivity are only maintained by the sound control of resources, continuous improvement and the effective management of people. Too often the role of staff was seen as serving a system which discouraged participation and excluded the important contribution of most of an organization's people resource.

Staff contribution

One result of the traditional organizational and job design approaches was that the overall contribution of staff was constrained. Invariably it constituted the specific 'doing' element of the task and what was delivered was limited by the structures and expectations in place. Although some organizations may have talked about a wider and fuller contribution, the statement was at best one of exhortation, with reality not matching expectation. These approaches were epitomized by the maxim that 'when staff came to work they left their brains at the gate'.

Job design

How job design was used to help overcome some of the outcomes of traditional approaches to organizational and role design are now reviewed. This provides the context for the later sections on how to manage people more effectively in order to retain valuable staff while maximizing their contribution to the ongoing success of a business.

Job enlargement

Job enlargement increases the scope of a job by adding to the number of operations to be performed by a person. This type of increase is horizonal in nature. The advantages include increasing the variety of both the work to be completed and the skills to be used, and to provide an opportunity for a person to be responsible for a set of tasks that constitute, where possible, an identifiable programme of work.

Job rotation

It is not always possible to enlarge jobs as a way of increasing their intrinsic interest. Also, in many service organizations certain jobs have to be performed throughout the normal day or over a 24-hour period, for example the checkout counter in a library or supermarket, and the night shift in fire, police and hospital services. In the first example, the task is monotonous but does not lend itself to enlargement. In the second example, although parts of the work often include areas of greater responsibility than tasks completed during other parts of the working day, the unsociable hours of the night shift make it undesirable to most people. In these circumstances, job or shift rotation is used periodically to change the job assignments or times of working. Exhibit 3.2 reviews Mr James's approach.

Exhibit 3.2 Mr James's introduction of job rotation needs a little more thought!

Job enrichment

Whereas job enlargement widens the scope of the job, job enrichment also increases job depth, giving people a greater responsibility to organize and control the work that has to be done. For meaningful control to take place, the necessary information on which to base sensible decisions must be made available to those now responsible for making decisions. In addition, the organizational climate necessary for a successful change of this kind must be provided by all concerned. In the early stages, at least, there will be some who will view job enrichment as including a measure of role reduction, leading to an erosion of their own responsibilities.

Changes to working schedules

Where job designs are difficult to alter, organizations introduced changes in the working week as a way to make work more interesting. In more developed economies, there is an ongoing call for a shorter working week. In response, changes have been introduced to achieve this end, for example the introduction of a working week comprising normal weekly hours but compressed into four days to allow a longer weekend. Another is the introduction of flexitime that allows employees a certain amount of freedom in selecting their hours of working. The basis of a flexitime arrangement is that each person is required to be at work during certain 'core' hours, but at other times people can choose, within certain procedural agreements, the pattern of working for a particular day or week.

New approaches to work design

With the context set, this section looks at how approaches to organizational, role and job design have changed and the rationale that underpins these developments. Again, the topics in this section overlap and are interdependent, in that for developments to be completed in one topic area, developments would need to be made in another topic area. However, organizations can and do move forward at the organizational, role or job level even where there is overlap and, having done so, make these developments self-sustaining. Moving towards better ways of designing work often has to be based on pragmatism – doing what the organization and people are ready for. This task is always a long haul and companies need to progress these developments as best they can.

Organizational redesign

This section looks at the ways that organizations are changing. These concepts and approaches form part of the way that progressive companies design their organizations and develop their people to help meet the demands of today's markets, while creating environments that provide those involved with the opportunity to contribute fully to the needs of a business.

The learning organization

The underlying argument and rationale for moving to an organization designed to purposefully and continuously improve and adapt to change is easy to recognize and overwhelming in its proposition. But designing and developing an organization that helps individuals as well as the business as a whole to embrace, and adapt to, change is as difficult as it is logical. Organizational commitment to such fundamental tasks is a prerequisite for success but often this is neither recognized nor forthcoming. Peter Senge puts forward the view that organizations, like individuals, can suffer from learning disorders. Learning disabilities are tragic in children... but are no less tragic in organizations, he observes.[5] Because of these disorders, few organizations live even half as long as a person – most die before the age of 40. Senge's view of learning organizations includes a framework for understanding why some organizations are unable to develop team-based management styles that can adopt a proactive attitude towards, and an acceptance of, the necessity for change. He highlights the need for organizations to embrace change as an ongoing feature if they are to grow and prosper.

But these capabilities are not inherent in organizations. They need to be built into the structure and developed on an ongoing basis. Management teams do not start out great but learn how to produce extraordinary results. Teams and organizations that learn faster than competitors can gain a competitive advantage. Creating a learning organization is not only fundamental to long-term success but also cannot be purchased or created as the need arises. It can only be developed over time and those organizations that have embraced change and nurture and reinforce these attitudes and environments can create a sustainable advantage over their competitors.

To create an organization that can 'truly learn', Senge puts forward five essential dimensions:

- **Systems thinking** highlights the need in a learning organization to understand and work at the 'big picture' level in order to evaluate developments and prioritize actions. The gestalt approach to learning emphasizes the need for organizations to understand the whole to better understand the parts, and firms need to develop a process for seeing the big picture in order to provide a context in which events, issues and developments are placed and evaluated.

- **Personal mastery** involves a reciprocal relationship between individuals and an organization. Developing the emotional and intellectual needs of people and directing their energies towards achieving personal goals and development targets will enhance them as individuals as well as enhancing their contribution to the organization in which they work.

- **Mental models** highlight one way in which individuals learn and carry forward experience and learning from the past into their current way of working. Deeply ingrained assumptions, generalizations and paradigms influence the way individuals see the world in general and the work environment in particular and influence approaches to current ways of completing tasks and making changes. Mental models often form barriers to personal development and organizational change. People in learning organizations must have open minds that are receptive to the need for change, be willing and able to recognize and assess their own perceptions and address the underlying assumptions that underpin their own mental models in order to reduce or remove any inherent barriers to how they think about and review situations and opportunities.

- **Building shared vision** involves developing common views of the future that foster genuine commitment and involvement rather than compliance. But developing a shared vision can only happen in an organizational structure where employees are truly empowered and learning takes place throughout. It's a long process underpinned by hard work. As Exhibit 3.3 illustrates, Mr James has much to do.

- **Team learning** requires people to set aside assumptions and stereotypes and instead address issues and problems in such a way that individuals, teams and the organization as a whole can learn and develop.

Exhibit 3.3   Mr James attempts to build a shared vision within his team

© AMD Publishing

Developing a change-oriented organization

As competition increases, it is paramount that organizations anticipate the need for change. Companies have to be on the lookout not only for competitive threats but also opportunities to change proactively in order to keep ahead.

A change-accepting culture stimulates and reinforces awareness of development opportunities by creating an environment where experimentation is encouraged without recrimination. As you will see later in Chapter 11 on quality management, one of Deming's 14 points for management urges organizations to drive out fear as a prerequisite for change.

Similarly, Senge[5] lists as one of the 'laws of the fifth discipline' that there should be a 'no blame' culture within organizations in order to encourage and stimulate a proactive response to change from inside companies. Too often managers create an environment that discourages individuals from proactively challenging current approaches and practices. The ensuing risk-averse culture is, at best, unproductive and, at worst, promotes political infighting to safeguard individual and functional boundaries. 'Turf protection', which refers to functions safeguarding the existing status, activities and responsibilities of staff in their part of a business, is the unproductive outcome.

Using external threats to prevent organizations becoming complacent can, however, be a constructive development. For example, Bill Gates, when he was CEO of Microsoft, frequently emailed staff to alert them to the ongoing threat of competition thereby helping to prevent complacency. In the same way, some organizations encourage staff to think 'outside the box' by making this activity an integral part of their work. For instance, 3M requires researchers to spend 10 per cent of their time on personal ideas that are not a part of the formal, corporate R&D agenda. Post-it notes are one example of the outcome of this initiative.

The changing role of managers

As with executives who manage other functions, operations managers are responsible for two distinct sets of activities:

- to organize, manage and control those areas of a business for which they are responsible – the internal operational dimension

- to develop and improve performance in operations with regard to the order-winners and qualifiers for which operations is solely or jointly responsible – the external, customer-facing, strategic dimension.

The first step is to separate the strategic directing tasks from those of managing and controlling the internal sets of responsibilities that concern making day-to-day, short-term events happen. With this separation in place, it is then necessary to recognize that managers do not manage people. On the contrary, people manage themselves. What executives manage and influence is the context and environment in which people work. The management task is to think through the structure and systems of an organization (that is, the way an organization works) in order to create the values, expectations and environment in which people can manage themselves more effectively.

The essential role of managers is to create conditions where people want responsibility, will learn and hence manage themselves in a way that maximizes their contribution to an organization as well as their own personal development. One result is that it makes the decision and action phases part of the same set of responsibilities. To bring this about, managers have to recognize that their role has to change from one of making decisions to one of, on the one hand, communicating a vision and confirming corporate objectives and, on the other, getting people to see their own behaviour, own their own problems and be responsible for putting things right.

To do this managers have to think through their own role and relationships as well as the roles of others. People interpret roles from their past experience of organizations and the sets of responsibilities, areas of decision making and status associated with roles and titles. Similarly, what a manager says or asks questions about has a symbolic as well as a literal meaning. At the very least what a manager asks questions about signals or implies interest, but typically most interpret such questions as pointing to an area of concern inferring responsibility and ownership – the symbolic dimension. The activities in which managers get involved (for example meetings) have the same two sets of meanings. Similarly, if managers answer the questions posed about an aspect of a business, they are perceived as owning the problem and consequently the decision-making role within that area of a business. Defining the areas of responsibility and boundaries for taking ownership of problems and solutions is part of the environment-setting task of managers, and a prerequisite for empowering people within an organization.

Flatter organizations

As mentioned earlier, in more developed economies, most organizations make extensive use of specialists to run a business. The typical approach adopted has been to create specialist

Exhibit 3.4 Organizational levels

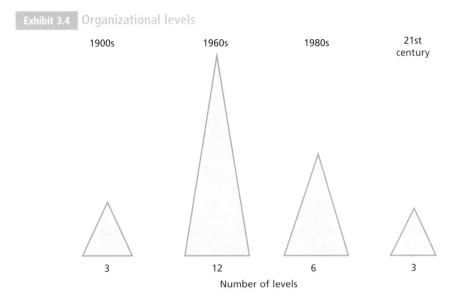

functions to supply expert advice, guidance and help in various relevant areas to the main functions in a business (such as operations).

The extensive use of specialists has resulted in organizations with too many layers, which increases overhead costs and makes good communications and effective collaboration all the more difficult to maintain. The results are reviewed in Exhibit 3.4, which illustrates the changes in number of layers of management through the twentieth century to today. The need to reduce the layers in most organizations is essential. But companies need to undertake this critical task with care. Avoiding across-the-board reductions is most important as this assumes that existing structures will be appropriate in a scaled-down form. Reshaping organizations is a job for a scalpel, not an axe. Reducing the size of organizations has to be carried out in line with business requirements, and must include top-down as well as bottom-up approaches. In the past, top-down approaches were most often employed, which merely added to existing layers. Reshaping an organization has to take into account the role of functions, establish the responsibility for decisions and boundaries of authority, and agree on which tasks are completed centrally and which are allocated to the providers of the organization's services and products. This approach ensures that truly specialist activities are left to specialists, while all other activities are undertaken by those functions and people providing the services and products involved.

A business-related approach, therefore, enables a company to develop its organization in line with its needs and the opportunity to change the perception and reality of who does what at all levels in a firm. In this way, the role of managers, the need to empower people throughout an organization and where tasks are best undertaken can reflect the needs of the business in today's increasingly competitive markets.

Role redesign

Superior organizational performance is ultimately provided by people. Appropriate infrastructure in the form of procedures and systems is essential, but the capabilities that enable an organization to best support the order-winners and qualifiers of its markets are those that come from people. These capabilities include the skills, technical know-how, ability to solve problems and make decisions, capacity for learning and motivation to make things happen.

Also, what makes it difficult for one organization to match the people capability within another organization is the time and mind-set changes involved. Creating an environment in which people can manage themselves more effectively is difficult and involves long timescales. The purpose of this section is to introduce some of the important dimensions in role design and highlight some of the issues involved.

Employee involvement

Within the organizational changes described in the last section the need to change people's roles to ones that involve them in relevant aspects of the organization was a common theme throughout.

Employee involvement is the process of pushing information, knowledge and power down to appropriate levels in an organization. In that way it is a management initiative designed to increase employee information about, and commitment to, the organization. However, the idea of employee involvement is not new. Columella, a Roman agriculturalist, reflecting on the ways of managing his estate workers, wrote in AD 100: 'Nowadays I make a practice to call them [his estate workers] into consultation on any new work... I observe they are more willing to set about a piece of work on which their opinions have been asked and their advice followed.'[6] Clearly, Columella understood the impact on the level of worker commitment by involving them in the decision-making process from the start.

Over the last 30–40 years, companies have increasingly recognized that involving people in aspects of work other than the prime role of completing their principal tasks is essential if the abilities of all employees are to be harnessed to help improve the overall business. Suggestion schemes and quality circles are two ways of achieving this aim.

Suggestion schemes

Such schemes encourage staff to come up with ideas that may lead to tangible savings or an improvement in the way something is done. In terms of the average annual number of suggestions per employee, results vary as does the success rate, but an organization can expect up to 20 ideas per year for each 100 staff employed and adoption rates of over 25 per cent. Some organizations do a lot better. Toyota for example, records success rates far in excess of these norms, with 48 suggestions per employee per year and an adoption rate of 96 per cent. To succeed, suggestion schemes need to meet the following criteria:

- They must be carefully planned and provided with the resources and management backing to sustain them over the long term.
- They require constant promotion. Linking them to other regular events helps. For example, Richer Sounds, a UK-based hi-fi chain, funds a monthly brainstorming session for the teams working in each of the company's stores and the venue is each team's local pub.
- They should be fun, for example T-shirts and coffee mugs with appropriate logos for all who contribute. Schemes can also be enlivened with short-term campaigns based on themes such as customer care, energy saving or the environment.
- Suggestions must be handled quickly and efficiently. If staff have a good idea and get excited, they should not wait more than a day or two at most for a response, and a decision should be made within a week. Also 'not adopted' rather than 'rejected' reduces the demotivational aspect of a turndown.
- Suggestions should be rewarded. Although views vary on the extent and type of the reward, one-off payments tend to average about 20 per cent of the annual savings that result.

Quality circles

Quality circles are improvement groups that comprise structured, voluntary work groups of around six or eight people from a particular work area. Meeting for about one hour on a weekly or fortnightly basis, they address and resolve work-related problems that the groups themselves have selected. Those taking part are trained in new skills, such as problem analysis, as well as developing their all-round abilities such as working in groups, problem solving and implementing change. Quality circles are a means of giving employees the opportunity to do something positive about the problems and issues they face, rather than just making suggestions for others in the organization to consider. They are based on the philosophy of making more effective use of an organization's most valuable asset, its people. The role of a group is to identify and select problems over which they have jurisdiction, while solutions that fall outside their remit are put forward as suggestions for change. Although generally having limited power, groups are able to fix certain problems that fall within their scope of activity.

The origins and development of quality circles have their roots in Japanese businesses. Many of the early problems facing Japanese companies concerned quality-related issues and this led to the term 'quality circles', whereas, in fact, the problems addressed concern all aspects of work. Hence many organizations use the term 'improvement groups' to better reflect their purpose. Case example 3.2 shows how these work at Unipart.

Case example 2   OPPORTUNITIES FOR INVOLVEMENT AT UNIPART

Unipart, the Oxford (UK)-based company with sales of over £1.2 billion, channels some 250 million items a year from about 5000 suppliers to about 30,000 individual customers including Vodafone, Hewlett-Packard, Virgin Trains, Jaguar and the UK's Ministry of Defence. Most of Unipart's 9500 staff work on the distribution side of the business. It has five large warehouses which, together with 500 small distribution operations, handle some 6500 different items a year.

Unipart's staff (whether in distribution or manufacturing) are grouped into 1500 small teams that meet daily to discuss problems and opportunities for improvement. These 'improve-

ment circles' include representatives of customers, suppliers and transport groups. In a circle, participants spend an hour or so a week discussing how to speed up deliveries or why part of an operation is not working properly and communicate their progress and end results to others in the company. Each work unit has a room fitted with IT systems linked to the internet and the rest of the company. This keeps everyone in touch, allows anyone to contribute to a circle's project and allows circles to check previous discussions and outcomes so that people don't spend a lot of time going over old ground.

www.unipart.com

Case questions   1   What are some of the ways that Unipart ensures that as many staff as possible contribute to the work of improvement circles, given the disparate nature of the group's structure?

2   Why do you think representatives from customers, suppliers and transport groups are sometimes included in an improvement circle?

Self-managed teams

For many organizations employee involvement is the start of a long journey. As Exhibit 3.5 illustrates, there are four stages in the redesign of jobs, beginning with staff involvement and collaboration through to where the job is designed around self-managed teams and the more extensive role that this comprises. Major redesigns at one level often require change at other levels and, in this instance, organizational design changes will need to reflect this fundamental job change within the management structure of a business. At stage 4, the business becomes virtually an organization without rank.

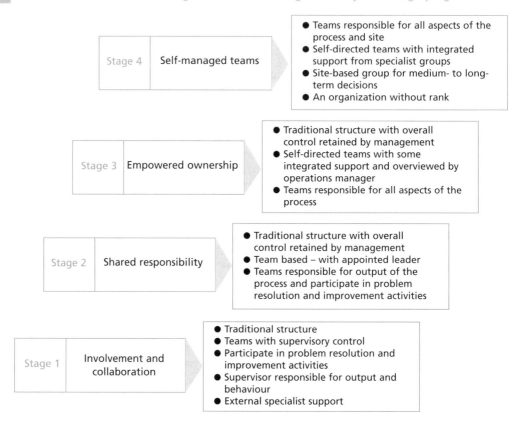

| Stage 4 | Self-managed teams | ● Teams responsible for all aspects of the process and site
● Self-directed teams with integrated support from specialist groups
● Site-based group for medium- to long-term decisions
● An organization without rank |

| Stage 3 | Empowered ownership | ● Traditional structure with overall control retained by management
● Self-directed teams with some integrated support and overviewed by operations manager
● Teams responsible for all aspects of the process |

| Stage 2 | Shared responsibility | ● Traditional structure with overall control retained by management
● Team based – with appointed leader
● Teams responsible for output of the process and participate in problem resolution and improvement activities |

| Stage 1 | Involvement and collaboration | ● Traditional structure
● Teams with supervisory control
● Participate in problem resolution and improvement activities
● Supervisor responsible for output and behaviour
● External specialist support |

Job redesign

Organizations are introducing extensive job redesigns so that employees use a variety of skills, often in teams. Under this development, staff have considerable freedom in deciding how to do the necessary tasks. Furthermore, work is designed to involve elements not directly associated with providing the services or products, such as aspects of planning, scheduling and evaluation. To bring this about requires organizations to rethink who does what. To illustrate let us see how the use of specialists has evolved.

Phase 1 of Exhibit 3.6 shows how activities that were originally undertaken by executive functions (such as operations) have been separated and housed under the auspices of a specialist function. For example, the tasks undertaken by a purchasing department may typically include supplier-related roles, contract negotiation, placing purchase orders and arranging for services and goods to be brought to site when needed. This is then reinforced by structures that create distinct reporting lines that separate the provision of an activity from the direct user, as shown in phase 2 in Exhibit 3.6.

The disadvantage of these arrangements is that whereas the first two tasks listed in the purchasing example above fall within the purchasing specialism, the other two tasks would be better undertaken by the function wanting the services and goods. In this instance, what services or products are required and when they are needed is best known and undertaken by the user. A central provision of these latter tasks results in additional procedures, additional communications and the potential for mistakes.

Exhibit 3.6 Evolution of specialist functions in an organization

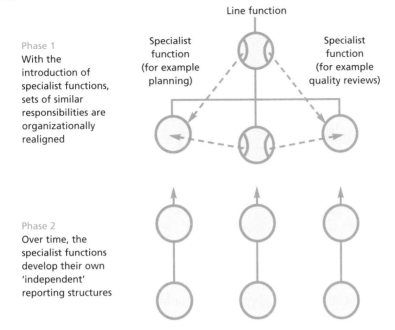

Line function

Phase 1
With the introduction of specialist functions, sets of similar responsibilities are organizationally realigned

Specialist function (for example planning)

Specialist function (for example quality reviews)

Phase 2
Over time, the specialist functions develop their own 'independent' reporting structures

In most companies the decision concerning who does which tasks results in operations staff completing the doing task (that is, providing the service or product). But a job comprises the three separate elements of planning, doing and evaluating. As shown in Exhibit 3.7, these three parts of work have been separated and are now in different reporting systems within an organization – a byproduct of the use of specialists and the development of support functions within a business. Exhibit 3.7 is, therefore, an extension of phase 2 in Exhibit 3.6. It illustrates a typical structure and shows the separation of important parts of the whole task into different functional responsibilities that report in different systems and the gap that results between the reporting lines of these three intrinsic parts of work.

This has led to situations where the contribution from those responsible for providing the services and products to activities such as continuous improvement and the day-to-day

Exhibit 3.7 Separation of the three facets of work

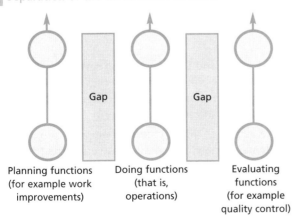

Gap

Gap

Planning functions (for example work improvements)

Doing functions (that is, operations)

Evaluating functions (for example quality control)

Exhibit 3.8   Integration of the three facets of work

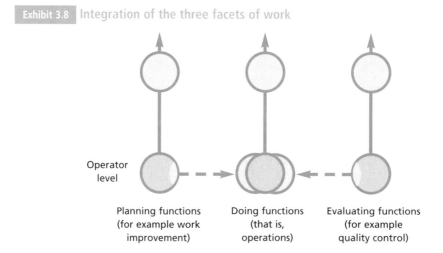

Operator level

Planning functions (for example work improvement)

Doing functions (that is, operations)

Evaluating functions (for example quality control)

scheduling of work has been lost, and the essential link between the responsibility for providing services and products and checking the quality conformance of the service or product involved has been severed.

Exhibit 3.8 illustrates how appropriate planning and evaluating activities (presently completed by specialist support functions) should be reassigned to those currently responsible for providing the services or products (that is, operations). Such actions lend support to the arguments put forward earlier and also provide a tangible, common-sense illustration of the effect this can have. Such actions switch activities so that they now form part of the task undertaken by those responsible for completing the services and products, thus facilitating productivity improvements, the day-to-day scheduling of work and consistent conformance to specification, while at the same time creating greater job interest for all concerned. On the one hand it releases specialists from undertaking non-specialist tasks, while on the other it gives those who provide services or products the responsibility for all three dimensions that make up meaningful tasks by broadening their activities and so allowing them to plan and evaluate the work they carry out.

Exhibit 3.9 includes the example of purchasing as well as other functions to illustrate possible reallocations of activities from specialists to those who complete the services or products involved.

In addition to the significant empowerment and involvement gains that come from increasing job scope by including indirect activities (that is, tasks that are not concerned directly with the provision of services or products) in the role of the providers, there are two further key advantages:

- Decisions on day-to-day scheduling and the checking of services and products against specification are best completed at the point where the services or products are provided. It is here that the up-to-date position is known and the interval between finding faults and correcting the delivery system is shortest.
- Where staff only undertake activities directly concerned with providing services or products, at times of low demand there are no alternative, indirect or non-providing tasks for them to undertake. The available choice is to make inventory or incur non-value-adding costs.

Given these sets of gains, many companies are reallocating activities previously completed

Exhibit 3.9 Examples of activities best undertaken by providers and those best completed by specialists

Aspect	Activities that are best undertaken by	
	Those providing services or products	Specialists
Purchasing	Placing orders or calling off deliveries of service or product against contracts	Supplier selection, supplier relations and contract negotiation
Operations planning and scheduling	Short-term operations control and day-to-day scheduling	Long-term planning and capacity planning
Quality assurance and control	Quality control including checking at all stages in the delivery system	Quality assurance including the development of sampling plans, customer reviews and material tests

by overhead staff to the role of service and product providers. Now these latter staff have a mix of work that is more rewarding, reflects more appropriately the demand patterns and customer expectations in today's markets, the costs of which are met by the reductions in overhead staff that follow.

Staff training and development

Naturally, these changes need to be underpinned by extensive training and staff development which would need to address three key areas:

- Multiskilling – most redesign initiatives need multiskilling to facilitate team-based working and other organizational and role changes.
- The use of technology as well as new skills in the planning and evaluating activities that work would now comprise.
- Skills that concern the change in style and approach involved, such as group working, analysis, decision-making and implementation skills.

Flexitime and job sharing

To help create conditions that meet the needs of organizations and their staff, companies are turning to other work arrangements and packages that better fit the availability of their staff or provide people with more choice.

Flexitime

Flexitime offers staff an opportunity to adjust their working day to meet their domestic or social life patterns on a permanent or as-needed basis. The principal purpose is to help staff manage both their work and home commitments – unlike the humorous interpretation given in Exhibit 3.10. In most schemes, the totalling and balancing of hours is made over a period of several weeks and allows for plus and minus balances to be carried forward within agreed limits.

Exhibit 3.10 Perhaps not the desired intention of flexitime

© Roger Beale

Flexible benefit schemes

These schemes require staff to take part of their salary as cash but allow them to use the rest to buy extra benefits. For example, PricewaterhouseCoopers, a large UK accounting firm, gives staff a reward package comprising a notional salary and benefits entitlement. At least 80 per cent of salary must be taken as cash but the rest can be used to purchase benefits. In the PricewaterhouseCoopers' scheme, the range of benefits includes:

- up to 10 days extra holiday
- childcare vouchers
- sports and leisure club membership with discounts
- pension plan
- luncheon vouchers useable at 30,000 outlets with 6 per cent discount
- leased car scheme
- substantial savings on group medical, dental and personal accident insurance.

Job sharing

This provides the opportunity for two people to meet the requirements of a job. These arrangements are usually on a 50/50 or 40/60 share basis.

Other people-related issues

This section provides an overview of several people-related issues and perspectives that form part of the task of managing people. While most are general in nature and application, some are specific to certain situations (for example, 'Culture in the workplace' and 'Managing operations overseas').

Recruitment

Recruiting the right people is a major factor in helping ensure that the attitudes, values and work ethics required are met from the start. The need to allocate the time and attention to this task is self-evident. Analysing recruitment and retention methods forms part of this investment, and for operations managers it is an essential part of their role at all levels in an organization. Although human resource support is typically provided within a business, the ultimate responsibility for recruiting people rests with the function where they eventually work.

In his time as CEO of General Electric, Jack Welch personally interviewed candidates for the top 250 jobs in the organization. There is no better time to communicate expectations and requirements than at the start.

The use of short-term contracts is one way to help, as an organization can try people out and vice versa. One element of this development is the growing use of holiday work as a way to help pre-select employees. It needs to be used for what it is – a 10-week interviewing process. Selecting summer interns needs to have one eye on the long term. The mutual opportunity to test skill need and culture fit can reduce fall-out levels later. For example, Merrill Lynch, the investment banker, uses its summer programmes in this way. It takes up to 190 third-year students on its summer programme and typically offers up to 80 per cent a job on graduation.

Staff retention

How do organizations keep their skilled and experienced staff? The first thought that often comes to mind is pay! But this is only one element of a reward system. Reward refers to all the monetary, non-monetary and psychological payments that an organization provides. The emphasis that staff place on each of these elements will differ by level in the organization and by individual at each level. What is sure is that paying more than the going rate rarely motivates for long and will not on its own retain staff. But, paying less will cause problems. The role of pay described here illustrates the insights provided by Hertzberg – the concept of hygiene factors and motivators. Pay too little and people are dissatisfied. Pay sufficiently well and the dissatisfaction factor is removed but will not in itself motivate. Other motivators need to be identified and provided, such as increased level of discretion in work-related situations and personal recognition.

Giving time and attention to people is at the root of understanding why they stay and why they leave and operations managers need to invest appropriately.

The growing use of temporary staff

Every working day, Adecco, a Swiss company and one of the world's biggest private employers, places nearly 700,000 temporary and full-time staff with businesses all over the world. Adecco is the 'temp industry' giant but it only has a small share of the total market. In the US alone there are thousands of such companies that together place some 2.5 million workers each day.[7] The outsourcing of staff and the growing use of temporary staff is an international trend. For instance, Adecco's biggest market is France and its second largest is the US. The task for operations managers is to recognize that much of its staff are either 'temps', employees of the outsourcer (for example a call centre) or older part-time staff working on specific assignments. The underlying rationale for temporary staff is lower costs. But the productivity of people depends largely on how well they are managed and motivated. The fact that the organization doesn't own some staff does not discharge them from being responsible for motivating them. The challenge for operations in particular is managing all the people in the new regime.

Staff appraisals

The formal process of appraisals is still widely practised in many organizations. Although it varies by country and by sector, their use is still a characteristic part of the way managers manage people. The most fundamental misunderstanding appears to be their perceived role, as Mr James found in Exhibit 3.11. Originally introduced as a way to help manage staff performance, in many organizations the annual appraisal round became the only time performance was discussed and resulted in a delay in addressing poor performance or praising good performance. Recognizing this, many organizations have now shifted ground on how best to use appraisals. Purposes range from making sure staff understand the aims of the business, identifying training needs, helping clarify roles and objectives and identifying ways to help improve performance and decisions on pay.

　Where appraisal systems are in place, operations managers need to think through their role in the context of managing people and then discuss with and communicate to all concerned their purpose. Any help in managing people should be used and developed. With appraisals (as with much else) keys to getting the best out of the system include keeping it simple with a clear purpose and seen to be fair so that expectation better matches reality.

Exhibit 3.11 Mr James reviews Gianni's performance while Gianni reviews his car's performance

© AMD Publishing

Managing operations overseas

The growing internationalization of large organizations brings with it the task of managing overseas. While many organizations base their international expansion on their brand name, South African Breweries (SAB) have based theirs on exporting people. SAB has recognized that what made it initially successful (currently, SAB has a massive 98 per cent of its home market) was its expertise and the experience of its people. As the company expanded overseas, it exported its home-grown technology, talent and management expertise to its operations around the world. But above all it exports its people – more than 140 South African expatriates work in the operations acquired abroad, with at least one (and sometimes as many as 20) in a business. SAB's focus is brewing beer in developing countries in Asia, Africa, Central and Eastern Europe and, most recently, Central America. Difficult emerging markets are where SAB honed its operations capabilities and business acumen. For example, it is now the second largest brewer in China but makes more profit than Tsingtao, the country's #1 brewer.

The key here is that SAB transfers essential expertise in operations to elsewhere in the world. Often there will be a process technology mismatch but earlier experience of such situations resides in the capabilities of the company's existing operations managers. Getting the basics right and the foundations in place has been fundamental to SAB's successful development of these growth opportunities.

Ergonomics

Ergonomics is primarily concerned with how the human body fits with its environment. Reviewing and matching the physiological aspects of job design to the person doing a job contribute to greater productivity while reducing fatigue and avoiding conditions that may lead to physical strain and other types of health risks. It represents an important element of one key task in operations, that of managing people. Care for people makes sense all round and placing ergonomics in the managing people chapter, rather than in a later chapter addressing topics such as layout and improving operations, signals its integral role in the central dimension of operations management.

Ergonomics addresses the three central factors:

- Workplace factors concern the interface between the physical attributes of people and the workplace. The dimensions reviewed relate to features such as reach, relative heights of equipment to body positions such as seating to monitor dials or use of PC screens. The purpose is to design workplaces that reduce strain and fatigue over a working day while eliminating conditions that could lead to physical injury over time.

- Environmental factors cover aspects of work that also impact job performance and could affect people's long-term health. Specified and supported by comprehensive occupational health and safety legislation, ergonomics lays down conditions concerning the temperature, lighting and noise levels for a variety of working environments.

- Behavioural factors highlight the role of these dimensions in effective workplace design. These factors link personal motivation and commitment to work design and build on to the change principles discussed earlier. Key factors include providing a meaningful set of activities that constitute a whole task, embodying aspects of planning, doing and evaluation within teams and establishing relationships, allowing staff to contact internal and external customers.

By combining these factors companies are able to design workplaces that improve productivity, motivate people, encourage involvement and provide safe and stress-free environments.

Reflections

The challenge to create a working environment that helps people to develop their full potential, want to do a good job and contribute fully to improving all aspects of work is central to the role of operations management. To bring this about will require businesses to fundamentally rethink their approach to organizational design and the structure of work.

One key to this is involving and empowering people. But this means more than employee participation. Even where companies delegate authority and resources, this does not, by right, lead to empowerment. Attempts to empower people from above will fail. The emphasis on empowerment needs to shift to one of providing the opportunity for staff at all levels to exercise increasing influence over their work and role. But, the giving of power itself without providing support in the form of training and direction will result in failure.

Where empowerment does exist it leads to power and control being exercised by individuals. Giving people more control over their own actions results in them accomplishing more and increasingly taking initiatives to get things done.

Creating the conditions where people are responsible for a meaningful set of activities is a key factor in these developments. This, however, can only be achieved with a fundamental reappraisal of work and organizational structures. Essential factors to making this happen include:

- **Self-managed teams** are not only responsible for given tasks but are capable of making and implementing their decisions, are held accountable for results and also influence the behavioural aspects of the job.

- **Sharing information** highlights the need for people to have full information about all elements of the job and ongoing performance. Without full information, teams cannot be held responsible for their performance as they do not know the full dimension of the company's problems. Aligning corporate and individual goals is a key factor here and is a two-way street as Mr James and Gianni need to work out (see Exhibit 3.12).

- **Creating autonomy** is essential and needs to be developed. To help do this, structure needs to be built into these arrangements as it enables people to handle the uncertainty they feel when trying out new behaviours. As teams evolve, more autonomy can be created which is essential for the sound and full working of teams.

Exhibit 3.12 Aligning corporate and individual goals – a two-way street on which Mr James and Gianni need to do more!

However, these developments are dependent on how well people and, in particular, organizations learn. People, like businesses, need to be continually reinvented. But self-learning is not easy. 'It is no accident', Senge concludes, 'that most organizations learn poorly. The way they are designed and managed (and) the way people's jobs are defined... create fundamental disabilities.'[8] However, progressive companies have been addressing these issues of change as they recognize the key role that people play within the success of organizations. The outcome of such changes will help companies to capitalize on their key resource – the people within the business.

Key Elements of Managing People

- Creating an environment in which people can fulfil their potential and one that meets both their needs and those of the business is a key operations management role. This is a difficult task, made more complex by the fast-changing nature of today's business in terms of market needs, level of employee commitment, the technical content of jobs, and the training and development needs this brings.

- General definitions concerning jobs set the scene while managerial philosophies of work and traditional approaches to managing people complete the introduction.

- The next section switched to the need for companies to create change-oriented business environments that, in turn, bring implications for the current role of managers and the traditional shape of organizations.

- Then followed the core section of the chapter that introduced developments such as employee involvement and empowerment and a range of key dimensions from staff training and development through to issues such as flexitime, job sharing and ergonomics.

Self-check

1 According to Hertzberg, hygiene factors are those that:
   a lead to staff dissatisfaction if not maintained ☐
   b prompt the motivation of staff ☐
   c both a and b ☐

2 The trend in the use of temporary staff in more developed economies is:
   a staying the same ☐
   b decreasing ☐
   c increasing ☐

3 Job performance is dependent on:
   a the size and depth of work ☐
   b a person's attitude to the job and the level of interest the job holds ☐
   c a person's ability and level of motivation ☐

4 Job enrichment concerns:
   a widening the scope of a job and also increasing the depth of a job ☐
   b increasing the scope of a job ☐
   c periodically changing the assigned job ☐

5 Quality circles refer to:
   a quality targets displayed as the target in archery with the bull at the centre ☐
   b voluntary work groups to address and resolve any work-related problems ☐
   c voluntary work groups to address and resolve only quality-related problems ☐

6 The trend in the number of levels in an organization is:
   a decreasing ☐
   b staying the same ☐
   c increasing ☐

7 In the stages of a job redesign programme which of the following is stage 4:
   a self-managed teams ☐
   b shared responsibility ☐
   c empowered ownership ☐

8 Flexitime means:
   a staff can work when they wish providing they get agreement ☐
   b staff contract to be at work in core hours but can change their work arrangements by agreement at other times ☐
   c neither of these ☐

9 Employee involvement concerns:
  a giving staff more jobs to perform ☐
  b making staff part of the decision
     process from the start ☐
  c neither of these ☐

10 Ergonomics refers to:
  a common-sense economics from the
     Latin *ergo* (therefore) and the Greek
     oikonomia (economy) ☐
  b ways to cut costs ☐
  c how the human body fits with its
     environment ☐

Study activities

Discussion questions

1 Name some factors that fall into the hygiene and motivator categories. How may these differ for blue- (for example shop floor) and white-collar (for example administrative) staff?

2 Using Exhibit 3.1 and the accompanying narrative, give two illustrations of service and manufacturing jobs that illustrate the difference between job depth and job scope.

3 Why are companies increasingly building indirect tasks into the remit of those staff primarily responsible for providing services and making products?

4 How are job satisfaction and motivation different? Illustrate your answer with an example.

5 Why, in the past, did companies build organizations based on 'control through specialists' and 'the specialization of labour'?

6 Can all jobs be enriched successfully? Illustrate your answer with examples.

7 Why is it imperative that businesses turn themselves into learning organizations?

8 What are the advantages and disadvantages of job enlargement, job rotation and job enrichment? Give an example in operations where these would be beneficial and an example where it would be better not to employ these approaches.

Assignments

1 Review a wine bar, supermarket and take-away restaurant in line with the following:
  ● How do these organizations each cope with the long opening hours involved?
  ● Do they use flexitime? If so, give details. If not, could they and how would it work?

2 Together with two others, draw up a list of factors that affect people's attitude to work. Then review 12 staff from an organization of your choice in terms of how they would classify these chosen factors into hygiene and motivators. Analyse the results and explain your findings.

Exploring further

Barlett, CA and Ghoshal, S 'Building competitive advantage through people', *Sloan Management Review*, winter (2002), pp. 34–41.

Bratton, J and Gold, J *Human Resource Management: Theory and Practice*, 3rd edn, Palgrave Macmillan, Basingstoke (2003).

Clarke, T and Dopp, S 'Challenging McWorld', Canadian Centre for Policy Alternatives, Ottawa (2001), p. 64.

Gates, B and Collins, H *Business @ the Speed of Thought: Using a Digital Nervous System*, Penguin Books, London (1999).

Gibson, R (ed.) *Re-thinking the Future*, Nicholas Brealey, London (1997).

Grief, M *The Visual Factory: Building Participation Through Sharing Information*, Productivity Press, Portland, OR (1991).

Gross, CM *The Right Fit: The Power of Ergonomics as a Competitive Strategy*, Productivity Press, Portland, OR (1996).

Hays, JM and Hill, AV 'A preliminary investigation of the relationship between employee motivation/vision, service learning and perceived service quality', *Journal of Operations Management*, **19**(3) (2001), pp. 335–49.

Lawler, EE, Mohramann, SA and Ledford, GE *Employee Involvement and Total Quality Management*, Jossey-Bass, San Francisco (1992).

Malone, TW 'Is empowerment just a fad?', *Sloan Management Review*, winter (1997).

Marchington, M, Goodman, J, Wilkinson, A and Ackers, P *New Developments in Employee Involvement*, Manchester School of Management, University of Manchester Institute of Science and Technology. Employment Department Research Studies No. 2 (1992).

Mayo, A *The Human Value of the Enterprise: Valuing People as Assets – Monitoring, Measuring, Managing*, Nicholas Brearley, London (2001).

Nilles, J *Managing Telework*, John Wiley & Son, New York (1998).

Noe, RA, Hollenbeck, JR and Gerhart, B *Human Resource Management: Gaining a Competitive Advantage*, 3rd edn, McGraw-Hill, New York (1999).

Ortega, B *In Sam we Trust; The Untold Story of Sam Walton and How Wal-Mart is Devouring America*, Times Business/Random House, New York (1998).

Osborne, DJ *Ergonomics at Work*, John Wiley & Sons, New York (1995).

Pfeffer, J 'Six dangerous myths about pay', *Harvard Business Review,* **76**(3) (1998).

Skapinker, M, Merchant, K and London, S 'A question of holding onto staff'. A feature on call centres, part 1, *Financial Times* (London), 4 October (2002), p. 13.

Storey, J 'Human resource management today: an assessment' in J Storey (ed.) *Human Resource Management: A Critical Text*, Thompson Learning, London (2001), pp. 3–20.

Notes and references

1   Drucker, PF 'They're not employees, they're people', *Harvard Business Review*, February (2002), pp. 71–7.

2   Jacob, R 'Absence of management', *The American Way*, February (1993).

3   Drucker op. cit., p. 73.

4   Hertzberg, F *Work and Nature of Man*, Cleveland, World Publishing (1966) and Hertzberg, F 'One more time: how do you motivate employees?' (with retrospective comment), *Harvard Business Review*, **65**(5) (1987).

5   Senge, PM *The Fifth Discipline,* New York, Doubleday (1990), p. 18.

6   Columella as quoted in Saskin, M 'Changing toward participative management approaches: a model and methods', *The Academy Review* (1976), pp. 75–86.

7   Drucker op. cit., p. 71.

8   Senge, op. cit., p. 18.

Part 2

Designing Services, Products and Delivery Systems

book map

Part

1

- 1 Managing Operations
- 2 Operations Strategy
- 3 Managing People

2

INPUTS

SUPPLIERS

PROCESSES

4 Designing and Developing Services & Products

5 Designing Service Delivery Systems

6 Designing Manufacturing Processes

7 Location and Layout

8 Managing Capacity

9 Technology Developments

10 Operations Scheduling and Execution

11 Managing Quality

3

12 Managing Inventory

13 Managing the Supply Chain

14 Process and Delivery System Reliability and Maintenance

4

15 Time and Productivity

16 Improving Operations

5

Managing Operations in Practice: Long Case Studies

OUTPUTS

CUSTOMERS

Designing and Developing Services and Products

Outline of chapter

Although operations is not primarily responsible for designing services and products, post-launch provision rests with this function. Identifying the cost, quality conformance and delivery implications of proposals, therefore, is a critical contribution by operations to design outcomes.

Why are designing and developing services and products important?

Executive overview

Growth and success are based to a large extent on an organization's ability to introduce new and develop existing services and products. While a natural market may exist for some essential needs (for example food and clothing), for many a market has to be created. In either case, most organizations have changed from an ad hoc approach to the planning of new services and products in the past, to one that is an organized activity involving a procedural cycle from generating ideas through to market launch. Here we examine the procedures involved and some of the important issues to be considered for both new and existing services and products.

This chapter covers the following topics:

- The research and development process from the phase of generating ideas through to final design.

- The key issues and considerations in service/product design including life cycles, portfolio analyses and design contributions to help support different service/product market segments.

- The input of technology, techniques and approaches related to design including standardization, modular design, Taguchi methods, value engineering, value analysis, simultaneous engineering and variety reduction.

Designing and developing services and products

Introducing new and developing existing services and products is the lifeblood of organizations. However, the task involves more than initiating new ideas, although that is where it typically all begins. The procedure is one of checking ideas and alternatives and verifying that what is proposed can be done within the context of the market, the organization's own objectives and the impact on other parts of the business, including operations. It concerns generating ideas, setting financial targets, providing detailed specifications and checking what will be involved in providing them prior to the marketing and provision of the services or products in question. Ideas come from internal or external sources depending upon an organization's allocation of resources (for example research spend), its approach to stimulating and processing contributions and its attitude towards the degree of risk it is prepared to take, for example whether to be a leader or follower in its chosen markets.

Some of the issues are now overviewed as a way of outlining what is involved. The sections that follow then look at the various aspects in more detail and address some of the key points to be considered throughout this core task. One thing is for certain, however; in many markets service and product design can have a telling impact on the success of an organization, as Case examples 4.1 and 4.2 show.

Case example 1 SERVICE AND PRODUCT DESIGN AT FIAT

In the latter part of the last and early part of this century, Fiat's products in the people carrier segment of the competitive European car market were the Multipla and Doblo. To most (and importantly the critics) their appearance was, at best, unattractive. As the UK's *Car Magazine* put it, the Multipla had 'boss-eyed swamp hog looks' while the Doblo was a 'Toytown-styled utilo-box' that is 'very big if you're desperate for space.' But you'd have to be – take a look at the Multipla in Exhibit 4.1.

Fiat's Western European market share has fallen from 10 per cent to 6 per cent in the last ten years, and in the first few months of 2003, European sales of Fiat's core brand cars fell a further 16 per cent to fewer than 300,000. So the Italian company is setting about building cars that, if not boring, are

at least mainstream. As Humberto Rodriguez, Fiat's director of design since 2001, explained, 'I have abolished all the strange things'. The first designs in the new era were launched at the March 2003 Geneva Motorshow. Both the Gingo (a smaller replacement for the Panda – see Exhibit 4.2) and the Idea (a new, small people carrier) have sweptback windscreens and near vertical rears. Similar, middle-of-the-road designs are planned for the Multipla. The aim is simple: to give it a normal exterior look so that customers only pay attention to the interior space and flexibility that led reviewers to rate it the best people carrier in Europe rather than cringing with embarrassment at its ugliness.[1]

www.fiat.com

Exhibit 4.1 Fiat's Multipla

© AMD Publishing

Exhibit 4.2 Fiat's Gingo

© AMD Publishing

Case example 2 SERVICE AND PRODUCT DESIGN AT ASAHI BREWERIES

Asahi Breweries, Japan's biggest beer company, is still revered as the company that transformed the Japanese beer industry when it launched Super Dry in the late 1980s. Developed in 1987, the country's first 'karakuchi' (dry) beer became an overnight success. Super Dry sold 13 million cases and quickly became Japan's #1 beer. By 2002, it had almost 50 per cent of the Japanese lager market, selling 2,100 million litres compared to the next most popular brand, Kirin Ichiban, at 632 million litres.

One of the secrets of this success was that its taste was developed to suit the Japanese market. As such, it was a new type of beer and the first new beer since World War Two. Furthermore, it was the first beer to be offered in cans, to sell in 3-litre containers and to be put together in seasonal gift packs.

And, Asahi Breweries is exporting. First to China, which consumes 20 billion litres of beer a year and later to the UK and then the rest of Europe.

www.asahibeer.co.jp/english/

Case questions
1 Is the role of design an order-winner or qualifier in the Fiat and Asahi Super Dry examples?
2 Explain the reasons for your view.

The research and development process

The objective of research and development (R&D) activity is to bring about technological change and innovation within both the services and products to be sold and the processes by which these will be produced. The total cycle of events to achieve this embraces programmes classified as being at the strategic and tactical levels.

Strategic programmes

Strategic programmes comprise activities concerned with both fundamental and applied research. Although it is convenient to highlight this split when defining what is involved, in reality the distinction between fundamental and applied research is often blurred:

- Fundamental research studies the basic relationship between cause and effect, with the aim of increasing knowledge, making discoveries and establishing new applications that may eventually be used on a commercial basis.

- Applied research is concerned principally with practical applications and solutions to practical problems. Its function concerns classifying and interpreting basic knowledge from fundamental research activities to facilitate problem solving. The return on this research investment is quicker and more assured than for fundamental research. Since applied research is directed towards solving particular problems in the later stages of service and product planning (for example advanced development work), the practical usefulness of the results is inherent in the activity. However, an organization may well subcontract some or all of this task until its own research demands can justify employing its own staff.

The level of commitment to strategic programmes is an important corporate decision. Organizations may decide to adopt either an offensive or a defensive design strategy, while others fall in between, making a moderate R&D commitment by, for instance, contracting out research or licensing other organizations' existing service and product designs.[2]

The offensive strategy brings with it a relatively large research spending commitment, with the objective of being a leader in service and product innovation within a given market. The defensive strategy usually limits the amount of research spending to a minimum and will be largely directed towards the development of existing knowledge to enhance service and product roles in a market or in response to customer requirements.

To help to explain these alternative strategies, the following categories are often used.[3] A 'first-to-market' posture focuses on cutting-edge research that leads to the introduction of new technologies ahead of competitors, whereas a 'fast-follower' posture requires a quick response to technical innovation by industry pioneers and may include modifying the technologies involved. A 'me-too' approach, on the other hand, is aimed at imitating widely available technologies by the introduction of close substitutes, while, finally, a 'late-entrant' approach is concerned with making incremental changes to existing technologies for limited applications. Case example 4.3 illustrates one approach.

Other strategic approaches also exist, such as manufacturing under licence or providing a service under a franchise. In the former, marketable products and products manufactured successfully elsewhere are produced under licence agreements. In the latter, invariably the products, methods of working and environment are highly specified and materials and other supplies are from prescribed sources (for example fast-food restaurants). In that way, a tight control on service and product specifications and their provision is maintained by the franchiser.

In early 2003, Bill Gates, Microsoft's chairman, announced that, while most of its rivals were cutting back on costs, the world's largest software company was going to increase its R&D budget by 20 per cent to $5.26 billion. That is not only big but is, in fact, more than the rest of the software industry's R&D budgets combined. This commitment to R&D has been a significant feature in Microsoft's strategy throughout.

It set up its R&D function in the early 1990s and has consistently increased its spend on this activity year on year – in fact, it more than doubled its budget between 1998 and 2003. On announcing the latest increase in research expenditure, Bill Gates highlighted its worthwhile and essential nature, explaining that customers underestimate the software's potential, and his belief that the industry and the market 'are going to be stunned at the advances we make'. Clearly Microsoft's intention is to maintain its cutting-edge technology position as it supports its belief in the significance of software in the future.

www.microsoft.com

Case questions   1   In which category of strategy would you place Microsoft?
                     2   Explain your choice.

Returning to what companies need to do in their R&D process, one further essential step is to ensure that research activity leads to the transfer of the resulting new technologies into services and products. Much investment is wasted if the fruits of the research are not adopted. Without this there is no commercial payback so essential to justify past and future R&D spend. But this transfer will not happen by itself. Companies need to create the organizational conditions, attitudes and expectations in order to facilitate this essential conversion, as Case example 4.4 illustrates.

Microsoft's awareness of the need to transfer research into product development is clear. Bill Gates reflected on Xerox's failure to do just this. 'In our industry the most famous story of all is that of Xerox's Palo Alto Research Centre (PARC)', he explained. '[It] managed to do amazing research but the company did not ... get the benefit of it. In fact, the few things they did from that research, like the Xerox Star (the first computer with windows, icons and a mouse), well, most of them lost money.'[4] To try to ensure that it would not suffer the same fate as Xerox's PARC, Microsoft has developed structures and approaches aimed to increase the transfer of research outputs into product development. Partly, its approach concerns organizational structure. Almost without exception, all parts of Microsoft's research organization are actively engaged in at least one product group. Specific approaches to improve the transfer of research activities include:

● The research organization has some eight dedicated programme managers. Their job is to spot technology that might transfer and show it to the product side at the right time. Too early and it won't have relevance, too late and it can't be incorporated. In fact, the research group measures its success by assessing the level of awareness of various technologies within the business and their take-up within product development.

● Off-site meetings (known as 'mind-swaps') are set up between research and product teams to discuss selected topics. Being located off site also means less distractions and a more relaxed atmosphere.

● Researchers organize annual fairs on site, known as 'techfests'. Attracting upwards of 20,000 staff, the research teams monitor the level of interest by staff in different ideas and developments. Also, visits to these fairs by top executives within the company signal the level of corporate importance and commitment to the broadcasting of ideas.

www.microsoft.com

Case questions   1   What are the key factors that Microsoft uses to aid the transfer of research ideas into product development?
                     2   From your list select the most important and give reasons for your choice.

Tactical programmes

Following these strategic activities come the tactical steps to develop a service or product. Although excellent and innovative services and products are conceived and designed by a whole range of businesses, a feature frequently experienced by many organizations is that the requirements of subsequent steps in the procedure are not adequately taken into account at the design stage. The result leads to higher than necessary costs. The typical view held is that design determines 70 per cent of costs.[5] While others may disagree with the percentage,[6] what is not contested is the significant impact on costs at this stage in the process. A good way to illustrate this relationship is provided by the Ford Motor Company's 'effectiveness lever', which illustrates the impact upon effectiveness that can be achieved at each of the principal stages in the procedure from design through to operations (Exhibit 4.3).

Exhibit 4.3   The Ford Motor Company 'effectiveness lever'[7]

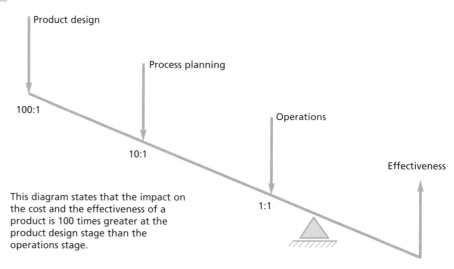

Tactical programmes cover all stages throughout the development of a service or product including its launch. They are concerned with the functional aspects of design and address basic questions covering:

- What will it do?
- How will it do it?
- How will it be made or provided?
- What is the maintenance and repair requirement?
- How will it be distributed?

The link between market need, technology, development, design and the operations delivery system is essential to the profitable provision of a service or production of a product and all the steps must be addressed.

The approach to development involves defining a service or product by a procedure of checking successive designs until the required specifications are met as economically as possible. This usually involves testing several designs to evaluate their feasibility in terms of functionality and cost. The following section looks at these steps in detail.

The design and development process for services and products

The first step in designing and developing a new or modifying an existing service or product is generating ideas. But a good idea does not necessarily indicate a successful outcome. A significant amount of development work is required before a service can be provided or a product produced and made available to customers. These steps are described as the service and product design and development process and are outlined in Exhibit 4.4. However, before discussing these in some detail, it is important to make two observations about Exhibit 4.4:

- **Sequential** – the process outline shows the steps as being sequential, whereas in fact parts of several stages will be completed in parallel one with another. This allows for a reduction in development lead times and so enables the earlier introduction of final designs to be made.

- **Reiteration** – although shown as being principally sequential, the steps actually involve much reiteration throughout. Questions are posed at each stage and these often take the proposal back one or more steps in order to clarify and resolve the fresh issues raised.

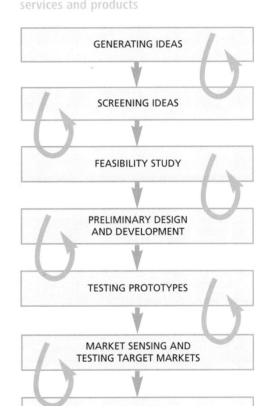

Exhibit 4.4 The design and development process for services and products

1 Generating ideas

The need to generate ideas is a key step in this process especially as the ratio between ideas and successful service and product introductions is often as low as 1 or 2 per cent. Ideas for new services and products can arise from a variety of sources within and outside a firm.

Internal sources

One important source of ideas comes from within the company. Some of these include:

- Employees – companies stimulate ideas in several ways. For example, suggestion schemes (where prizes of various values are awarded for useable ideas) or including the generation of ideas as part of employee evaluations have long been effective ways of getting ideas on the table.

- **Research and development** – investing in resources solely committed to generating ideas as discussed earlier.

- **Market research** – the systematic process of discussing with or using customers to identify needs and ideas. For example, part of the procedure used by Asahi Breweries when launching its Super Dry beer (see Case example 4.2) was to visit pubs, restaurants and parks asking drinkers what they wanted from a beer. As well as confirming that people mainly wanted something to drink with food, the company also received a resounding message: people wanted a beer that was 'nodogoshi' (easy to drink) with a somewhat dry bite. So, Asahi Super Dry was launched to meet these characteristics. A new taste was developed and a success story was born.

- **Sales force** – by remaining alert to potential customer needs and systematically recording and evaluating customer comments and discussions, sales staff can consistently add to the stream of ideas at this stage in the design and development process.

- **Reverse engineering** – this involves taking existing services and products (competitors as well as the company's own) and systematically analysing them to check the design concepts and principles being used. In this way existing thinking and current approaches are challenged, and the transfer of concepts used in one application to another helps to create a source of new ideas.

The need to rethink approaches at this stage in the design and development process has been recognized by many organizations, as Case example 4.5 illustrates.

Case example 5   DESIGN AND DEVELOPMENT AT GLAXOSMITHKLINE (GSK)

The pharmaceutical industry, where new product introduction is a key factor for success, has seen 'a quantum leap in the mechanics of drug research [that] promises to revolutionize pharmaceuticals in the way PCs reinvented the computer industry'.[8] GSK has started to use 'combinatorial chemistry' which creates tens of thousands of new molecules – the building blocks of new medicines – within a few hours, compared with conventional chemistry that results in an average of some 40 new molecules a year. Linked to this is a robotized screening station that evaluates a compound's effectiveness against specific disease-causing genes at the rate of 50,000 a week. As only one in 4000 synthesized compounds ever make it to market, and only 30 per cent of these earn back their full development costs, creating new compounds in a cost- and time-effective way is essential. Molecule selection is the essence of the pharmaceutical business and effectively generating ideas is the essential first step.

www.gsk.com

Case question   What is the fundamental change in approach adopted by GSK?

External sources

Equally important, and sometimes more important than ideas from internal sources, are those ideas generated outside the firm. These sources include customers, legislative requirements, environmental pressures and technology advances.

Customers[9]

There has been a marked change in the last 30 years regarding the source and approach to new service and product design. Gone are the days when the role of researchers was to come up with ideas that then went into the services and products that customers were encouraged to buy. Although this still happens (see for example the section on technology below), there has been a recognition that customer involvement, through focus groups being given the opportunity to express preferences and ideas and interfacing on the design process of products such as vehicles and housing, brings consumer-led ideas into the design arena. For example:

- Having closed their doors on a Saturday for over 30 years, UK banks, recognizing the changing lifestyles of many customers, asked how they could better meet their needs. One outcome was that selected high street branches reopened on a Saturday morning and stay open later on at least one day per week. In this way they provide services at times that best suit many customers. The service provision has now increased to a point where in all UK banks an almost full service is on offer when many customers are best able to use it.

- Over the last decade the number of US business trips involving children has grown to 15 per cent. Several factors are fuelling this trend (including two-career families and more single-parent households) and many working parents see business trips as a way of squeezing in precious time with their families. When the travel industry monitored these trends and also sought customer opinion on what changes would improve overall travel provision, the answer was to develop service delivery systems to meet these changing requirements. Hotels and airlines are now tailoring services to do just that – licensed babysitter booking, children's menus and sightseeing programmes for children illustrate some of the service development responses in many hotels.

- In more developed economies, the growing awareness of consumers to eat healthily has resulted in changes to the range of food being offered. Vegetarian options are now typically included while many fast-food restaurants now include non-beef main courses together with a wide range of fruit and salad options.

Legislative requirements

Government legislation invariably requires organizations to adapt and change, often necessitating new services and products to meet new requirements. For example:

- The European Commission's year on year higher targets for waste management continue to impact packaging design and stimulate change to meet these future requirements.

- Citizens' Charters introduced by many governments will increasingly have an impact on service design within several industries.

- Legislation concerning issues such as noise and pollution has required product design changes to meet the new requirements. The increasing use of active noise cancellation in turboprop aircraft to reduce noise levels, the pressure on emission levels in vehicles and the research work on battery-driven vehicles illustrate the impact of legislation on design.

Environmental pressures

Concerns and pressures from the 'green lobby' are forcing change often independent of government action. For example:

- Over 400 German companies have set up the Duales System Deutschland (DSD) to establish the infrastructure needed to recover and reuse packaging waste. At an estimated set-up cost of £3.5 billion and annual running costs of £0.7 billion, DSD is in response to growing consumer awareness about waste. These recycling targets are influencing European standards and the impact on packaging and waste collection services is already widespread.

- The sales growth in rechargeable batteries (a nickel–cadmium battery can be recharged 1000 times) reflects concerns not just about price but also the environment.

Technology advances

Technology shifts have far-reaching effects on service and product design. In some instances the changes revolutionize design and in others provide a plethora of new offerings. Dupont's invention of nylon and the impact of plastics, semiconductors, integrated circuits and computing on new service and product opportunities have been significant. The examples of the new services and products spawned from these new technologies are numerous – telephone and internet banking, internet shopping and the purchase of air tickets, theatre tickets and holidays online.

Enhancing services and products by incorporating new technologies is also widespread. For example, Federal Express interlinks stages in the service system by using computers to monitor and track deliveries throughout its whole delivery system. On receipt of a customer call a Federal Express operator enters details onto a computer. This information is then radioed to a courier and displayed on a hand-held computer terminal. After pick-up, the package is logged into the company's central computer in Memphis. With the use of industrial bar codes, packages can be tracked in the system and customers can access these details at any time on request.

2 Screening ideas

The purpose of screening ideas is to eliminate those that do not appear to have high potential and so avoid the costs incurred at subsequent stages. Proposals, supported by graphics, models and an outline specification, are then judged against a set of criteria to enable each design to be evaluated overall. The criteria used in such assessments include the potential impact of the idea on a firm's future success or survival, its role in filling out an existing service or product line, the degree of overlap with existing services and products, the utilization of existing delivery systems, processes and capabilities, a reflection of the firm's core interests and expertise and the overall impact on estimated sales and profits.

To provide greater insight, organizations often score each dimension of each idea on a 0–10 scale and then apply weights to each of these dimensions. The resulting aggregate score helps when deciding which ideas to progress and which to terminate. Unfortunately, it's too late with Mr James's approach (see Exhibit 4.5)!

Exhibit 4.5 The need to screen ideas!

© AMD Publishing

3 Feasibility study

The next step is to complete a more detailed check on the ideas still being considered. This part of the process will look at a whole series of dimensions that relate to a service or product idea and its intended markets, for example:

Service and product development

- development lead time – how long to develop a service or product from idea to provision
- previous experience
- anticipated length of life cycle – how long will the sales levels of a service or product be sufficient to justify keeping it on the sales list
- uniqueness of design

Market(s)

- relevant order-winners and qualifiers
- selling price
- sales volumes over time
- fit with a company's corporate strategy
- level of existing and future competition
- stable or seasonal nature of forecast patterns of demand
- advertising required
- technical demands on support staff in both the selling and after-sales stages

Operations

- degree of match with existing capabilities
- quality conformance requirements – the need to provide the service or product specification
- ability to support relevant order-winners and qualifiers
- capacity needs
- process investments

Financial

- capital outlays
- return on investment
- cash flows

Whereas the scoring model adopted in the initial screening stage provides a rough, quantitative measurement, the purpose of the analysis at this stage in the design process is to determine more specific qualitative measures on all important dimensions. This is necessary in order to help decide whether or not to commit further resources to the development of an idea. From this stage forward development costs tend to increase significantly.

4 Preliminary design and development

This stage of the process involves developing the best design for a new idea. Here the outline of the new service or product will need to be specified in much greater detail. Many trade-offs will have to be made concerning features, costs and producibility. Reconciling these, often conflicting, demands is a difficult task and one that needs to be resolved at this stage.

Computer-aided design (CAD) and later IT-based developments have made significant contributions to facilitating these decisions and are dealt with in more detail in a later section addressing the impact of technology on design.

5 Testing prototypes

The physical embodiment of the functional and aesthetic requirements of a service or product is known as the 'prototype'. Using this step in the process serves many ends. In addition to illustrating the aesthetic dimension, it serves to check the functionality of the idea, its robustness and the operations implications of its provision. In this way it tests the specification of the service or product, its physical or other dimensional properties or use under actual operating conditions. Part of this involves questions about the need for specific capabilities, material requirements, use of standard components, process steps, layouts, packaging and despatch implications. Typically there will be several, if not many, prototypes. It is a way of checking reality beforehand and enables savings in both time and costs to be secured.

6 Market sensing and testing target markets

The last section explained the need to test the functionality of an idea and undertake the continuous and critical task of checking prototypes. At the same time assessing potential demand needs to continue. That the idea works and can be reproduced is one side of the

Exhibit 4.6 Designing products around customer research – the approach to avoid

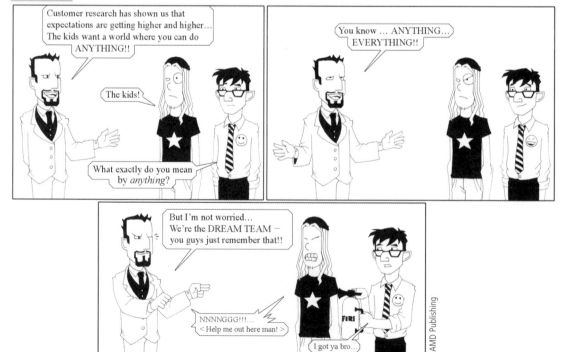

© AMD Publishing

coin and whether customers will buy it is the other. As with prototype testing, this step is an ongoing task and not the Gianni way (see Exhibit 4.6).

For example, a prototype may constitute the introduction of a new or revised service in one or more test sites where the concept can be evaluated and modified as necessary. Once a new service and its delivery system has been tried and proved to be successful it can be introduced into other outlets. This would typically be the approach adopted in national retail and fast-food restaurant chains. Here, a new range of clothing or a new line of meals would be trialled in selected outlets and, if successful, then launched throughout the rest of the business.

In the same way, product prototype testing is a way of verifying the technical perform- ance and sales potential of a new idea. Test marketing in a selected geographical area is a similar approach to that outlined above for services. Throughout, screening and testing is a continuous activity aimed at checking and rechecking in order to reduce uncertainty before large capital investments are committed.

7 Final design

Prototype testing often identifies necessary changes to the initial design. During the final design phase these will be incorporated. At this stage, specifications will be completed and the essential tasks of marketing plans, material supply, operations tasks and associated investments will be initiated.

Design – the reality

As mentioned earlier, the design process is characterized by reiteration and a non-sequential nature. Steps into the unknown embody uncertainty and the rigours of the process are intended to flush out questions essential to arriving at a viable design. Two further issues that are also part of the reality of the design process are now highlighted.

The decision

The final decision as to whether or not to go ahead rests with top management. The levels of investment, corporate profile and reputation, and the strategic direction of the firm are invariably central to the decision. Rejection stems from a combination of experience, judge- ment and placing a decision in the context of other investment opportunities. Approval commits a firm's efforts and resources one way and to a course of action, the success of which may not be measurable for months, even years later and yet may harm a company's success or even jeopardize its very survival.

Service/product design and delivery system/manufacturing process design

The design of services or products and the design of the service delivery systems or manu- facturing processes to provide them are interlinked. However, the separation of these aspects by addressing them in different chapters has been deliberate. Providing detail on both is essential, but incorporating them in a single set of statements can often be confus- ing. Separating the two aspects adds clarity without significant disadvantages. In the discus- sions on service delivery system and manufacturing process design in Chapters 5 and 6, links to service and product design will be recognized throughout.

Corporate strategy issues

All organizations have a range of services or products at a given time. To be competitive, it is necessary to have a set that is complementary, relates to the organization's strategic decisions that are associated with issues such as growth and market share, and takes account of tactical considerations such as completeness of range, process capability and distribution costs. Furthermore, the mix is always undergoing change. New services or products are necessary for survival and growth. It is essential, therefore, for an organization to review its service and product mix as a whole. When undertaking this review, there are three important factors to be considered:

- The development and introduction of new services and products are both risky and costly.
- Services and products tend to follow a life cycle.
- Some services and products are or have the potential to be more successful than others – service/product portfolio analysis.

The issues around the first point have been addressed earlier. Here we look at service/product life cycles, service/product portfolios and designing services and products to meet the needs of different market segments

Service/product life cycles

The extent and rate of new service and product introductions can make a significant impact on a business. However, of equal concern in these decisions is the life cycle pattern anticipated or experienced once the service or product has been introduced. Market pressures require that designs never remain static and continuous endeavours are made to increase the fit with customer needs while scrutinizing the relationships between cost, quality and value. Despite the attention given by most organizations, many services and products enter the market and are then quickly phased out due to a lack of sales.

The process of introduction, initial growth, maturity and eventual decline in sales is referred to as the 'service/product life cycle' (see Exhibit 4.7). It outlines the phases through which a service or product may go as it moves into and out of its market. New services and

Exhibit 4.7 The generalized service/product life cycle

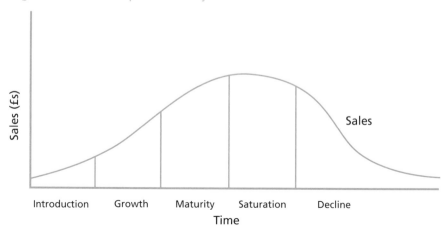

products are required to replace those already in the cycle, no matter how extended the timescale may be. The phases detailed in Exhibit 4.7 are now explained.

Introduction

Initially the sales pattern of many services and products shows a slow rate of growth. Market awareness is low and acceptance has not yet been achieved. The concept is often new, and initial teething troubles are usually experienced. This makes for low sales with slow growth.

Growth

In the growth phase, the market has now been conditioned to the service or product. With acceptance comes a rapid growth in sales resulting from promotion, increased dependability, past sales and often a lower selling price.

Maturity

At the maturity stage, the rate of sales increases begins to slow. This is due to the competitors who have entered the market because of increased demand as the service/product is now well known and established within its market segment.

Saturation

In the saturation stage, most of those who want the service or product have typically now bought it. Market demand is restricted to replacement demand plus a small quantity of new sales. Service and product promotion is often used more extensively here, not to publicize the item but to differentiate it from its competitors.

In service firms, this phenomenon is often not as marked. For example, restaurant chains still keep selling but often the sales levels plateau because of overcapacity in their sector or the reasons stated earlier. Also, some decline may take place as alternatives enter and prosper. For example, Kentucky Fried Chicken sales have declined in the last decade even though overall sales in the fast-food sector have grown. This is due to the success of fast-food alternatives.

Decline

In the decline phase of a life cycle, sales continue to fall off, invariably at a rapid rate. The introduction of competing services and products, either as improvements or substitutes, accelerates the decline to the point where it becomes obsolete. For example, the traditional telephone had been in the mature/saturation stage for a long time but over the last ten years has increasingly been replaced by, first, the cordless and, more recently, mobile phones. Similarly, in more developed economies, public transport services in many country areas have been replaced by private car ownership.

Reporting current and forecast sales of services and products in terms of the stage in their life cycle provides an insight into the spread of sales by phase, future patterns and the levels of new services and products that need to be targeted in the future. Also, different strategies are more relevant to one cycle stage than another. For example, an applications-oriented strategy is appropriate in the mature stage by offering modifications to existing services and products in order to serve particular market segments, whereas the emphasis on reducing costs and keeping designs fixed is most appropriate in the saturation phase of a typical cycle.

Service/product portfolio analysis

Portfolio analysis provides another way of helping companies to look forward and decide on the allocation of resources. As shown in Exhibit 4.8, services and products can be separated into four classes, with the market share held by an organization being measured horizontally and the growth rate within the market measured vertically.

Services and products are then placed throughout or across two or more of the four segments to illustrate their relative positions against these two dimensions. The resulting 'portfolio' of services and products serves as part of the basis by which an organization can determine the appropriate allocation or concentration of corporate resources and particularly research and development funding. These quadrants are explained below.

An organization that has analysed its services and products in this way is then able to look at its current or proposed mix in terms of cash and profits. This will help it to ensure continuity of a suitable service or product mix by determining a series of corporate issues. These include which markets to aim for and the degree of support required, particularly with regard to decisions on research and operations investment.

Exhibit 4.8 Service/product portfolio analysis

Growth rate of the market (cash use)	Service/product market share (cash generation)	
	High	Low
High	☆ Stars Cash generated is equal to or less than the cash used	❓ Dilemmas Cash generated is less than the cash used
Low	£€$ Cash cows Cash generated is greater than the cash used	🐇 Pets Cash generated is less than the cash used

Dilemmas

Dilemmas are services/products with a small percentage of a high growth market. In order to maintain or improve its position, an organization will have to allocate more cash than the services and products generate. Although the environment is favourable, current performance is questionable, thus requiring close examination and often remedial action. Consequently, it will be uncertain as to whether a service or product in the future will become a star or a pet.

Stars

Stars are services/products with a high market share (typically a market leader) in a high growth market but often in a position where the cash generated is, at best, equal to (and often less than) the cash needed. Stars will eventually become cash cows if they hold their market share; they will become pets if they do not.

Cash cows

Cash cows are services/products with a high percentage of a low growth market and in the latter half of their life cycle. These are the principal generators of funds. The cash cow can be 'milked' to generate more cash than can be profitably reinvested. However, they can in no way be forgotten: they have to be managed efficiently, new developments within a service or product range have to be made and customers have to be carefully tended, with the emphasis on cash flow rather than building market share.

Pets

Also known as cash traps, cash dogs and cash coffins, pets describe services/products where individual market share is low, market growth is low and they are cash absorbers, with little or no hope of changing the situation. For many organizations the majority of their services/products fall into this category. They may show an accounting profit but the profit must be reinvested to maintain market share. They leave no cash surplus for investment elsewhere and often absorb cash surpluses created by other services and products. As a rule, they should be deleted from the range.

The service/product portfolio analysis is essentially static but is a useful selection technique to help organizations to both understand more fully their current position and reposition their service/product portfolio in the future. Its primary functions are to aid resource allocation and cash management by pinpointing those services and products with greatest potential and maintain a balance within the current mix. On the other hand, the service/product life cycle is a dynamic model with associated market-related strategies built in. Thus, combining the two analyses allows companies to assess their service or product mix on both dimensions which, in turn, gives further insights to help determine decisions such as investment priorities and where best to harvest existing services and products.

Designing services and products to meet the needs of different market segments

Firms invariably compete in more than one market segment, and recognizing and addressing the differences involved in terms of service or product development, as well as marketing, operations and other functional tasks, is essential. To illustrate how companies have developed different services and products to meet the needs of different market segments, take a look at Case examples 4.6 and 4.7.

Case example 6   PRODUCT DESIGN FOR DIFFERENT MARKET SEGMENTS AT HANDELS BANK NW

Handels Bank NW of Zurich provides a different service offering for the following market segments:

- Institutional investors
- Portfolio management clients
- Large investors
- Standard investors
- Medium investors
- Small investors.

These segments reflect the needs of its investors, the appropriate investment tools to be used and the differential costs the bank applies in providing its different services. In this way, the bank more clearly identifies the type and level of service to be provided and the operations support required in that provision.

In the same way, UK banks have been segmenting their market and developing services to meet the needs of 'high earners'. Tailoring products and allocating more management time are high on the agenda and linked to different segments.

Natwest, for example, divides its customers by age, family status and income, and addresses each segment differently.

www.lhb.de

Case questions

1 For the six market segments above, identify three elements of service where the level or type of provision would not be the same for each segment.

2 For two of the six segments above, suggest how the three elements you selected could differ.

Case example 7   MARKET SEGMENTATION IN THE HOTEL INDUSTRY

Hotels continue to emphasize segments within their offering and support these with appropriate service developments. In the 1970s it was in-room mini-bars, while health clubs were all the rage in the 1990s. Now executive floors have emerged in the top business hotels in North America and Europe. Billed as a hotel within a hotel, the premium floors have their own check-in and check-out facilities, an executive lounge and sometimes a dedicated, express-elevator service. For five-star hotels, executive floors are a way of differentiating themselves at a time of intense competition in downtown and airport sites. For example, the Hilton Hotel in the Boulevard des Waterloo, Brussels offers for a $60 supplement, an executive floor room which includes the complimentary breakfast (normally $27), free drinks in the lounge until 2200 hours, butler service,

a library of CDs and videos for guests to play in their room and a mobile phone loaned free, for which they can obtain their individual phone number three days in advance.

Finally, with the growing number of guests who are businesswomen travelling alone, hotels are providing services to reflect this. The Meridien Hotel, Piccadilly, London offers a female executive traveller package including female room service attendants and increased awareness of security at all stages in the hotel process. The Thistle Hotel chain includes special features in its rooms allocated to women and some of its hotels offer women-only wings. A recent survey showed that 35 per cent of all business travellers are women, with the number expected to rise rapidly to more than 50 per cent.

Case questions

1 What are the three most significant ways in which hotels have addressed the 'executive' and 'female guest' segments described above?

2 Explain your choice.

Operations strategy issues

As highlighted in Chapter 2 on Operations Strategy, the need to link decision areas within functions to one another is essential. This section continues this theme and, in particular, looks at how the development of a specification (what a service or product comprises) has to be detailed from several perspectives. That services and products need to be defined in terms of what they comprise is self-evident. What is equally important, however, is to identify within the development process those aspects of the design that will later impact other functions tasked with selling and providing it. Here we deal with the perspectives of operations.

The inherent nature of services and products

The physical nature of products brings with it an inherent need to specify what a product comprises when it is being developed. Services, on the other hand, are less tangible and consequently the task of defining what a service comprises needs to be a more specific undertaking. Without this recognition, the rigour necessary to define a service may not be applied and the required detail not provided.

In manufacturing, products and customers are invariably decoupled in the system, for example through inventory or the wholesale and/or retail stages in the total supply chain. In services, however, the provider and customer are invariably linked at the point of provision. The result is that the opportunity to interpret what is meant by 'service' is also at the point of provision. It is necessary, therefore, for organizations to determine the level of discretion to be allowed in the service delivery system. This concerns what a service comprises and what a server can provide as part of a service specification.

The service/product mix

As highlighted earlier in Chapter 1, most offerings comprise a mix of service and product and Exhibit 1.6 provided some examples. This mix together with other factors make up a specification and these various elements are now explained.

The mix itself

When detailing a specification, it is useful to identify the nature of the service and the nature of the product within the mix. One way to highlight the corresponding roles of the service and product elements in the mix is to ask: is this a service within which there is a facilitating product or is this a product that also involves a facilitating service? This helps to clarify the mix issue and identify which elements are an integral part of the specification, which would enhance the offering in the eyes of the customer and which can be challenged.

A look back at Exhibit 1.6 is a reminder that what is purchased is a combination of services and goods and the mix will vary, for example purchasing a television set compared to tailored kitchen units requiring installation, or a meal provided by a high-class restaurant compared with a fast-food outlet.

The explicit and implicit benefits of the offering[10]

When developing a specification, the process followed needs to scrutinize the principal elements, so as to identify these requirements in sufficient detail. Only in this way will the offering be adequately specified and the perspectives of all the functions that contribute to its design and provision be identified and embraced. One approach is to separate the elements of the specification into explicit and implicit dimensions. When customers purchase services or products, they perceive that they are receiving one or more explicit services. For example, a bank provides the explicit service of money transactions; a hotel provides food and accommodation; and a hairdresser, the styling of hair. Customers may choose from a range of quality levels concerning the provision of a service and this will typically influence their selection of the providing organization. In addition, the offering may also include a range of implicit dimensions. For example, security and privacy within a banking system; level of attention, promptness and recognition of a regular customer by hotel staff; magazine and hot/soft drink provision and levels of cleanliness within a hairdressing salon. In fact, in many markets the implicit services may well be as, if not more, important a factor in customer selection as the explicit service that is at the core of the purchase. However, no matter what comprises the relative importance of the explicit and implicit dimensions involved, recognizing those differences facilitates developing a specification and signalling in detail what the offering should comprise and the functional perspectives that need to be taken into account in terms of design, development and provision.

The supporting structural facilities

This concerns a recognition of the need to determine support facilities that reflect the nature and customers' perceptions of the service or product provided. Typical examples are the quality of buildings, reception areas, meeting rooms, furniture, fittings and equipment, appropriate decor, level of maintenance and general upkeep, delivery vehicles, appearance and technical know-how of after-sales support staff.

The implications of the non-repeat or repeat nature of a service or product

The design of a service or product must also reflect the market characteristics in which it is to be sold. At one extreme a service or product may comprise an offering that is not repeated, that is, it is designed specifically for one customer. This is termed a 'special' service or product, referring to its unique, non-repeat nature. Examples include in-depth financial advice regarding a multinational takeover, the interior design for corporate offices, the logo for a blue-chip company, the public relations campaign for a political party, the garden design for a large country house and an ocean-going yacht designed to compete in the Melbourne to Hobart race or America's Cup. As you will see from these examples, markets characterized by non-repeat offerings are unusual and not the norm.

Most services and products are of a repeat nature (provided more than once and to more than one customer) and at the extreme will be high volume. Examples of repeat offerings include post office services, petrol or gas stations, supermarkets, sandwich bars, fast-food outlets and cash machines in the service sector, with computers, mobile phones and T-shirts providing examples in the manufacturing sector. With this fundamental change, dimensions of the service and product such as volumes, order size, level of change required and typical order-winners and qualifiers will also differ, as shown in Exhibit 4.9.

Exhibit 4.9 The implications of the non-repeat and repeat nature of a service or product

Aspects		Non-repeat	Repeat	
			Low volume	High volume
Service or product	type	Special	——————→	Standard
	range	Wide	——————→	Narrow
Customer order size		Low	——————→	High
Level of service/product change required in the process		High	——————→	Low
Design predominantly determined by		Customer	——————→	Provider
Orientation of innovation – process or service/product		Service or product	——————→	Process
What does the company sell?		Capability or skill	——————→	Standard offering
How does the company win orders?	order-winners	Unique capability, repeat business or recommendations	——————→	Price
	qualifiers	Price, delivery on time, quality conformance	——————→	Delivery on time, quality conformance

Exhibit 4.9 illustrates some of the aspects that relate to service and product design issues that, in turn, will have implications for operations. The special (non-repeat) or standard (repeat) nature of the service or product is reflected in the width of the range offered. As a capability or skill seller, companies in non-repeat design markets offer a range, the width of which is only limited by the skill base available. On the other hand, companies selling high volume, repeat services or products will typically restrict the range. The higher the volume, the less the choice. And the dimension of range is not service- or product-related but reflects the volumes involved. For example, the options available on a Honda Accord are significantly less than those available on a Rolls-Royce or Mercedes Benz. Although both products are automobiles, they represent very different markets, differences which are duly reflected in the design-related features highlighted in Exhibit 3.6. Hence, in non-repeat markets, service and product designs are predominantly determined by the customer, while with repeat service/product offerings designs (including options available) are determined by the provider – a customer's choice is limited to what is on the option list. Finally, the way a company wins orders will similarly reflect these non-repeat/repeat and volume dimensions and the role of design is to contribute to these strategic requirements. Innovation of the offering and the potential order-winning role of unique capability will progressively be replaced by the design task of taking out cost and contributing to the need for a simple-to-provide offering that helps reduce costs while making repeatability an easy-to-achieve characteristic.

Operations techniques and approaches related to design

This final section outlines some of the operations techniques and approaches used to help improve the design process in the overall context of a business:

- standardization
- modular design
- mass customization
- Taguchi methods
- quality function deployment and the house of quality
- value engineering and value analysis
- simultaneous engineering
- variety reduction.

Standardization

As shown in Exhibit 4.9, the service/product continuum ranges from specials, where each item is unique, to offerings where there is little if any choice – the Model T Ford 'any colour as long as it is black' syndrome. For the most part, today's markets lie between these extremes. To help enhance volumes, designers, where possible, use the same components, ingredients or materials to provide a range of offerings. For example, designers use the same chassis in more than one car and, similarly, the same engines in more than one model. In the same way, suppliers of prepacked food use much the same packaging from one item to another, while fast-food restaurants use the same containers, food items and disposable packaging wherever possible. In doing so, the volume of the standard item is enhanced which helps to reduce costs.

Thus, the concept of standardization helps provide a range of options, while enhancing the volumes of parts from which end services and products are built. The concept can be applied to components, materials, processes and delivery systems to great effect, as Case examples 4.8 and 4.9 illustrate.

Case example 8   OPERATIONS TECHNIQUES: OIL AND GAS

Oil and gas production platforms, historically custom-built to a bespoke specification, are moving towards standard designs built on a modular basis as part of a cost-cutting orientation to ensure the future profitability of big oil companies.

Case example 9   OPERATIONS TECHNIQUES: TOYOTA

Toyota launched its smaller, recreational vehicle Rav 4 at around half the price of most vehicles in this segment in part by using existing components and subassemblies from other cars – the engine and steering wheel from Celica, a sports car, and door mirrors from Corina, a four-door sedan.

www.toyota.com

Case questions   1 Why were oil and gas platforms originally custom-built, non-repeat products?

2 Compare the use of standardization in the two examples. What similarities do you find?

Modular design

The use of modules as standard building blocks in designing and providing products and services is an extension of the concept of interchangeable parts. Using common sets of parts enhances volumes, lowers costs and reduces inventory levels, as Case example 4.10 illustrates.

Case example 10   OPERATIONS TECHNIQUES: SONOCO

Offering modular services in support of products enabled Sonoco's (a large US packaging company) industrial products division to customize its packaging of support services 'to meet more precisely the requirements of its spectrum of customers'. The concept of offering only essential services as part of the sales package and then offering modular services at set prices enables companies such as Sonoco Products, Baxter Healthcare International, Asea Brown Boveri (ABB) and AZKO to tailor packages to customer needs and keep prices lower.

www.sonoco.com

Case question   How is modular design used by Sonoco and others?

Mass customization

The increasingly competitive nature of today's markets has increased the need to provide customers' requirements without prohibitive price and lead time implications. While process investment is at the core of this provision, the decision to customize products as the way to run a business will mean substantial changes throughout an organization. Ever since General Motors (GM), by offering choice and alternatives, took over the world leadership mantle from Ford and its 'no choice' strategy in the 1920s, the car industry has offered a wide choice on many dimensions. The result is that the potential number of different car configurations (engine types and size × colours × options) for most models runs into six figures and they are all assembled on the same process. This development is now spreading to other markets.

The proliferation of faster, smarter and more affordable computers, software and telecommunications allows more choice or customization on a mass (that is, high volume) scale. Aspects of modular designs and interchangeable parts offer choice to the customer and, with the necessary process investment required in place and an organization geared to meet these offerings, the ability to customize a standard product is a viable activity. Whereas mass customization is not in itself new (the GM strategy was launched in the late 1920s), its application to a wider range of product offerings is, and the phrase 'mass customization' is intended to herald this growing phenomenon.[11]

Taguchi methods

The approach to design developed by Japan's Genichi Taguchi[12] received considerable attention in the early 1990s and now forms an integral part of the approach to design. His principle is simple. Instead of constantly directing effort to control a process so as to assure consistent quality conformance, it is better to design the service or product to achieve desired levels of quality conformance, despite the variations that will occur in the service delivery system or production process. Based on his work in manufacturing, Taguchi's approach uses statistically designed experiments to optimize design and operations costs. This approach requires a service or product to perform to specification in extreme conditions. For example:

- **above-average demand** – ability of manufacturing to provide capacity uplifts
- **absenteeism** – staffing plans to provide short-term cover
- **dietary needs** – range of options to provide alternative menus
- **weather shifts** – alternative activities to meet changeable weather patterns
- **unexpected demand** – plans to meet early arrivals
- **working conditions** – developing products to withstand harsh climates or extreme patterns of use.

The effects of this approach on design procedures and objectives continue to be most noticeable. In part it forces the service delivery system/manufacturing process and service/product design to come together and agree the parameters to meet a range of conditions and build these into the specification. In so doing, it moves to a more proactive approach that emphasizes prevention of defects and enables organizations more consistently to meet the design specification and achieve higher levels of quality conformance, a key factor in many of today's markets.

Quality function deployment and the house of quality

There are two dimensions that affect the success of the design effort – the extent to which a service or product design meets customers' needs and how well an organization can produce or deliver the design. Quality function deployment (QFD) is a way to evaluate how well the service or product design and the operations process meet or exceed the needs of customers. Using competitors' offerings as an additional part of the assessment helps organizations to identify both where they need to improve and also the service and product features and activities that are non-value adding.

QFD had its origins in Bridgestone Tire Corporation and Mitsubishi's Kone (Japan) shipyards in the late 1960s. Professor Yoji Akao (Tamagawa University) and Shigeru Mizuno gave QFD its name in the late 1970s and popularized the concept of formalizing customer inputs into service and product design procedures. The complete QFD approach involves a sequential set of matrices (see Exhibit 4.10) through which the links between

Exhibit 4.10 How quality function deployment links customer needs to operations requirements

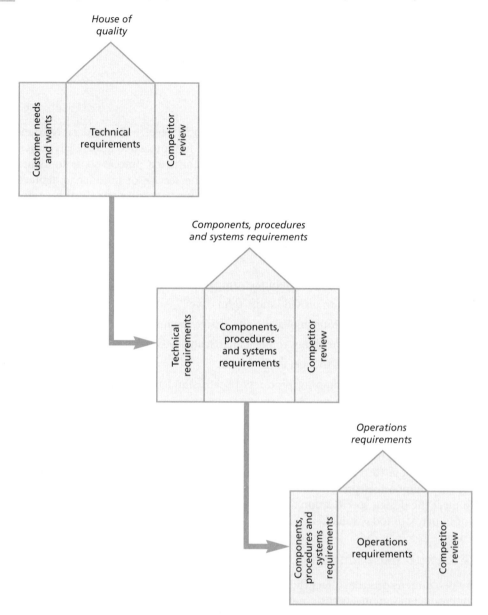

customer needs and the technical, component/material and operations requirements are identified and maintained.

The most commonly used phase of QFD is the stage 1 matrix, often called the 'house of quality'. Exhibit 4.11 illustrates the general steps involved and will be used to show how the approach is applied, in this instance to a fast-food restaurant.

1   Customers' needs and wants – establish what customers need and want and the characteristics and attributes of the services and products involved. Furthermore, the relative importance of these must then be established and weights agreed as a percentage, as shown in Exhibit 4.11.

2 **Establish the customers' view of competition** – establish how well this facility is satisfying customers' needs compared with competitors' outlets. In Exhibit 4.11, three competing restaurants are compared, with OP (own performance) representing this outlet and A, B and C representing the competitors' facilities. Where 1 is the worst and 5 the best, category comparisons are made and areas that potentially need improving are revealed.

3 **Identify the technical requirements** – identify the technical requirements necessary to provide customers' wants and needs. For example, fast service may be achieved, in part, by making food ahead of time or reducing the process lead time involved. Measuring the

Exhibit 4.11 Using quality function deployment matrix I: the 'house of quality'

Customers' needs and wants		Weights %	Increase grill area	Increase server staff at peak times	Increase server stations	Increase kitchen staff at peak times	Decrease average time food is stored	Decrease maximum time food is stored	Decrease process steps – main meal	Best 1	2	3	4	Worst 5
Decor and layout		5									OP B	A&C		
Menu variety	Child	5	+			+					OP C	A&B		
	Adult	10	+			+				C		B	OP A	
Service speed		30	+	+	+	+	−	−	+	C		OP A	B	
Food	Tastes good	15	+	+	+	+	+	+	+		OP C	A&B		
	Served warm	10	+	+	+	+	+	+	+	C	A	B	OP	
	Ingredients	5									OP C	B	A	
Low price		20	−	−		−	−	−			OP	A&B		C

Technical evaluation of competitors		m²	#	#	#	mins	mins	#	Comments
Own performance (OP)		2.5	5	5	7	6	9	8	
Competitors	A	2.4	5	5	7	6	8	6	
	B	2.7	5	5	8	6	7	6	
	C	3.0	6	7	8	4	7	5	
Target technical specifications		2.9	6	7	8	4	7	5	

factors that affect these and other dimensions would then be completed as an input into step 5.

4 Look for links between customer needs and technical requirements – look for links between the technical requirements and their effect on the different customers' needs and wants. These are recorded in the body of the house of quality with a + or – sign indicating the extent to which it would potentially improve or harm relevant service or product attributes. For example, let us consider the technical requirement 'Decrease average time food is stored' in Exhibit 4.11. While decreasing the average storage time of food is potentially harmful to service speed (the chance of being out of stock increases and customers would have to wait), it is also recognized as potentially helping the attributes 'food tastes good' and 'food served warm'. Obviously, if we changed this technical requirement from 'decrease' to 'increase average time food is stored', the + and – signs would be reversed.

5 Complete technical comparisons – check the extent of your technical provision with that of your competitors. The actual figures involved or using a scale of 1–5 help in drawing comparisons and making subsequent assessments. In Exhibit 4.11, actual figures are used throughout.

6 Evaluate the trade-offs for different design features – in the 'roof' section of the house of quality, record the information relating to the trade-offs of different design features, using + or – signs. This highlights the effect of changing the extent of one requirement on the other technical dimensions in the process. In Exhibit 4.11 you will see a + sign recorded between the first and fourth technical requirements. This highlights the need for both these requirements in order to increase menu variety and improve delivery speed. You will, however, see a – sign between the first and fifth and the first and sixth technical requirements – whereas increasing the grill area will help to improve service speed, decreasing storage times will have the reverse effect.

Value engineering and value analysis

In 2002, the cost of purchases made by all the manufacturing industries totalled £287 billion. Not only is this high in itself but also many times larger than both the employment costs and net capital expenditure for these industries. As Exhibit 4.12 shows, the ratio of purchases to employment costs remains more than three times higher while the ratio of purchases to net capital expenditure was more than twenty times greater in 2002. It makes sense, therefore, for companies to give time and attention to reducing material costs so as to secure the significantly higher potential benefits and savings.

The size of the purchasing bill comprises two elements – the price of the materials, components and services purchased and the amount of materials, components and services used. While the former is the concern of the purchasing function (which to some extent will be influenced by world markets, competition and usage volumes), the latter is influenced by service and product design (the specification itself) and how well it utilizes these purchased items. The approaches to checking the amount of materials, components and services used are now reviewed.

An important, but often underused technique to help provide this systematic approach to reducing the cost of a service or product without impairing its function is *value analysis*. Each product, component or service is methodically examined with the purpose of minimizing its cost without reducing its functional value.[13] Although value analysis was applied initially to existing manufactured products, it is now applied with equal success to the

Exhibit 4.12 Ratio of purchases to employment costs and net capital capital expenditure for selected sectors

| Sector[1] | Ratio of purchases[2] to employment costs and net capital expenditure | | | | | |
| | 2002 | | 1988 | | 1995 | |
	Employment costs	Net capital expenditure	Employment costs	Net capital expenditure	Employment costs	Net capital expenditure
Food, beverages and tobacco	4.5	18.5	4.9	16.8	5.7	18.8
Chemical products	3.9	15.1	4.2	9.7	4.3	12.3
Electrical and optical equipment	3.2	42.0	3.6	15.6	3.6	13.4
Transport equipment	4.2	21.8	4.2	15.5	4.0	14.3
Textiles and textile products	2.6	25.2	2.3	19.1	2.7	23.4
Leather and leather products	3.5	53.4	2.8	31.1	2.4	23.8
Wood products	2.8	24.6	2.6	13.9	3.4	26.7
Rubber and plastic products	2.6	17.9	2.6	11.3	2.8	12.1
Paper, publishing and printing products	2.4	17.9	2.4	12.5	2.7	10.9
All manufacturing industries	3.3	21.1	3.3	14.2	3.6	15.1

Notes   1   Industry categories were revised in 1986.
2   Includes materials for use in production, and packing and fuel: these include the cost of raw materials, components, semi-manufactured goods and workshop materials, replacement parts and consumable tools not charged to capital account, packaging materials of all types, stationery and printed matter, fuel, electricity and water materials.

Source HMSO Business Statistics Office, PA 1002 Business Monitor Report on the Census of Production and Annual Business Inquiry for relevant years.

service sector and the overhead costs within all types of organization. The term *value engineering* is often used synonymously with value analysis but, strictly speaking, it refers to the use of this technique in the initial stages of service or product design.

Value analysis, like other methods of continuous improvement, aims to reduce costs. However, its orientation is different. Continuous improvement methods (discussed in detail in Chapter 16) tend to accept the service or product as a given and instead concentrate on the way it is provided or made. Thus, the principal aim is to reduce aspects such as staff costs, rejects, wastage and lead times. Value analysis, however, considers the functions that the components, products or services are intended to perform. It then reviews the present design in order to provide these functions at a lower cost, without reducing the value, that is, the specification of a service or product to meet a given customer requirement will be maintained and will be met by any proposed changes.

The need for value analysis to be introduced and maintained throughout an organization is an essential part of any strategy to systematically reduce costs. As Lawrence Mills, who developed these concepts in 1961, said: 'On average, one fourth of manufacturing cost is unnecessary. The extra cost continues because of patterns and habits of thought, because of personal limitations, because of difficulties in promptly disseminating ideas and because today's thinking is based on yesterday's knowledge.'[14]

Value can be classified under two headings:[15]

●   **Use value** – the properties and qualities that accomplish the function of a service or product.

●   **Esteem value** – the properties, features or attractiveness that cause people to want to own or use it.

Value, therefore, consists of a combination of use and esteem properties related to the cost of providing them.

The analysis of value

In attempting to analyse value, three aspects of operations are reviewed:

1   Design of the service or product.
2   Purchase of materials or services.
3   Service delivery system/manufacturing process methods.

Design

Too often design decisions are made without due consideration of the effects on service or product costs. There are a number of reasons:

- Designers are often preoccupied with the initial task of designing to meet the functional requirements involved.
- Traditional designs are often concerned with reliability and quality and do not ask value-for-money questions.
- Designers often adopt a safety-first policy and thereby overspecify compared with what is required.
- Too often there is a lack of current information available to designers and therefore they design too much from yesterday's principles and information sources.
- The functional specialisms that exist help to create barriers between design, purchasing, operations and sales.
- In the case of services, too often the specification is not clearly determined, as explained in an earlier section.

Purchasing

In many organizations too little attention is given to the need to obtain services and materials that meet design requirements at lowest cost. This is because:

- In most organizations purchasing is still seen largely as a paper-processing task and so the resources allocated and importance attributed to this critical role tend to be insufficient. As a result the essential cost-reduction and value-oriented approaches tend not to be forthcoming.
- It is too easy to: (a) rely on previous or known suppliers, or allow other functions to specify the source for items; (b) avoid investigation and questioning as an integral part of the purchasing procedure, and (c) be reactive in this role.
- As in other areas, purchasing also suffers from the barriers created by functional specialisms.

Operations

Many firms are increasingly looking to improve all aspects of their organization. This has long been so in the operations function. But in the past, reviews of working procedures have been limited:

- The investigation has been based on an operation or department rather than the service or product through all its stages including design.
- Study has usually concentrated on the process, the way the work is completed. In so doing, it has failed to ask essential questions regarding design and materials.

Value analysis procedure

Value analysis comprises two parts: (1) those responsible for completing the analysis, and (2) the procedure to be followed.

The make-up of those responsible for completing the analysis work is quite wide-ranging. The classic structure is to have a group comprising a full-time specialist (the value analyst) and representatives from design, purchasing, costing and operations. However, other forms have proved equally successful and, in the case of many Japanese companies, include groups constituted under the title of 'quality circles'. In each instance, prerequisites to the successful application of value analysis are that those concerned are trained in the procedures involved and that corporate goodwill is demonstrated at all points throughout, including time to complete the tasks, access to cost and other data and liaison with outside suppliers. The steps involved are:

1 Select the service or product.

2 Gather information about it.

3 Analyse its function and its value for money.

4 Generate alternative ways to provide the same function through speculation and brainstorming.

5 Assess the worth of these ideas.

6 Decide what is to be done.

7 Implement the decisions.

8 Evaluate the results.

In step 4, it is essential to use someone with experience (the value analyst) and carefully select the group involved. The selection should avoid the potential problems of seniority and provide a wide range of disciplines within the group. This stage is key to the successful application of this technique and needs to be used with care.

The items selected are usually known to be of high cost and the use of the 80/20 rule will help in the procedure.[16] However, it is important not to select a service/product that is nearing the end of its life cycle. Value analysis is not a prop to help non-viable services or products become viable. It can, however, form a legitimate part of extending the life cycle of existing services or products.

When introducing value analysis, the procedure should in no way bring with it an air of recrimination. Those concerned need to contribute to the process in an objective way without implying criticism of any department's or person's previous work. The following questions will help when applying value analysis to each item or part of the service or product:

- Does it contribute to the esteem or use value of the service/product? If so, how?
- What is its cost? Does the cost of each part or feature appear to be in proportion to its function?
- Are all the features essential? Which ones are questionable?
- If it is necessary, what else could provide the same function:
  (a) standard part?
  (b) alternative part?
- Is the way in which the service/product is currently provided or made in line with current volumes? Often volumes change, but the delivery system or process does not.

- Has anyone asked the supplier if an alternative is available to provide the same function?
- Have alternative supplies been sought recently in terms of current volumes and prices?

Value analysis consists of taking each part of a service or product and looking in detail at its function. Every feature, tolerance, hole, degree of finish, piece of material, part of the service is vetted to ensure that none of these is adding to the total cost without providing a useful function.

The application of value analysis principles to products can be readily visualized. However, these principles are increasingly, and appropriately, being applied within service industries. One example is provided in a review of the Paul Revere Life Insurance Company's application of value analysis as part of achieving its corporate strategic objective of improved quality.[17] Management groups formed value analysis workshops to address the question, 'Are we doing the right thing?',[18] which resulted in recommendations to improve basic work functions and processes. The responsibility for implementing these organizational and work process changes was delegated to those running the individual sections, with department managers themselves eventually taking part in the value analysis workshops. Having identified the more important departments and the functions within a department, standard value analysis procedures were applied. Annual savings in the first six months were $6 million.

The sources of savings from value analysis come principally from steps in a system and materials. They include:

- Eliminate parts (for example components, transactions and steps in a service system) without reducing the functional qualities involved.
- Combine the functions of two or more components or services by redesign.
- Reduce tolerances that are unnecessarily tight and make for higher operations costs.
- Extend the concept of standardization.
- In conjunction with many of these savings, it will be possible to simplify the system or process and consequently reduce staff costs.

Simultaneous engineering

The speed with which services and products can be designed and introduced into a market directly affects sales revenues and profit. Simultaneous engineering is an organizationally based approach to reducing design lead times. It involves all relevant functions within a business (for example design, marketing, IT and operations) as well as suppliers. The purpose of the approach is to undertake tasks, in part or in total, in a parallel rather than sequential way. Receiving early inputs from various functions also reduces time-consuming redesigns and consequent delays. Teamwork encourages co-ownership of design and a greater commitment to making a service/product succeed. Jobs are enriched and creativity is stimulated. Because everyone is communicating with everyone else throughout the design process, service/product quality increases, service/product lead times are dramatically shortened and service/product costs are cut. What happens in principle is shown in Exhibit 4.13.

To achieve reductions similar to those outlined in Exhibit 4.13, companies use a number of approaches to help speed up the process of designing and introducing services and products. These new methods (some of which have been mentioned earlier) include:

- Contracting out activities – using external resources for one or more of the stages increases capacity and reduces delays. The areas of activity could include a range of tasks from design, marketing and IT through to prototypes, initial launch and public relations.

Exhibit 4.13 Reducing service/product development lead times by undertaking tasks in parallel

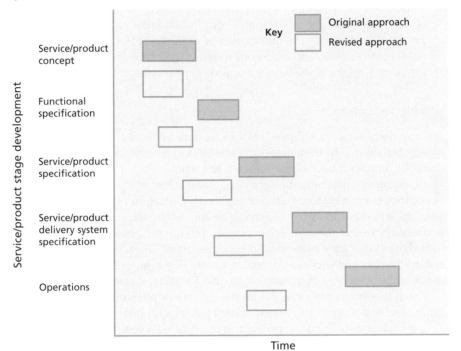

- Increased use of suppliers – as explained later in Chapter 13 on Managing the Supply Chain, suppliers are increasingly being asked to take on several of the design and service or product introduction phases as part of the supplier package, especially those elements of the service or product they will later supply. This reduces the overall demands on a company's own design team and shortens the total time taken to complete the design tasks.

- Teamwork – forming service, product and process teams not only stimulates ideas but also speeds up the process and eliminates problems.

- Combining or eliminating stages – combining or eliminating stages by re-examining the need to undertake all or part of the existing procedure not only rigorously tests current practices but also reduces lead times throughout.

- Overlapping stages – as illustrated in Exhibit 4.13, identifying opportunities to begin the next phase before the current stage is complete moves the overall procedure away from a sequential to a parallel activities format. Delays are reduced and the overall lead times improve dramatically.

- Incremental vs breakthrough innovations – in the past breakthrough innovations have often been the desired goal of designers. Breakthroughs are harder to come up with, typically have longer lead times in all phases of the design process and result in a higher failure rate. Switching the emphasis to incremental improvements and introducing clusters of these at the same time still leads to significant service and product improvements but reduces the lead times to bring them about.

- Using standard parts and modular designs – an earlier section introduced the principles and benefits of using standard parts and components and modular approaches to designs. A further advantage is also made available as improvements in 'common' parts can be introduced into relevant existing designs with corresponding benefits.

- Using new technologies – employing technologies such as computer-aided design (CAD) and computer-aided engineering (CAE) reduces lead times within the overall process as well as eliminating stages. For example, CAE takes CAD designs and subjects them to stress, loads and vibrations to assess their strength and reliability, thus eliminating later elements of the design and prototype phases.

Variety reduction

The approaches and techniques listed so far have addressed issues around the design itself. Variety reduction, however, questions whether or not retaining all the services and products currently on offer is best for the business as a whole.

In the service/product range provided, some items will generate more sales, more profit or contribute more to the fixed costs of the organization than others. Moreover, the costs incurred and effort involved in providing and selling these lower contributors are disproportionately higher than for other services/products. Consequently, looking closely at the contribution that they make should become part of the tactical approach to reduce uneconomical variety and increase control of variety in the future. A more quantitative appraisal of the range of services and products on offer by a firm is that of variety reduction.

Using the Pareto principle, list all the services or products into order with highest total value of sales at the top and lowest at the bottom. This often reveals that about 20 per cent of items account for about 80 per cent of the total sales revenue – the 80/20 rule. In Exhibit 4.14, the top 6 of the 24 products account for about 74 per cent of total sales (see note 3 to the exhibit), whereas the bottom 15 products account for only 17 per cent. In addition, these top 6 account for some 76 per cent of the total contribution (see note 1 of the exhibit), whereas the bottom 15 (or 62 per cent) contribute only £375,000, about 13 per cent.

The next step is to check the relative performances of the items with a low percentage of the sales revenue over the last three or four years in order to determine if the individual trend is going up, staying the same or going down. Further checks are then made on the level and downward trend items to see if their contribution can be improved by reducing variable costs and/or increasing the selling price. If this action does not bring about the required changes in terms of percentage contribution to selling price, then phasing out the service or product should be considered.

The advantages of variety reduction are many, including:

- Longer operations runs, with less downtime through changeovers.
- Potential savings in plant/equipment requirements.
- Reduced inventory, with the advantages in capital, control, space and costs.
- More activity in development and design, sales effort and after-sales service.
- Easier operations planning and control.
- Appropriate reallocation of capacity (particularly scarce resources) to the overall benefit of a business.

The disadvantages of this approach are the reduction in service or product range in terms of the number of individual items provided or produced, the reduced range available and the danger of cutting out services/products that serve as loss leaders. Thus it is variety reduction's net corporate effect that needs to be considered and on which such decisions should be based. Case example 4.11 highlights the issues.

Exhibit 4.14 Product analysis by annual sales revenue

Product reference number	Sales revenue (£000)	Percentage of total sales	Total variable costs (£000)	Total contribution (£000)	Percentage of total contribution
054-19	2480	19.5	2128	352	12.7
303-07	2134	16.8	1684	650	23.4
691-30	1720	13.5	1372	348	12.5
016-10	1440	11.3	1028	412	14.8
418-50	980	7.7	676	304	10.9
402-50	620	4.9	580	40	1.4
155-29	428	3.8	390	92	3.4
900-01	360	2.8	240	120	4.3
308-31	308	2.4	220	88	3.2
341-17	280	2.2	212	68	2.4
540-80	260	2.0	200	60	2.2
701-91	232	1.8	160	72	2.6
650-27	220	1.7	202	18	0.6
712-22	192	1.5	140	52	1.9
137-29	180	1.4	152	28	1.0
003-54	172	1.4	168	4	0.1
541-21	140	1.1	122	18	0.6
543-61	136	1.1	112	24	0.9
305-04	96	0.8	86	10	0.4
097-54	88	0.7	86	2	0.1
323-34	72	0.6	68	4	0.1
542-93	68	0.5	62	6	0.2
386-07	44	0.3	36	8	0.3
440-18	20	0.2	19	1	–
Total	12,724	100.0	7463	2781	100.0

Notes   1   Contribution = selling price less variable costs.
2   Further analysis could be complemented by grouping like products together and showing the product group totals for columns 'percentage of total sales' to 'percentage of total contribution' inclusive.
3   The 80/20 relationship implied in the rule is only an indication of the size of the actual figures involved. Thus in the example here, 25 per cent of the products account for 74 per cent of sales, illustrating clearly the concept of a relatively small number of products accounting for a high percentage of the sales revenue.

Case example 11   CAPITALIZING THROUGH VOLUME AT ASSA ABLOY

Few products have resisted standardization as much as the humble door lock. In Europe alone, several hundred thousand types are sold – a product range diversity that reflects the doors and buildings that have evolved in different countries over several centuries.

Today demand for security is growing and prospects are good. Assa Abloy (the Swedish lock maker with worldwide sales of £12.5 billion) is now #1 worldwide with 6 per cent of total sales. This growth was partly generic and partly by takeover, as in the 1990s Assa spent £400 million on 20 lock companies worldwide. Its current sales profile is 50 per cent in Europe, 35 per cent in the USA, 10 per cent in the Pacific Rim and the remaining 5 per cent in the rest of the world. Despite this international breadth, products sold in more than one country account for only 25 per cent of sales.

Where possible Assa tries to capitalize on the potential

high volumes involved, for instance all exit bars for its fire and emergency doors are made in one plant in France. But this is more the exception than the rule. The outcome is over 40 manufacturing plants around the world, each mainly supplying its domestic market.

www.assaabloy.com

Case questions
1 Why are some product ranges less open to variety reduction than others?
2 Choose a product suitable for standardization and variety reduction. Compare and contrast this with the example above on locks.

Reflections

All organizations have a range of services or products at a given time. To be competitive, it is necessary to have a set that is complementary, relates to the organization's strategic objectives, such as growth and market share, and takes account of tactical considerations such as completeness of range, process capability and distribution costs. Furthermore, the mix is always undergoing change, as organizations are continuously faced with the need to introduce new services and products in a never-ending requirement to keep a mix that meets the needs of their customers. On the one hand, developing and introducing new items is typically expensive, risky and involves a long time horizon, while on the other hand, it is the very lifeblood of business, as new services and products are necessary for survival and growth.

Attitudes and norms concerning the level of innovation and the introduction of new services and products are affected by internal and external forces. Decisions to invest in R&D or to seek to exploit developments in technology will vary from industry to industry and company to company, often markedly so. In product-based companies, the tradition of investing in R&D and actively seeking to introduce new products has noticeably increased over the past few decades. This varies from superficial modifications (for example, in markets such as customer durables, there is a traditional 'facelift' to existing models/products on a regular basis) to major product changes.

A review of service industries also highlights the changes over the past decade in what is on offer. Protected for a long time by geographical distance, commercial legacies and legal constraints, many service industries remained conservative and insensitive to the needs of their customers. They competed in what are known as 'sheltered markets'. However, the impact of deregulation, advances in data processing and increased global competition in many areas of the service industry have moved many sectors into what are known as 'traded markets'. For instance, deregulation and advances in data processing have had an enormous impact upon the travel industry. Whereas 20 years ago high street travel agents commanded a prime position (as a sheltered market), the advent of online selling has moved much of the industry into a traded market, bypassing high street outlets and, in some instances such as airlines, bypassing the travel agent altogether. In the same way the limited competition that banks enjoyed from the very beginning changed with the alterations to trading rules, the opening up of financial markets, investments in data processing and the entry of non-finance organizations (for example supermarket chains, other retailers and a wide range of other businesses) into credit sales, personal loans and the like. One outome has been a dramatic alteration to the basis and form of competition in the finance sector.

A tough business lesson that top managers need to draw from the history of progress is that most services, products and technologies will be replaced and most efforts to replace them will fail. This is somewhat a game of Russian roulette in which companies need to participate if they wish to grow and prosper. The stakes, however, will vary with the nature of the service and product and the level of change involved. But it is easy to be misled. Changes to existing, well-established markets of a non-dramatic nature can result in major shifts in success as Case examples 4.12, 4.13 and 4.14 illustrate.

Case example 12   INCREASING THE FRESHNESS OF BREAD IN SUPERMARKET BAKERIES

A small change in existing specifications is enough to make a significant impact. For example, increasing the freshness of food provision has enabled supermarkets not only to match local high street outlets but outperform them. Bread technologies now enable doughs to be held for several days without deterioration. This enables in-store, supermarket bakeries to produce bread several times each day, thereby increasing product freshness. In addition, part-baked breads to be oven-finished at home have opened up a new dimension to fresh bread provision.

Case example 13   PRODUCT DESIGN CHANGES AT ALTRACK

Traditional markets are as vulnerable to the impact of design changes as any other. For example, alternatives to pneumatic tyres for off-road vehicles in order to reduce punctures and the costs involved have been long needed. Traditional solutions of solid and foam-filled wheels have the drawbacks of lack of comfort for the driver and wear on vehicle suspension due to increased rigidity. In the 1990s Altrack, an Australian tyre company, introduced a puncture-free wheel for construction equipment where punctures are up to 10 times more likely than on other vehicles. The new tyre design comprises a number of hollow-moulded, rubber segments that bolt on to a special wheel rim. A damaged rubber section takes only 15 minutes to replace with the vehicle (and its load) still in place.

Case example 14   FLYING FIRST AND BUSINESS CLASS AT BRITISH AIRWAYS AND VIRGIN ATLANTIC

Typically, full-service airlines derive about half their profits from business and first-class travellers. With the terrorist attacks in the US and, more importantly, the downturn in the Asian economies, particularly that of Japan, there is more capacity in the sky than demand. Airlines need their high-paying customers more than ever. While these tickets are not cheap, if you've got to fly long distances and you're either rich or an executive with a full and busy schedule, then a good night's rest is worth its weight in gold (well, not quite). In this context, the value-added luxury of flat-bed seats introduced in the past few years by British Airways and Virgin Atlantic have acquired a new significance. These expensive innovations (BA's Club World project to re-equip its Boeing 747s and 777s cost about £200 million) were launched to protect and grow market share. British Airways scored a public relations success by winning the grand prix in the Design Business Association's Design Effectiveness awards for its Club World seat introduced in 2000. The seat, which BA calls the 'lounge in the sky', was aimed at redefining business travel. Not just a bed, it is designed to meet the several needs of the executive. The seat units are in facing pairs, with removable footstools that clip on to make a fully flat 6ft bed. They have electronic adjustment, built-in power for laptops and in-flight entertainment. The design used data from NASA on sleep posture, while the additional privacy of the fore and aft layout was valued by female passengers in particular. Finally, one dimension that impressed the panel of judges was the speed with which BA put the new seat into service – just 16 months from drawing board to installation.

www.ba.com
www.virgin-atlantic.com

Case questions

1   List what you think are the two most significant aspects of the design changes for each of the three examples above and explain your reasons.

2   What design aspects in the three examples are similar to one another? How do they link to the issues, concepts and approaches discussed in this chapter?

After the cost cutting, rationalization and restructuring of the 1980s and 90s, the corporate agenda has recognized the key role of innovation in the quest for growth. In part, this stems from a recognition that improved efficiency is no substitute for growth. Some organizations are experiencing anxious times as they are having difficulty in moving back towards an innovative culture. Many are stressing innovation as a corporate goal, while others (for example BP Chemicals, 3M, Elf Aquitaine, Siemens and British Airways) are introducing innovation schemes as a way to stimulate further these essential activities. But the area of innovation is as difficult to embrace as it is essential for continued success. Some pointers to these issues and ways forward include the following:

- Encouraging more creativity only addresses part of the problem. Much of the difficulty lies in establishing a clear link between innovation and corporate success.

- One common mistake is to believe that innovation can compensate for competitive disadvantages elsewhere.

- It is a misconception to think that innovation is a technical issue. Akio Morita (the founder of Sony) dismissed descriptions of the Walkman as an innovation marvel. 'Frankly', he observed, 'it did not contain any breakthrough technology. Its success was built on product planning and marketing.'

- There is a need to move away from a preoccupation with R&D to the totality of innovation, in terms of scope (the Sony Walkman syndrome) and organizational style. Innovation is potentially in everyone and everywhere.

- Using customers is essential. One-third of the toy company Hasbro's annual sales come from new products. To ensure this trend continues, Hasbro goes to great lengths to keep its designers in touch with children. To this end it has built a crèche (known as the 'fun lab') for 25 children next to its R&D department.

- The task is to generate good services and products on a continuous basis. A culture of innovation is essential for this to happen. Ways of engendering the need to spend time on creating ideas has to become part of the corporate culture. 3M allows designers to spend up to 15 per cent of their time on any research project they wish. The Post-it note pad had bottom-up origins. Other organizations need to break down the status quo dimension that traditionally goes with innovation. They need to create a culture that encourages and develops innovation in order to bring everyone and their ideas on board.

Key Elements of Designing and Developing Services and Products

- The introduction of new and the development of existing services and products is the lifeblood of organizations. For this to become an integral part of the way in which companies grow and prosper, they need a way to generate ideas and then translate them into reality.

- While breakthroughs will always gain the spotlight, most companies will typically sell today what they sold yesterday and the same for tomorrow. This does not imply that thinking outside the box is not required. On the contrary, nothing could be further from the truth. The key is more to do with where to focus attention, which for many companies concerns thinking differently about what they currently provide and the markets in which they currently compete.

- With ideas being the spark that ignites development, companies are realizing that they need also to seek perspectives from less traditional sources. Key areas among these alternatives are the staff who provide the service or make the product and customers who buy the offering. Breaking the mould of past approaches is difficult but in today's competitive world it is essential.

● While the first step is essential, getting from idea to market reality is critical. For much of the time this part of the process changes from being one of inspiration to one based on hard work. Systematically checking and rechecking needs time and effort.

● Finally, while new services and products create tomorrow's success, a company needs to get the most out of today's offerings. On the scale of being inherently interesting, generating ideas is at the top, with developing existing services and products much lower down. However, on the scale of what impacts corporate success and prosperity, the order is often the reverse. The attraction of stars and the mundane nature of cash cows often results in an imbalance of time, attention and recognition. Keeping all the corporate balls in the air is an essential element of successfully managing the process for the design and development of services and products.

Self-check

1 The objective of research and development is to bring about technological change and innovation within:
  a Services and products to be sold ☐
  b Service delivery systems and processes used ☐
  c Both a and b ☐

2 Applied research is concerned with:
  a Practical applications and solutions to practical problems ☐
  b Increasing knowledge, making discoveries and establishing new practices that may eventually be used on a commercial basis ☐
  c Both a and b ☐

3 The third step in the design and development process for services and products is:
  a Generating ideas ☐
  b Testing prototypes ☐
  c Feasibility study ☐

4 One purpose of testing prototypes is to:
  a Eliminate those ideas that do not appear to have high potential ☐
  b Understand whether customers will buy the service or product ☐
  c Illustrate the aesthetic dimension and check the functionality of an idea ☐

5 If the cash generated is greater than the cash used by a service or product, it is considered to be a:
  a Cash cow ☐
  b Star ☐
  c Dilemma ☐

6 With a repeat service or product, the company typically wins orders on:
  a Unique capability ☐
  b Repeat business or recommendations ☐
  c Price ☐

7 Which of the following is **not** an operations technique or approach related to design:
  a Quality functional deployment and the house of quality ☐
  b Statistical process control ☐
  c Taguchi method ☐

8 'Use value' can be classified as:
  a The properties and qualities that accomplish the function of a service or product ☐
  b The properties, features or attractiveness that cause people to want or own a service or product ☐
  c Both a and b ☐

9 Which of the following is **not** typically a method used to speed up the process of designing and introducing services and products:
  a Using standard parts and modular design ☐
  b Overlapping development stages ☐
  c Quality functional deployment ☐

10 An example of an advantage of variety reduction is:
  a Reduced inventory ☐
  b Reduced operations runs ☐
  c Increased downtime through changeovers ☐

Study activities

Discussion questions

1 The section 'The service/product mix' explained that a service or product can be expressed as a combination of dimensions (that is, 'a service within which there is a facilitating good', 'the explicit and implicit dimensions of an offering' and 'the supporting structural facilities'). Analyse the following businesses in line with these dimensions:
  ● a supermarket
  ● a high street post office
  ● an upmarket restaurant.

2 Select a service and a product that are at different points of their life cycles. Explain their progress to date, where they are now and what you expect will happen in the future.

3 In what types of organization might new ideas have:
  ● a low mortality rate (that is, they last for a long time)
  ● a high mortality rate (that is, they last for a short time)?

4 Since markets for services typically have lower entry barriers than product markets, why do overseas companies not start with services when they first begin to compete in foreign markets?

5 A major German shoe company launched a new range of tennis shoes. There were two styles, one for men and one for women. Within each of these two styles there were six colour combinations and the shoe sizes ranged from size 7 to 14 for men and 4 to 9 for women. How many shoes would a store have to stock to have one pair of each shoe within both ranges?

6 Give two examples (with supporting details) for each of a service and manufacturing firm of the impact of technology in service and product design.

7 Give one example of the use of standardization and modular design for both a service and product of your choice.

Assignments

1 Apply the value analysis principles to a service or product and see if you could identify opportunities for cost reduction without reducing the value.

2 Complete a review of two fast-food restaurants of your choice using the quality functional deployment approach. In this task use the outline in Exhibit 4.11 but check, where possible, the detail re:
  ● customers' needs and wants and weight percentages
  ● technical requirements
  ● customers' ratings for each restaurant.

Exploring further

Akao, Y (ed.) *Quality Function Deployment: Integrating Customer Requirements into Product Design*, Productivity Press, Cambridge, MA (1990).

Alström, P and Westbrook, R 'Implications of mass customisation for operations management: an exploratory survey', *International Journal of Operations and Production Management*, **19**(3/4) (1999), pp. 262–74.

Baldwin, CY and Clark, KB *Design Rules:* Vol. 1: *The Power of Modularity*, MIT Press, Cambridge, MA (2000).

Bangle, C 'The ultimate creativity machine: how BMW turns art into profit', *Harvard Business Review*, January–February (2001), pp. 47–55.

Baxter, M *Product Design*, Chapman & Hall, London (1995).

Bruce, M and Bessant, J *Design in Business: Strategic Innovation through Design*, Financial Times/ Prentice Hall, London (2002).

Chase, RB 'The service factory: a future vision', *International Journal of Service Industry Management*, **2**(3) (1991), pp. 60–70.

Christensen, CM *The Innovators' Dilemma*, Harvard Business School Press, Boston (1997).

Cohen, L *Quality Function Deployment*, Addison-Wesley Longman, Wokingham (1995).

Cooper, R and Chew, WB 'Control tomorrow's costs through today's designs', *Harvard Business Review*, January–February (1996), pp. 88–98.

Duke, L, Johnson, MD and Renaghan, LM 'Adopting the QFD approach to extended service transactions', *Production and Operations Management*, **8**(3) (1999), pp. 301–17.

Fitzsimmons, JA and Fitzsimmons, MJ (eds) *New Service Development*, Sage, Thousand Oaks, CA (2000).

Hauser, JR 'How Puritan – Bennett used the house of quality', *Sloan Management Review*, **34**(3) (1993), pp. 61–70.

Hauser, JR and Clausing, D 'The house of quality', *Harvard Business Review*, May–June (1988), pp. 63–73.

Henkoff, J 'Service is everybody's business', *Fortune*, June (1994), pp. 48–60.

Heskett, JL, Sasser, WE and Hart, CWL *Service Breakthrough: Changing the Rules of the Game*, Free Press, New York (1990).

Krishman, V and Ulrich, KT 'Product development decisions: a review of the literature', *Management Science*, **47**(1) (2001), pp. 1–21.

Lowe, A and Ridgway, K 'A user's guide to quality functional deployment', *Engineering Management*, January (2000).

Pine, JB II *Mass Customisation: The New Frontier in Business Competition*, Harvard Business School Press, Boston (1993).

Quelch, JA and Kenny, D 'Extend profits, not product lines', *Harvard Business Review*, September–October (1994), pp. 153–60.

Ramaswammy, R *Design and Management of Service Processes*, Addison-Wesley Longman, Reading, MA (1996).

Schilling, MA and Hill, CWL 'Managing the new product development process', *Academy of Management Executive*, **12**(3) (1998), pp. 67–81.

Stuart, FI and Tax, SS 'Planning for service quality: an integrative approach', *International Journal of Service Industry Management*, **7**(4) (1996).

Taylor, GD, English, JR and Graves, RJ 'Designing new products: compatibility with existing production', *Integrated Manufacturing Systems*, **5** (1994), pp. 13–21.

Zeithaml, VA, Parasuraman, A and Berry, LL *Delivering Quality Service: Balancing Customer Perceptions and Expectations*, Free Press, New York (1990).

Notes and references

1 Mackintosh, J 'Fiat facelift ditches ugly cars', *Financial Times*, 29 May (2003), p. 12.

2 This explanation of design strategies was put forward by Schonberger, RJ in *Operations Management*, Plane, Business Publications, Texas (1981).

3 Zahara, SA, Sisodia, RS and Das, SR 'Technological choices within competitive strategy types: a conceptual integration', *International Journal of Technology Management*, 9(2) (1994), pp. 172–95.

4 Abrahams, P 'A meeting of Microsoft's minds', *Financial Times*, 5 February (2003), p. 11.

5 For example, Daetz, D 'The effect of product design on product quality and product cost', *Quality Progress*, (20) (1987), pp. 63–7; Sheldon, DF, Perks, R, Jackson, M, Miles, BL and Holland, J 'Designing for whole life costs at the concept stage', *Journal of Engineering Design*, (1) (1990), pp. 131–45; Suh, NF *The Principles of Design*, Oxford University Press, Oxford (1990).

6 Barton, JA, Love, DM and Taylor, GD 'Design determines 70 per cent of costs? A review of implications for design evaluation', *Journal of Engineering Design*, 12(1) (2001), pp. 47–58.

7 The graphical representation of the relationship between the functions in the design production procedure and their impact on effectiveness is a product of the Ford Motor Company.

8 For example, see Moore, SD 'Glaxo accelerates pursuit of new medicines; Glaxo lab initiates a high-speed chase in the drugs industry', *Wall Street Journal*, Europe, 6 December (1996), pp. 1 and 5.

9 For example, see Thomke, S and von Hippel, E 'Customers as innovators: a new way to create value', *Harvard Business Review*, April (2002), pp. 74–81.

10 These concepts were first introduced by Sasser, WE, Olsen, RP and Wyckoff, DD in *Management of Service Operations: Text, Cases and Readings*, Allyn & Bacon, Boston (1978), pp. 10–11.

11 Articles giving different perspectives on mass customization include Berman, B 'Should your firm adopt a mass customization strategy?', *Business Horizons*, July–August (2002), pp. 51–60; Feitzinger, E and Hau, LL 'Mass customization at Hewlett-Packard: the power of post-ponement', *Harvard Business Review*, 75(1) January–February (1997), pp. 116–21; Gilmore, JH and Pine II, BJ 'The four faces of mass customization', *Harvard Business Review*, 75(1) January–February (1997), pp. 91–101; Kasanoff, B 'Mass customization and customer intimacy pay off for Dell' @ www.1to1.com/articles/ il–4–10–97 (1997); Salvador, F, Forza, C and Rungtusanathan, M 'How to mass customise: product architectures, sourcing and configurations', *Business Horizons*, July–August (2002), pp. 61–9; Zipkin, P 'The limits of mass customisation', *Sloan Management Review*, 42(3) (2001), pp. 81–7.

12 References include Noori, H 'The Taguchi methods: achieving design and output quality', *Academy of Management Executive*, November (1989), pp. 322–6; Taguchi, G and Clausing, D 'Robust quality', *Harvard Business Review*, January–February (1990), pp. 65–75.

13 Value analysis is defined in BS 3138 as: 'a systematic interdisciplinary examination of factors affecting the cost of a service or product, in order to devise means of achieving the specified purpose most economically at the required standard of quality and reliability'.

14 Miles, LD *Techniques of Value Analysis and Engineering*, McGraw-Hill, Maidenhead (1961).

15 In Chapter 4 of *The Four Kinds of Economic Value*, Harvard Business Press (1926), Walsh, CM describes four kinds of value: 'Use-value is a thing's power to serve our ends. Esteem-value is its power to make us desire to possess it. Cost-value is its power to impose upon us effort to acquire it. Exchange-value is its power to procure other things in its place'.

16 This refers to the principle put forward by Vilfredo Pareto (1848–1923) that a few items in any group contribute the significant proportion of the entire group. Pareto was an Italian sociologist and economist, who used this law to express the frequency distribution of incomes in society. Chapter 12 provides another example of its application.

17 *The Paul Revere Life Insurance Company*, Case Study no. 42, Houston: American Productivity Center, February (1984).

18 Ibid., p. 1.

book map

Part

1
- 1 Managing Operations
- 2 Operations Strategy
- 3 Managing People

2

INPUTS

SUPPLIERS

PROCESSES

OUTPUTS

CUSTOMERS

- 4 Designing and Developing Services & Products
- 5 Designing Service Delivery Systems
- 6 Designing Manufacturing Processes
- 7 Location and Layout
- 8 Managing Capacity
- 9 Technology Developments
- 10 Operations Scheduling and Execution
- 11 Managing Quality

3
- 12 Managing Inventory
- 13 Managing the Supply Chain
- 14 Process and Delivery System Reliability and Maintenance
- 15 Time and Productivity

4
- 16 Improving Operations

5
- Managing Operations in Practice: Long Case Studies

Designing Service Delivery Systems

Outline of chapter

The essence of a service business is to provide and sell services. Therefore, how a company delivers the services it offers will impact customer experience and directly influence repeat purchase decisions. Consequently, how services are provided is central to both sales revenue and profit growth.

Why is designing service delivery systems important?

Executive overview

This chapter concerns designing service delivery systems, with the next chapter doing the same for manufacturing processes. The principal sections here are now outlined:

- **Distinctive service characteristics** – this initial section overviews the distinctive characteristics of services from their intangible nature and simultaneous provision and consumption to the time-dependent nature of service capacity and the role of customers in the delivery system.

- **Factors involved in the delivery of services** – this section highlights several factors, including the mix of technology and people within delivery system design, the categories of services that exist from professional to mass services, the volumes involved and order-winners/qualifiers that need to be met.

- **Overall and detailed design of service systems** – the next two sections look at the overall and detailed design features respectively and introduce key factors including front-, middle- and back-office dimensions, the level of customer interface within a delivery system, the non-repeat and repeat nature of the offering and the single or multi-step design of the system.

- **IT and alternative designs** – the impact of IT and alternative design characteristics are then reviewed and developments in e-commerce and the increasing use of call centres are discussed.

- **Service profiling delivery system alignment** – the final part of the chapter shows how alignment checks need and can be made to check the level of fit between the requirements of markets and the characteristics of the organization and its delivery systems.

Introduction

As explained in Chapter 1 and illustrated in the book overview at the beginning of each chapter, central to the operations management task is the operations process that involves transforming inputs into outputs. This chapter considers the different methods available to an organization by which it provides services to customers – the task of choosing and designing a service delivery system.

As the examples given later illustrate, the methods used to provide services will often comprise different designs and each of these will have been selected to meet the particular requirements of the service involved. Two dimensions of a service that will affect the design of an appropriate delivery system are the complexity of the offering itself and the characteristics of the market in which the service is sold:

- Service complexity – the complexity of a service will directly impact the number of steps it takes to complete it. In many organizations the provision of a service is completed as a single step (for example borrowing books from a library or paying in a cheque at a local bank), whereas the processes involved to meet the needs of different patients in a hospital will comprise several steps and several combinations of steps. The design of the service delivery system will, therefore, reflect this complexity factor.

● The market – a delivery system needs to provide the following dimensions:
  – **the technical dimension** – concerns what the service comprises. For example, bread is baked and cheques are processed. To complete these tasks requires appropriate technology (in the form of skills and equipment) within the delivery system, in this instance a baker and ovens and skilled staff and cheque processing equipment.
  – **the business dimension** – how operations decides to provide a service will reflect the volumes involved and the market drivers (order-winners and qualifiers) to be supported.

To illustrate how these differ, let us take the example of baking bread. A village baker will choose different oven arrangements and auxiliary equipment from a large bakery company that bakes and delivers bread throughout a city and its suburbs. In both instances the product to be made (namely, bread) is the same in a technical sense but the requirements are totally different in a market sense. Hence, the process chosen will reflect these business-based differences. It is this latter dimension that constitutes the operations management task and which this chapter addresses.

The chapter reviews the operations management task of using delivery systems to meet the needs of markets. In undertaking this an operations executive requires and will call on the support of technical specialists such as systems and IT specialists. For example, operations managers of call centres would not resolve the technical dimensions of the systems their staff use but would look to specialists to fix technical problems and undertake technical developments as necessary. In this way, operations management is not a technical role. Instead operations management uses the necessary system technology together with other inputs, particularly staff capabilities, to meet the needs of markets and the cost profiles and profit targets of the business. The essential technical role of operations management concerns, therefore, the choice and development of the process used to provide services that best meet the needs of customers and markets – the service delivery system. Working with technical experts is a key operations management role. Each is responsible for providing different but essential inputs – namely the technical and business perspectives of the service offerings involved.

The need to help other functions in an organization to understand these alternative choices and their implications for the business is an integral part of an operations manager's role. Each delivery system will have trade-offs (things it can do well and less well) and these need to be understood by a business and form part of making these key investment decisions.

Distinctive characteristics of service operations

Before discussing the design alternatives for service delivery systems, let us first look at some of the distinctive characteristics of service operations that will form part of the delivery task, will need to be accommodated by the process and will influence the design of the delivery system itself. The extent to which these characteristics will impact the design will, as you would expect, differ from one service offering to another.

Service/product mix

Earlier in the book, two important dimensions of services were highlighted and it is important to bear these in mind when discussing delivery system design:

- Customer purchases are a mix of both services and products. As Exhibit 1.6 illustrated, the ratio between these two elements within the mix will vary. In some instances there can be a heavy accent on services, while in others, the reverse.

- The service component of the mix is a package of explicit and implicit benefits performed within a supporting facility. The need to identify these three elements was highlighted in the last chapter.

Customers receive impressions about an organization through their experience of the way a service is delivered. These impressions will be created both by the product (how well the design specification itself and delivery to this specification meets a customer's expectations) and the service experience which a customer undergoes and which is uniquely linked to the service delivery system.

Intangible nature of services

While products are tangible (a customer is able to see, feel, inspect and even test a product before purchase), services are not. This presents a problem for both providers and customers. While the latter rely on a firm's reputation, recommendations or 'pot luck', the provider needs to develop a service delivery system that provides the service dimension of the package such that existing customers purchase again and new customers are attracted by factors such as reputation and recommendation. In this way the delivery system creates the intangible customer experience that constitutes the service element of the purchase, and so becomes a critical element of the sale.

Simultaneous provision and consumption of services

The simultaneous provision and consumption of most services precludes the use of inventory as one way to help absorb fluctuations in demand. Whereas manufacturing companies may use inventory as a way of transferring capacity from one time period to be sold in a later time period, most service companies cannot. In a manufacturing firm, inventory serves as a convenient boundary line, allowing the overall system to separate the management of the internal process from the external environment of the market. The result is that inventory can be used to cushion the process at both ends: it decouples the system from suppliers by holding materials and parts at the beginning and from fluctuations in customer demand by holding finished products at the end. The manufacturing process can thus operate as a closed system and, as a consequence, at a level of output that is deemed most efficient for the overall business. Services, on the other hand, operate as open systems and are thus exposed to the full impact of market demand variations.

For delivery systems, the decoupling role of inventory is typically less available. In some situations, inventory of the product element of the offering is used in various forms. For example, a sandwich bar holds ingredients, pre-makes a range of fillings for sandwiches and makes and packages some sandwiches ahead of demand. But the most universal way to cushion a delivery system in a service firm is by using a combination of capacity and customer queues. For example, the number of beds in a hospital or teller windows in a bank are designed to exceed average demand. In so doing, above-average demand levels, when they occur, can be met. In such situations, operations managers need to balance excess capacity provision and queue lengths, while meeting the needs of customers.

The simultaneous provision and consumption of services also reduces (and often eliminates) the opportunities for controlling the quality of the service provision in terms of meeting the service/product specification. Unlike manufacturing where a product can be checked before delivery, services must build other ways into the system to ensure that the specification is met as it is delivered.

Time-dependent capacity

Linked to the last point is the fact that the usefulness of capacity in a service firm is time-dependent. If a hotel room, passenger airline seat, space on a container ship, goods train or truck is not used at the time, the capacity is lost forever. Similarly, if a restaurant cannot seat you for dinner, the sale is lost forever. Therefore, a service firm has to find ways to handle the fact that unused capacity is perishable while insufficient capacity will lose sales.

Capacity is not only expensive but also involves a complex set of issues, as a decision on how much is needed has to be made in the different phases of a delivery system. These design issues include not only how much capacity in terms of structural facilities (for example teller windows in a bank) and people, but also the shape of the capacity, for example the mix of part- and full-time staff and which sizes of aircraft best meet the demand profiles of a bank and a passenger airline's routes respectively.

Customers as participants in the service delivery system

In most service firms the customer forms part of the delivery system and is often actively engaged in the system itself. The popularity of supermarkets, self-service stores, internet purchasing and online banking are illustrations of this phenomenon.

For the firm, the customer provides capacity within the system that helps lower costs and also facilitates some aspects of operations management. For example, where customers undertake part of the role of a server, staff costs and the need to plan staff capacity in this phase of the delivery system are both reduced.

Customer management

Relating to the last point, the design of the delivery system is such that customers and staff are linked. Customers are not just onlookers; their presence creates a dynamic that needs to be managed. For example:

- The supporting structural facilities (such as decor, furnishings and cleanliness) need to meet customer expectations.
- Staff need to be conscious of their roles and impact on the experience of and sense of participation by the customer and the lasting impression that is made (see Case example 5.1).
- The level of server discretion (the extent to which staff are permitted to customize the offering) in what constitutes the service specification needs to be identified, agreed and managed.
- The social dynamics of the customer experience, from entering to leaving the delivery system, need to be accommodated by and accounted for within the system itself, and the approach to meeting these dimensions needs to form part of the system design, part of the people skills development and part of the operations management task.

Case example 1   TIPPING AS A MEASURE OF CUSTOMER SERVICE

Tipping is not a trivial business. For staff it often represents a substantial portion of their income while for the organization it provides a tangible measure of customer service. Research on what makes customers tip at the end of a service encounter such as a meal in a restaurant highlights certain aspects of customer management that can have general application elsewhere. Some of the key findings include:

1   Interacting with a customer throughout the delivery of a service. For example:
   - Making initial eye contact and then reinforcing this contact throughout the service encounter
   - Personalizing the service – introducing oneself by name works better than a badge, while even gestures such as writing 'thank you' or drawing a cartoon on a bill together with one's name help personalize the service
   - Smiling warmly and genuinely when greeting a customer and being pleasant throughout
   - Making additional, discreet non-task visits to check all is well and checking that nothing extra is required.

2   Speed of service – there are four occasions when speed of response is important:

   - Delivery of the menu and pre-dinner drinks
   - Taking the food order
   - Delivery of the food
   - The payment process from presenting the bill to conclusion.

But the key is to gauge the optimum speed rather than the maximum speed, and this concerns trying to understand the level of speed a customer wants. Getting the timing right is an essential part of the overall service specification and the clues are not hard to find.

3   Goodwill gestures. Providing symbols of goodwill such as the complimentary aperitif, bite-size nibbles, pre-meal nibbles or the truffle with the bill, or the overtly generous measure of pre- and post-dinner drinks all help create an impression of goodwill and good value.

To an extent, tips reflect fulfilling expectations about the quality of food and the service provided. Getting these right not only leads to satisfied staff but also satisfied customers and repeat business.

Case questions   1   What makes up the total service offering for a customer during an evening meal at a restaurant?
2   How would the examples here translate into customer management in a boutique clothes shop or hairdressing salon?

People skills

In service organizations, some staff deal directly with customers. The customer/server interface that takes place can often combine the business dimensions of both provision and sale. One consequence is that the range of people skills that staff need to develop as part of the delivery system will have a significant effect on the perceived value of the service by the customer.

Also, part of the skill set essential to staff that serve customers is the effective exercise of the levels of discretion. Ensuring that the systems reflect the varying needs of customers as and when necessary is a critical feature of a responsive system in which agreed degrees of customization can be provided.

Effective services are reproducible

One of the reasons for the emergence of large service companies in sectors that used to be regarded as local lies in the improved method of reproducing service delivery systems. Franchise companies, for example fast-food chains, are classic examples of this. Here, control over key elements of the offering and delivery system such as the physical layout, internal and external decor, range of offerings, purchasing of inputs (for example food ingredients), service delivery system design, training and equipment is held and routinely checked by the originating company. This approach allows companies to expand beyond their initial geographical area using the same model and tried and tested approach.

Site selection: proximity to the customer and multi-site management

Whereas products are shipped to the customer, in many companies the service provider and customer must physically meet for a service to be performed. As a consequence, many service organizations are made up of small units of capacity sited close to prospective customers. Either the customer comes to the facility (as in a restaurant, retail store, hairdresser or hospital) or the service provider goes to the customer (as in a mobile library or ambulance service). Of course, there are exceptions (for example distance learning) and even more so with the growing use of IT systems (for example telephone and internet banking, online shopping and passenger airline, holiday and theatre ticket sales).

Travel time and costs are thus reflected in the economics underpinning site selection, with many small units of capacity bringing the added task of multi-site management. The resulting challenges for an organization include the fact that services are performed in the field, so to speak, and not in a controlled factory environment. To achieve and maintain consistency across multiple locations requires a combination of standardization within the service delivery system, extensive training, licensing and third-party or peer reviews.

No patents on services

Firms that design their own products have the advantage of patents and licensing agreements to protect them. The intangible portion of the service element of the package is more difficult to protect using these legal formats. Although some protection of a service may be afforded by copyright and trademarks, most service firms need to recognize and highlight the service delivery system's role in protecting the service concept. Capturing and retaining market share by designing robust delivery systems that meet the needs of customers and respond and proactively lead change and development are essential dimensions of many successful service organizations. The operations management role to recognize this dimension of service delivery system design and development is an essential contribution to the long-term success of a business.

Factors involved in delivering services

The services that companies provide and sell are different and these differences will impact the design of the system used to deliver them. It is important, therefore, to clarify at this early stage those differences that impact service delivery system design and then reflect on these in the rest of the chapter as alternatives and approaches to process design are reviewed.

The technology/people mix

There are several perspectives to be taken into account in understanding the alternative choices of delivery system that can be made, but first let us recap on the technology dimension of service provision.

Exhibit 5.1   Range of operations requirements within the service delivery system

Predominant base	Level of automation and people skills	Examples
Technology	Automated	Cash dispensing
		Photocopying
		Vending machines
		Car wash
	Monitored by unskilled/semi-skilled people	Photocopying
		Dry-cleaning
		Gardening
		Tree surgery
		Taxis
	Operated by skilled people	Airlines
		Computer time-sharing
		Word processing
People	Unskilled	Cleaning services
		Security guards
	Skilled	Catering
		Vehicle maintenance
		Appliance repairs
	Professional	Lawyers
		Management consultants
		Accountants

A company needs to select the delivery systems by which it will provide the services it sells. In part this concerns the technical dimensions of the items involved, for example:

- A restaurant would need to prepare food in line with the menus on offer and customers' requirements. It would, therefore, need the equipment and skilled staff to undertake the food preparation involved.

- A computer services bureau would need the hardware and skilled staff to enable it to process the information requirements of customers.

This requirement is obviously fundamental. However, as will be explained later in the chapter, the level of process investment will also reflect issues such as volumes, as these market dimensions underpin the business case for committing different levels of resources. The lower the sales levels, the less justification there is for investing in equipment and processes to complete the delivery of a service, and this will need to be reflected in the technology/people mix selection. The mix of process technology and people skills will not only need to be reflected in the service delivery system design but will also require a different operations management orientation and capability set.

Separating services into those based principally on technology or people illustrates this point (see Exhibit 5.1), and the impact on the service delivery system in terms, for example, of how it will be designed, the interface between customers and staff and the different levels of customer involvement can be envisaged.

The nature of the services to be delivered

The services to be processed by the operations system are different not only in themselves (fast-food and high-quality restaurants provide a different service and product mix, as illustrated in Exhibit 1.6) but also by the nature of what is involved. Exhibit 5.2 highlights these differences. The key dimensions illustrated by these examples are:

- the complexity (that is, the number of steps to complete) of the service to be provided
- what is processed in the delivery system – customers, customer surrogates, products or information.

Understanding how services differ is, therefore, an important prerequisite when designing the delivery systems to be used. Organizations typically design and develop a number of delivery systems to meet what they sell. Additional ways of categorizing services will help explain this still further and these are provided in the next section.

Exhibit 5.2 The nature of service processing

Nature of the service	Examples
Customers	Hairdressing, passenger airlines and healthcare
Customer surrogates	Car maintenance and repair, dry-cleaning and furniture restoration
Products	Retail grocery, laundry and automated banking services
Information	Mortgage application, insurance claim and tax advice

Categories of services

Exhibit 5.3 Service categories

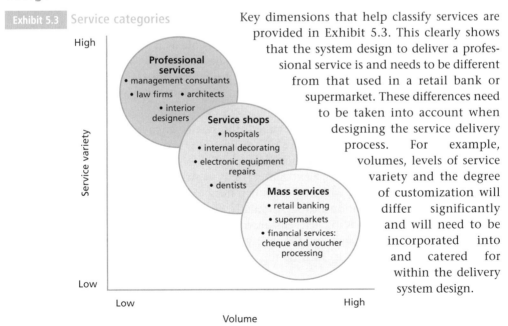

Key dimensions that help classify services are provided in Exhibit 5.3. This clearly shows that the system design to deliver a professional service is and needs to be different from that used in a retail bank or supermarket. These differences need to be taken into account when designing the service delivery process. For example, volumes, levels of service variety and the degree of customization will differ significantly and will need to be incorporated into and catered for within the delivery system design.

Complexity of the service

Many customer-based services are relatively simple in terms of the operations process involved and can be delivered as a single-step transaction, for example the front-office process in a retail bank and a takeaway food restaurant. Other services need multi-step process provision. For example, whereas a 'dry cut' in a hairdressing salon is a single trans-action, a cut and blow-dry would require two or more processes depending upon what was involved. Similarly, the delivery system to provide dinner at the Ritz in London would involve many more stages than having dinner in a fast-food restaurant.

Volumes

The critical nature and impact of volumes on service delivery system choice and design has already been introduced and forms part of the illustrations given in Exhibit 5.3. A glance at this exhibit shows the relationship between different categories of services and levels of volume and service variety. The key factors concern the non-repeat or repeat nature of the service offering and the volumes involved. The design of the delivery system will then need to reflect these fundamental dimensions.

Order-winners and qualifiers

Service delivery system design needs to reflect the order-winners and qualifiers for which operations is responsible. These comprise the business dimension of the offering and the system design needs to be built around this as well as the technical aspect of a service specification.

Service delivery systems – overall design

This and the next section now take a closer look at service delivery system design. Exhibit 5.4 provides a way of analysing and developing the overall design of a service delivery system and the principal phases are now discussed:[1]

- The market – the market provides the external context in which the service delivery system needs to be set and where the process of design and development starts. Identifying volumes, the relevant order-winners and qualifiers to retain and grow share in chosen markets, together with the service mix and design specifications, become the specification for the design of the system.

- The service encounter and experience – the service encounter (where and what is delivered) and the service experience (the reality of the service delivered) are the essence of the delivery system. But each dimension, as Exhibit 5.4 shows, needs a checks and balances approach. The service encounter needs to ascertain customers' expectations of what the service offering will provide, which need to be set against the operations standards that the organization has set. Similarly, the reality of the service delivered (the service experience) needs to check customers' perceptions with operations performance. In this way, customer needs and the reality of provision (what the company sets out to do and how well it does it) provide the essential inputs into the continuous development of the services on offer.

- Retention – one aim of the service delivery system is to help retain and grow market share. The delivery system design, therefore, needs to monitor its level of success while determining what to do to recover failure situations.[2] As Exhibits 5.5, 5.6, 5.7 and 5.8 show, while failure impacts retention rates, service recovery by satisfying complaints can help redress the loss of repeat business that follows. On the other hand, getting it wrong and leaving customers dissatisfied with the outcome or being too slow or too involved spells trouble![2]

Exhibit 5.4 Elements within service delivery system design

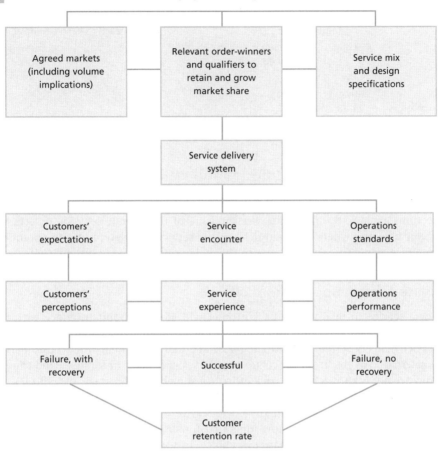

Exhibit 5.5 Customer problems and retention rates

Sector	Percentage total of customers experiencing problems	Retention rates (percentage total) for customers having	
		no problem	problem
Consumer goods	22	83	54
Appliance repairs	44	73	40
Car rentals	47	92	75
Branch banking	49	86	76
High-tech (business customers)	60	91	81
Air travel	69	91	77

Exhibit 5.6 Dissatisfied customers' repurchase intentions

Level of service recovery	Percentage of customers who will buy again by level of compaint	
	major	minor
Compaint not resolved	19	46
Complaint resolved	54	70
Complaint resolved quickly	82	95

| Exhibit 5.7 | Customer satisfaction: response time |

Response time	
# of days	% Customers satisfied
1–7	52
8–21	42
22–28	38
29+	23

| Exhibit 5.8 | Customer satisfaction: number of contacts |

Contacts to handle complaints	
#	% Customers satisfied
1	58
2	37
3	32
4	29
5+	11

Service delivery system – detailed design

Designing the detail of a service delivery system comprises two principal phases. As the next sections explain, the first addresses the issue of the overall delivery, reflects the decision about how and where a system delivers the service and determines the point of customer interface, while the second concerns the design of the delivery system itself.

Phase 1: back office or front office

For a service to take place, the customer will at some point interface with the delivery system. But at which point and for how long a customer is involved is an important part of service delivery system design. The phase of a delivery system where customers are present is referred to as the 'front office' (or sometimes, 'on stage' or 'online') and the phase where they are not is known as the 'back office' (or sometimes, 'off stage' or 'offline').

In some instances (for example a hairdresser and restaurant) a customer's involvement is not the subject of a decision. Here, the service can only be provided with the customer present. In other instances how long a customer is involved in the delivery system front office is, to some extent, a matter of choice. In some circumstances, a company decides to limit the front-office service provision to what is essential and complete as much of the service as possible in the back office. For example, paying a cheque into your bank account at your local high street branch has both front- and back-office elements. In the front office, the cheque and paying-in slip are presented and checked by the teller and set aside. The remainder of the transaction (for example the transfer of funds from the bank accounts involved) is completed in the back office. Similarly, taking garments to be dry-cleaned involves the front-office tasks of the customer explaining what is required, payment and the issue of a receipt. The cleaning takes place in the back office and collection of the garment takes place in the front office.

What then are the characteristics of the back office and front office that influence service delivery system design?

Back office

The key distinction between back office and front office is that in the former the activities take place without the customer being present or involved. For this reason, the separation of front and back office is sometimes referred to as the 'line of visibility', thus highlighting what of the delivery system a customer can and cannot see. Some of the advantages of completing work here include:

● Easier scheduling – undertaking tasks in the back office means that the system is not required to respond immediately to customer demands and so allows the completion of work to be planned when it best suits the system itself. For example, the choice to delay completing work means that scheduling what to do and when to do it can be in line with staff availability, when it best fits in with other work priorities and so on.

● **Higher processing volumes** – similarly, delaying completion allows the back-office system to cumulate volumes and provides the opportunity to undertake tasks more efficiently as all the work can be done at the same time. Furthermore, in a bank, for example, back-office tasks such as cheque clearance and bank statement preparation can be cumulated still further by bringing together the demands of many high street bank branches. Using regional or even national centres for these tasks creates even higher volumes that justify more process investment leading to lower processing costs overall.

Front office

On the other side of the line of visibility is the front-office portion of the system in which customer contact occurs. The characteristics inherent in this part of the system include:

● **Structural facilities** – as the customer is present in this part of the system, the structural facilities need to reflect the standards of the organization and meet the needs of customers. Ambience, decor, staff presentation and the efficient and responsive dimensions of the organization need to be created in line with its market position, its desired image and its customers' expectations.

● **Lead times** – as customer contact occurs here, the system needs to be able to meet the service specification involved while ensuring sufficient capacity to meet the service targets concerning queues (the time a customer waits) as well as the length of time it takes to deliver the service and the costs of overcapacity provision.

● **Ease of customer use** – the design must allow easy access (that is, it must be easy for customers to interface with the system). In this way, customers are encouraged to use the system design which is the organization's preferred method of delivering the service. If not, customers will choose delivery systems which, from a provider's viewpoint, are less preferred in terms of effectiveness and cost, for example getting cash from an ATM vis-à-vis cashing a cheque in the bank.

● **Staff roles** – the skills and roles of staff are essential to the effective working of delivery systems. This addresses the need for staff to be trained in the delivery of the service specifications involved, as well as the level of multiskilling desired, the role of staff in the task of cross-selling other services or products and the scope of server discretion (the extent to which a server can customize an offering).

Back office, middle office or front office

To help give sufficient insight into delivery system design, some organizations recognize that in their businesses there is a middle-office phase, as illustrated in Exhibit 5.9. Whereas in the back office there is no customer contact and in the front office the customer is involved, the middle office recognizes the indirect impact that certain tasks in this phase have on customers.

The purpose of identifying a middle-office stage is to facilitate delivery system design. By not recognizing this dimension in the examples provided in Exhibit 5.9, the activities listed under this category would have been allocated to the back-office function. One outcome of this is that the need to recognize the customer-facing dimension of these tasks may not have been adequately recognized by or incorporated into the system design itself.

Exhibit 5.9 Examples of front-, middle- and back-office activities in selected service organizations

Part of the delivery system	Illustrations		
	Passenger airline	Hotel	Fund management
Front office – direct customer contact	• Reservation and booking changes • Check-in • Departures and arrivals lounges • In-flight attendance • Flight transfers • Airport information desk	• Sales agents • Reservations • Reception • Concierge • Restaurant and bar staff • Switchboard	• Pre-trade compliance and and decisions • Trade order management • Client reporting • Client extranets
Middle office – indirect customer contact	• Ticket pricing • Flight schedules • Self-check-in system development • Frequent flier programme • Holiday and flight offers	• Marketing • Pricing – rooms and banqueting • Menu fulfillment • Wine selection • Housekeeping • Maintenance	• Transaction reconciliation • Compliance checks • Trade support • Risk management
Back office – no customer contact	• Aircraft maintenance • Flight preparation • Accounts • Refunds • Administration • Self-check-in system maintenance	• Administration • Accounts • Human resources • Kitchen	• Custody of assets and documents • Fund accounting • Fund administration • Transfer agency

Determining the customer interface within the delivery system

Some services are inherently online and do not allow the server to be separated from the customer (for example hairdressing and passenger transport). However, other service businesses do allow for a measure of server/customer decoupling. Where this is so, online services can be done offline if desired.

Furthermore, once parts of a service are offline they can also be transferred from the front office to the back office. This not only allows them to be completed using different methods and at different times (thus enabling low-cost opportunities to be exploited by cumulating demand and thereby increasing volumes prior to processing) but also allows firms to improve customer perceptions of the service itself, as illustrated in Case example 5.2.

Case example 2   **INFLUENCING CUSTOMER PERCEPTIONS AT THE ROYAL BANK (CANADA)**

The Royal Bank (Canada) believes that customers' perceptions are a critical factor in service provision. The bank considers that when queues form, customers' attitudes to waiting are affected by both the server's attitude when they are eventually attended to, and the fact that when waiting, customers judge service by the level of staff attendance shown in the front office. Thus, if bank staff are doing jobs other than attending to customers, and the queues are long, customers' attitudes to the bank's overall regard for service quality are affected. Thus, the bank's aim is to transfer as much paperwork as possible to head office or the back office.

www.royalbank.com

An electrical repair shop recently changed the customer interface point in the delivery system. Whereas previously the customer explained the repair needs to those in the front office, the customer now takes the repair to the back office and discusses the problem with the person who will complete the repair. Everyone gains. The repair person can now ensure that all pertinent questions are covered and the customer is able to discuss the repair both before and after the service is completed. This, of course, has long been the arrangement in many good quality dressmakers and tailors.

Case questions   1 How do these two examples differ?
2 What are the benefits and disadvantages of the alternative approaches in the two examples?

However, there are times when interfacing the back office and the customer brings significant benefits. One example where coupling the front office and back office together is provided in Case example 5.3.

Phase 2: The delivery system

Earlier Exhibit 5.3 introduced the principal ways to categorize services as 'professional services', 'service shops' and 'mass services', which provides a useful starting point. But, in reality, many organizations provide a range of services that fall into more than one of these three categories. For example, within a law practice, house conveyancing is a set of standard procedures typically completed by junior staff. The process is known, there are well-documented steps to be followed, with clear guidelines and preprinted forms containing questions that need to be answered by third parties as well as internal staff themselves. At the other end of the spectrum there will be one-off, non-repeat, complicated cases requiring technical and legal advice in a specialist area. Clearly these two tasks do not fall within the same service category. Similarly, the services in a hospital range from refreshment facilities through reception to surgery, postoperative care and rehabilitation. There will be outpatient clinics, accident and emergency provision and ambulance services that range from paramedic tasks at the scene of an accident to routine collection services for disabled or elderly patients. Although categorized as a service shop, the full scope of services provided by a hospital will need to be allocated to all three broad categories.

It therefore follows that as services differ, so will their delivery system designs. This section describes the different systems that are used and which types of service they are used to support. The key characteristics that underpin these differences are the non-repeat or repeat nature of a service and the range of volumes involved in the latter and whether the delivery system is designed as a single-step or multi-step process

Non-repeat services

As the name implies, services in this category are unique (known also as specials) and will not be provided in the same format a second time. Examples include interior design, legal advice for a business merger or takeover, financial advice for a stock exchange placement, executive development by one-to-one coaching, board-level consultancy advice regarding future corporate strategy decisions and the design and installation of a tailor-made IT system.

Providers of non-repeat services sell their skills and capabilities to meet the specific needs of a customer. In this way, the service specification is determined by the customer, with changes to what is required being made throughout its delivery. Typical order-winners include having a unique set of skills (being the best), with referrals and repeat business characteristic of the way this type of market works. Although customer orders will not be price-sensitive, the price for a service will need to be competitive (that is, in an acceptable price band) but yielding high margins.

The delivery system used for non-repeat services comprises one or a small group of skilled people providing all the service. The provider's role will include helping to determine what is required, determining the best process to follow and undertaking all the other steps involved through to and including implementation. As the service does not repeat, the opportunity to invest in the delivery system is not available and could not be justified, given the volumes involved. What is transferred from one service provision to the next is the provider's capability, skill base and the experience gained from providing other one-off services in the past.

Repeat services

Most organizations provide services that are deemed standard (that is, they have been provided before) rather than special. The repeat and higher volume nature associated with standard services signals a need to consider a different delivery system designed to take advantage of these characteristics. The volumes involved, however, can range from low to very high and this factor will be reflected in the design of the service delivery system used. To illustrate, let's take a transcontinental air flight. At the extremes there will be first-class and economy cabins. Although all passengers are travelling to the same destination and both classes of seat are repeat service offerings, the delivery system will show marked differences. Check-in arrangements, pre-boarding lounge facilities, carry-on luggage allowances, cabin staff/passenger ratios, range of food, drinks and beverages, the level of customization provided, choices of in-flight entertainment, and disembarkation and luggage collection priorities will all differ and the service delivery system design reflects these differences.

Exhibit 5.3 provides other examples of repeat services and illustrates the key factor of the different volume levels associated with these different offerings. The higher the volume then factors such as service variety, level of price sensitivity and degree of customization will change. Higher volumes justify the higher levels of process investment necessary to support

Exhibit 5.10 Implications in delivery system design for non-repeat and repeat services

Factors reflected in service delivery system design		Non-repeat services	Repeat services	
			Low volume	High volume
Service variety		Wide	→	Narrow
Level of customization		High	→	Low
How are orders won?	typical order-winners	Design, response to change	→	Price
	typical qualifiers	Price, on-time, quality conformance	→	On-time, quality conformance
Volumes		Low	→	High
Delivery system	design	General and unspecified	→	Specified and dedicated
	levels of flexibility	High	→	Low
Ability of delivery system to cope with	service change	High	→	Low
	new services	High	→	Low
Dominant factor of utilization		Staff	→	Process
Prior knowledge of the operations task		Not well defined	→	Well defined
Level of process investment		Low	→	High
Staff skill levels		High	→	Low

the associated order-winning nature of price. Where possible, work is deskilled, with the process investment completing more of the task which, in turn, results in less staff costs both in terms of skill levels and work content. Exhibit 5.10 summarizes some of the principal factors in delivery system design that reflect the non-repeat/repeat nature of the service offering and the level of volumes involved.

Single-step or multi-step process

A key decision in the design of a system concerns the number of steps to be taken in delivering the service. A single-step design implies that the complete service is delivered as a single transaction, for example getting cash from an ATM and purchasing a newspaper from a retail outlet. A multi-step delivery system means that the service is delivered in two or more steps. In a multi-step system the first part of the design process is to break down the service into a number of steps. How many stages will depend on the complexity of the service involved. The activities at each stage that make up the whole will then be completed. They will be done separately, by different staff and normally in different parts of the system. The purpose of splitting the task into a number of smaller steps is a form of investment in itself, and is one way to help undertake the task more efficiently by cumulating similar activities from a range of services and completing these in the same part of the delivery system (for example the reception and X-ray functions in a hospital). This provides an opportunity to undertake the tasks more efficiently and introduces the potential for staff specialization and process investments. For example, customers would enter a service delivery system such as a hospital. The patients (that is, the customers) would initially go to reception and the staff would process them, such as recording relevant details. Patients would go to the next stage in the process (for example to see a specialist consultant) and, having waited, would go through that stage of the treatment. They would then go through the next stages in the same way until the total service was completed. A similar example is provided in Exhibit 5.11 which outlines the steps in two delivery systems in a dental surgery.

With information processing, the procedure is broken down into a number of stages, the total of which completes the whole process. As in the hospital example, the documents then go from stage to stage, with each step typically involving waiting time, a single set-up or preparation stage and the processing of all the documents at the one time. This waiting between stages allows processes to work independently of one another (known as decoupling) and hence more efficiently, while the processing of all the documents at one stage reduces the number of set-ups involved and increases the volume processed in any one step at any one time.

You will see from these examples that similar steps for all customers are undertaken in the same function, hence increasing overall volumes at each stage and providing the opportunity to reduce costs to complete this step by, for example, process investment.

Now let's address the question of why organizations choose a multi-step rather than a single-step delivery system design. The factors to be taken into account include the following:

- The service comprises a range of staff skill levels – where a service comprises a range of skill levels, organizations seek to keep costs low by allocating the activities and tasks involved to the relevant staff skill sets. If a hospital was set up as a single-step system, the healthcare specialist would record a patient's details, undertake the consultation, complete the X-ray, check to confirm the nature of the broken limb, apply the plaster and make the next appointment. But this service system is much more suited to a multi-step design where these various tasks are performed by different staff who specialize in different areas to deliver different parts of a service. Thus, healthcare specialists restrict their involvement to their area of specialism, with other tasks being completed in a more cost-

Exhibit 5.11 Patients visiting a dental surgery – an example of a multi-step delivery system

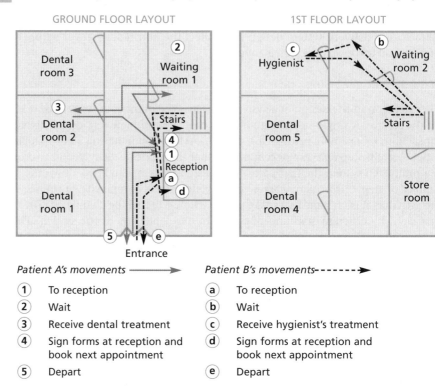

Patient A's movements ——————➤		Patient B's movements------➤	
①	To reception	ⓐ	To reception
②	Wait	ⓑ	Wait
③	Receive dental treatment	ⓒ	Receive hygienist's treatment
④	Sign forms at reception and book next appointment	ⓓ	Sign forms at reception and book next appointment
⑤	Depart	ⓔ	Depart

effective way in terms of staff skill and with each step of the process developing specialized and more effective procedures and approaches to completing the tasks involved. By
processing customers operation by operation, the capacity at each stage in the process is
used and reused to meet the different requirements of different customers, with volumes
justifying process investment leading to a more overall cost-effective provision.

● **The service specification is complex** – where services are relatively simple they lend
themselves to being delivered by a single-step system. Where services are more complex
companies provide them in a multi-step format. One reason is that matching the task
requirement to the appropriate skill set is easier. Similarly, companies often prefer to
complete as much of the service as makes sense in a back-office rather than front-office
environment.

● **To enhance volumes** – using a multi-step design to provide a number of services brings
together similar steps from two or more services to be completed in the same function or
area. The higher volumes that result provide scope for cost reduction by creating the
opportunity to invest in the process, develop specialist skill sets and match each step in
the service to the required skill levels and salary grades that go with these. As a result,
work content is reduced, staff become better in specialist skill areas and aspects of the
service are delivered by the appropriate level of skilled person.

IT-based and other service delivery system designs

When designing delivery systems, many organizations have used developments in information technology (IT) to rethink approaches while others choose different ways to deliver the services they offer. Before looking at some of them let's first reflect on the key interface between technology developments and delivery systems. Within the delivery system design process, operations managers have the task of interfacing with technical specialists whose predominant perspective is typically that of technology rather than markets. As the operations task is to use and manage technology to supply services, putting forward the business dimensions of these developments falls clearly and appropriately within the remit of operations. The danger is that technology is left with experts and is not recognized as needing to be driven by business requirements – behind the humour in Exhibit 5.12 is a serious but often neglected message!

Exhibit 5.12 Technology is a business as well as a technical issue

© Roger Beale

Information technology

IT developments have not only reduced costs and lead times within systems and procedures but have also enabled organizations to redesign many of these delivery systems as the following examples illustrate:

- Automated banking – banks are continuing to cut costs by automating more of their services, for example ATMs are now the principal way to get cash from your bank account. Increasingly banks are adding video disc displays selling insurance, providing details on loans and screens offering share quotations. In parts of Europe and the USA fully automated bank branches are replacing traditional set-ups, offering all the usual range of services but without tellers.

- Teleworking – since the early 1980s, companies have been experimenting with teleworking, the practice of using computers and telephone links to work away from the office. Home offices are part of this growing trend while companies are making increasingly heavy use of telecommuting, a policy that allows employees to work in the office one or two days a week and spend the rest of the time with clients and working from home. Jack Nilles, the 'father of teleworking', coined the phrases 'teleworking' and 'telecommuting' in 1973 while leading a research project at the University of Southern California into the impact of IT at work.[3]

Teleworking brings benefits including productivity increases of 20 per cent or more, reduced office space requirements and lower staff turnover levels.[4] In addition, benefits to a nation's economy are significant. It is estimated that traffic congestion costs the UK economy more than $100 billion in lost productivity while London commuters waste more than 10 hours per week going to work. In the USA, clean air legislation is obliging large firms to reduce their commuter workforce. AT&T, for instance, had a telecommuting workforce of over 40,000 by 2002. While in the late 1970s there were very few tele-workers, by the late 1990s this had grown to 20 million worldwide and it is predicted to reach 200 million by 2016.

In addition, automated or 'predictive' dialling (that connects agents to customers just as the incoming call rings out) is being increasingly installed to cut the time to answer and also reduce the number of times a customer rings off. Favoured locations for call centres in Europe are Ireland and Scotland due in part to wage rates in a service where labour accounts for 45 per cent of total costs. For example, American Airlines relocated its European reservation centre to Dublin in the late 1990s where it estimated that staff costs were half those in Switzerland. In fact, in the late 1990s it was estimated that Ireland alone accounted for 30 per cent of all pan-European call centres in the EU. The problem, however, that Dublin, Edinburgh, Glasgow and their immediate hinterlands now face is how to keep staff. The concern is not so much one of losing staff to competitors but to other job opportunities.[5]

E-commerce

The internet offers the capability to personalize the service to customers. It has the ability to tailor itself to every one of its 100 million users.[6] Furthermore, the internet crosses borders, which means that pressure on prices is going to increase almost overnight. For example, European companies will find it tough competing with US competitors in many retail markets – books in the UK and CDs in Europe and Japan are both about 30 per cent more expensive than in the US.

The benefits on the retail end of the spectrum have also been increasingly embraced by company inter-trading. But e-commerce is not just shopping by another name. It encompasses companies' relationships with their suppliers as well as their customers. Corporate intranets will be linked in order to provide a safe, secure, manageable, business-to-business environment, and e-commerce will be an integrated part of the customer/supplier partnership. These issues are discussed in more detail as part of Chapter 13 on supply chain management.

Dealing with customers and suppliers through e-commerce has profound implications for the way companies operate and, as more users gain access to the internet, the need for organizations to embrace relevant technologies into the design of their delivery systems is critical. Here are some examples of online service developments.

Travel booking

Since its early days, online travel booking has grown rapidly. The European online market is forecast to continue to grow by 20–30 per cent a year in the period 2003–07 compared with single digit growth for the travel industry as a whole. Part of this growth has been boosted by the no-frills passenger airline phenomenon. By 2003, 90 per cent of easyJet's and 94 per cent of Ryanair's bookings were made online. Their success has encouraged more traditional airlines to move to increase online bookings. By 2003 Aer Lingus handled 30 per cent of its bookings online (up from just 2 per cent a year earlier) and British Airways now completes 35 per cent of all short-haul bookings this way.

Call centres

Whether the vendor is a PC manufacturer providing a help desk for users, a gas or electric distribution company answering queries or a financial services company handling account, policy or general enquiries or mortgage and personal loan applications, a call centre has become the preferred solution.

The advances in computer telephony integration have enabled call centres to replace traditional service departments by linking the telephone to a computer that routes calls to the most appropriate agent, prompts the agent with caller data (known as 'screen popping') and leads the agent through a script to produce answers to thousands of different questions. Call centres cut staff costs compared to multi-site arrangements, both in terms of the number of staff required and the opportunity to locate centres in lower wage rate areas. With call centres, customers are offered free or low-rate calls to encourage their use, and international centres allow customers to call a local number while the system then transfers them to an overseas agent who speaks their own language.

In addition, some companies (for example Dell) transfer calls from one region to another (for example mainland Europe to the UK or Ireland and then to the eastern seaboard of the USA and so on) as a way of efficiently handling the times during a 24-hour period when the number of calls are low. For example, bookings and enquiries for Radisson Hotels in Europe and the Middle East are handled by the group's call centre in Dublin from 7am to 7pm. The operation handles more than 1000 calls daily, with 22 incoming telephone lines (all free phones) operated by 25 staff speaking 11 different languages. From 7pm the service switches to operations in the USA. The range of services suited to call centre provision is well illustrated in Case examples 5.4 and 5.5.

Case example 4 **TELEPHONE SERVICE DELIVERY AT THOMAS COOK/WEST DEUTSCHE LANDESBANK**

Thomas Cook AG has been providing travel services since 1808 and operates the world's largest network, with over 3000 travel agencies and 26,000 staff worldwide. Now owned by West Deutsche Landesbank, it serves 12 million customers each year, with sales in 2003 of €7.2 billion.

Thomas Cook has now added Global Services to provide value-added travel emergency assistance services. This entails providing detailed assistance at the end of a telephone line with the use of computer telephony integration that identifies a caller's number and places that call in the queue for a call centre agent with appropriate skills. Further developments link a caller in Shanghai (say) with a map showing the location of the caller and the closest medical services displayed so the agent can talk the caller through. Details of all incidents are also stored, allowing an agent to pull up a full history of customer's problems on future occasions. The main site in Peterborough (UK) can handle queries in 60 languages. The £20 million investment is attracting a new group of corporate customers and is now being offered to third parties such as airlines and government agencies.

www.thomascook.co.uk

Case questions
1 Why would corporate customers be attracted to this service?
2 How is a call centre uniquely appropriate for providing these services?

First Direct, HSBC's telephone banking business, was the first to challenge the traditional bank-based provision that characterized the banking industry in the last century. Based on call centre provision, First Direct presents itself as a gateway through which customers pass to access their money, obtain advice and control their financial affairs. Conventional banks, First Direct's staff are told, are a brick wall in comparison – resolute, restrictive, secure but unresponsive. A basic tenet is to offer customers an equal relationship with their bank manager. To inculcate this into their behaviour and values, staff are themselves treated with equality in the workplace. First, recruitment is based on behavioural rather than banking skills – only 5 per cent of staff have worked previously in banks. Second, the 24-hour banking service is run on flexible shift patterns where staff choose their own patterns (anything from 16 to 32 hours) while recognizing the peaks and troughs in demand. Staff also decided themselves how they should dress for work and opted for a smart dress code to better reflect the way they needed to carry out their jobs. Crèche facilities at the Leeds (UK) centre have always been available, allowing staff to mix family and work commitments. Basic pay relates to an employee's skills which are heavily weighted towards the behavioural (communicating, handling stress, influencing, assessing information, judgement and decision making) end of the skill continuum. Staff are also required to match certain standards covering call duration, availability and signed on times.

www.firstdirect.com

Case questions
1 Why are call centres attracting customers away from conventional bank branch provision of services?
2 What aspects of First Direct have helped make its call centre a success?

Grocery shopping

After its first tentative steps, online grocery shopping is gaining ground. Competitors in the field have, however, chosen different ways to provide this service. Ocado, the UK's first e-grocer, has taken a warehouse-based approach. Its dedicated picking and delivery system is based at its depot in Hatfield, north of London, which is the size of seven soccer pitches or about 20 average supermarkets. Others using the warehouse model include Simon Delivers in Minneapolis, Greengrocer.com in Australia and Carrefour, Europe's biggest retailer based in France.

Tesco (the UK's largest supermarket), among others, has taken a different approach. It developed its own technology to enable it to use store-based picking – a low-investment route to this new type of shopping. This approach is now gaining ground in the USA, with Safeway, California's biggest supermarket group, being one of the early adopters. In 2003 Tesco's internet sales had risen to close on £500 million, with profits exceeding £12 million. With 250,000 customers, Tesco processes 110,000 orders per week and has 65 per cent of the UK market. Using this model, Tesco estimates that it can service £2–3 billion of sales through its existing stores. On the other hand, Sainsbury's (a large UK supermarket) has chosen a hybrid model, with a warehouse in north London but most sales done through store-based picking. Now take a look at Case example 5.6 for a further illustration.

Jeri Capozzi only shops for plants at the online nursery Garden Escape. The reason is not just that the website offers unusual plants, but also because Garden Escape created a personal store just for her. Greeted by name on her personal page each time she visits, Capozzi can make notes on a private online notepad, tinker with garden plans using the site's interactive design program, and get answers from the Garden Doctor. So far, Jeri has spent $600 in less than 12 months and has no plans to shop elsewhere. With service that personal, she says, 'I probably will never leave it'.[7]

www.burpee.com

Case question What are the advantages of shopping on the internet? Do you see any problems?

Alternative approaches

Many organizations choose alternative approaches to designing their delivery systems. Each has its own merits and similarly its own disadvantages. Case examples 5.7 and 5.8 illustrate different approaches and the trade-offs involved.

Case example 7   **SERVICE DELIVERY AT A LOCAL HIGH STREET BANK BRANCH**

If you go into the local high street branch of your bank and wish to collect foreign currency, pay in a cheque and discuss some detail of your account, then you will have to use three different, single-step delivery systems to meet your needs.

Each of these will only deal with a limited number of the total range of services the bank provides. On the other hand, if you go into a post office, you will stand in one queue and all the services you require will be delivered by the one teller.

Case question   1   What is the fundamental difference in service delivery design in these two examples?

Case example 8   **SERVICE DELIVERY AT THE MOSCOW SCIENTIFIC INSTITUTE FOR EYE MICROSURGERY**

For most, the perception we have of hospital surgery is one of delicate and sensitive operations. In reality, many surgical approaches are routine and comprise a series of standard steps and procedures. One surgeon who has taken this dimension to an extreme is the Russian eye surgeon, Dr Svyatoslav Fyoderov. In his Institute for Eye Microsurgery,[8] Fyoderov's surgical treatment of myopia (short-sightedness) is radical keratotomy. As

Exhibit 5.13 illustrates, patients lie on moving theatre tables. Six surgeons perform their part of the operation and then each patient moves on to the next stage. Surgeons check the previous step(s) in the surgical process, perform their step and the process continues. TV screens, microphones and headsets enable visual and voice contact to be maintained throughout.[9]

eng.mntk.ru

Exhibit 5.13 Dr Svyatoslav Fyoderov's eye microsurgery unit

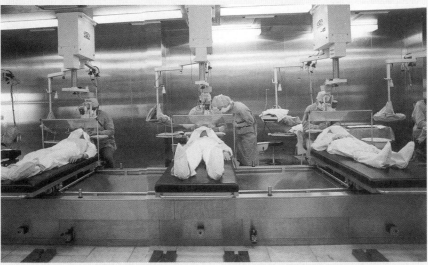

Case question   1   What advantages and disadvantages does this approach bring compared to alternative design approaches?

Other issues that may be considered in delivery system design

This section introduces some additional issues that organizations may consider when developing the overall design of their service delivery systems.

Enhancing services: making the intangible tangible

Companies basing their approach on service differentiation employ several strategies to enhance the service provided. One way is to bring the intangible facets of a service to the attention of a customer by making them tangible. By doing this, parts of a service package that may go unnoticed by the customer now become a visible part of the provision. For example:

- Maid service in a hotel bedroom to include collars placed on toilets with words similar to 'sanitized for your personal use', end-folding toilet roll paper, folding down the bed in the evening, with a personalized note and guest room checklist duly completed (see Exhibit 5.14).

Exhibit 5.14 A personalized note

THE
AMBASSADOR
★ ★ ★ ★
HOTEL AND EXECUTIVE SUITES

To My Special Guest

My name is ...Constance...
I have made a commitment to ensure that your
room is spotlessly clean and well made up.
Should anything not be quite right may I ask
you to please call the duty manager.

Exhibit 5.15 Informing customers about standards

Lloyds TSB

3 MINUTE WARNING
We at SOLIHULL Branch feel
that you shouldn't be waiting
any longer than 3 minutes
in this queue.

If you feel that you have been
waiting longer than this, please
complete your details below and
hand to a member of staff.

Thank you

Name...

Account Number.....................................

Time.......................... Date.......................

Enquiries or Cashiers Queue......................

- Fast, attentive service is signalled by prominent positioning of the '3-minute warning' notice in some high street branches of the UK bank Lloyds TSB (see Exhibit 5.15). Supported by the prompt opening of additional tellers when queues start to form, this draws customers' attention to this dimension of service provision.

- Hotels are increasingly making in-room hot drink provision a feature. Moreover, many also provide the highest quality amenities such as French-milled and smooth facial soaps, shampoo, conditioner, bath foam, hand lotion and shower caps; aftershave for male travellers, and make-up remover and styling preparations for their female counterparts. All designed, in part, to give a tangible feel to the hotel's quality of service provided elsewhere.

- In a similar vein, some hotels now display notices in the en-suite bathrooms informing guests that should they have forgotten any essential toiletry item, to telephone reception for complimentary provision (see Exhibit 5.16).

Exhibit 5.16 Complimentary provision notice

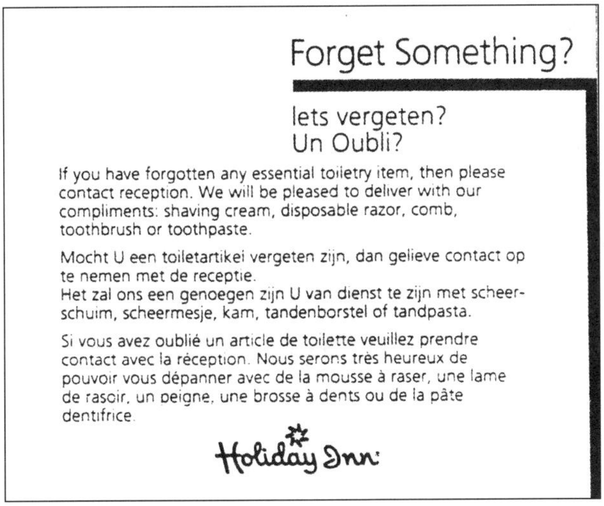

Forget Something?

lets vergeten?
Un Oubli?

If you have forgotten any essential toiletry item, then please contact reception. We will be pleased to deliver with our compliments: shaving cream, disposable razor, comb, toothbrush or toothpaste.

Mocht U een toiletartikel vergeten zijn, dan gelieve contact op te nemen met de receptie.
Het zal ons een genoegen zijn U van dienst te zijn met scheer-schuim, scheermesje, kam, tandenborstel of tandpasta.

Si vous avez oublié un article de toilette veuillez prendre contact avec la réception. Nous serons très heureux de pouvoir vous dépanner avec de la mousse à raser, une lame de rasoir, un peigne, une brosse à dents ou de la pâte dentifrice.

Holiday Inn

● Prompt service is also made tangible in one of several ways – many hotels guarantee an in-room breakfast that will be delivered within ten minutes of the requested period or it will be provided free of charge. Domino Pizza's promise to deliver an order to your home within 30 minutes (normal times) or 40 minutes (peak demand times) or it will be replaced or money refunded. In practice, this means that if a delivery is late, customers would be asked to pay for the pizza(s) but not (say) the soft drink(s) or dessert(s). Further-more, if a delivery is considered very late (20 plus minutes), the whole order is offered free of charge. Domino Pizza's replace or refund policy also applies to its quality guarantee.

Exhibit 5.17 The time stamp as a tangible symbol of freshness

The Upper Crust

If you are not satisfied with the quality of this baguette return it to the store of purchase and we will replace it or give you your money back. Your statutory rights are not affected.

We ≡ guarantee ≡ you'll enjoy this.

FRESHLY BAKED TODAY AND FILLED AT:

17·30

● In maintenance work, cleaning up after completion provides a 'reverse' example of this same perspective. Similarly, a car wash given free with a routine service or paper covers left inside the vehicle demonstrate to the customer the level of care taken by the company when providing the core element of the service.

● Guarantees on quality are now standard for most products where reimbursement of price and postage is prompt and is encouraged by companies where a customer has any concerns whatsoever. With food, the time of preparation also signals freshness, as demonstrated in Exhibit 5.17.

Determining the level of customer participation in the delivery system

When designing the delivery system organizations need to decide the extent to which customers will or will not participate in the creation of the service. The degree of customer involvement in the system affects many

Exhibit 5.18 Customers as participants in the delivery system – not quite the experience that Wiggins expected!!

© AMD Publishing

factors including the provision and management of capacity, service levels, staff training requirements and costs.[10]

Higher levels of customer participation in the delivery system make capacity management easier and reduce the cost of its provision, while lower levels decrease the degree of customer contact and the opportunities to personalize the service and encourage customer loyalty. The trade-offs involved need to be understood and the operations implications for supporting the alternative service delivery system designs need to be fully assessed. For example, while banks in Europe are increasingly standardizing procedures for bank loan applications, in Japan the procedure has already progressed to the use of a score sheet. Answers to several questions are graded and if the customer's score is above a certain level, the loan application is handled quickly. The impact upon operations provision is significant.

However, for the use of do-it-yourself approaches to be successful, companies must assess the total operations requirement of the service delivery system and carefully complement the customer inputs by well-trained staff, reliable equipment and appropriate and well-maintained systems and procedures. Exhibit 5.18 gives one approach!

The use of the do-it-yourself concept in service delivery systems has been gaining ground over the last few decades. Examples of service industries increasingly using this approach include:

- **Supermarkets** control over 80 per cent of the gross retail market and sell principally on a self-service basis.
- **Fast-food outlets** form a growing part of overall restaurant provision.
- **Telephone services** are principally based on subscriber dialling, with most telephone calls now being made by customers.
- **Petrol stations** use self-service as the basis for providing fuel, screen washing, and oil, water and tyre pressure checks.
- **Online shopping** is a major provider in the retail industry. It requires a customer to complete the selection, application and payment parts of the procedure, with the business providing fast delivery once the transaction is fed into the service system.
- **Financial services** provide a growing range of products through self-service delivery systems from ATMs, general banking, insurance, mortgages and personal loans.

The reasons for the growth in these sectors vary. Exhibit 5.19 summarizes some factors that relate to their success, while Case examples 5.9 and 5.10 provide illustrations.

Exhibit 5.19 Success factors of self-service approaches

Success factors	Selected service sectors					
	Supermarkets	Fast-food outlets	Telephone services	Petrol stations	Online shopping	Financial services
Faster service	✓	✓	✓	✓	✓	✓
Lower price	✓	✓	✓	✓	✓	✓
Improved product quality	✓	✓				
Increased product variety	✓				✓	
More convenient	✓	✓			✓	✓
More control within the delivery system	✓	✓	✓	✓	✓	✓

Case example 9   SELF-SCANNING IN SUPERMARKETS

The downside of supermarket shopping is queuing to pay. To speed up this part of the delivery system, retailers are looking for ways to involve customers in this last step of the process. For some time now, the facility for self-scanning your purchases as you go and then paying at a designated checkout has been available. Now, further help is on the way. Developed in the US, a touch-screen system (those provided by NCR and Optimal Robotics are leading the charge) enabling self-service checkouts by customers is gaining ground in UK retailers such as Marks & Spencer, Sainsbury's, Waitrose and Safeway. The way it works is that the system uses visual and voice commands to talk customers through the process. Once an item is swiped at the checkout, it is put in a shopping basket sitting on sensitive weighing scales. The precise weight and price of every item (loose vegetables and fruit are scanned at the point of purchase and given a bar code sticker) is stored on a database. An item when scanned is verified by its weight when placed on the sensitive scales. If an item does not register properly, the voice system asks the customer to scan it again.

To guard against dishonesty there are several in-built checks. For example, the weighing system is so sensitive that it can even identify different types of the same product, for example different grades of lemonade, bottles of wine or bottles of spirit and so guards against attempted substitution of a higher priced alternative. CCTV cameras are installed to catch anyone who fails to scan every item and if a customer fails to pay an alarm goes off. Payment is by credit or debit card. To pay customers sign on a computer screen pad which is cross-checked electronically with the one on the back of the card. No pre-registering and being easy to use appeals to those who simply wish to shop and go! With the average person in the UK spending two hours in queues every week (even with internet banking and shopping), user-friendly forms of self-service are gaining ground.

www.ncr.com; www.safeway.com
www.sainsbury.co.uk; www.optimalgrp.com
www.marksandspencer.com; www.waitrose.com

Case questions

1 Why are supermarkets introducing self-checkout systems?

2 In 2003, consumers ranked self-checkout technology second only to cash machines as the self-service they are most likely to use. Why?

Case example 10 SERVICE DELIVERY AT DIRECT LINE

There are over 20 million private motorists in the UK and car ownership continues to grow. As a result, motor insurance is big business, with an £8 billion annual premium spend. Launched in 1985, Direct Line was the first insurance company to use the telephone as its primary medium for sales and other transactions. Cutting out the middleman and commissions enabled it to speed up the application process and reduce premiums. Now, in 2004 Direct Line is the UK's largest private motor insurer, with over ten million policy holders. Direct Line has also successfully expanded its product range and the Direct Line Group (a wholly owned subsidiary of the Royal Bank of Scotland) now offers the following:

- Direct Line Insurance plc – motor, rescue, home, travel and pet insurance and a 24-hour home emergency call-out service

- Direct Line Financial Services Ltd – mortgages, savings, personal loans and credit cards

- Direct Line Life Holdings Ltd – personal pensions, life insurance and ISAs.

In 1995 Direct Line opened its first industrial-scale Accident Management Centre. By 2004, it operated seven throughout the UK together with a further 278 approved garages in its network that contribute to the quality and efficiency of the service within its overall claims business.

A strong feature of the early years was Direct Line's speed of growth. By year three it was profitable even though it offered premiums that were typically 20 per cent lower than competitors. The concept of the telephone as its primary tool enabled Direct Line to deal directly with the public and use the advantages afforded by its technological efficiency and underwriting precision to cut costs. Less than a decade after its entry, Direct Line became the UK's largest private motor insurer.

Direct Line's entry set new service standards for the insurance industry. It offers extended hours, with lines open from 8am to 8pm on weekdays and 9am to 5pm on Saturdays. It enables customers to register and complete their claims by telephone and provides 24-hour emergency help lines. The idea brings greater simplicity, improves the level of customer support through the process and results in better value for money.

In 1993, when the company's flagship products were both the fastest growing in their respective markets, Direct Line extended its range, adopting the same tactics of low prices, straightforward products and telephone-based service delivery systems. As the company transacts the vast majority of its business by telephone, operations is at the core of the Direct Line service proposition. To ensure standards are maintained, the company provides extensive customer care training and re-engineers processes to cut out complicated forms and jargon. One of its first revolutionary moves was to eliminate cover notes (that were traditionally sent to customers as confirmation of insurance cover but were not the official documents) by laser printing and mailing policies, insurance certificates and other documents the same day.

Innovative technology helps Direct Line keep down costs. For example, most products are paid for by credit card or direct debit, allowing payments to be processed electronically and so reducing staff and overheads. Similarly, automated call handling systems ensure that the 15 million calls received each year are quickly and effortlessly rerouted between Direct Line's different call centres to minimize customer waiting time.

Today, Direct Line continues to improve its operations so as to offer additional customer benefits and better customer support. These range from the use of daily interest calculations for mortgages to a 'pet bereavement' helpline for pet insurance customers. Staff development is also a key activity, with initiatives such as cross-training sales and claims staff so that the same people can handle both sets of tasks. The result is that work interest increases while customers are served more quickly.

www.directline.com

Case questions	1	Why is Direct Line so successful and how has operations supported the business growth?
	2	How do (if at all) the products offered by Direct Line differ from its competitors?
	3	Analyse Direct Line in terms of the 'factors for success' introduced in Exhibit 5.19.

Maximizing the use of skilled staff

Businesses that offer a wide range of services will also typically employ a wide range of skilled staff. As higher skilled people are more difficult to find and command higher salaries, ensuring that there is a match between the level of difficulty and the level of staff skill needed to deliver the task is an important factor in delivery system design. The approach is

referred to as 'maximizing the leverage of scarce resources', with scarce resources here referring to the skill and experience level of staff. This concept is designed to highlight the need
to ensure that staff do not undertake tasks for which their skills are too high.

For example, the auditing divisions of big accounting firms employ large numbers of
juniors or associate staff on relatively low salaries and these junior staff make up the majority of the audit teams. In this way, the less difficult tasks are completed by less experienced
staff, with more senior staff leading the team and partners responsible for more than one
team. One result is that the sales and profit per partner are enhanced. Furthermore, with
little opportunity for advancement, the staff turnover at this level is high and so junior and
associate staff are continuously being replaced by new entrants so helping to maintain the
sales and profit levels per partner.

Determining the level of server discretion within the delivery system

The system–customer interface allows for servers to exercise discretion. It is important,
therefore, for organizations to establish the appropriate level of discretion to be exercised
within each service category and delivery system (that is, the extent to which it is desired or
appropriate that a server is allowed to interpret what should constitute the service specification actually provided). Earlier issues concerning customer participation, service enhancement, the non-repeat or repeat nature of a service and the level of customer interface within
the system will impact server discretion levels. Firms need to recognize these factors as ways
of reducing or increasing customization and use them to develop a service delivery system
that supports the desired level of customization. In so doing, organizations can improve
their control of quality conformance within a service delivery system with given levels of
customer contact and staff skills.

Service profiling

Organizations need to have a clear understanding of the implications for their business as
alternative delivery systems are chosen. When companies invest in systems they need to
incorporate into that decision the business trade-offs involved. Similarly, as markets change
or as companies enter new markets with different competitive needs, they must check
whether the changing or different needs of their markets can be supported by the operations investments already in place. The critical nature of these checks stems from the fact
that whereas markets are characterized by change, investments in operations are characterized by their large size and fixed nature, so to make changes in operations typically takes a
long time and a lot of money. Thus, if market needs and operations capabilities are not
matched a company can be strategically disadvantaged.

Now place these considerations in the context of today's competitive environment.
Markets are changing faster and are increasingly different rather than increasingly similar. For
operations to align its capabilities to the needs of the company's markets today and tomorrow,
it needs a way of assessing the level of current alignment and being alerted to future changes
that may reduce this essential support. Similarly, in its market-driving role it needs to agree
with a business, ahead of time, those order-winners and qualifiers it must improve to maintain
or grow share in current markets or enable it to successfully enter new markets.

The concept for undertaking this check is called service profiling.[11] It offers an organization the opportunity to test the current or anticipated degree of fit between the characteristics of its market(s) and the characteristics of its existing or proposed process and

infrastructure investments. The principal purpose of this assessment is to provide a method to evaluate and, where necessary, improve the degree of fit between the way in which a company qualifies and wins orders in its markets and operations ability to support these criteria.

The ideal is to achieve this fit. In many instances though, companies will be unable or unwilling to provide the desired degree of fit due to the level of investment, executive energy or timescales involved to make the necessary changes. Sound strategy concerns improving the level of consciousness an organization brings to bear on its corporate decisions. In such circumstances service profiling will increase corporate awareness and allow a conscious choice between alternatives.

Inconsistency between the competitive factors in markets and an organization's capability to support them can be induced by changes in either market needs or delivery system investments, or a combination of the two. Potential mismatches emanate from the fact that while investments within operations are both large and fixed, markets are affected by competition that brings about change and the fact that corporate marketing decisions can sometimes be relatively transient. While the latter allows for change and repositioning, operations decisions can bind a business for years ahead. Thus, linkage between these two parts of an organization is not just a felt need but an essential requirement.

Procedure

Alignment involves checking how well the requirements of markets are matched by the characteristics of the operations systems used to provide them. The purpose of the check is to assess the level of business fit that exists. It also serves to alert companies to future potential alignment issues that could arise as a result of current strategies in a business.

Completing a check links aspects of the last two chapters on operations strategy and service design and development respectively to aspects of this chapter that concern service delivery system design. The procedure for developing a service profile involves the following steps and analyses:

1   Select aspects of the business (some are given in Exhibit 5.10) that are relevant to the situation under review. The key here is to keep the number of chosen dimensions small and so keep the insights sharp. Remember, this approach is a mechanism for communicating strategic issues within a business. Keeping to the point highlights the message, avoids digression and concentrates discussion on the strategic issues under review.

2   Next, put down the characteristics associated with each chosen dimension in the same way as they are displayed in Exhibit 5.10. Exhibit 5.20 is an example of the outcome of service profiling and a glance at this will show you how to proceed.

3   Now profile the service(s) by positioning them on each of the characteristics selected. Where the circle is drawn indicates the relative position of a service on a dimension. The example in Exhibit 5.20 shows the resulting profiles for two of the three segments within a part of a large utilities company. The dogleg nature of both profiles provides a way to identify the lack of fit between some key activities and dimensions of the total business with the different market needs of these two market segments. Note that to help clarity only two of the three segments of the company have been profiled.

The story behind Exhibit 5.20

To better meet the needs of its markets in the face of growing competition, the company was set up as a stand-alone business. With some 3000 staff, it meets the requirements of over 0.25 million new customers each year split into three segments (see Exhibit 5.21):

Exhibit 5.20　Service profiling

Aspects		Typical characteristics		
		Non-repeat	Repeat	
			Low volume	High volume
Customer value (£)	per job	High		Low
	percentage total sales	High		Low
Customer relationship	frequency of contact during job	High		Low
	type of contact	Define/understand data, complete work		Exchange data
	repeatability	Ongoing		One-off
Order nature	order volume	Low		High
	technical similarity	Low		High
What does the company sell?		Capability		Fixed service
How are orders won?	order-winners	Design capability		Price
	qualifiers	Delivery reliability, price		On-time, quality conformance
Key task	business centre	Respond to needs of customer		Cost reduction
	management centre	Technical meeting schedules		Efficiency
Service delivery system flexibility		High		Low
Organizational structure		Decentralized		Centralized
Performance measurement orientation		Level of customer support		Cost reduction
Customer management	satisfaction measurement	Face-to-face interview		Questionnaire
	relationship measurement	One-to-one relationships		Database

○ ◑ Position of Segment 1 on each of the chosen dimensions and the resulting profile ————————

● ◐ Position of Segment 3 on each of the chosen dimensions and the resulting profile ------------- .

Exhibit 5.21　The nature of work, customer relationships and key management tasks within each market segment

Market segment	Nature of work completed	Customer relationships to be managed	Key management task
1	Short duration High volume Repeat tasks	One-off Non-repeat	Cost reduction
2	Long duration Medium volume Repeat tasks	Ongoing High contact during project	Project management
3	Long duration Low volume Non-repeat tasks	Ongoing High contact during project	Product development

● **Segment 1** – with 110,000 domestic and small business customers, service provision is of a once-and-for-all nature, typically completed in less than a day and differs little from customer to customer. The work is price-sensitive and the key task is to take advantage of the high volume, repeat nature of the business to reduce costs.

- **Segment 2** – involves larger projects in the course of which the company needs to respond to short lead times and meet customers' schedules. These larger business customers typically have several locations and are involved in site development. The result is the opportunity to undertake repeat contracts.

- **Segment 3** – comprises a small number of very complex jobs of a highly technical nature. Meeting customer specifications and schedule deadlines is essential and may lead to additional large contracts.

To meet the needs of its market the company had developed a single organizational approach. The rapid growth in sales revenue during the last few years had put increasing strain on the company's ability to support these diverse needs. Profiling these businesses as shown in Exhibit 5.20 enabled the company to identify the source of its problems and realign key aspects of the business to these different sets of needs.

Reflections

Although how a company chooses to meet the technical specification of its service offerings will impact delivery system design, operations managers must also ensure that those design decisions

- are aligned to the order-winners and qualifiers of its chosen markets
- reflect the internal requirements of the organization such as capacity utilization, control of costs, queue lengths and the interface with customers

Exhibit 5.22 Factors in reactive and proactive service delivery system design

Factors		Service delivery system design	
		reactive	proactive
Delivery system design	objective	Streamlined and efficient	Customer focused
	structure	Rigid	Responsive
	design premise	Events are consistent and unchanging	Change acknowledged and built into design
	approach to service failure	Prevention	Recovery
	response to service failure	Not designed in the system	Integral part of system design
	role of server in quality provision	Procedures specify server behaviour	Proactive response expected
Achieving quality conformance	systems design	Built into system	Built into staff
	error handling	Refer to another level	Dealt with on the spot
	level of recovery	Low and slow	High and immediate
	response to failure	Back-office management	Frontline staff
	quality objective	System has zero defects	Customer-centric
Staff	attitude	Lack of involvement	Part of provision and solution
	level of discretion	Low and not encouraged	High and encouraged
	attitude to failure	Part of failure	Part of recovery solution then part of success
	level of motivation	Frustration leading to lack of interest	Part of service provision leading to becoming involved and motivated

• incorporate IT and other development opportunities to help keep the business competitive and improve its ability to meet customer requirements.

This chapter has emphasized how businesses must recognize the key differences that exist between services and then incorporate these differences into delivery system design. A range of dimensions are highlighted including order-winners and qualifiers, volumes, variety, level of customer contact and back-, middle- and front-office provision. One further dimension concerns how reactive or proactive the service delivery system design should be. Organizations need first to recognize the fundamental differences in approach that result (see Exhibit 5.22), check the desired position on relevant factors and then incorporate these approaches into its delivery system designs.

What underpins the drive to develop delivery systems that meet the needs of customers is the impact they have on market share, retention and growth. Online retailers estimate that the initial cost of customer acquisition is $100 and there is no overall profit on transactions until a customer has returned three or even four times. Similarly, as Exhibit 5.23 shows, keeping customers grows profit. Aligning delivery systems to markets is a key task, therefore, and requires sound corporate understanding on what is needed and how systems are to be developed.

Exhibit 5.23　Trends in annual profit per customer

Sector	Annual profit/customer				
	1	2	3	4	5
Car servicing	100	140	280	350	350
Credit cards	100	250	283	290	309
Distribution	100	220	270	320	373

Note　Figures indexed on year 1.

Key Elements of Designing Service Delivery Systems

• At the core of any company is the decision how to deliver its services so as to meet both the requirements of its customers and the objectives of the business. Factors that need to be embraced by these decisions and developments comprise the technical (what the service comprises) and business (the order-winners and qualifiers of a market) dimensions that make up the service offering.

• This chapter overviewed these decisions while highlighting a range of issues that make up the context in which these developments need to be set. These included the distinctive characteristics of services, the features of overall and detailed service delivery system design and the impact of IT and other developments on design alternatives.

• The final section linked back to the opening statements that highlighted the core nature of these decisions by providing a way to check the level of alignment between the requirements of customers and markets and the characteristics of an organization's service delivery systems. The worked example shows how service profiling enables companies to check the level of current or future fit and allows it to discuss current and future strategic direction and the nature of operations developments to maintain or improve its ability to support the needs of its markets.

Self-check

1 The design of an appropriate service delivery system will reflect:
  a The complexity of the service ☐
  b The business and technical dimensions of the market ☐
  c Both a and b ☐

2 Which of the following is a distinctive characteristic of service operations:
  a Services are produced and consumed separately, so it is possible to use inventory as a way to help absorb fluctuations in demand ☐
  b Customers do not form part of the delivery system ☐
  c The intangible nature of services means that customers are not able to see, feel, inspect or even test a service before it is purchased ☐

3 Which of the following statements is true about service organizations:
  a Some staff will deal directly with customers ☐
  b All staff will deal directly with customers ☐
  c None of the staff will deal directly with customers ☐

4 An example of an automated service is:
  a Dry-cleaning ☐
  b Cash dispensing ☐
  c Word processing ☐

5 The key dimensions that help to classify services into professional services, service shops and mass services categories are:
  a Volume ☐
  b Service variety ☐
  c Both a and b ☐

6 A key element within the service delivery system design is the service experience. This concerns:
  a The reality of the service that is delivered ☐
  b Where and what is delivered ☐
  c Identifying volumes and the relevant order-winners and qualifiers to retain and grow market share ☐

7 Which of the following statements is true:
  a Retention rates are higher for customers having no problems during service delivery ☐
  b Retention rates are higher for customers having problems during service delivery ☐
  c Retention rates are not affected by whether a customer experiences a problem during service delivery ☐

8 The front-office tasks of the service delivery system are conducted:
  a In the presence of and involving the customer ☐
  b Away from and not involving the customer ☐
  c Both a and b ☐

9 An advantage of completing work in the back office is that:
  a Processing volumes are lower ☐
  b Work is easier to schedule ☐
  c The customer can process some of the activities ☐

10 Alignment involves:
  a Ensuring that all operations processes are in a line ☐
  b Checking how well the requirements of markets are matched by the characteristics of the operations systems used to provide them ☐
  c Checking that the skill level of people delivering the service is the same for each step of the delivery system ☐

Study activities

Discussion questions

1 Choose a service company that uses at least two of the delivery systems detailed in this chapter. Explain why a company would have made such choices.

2 Give an example where you consider that an operations delivery system is not aligned to an organization's market(s). Explain key aspects that illustrate this. What steps would you take to improve the level of fit between market needs and operations capabilities?

3 Select a single-step and multi-step service delivery system in a service organization of your choice.

Explain how they work and why you think that the design was the one chosen.

4 Why is queuing often an integral part of a service delivery system design?

5 For a service company of your choice explain:
● the service delivery system design
● how the company could reduce queues within the system.

6 Review the data in Exhibits 5.5, 5.6, 5.7, 5.8 and 5.23. Why do the results seem to make sense?

Assignments

1 Envisage going to the emergency unit of your local hospital with a suspected broken wrist. List the key steps in the delivery system in which you would be involved. What type of system is used at each step?

2 Select a company (other than the examples provided in the chapter) to illustrate a:
● non-repeat business
● repeat business – low volume
● repeat business – high volume.

For each, outline the service delivery used.

Exploring further

Collier, DA *Service Management: Operating Decisions,* Prentice Hall, Englewood Cliffs, NJ (1987).

Fitzsimmons, JA and Fitzsimmons, MJ *Service Management: Operations, Strategy and Information Technology,* McGraw-Hill International, New York (2000).

Fitzsimmons, JA and Fitzsimmons, MJ (eds) *New Service Development,* Sage, Thousand Oaks, CA (2000).

Fitzsimmons, JA and Fitzsimmons, MJ *Service Management, Service Development and Process Design,* 3rd edn, McGraw-Hill, New York (2001).

Groucutt, J and Griseri, P *Mastering E-business,* Palgrave Macmillan, Basingstoke (2004).

Harrington, HJ, Esseling, EKC and Nimwegen, HV *Business Process Improvement Workbook: Documentation, Analysis, Design and Management of Business Process Improvement,* McGraw-Hill, New York (1997).

Henkoff, R 'Service is everybody's business', *Fortune,* 27 June 1994, pp. 48–60.

Jones, TO and Sasser Jr, WE 'Why satisfied customers defect', *Harvard Business Review,* November–December (1995) pp. 88–99.

Kingsman-Brundage, J, George, WR and Bowen, DE 'Service logic: Achieving service system integration', *International Journal of Service Industry Management,* **6**(4) (1995) pp. 20–39.

Levitt, T 'Production line approach to service', *Harvard Business Review,* September–October (1972) pp. 41–52.

Moon, Y and Frei, FX 'Exploding the self-service myth', *Harvard Business Review,* **78**(3) (2000) pp. 26–37.

Prahalad, CK and Ramaswamy, V 'Co-opting customer competence', *Harvard Business Review,* **78**(1) (2000) pp. 79–85.

Reinhart, A 'Tesco bets small – and wins big', *Business Week,* e.biz, 1 October 2001 (EB14–18).

Rowley, J *E-business: Principles and Practice,* Palgrave Macmillan, Basingstoke (2002).

Schneider B and Bowen, DE *Winning the Service Game,* Harvard Business School Press, Boston, MA (1995).

Singh, T, Jayashankar, JV and Singh, J 'E-commerce in the US and Europe – is Europe ready to connect?', *Business Horizons*, **44**(2) (2001), pp. 6–17.

Verma, R, Thompson, GM and Loviere, JJ 'Configuring service operations based on customer needs and preferences', *Journal of Service Research*, **1**(3) (1999) pp. 262–74.

Wall Street Journal Europe, 'Business utilization of information technology', 1/2 August 1997.

Wall Street Journal Europe, 'Evolution of the net', 12 October 1999, p. viii.

Notes and references

1 Also refer to the approach to service delivery system design in Heskett, JL, Jones, TO, Loveman, GW, Sasser Jr, WE and Schlesinger, LA 'Putting the service–profit chain to work', *Harvard Business Review*, March–April (1994), pp. 164–74.

2 Also refer to Hart, CWL, Heskett, JL and Sasser Jr, WE 'The profitable art of service recovery', *Harvard Business Review*, July–August (1990), pp. 148–56 and Reinartz, W and Kumar, V 'The mismanagement of customer loyalty', *Harvard Business Review*, July (2000), pp. 4–12.

3 J Nilles' books include *Managing Telework,* John Wiley, New York (1998).

4 Niam, G 'The Future of Work', *Financial Times Information Technology Review*, 8 January 1997, p. x.

5 Brown, JM 'Call centres: keeping staff is a problem', *Financial Times Survey*, 21 May 1998, p. v.

6 *Business Week* Special Report 'Now its your web', 5 October 1998, pp. 68–76.

7 Adapted from *Business Week*, October (1998), p. 68.

8 Smoland, M and Cohen, D *A Day in the Life of the Soviet Union*, Collins, London (1987), pp. 66–7.

9 See Pean P 'How to get rich on perestroika', *Fortune*, 8 May 1989, pp. 95–6 and 'Vision factory', *National Geographic,* November (1993).

10 Collier, DA *Service Management: Operating Decisions*, Prentice Hall, Englewood Cliffs, NJ (1987), p. 43.

11 Based on Hill, A and Hill, T 'Customer service: aligning business to markets', Templeton Executive Briefing, University of Oxford (2003).

book map

Part	
1	

PROCESSES

INPUTS

SUPPLIERS

CUSTOMERS

OUTPUTS

1 Managing Operations

2 Operations Strategy

3 Managing People

2

4 Designing and Developing Services & Products

5 Designing Service Delivery Systems

6 Designing Manufacturing Processes

7 Location and Layout

3

8 Managing Capacity

9 Technology Developments

10 Operations Scheduling and Execution

11 Managing Quality

12 Managing Inventory

13 Managing the Supply Chain

4

14 Process and Delivery System Reliability and Maintenance

15 Time and Productivity

16 Improving Operations

5

Managing Operations in Practice: Long Case Studies

Designing Manufacturing Processes

Outline of chapter

The essence of a manufacturing company is to produce and sell the product it makes. Central to this is the design of the manufacturing process and the level of fit provided by the process and the needs of the market. Initial design and subsequent checking and realignment thus form an integral part of the operations role.

Why is designing manufacturing processes important?

Executive overview

The last chapter looked at the design of delivery systems for services and this chapter does the same for manufacturing. The principal sections covered by the chapter are as follows:

- The factors involved in making products, including product categories (from special to mass products), the complexity of a product and the volumes involved.

- The types of process (from project through to continuous processing) are then explained, with examples to illustrate each together with a summary of the key characteristics involved.

- Then follows a section which links together the previous sections and summarizes the key points in Exhibit 6.10. In addition, several reflections are also provided to help illustrate the product categories and process types and how they relate to one another.

- The next section looks at the business implications involved when the different types of process are selected and those are summarized in Exhibit 6.16.

- Many companies choose to develop processes that are, in effect, a mix of the classic process forms highlighted in an earlier section. Known as hybrid processes, these include cells, linked batch, Nagare production system and transfer lines.

- The need to align manufacturing processes to the needs of a company's markets is paramount. The section entitled 'Product profiling' provides a way to undertake this check, with an illustration of its use in Exhibit 6.21.

Introduction

The products that companies make and sell are different and these differences will impact the design of the manufacturing (or production) processes used to make them. As these are an integral part of the operations process, their design is a key responsibility and central to the continued success of a business.

As examples given later in the chapter illustrate, the methods of transformation or conversion of inputs (materials, people skills and so on) into outputs (the products) will often be an interrelated set of processes feeding into one another as part of the total transformation. In turn, the design of these processes will need to embrace two related but distinct dimensions:

- The **technical dimension** concerning what has to happen in a technical sense to the product. For example, packaging would need to be produced on printing machines and then cut to size using slitting machines. Plastic containers, on the other hand, would need to be produced by loading the appropriate tooling (designed to give the shape and detail of the product) onto a machine and then injecting material under pressure to fill the cavity within the mould – a process known as injection moulding.

● The **business dimension** concerning how operations decides to make a product. This choice is designed to best reflect the volumes involved and the order-winners and qualifiers that it needs to support.

This chapter is concerned with the operations management task of using processes to meet the needs of markets. In undertaking this, operations executives require and will use the support of technical specialists such as process engineers and IT specialists. Thus, operations is a business function not a technical function, as it is a user rather than a provider of technology to meet both the needs of customers and the objectives of the business.

Factors involved in making products

The products that companies make and sell are different and these differences will need to be taken into account when designing the manufacturing process. As highlighted earlier, the process technology used will need to reflect the technical specification of the product itself (the technical dimension). And, just as the technical differences require appropriate (and different) process technologies, the business differences will need appropriate (and different) choices of manufacturing process. To explain what this means, this section provides an overview of the key factors involved.

Categories of product

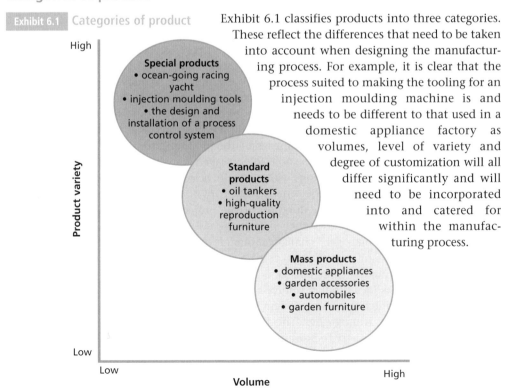

Exhibit 6.1 Categories of product

Exhibit 6.1 classifies products into three categories. These reflect the differences that need to be taken into account when designing the manufacturing process. For example, it is clear that the process suited to making the tooling for an injection moulding machine is and needs to be different to that used in a domestic appliance factory as volumes, level of variety and degree of customization will all differ significantly and will need to be incorporated into and catered for within the manufacturing process.

Special products
• ocean-going racing yacht
• injection moulding tools
• the design and installation of a process control system

Standard products
• oil tankers
• high-quality reproduction furniture

Mass products
• domestic appliances
• garden accessories
• automobiles
• garden furniture

Product variety — High / Low

Volume — Low / High

Product complexity

The complexity of a product varies. A plastic screw top for a soft drinks bottle is a much simpler product to make than a decorated coffee mug, and a jet engine is a much more complex product to make than a coffee mug. For example, the number of steps to make the Rolls-Royce Trent 800 and 900 engines for the Boeing 777 and Airbus 330 passenger aircraft respectively each run into hundreds. As the product complexity increases, the number of steps and different processes involved will also increase, which will have an impact on the process design.

Volumes

Exhibit 6.1 shows the important relationship between the three categories of product and the levels of volume involved. The fundamental nature of this dimension is central to this chapter and the following section shows how it is reflected in the manufacturing process design.

Types of manufacturing (or production) processes

Now let's turn our attention to the types of production process design that manufacturing companies use to make products. The choice of design can be made from five classic process types (project, jobbing, batch, line and continuous processing), together with a number of hybrids (processes that are a mixture of two of the classic process types). This section explains these classic processes and provides examples to help illustrate the differences involved.

Project

Organizations selling large-scale, complex products that cannot be physically moved once completed will normally provide them using a project process. Examples include civil engineering contracts to build reservoir dams, housing, roads, tunnels and bridges. It can involve the provision of a unique product (for example the Sydney Opera House or San Gottardo Tunnel through the Alps linking Italy and Switzerland), or a standard product such as estate housing. The former examples are made to unique, specific requirements while the latter are of a standard design with limited options. But, in each instance, the resource inputs will be taken to the point where the product is to be built. If you reflect on these examples, you will probably be able to envisage what the process looks like. All the activities, including support functions, will normally be controlled by a total system for the duration of the project and under the direction of the coordinating team, Similarly, resources will be allocated for the duration of the project and these, like the supporting functions, will be reallocated once their part of the task is completed or at the end of the project. The operations manager's challenge, then, is one of coordinating a large number of interrelated activities and resources so as to achieve the customer's requirements while minimizing costs throughout the process.

This choice of making a product is forced upon an organization because the product has to be made on site, which is not an efficient way of working, as resources need to be moved to and from the job as it progresses. This incurs costs and militates against achieving efficiencies. Hence, companies try to produce as much as possible of the product off site, which allows a more efficient process to be used, with the parts then being transported to the site. For example, concrete sections and timber framing for buildings will be made off site and

Exhibit 6.2	Project – key characteristics	
Products	Made or provided on site as it is too large or difficult to move after completion. Examples include building reservoir dams, tunnels, roads, bridges and houses.
Process	Resources to make the product are brought to the site, allocated for the duration of the project and then reallocated once their part of the task is complete or at the end of the job.

assembled or arranged on site as required. Overall, the improved process efficiency of making off site outweighs the additional transportation costs of getting parts to the site. Exhibit 6.2 summarizes the main points.

Jobbing

Once products are transportable, companies look to another process to make them. The jobbing process is designed to meet the one-off (that is, unique) requirements of customers, where the product involved is of an individual nature and tends to be of a smaller size (and, therefore, transportable) than those provided by a project process. Product examples include a purpose-built piece of equipment (for example injection moulding tools), hand-made, built-in furniture to meet specified customer requirements, a customer-designed and specified control unit and hand-crafted shoes and clothing. Although some elements of these products may be provided on site, usually they are completed in-house and transported to a customer. The producer then often installs and commissions the product before it is accepted by a customer. Jobbing, however, requires that the providing organization interprets the design and specification of the job, applying high-level skills in the conversion process.

Normally, one person or a small group of skilled people will be responsible for completing all or most of the product. It is a one-off provision, which means that the product will not usually be required again in its identical form or, if it is, the demand will tend to be either irregular or with long periods between one sale and the next. Exhibit 6.3 summarizes the main points.

Exhibit 6.3	Jobbing – key characteristics	
Products	Special (that is, will not be repeated) products. Examples include the design and installation of a control system, purpose-built piece of equipment, handmade, built-in furniture and hand-crafted shoes and clothing.
Process	One person or a small group of skilled people do everything, including interpreting the product specification, clarifying issues with the customer and ensuring that what is delivered meets the specification.

Batch

Most organizations provide products that are deemed standard (that is, they have been provided before) rather than special. The repeat and higher volume nature associated with standard products signals the need to consider a different process designed to take advantage of these characteristics. A batch process is one alternative.

As the product has been provided before or will be provided again in the future, it makes sense to invest in the process in order to simplify and reduce costs. The level of investment that can be justified will relate to the repeat nature and total volumes involved. This investment can range from recording and establishing the best way to complete a job through to substantial investment in equipment to help make the provision of the task more efficient.

When using a batch process, the first step is to break the job into a number of stages. How many stages will depend, in part, on the complexity of the product involved. The provision of a product may be completed by a single-step batch process where the requirement is simple; more complex products will be provided by a multi-step batch process, as shown in Exhibit 6.4. In a batch process, each operation making up the whole product is

Exhibit 6.4 Printing – a multi-step batch process

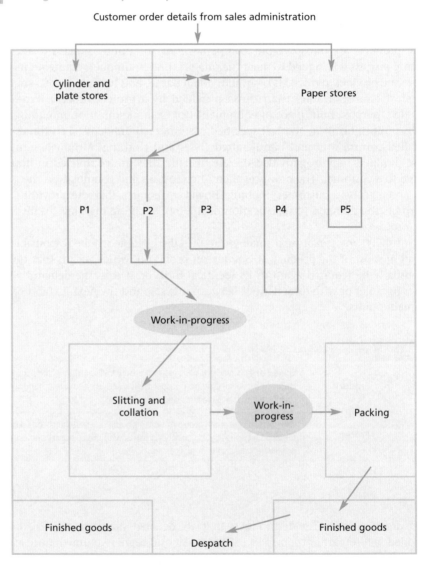

Notes 1 The 'P' in P1 to P5 is an abbreviation for printing machine.
        2 ———▶ Movement of a typical order.

completed separately, by different people/equipment and normally in a different part of the process. The purpose of splitting the task into smaller operations is a form of investment in itself, and is one way to help undertake the task more efficiently and introduce the potential for specialization.

The following example helps to explain how a batch process works. In principle, the product would first be split into an appropriate number of operations and the decision taken on how best to complete each of these. The order quantity to be produced (which may reflect the size of a customer's order, production rules concerning the quantity to be produced at any time or forecast sales projections) would then go to the process in which the first operation is to be completed. The appropriate process is set up to undertake the first operation and the whole order quantity is completed. In this way, each process is only set up once per order quantity. This reduces the amount of lost capacity due to set-ups/changeovers which, in turn, reduces costs. With operation 1 completed, the whole order quantity then moves on to the next process in which operation 2 will be completed. Typically, the order quantity would wait for this process to become available, as often there are other products being, or waiting to be, completed. When available, this process is set up to complete operation 2 of the given product and the whole order quantity is processed. Meanwhile, the process needed to complete operation 1 is available to be reset to complete a given operation on another product. Thus, a product goes from process to process until all the operations necessary to complete the job have been undertaken.

The key features that distinguish a batch process are:

- The volumes for a particular product are not sufficient to justify dedicating processes to this product. If they were sufficient, another process such as line would be the appropriate choice. As a result, batch processes are designed to be used and reused by different products.

- To use and reuse a process it will need to be reset each time in line with the requirements of each product.

- Having set up a process, the whole of the agreed quantity is produced. The process is then available to be reset for the next product.

- As different products use some of the same process as others, one product will often have to wait in a queue until the process is available. The outcome is part-processed products throughout the total production system waiting to be processed, known as work-in-progress inventory.

Exhibit 6.4 shows a repeat order for an existing flexible packaging product (for example a toffee bar wrapper). In this instance, a roll of film is loaded on the front of the print machine. The choice of machine reflects the quantity required and the number of colours on the packaging product. These colours are transferred onto the film at each station on the printing machine by means of a flexographic mat. Between each application of colour the ink is dried. When the product quantity is completed, the toffee bar wrapper or other product is taken off the machine in roll form.

With an understanding of how the process technology works, let us look at how a product would be printed using these batch processes. The flexographic mats, paper and inks would be made available in line with a customer's delivery date. At the scheduled time, the paper, mats and ink would be loaded onto the printing machine as an integral part of the set-up. Typically, the wrapper design would be printed (for reasons of lower cost) two or more times across the width of the film. The order quantity would be produced and the roll(s) of printed film would go into work-in-progress inventory waiting to be loaded onto

Exhibit 6.5   Batch – key characteristics

Products	Standard, repeat products, the volume demand for which justifies the process investment. Examples include machined parts, injection mouldings and printing.
Process	Having broken down the products into different operations, the order quantity is taken to the process where the first operation is to be undertaken. The process is made ready/set up and the whole order quantity is completed. The part-made product typically goes into work-in-progress inventory awaiting the next process that will complete the second operation. When available the process is made ready, the whole order quantity is processed and so on or until the whole product is completed.

Exhibit 6.6   Different stages on the Land Rover vehicle assembly line

the slitting process. This will cut the rolls so that there will be one design per smaller roll in line with the customer's own packing requirements. Following slitting, the product would go into work-in-progress inventory awaiting packing, then in and out of inventory before being despatched. The role of inventory here is to decouple the various processes. This allows processes to work independently of one another (that is, one process is not waiting for another process to finish its stage on a product). There will typically be several products that have already been processed to the required stage and from which a process can draw. This and the other characteristics of batch processes are summarized in Exhibit 6.5.

Line

With further increases in volume, investment is made to provide a process that is dedicated to the needs of a given range of products. While often the range of products is narrow, this is not always so. For example, the number of different vehicles that an assembly line can handle will often be tens, even hundreds, of thousands. In car manufacture, for example, when the number of engine types is multiplied by the number of colours and this is then multiplied by the typically wide range of options, the result is a very large number of potentially different vehicles.

As with batch the product is split into a number of steps and the process is arranged to complete these sequentially. As the process steps follow each other they are set out in a line, hence the name. Products are then processed, with each product passing through the same sequence of operations. The result is that operation 1 is completed on the first product which goes immediately to operation 2. Meanwhile, operation 1 is being completed on the next product and so on. The line has also been designed to cope with any item within a given range and, therefore, the essential characteristic of line is that, in order to produce another product, the process does not have to be stopped and reset. Examples include domestic appliances and motor vehicles. Exhibit 6.6 shows part of the vehicle assembly plant at Land Rover, Solihull, UK, while Exhibit 6.7 provides a summary of the key characteristics of line processes.

Exhibit 6.7	Line – key characteristics
Products	Standard, repeat, high volume, mass products. Examples include motor vehicles and domestic appliances. Not often found in manufacturing today, as the required volumes to justify the investment are not typical of current markets.
Process	Products are separated into different operations. These are met by a series of sequential processes through which all items in a selected range pass. To the process, all the products are the same and, therefore, the line does not have to be stopped and reset to accommodate a change in requirement. However, the line can only cope with the predetermined range for which the process has been designed. To widen the existing range would require additional investment.

Continuous processing

With continuous processing, one or several basic materials are processed through successive stages and refined into one or more products (for example petrochemicals). Because the costs of stopping and starting up are very high (often prohibitive), the process will have been designed to run all day and every day with minimum shutdowns. The materials are transferred automatically from one part of the process to the next, with the staff tasks being

Exhibit 6.8   ExxonMobil's ethylene cracking plant – Fife, Scotland

predominantly ones of system monitoring. Exhibit 6.8 gives an example of continuous processing – ExxonMobil's ethylene cracking plant in Fife, Scotland. To close down and restart the plant would take several days, due to the complex process and safety requirements involved. Exhibit 6.9 provides a summary of the key characteristics.

Exhibit 6.9   Continuous processing – key characteristics

Products	Standard, very high volume (mass) products. Examples include oil refining and some petrochemicals.
Process	Materials are processed through successive stages, with automatic transfer of the product from stage to stage. The costs of stopping and restarting are typically so high that the process is not stopped, hence the name – continuous processing.

Product categories and production processes reflections

Exhibit 6.10 summarizes the last section and also relates the different processes to the product categories introduced in Exhibit 6.1. You will see from this that the transition from special through to mass products given in Exhibit 6.1 relates, in general, to the types of process used. This section now reflects on this link between product type, process type and volumes.

1   Project for special and standard products – as shown in Exhibit 6.10, both special and standard products may choose project as the appropriate process. For example, a new estate of 120 houses comprising six designs would, for the builder, be a standard offer-

Exhibit 6.10 Manufacturing processes and their relationship to product categories

Process type	Product		Process description
	Category	Examples	
Project	Special	• Sydney Opera House • Oresund bridge connecting Denmark and Sweden • San Gottardo Tunnel in the Alps	Products that cannot be physically moved once completed use a project process. Here resources (materials, equipment and people) are brought to the site where the product is to be built. These resources are allocated for the duration of the job and will be reallocated once their part of the task is completed or at the end of the job.
	Standard	• Estate housing • Prefabricated industrial and warehouse units	
Jobbing	Special	• Ocean-going racing yacht • Injection moulding tools • Formula One and Indy racing cars • The design and installation of a process control system	Once a product can be moved, companies will choose to make it in-house and then despatch it to the customer. Jobbing is the name of the process that is used for special (that is, unique) products that will typically not be repeated. Here, one person or a small group of skilled people will complete all the product. Often the task requires the provider to install and commission the product as part of the job.
Batch	Standard ↓ Mass	• Business cards • Golf tees • Wheel rims • Packaging • Plastic bottles	The repeat and higher volume nature of standard products requires a process designed to take advantage of these characteristics. Batch, line and continuous processing are the alternatives. Which one to use depends on the volumes involved. Batch can be appropriately used for low through to high (mass) volumes. As how to make the product is known, the steps involved are predetermined and products move from step to step until complete. Batch is chosen for standard products with volumes insufficient to dedicate processes. Thus, different products share the same processes by setting and resetting each time. Consequences of this include waiting between steps and the prioritizing of jobs using the same process.
Line	Mass	• Domestic appliances • Cans of Coca-Cola • Automobiles • Pet food • Mobile phones	Higher volumes mean that processes can be dedicated to the needs of a given range of products. Whereas in batch a process has to be reset each time a new product is to be made, in line the process does not have to stop as it has been designed to make the range of products required without being reset. As with batch, the products are standard. The steps to make them are sequentially laid out in line and a product goes from step to step until completed. Although the range of products will vary, to the process they can be made without stopping and resetting the line.
Continuous processing	Mass	• Petrochemicals • Oil refineries • Some chemical plants	For some products, the high volumes involved are best handled by continuous processing. In addition to high volume, these products will need to be transferable through piping or in liquid form. Continuous processing is similar to line in that it handles mass products without being stopped and reset. Its distinguishing feature is, however, that to stop and restart the process is lengthy and expensive and consequently it is designed to be run continuously.

ing – that is, the house specifications would be known, the method of build would be decided ahead of time and any possible options to the basic design would be fixed. However, the houses would need to be built on site as they cannot be moved. On the other hand, a large country house built to a unique design would, for the builder, be a special but again would need to be built on site.

2 Project and continuous processing are specific to certain product types – typically, project would only be used when a product has to be built on site. Setting up and dismantling a site, moving equipment and people to and from a site increase costs and make the management task more difficult compared to making a product in-house. As a consequence, project is typically only used where the product has to be made in situ.

Similarly, the use of continuous processing is limited. The products best suited to this process would be high volume, with the physical characteristics that allowed them to be moved from step to step in the process using pipework, such as the refining of oil and the production of petrochemicals.

So, the appropriate use of project and continuous processing is restricted (as shown in Exhibit 6.11) and most organizations choose from jobbing, batch and line for their business needs.

Exhibit 6.11 Process choices

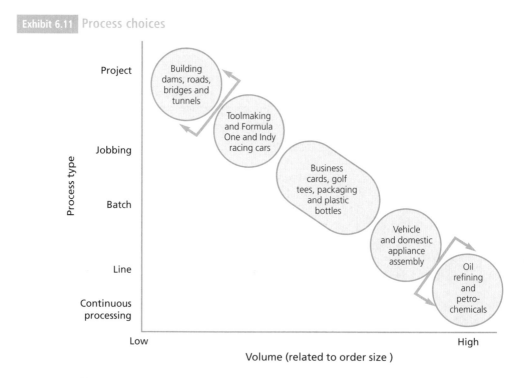

Note   The elongated shape of batch reflects the range of volumes (from standard to mass) that this process covers.

3 Combinations of processes – often companies will use more than one process type to meet the overall needs of their business. The reason is that one process best meets the different needs of a product or parts of a product. For example, building the 120 new houses in point 1 above would use a combination of processes:

- **project** to meet the overall requirements of bringing resources to and from the site, with one person having the overall management responsibility to undertake this task in line with the effective use of the resources and cost budgets involved.
- **batch** would typically be used to meet several phases of the work. For example, once the footings had been completed on a number of houses, the concreting of the ground floor areas for these houses would be completed consecutively. In this way, one phase would be completed on one house and this same phase would be completed on the next house and so on until this task was completed for a number of houses. Other phases in the building of several houses would be cumulated by completing them one after another (for example roofing, glazing, electrics, plastering, bathroom fitting and kitchen installation). In this way a builder would take advantage of the increased volume associated with the repeat nature of each phase by looking to reduce costs and make the management task easier. So, all roofing tiles for several houses would be delivered to site at the same time, similarly the materials for the glazing, electrics and other phases. Also, contractors to complete each phase would be less costly as they would undertake several consecutive days (even weeks) of work which, in turn, reduces their set-up costs on a job.
- **jobbing** – where specific alterations or additions to a standard design were requested and agreed, they would be completed using jobbing as the appropriate process. Here, skilled staff such as bricklayers and joiners would receive drawings, interpret these and be fully responsible for fulfilling the specification(s) and checking the results.

4 Jobbing, batch and line – these are the processes from which most companies choose, and again they often choose more than one to best meet their needs, as illustrated in Exhibit 6.12. This shows that typically companies make components or parts in batch processes, while using line to assemble products. For example, the body panels for an Opel Astra will be made on a press. This will be set to make the left body panel, stopped and reset to make the right body panel, and so on. However, Opel uses line to assemble the car.

Exhibit 6.12 Tasks undertaken by jobbing, batch and line processes

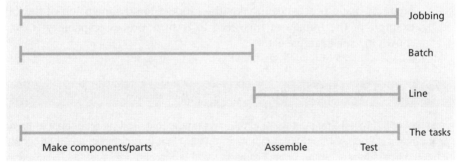

5 What comprises volume? – as volume is one of the fundamental factors in choosing appropriate processes, it is important to clarify the meaning. When choosing an appropriate process, the following dimensions of volume are involved:
- order quantity, that is, how many products are to be made at one time on the process. As jobbing typically involves making an order quantity of one for each product ordered, the order quantity volumes are low, whereas line is high volume because the order quantity comprises the total volume made during the life of the

Creating a high volume process

process. In vehicle production the order quantity is the total number of automobiles processed over the length of time the assembly line is in place. The order quantity, in reality, is the combined volumes over that time period – not quite Lloyd's rationale (Exhibit 6.13).

● volume is a combination of order quantity × unit time. The time taken to make the left body panel of the car is far less than to assemble the car itself, and so, although the quantity of panels and cars is the same, the panel is lower volume than the car and hence more suited to batch.

6   Widening the product range to increase volumes – several factors in today's markets have eroded demand for individual products and with it the volume to be processed by manufacturing. Foremost among these factors is overcapacity within market sectors and the increasing difference rather than increasing similarity of today's markets. One result is that companies have had to rethink process configurations, both in terms of the overall capacity (how many products in total a facility can produce) and the range of products that a process can make (the product range dimension of flexibility. A classic example of the impact of this need to rethink process capability is car assembly, as shown in Case example 6.1.

Case example 1   OLD AND NEW CAR PLANTS

No one is ever likely to build again a car plant similar to Volkswagen's Wolfburg plant in Saxony, Germany that is capable of building 750,000 vehicles a year or another Toyota City, near Nagoya in Japan. Most new factories are now built to make around 200,000 a year and, some believe, many future plants could be a quarter of this current size.

To create the volume required to justify these new plants, the process is designed to handle a wider product range. For

example, Ford's new assembly plant at Rouge in Dearborn, Detroit makes light trucks, sport utility vehicles and the like and can handle three basic platforms (the chassis and underpinning of a vehicle) and nine different model variations built on them. The mix scheduled to be made will depend on which models are most in demand.

www.volkswagen.de; www.toyota.com; www.ford.com/en/default.htm

Case questions   1   The process type used at Ford's new assembly plant at Rouge is line. Why?
2   Why would you classify the Rouge plant as inflexible (see Exhibit 6.7)?

7 The dimensions of flexibility – one recent trend is to describe process capability as 'flexible' and 'agile'. Although these words capture the essence of the overall process capability dimension being described, such descriptions embody several important distinctions. It is better, therefore, to set aside these single-word descriptions and use one that reflects the specific dimensions of process capability involved (as Mr James needs to recognize – see Exhibit 6.14). As you will see from the list below, the dimensions differ markedly one from another, both in terms of their strategic relevance (the aspect of market advantage to which they relate) and how the investment spend would be directed. To achieve an improvement in any of the following aspects will result in more investment, so knowing the cost/benefit mix involved is an essential part of the decision.

Exhibit 6.14 Mr James introduces his idea of flexible and agile processes

In each of these dimensions of flexibility, companies need to assess how well a process can, and needs to, respond to the aspect of change involved, while recognizing that the flexibility factor will typically have both process and people skill implications:

- **Introduction of new products** – this aspect of flexibility concerns the ability of the operations process to handle new product introductions. These are vital to the long-term success of any business and operations is one of the functions that plays a key role in this overall process.

- **Handling a range of products** – most, if not all, companies produce a range of products and product options. Even Ford with its Model T car and 'any colour as long as its black' approach of the 1920s was soon replaced by General Motors and its willingness to provide choice. The process flexibility to handle these dimensions is, in most markets, a key factor in the successful growth of a business as it reflects the nature of today's demand profile.

- **Handling a range of volumes** – as explained earlier, the level of volume required to justify the dedication of processes to a given range of products is typically not available. For this reason batch is the most commonly used process as it is designed to be used and reused by a range of products. One key feature that results is the ease (that is, how long it takes) with which a process can cope with different levels of volume. The volume requirements of products will not only differ from one to the next but will also often differ for the same products in different time periods. How quickly a process can be changed from one product to another will directly impact the loss of potential outputs while the process change is taking place. The shorter the changeovers, the more flexible the process.

- **Meeting demand peaks** – the demand for many products has a seasonality dimension. This aspect of flexibility concerns how easily the process can be ramped up to cope with sudden increases in demand.

Finally, other non-process dimensions of being responsive (such as meeting changes in customer delivery schedules) are accomplished not through process investment but through, for instance as in this example, developing a system that can handle the rescheduling of delivery dates.

The key factors in managing the need for flexibility are:

- Specify what dimension is involved – it brings clarity in analysis and prevents confusion in communication through a business.

- Identify where the investment needs to be made. This helps ensure that the investment is appropriate to the need and that unnecessary investment is minimized.

8 The use of batch to best meet the requirements of most companies – as explained in points 2 and 4, for most companies the choice is between jobbing, batch and line and, of the three, batch is the most commonly used process. The reason is the nature of today's markets. Special products (using jobbing) and mass products (using line) are not commonplace. Demand for specials is limited, while the increasing level of difference required in today's markets has eroded volumes. For these reasons batch is most suitable as most companies make standard products but not in volumes that would justify investing in line. Instead, companies invest and develop processes that can be used and reused by a range of products. In this way, it is able to make a range of products whose volumes vary.

Finally, it is useful here to explain that as the process is stopped and reset for each different product, the use of the process capacity is categorized in three ways:

- **unproductive time** – the utilization of the capacity is unproductive in nature. A classic example of this category is a machine breakdown.

- **non-saleable productive time** – the capacity is being used in a productive way but the outcome is non-saleable. Examples here include making samples and resetting the process for the next product. The time spent on samples is a productive use of the resource but the output cannot be sold. Similarly, setting up a process for another product is productive (it has to be done) but again the outcome does not result in saleable output.

- **saleable productive time** – completed products that will be sold to customers.

The non-saleable productive time element of this mix of outputs is a characteristic of batch as the process will need to be reset for each different product. Keeping the ratio between non-saleable and saleable productive time in balance is most important for a business. If the non-saleable percentage increases, saleable output goes down which will have an adverse effect on sales and profits. Now look at Case example 6.2 which illustrates several of these isssues.

Case example 2 MANUFACTURING PROCESSES AT MEINDORF GMBH

Meindorf GmbH is part of a large German cable company that manufactures compounds (the material used to cover the copper or aluminum conduit) to meet inter-group and external demand. It has four process units that heat and mix the various fillers and oils that make up a range of standard product specifications. Order sizes from customers range from 1 to 40 tonnes. To meet a customer order typically requires several mixings:

- **process unit 1** produces natural and coloured elastomers
- **process unit 2** manufactures the whole range of thermo-plastics
- **process unit 3** makes black elastomers
- **process unit 4** produces small order quantities of thermo-plastics and experimental compounds for the R&D department. This unit is not fully utilized.

On leaving these process units, the compounds move onto the next stage that involves shaping, cutting and packaging.

The mixing stage lasts 8–14 minutes and the number of mixes required to meet a customer order are completed one after the other. At the end of a run the process units are changed to make the next product. The colour and compound change-overs take 40–120 minutes. The most difficult colour changes involve moving from a dark to a lighter colour. In order to minimize changeovers, similar colours and similar compounds are run together wherever possible and in line with customer schedules. Typically, changeovers for process unit 2 account for 20 per cent of available time and those for process units 1 and 3 each account for up to 10 per cent of available time.

Delivery reliability is an order-losing sensitive qualifier for most customers and the trend towards smaller customer orders is giving concern to operations in terms of meeting schedules.

Case questions
1. Which process type (project, jobbing, batch, line or continuous processing) is used to heat and mix compounds in this plant?
2. Give reasons for the different changeover levels (10, 20 and 10 per cent respectively of available time) for process units 1, 2 and 3.
3. Why are reducing order quantities of concern to operations?

Implications reflected in manufacturing process alternatives

Investing in the way to make products takes many forms. It can range from process equipment through to the task of determining how best to make a product and preparing the necessary process details, procedures to follow and supporting information. However, no matter what form the investment takes it will invariably be costly to change. For this reason companies

Exhibit 6.15 Potential transitions between manufacturing processes

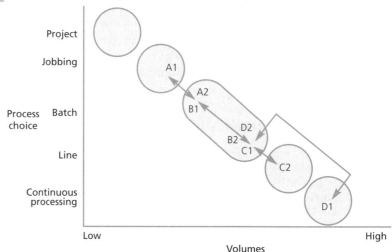

This shows four potential volume transitions that may typically face a business. The first transition shows a move from one-off* low volume (A1) to repeat order, low volume demand (A2) for a product/service or vice versa and the change in operations process which should ideally accompany this movement. Transitions B1 to B2, C1 to C2 and D1 to D2 show similar demand changes at different points on the volume scale, requiring similar decisions concerning the realignment of the choice of process.

* One-off is a description of uniqueness, not order quantity.

Source: Terry Hill, *Manufacturing Strategy: Text and Cases*, 2nd edn, Basingstoke, Macmillan – now Palgrave Macmillan (2000).

choose the process they judge best, with the intention of not changing the decision and thus avoiding future additional investment. Exhibit 6.15 illustrates and reinforces the point that the transition of processes from one to another does not typically occur. Organizations do not, for instance, choose project and later replace it with jobbing; similarly, companies rarely move from jobbing to batch then line. However, as Exhibit 6.15 illustrates, some marginal transitions may take place between jobbing and low volume batch, low volume batch and higher volume batch and high volume batch and line. But these are unusual and not the norm.

Finally, you will notice in Exhibit 6.15 that batch is depicted as an elongated shape, highlighting the fact that batch covers a wide range of volumes and other factors, as the next section explains.

As implied throughout the chapter, each process carries different characteristics and alternative sets of trade-offs (things a process can do well or less well). To illustrate these, an overview of some factors is provided in Exhibit 6.16 and recognizing and understanding these needs to form part of the decision on which process to buy. You will note in Exhibit 6.16 that the format used to reflect the elongated shape depicting batch in Exhibit 6.15 is that of an arrow. In this way the wide range of volumes and other characteristics that the process of batch spans is again appropriately depicted. Finally, the format of Exhibit 6.16 also reflects the specific nature of the type of businesses where project and continuous processing would be used.

Some comments on Exhibit 6.16 will help explain the trade-off alternatives and different characteristics that go hand in hand with each type of manufacturing process. The first half of the table illustrates the fact that as the choice moves to the right, high volumes justify more dedicated processes which, by their nature, are less flexible and less able to cope with the introduction of new products or changes to existing products.

In essence, it is the process that makes the product here which, in turn, requires a high

Exhibit 6.16 Implications reflected in manufacturing process alternatives

Factors		Project	Jobbing	Batch	Line	Continuous processing
				Typical characteristics of manufacturing process alternatives		
Process	nature	General purpose	General purpose	→	Dedicated	Dedicated
	flexibility	Flexible	Flexible	→	Inflexible	Inflexible
Level of process investment		Variable	Low	→	High	Very high
Ability of the process to cope with	product changes	High	High	→	Low	Nil
	new products	High	High	→	Low	None
How are orders won?	typical order-winners	Capability	Unique capability	→	Price	Price
	typical qualifiers	Delivery on-time Price	Delivery on-time Price	→	Delivery on-time, quality conformance	Delivery on-time, quality conformance
Operations volumes		Low	Low	→	High	Very high
Set-ups or changeovers	number	Many	Many	→	None in life-time of process	None in life-time of process
	expense per	Variable	Inexpensive	→	Prohibitive	Prohibitive
Dominant utilization		Predominantly people	People	→	Process	Process
Pre-knowledge of the	operations task	Variable	Known but often not well defined	→	Known	Well defined
	material requirements	Known at tendering stage	Some uncertainty	→	Known	Well defined
Level of waiting time in the process		Varies	Low	High	Low	Low
Difficulty of the day-to-day scheduling task		Complex	Complex	Very complex	Easy	Easy
Process layout		Fixed position	Function	Function	Product	Product
Operations key strategic task		Respond to product and schedule changes	Respond to product and schedule changes	→	Low cost	Low cost

level of pre-knowledge in order to design and develop it. One outcome is that process utilization becomes more important than that for people as the process is, in fact, the key resource.

You will note that three of the last four dimensions in Exhibit 6.16 do not conform to the arrow principle. Regarding waiting time, there can be some occasions in project where one group of skilled people have to wait for another aspect of the job to be completed. But in all other processes, the waiting time between one part of the system and the next tends to be low except for batch. In jobbing, the skilled person is always moving the job forward, whereas with line and continuous processing the product moves automatically from one part of the system to the next. In batch, on the other hand, because products use the same processes, priorities need to be determined and, as a consequence, some products will have to wait. This need to prioritize means that day-to-day scheduling is most complex in batch. Once materials are brought to a line or continuous process, on the other hand, the scheduling of products through the system is straightforward. At the other end of the process spectrum, the person making the product schedules the work but the unknown (that is, a new product) brings a level of complexity. In project, the building of a product on site, the uncertainty of resource and material supply, together with potential problems of weather, bring scheduling difficulties. Finally, process layout is functionally based in both jobbing and batch processes and product based in line and continuous processing.

Now test your understanding of these insights and issues by analysing Case example 6.3.

Case example 3   MANUFACTURING IN SMALL QUANTITIES AT TOSHIBA

At Toshiba's computer factory in Ome, 50 km from downtown Tokyo, a computer-based system networks the office, engineering and factory operations, providing just-in-time (JIT) information as well as JIT parts. Ome workers assemble nine different word processors on the same line while on an adjacent one, 20 varieties of laptop computers are assembled. Usually they make 20 of one product and then change. Workers on the line have been trained to make each model and they are further supported by a computer display at every work station that shows a drawing and provides detailed instructions. When the model changes, so does the display. Product life cycles of some models are measured in months, so making in small order quantities helps guard against being unable to support sales peaks and overproducing when sales fall off.

www.toshiba.com

Case questions

1 What type of process does Toshiba use to manufacture its word processors and laptop computers?

2 What key operations developments have enabled the company to match process capability to its market needs?

Hybrid processes

Given the increasing difference in markets, companies have responded by developing processes to reflect these changing demands. Line processes are often developed to produce a relatively wide range of products, with a marked increase in investments typically associated with these decisions. Similarly, numerically controlled (NC) machines or machining centres provide programmable systems that can better handle the repeat, low volume demand of certain markets.[1]

In addition to investing directly in the process itself, companies often choose to rearrange or use existing processes in a different way. Some of the more common examples of these process redesigns (cells, linked batch, Nagare production system and transfer lines) are now explained. They are called hybrid processes as they are a mix of processes and are developed to provide a different set of trade-offs than was delivered by the process arrangements from which they originate.

Cells

Exhibit 6.16 illustrated how the trade-offs on a range of dimensions changed depending on the process chosen. Companies may seek to alter some of these trade-offs by rearranging existing processes. One such example is changing from a batch process to cells.

As a company choosing batch processes would be providing standard products, the only practical alternative to a batch process is line. The reason why companies choose batch rather than line is based on volumes. Where products do not have sufficient volumes to justify the investment involved in dedicating processes, then batch is used. These processes are designed to allow products to share processes and thus make more sense of the utilization/investment equation. However, batch processes embody trade-offs, some of which companies look to change. In particular, these include the complex scheduling problems and the high incidence of waiting that result (see Exhibit 6.16). Cells are a hybrid process that, although still batch in origin (the process will still have to be stopped and reset to handle a product change), are in fact a mix of batch and line, offering changes on some key variables. First let us discuss what cells are and then review the key trade-off changes that result.

Exhibit 6.17 Batch layout

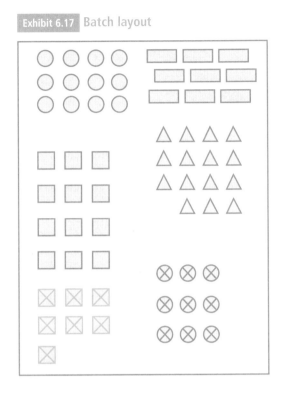

Exhibit 6.17 shows the functional layout of the batch process (similar processes are grouped together in the same geographical area). Now the rationale underpinning cells is that grouping products together and treating them as being the same leads to an increase in volume (the volumes of all the products under consideration are added together and the aggregate is viewed as a whole) and hence allows processes to be allocated to these products for their sole use. What happens, therefore, in cells is that the necessary processes, both in terms of capability and capacity (that is, they can provide the product requirements both in terms of its technical and demand dimensions), are allocated to the sole use of these products, with the 'dedication' being justified by the enhanced level of volume that results – see Exhibit 6.18.

Exhibit 6.18 Cellular layout

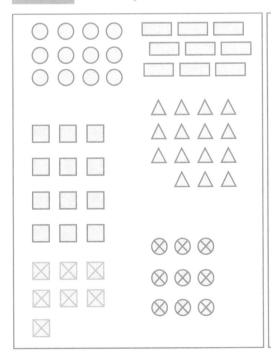

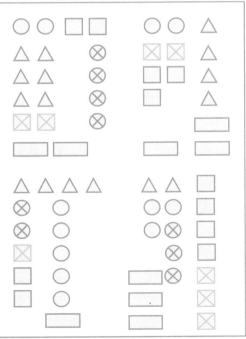

Process or functional layout
Six process types functionally laid out

Cellular layout
Four cells with processing allocated to each cell

Compared to batch, this rearrangement brings with it changes in certain key dimensions, for example:

- process waiting time is reduced
- work-in-progress inventories are lower
- day-to-day scheduling of operations is made easier.

The question is why? Well, it is bound up with the allocation of processes which moves this hybrid process towards line (although still on the batch process dimension) as shown in Exhibit 6.19. The production process will be laid out within a smaller physical area and handle a reduced range of products. This, in turn, simplifies the day-to-day scheduling task and enables lead times and work-in-progress inventory to be reduced, as waiting time between processes is more easily managed.

Exhibit 6.19 The position of cells and linked batch relative to batch and line processes

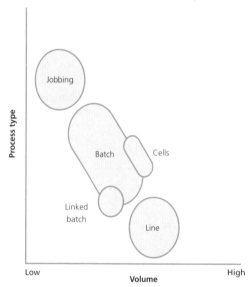

Just as these 'gains' come from moving the hybrid towards line, cells, compared to batch, also incur certain disadvantages associated with their repositioning on the process continuum. Compared to batch, cells are:

- less flexible
- result in lower utilization of equipment that may require additional process capacity investment.[2]

Both these are characteristic of line rather than batch.

Linked batch

Companies investing in line processes often find that, over time, the demand for the products may decline. With spare capacity resulting from this change in demand, companies seek to reuse the available process capacity by making other products. The outcome of this decision is that whereas originally the process would not have to be stopped and reset to accommodate a product change, now it would, as the added products fall outside the original process arrangement. The result is that the process, although it still looks like a line (with processes set out sequentially), is, in fact, a batch hybrid known as linked batch (see Exhibit 6.19). The key change resulting from this move from line to a hybrid batch process is the impact of set-up or changeover times now incurred to provide the revised range of products. As the stages in a linked batch process are coupled (as it was originally configured as a line process), a changeover will involve resetting all the parts of the total process before the process can begin to make the next product. Thus, although in batch, all the different processes to make a product would have to be reset before each operation could be completed, all the set-ups would not have to be done at the same time. The total set-up time in linked batch, therefore, would be high, as not only do all parts of the process need to be reset at the same time but there will be an interference factor during the changeover between one part of the process and another, adding to the total length of changeover time involved.

Nagare production system

The Nagare production system was developed within the disc brake division of Sumitomo Electric. The layout is a derivation of cells and, in the same way, provides an alternative to the process layout used in batch, as illustrated in Exhibit 6.20. The key differences between this system and cells are:

- The sequence of steps reflects the flow of materials in making the product.
- Operators move the part from step to step and hence complete a whole product.
- Operators typically produce to a JIT system using a *kanban*-type arrangement (this and JIT systems are explained fully in Chapter 10).
- The quantity of products produced at any one time is relatively small.
- The Nagare production system is ideally suited to making products that are similar to one another. This helps keep the level of change involved low and hence set-up times are reduced.

Exhibit 6.20 Changing from process to Nagare cell layout

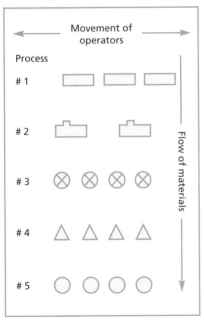
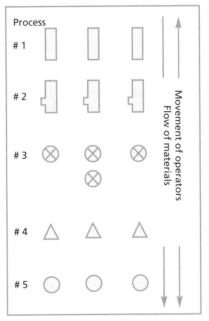

Process layout   Nagare cell layout

Transfer lines

Where the volume demand for products is very high, further investment is justified. Transfer lines are a hybrid between line and continuous processing. The high demand leads to investments designed to reduce the manual inputs associated with a line process and move more towards a process that automatically transfers a part from one station to the next, positions it, completes the task and checks the conformance quality. Furthermore, deviations from specified tolerance levels will be registered within a process and automatic tooling adjustments will often be part of the process capability.

Product profiling[3]

When companies invest in manufacturing processes, recognizing the implications for their business has to be part of the evaluation and decision. Similarly, as markets change or companies enter new markets with different competitive needs, checking whether existing processes can meet the business dimensions of these changes is part of the strategic task.

As emphasized earlier, investments in operations are large and fixed, whereas today's markets are fast changing and becoming increasingly different rather than increasingly similar. For operations to align its capabilities to the needs of a company's markets today and tomorrow, it has to have a way of assessing the current level of alignment and being alert to future changes that may weaken this essential support. Similarly, in its market-driving role, operations needs to agree with the business ahead of time those order-winners and qualifiers it has to improve in order to maintain or grow share in existing markets or enable it to successfully enter new markets.

As explained earlier, on the one hand, investments enable operations to meet the technical dimensions of the products to be provided, while on the other hand, they enable operations to meet the business dimensions (that is, the order-winners and qualifiers for which operations is solely or jointly responsible, for example delivery speed, on-time delivery and price) that comprise the other part of the market requirements. This section explains how organizations can check alignment, that is, how well market needs are matched by what operations is set up to provide.

The concept of undertaking this check is called 'product profiling'. It offers an organization the opportunity to test the current or anticipated degree of fit between the characteristics of its markets and the characteristics of its existing or proposed process and infrastructure investments. The principal purpose of this assessment is to provide a method to evaluate and, where necessary, improve the degree of fit between the way in which a company qualifies and wins orders in its markets and the ability of operations to support these criteria.

The ideal is to achieve fit. In many instances, though, companies will be unable or unwilling to provide the desired degree of fit, due to the level of investment, executive energy or timescales involved to make the necessary changes. Sound strategy concerns improving the level of consciousness an organization brings to bear on its corporate decisions. Knowing what needs to be done and implementing the necessary changes is the aim, but knowing what needs to be done while being unable to justify the change still constitutes sound strategy. Product profiling increases corporate awareness of what strategic changes need to be made and allows a conscious choice between alternatives.

Procedure

Alignment involves checking how well the requirements of markets are matched by the characteristics of the operations process used to provide them. The purpose of the check is to assess the level of business fit that exists. It also serves to alert companies to future potential alignment issues that could arise as a result of current strategies in a business.

Completing a check links aspects of Chapter 2 on operations strategy and Chapter 4 on product design and development to aspects of this chapter concerning the design of the manufacturing process. The procedure for developing a product profile involves the following steps:

1   Select aspects of the business (some are given in Exhibit 6.16) that are relevant to the

business situation under review. The key here is to keep the number of dimensions to a few and so keep the insights sharp. Remember, this approach is a mechanism for communicating strategic issues to other parts of the business. Keeping to the point highlights the message and avoids digression.

2   Next, put down the characteristics associated with each chosen dimension (see Exhibit 6.16 for some illustrations). Exhibit 6.21 is an example of the outcome of product profiling and a glance at this will show you how to proceed.

3   Now profile the product(s) by positioning them on each of the characteristics selected. Where the circle is drawn indicates the position. The example in Exhibit 6.21 profiles two plants to illustrate why one was successful and the other was not. Different circles represent the two different plants. Profiling the product and market characteristics served by both plants and also profiling the operations and investment characteristics involved is the procedure used to check alignment. Thus, these profiles show the needs of the markets under review and the capability of operations to provide these requirements. In this way it tests the fit (current or future) between market requirements and operations characteristics.

Exhibit 6.21 Profile analysis for two plants

Some relevant aspects for this company			Typical characteristics of process choice		
			jobbing	batch	line
Products and markets	Product	type	Special		Standard
		range	Wide		Narrow
	Customer order size		Small		Large
	Level of product change required		High		Low
	Rate of new product introductions		High		Low
	Order-winner		Delivery speed/ unique capability		Price
Operations	Process	nature	General-purpose		Dedicated
		flexibility	High		Low
	Operations volumes		Low		High
	Operations key strategic task		Meet specification/ delivery speed		Low cost operations
Investment	Level of capital investment		Low		High

○ ◑ Position of Plant A on each of the chosen dimensions and the resulting profile ————

● ◑ Position of Plant B on each of the chosen dimensions and the resulting profile -- -- -- --

This figure reflects the consistency of products and processes for Plant A and the inconsistencies for Plant B, reflected by a straight-line and dogleg shape, respectively.

Source Terry Hill, *Manufacturing Strategy: Text and Cases*, 2nd edn, Basingstoke, Macmillan – now Palgrave Macmillan (2000), p. 152.

4   The resulting profiles illustrate the degree of consistency between the requirements of the market and the operations strategy to support these needs. The higher the level of consistency, the straighter the profile. Inconsistencies will be shown by a dogleg profile.

Product profiling, therefore, is a way of illustrating the level of fit between a company's markets and operations capabilities, in terms of current or future requirements. The lack of alignment can be caused by a strategy that moves the company in part or in total to new markets and new requirements or an operations strategy that is not in line with the needs of current and/or future markets.

The story behind Exhibit 6.21

Faced with a decline in markets and profits, the company illustrated here undertook a major internal review of its two manufacturing plants. To provide orientation to its business, it decided to manufacture different products at its two sites. Two or three years later the number of product types handled by Plant B was eight times as many as Plant A and, as one would expect, product volume and order size differences resulted from this decision. While in Plant A, average volumes for individual products rose by 60 per cent, in Plant B they decreased by 40 per cent. To further help redress the overall decline in profits, the company also embarked on major operations developments at each plant, involving identical process investments and infrastructure changes. Exhibit 6.21 illustrates how these changes fitted Plant A's markets while they led to a significant mismatch for Plant B.

The procedure followed to complete Exhibit 6.21 is the one given in the previous section. Again, the first step is to choose the characteristics of markets and operations pertinent to this business. Next, the characteristics that reflect the change between jobbing, batch and line are described. On the one hand, the product range associated with jobbing is wide and becomes increasingly narrow as it moves through to line. On the other, customer order size is small in jobbing and becomes increasingly large as it moves through to line and so on. These dimensions represent the classic characteristics of the trade-offs embodied in choosing a process, as illustrated in Exhibit 6.16. Plant A's profile shows a straight-line relationship between the markets and the process and infrastructure provision, that is, the requirements of Plant A's markets are matched by the characteristics of its operations investments and capabilities (its operations strategy). However, Plant B has a dogleg profile because the process and infrastructure investments, although similar to those in Plant A, did not relate to the requirements of Plant B's market and hence a mismatch occurred. That is, the needs and characteristics of Plant B's markets are not matched by the characteristics of its operations investments and capabilities (its operations strategy).

When using product profiling it is important to note the following:

● As companies are often in more than one market, profiles will need to be drawn on a market-by-market basis.

● Another cause of non-alignment may be that market changes are not matched by the developments in operations necessary to support these new requirements. As changes in markets are often incremental, the impact of the aggregate changeover time often goes undetected and an increasing lack of alignment is the result. Whereas in Exhibit 6.21 the comparison made was between two plants in the same time frame, a review of one business over time compares one time period to another. If, during this period, the strategic position of operations continues unaltered, alignment problems would result. These reviews should form part of a forward look by organizations to detect potential mismatches, and hence avoid them.

- Product profiling is an important and constructive way to illustrate current or future alignment problems. The picture format is the key to providing this insight and needs, therefore, to be kept focused on the underlying issues within a business. Keeping the number of dimensions small and relevant is essential.

- One fundamental reason why alignment problems develop is that companies wish to invest in processes just once. Propositions that companies link process investment to stages in the life cycle of products[4] are not borne out in reality.[5] Although theoretically attractive, this proposition is not followed because of associated investment costs. To invest and reinvest as volume grows would involve very high overall investment. Although companies use different processes at the R&D phase, once a product enters operations to be provided commercially, investment decisions are made on the basis of forecast volumes, with the aim of minimizing associated costs. That is, they intend and plan to invest only once unless, of course, sales grow to the point where extra capacity is needed. Any transitions, therefore, will tend to be restricted, as explained in Exhibit 6.15.

Reflections

Markets are different and they change over time. The main issue in this chapter concerns understanding markets in terms of volumes and requirements and processes in terms of what, in relation to market support, they can do well and less well. Thus, as markets are different so will be the nature of operations support. The reality in most businesses is that this essential link between operations and market need is not adequately provided. One source of this problem comes from the structure of organizations themselves.

When most organizations start to grow, the initial functional division that usually takes place separates operations from other functions. With further growth, procedures and systems are developed, and support and specialist functions are introduced to link the marketing dimension with the operations dimension. Exhibit 6.22 illustrates this development.

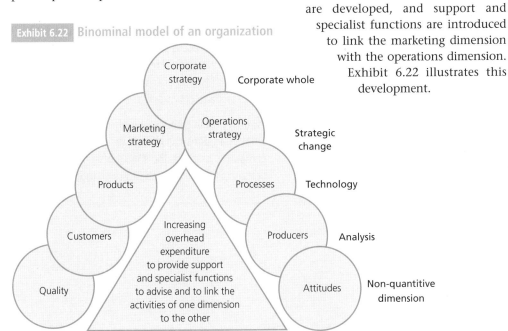

Exhibit 6.22 Binominal model of an organization

Source Developed from NK Powell, 'Steps towards a definition of operations management', *Management Education and Development*, **9**(3) (1979), pp. 162–7.

The task facing operations is to ensure, through its joint ownership of the links between products and processes, between customers and producers, and between quality and attitudes, that it makes its essential contribution towards the improvement of these within an organization. In many instances, operations managers have shed this major responsibility to the detriment of the operations function, their own managerial role and the business as a whole. Given the important strategic role to be provided by operations and the essential task within this of supporting agreed markets, understanding and explaining to the rest of a business the trade-offs being faced is a prerequisite in the strategy debate and its outcomes.

With organizations typically being developed on the basis of functions and specialists, the key links between products and processes and between customers and producers have been separated in their essential task of providing and selling products to customers. The task of any business is to provide products and sell them in chosen markets, but using functions and specialisms as the basic building blocks of organizations has separated the provision from the sale. The key links between products and processes and between customers and producers have been severed. As highlighted in Chapter 2, operations (as with other functions) needs to proactively close this gap. Providing the necessary insights to do this is a key role of all functions.

Key Elements of Designing Manufacturing Processes

- A key role in operations is to determine how best to make the products an organization sells to its customers, which comprises a technical and business dimension.

- Meeting the technical characteristics leads to certain, often given, choices – commercial bread-making requires ovens of a given size, plastic mouldings need injection moulding machines and so on. While this is a key issue, alternative process technologies normally form part of the role of the engineering and other technical functions. Operations must use these technologies to make products in line with the needs of chosen markets.

- Operations has to choose the type(s) of manufacturing process to best meet the demands of customers. This chapter described the process choices and their associated trade-offs.

- When you prepare one of the case studies at the back of the book or analyse operations in a real-life setting, process choice is one of the first questions you should resolve. It will give you important insights into operations, in terms of trade-offs and characteristics.

- Product profiling checks alignment between what operations can do and the needs of a company's markets, the source of alignment problems and helps with future changes.

Self-check

1 Which of the following is an example of a special product:
   a Automobile
   b Oil tanker
   c Ocean-going yacht

2 The essential difference between a batch and a line process is:
   a A line process is always straight
   b When changing from one product to another, a batch process has to be stopped and reset whereas a line process does not
   c A batch process can be stopped but a line process cannot be stopped

3 The differentiating feature of a continuous process is:
   a The processes are laid out sequentially
   b It is another name for a line process
   c It is very expensive (often prohibitively so) to stop and restart

4 In operations management, the definition of volume is:
   a Order quantity for a product × unit time
   b Sales revenue value (£) of an order
   c Annual quantity sold of a product

5 Which of the following is a definition of flexibility:
   a Handling a range of products
   b Meeting demand peaks
   c Both a and b

6 Which of the following is a definition of the saleable productive time of production capacity:
   a Time spent not producing products

   b Time spent producing products that will be sold to customers
   c Both a and b

7 Which of the following is true:
   a Process investments tend to be inexpensive to change
   b Companies choose a process with the intention of not changing it in the near future
   c Both a and b

8 The essential difference between cells and batch manufacturing is that:
   a In cells, processes are allocated to the sole use of a group of products
   b In cells, similar processes are grouped together
   c In cells, equipment utilization tends to be higher than in batch

9 Which of the following is **not** true for a linked batch manufacturing process:
   a Changeovers involve resetting all parts of the process
   b The process no longer looks like a line process
   c Processes are coupled together

10 Potential cause(s) of non-alignment between a company's markets and its operations capabilities are:
   a The company is trying to meet the differing needs of several markets with a single process
   b The needs of the market have changed over time
   c Both a and b

Study activities

Discussion questions

1 Select a simple (involving one or two steps) and more complicated (three or more steps) batch process in manufacturing companies of your choice. Explain how they work.

2 What are the essential differences between:
   - project   and   jobbing
   - jobbing   and   batch
   - batch   and   line
   - line   and   continuous processing?

3 When assembling a car there will be five tyres (four plus a spare) to each vehicle. Why is it that tyre-making would use a batch process, while a car is typically asssembled using a line process?

4 Select an example to illustrate the make components/parts, assemble and test tasks typically completed by jobbing, batch and line processes, as shown in Exhibit 6.12.

5 For the example given in Exhibit 6.21:
   - What are the key reasons for the underperformance of Plant B?
   - What steps could you take to improve the existing level of fit?
   - Choose the one most appropriate action to follow to bring about improvement.

6 Why is waiting time an integral part of a batch process design? Illustrate with two examples.

Assignments

1 Check the internet to review one of the major petrochemical companies. Analyse one of its oil refineries and explain:
   - how it handles the product range that is processed in the plant
   - how often the plant is shut down and why.

2 Select a business/organization (other than the examples given in this chapter) to illustrate the five types of process – project, jobbing, batch, line and continuous processing. For each example, briefly explain how the process works.

3 Give an example where you consider that the production process is not aligned to the organization's market(s). Explain key aspects that illustrate this. What steps would you take to improve the level of fit between market needs and operations capabilities?

4 For a manufacturing company of your choice, explain:
   - the process design
   - how it fits/does not fit the needs of its markets
   - draw the resulting product profile.

Exploring further

Benders, J and Morita, M 'Changes in Toyota Motors' operations management', *International Journal of Production Research*, **43**(3) (2004) pp. 433–44.

Conti, R and Warner, M 'Taylorism, new technology and just-in-time systems in Japanese manufacturing', *New Technology, Work and Employment* **8**(1) (1993) pp. 31–42.

Ford, H *Today and Tomorrow*, Productivity Press, Cambridge, MA (1988).

Fujimoto, T *The Evolution of the Toyota Production System*, Oxford University Press, New York (1999).

Golden, W and Powell, P 'Towards a definition of flexibility: in search of the holy grail?', *Omega* **28** (2000) pp. 373–84.

Goldratt, EM *The Goal*, Crocton-on-Hudson, North River (1984).

Shingo, S 'Study of Toyota Production System', *Japan Management Association (Tokyo)* (1981).

Womack, JP, Jones, DT and Roos, D *The Machine that Changed the World*, Rawson Associates, New York (1990).

Notes and references

1   NC refers to the operation of machine tools from numerical data stored on magnetic tape, computer storage or direct information. The development of machining centres results from the concepts of NC. In a machining centre, a range of operations is provided using a carousel with up to 150 tools or more (that is, embodied in the centre) from which the program will select as required, with some operations taking place simultaneously. Consequently, a machining centre is not only able to cope with a wide range of product requirements, it can also be scheduled to complete single products in any desired sequence.

2   If you compare the batch layout to the cellular layout in Exhibit 6.18, you will notice that additions to some process types have been made. This is because when similar processes or capabilities are brought together and managed as a single group, utilization and reutilization will be facilitated, and this is what happens in process layouts. Process design in cells, on the other hand, moves away from the principle that underpins batch processes of grouping all similar processes together and one outcome is that process utilization levels fall. At one extreme, if a company has a single process or capability

and moves from a process-based arrangement to (say) two cell-based arrangements that both require this capability, a company would have to buy another process to have a source of capacity in each cell.

3   The concept of product profiling is more fully explained in Terry Hill's books *Manufacturing Strategy: Text and Cases*, 3rd edn, McGraw-Hill/Irwin, Burr Ridge, IL (2000), Chapter 6 and *Manufacturing Strategy: Text and Cases*, 2nd edn, Macmillan, Basingstoke – now Palgrave Macmillan (2000), Chapter 6.

4   The proposition of linking process life cycles and product life cycles was most noticeably argued by Hayes, RH and Wheelwright, SC in, 'Link manufacturing process and product life cycles', *Harvard Business Review*, January/February (1979), pp. 133–40.

5   A comparison between how useful the insights in note 4 are in evaluating the source of alignment problems between markets and operations strategy, compared with those of product profiling, was reported in an article by Hill, T, Menda, R and Dilts, DH 'Using product profiling to illustrate manufacturing–marketing misalignment', *Interfaces*, **28**(4) (1998), pp. 47–63.

book map

Part

1

- 1 Managing Operations
- 2 Operations Strategy
- 3 Managing People

2

SUPPLIERS

INPUTS

PROCESSES

OUTPUTS

CUSTOMERS

- 4 Designing and Developing Services & Products
- 5 Designing Service Delivery Systems
- 6 Designing Manufacturing Processes
- 7 Location and Layout

3

- 8 Managing Capacity
- 9 Technology Developments
- 10 Operations Scheduling and Execution
- 11 Managing Quality
- 12 Managing Inventory
- 13 Managing the Supply Chain

4

- 14 Process and Delivery System Reliability and Maintenance
- 15 Time and Productivity
- 16 Improving Operations

5

- Managing Operations in Practice: Long Case Studies

Location and Layout

Outline of chapter

Where best to locate operations and how best to layout the people, delivery systems, processes and facilities involved will directly impact the revenue and profit performance of a business. Factors influenced by these decisions include inital and repeat sales, costs, speed of service, ease of provision and level of customer support.

Why are location and layout important?

Executive overview

This chapter addresses the two issues of location and layout – where best to position a facility or outlet and how best to layout the processes, equipment and staff used in providing the services or making the products.

Location decisions aim to secure the best net gains for an organization now and in the long term and embrace the following criteria:

- initial and later development costs

- trading costs when providing the services or products to customers

- impact on sales revenue

- level of service a facility is able to provide to its customers.

For many larger organizations where to locate a facility may involve decisions at several levels including:

- continent or region

- country

- area or city

- the site itself.

The factors influencing location decisions are then reviewed and are separated into:

- general factors such as the origin of existing decisions, political constraints and need for market access

- specific factors including existing infrastructure, proximity to markets and suppliers, staff availability, costs and favourable government policies.

The final part of this section introduces some of the techniques used in making these decisions (weighted-factor and centre of gravity method) together with examples.

Layout – this section addresses the task of how best to arrange the processes, systems and staff used. First, background factors such as existing space, health and safety and aesthetics are discussed. Then the basic types of layout (fixed position, process or function and service or product) are described, together with examples of where they are used. Hybrid delivery system layouts are discussed, together with other formats such as flexible office layouts.

The final section looks at detailed layout design and the approaches used for each of the basic types of layout.

Location

Location, whether concerning, for example, hospitals, offices, retail outlets, warehouses or manufacturing plants, is a significant corporate decision because, once built, organizations have to live with the consequences for a long time. Such decisions are, therefore, not easily taken and usually are resolved only after a long and careful review of all aspects, including due regard for the future uncertainty factor that comes with the long timescales involved. What might have been a sensible decision at the time may prove to be less appropriate in the future!

Much time and effort needs to be put into identifying and assessing the key variables that make up these decisions as the size and binding nature of the investments make relocation hard to justify. In fact, the magnitude of these decisions is such that some organizations are, in reality, committed indefinitely to a location once it has been chosen.

Overall objective

The overall objective in choosing one location over alternatives is to secure the best net gains for an organization now and in the long term. In essence this concerns:

- initial and later development investments, and the trading costs when providing services or products to customers
- the impact on sales revenue that the facility is able to make
- the level of service the facility is able to provide to its customers.

Although the last point is linked to commercial companies, this factor would also be an appropriate objective for non-profit-making organizations.

The levels of decision

A location for an outlet or facility might involve decisions concerning which continent or region, country, area or city and finally which street. Depending on the type of outlet, the number of decision levels and the importance attached to the factors that determine the choice at each level will change. For example, the factors that Disney's management considered when deciding where to locate a new theme park in Europe would have been at all levels and embraced more factors than Burger King's decision on where to locate its next outlet in Stockholm. While Disney would place great importance on factors such as staff availability, transport infrastructure, proximity to potential customers, climate and level of government support, for Burger King's local management factors such as local customer density, location of competitors, zoning and building regulations, space availability and ease of access would have been more important.

Not only do the number of levels involved differ by decision but the factors relevant to location decisions will also change. First, let's briefly look at each possible decision level and afterwards review the factors that organizations may have to take into account when deciding where to go.

Choosing the continent or region

For many larger organizations, where to locate a facility increasingly has a regional dimension. While over the years many manufacturing companies have chosen to make products in one region to sell in another, in more recent times many service companies have also been locating in different regions. For some companies (for example hotel chains such as Marriott and Holiday Inn, coffee outlets such as Starbucks and Coffee Republic, accountancy firms such as PricewaterhouseCoopers, Ernst & Young and Touche Ross and retailers such as IKEA and Wal-Mart) the prime reason is access to new markets. For other companies (for example by 2008 the estimated relocation of call centre jobs in financial services to India, Malaysia, China and other Asian countries will be as many as 3.3 million from the US and 2.0 million from Western Europe) the prime reason is to lower costs. While for other organizations (for example management consultancy companies such as Accenture, Booz Allen Hamilton and McKinsey) it is a combination of market access (through a local presence) and less expensive service provision, with local consultants commanding lower salaries and the lower living costs of local vis-à-vis expatriot staff provision.

Choosing the country

For some companies, the choice of country is an integral part of the last decision. For example, where the prime location aim is to access markets, often the region and country decision are part of the same whole. In other instances, however, it will be a separate issue. Disney's decision to build a theme park in Europe was only step #1. While choosing Europe may only have involved selecting from a very few options, which country in Europe would have meant choosing from several viable alternatives and achieving a shortlist of two would have involved considering a whole range of alternatives. Similarly, choosing France ahead of Spain would have meant carefully judging the relative importance of a number of variables, while weighting the relevant criteria over the timescales involved.

Similarly, the decision by financial service companies to locate call centre services in Asia would involve the decision of which country, where alternatives such as India and Malaysia have now been joined by countries such as China.

Choosing the area or city

For Disney, the decision of choosing France over Spain still left a long way to go. Similarly, choosing northern France still left the decision of which area or city would best meet the objectives of the company. Again, trade-offs between factors such as climate, availability of staff and density of potential customer catchment areas would have come into play. No doubt analyses would be made and models used to provide options and identify one or more possible optimal locations. The parameters used in modelling alternatives would include a whole range, as discussed in the next section, and different scenarios could be considered to test the impact of changes to key variables on alternative sites.

For companies where locations comprise smaller sized outlets, this level of decision is often more self-defining, with the 'which site?' decision becoming the one that needs greater care and is more difficult to make.

Choosing the site

Selecting the actual site requires other considerations to be taken into account. This is the domain of the micro-scale decision that deals with the precise location within a city centre, regional centre, retail warehouse, business or industrial park or site in relation to major roads, rail links, airports or seaports. At this level of detail, a whole range of factors come into play as discussed in the following sections.

General factors influencing location decisions

Before looking at the specific factors to be considered when addressing location decisions, we start by recognizing that although the choice of where best to locate should, as with other management decisions, be set against objective criteria, reality is often a major factor in determining what is and is not feasible. This section now looks at six general factors; 1 and 2 are possibly of an overriding nature, 3 and 4 result from recent technology changes and globalization trends, while 5 and 6 are of an economic nature.

1   The origin of existing locations – many organizations are located where they are now as a result of decisions made in the past and the cost of changing to a more suitable location cannot be justified. Being close to a founder's residence or near to the source of materials or customers for the original business are typical of the historical decisions that have underpinned past choices. As organizations grow and the investment to meet that expansion also grows, the cost of relocation compared with extending an existing site can often become prohibitive. As a result, organizations stay where they are.

2   Politically based constraints – countries wish to develop their own industrial and service sectors in order to create the wealth essential for national prosperity. To this end one step being taken by governments is to require multinational companies (MNCs) to build facilities within their own country so as to reduce imports and create value-adding activities. Joint ventures are an increasingly common way of meeting these requirements. Such arrangements dictate the location and often the size of facilities as MNCs seek to increase global presence.

    These pressures relate not only to developing nations; marked balance of payment deficits result in governments putting pressure on foreign competitors to locate facilities locally. This is one reason why Japanese car makers have located plants in the USA and Europe and are continuing to increase the capacity of these over time.

3   Technology developments – technology is not specific to a location and, in that way, is redefining what makes a location feasible. While physical proximity to aspects such as customers and raw materials will invariably remain important factors, advances in technology and electronic communications may set aside the emphasis placed on such factors in the past. The opportunities that these technologies provide have already changed the pattern of locations in several industries.

4   New countries are opening up – areas of the world that for decades had been closed to investments due to political dogma and/or social/economic instability have now opened up. Notable examples were parts of Southeast Asia in the 1980s and China and Eastern Europe in the last decade. Being close to new markets, low labour costs and the opportunity for companies to take over existing, often not well-managed, facilities have driven many recent location decisions.

5   Market access/local presence in large consumer markets – there is no more clearcut example of how large markets are attractive locations for businesses than the recent and continuing investments in North America and Europe. The reason primarily concerns market access. The USA is a very large market in its own right. The North America Free Trade Agreement (NAFTA) has swelled the consumer base by over 40 per cent to 360 million consumers. Becoming direct participants in this highly competitive and innovative market is one reason that led Honda and Toyota to build plants and establish joint venture agreements in the 1980s and to continue to expand these facilities through to the present day. This was also part of the rationale for BMW and Mercedes-Benz building

their first manufacturing plants outside Germany, locating them in South Carolina and Alabama respectively. Similar patterns are also present in Europe where the total market continues to grow as EU membership increases. One outcome reflecting the growing importance of this combined market is the level of foreign direct investment within Europe. Since the mid-1990s this has consistently been more than 40 per cent of the world total.

6   Currency value fluctuations – as the relative values of currencies change, the impact on costs may force a company to rethink the location of its manufacturing plants, particularly those serving local markets. The most marked example of this is Japan. In order to enable it to remain competitive, particularly in export markets, a whole range of Japanese companies have moved the location of their manufacturing plants to the regions in which they export. The motor industry examples above were also influenced by this factor. Other examples include electronics and consumer products companies.

Specific factors influencing location decisions – continent/region, country and area/city

The specific factors influencing the choice of where to locate have been separated into those relating to the continent/region, country and area/city decision levels and those that relate to the choice of the site itself. This section discusses the factors to be considered when making the three higher levels of decision, with the site choice issues to follow:

● Well-developed infrastructure – ease of access to road and rail systems and sea and air links will often be high on a company's list of requirements, particularly where the inputs and outputs of the transformation process are high volume and bulky. Similarly, other aspects of infrastructure such as communication and power systems will be important factors in deciding where, in general, to locate. In addition, the availability of appropriate support services is an increasingly important factor in location decisions. For example, the growing technology base, particularly the role of IT that characterizes many businesses today, places great emphasis on the need for local technical support.

● Proximity to markets – it is inherently sensible that services and goods are produced as close to the market for them as possible. The gains include lower distribution and provisioning costs and shorter distances where aspects such as product freshness are involved. Furthermore, where the delivery of a service involves direct interface with customers, being close to potential users will be a high priority in the selection process.

● Proximity to suppliers – as well as the obvious cost implications of distance, being a long way from suppliers also incurs longer lead times and introduces a higher level of uncertainty. Longer lead times reduce a supplier's ability to respond quickly. Regarding uncertainty, although longer lead times may, in effect, be no more variable than shorter lead times, the holdings of material and other inputs to the transformation process will typically be greater so as to provide added insurance against potential failure to deliver and the likely knock-on effect on a company's own business activity.

● Hospitable business climate – the long-term nature of location decisions places the business climate high on the agenda. The combination of an environment of free trade, free thought and the opportunity to create wealth are key factors in attracting investors. For this reason, Europe and North America continue to attract a high percentage of global foreign investment.

● Availability of staff – recent surveys of the factors cited by executives when making location decisions all point to suitable and sufficient staff as one of the most important. Concerns about the skill levels and flexibility of staff are high on the location agenda, given the long-term nature of these decisions. In addition, multinational companies will also take into account the traditional attitudes to work (the work ethic) within different regions.

- Quality of life for employees – it is not enough that sufficient skilled staff are to be found in the region or area, but a prospective employer must be satisfied that the facilities are or will be made available to a level that will retain the staff required. Factors concerning schools, accommodation and social infrastructure have an impact on the quality of life for employees, particularly expatriates whose skills and experience may be particularly critical in the earlier phases of the project. As concerns about and recognition of the family dimension of executives' lives have grown, these factors have become increasingly important.

- Variable cost structures – these remain a critical issue in location decisions and concern the several dimensions that make up total variable costs:
  - **staff costs:** locating in lower staff cost areas of the world such as Mexico, Eastern Europe, China and parts of the Asia Pacific region is often fundamental in the decision process. Typically, these decisions concern less skilled staff but developments in IT and communications systems have extended this location alternative to higher skilled people
  - **energy costs:** where energy costs of processing are high, companies may often choose to locate near to a less expensive source of power such as hydroelectricity
  - **transportation costs:** these costs concern incoming materials and the distribution of finished goods. They involve not only the actual costs of haulage but also excise duties and tariffs that may vary depending on the country of origin.

- Fixed costs and investments – these are the costs of getting started and also the fixed costs of doing business in a country or region:
  - **investment factors:** sizeable inducements to locate in a country or area in order to stimulate economic activity can be offered, including government financial assistance in the form of special grants, low-interest loans and tax allowances on building and material imports. For example, in 2004, AMD, the US chip maker, confirmed it would build a second chip plant in Dresden, Germany, after winning US$1.5 billion in German government-backed funding. The US$2.4 billion plant will begin production in 2006 and employ about 1000 people. It is one of the biggest investment projects in the former East Germany since reunification in 1990
  - **fixed costs** – can include inducements in the form of low local rates, low rents and low employment taxes.

Case example 7.1 provides an illustration of some of the factors that influence location decisions.

Case example 1   GROWTH AT SOFTWARE TECHNOLOGY PARKS OF INDIA

Until the late 1990s, Noida, a suburb north of Delhi, was a sleepy haven for pensioners wishing to escape the hustle and bustle of India's capital city. Now it is a boom town, with shopping malls, multiplex cinemas and chaotic traffic reflecting its growth and the lifestyle that its well-educated workforce is demanding.

At the centre of Noida's rapid expansion is the office that houses Software Technology Parks of India (STPI), the quango at the centre of India's rapid IT growth. STPI is the licensing authority for companies wanting to export IT or IT-enabled services. Formed in 1991, STPI has been central to the rapid growth in India's IT exports that were close to US$10 billion at the beginning of 2004.

As well as its licensing role, STPI has pushed hard on developing the necessary IT infrastructure including setting up broadband networks across the country. Now it receives 10 applications per week from companies wanting to join the IT phenomenon. While it expects this rate to increase in the future, it is sure that it can still turn around the paperwork inside a month.

www.stph.net

| **Case questions** | 1 What are the reasons for the rapid growth in Noida's IT-based services? |
| | 2 Relate your answer to question 1 to each of the 'Specific factors influencing location decisions' given earlier and comment. |

- **Favourable government policies** – in addition to investment and cost inducements, national and local government departments can facilitate the siting of a new business by how easy or difficult it makes the process involved. These include the political stance towards:
  - environmental concerns: the extent to which building and planning regulations embody stringent regulations regarding all forms of pollution including noise, toxic emissions, odour and the types and levels of effluent
  - political attitudes towards inward investment
  - barriers and licences: individual countries and trading blocs may impose restrictions in the form of quotas or increased tariff levels for different importers. The task of overcoming or circumventing such restrictions often leads MNCs in particular to choose locations that reduce or even eliminate such disadvantages
  - capital movement restrictions
  - government planning assistance
  - availability of suitable land: an important constraint on relocation activity in certain areas of the world is the availability of suitable land. In densely populated regions such as Europe, the failure of some governments to identify and account for this factor has curtailed opportunities and hence attracted less relocation investments. While Eire, France and the Netherlands, for example, can supply land to suit most requirements, Denmark, Greece and Italy are seen to be short of suitable relocation sites and consequently are not considered attractive areas.

- **Being near to other company facilities** – the level of integration with other parts of the same organization may influence the general area for a new location. The ease of giving support to one another, switching staff to meet short-term needs or integrating the work across associated business units may be a significant factor for companies where the gains of managing the whole company as one entity may outweigh other considerations.

- **Being near to the customer** – increasingly customers, especially those requiring frequent deliveries of materials in a just-in-time (JIT) context, require suppliers to build plants close by. In this way deliveries can be made, sometimes several times a day, thus keeping inventories low. Also, being close to your customer signals commitment and provides reassurance, as Case example 7.2 illustrates.

- **Individual preferences** – senior executives within an organization may prefer a new site to be in one region, country or city for their own convenience or preferences and this can have a substantial bearing on the eventual choice.

Case example 2   GROWTH AT PLASTIC OMNIUM

In 1947, Pierre Bureller, founder of Plastic Omnium, a parts supplier, published his strategic blueprint. It was a drawing of an automobile showing all the components then made of metal that he thought could be replaced by plastic. More than half a century on and guided by his earlier strategic vision, Paris-based Plastic Omnium is, through a joint venture, the world's biggest maker of plastic fuel tanks and second largest supplier of bumpers for automobiles.

In 1987 the company had just four factories, three of them in France. Now the company has 60 plants, 14 of which have opened since the turn of the century. The key to this growth is principally the company's willingness to build plants next to its customers' premises. It all began in 1990 when Plastic Omnium agreed to build a plant near to BMW's Munich assembly plant and, in that way, gain second supplier status. Since then it has adopted the same location strategy many times over, for example with VW in Slovakia and General Motors, VW and others in Mexico. Of its £1 billion sales in 2003, revenue from Mexico and the rest of North America now accounts for over one-third and is vying for the #1 spot with France.

www.plasticomnium.fr

Case question   How is plant location central to Plastic Omnium's rapid growth in the last 12–13 years?

Specific factors influencing location decisions – the choice of site

The final step is that of deciding the precise location within the chosen city centre, regional shopping centre, business park, industrial complex or street. At this micro-level, an array of factors specific to this decision come into play. To help review these, the different factors have been grouped under two headings; the site and impact of site location on potential demand.

The site

The factors that fall under this category comprise a whole range of issues including:

- adequate, off-street parking for both staff and customers
- attractive building in terms of the external impact and the internal arrangements regarding the basic tasks involved and the front-office space where customers interface with delivery systems
- attractive rental costs and local taxes
- the appropriateness of the existing space to meet the specific needs of the business including the amount of time and investment to bring it to the required level
- proximity to support services
- a fully developed site increases overall convenience, in that access is defined and developed, site-based facilities (for example roads, street lighting and telephone lines) are in place and construction work elsewhere on the overall site is minimized
- room for future expansion and associated development costs
- high traffic volumes may be a plus factor re demand but may be an unwelcome factor regarding customer access
- being visible from the street or highway would be of particular relevance where call-in trade is an important factor in a business
- convenient entry and exit to major road systems through to the closeness of a site to public transportation for customers and employees will be important in many businesses.

© AMD Publishing

Exhibit 7.1   There's more than one factor when choosing where to locate!

Impact of site location on potential demand

The factors here include:

- high levels of customer traffic in the area will be an important factor influencing demand in a whole range of businesses such as hotels, restaurants and retailing

- proximity to competitors – when shopping for services such as banking, hotel accommodation, clothes, shoes, accessories and restaurants, customers prefer to be able to choose from a range of options – the concept of competitive clustering. For example, research[1] has shown that hotels or motels located in areas with many competitors nearby experience higher occupancy rates than those in isolated locations. Furthermore, many budget hotels are located by motorways or major highway intersections to reflect the fact that their market is not the local population but businesspeople and others travelling by car.

- market saturation – the basic principle behind this strategy is to group outlets closely together in urban and other high traffic areas. In Europe and North America this unconventional strategy is gaining ground. Examples include Benetton, the Italian clothing company and Au Bon Pain cafés in the US. The idea is to locate the same outlets close to one another in the same area. For example, Au Bon Pain's 132 US cafés are concentrated in Boston, New York, Philadelphia, Miami, Pittsburg and Washington DC. As Exhibit 7.2 illustrates, its deliberate policy is to locate several cafés, all selling a wide range of gourmet sandwiches, salads, muffins, croissants, bread and soups, in the same area. As you can see, the pursuit of this strategy is a key factor in the company's location decisions.

Exhibit 7.2   The location of Au Bon Pain's outlets

Locations		Outlets
New York City		25
Boston		18
Chicago		10
Philadelphia		8
Miami		7
Pittsburg		6
Airports	Dallas Fort Worth	6
	Logan International	3
	JFK	2
	Atlanta	2

Before moving on to the next section, take a look at Case example 7.3, which illustrates a growing phenomenon in call centre location and review the case questions.

Case example 3   HSBC RELOCATES CALL CENTRE OPERATIONS

HSBC, the world's second largest bank, is to cut 4000 UK staff as it relocates work to India, Malaysia and China. The decision by the bank follows similar moves by other companies including BT, Goldman Sachs, Abbey and Prudential. The jobs would principally be processing work and telephone enquiries and the transfer would take place between 2004 and 2006.

The number of offshore operations belonging to UK financial service companies grew from 200 employees in 1996 to 3700 by the end of 2003, rising to an estimated 200,000 by the end of 2008. HSBC already runs a number of global processing hubs in Hyderabad and Bangalore in India and also in Malaysia. It is thought that much of the UK work will be relocated to these sites. India, in particular, has emerged in the past decade as a new location for call centre operations, given its large number of well-educated, English-speaking young people and lower staff costs. By the end of 2006, about 7000 (some 13 per cent) of HSBC's staff are expected to be in service centres in Asia.

www.hsbc.com

Case questions	1	HSBC's chief executive is quoted as saying that this move is essential to the bank's continued success and to help ensure job security for the bank's staff worldwide. Why?
	2	Why will HSBC relocate the work to its existing hubs in India and Malaysia?
	3	Explain the steep rise in the relocation of jobs expected in the UK's financial services sector.

Location techniques

Although site selection is often based on opportunistic factors such as site availability and cost benefits such as government grants and favourable tax rates, a quantitative analysis brings an important perspective to the decision and helps identify the optimal location based on the key benefits an organization is seeking. To help companies make decisions regarding the choice of optimal location, a number of approaches have been developed. This section introduces the more commonly used techniques but first let's look at the basic ideas on which they are built.

The underlying objective of choosing the optimal location is to maximize some measure of benefit. Which aspect of benefit an organization wishes to maximize will differ. In the private sector the driver will either be to maximize sales revenue, in the case of a retail outlet or restaurant, or to minimize cost, as in a distribution centre or courier service company. In the public sector, on the other hand, the drivers will reflect the needs of the community which a facility serves. For example, a hospital may be located to offer the easiest access by local people, such as distance and availability of public transport.

Each facility will approach the problem of where best to locate by assessing the various factors involved. For example, a company building a distribution centre would focus on the trade-offs between building costs and operating costs of the centre and the transportation costs to its various sites. For a retail outlet the trade-offs would include building and operating costs and also the attractiveness of different sites to potential customers and the impact on sales revenue. In the public sector, location decisions are often more difficult to assess as the factors involved are not as easily defined. However, two of the more commonly used factors to maximize the location benefits for a community are:

- distance per visit – to minimize the average per-visit distance to the facility by potential users (for example a hospital or health centre)

● utilization level of the facility – to maximize the total number of visits to a facility by choosing a location that will make visiting easier where the use of a facility is optional as, for example, in the case of a library.

Now let us look at two of the more commonly used techniques to help determine the optimal location of a facility.

The first task in location analysis is an accurate assessment of the spatial demand for a service, that is, the demand by geographical area. To establish this the target population needs to be defined. For a distribution centre, the company's sites that the centre is intended to serve will be known. For a community health centre, on the other hand, the target population could be the total number of people it is intended to serve, broken down by groups to reflect the level and type of service to be provided (for example family units and age groups). The area being served would then be split into smaller geographical units for which demand would be assessed and from them a complete picture established of the spatial demand requirements for the whole community to be served by the health centre in question.

The second task is then to use one or more of the techniques to evaluate how best to meet the demand requirements against selected criteria. Of the several facility locations techniques and models that exist, the appropriate one to use will reflect the nature of the location problem on hand. Here, two techniques are reviewed – the weighted-factor and centre of gravity methods.

Weighted-factor method

Consider the example of a chain of coffee and sandwich bars choosing between three potential sites in Paris. The company's experience in what makes a good location has highlighted the factors that influence sales and the relative importance of these one to another. To assess each site, these factors are then scored on a scale of 0–10 and a weighted average score for each site is then calculated, as shown in Exhibit 7.3. The individual scores are multiplied by the weight (%) given to each factor and the highest total is the best potential site based on this measure. For example, site 1 gets a score of 630, as shown below:

$$(40 \times 6) + (20 \times 7) + (15 \times 5) + (10 \times 8) + (10 \times 6) + (5 \times 7) = 630$$

In the example given in Exhibit 7.3, site 2 is clearly the best potential location for the proposed coffee and sandwich bar.

Exhibit 7.3 Weighted-factor method of choosing a coffee/sandwich bar site

Factor	Weight	Site 1		Site 2		Site 3	
Closeness to office customers	40	6	240	8	320	7	280
Visibility from street	20	7	140	7	140	6	120
Near to metro station/but stops	15	5	75	8	120	8	120
Closeness to tourist attraction(s)	10	8	80	5	50	5	50
Ease of access/width of sidewalk	10	6	60	8	80	6	60
Ease of parking for suppliers	5	7	35	7	35	7	35
Totals	100	–	630	–	745	–	665

Centre of gravity method

Where the choice of site needs to be made in relation to a number of existing locations, the centre of gravity method provides a way to address the factors involved. As the name implies, the outcome will be the location point which strikes the optimum balance between the set of variables involved.

The best way to explain this approach is to provide a worked example of the steps to follow. A German supermarket chain is planning to build a distribution centre to serve the Bavarian region where over the last five years it has built seven supermarkets. Until this time, it has supported these outlets with a combination of approaches including direct supply and deliveries from its existing distribution centres located further north. Several ranges of product will continue to be delivered directly from producers but the company's past experience has found that a combination of direct and distribution centre supply works best. The location of the seven supermarkets is shown in Exhibit 7.4.

Exhibit 7.4 Centre of gravity method of siting a new distribution centre

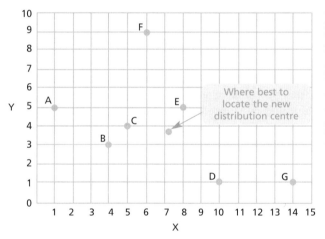

Site	X	Y
A	1	5
B	4	3
C	5	4
D	10	1
E	8	5
F	6	9
G	14	1

You will see from the exhibit that a reference grid has been superimposed on the map. The centre of gravity method identifies the lowest distribution cost location for the new distribution centre by calculating the mean of X and Y. Exhibit 7.5 shows the number of weekly van deliveries to each supermarket. The information in Exhibits 7.4 and 7.5 is combined in the following way in order to identify the optimum position for the new supermarket:

Exhibit 7.5 Number of weekly van deliveries to each supermarket

Supermarket	# Weekly deliveries
A	6
B	14
C	14
D	10
E	8
F	12
G	14
Total	78

Mean of X $\quad = \quad \dfrac{\Sigma XiAi}{\Sigma Ai}$ $\qquad$ where Xi = site locations on the X axis

$\qquad\qquad\qquad\qquad\qquad\qquad\qquad$ Ai = weekly van deliveries to each supermarket

Mean of Y $\quad = \quad \dfrac{\Sigma YiAi}{\Sigma Yi}$ $\qquad$ where Yi = site locations on the Y axis

$\qquad\qquad\qquad\qquad\qquad\qquad\qquad$ Ai = # weekly van deliveries to each supermarket

In this example

Mean of X $\quad = \quad \dfrac{(1\times 6) + (4\times 14) + (5\times 14) + (10\times 10) + (8\times 8) + (6\times 12) + (14\times 14)}{78}$

$\qquad\qquad = \quad 7.23$

Mean of Y $\quad = \quad \dfrac{(5\times 6) + (3\times 14) + (4\times 14) + (1\times 10) + (5\times 8) + (9\times 12) + (1\times 14)}{78}$

$\qquad\qquad = \quad 3.85$

Layout

This section addresses the task of how best to arrange the processes, systems and staff used in providing a service or making a product. First, the general background factors to be taken into account in layout design will be reviewed. This is followed by an overview of the basic types of layout and where and how each is used, together with an explanation of a number of hybrids (mixes between one basic type of layout and another) and a review of the techniques and approaches used in layout design.

Background factors

This section highlights a number of background factors that will dictate some of the design parameters in a facility layout. The relative importance of these will differ from one organization to another, but they will need to be incorporated into the organization's layout design.

Nature of the core task

The nature of the core task of an organization will dictate some of the parameters in a facility layout. A supermarket will need to incorporate sufficient customer parking as well as adequate access for the delivery of goods. Similarly, it will need to have a stockholding area which would need to include cold storage facilities for fresh dairy, meat and fish products. The branch of a bank would need to incorporate an area for ATMs that could be accessed by the public in non-opening times, teller facilities inside the bank that afforded sensible levels of security and areas that would provide privacy when customers sought advice on personal finances from banking staff. And so on.

Available space

Often the space available for a facility comes with a mix of constraints including ease of access, building regulations, land costs and the actual area itself. The facility design will need to accommodate these. For example, where land is at a premium (either in terms of availability or cost), a facility incorporating several floors would be a design prerequisite. For instance, while the classic McDonald's outlet is a single storey, free-standing facility, in cities such as Stockholm, Copenhagen and Madrid, the outlets are designed with several floors.

Designing-in the need for future flexibility

Organizations are dynamic and so need to adapt to future changes in terms of space requirements and facilities' layout. It is important, therefore, to incorporate the possible need for change during the design phase of a facility. The dimensions of these future changes may include:

- **activity volumes** – how many passengers to be handled by an airport in the future, or customers to be served in a retail outlet or accommodated in an upmarket restaurant if the businesses are a success

- **range of services and products** to be provided

- **nature of the services or products** on offer. For example, whether a bank or fast-food outlet will incorporate a 'drive-thru' option in the future.

Health and safety

The increasing and appropriate emphasis on health and safety in the workplace has to be incorporated into facilities' design, both in terms of staff and customers. Factors range from chemical and other pollution hazards and fire risks through to eliminating possible accidents in terms of flat walking surfaces, the width and depth of stairwells, provision of handrails and adequate entrances and exits.

Aesthetics

Decisions may be required about staff areas of work (the back office) and areas where customers interface with the delivery system (the front office) or business in general such as the main reception. In the staff work areas decisions on a range of features need to be made such as the size and number of windows, lighting, height of partitions, floor coverings, floor surfaces, the size and number of break or refreshment areas as well as decisions about open plan versus half-height dividers versus private office arrangements. In the front-office phase of the delivery system, decisions would need to be made on several factors including lighting, decoration, wall coverings, space and formal versus informal layouts. The response by customers and staff to these aspects of layout are split into three categories:[2]

- cognitive response refers to the affect on customer and staff perceptions and expectations of the organization. Dimensions such as decor, fittings and fixtures and staff dress code will communicate a sense of the level of service or product to be provided. For example, smart/casual and matching clothes in a hairdressers will give a feeling of uniformly high quality.

- emotional response comprises the characteristics of pleasantness and excitement generated by the aesthetics of a facility. The immediate surroundings on entering a restaurant will help create an appropriate emotional response that will set the mood for customers while helping to motivate staff to meet their expectations.

- physiological response – characteristics such as decor, space, furniture and level of privacy will affect a customer's response to the service experience that is, in turn, reflected in their behaviour. For example, how relaxed a customer feels and the length of stay over dinner in a restaurant.

Now take a look at Case example 7.4 to reflect on some of the background factors we have just covered.

Case example 4   CREATING SPACE ON PASSENGER JETS

When push comes to shove, more than 50 per cent of airline passengers cite elbow room (having an empty seat next to them is the ideal) as their first choice when it comes to extra space. By 2001, the percentage of seats filled on US internal flights had risen to almost three-quarters. Economy seats are about 17 in or 42 cm wide, the same as they have been for years. Making aisles dangerously narrow or putting fewer seats in rows and sacrificing revenue are difficult calls to make.

But, more elbow room is starting to influence airline choice. Denver-based Frontier Airlines cited the extra 7 in (17 cm) wider interior as 'a big selling point' in ordering twenty Airbus 318s and 319s over the new-generation Boeing 737s. Also, Continental Airlines specifically designed the coach-class seating in its new Boeing 777s in a way that increased the chances that passengers would have an empty seat next to them. As the table below shows, seat layouts in today's passenger jets have taken these issues on board.

As most airlines report, one of the biggest drivers for satisfaction is whether the seat next to a person is empty. When the seats filled crosses the 60 per cent line, customer satisfaction plummets, while at a 70 per cent load factor only 25 per cent of passengers view a flight as being satisfactory.

Seat arrangements	Airplane	Percentage of seats filled before a passenger must sit next to another
3–2	● Boeing MD80, 88, 90 ● DC9 and Fokker F100	51
3–3	● Boeing 727, 737, 757 ● Airbus A-319, A-320 ● DC10	54
2–5–2	● Boeing MD11 ● Lockheed L-1011	34
3–3–3	● Boeing 777	54
3–4–3	● Boeing 747	52

Source Boeing.

Case questions

1 Why is elbow room on passenger airlines an increasingly important factor in the new millennium?

2 Why is legroom often easier to provide than elbow room in passenger jet design?

3 Link this case example to Exhibit 5.4 and highlight the key dimensions it illustrates.

Basic types of layout

The objective of a layout is to develop an arrangement of the processes and related equipment, work areas, systems, storage areas and staff needed to provide a service or make a product such that these resources operate at peak effectiveness and efficiency. This section looks at the three basic types of layout – fixed position, process or functional and service or product. Some organizations seek to improve the level of effectiveness and efficiency of these basic types by mixing elements one with another. Such hybrids are discussed in the next section. The appropriate basic layout type reflects the service and product characteristics involved, as is now explained.

Fixed position layout

Some services and products have to be provided or made on the customer's site. The reason is one of necessity. Where the service needs to be undertaken on a customer's site (for example a management consultancy assignment, the regular or breakdown maintenance of a mainframe computer or other large piece of manufacturing equipment), the completed product cannot be moved as it is not feasible (for example a highway) or it is too large (for example a bridge or office block), the layout arrangements is known as fixed position (see Exhibit 7.6). Thus, where the service or product to be provided is in a fixed position, that is, it cannot be moved, it requires staff, equipment, materials and other resources to come to or be brought to the place or site where the service is to be provided or product is to be made.

Exhibit 7.6 Types of layout used by different types of service delivery system and manufacturing process

Types of		
service delivery system	layout	manufacturing process
Non-repeat	Fixed position	Project
Repeat — low volume ↓ high volume	Process or functional	Jobbing Batch
	Service or product	Line Continuous processsing

As a consequence of the fixed position nature of this provision, the layout design requires the scheduling of materials, equipment, skilled staff and other resources to a site and the rescheduling of these to other jobs on completion of their phase of the work or at the end of the job. The consequence is that the capabilities and resources to complete a service or product are brought to and arranged on site, are managed on site and then dismantled or redistributed during and at the end of a task. The layout, therefore, needs to:

- reflect the space requirements of each part of the task while recognizing the varying levels of activity throughout the time involved
- provide for the delivery and storage of materials
- accommodate the staff and equipment needs over the time it takes to provide the service or make the product
- facilitate the movement of staff and equipment on the site
- minimize the total movement of resources on site.

The fixed position layout is complicated by a number of factors including:

- typically there is limited space. When building an office block, the total site is limited in area while needing to cope with the several activities involved. Similarly, when completing the maintenance programme on a large piece of equipment, the space available for accommodating the tasks restricts the optimum layout

- the tasks that make up the service or product will vary in nature and volume during the provision and the layout needs to accommodate these often sizeable differences in requirements

- often the steps involved are uncertain and plans change due to delays. The outcome is that the schedule is rearranged and the layout needs to be designed to cope with these types of changes.

Process or functional layout

The term process or functional layout reflects the fact that the layout arrangement is based on putting together similar processes or functions in one geographical area, then, to be processed, the services (customers or information) or products move to the various process or functional groups in a given order. So, in fixed position layout the resources (for example staff and equipment) move to the point where the service or product is to be provided, while with process or functional layouts the reverse happens – the resources stay still and the service or product moves to them in a given sequence. Once the service or product does not have to be provided or made on site, companies typically prefer to use process or functional layout.

The advantages of this delivery system layout include:

- similar skills are grouped together which allows for skill levels to be enhanced and experience to be transferred.

- the utilization of processes, skilled staff and equipment is improved as accessing the availability of this total resource is made easier as it is grouped in the same area.

- a wide range of services and products can be provided.

- the delivery system can handle many customer requirements at the same time.

As indicated in Exhibit 7.6, a process or functional layout is used for both non-repeat (special) and repeat (standard) services and products. The examples that follow illustrate how the delivery system and layout would work for these types of services and products.

Non-repeat (special) services and products

As these services and products are unique and will not typically be repeated, the skilled person or team undertaking the job will determine and then follow the best sequence of steps to complete the service or product and then access the relevant processes, functions or other resources as appropriate.

In the service sector, the analysis phase of the design and implementation of an IT system would be completed by an information systems specialist. Here, the consultant may initially stay in the same location and would access or compile the relevant data and complete the appropriate analyses to meet the varying outcomes of each phase of the assignment. In addition, when discussions with executives and staff are necessary, the systems consultant would typically meet with them in their own office, area or location. Similarly, analysis of procedures, systems and facilities would typically be completed in the various functions or areas involved. In this way, the skilled person takes a job or task to the appropriate process, completes the work, moves to the next process to complete the next step and so

Exhibit 7.7 Process layout for a tool-making company

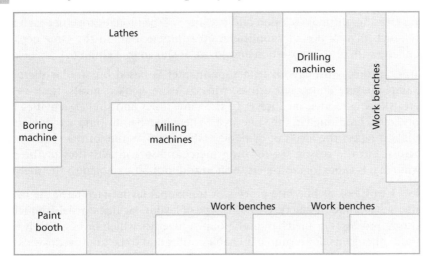

on until the job is completed. A further illustration of a company using a process layout to complete a non-repeat job is given in Exhibit 7.7. This is a tool-making company that builds unique tools, moulds and dies for customers. Having reviewed and discussed the details of a customer's drawing, a skilled toolmaker completes the whole task of machining and building the tool to the design specification required. To do this the toolmaker completes the machining requirements by taking the part-finished die from work bench to machine and from machine to machine to undertake each appropriate step until it is completed. Here, just as with the information systems consultancy example given earlier, both product and skilled person move from process to process until the work is completed.

Now you understand what happens, why does a process or functional layout best suit these requirements? The principal reason is that this layout design enables any skilled person to access the resources (processes or people in a function) in any chosen sequence to complete the whole of the task. In the tool-making example above, there will be several skilled toolmakers machining and building customer-specific tools, moulds or dies. With this layout, each can access a specific resource in the order that best meets the task on hand and, as the sequence of steps will differ by product, the layout must facilitate the use of the various machines and other equipment to meet these various work patterns.

Repeat (standard) services and products

As explained in the last two chapters, when services and products are completed more than once, the higher volumes and repeat nature of these requirements are more appropriately provided by a different delivery system. What is processed (that is, customers, information or products) will impact the people skills and equipment required but the layout of the delivery system will be designed on a process or functional basis (see Exhibit 7.6).

Examples of process layouts for delivering standard services and products include:

- Hospital – the functions in a hospital (for example operating theatres, pharmacy, consulting rooms, reception area, X-ray facilities, wards and laboratories) are laid out functionally. That is, the facilities and staff that constitute pharmacy services will be put together in one department, all operating theatres will similarly be located in the same area and so on.

- **Printing company** – the activities in a printing company that comprise design, plate preparation, ink laboratory and stores, printing and post-printing tasks such as cutting and creasing, slitting, collation and packing will be brought together each in their own area such that all designers and relevant equipment are in the same department, and similarly with plate preparation and so on, as shown in Exhibit 6.4.

- **Supermarket** – the layout in a supermarket is based on similar merchandise (for example bakery items, soft drinks, wines, cheese, cooked meats, fresh vegetables and cereals) being located on shelves in the same aisles and similar activities (for example checkouts) positioned in the same area. Where merchandise and activities are positioned will also reflect the levels of demand, traffic flows, nature of the purchase and similar factors. But the reason for locating merchandise and activities in the same area is twofold: it is easier for customers to shop and for staff to replenish the shelves.

Now let us look at how the process or functional layout facilitates the delivery of the required services and products. With this type of layout, facilities are laid out with like kinds (functions, processes or merchandise) grouped together which brings with it economies of scale and other gains, for example it enables utilization to be improved, keeps skills groups together and reduces investment (due to higher utilization and minimizing unnecessary process, equipment and space duplication) and operating costs. Second, the total service or product is often provided by two or more steps. In such instances the task is broken down into a number of steps and each step is completed by a different process. This is achieved by the customer, information or product going to each function or process group in the appropriate order and the required task is then completed. In some service delivery systems, for example a fast-food restaurant, the total requirement is provided as a single step. But, the principle is the same as in a multi-step provision. The food preparation processes and counter service operation are laid out in their own area. A customer then goes to a server at the counter and is 'processed' (that is, orders, pays and is given the food). For a multi-step process, let's take the example of you going to a hospital with a suspected broken arm. You would typically be 'processed' by the hospital in the following way and with potential delays (queues) between steps, as shown in Exhibit 7.8:

1   Go to hospital reception, queue and then provide details.

2   Go to orthopedic consultant and wait for your turn. Consultant assesses that you have a broken arm and asks you to go for an X-ray for confirmation and details of the break.

3   You queue and then an X-ray is taken of your arm.

4   Return to the consultant with the X-ray plates and wait. Consultant reviews plates and instructs the plaster room on how the arm is to be bound and supported.

5   To plaster room where you wait and then your arm is treated.

6   Back to reception to arrange your next appointment.

As you will see from this, the processes or functions (in this instance, skilled staff and equipment) remain in place and patients (that is, the hospital's customers) move from function to function to be processed. This movement by the customer, information or product is an underlying characteristic of this type of layout design. Furthermore, they will typically wait between steps for a process to become available. In this way, several of the advantages of this type of layout that were highlighted earlier are provided. For example, utilization of skilled staff is enhanced as the layout design requires that patients wait (queue) for skilled staff. In this way these key resources do not have to wait for patients and utilization is thereby increased. Also, this type of layout allows the hospital's delivery system to treat a

Exhibit 7.8 Overview of one delivery system in a hospital based on a process or functional layout

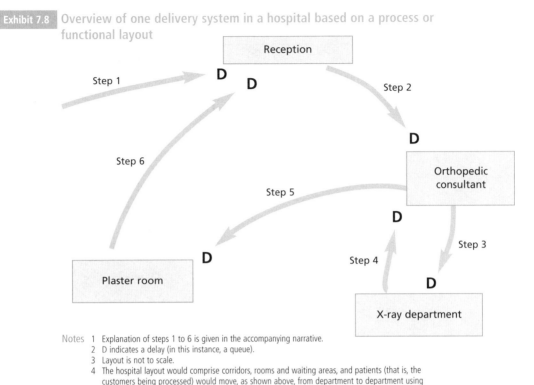

Notes 1 Explanation of steps 1 to 6 is given in the accompanying narrative.
       2 D indicates a delay (in this instance, a queue).
       3 Layout is not to scale.
       4 The hospital layout would comprise corridors, rooms and waiting areas, and patients (that is, the customers being processed) would move, as shown above, from department to department using corridors, stairs and lifts.

wide range of requirements at the same time, with each patient going through their own set of steps. In this way, the system can handle different customer needs requiring different combinations of skilled staff and equipment, with the amount of any resource required at each step being variable and unknown. These characteristics are those associated with low to relatively high volume repeat (standard) services and products.

Similarly, in the example of a supermarket, customers move from aisle to aisle selecting the food items they wish to purchase. This functional layout facilitates the serving of many customers.

In manufacturing, the process layout and the way in which a product is completed follow the same format as the last examples. Similar processes are grouped together in the same geographical area (see Exhibit 7.9). Products are broken down into a number of steps and a product moves from process group to process group to be completed. So, looking at Exhibit 7.9, a product that required moulding, sonic welding, hot roll stamping and final assembly would go through the necessary series of steps with periods of waiting between one step and the next.

Finally, with functional layouts the position of processes may reflect the flow of the services or products through the different steps or stages. This would only be the case where the services or products involved all follow (at least in part) the same sequence. Hence of the examples provided so far:

● Exhibit 6.4, a printing company. You will see when you glance back at this that the functional layout reflects the sequence involved. That is, all products will start with cylinders/plates and paper stores, through printing then possibly to slitting and collation (if required), to packing and on to finished goods.

Exhibit 7.9 Example of a product going through the process layout of a manufacturing company

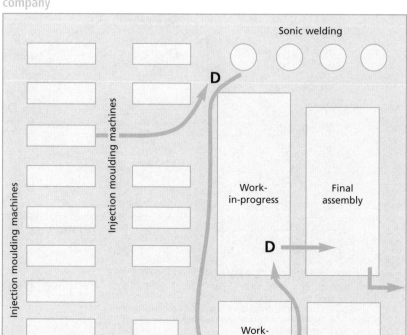

Notes 1 D indicates a delay: a product here is waiting its turn to be processed.
2 ➡ indicates product movement from injection moulding to sonic welding to hot roll stamping to work-in-progress to final assembly.

- Exhibit 7.9 is similar to Exhibit 6.4.

- Exhibit 7.7 on the other hand, does not reflect service/product flow as here products will have very different routings to one another and may, in fact, go back to earlier processes at some stage. This lack of similarity in process sequence is also well illustrated in the hospital example overviewed in Exhibit 7.8. As you can envisage, the sequence of steps for one patient's treatment will differ greatly from that for another patient and consequently the route for patients will also differ.

Service or product layout

Like the last type of layout, this layout type is oriented around similar services or products, but the volumes will be higher, demand patterns would be more stable, the services or products would be standardized and the inputs into the transformation system or operations process would be of a uniform level of quality conformance (that is, they consistently meet the material specification). Line and continuous processing use product layout in manufacturing. As explained in Chapter 5, examples in the service sector are most infrequent, with Dr Svyatoslav Fyoderov's eye microsurgery unit (see Exhibit 5.13) being one of the exceptions.

As the facilities are oriented about the service or product, the steps involved in providing a service or making a product are first determined and then the process is designed to complete each step at a different work station. For example, an assembly line is designed with several work stations and at each of these the parts making up the product are put together in a given order. To design a continuous processing system, for example to refine oil, the steps to complete this task are determined and the process is then designed to complete these in sequence. Both the examples used here illustrate the high volume and standard nature of the products involved (they all go through the same steps in the same sequence). As highlighted before, the high volume justifies the dedicated nature of the investment and the standard nature means that the process design involves the same sequence of steps. Finally, this leads to the fact that both line and continuous processing need to be balanced. That is, the work performed at each station must be balanced (take the same time) with the work at all the other stations. While assembly lines tend to be paced (how long to complete the work at a station) by people, continuous processing systems will be paced by the processing equipment.

Going back now to the Fyoderov eye clinic, the radial keratotomy treatment for myopia (short-sightedness) illustrates all the features of a service-oriented layout. The patients to be treated fit the medical specification for this treatment procedure, the eye operation performed is the same for each patient, the surgeons each complete their designated step in the total procedure, the patients who lie on operating tables are all then indexed one step further and the process continues. At each step the work involved takes a similar time to all the other steps, with the activities monitored on TV screens and the surgeons linked to each other through an audio system.

Other examples include:

- Automobile assembly – the steps to assemble a car form the basis for the process design of an automobile assembly line, with each vehicle passing along the same track where it is systematically built in line with the colour, type, engine size and other options from which customers can select.

- Fast-food restaurant – burger preparation in the back stage of a fast-food restaurant is often designed as a line process. The preparation is separated into a number of steps and each burger is completed by going through each step at a time.

- Self-service restaurant – customers entering a self-service restaurant will walk through the service line and select the food they wish to purchase and pay the bill at the end.

- Petrochemicals – the steps to process oil into a range of chemicals provide the blueprint for the design of a petrochemical plant. The refining process diverts part-processed products into different routes, with each going through its own required set of steps to complete the range of end-products.

Hybrid delivery system layouts

Given the increasing difference in markets, companies have responded by developing alternative delivery systems to reflect these changing demands. One outcome is that companies often choose to rearrange the layout of their facilities to create a better fit to the modified delivery system. Some of the more common examples of these layout redesigns are now discussed. This section reflects on the nature and rationale of the layout changes that go hand in hand with the delivery systems developments.

Cellular layout

As explained earlier, process or functional layouts are based on grouping similar processes or functions together in the same geographical area. Without sufficient volumes to justify the investment involved in a service or product-oriented layout such as line, process or functionally based layouts allow a range of services and products to share skilled staff and equipment thus making sense of the utilization/investment equation. What cells do is mix the process or functional and service or product layouts to create a hybrid as was illustrated earlier in Exhibit 6.18 and has been reproduced here as Exhibit 7.10. A look at this exhibit shows that the cellular layout comprises processes allocated to one of four cells based on the skills and equipment required to make the products within a cell (thus reflecting the service or product layout principle) and with like skills and equipment in a cell positioned in the same geographical area (thus reflecting the process or functional layout principle). Hence it is termed a hybrid.[3]

The same use of the cellular layout is now gaining ground in the service sector, as Case example 7.5 illustrates.

Exhibit 7.10 Cellular layout

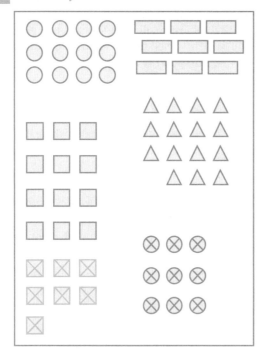
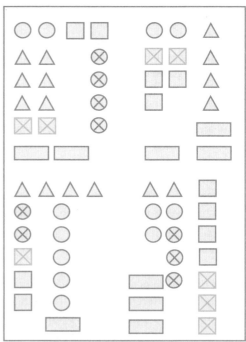

Process or functional layout
Six process types functionally laid out

Cellular layout
Four cells with processing allocated to each cell

Nagare cellular layout

As explained in Chapter 6, the Nagare production system is a derivation of cellular manufacturing. You will see the similarity to a cellular layout when you look back at Exhibit 6.20. This illustrates the change from a process or functional layout to a product-oriented layout. It is designed to facilitate a skilled person to take a product through all its process steps. The

---

Case example 5 **FUNCTIONS AT A TELECOMMUNICATONS COMPANY CALL CENTRE**

A large US telecommunications company organized its call centre on a functional basis. Using three tiers of support groups, customers' correspondence, requests and queries were initially handled at the Tier 1 level. Any issues that could not be resolved here would be passed to a Tier 2 technician. Delays on transfer between Tier 1 and Tier 2 staff frequently occurred and where a Tier 2 technician could not resolve an issue it would be passed back to the Tier 1 originator. This passing back and forth often happened two or more times. The result was that an issue requiring half an hour to resolve would take up to two days before a reply was given to a customer.

The company decided to reconfigure its call centres. Each centre retained four functional areas – inbound (payment collections), outbound (sales), technical support and research agents – and three tiers of support. However, cells were formed to handle specified groups of customers, with two of the three support tiers now contained within each cell. Hand-off between Tier 1 and Tier 2 staff now occurs within a cell and this means that over 90 per cent of customer queries are resolved within a single team leader's span of control. The cell team leader is ultimately responsible for ensuring that every customer query is followed through to a satisfactory conclusion.

Case questions
1 How did the original call centre structure result in delays?
2 How did the cell-based redesign reduce delays?
3 What could be the different ways of routing calls into the cells?
4 What other advantages or opportunities would a cell-based structure offer this company?

---

products in question are of a repeat and low volume nature and are typically produced on a make-to-order basis.

Transfer line layout

For high volume products the hybrid process known as a transfer line is sometimes developed. The process layout is product-oriented, with the basic line process enhanced by the inclusion of systems that automatically complete process steps and are typically self-adjusting for any deviation from the specification. The resulting layout is thus a hybrid between line and continuous processing and has been designed to reflect the high volume, standard nature of the products involved.

Other layout formats

The previous sections have addressed the concepts and issues that relate to the general approach to layout design. This section highlights other dimensions and formats that, while relating to more specific delivery system layouts, provide additional approaches and insights to meet the needs of particular markets and organizational requirements.

Flexing process layouts to reflect varying levels of demand

In many companies, sales demand can vary significantly. To meet these changes in activity levels, companies incorporate these factors, where possible, into their layout design. For example:

- Car assembly plants are often able to increase the number of positions on an assembly line layout thus decreasing the work content per station and thereby allowing operations to increase the speed of the process and raise output levels.

Exhibit 7.11 Delivery system layouts permitting adaptations for peak and non-peak demand periods

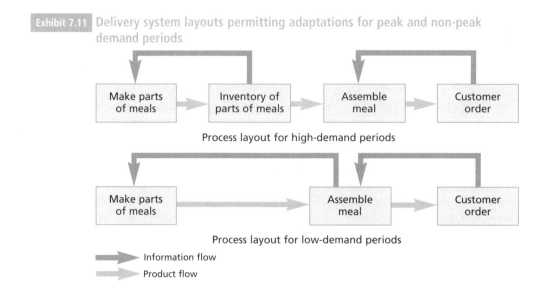

Process layout for high-demand periods

Process layout for low-demand periods

→ Information flow
→ Product flow

- Bank and post office branch layouts have several more teller positions than are normally required so enabling them to 'flex' capacity in line with queue lengths.
- Some fast-food restaurants have developed a process layout that can be altered to meet the requirements of peak and non-peak sales periods, as shown in Exhibit 7.11.

Exhibit 7.12 Mr James introduces his version of hot desking

© AMD Publishing

Flexible office layouts

For jobs such as consultants, service engineers and sales staff, the need for an office layout with dedicated desks occupying expensive floor space is often unnecessary. Companies now provide an office where the layout comprises a number of desks that can be used by staff on an as-needed basis. The combination of variable space to work and somewhere to hang a coat provides the alternative layout described as the 'virtual office', 'hot offices' and 'hot desks'.

Examples of other dimensions of the concept of flexible office layouts are mobile desk base units that can be put out of the way when the owner is out and computer screens that descend from the ceiling on demand. Add to these changes the growing trend towards flex-itime, working from home and the increasing use of part-time staff, then the need for a more flexible office layout to accommodate fewer permanent staff will be a growing phenomenon of the new millennium. Arriving at the office, picking up their personalized mobile phone from the recharging rack and then finding a place to work is the layout design that many staff will be using in the future.

Impact of IT on delivery systems and layouts

IT developments have not only reduced costs and lead times within systems and procedures but have also enabled companies to redesign many of these delivery systems. These changes also bring layout changes, as the following examples illustrate:

- Automatic banking – high street banks are continuing to cut costs by automating more of their services. ATMs are now the principal way of withdrawing cash from a bank account. Increasingly, automated branches are adding video disc displays selling insurance, providing details of loans and screens offering share quotations. In parts of Europe and the USA fully automatic branches are replacing existing arrangements. These offer all the usual customer services but no tellers. These changes necessitate layouts that accommodate these new delivery systems. The space needs to provide for varying numbers of customers, informal queries, areas to complete paying-in slips and the like, sufficient space to allow secure transactions to take place and a layout that allows access when the branch is closed.

- Call centres – telephone access has had a significant impact on the delivery of several services over the last 20 years. Sectors such as financial services, utilities, hotels and travel have made extensive use of telephone-based provision through call centre oper-

 **Exhibit 7.13** Layout of a typical call centre

ations. The principle on which these are built is that customers telephone the centre (usually free or local rate charges) and either call centre staff or computer systems handle queries and requests in a fast and customized manner. Call centre staff are linked to sophisticated telephone and computer systems, with the latter providing up-to-date information on the current position and past transactions of customer accounts and dealings so that requests can be handled promptly and accurately. Telephone calls handled by a computerized system use either voice or key pad responses to questions or to complete a transaction.

Extended opening hours facilitate the use of these services particularly for customers who are unable to visit the high street branches or offices of the service provider. Exhibit 7.13 illustrates the layout features that typify a call centre. With the service delivery system now front-office based and opening hours up to 24 hours a day, layouts need to be able to meet peak demands and the several staff changeovers and staff combinations that will occur.

At this point take some time out by looking at Case example 7.6 and review the case questions.

Case example 6   BUILDING COMMUNAL LEARNING SPACES AT VARIOUS NORTH AMERICAN UNIVERSITIES

North American universities are constructing a whole series of new buildings to house their existing business schools, with the underlying design aimed at encouraging creative, open, flexible, informal and interactive learning. To do so, these new building layouts include 'forums', 'marketplaces' and other communal areas. Current learning approaches mean that students spend much more time working together on campus and the new layout designs reflect this. Here are a few examples:

● **University of Chicago, Graduate School of Business** opened in September 2004 at a cost of £78 million; the layout allocates just over 30 per cent of the 415,000 square feet facility to space for students with lounges, a dining area, 34 group study rooms, 18 classrooms for MBAs and PhDs and 36 interview rooms where corporate recruiters can meet students.

● York University's Schulich School of Business in Toronto moved to a new £43 million, 335,000 square feet home in late 2003. The basic layout is designed to increase the level of interaction between faculty and students by, for example, making it impossible to get into or out of the

school without passing through the main space known as the marketplace. In addition, the marketplace is packed with everything from high-tech information screens around the lobby to a cluster of internet cafés and shops.

● **Wharton's Jon M Huntsman Hall** opened in September 2003 and comprises 324,000 square feet at a cost of £90 million. Here, lecture halls, study areas and classrooms brim over with technological connections including high speed networking and video conferencing that links the Philadelphia campus with Wharton West in San Francisco. Classroom podiums all have a microphone, computer keyboard, audiovisual control system and laptop computer link-up. Multi-screen systems facilitate video projection and teleconferencing, with all video and audio equipment linked to the internet. The 57 group study rooms are equally geared up.

● **At the Ohio State University's Max Fisher Business School**, the final phase of a six building development project is the residence for the college's executive education programme and includes a 151 bedroom hotel, an executive education centre and an upmarket restaurant.

Case questions
1 Buildings are a big part of moving forward. How do the above examples illustrate this?
2 How does the space created by the new designs challenge business schools to consider alternative ways of doing things?
3 Building layouts can have a big impact on human behaviour. How?

Detailed layout design

Having selected the appropriate basic layout, the next step is to design a detailed layout. The objectives of this phase are to decide:

- where to position the staff, processes, equipment and other facilities involved in providing the services and products
- the position and size of the other facilities that are not part of the delivery system such as meeting areas, rest rooms and cafeterias
- the number and dimension of other aspects such as entrances, exits, emergency routes, walkways, corridors, stairways and elevators
- the space to be allocated to each of the above.

In parallel with the detailed design phase, the steps involved in providing the services or making the products, the sequence to be followed and where these steps are ideally positioned will need to be determined. As space restrictions or layout advantages may influence the preferred sequence and position of the steps involved, the process routes will need to be considered at the same time as finalizing the layout and then be integrated into the detailed design.

The features of good layouts

Before discussing the techniques and approaches we can use to help in detailed layout design, let's first look at the aspects and features to be considered when developing a good detailed layout. The list below provides a comprehensive review of what needs to be addressed but the relative importance of these will change depending on the type of organization involved:

- System flow charting – system flow charting is a visual aid to help determine and clarify the sequence of steps involved in providing services and products in parallel with the detailed design. With service delivery system design, the flow chart (also known as a 'service blueprint'[4] would also establish what is known as 'the line of visibility' that separates front-office and back-office activities.
- Use of space – identifying space requirements is a prerequisite to developing a good layout. It helps ensure the effective use of the office, building or warehouse space available while accommodating any possible future long-term flexibility as needs change.
- Use of equipment – decisions about the equipment to be used including elevators, conveyors and automatic carts.
- Cost of movement – in many delivery systems an overriding objective of the detailed layout is to minimize the distance travelled and hence the overall cost of movement. In others, the overriding objective would be to maximize sales revenue by, for example, routing customers through a retail store in such a way as to increase exposure to the products on offer.
- Health and safety – a key feature in good layout design is to incorporate essential health and safety features (for example emergency exits and access points) while also designing-in other dimensions that will contribute to the overall health and safety considerations for both staff and customers, for example adequate lighting and ventilation, width of aisles, corridors and walkways and the number and size of entrances and exits.
- Aesthetics and the quality of the working environment – linked to the last point are

decisions that will affect the quality of the staff's working environment, including the levels of natural light, wall colours, use of planters, height of partitions and ways to increase airflow, reduce noise and provide privacy.

- Communications – a good layout needs to facilitate essential verbal and visual communication between the parts of an organization and different steps in a delivery system or process. Proximity of staff and the essential nature of the layout design (for example open plan versus enclosed offices) are typical of the features to be considered.

- Image and brand – some organizations use the detailed layout of their outlets as one way to reinforce the image and brand of the business. Fast-food companies such as McDonald's and Burger King and hotel chains such as Budget Inns and Holiday Inn Express are examples of this practice. Having the same entrances, reception areas, room layouts and front-office arrangements from decor to carpets and fittings to furniture provides familiarity for the customer, maintains standards (including franchisees) while reinforcing the company's image and brand.

Fixed position layouts

Having reviewed the aspects and features to be considered when developing a good detailed design, let's now look at specific detailed layouts. The first of these is a fixed position layout. The techniques and approaches for addressing this type of layout are not well developed and often the layout issues are addressed on a somewhat ad hoc basis because of the level of uncertainty inherent in this type of service or product provision.

Even where the task has been completed before (for example building set house designs on an estate), many variables are liable to change. Delays in material shipments, design alterations and adverse weather conditions are some of the dimensions that can create uncertainty. Add to this the limited space on site, the changing availability of this space as the work progresses (for example an area may be available for material storage at one stage but has been designated as a roadway or site for a building at a later stage), the varying volumes of materials and storage areas required and the changing priorities as a job progresses create uncertainty and impact layout decisions. Similarly, in a management consultancy assignment, the availability of suitable on-site office space at a client's premises and the changing need for and availability of consultancy staff throughout an assignment, particularly where the orientation of the assignment changes, make what ought to be relatively simple layout decisions more complex.

These uncertainties seldom yield an optimum solution, as the decisions are often more expedient than analytical and are handled on an ad hoc basis that reflects the position, progress and current dynamics of the task and situation.

Process or functional layouts

The objective is to arrange these processes or functions in line with the aspects and features of a detailed layout design described earlier.

The procedure involves the following steps:

- Clarify the total space on hand and the costs of any possible extensions
- Identify any constraints that exist and the possibility of reducing or eliminating these and the costs involved
- Determine the area required by the different facilities, processes and functions

- Determine the size of other facilities that are not part of the delivery system such as meeting areas, rest rooms and cafeterias
- Assess the number, size and position of the entrances, exits, corridors, gangways and walkways required
- Assess the direction and flow of staff, information and materials through the processes and functions.

The detailed design of these layouts is made more difficult by the large number of different services or products typically handled by the same set of processes or functions. As often one of the fundamental tasks in designing these layouts is to minimize the cost of movement, determining where the different processes or functions are best positioned relative to one another is essential. The common approaches to help resolve this step in the procedure are now described.

Load, movement or trip frequency charts

To help in the evaluation of alternative process or functional layouts, use is made of load, movement or trip frequency charts. This approach analyses the existing number of movements or trips between the processes or functions involved. In the example in Exhibit 7.14, this is titled Step 1. So, the number of movements or trips from Department 1 to 2 was 12 and the number from Department 2 to 1 was 20 and so on.

Exhibit 7.14 Collecting data using a load, movement or trip frequency chart

Step 1 – Analysis of # trips

From \ To	1	2	3	4	5	6
1		12	26	44	2	18
2	20		10	–	41	20
3	14	6		–	60	15
4	29	–	–		–	3
5	6	40	51	–		68
6	32	25	17	2	72	

Step 2 – Distance travelled (m)

From \ To	1	2	3	4	5	6
1		9	15	28	10	16
2	9		20	16	38	2
3	15	20		12	8	25
4	20	16	12		18	17
5	10	26	8	18		19
6	16	2	25	17	29	

Step 3 – Combine these two to give the total distance travelled (m)

From \ To	1	2	3	4	5	6	Total
1		108	390	1232	20	288	2038
2	180		200	–	1558	40	1978
3	210	120		–	480	375	1185
4	580	–	–		–	51	631
5	60	1040	408	–		1292	2800
6	512	50	425	34	2088		3109
Total	1542	1318	1423	1266	4146	2046	11741

The next step is to select the dimension that the detailed layout design seeks to mini-mize, for example total distance travelled or total cost of the movements. In Exhibit 7.14, distance travelled is the dimension to minimize and Step 2 provides this data for the exist-ing layout. In most instances the distance travelled between two departments one way is the same as the distance travelled going in the opposite direction. However, in three instances this is not the case due to a one-way system introduced for reasons of safety:

From/To	1 to 4	2 to 5	5 to 6
Distance (m)	28	38	19
From/To	4 to 1	5 to 2	6 to 5
Distance (m)	20	26	29

If the distance travelled both ways between all departments was the same, the procedure could be simplified by combining the number of trips between Departments 1 and 2 and Departments 2 and 1 and so on, as shown in Exhibit 7.15 and then using the total trips in subsequent calculations. However, it would always be best first to complete the analysis given in Step 1 of Exhibit 7.14 as subsequent layout options may need to use this data split.

The outcome of this analysis is given in Step 3 of Exhibit 7.14. The 633 trips involved a total distance travelled of 11,741 metres. This would then be used as a benchmark against which to measure alternative layouts and the gains to be made in terms of reduced travel distances. When considering possible changes, this factor as well as aspects such as the cost of changing an existing layout would then help to evaluate alternatives.

Exhibit 7.15 Simplified analysis of # trips in Step 1, Exhibit 7.14

To From	Department					
	1	2	3	4	5	6
1		32	40	73	8	50
2			16	–	81	45
3				–	111	32
4					–	5
5						140
6						

(Department label on left axis)

Relationship chart

A second approach to help in detailed layout design that also uses a matrix format is the rela-tionship chart. This helps identify the relative closeness of one department to another. As the example in Exhibit 7.16 illustrates, this approach makes use of a priority code to show the preferred proximity of two departments (shown as the 'degree of closeness') and a justi-fication code specifying the 'reason' for the desired proximity.

As the complexity of the detailed layout design task increases, these approaches to detailed layout solutions are unable to cope with the number of multiple flow patterns and constraints involved. Several computerized methods are available to overcome these limita-tions. In a way similar to that used by the manual methods, they use logical rules to list alter-natives and then evaluate them against relevant criteria. The link to a computerized system allows more variables to be included, refinements to alternatives to be assessed and more layout alternatives to be considered. Some of the 3D layout packages available include:

● Catia PlantLayout2
● E-factory
● Plant 4-D
● Plantspace
● Smart Plant.

Exhibit 7.16 A relationship chart used in the detailed layout design of a hospital

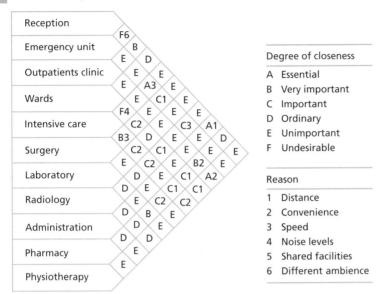

Degree of closeness

A Essential
B Very important
C Important
D Ordinary
E Unimportant
F Undesirable

Reason

1 Distance
2 Convenience
3 Speed
4 Noise levels
5 Shared facilities
6 Different ambience

For those wishing to study these computer-based approaches further, website references[5] are given at the end of the chapter.

Service or product layouts

As explained earlier, this type of layout is oriented around similar services or products and its appropriateness is based on the following assumptions:

- the services or products are standardized and involve the same sequence of activities
- the volumes are sufficient to give adequate levels of staff or process utilization
- demand is stable and predictable.

Invariably, the services or products using this type of layout would involve a multi-step process. Two essential layout design outcomes of this are:

- the layout design will mirror this sequence of steps
- the work content at each step will be similar in length – the concept of 'line balancing'.

Some high volume repeat service delivery systems and both line and continuous processes in manufacturing use this type of layout. As with a fabrication line and continuous processing plant, the machines or equipment make the products, then the work performed at one machine or stage in the process must match that performed at the next step in the process and so on. In assembly lines where parts of products are put together and in service delivery systems where people provide the services, the work content at one step must match the work content at the next step and so on. Hence the concept of line balancing. If the work content at each step is not similar, delays and waiting will occur. Exhibits 7.17, 7.18 and 7.19 provide an example.

Of concern to the cafeteria staff were the long queues that formed at lunch times and also in the early evening when most students took their main meals of the day. On checking, the

Exhibit 7.17 Cafeteria process times

Step	Activity	Served by self	Served by staff	Average time (seconds)
1	Collect tray/take water	✓		15
2	Select cold drink	✓		15
3	Select salad	✓		10
4	Select dessert	✓		10
5	Serve main course		✓	30
6	Serve vegetables		✓	20
7	Pour hot drinks		✓	15
8	Pay cashier		✓	55

Exhibit 7.18 Cafeteria flow diagram – current arrangements

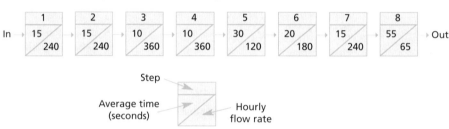

Exhibit 7.19 Cafeteria flow diagram – proposed arrangements

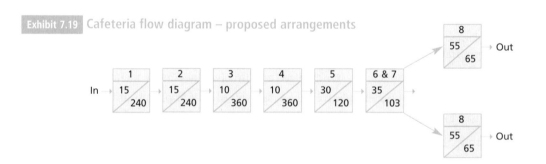

team found that the work was unevenly divided between the four staff. A flow diagram (see Exhibit 7.18) clearly illustrated this. A glance at the hourly flow rates for the staff providing Steps 5 to 8 shows the imbalance of the current arrangements. The bottleneck is at Step 8. Here the flow rate is 65 students per hour, almost half that of the next lowest rate, 120 students/hour at Step 5. Bottlenecks are due to the imbalance of capacity in relation to the amount of time taken to complete the task at one step or stage in a delivery system or process compared to that at other steps or stages. Here it is staff capacity at Step 8 in relation to the time to complete the 'pay cashier' task compared to the same ratio at other steps.

The team recognized that to increase the flow rate an additional cashier would need to be added. If Steps 6 and 7 were combined and undertaken by one member of staff, this would release someone to create an additional cashier slot. As the flow diagram in Exhibit 7.19 shows, the flow rates at the four staffed positions are now more in balance and the hourly flow rate increased from 65 (the bottleneck or limiting factor at Step 8 in the current arrangements) to 103, with the bottleneck or limiting factor now at Steps 6 and 7. The two staff now at Step 8 together can handle 130 students per hour.

The above example illustrates how, in principle, line balancing works. As you would imagine in high volume manufacturing or chemical plants, the line balancing requirements of these processes would be more finely tuned than the cafeteria example above. This would involve small adjustments and readjustments to the process layout until the optimum balance had been achieved and the line or continuous process would then be designed and built in order to maximize daily output and hence improve productivity and reduce the unit cost of the product. But the principles involved would be the same.[6]

Hybrid layouts

As explained in Chapters 5 and 6, hybrid systems will have their origins in one of the basic types of process. Of the four hybrids illustrated in the last chapter, three have their origins in a batch process and the fourth in a line process, as shown in Exhibit 7.20.

In horticulture, when grafting one tree onto the rootstock of another tree to produce a hybrid, it is the latter tree type that is the dominant factor in the resulting mix. This is also the case with process hybrids. Thus, the techniques and approaches used to help develop a detailed design for process or functional and service or product layouts will also be used for the hybrids which have a similar process origin.

Exhibit 7.20 Hybrids and their process origins

Type of hybrid	Process origin	Approach to layout design
Cells Linked batch Nagare production system	Batch	Process or functional
Transfer line	Line	Service or product

Reflections

Where best to locate and how best to arrange the people and processes within a facility and throughout the delivery system impact both sales and costs. Consequently, to reflect both the external, customer/market and the internal, operational dimensions in these key decisions is essential. As with many operations investments, their large and fixed nature embodies high costs and long timescales to change, so getting it right needs care and analysis.

Though expediency will often play a part in location and layout choices, organizations need to be aware of any sub-optimal aspects of their decisions and factor these into their expectations and day-to-day running of the business. Expectations will then be grounded in reality and performance measured against attainable targets. In that way control will be exercised and developments set in the context of the short- and long-term objectives of the business.

Key Elements of Location and Layout

Linking the topics of location and layout enabled you to review two distinct yet related questions. Distinct in that location concerns where best to site a facility whereas layout concerns how best to arrange staff, processes and equipment within the facility. But they are related, in that the topics address the two parts of the key decision of how best to position facilities in relation to undertaking the operations task to meet the needs of a business.

The key elements in the section on location included:

- highlighting the different levels at which location decisions may need to be taken from that of continent or region down to the site itself.

- the factors to be taken within these choices were then categorized. Those of a general nature looked at broad-based issues that could influence or even override other factors such as the origin of existing sites and politically based constraints and those that had economic implications such as market access.

- a number of specific factors such as infrastructure and proximity to markets and suppliers were then discussed in relation to each level at which location decisions may need to be made.

- the final section reviewed, with examples, the weighted factor and centre of gravity methods of helping make these key decisions.

The key elements in the section on layout covered the following topics:

- relevant background factors such as the availability of space and meeting the need for future flexibility.

- an explanation of the basic types of layout followed – fixed position, process or functional and service or product and these were related to the type of service delivery system and manufacturing process. Examples were given and a link back to other illustrations in Chapters 5 and 6 was provided.

- the development of hybrid delivery system layouts was then explained and illustrated.

- the final section looked at approaches to detailed layout design. A general section on the features of good layouts was followed by an overview of detailed design approaches used in the three basic layouts. These included an explanation of layout issues with fixed position, the use of frequency charts and relationship charts for process or functional layouts and line balancing within service and product layouts.

Self-check

1 The levels of decision when locating a business include:
   a The region and country ☐
   b The area or city and site ☐
   c Both a and b ☐

2 The following are changing the levels of freedom as to where an organization can locate:
   a New countries are opening up ☐
   b Reduced levels of currency fluctuations ☐
   c Technology developments ☐

3 Competitive clustering refers to:
   a Market saturation ☐
   b Customer ability to choose from a number of options (for example hotel accommodation or restaurants) ☐
   c Neither of these ☐

4 Which of the following is a technique used in deciding where to locate?
  a Weighted-factor method ☐
  b Centre of gravity method ☐
  c Both a and b ☐

5 Which of the following is a basic type of layout?
  a Fixed position layout ☐
  b Sequential layout ☐
  c Multi-step layout ☐

6 A typical hospital provides an example of which of the following types of layout?
  a Service layout ☐
  b Functional layout ☐
  c Repeat service layout ☐

7 A self-service restaurant provides an example of which of the following types of layout?
  a Service layout ☐
  b Functional layout ☐
  c Repeat service layout ☐

8 A trip frequency chart is also known as:
  a A load frequency chart ☐
  b A movement frequency chart ☐
  c Both a and b ☐

9 The purpose of a relationship chart is to:
  a calculate the distance between one department and another ☐
  b Identify the relative closeness of one department to another ☐
  c Neither of these ☐

10 Line balancing refers to:
  a Keeping the design of a line process flat so as to maximize the use of gravity rollers ☐
  b To balance the work content (time) across all steps in a process ☐
  c Neither of these ☐

Study activities

Discussion questions

1 Select a service outlet and identify the good and bad points of its chosen location.

2 Review the layout of a high street branch of three different banks. List the principal similarities and differences of each layout. Why do you think these similarities and differences exist?

3 Lord Sieff, when CEO of Marks & Spencer, the UK-based clothing store, is reputed to have said: 'There are three important factors in retailing – location, location and location.' Why would such a comment be made?

4 What are the advantages and disadvantages of a qualitative (as opposed to a quantitative) approach in location choices?

5 One location adage is: 'Manufacturers locate near their resources while retailers locate near their customers.' Discuss.

6 Contrast the location of a food distributor with one of the supermarkets to which it delivers products. Which important factors are similar and which are disimilar in their respective choice of location?

7 Review the layout of a service organization of your own choice and identify examples of 'The features of good layouts' given in this chapter.

8 What are the advantages and disadvantages of hot desking?

9 Complete a similar exercise to that given in Exhibits 7.18 and 7.19. How well balanced is your cafeteria service delivery system? What improvements could you suggest?

Assignments

1 As a team of three, select two supermarkets and individually assess them against the criteria listed in the section 'Specific factors influencing location decisions – the choice of site'. Then review each of your individual ratings against each others, discuss and list the key areas of agreement and disagreement.

2 As a team of three, individually select one of the following facilities to review: a large retail chemist, a large bookstore and a multiplex cinema.
   (a) In your team agree for each location the factors to be used to review each site.
   (b) As individuals assess one of the three locations using the agreed factors.
   (c) Discuss the three sets of findings and then identify the two most important factors that each facility shares and the two most important factors that are facility-specific.

3 Complete a similar exercise to the last assignment, but this time analyse the layout of each location with particular reference to customer flows and the type of layout used. Compare and contrast your results. What were the key determinants on layout design for each outlet?

4 A US-based engineering firm has been awarded a contract to build the assembly and fabricating facilities for a new automobile plant in Mexico. The need to complete the project on time is critical, given the proposed vehicle launch, and, as with all such assignments, staying within budget is essential. For these reasons the project manager needs to be continuously kept up to date. The client has assigned its own on-site staff to handle issues as they arise. The desired relationships for the specialist areas involved in completing the project are given below. The space allocated to the project team comprises an office for each of the seven sections (see below), together with an office for the client's own staff.
   (a) Using a relationship chart complete a suggested layout.
   (b) Give reasons for your layout proposal.
   (c) Why do the reasons above differ to the reasons used in the chapter example, Exhibit 7.16?

5 Electronic Controls International (ECI), a US-based technology group, has narrowed down its location choices to four possible sites in Europe. ECI will need to train relevant staff, and the key factors, their weights and ratings for each location are shown in the table opposite. High scores represent favourable values.
   (a) Calculate the weighted-factor score for each of the four sites.
   (b) Which site would you choose?
   (c) Would you reach the same conclusion if the weightings for operating costs and labour costs were reversed?

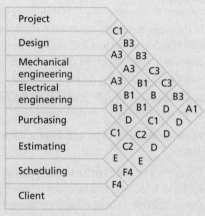

Project							
	C1						
Design	B3						
	A3	B3					
Mechanical engineering	A3	C3					
	A3	B1	C3				
Electrical engineering	B1	B	B3				
	B1	B1	D	A1			
Purchasing	D	C1	D				
	C1	C2	D				
Estimating	C2	D					
	E	E					
Scheduling	F4						
	F4						
Client							

Degree of closeness

A	Essential
B	Very important
C	Important
D	Ordinary
E	Unimportant
F	Undesirable

Reason

1	Convenience
2	Shared facilities
3	Day-to-day working
4	Potential interference
5	Different ambience

The eight offices are of similar size and comprise four offices on both sides of the same corridor and facing each other

Factor	Weighting	Location			
		A	B	C	D
Staff availability	15	7	8	7	8
Operating costs	25	8	6	8	6
Government incentives	15	8	8	7	6
Land, construction, other set-up costs	15	7	6	7	7
Labour costs	10	8	8	6	6
Local technical infrastructure	10	4	7	8	7
Transport	10	4	8	8	7

6 The accountancy firm Thomas and Mason comprises six main sections. Due to the growth of the business over the last five years, the partnership is planning to move into new premises. These comprise six offices of equal size on each side of a corridor, as shown opposite. The distance between the six offices is shown below, as are the number of trips between each sector. From this information, assign each of the six sections to an office in a way that minimizes the total distance travelled.

Office layout

Corridor

	Office	1	2	3	4	5	6
Distance between offices (metres)	1	–	8	16	24	16	8
	2		–	8	16	8	16
	3			–	8	16	24
	4				–	8	16
	5					–	8
	6						–

	Office	1	2	3	4	5	6
# trips between offices	1	–	26	31	82	64	14
	2		–	45	29	40	101
	3			–	20	39	27
	4				–	30	46
	5					–	56
	6						–

Exploring further

Almanza, BA, Kotschevar, LH and Terrell, ME *Food Service Planning: Layout, Design and Equipment*, 4th edn, Prentice Hall, Upper Saddle River, NJ (1999).

Ardel, T 'Site selection tools dig data', *Transportation and Distribution*, **37**(6) (1996), pp. 77–81.

Bartness, AD 'The plant location puzzle', *Harvard Business Review*, **72**(2) (1994).

Brandon, JA *Cellular Manufacturing: Integrated Technology and Management*, John Wiley, New York (1996).

Craig, CS, Ghosh, A and McLafferty, S 'Models of the retail location process: a review', *Journal of Retailing*, **60**(1) (1986), pp. 5–36.

Drezner, Z *Facility Location: A Survey of Applications and Methods*, Springer-Verlag, Secaucus, NJ (1995).

Ferdows, K 'Making the most of foreign factories', *Fortune*, March–April (1997), pp. 73–88.

Francis, RL, McGinnis LF Jr and White, JA *Facilities Layout and Location: An Analytical Approach*, 3rd edn, Prentice Hall, Upper Saddle River, NJ (1998).

Green, TJ and Sadowski, RP 'A review of cellular manufacturing assumptions, advantages and design techniques', *Journal of Operations Management*, **4**(2) (1984).

Heim, C 'From front to back with e-business, *APICS – The Performance Advantage*, **11**(2) (2001), pp. 28–31.

Houshyar, A and White, B 'Comparison of solution procedures to the facility location problem', *Computers & Industrial Engineering*, **32**(1) (1997), pp. 77–87.

Hyer, NL and Brown, KH 'The discipline of real cells', *Journal of Operations Management*, **17**(2) (1999), pp. 557–74.

Karlsson, C 'Radically new production systems', *International Journal of Operations and Production Management*, **16**(1) (1996).

Maister, DH 'The psychology of waiting times', Harvard Reprint No 9–684–064, May 1984.

Mellor, RD and Gan, KY 'The facility layout problem: recent and emerging trends and perspectives', *Journal of Manufacturing Systems*, **29**(5) (1996).

Owen, R 'Modeling future factories', *IIE Solutions*, August (2001), pp. 24–35.

Phillips, E 'Manufacturing plant layout: Fundamentals and fine points of optimum facility design', Society of Manufacturing Engineers (1997).

Price, WL and Turcotte, M 'Locating a blood bank', *Interfaces*, **16**(5) (1986), pp. 17–26.

Render, B, Stair, RM and Hanna, M *Quantitative Analysis for Management*, 8th edn, Prentice Hall, Upper Saddle River, NJ (2003).

Schmenner, RW 'Service firm location decisions: some mid-western evidence', *International Journal of Service Industry Management*, **5**(3) (1994), pp. 49 and 52.

Schmenner, RW 'The location decision of new services' in Fitzsimmons, JA and Fitzsimmons, MJ (eds) *New Service Development*, Sage, Thousand Oaks, CA (2000) pp. 216–38.

Teicholz, E *Facility Design and Management Handbook*, McGraw-Hill, New York (2001).

Notes and references

1 Kimes, SE and Fitzsimmons, JA 'Selecting profitable hotel sites at La Quinta Motor Inns', *Interfaces*, **20**(2) (1990), pp. 12–20.

2 For a comprehensive overview of location models refer to Brandeau, ML and Chiu, SS 'An overview of represented problems in location research', *Management Science* **35**(6) (1984), pp. 648–74.

3 Shambu, G, Suresh, NC and Pegels, CC 'Performance evaluation of cellular manufacturing systems', *International Journal of Operations and Production Management* **16**(8) (1996).

4 Shostack, GL 'Designing services that deliver', *Harvard Business Review*, January/February (1984), pp. 133–9; Hunt, VD 'Process mapping', Harvard Reprint No 9–693–065, November (1992).

5 Website details for the listed examples of 3D layout tools are: Catia PlantLayout2 (www.delmia.com); E-factory (www.eds.com); Plant 4-D (www.cea.com); Plantspace (www.bentley.com); Smart Plant (www.intergraph.com).

6 More detailed reviews of approaches to line balancing include Steyn, PG 'Scheduling multi-model production systems', *Business Management*, **8**(1) (1977); Gunther, RE, Johnson, GD and Peterson, RS 'Currently practised formulations of the assembly line balance problem', *Journal of Operations Management* **13**(3) (1983); Mabs, GH 'Assembly line balancing – let's remove the mystery', *Journal of Industrial Engineering*, May (1990).

Part 3

Managing and Controlling the Operations System

book map

Part

1
- 1 Managing Operations
- 2 Operations Strategy
- 3 Managing People

PROCESSES

2

INPUTS

OUTPUTS

CUSTOMERS

SUPPLIERS

- 4 Designing and Developing Services & Products
- 5 Designing Service Delivery Systems
- 6 Designing Manufacturing Processes
- 7 Location and Layout
- 8 Managing Capacity
- 9 Technology Developments
- 10 Operations Scheduling and Execution
- 11 Managing Quality

3
- 12 Managing Inventory
- 13 Managing the Supply Chain
- 14 Process and Delivery System Reliability and Maintenance

4
- 15 Time and Productivity
- 16 Improving Operations

5
- Managing Operations in Practice: Long Case Studies

Managing Capacity

Outline of chapter

Having sufficient capacity ensures that customers are served and products made in line with business plans and schedules. Too little results in delays and customers' expectations not being met. Too much incurs unnecessary costs. Therefore, effectively managing this core element of operations is critical to the continued success of an organization.

Why is managing capacity important?

Executive overview

This chapter provides an understanding of how capacity is measured and what the statements of capacity look like before addressing the planning and management of capacity and the systems for doing this. The order of the principal sections is as follows:

- **Capacity** – measurement, definitions and expressions of output are discussed. In order to further help your understanding of these aspects, examples from both the service and manufacturing sectors are provided.

- **Defining capacity** – factors affecting the definition of capacity including make vs buy, service/product range and the service delivery system or manufacturing process chosen to complete the task.

- **Determining how much capacity** – when determining capacity, both demand- and capacity-related issues need to be addressed.

- **Planning and managing capacity** – the essential task of matching capacity levels to demand is discussed and the factors of uncertainty and timescales are reviewed in the context of alternative approaches and execution.

- **Resource planning** – typically looking some two to five years ahead, this embraces general issues such as global capacity through to factors influencing the choice of region or country.

- **Rough-cut planning** – typically concerns the one- to two-year time frame and details the options available to achieve the plan.

- **Managing demand and capacity** – this section looks at ways of managing demand (for example through changing demand patterns, using service or product design features and scheduling) and managing capacity (for example through short-term adjustments and flexible work patterns).

Finally, this chapter addresses the important operations perspectives of capacity investment decisions that need to be considered by a business. By taking this orientation it is recognized that other aspects (outside the scope of this book) need to form part of these decisions. Notable among these is investment appraisal that covers the various ways in which the necessary financial assessment of investments can be made.[1]

Introduction

Capacity comprises the resources to serve customers, process information or make products and is a mix of the people, systems, equipment and facilities needed to meet the services or products involved. A bank needs staff to serve customers, IT systems to process transactions and cash machines to enable customers to draw out cash from their accounts. Similarly, a manufacturing company needs people and processes to make the products it sells. These elements constitute capacity. Consequently, when organizations develop their short- and long-term business objectives, one important consideration concerns the provision of appropriate levels of capacity to meet current and future sales. In turn, these capacity decisions will need to relate to:

- **delivery systems and process capability** – to ensure that the technical specification of the service or product can be met
- **volumes** – how many services to be processed or products to be made. Simple though it seems, this is a challenging task.

The capability provision will vary depending on the nature and range of service and product designs involved. Similarly, actual and forecast sales will determine how much capacity is needed. However, the uncertainty of forecasts and the certainty of reality will continue to create situations of false starts, underutilization of capacity or an inability to cope with actual demand. Furthermore, capacity considerations in service industries and the perishable nature of service capacity create their own set of difficulties. All in all, these variables and uncertainties create a challenging operations task that needs to be well managed for its own sake (it is sizeable and expensive) while meeting the needs of customers.

The costs incurred by investing forward when increased sales do not materialize and the lost sales involved in not being able to meet demand support both argument and counterargument for alternative business strategies concerning whether capacity investment should lead or follow demand. Even successful strategies place substantial strain on organizations as they attempt to change direction. To be successful therefore requires responses to be coordinated at both the strategic and tactical levels.

The initial steps in capacity investment will always command corporate attention. New markets, new customer contracts, new services and new products are high profile by nature, while decisions concerning additional staff and new plant, equipment, buildings and site locations are characterized by investments of large size. As such, this phase is approached with thoroughness and care due to the vetting and control exercised in corporate appraisal systems and the level of executive self-interest in making sound decisions that normally accompany such proposals. And rightly so.

Similarly, when companies need to change existing capacity levels in either growth or downsizing scenarios, the same degree of rigour needs to be applied.[2] While these decisions may not gain the same level of corporate attention as initial investments tend to attract, the outcomes are the same. Delays or inadequate reviews can result in an inability to respond to demand and lead to lost opportunities to retain or grow market share. Moreover, the need for rigorous reviews is also essential in times of downsizing. Cutting staff without either assessing the tasks that no longer need doing or re-engineering current practices will lead to responses that will inadequately support customers in times when retaining current sales is essential to business performance.

Capacity – general factors

There are two common denominators used in businesses to express, calculate and measure activities – time and money. In most parts of a business, money is the dimension used to express and evaluate activity, for example sales revenue and profit. In operations, the common denominator is time. Statements and measures of performance regarding capacity and output are calculated by using time as the base. So, all services and products will need to be measured in terms of the time taken to complete them. Checks can then be made, for instance, to assess how much capacity is needed and how well it has been used. The second aspect to be clarified concerns whether a firm should use staff or plant/equipment as the basis of these capacity statements, particularly where both are used in providing the same services and products. The sections that follow explain the aspects around measuring capacity but, before addressing the principles involved, it will be useful to discuss capacity statements and measurements in general.

Capacity – overall measurement

Statements and measurements of capacity will often differ within and between the various parts of an organization to reflect the issues and dimensions involved. Taking a hospital as an example, let us clarify what this means:

● Overall size – a hospital will typically use the number of beds it has as one indicator of overall size. This provides a useful statement about an important dimension of its capacity.

● Emergency unit – capacity in the emergency unit of the same hospital would relate to the expected levels of demand at different times through each day of a week. This would then be translated into the number and mix of staff (the ratio of doctors, nurses and support staff) required at different times of a week, month and year.

● Consultant clinics – based on the average length of appointments, a clinic would be arranged on a number of days each week or each month. Appointments would then be made in line with the scheduled capacity. The number of clinics would reflect known and future demand levels and this would be adjusted to reflect changes in demand over time.

In this way, expressions of capacity will differ, with each emphasizing the dimension that underlines the aspect of capacity being described. However, you will notice from the three examples above that the last two use a time base. Assessing how many emergency staff and how many clinics are required will use time as the means of calculating appropriate numbers.

Capacity – definitions

There are several definitions that surround the provision and use of capacity. Recognizing and recording these is a necessary step to avoid confusion and allow the expressions of 'how much' and 'how well' to be made with both understanding and insight:

● Planned (or available) capacity – although theoretically operations could run or be open 24 hours each day throughout a year, in reality this is not normally required nor does it typically make sense. An exception to this are those companies using continuous processing (such as an oil refinery) where the costs of stopping and starting a process are so high that the process is run continuously (see Chapter 6). Planned (or available) capacity, therefore, is a statement of the intended or planned number of hours to be made available in a given period.

● Utilization – this measures the actual number of hours staff worked, a plant was used or a department or firm was open compared with the planned hours.

● Efficiency – this compares actual output to the level of output expected, given the number of hours worked.

You will detect from these definitions that there are some important nuances that need to be clarified. The next section also concerns definitions. After this, two simple examples will be provided to illustrate these points and highlight the differences.

Capacity – unit of measurement

A question posed earlier was whether the measurement of capacity should be based on staff or plant/equipment. The approach to be used will reflect the delivery system or process involved, as follows:

- Non-repeat service delivery system, project and jobbing – in these businesses, skilled staff provide the service or product, with systems and equipment helping them to complete the task. Here, staff hours would be the measure of available capacity.

- Line and continuous processing – with these processes, the plant or equipment makes the product and people support the plant or equipment in this task. Although the speed of a line process can, within certain limits, be adjusted to reflect demand, the statement of capacity in these businesses will typically be based on the quantity the process is able to produce per hour.

- Repeat service delivery systems – high volume repeat service delivery systems are often more like line, with the equipment providing the service (for example a cash or cheque processing machine) and so equipment hours are typically the basis used to express levels of capacity. Where staff provide the service, staff hours would be used to calculate capacity.

- Batch – high volume batch is more like line and so plant/equipment hours are typically the basis used for statements on capacity. Conversely, businesses more towards the low volume end of batch will use staff hours as the basis of capacity calculations. This is because people rather than equipment will be the factor governing output.

So, the measure of capacity will reflect which input (people or equipment) into the delivery system or process is key in the provision of the services and products involved.

Capacity – expressions of output

The earlier section on units of measurement pointed to time as the common denominator used in operations. How much operations capacity is necessary will be assessed in relation to the size and type of expected demand and these dimensions are then translated into time as the way of comparing like with like. For example, a postal service concerns delivering letters. However, the time taken to deliver letters in the centre of a town would be considerably shorter than that in rural districts. Using the number of letters posted would not reflect demand or capacity. The time taken would need to reflect the number delivered, distances and other variables. The use of time as the basis for calculating demand and capacity is appropriate for most organizations as the services or products provided will incur different levels of resource. But whereas the number of units is known (for example letters delivered) the time taken has to be calculated (note, the approaches used to undertake these calculations are covered in detail in Chapter 15). As a consequence, the calculations or assessments need to be a true reflection of the time it takes to complete a task and not Mr James's approach (see Exhibit 8.1).

In some organizations while time is the underlying means of assessment, discussions do not typically use time as the means of expression or the form of calculation for either

Exhibit 8.1   Time needs to be calculated and not plucked from the air

© AMD Publishing

output or performance. Where the services and products are similar (for example vehicles produced in a car plant or meals served in a fast-food restaurant) or it is more meaningful to analyse a business in terms of the services and products involved, then units would be more appropriately used as the statement of capacity. For example, the capacity of an oil refinery would be expressed as the number of gallons or litres processed per day, the capacity of a car plant by the number of vehicles assembled per day, the capacity of a restaurant by the number of meals served at given times in a day and the capacity of a hairdresser by the number of appointments handled in a day. In turn these would form the basis for statements on capacity and calculations made on utilization and efficiency.

Capacity and output – examples

The two examples that follow are provided to help you understand the issues raised earlier in the chapter. They are based on real examples although they have been simplified to help get across the key points.

Example 1 – Conform

Conform is a small manufacturing business with five machines. One is often fully used but the other four machines always have spare capacity. Conform's business is subcontract work for a number of customers whose work is typically completed on two or more of the machines. The manufacturing process is simple, with all products being completed as a single operation on one machine. Following machining, the products are packed before being designated to customers against schedules or in line with orders. Conform employs three machine operators who complete the necessary set-ups on machines and undertake all the machining operations. In addition there is one full-time and one part-time packer. The former is also responsible for despatch.

Planned machine operator capacity – from Monday to Friday the three machine operators each work a single shift of seven and a half hours:

Planned capacity = Normal working hours
                   = 3 operators × 7.5 hours × 5 days = 112.5 hours

Machine operator utilization – week 1

In week 1, the company arranged overtime of one hour on four days for two machine operators. The utilization of operators in this week is shown below. As you will see, it compares total hours against planned capacity. In this way, it signals to the company that the number of hours required is higher than planned and allows the company to monitor capacity and adjust accordingly.

$$\text{Machine operator utilization} = \frac{\text{Actual hours worked}}{\text{Planned hours of work}} \times 100$$

$$= \frac{120.5}{112.5} \times 100$$

$$= 107 \text{ per cent}$$

Machine operator utilization – week 2

In week 2 no overtime was worked and there was a period of three hours without machining work for one operator. This operator (as was normal in these circumstances) was reassigned to packing. Utilization, therefore, was

$$\text{Machine operator utilization} = \frac{\text{Actual hours worked}}{\text{Planned hours of work}} = \frac{109.5}{112.5} = 97 \text{ per cent}$$

Machine utilization – weeks 1 and 2

The company has five machines on which the three operators make a range of products. The hours worked on each machine vary. The calculations on machine utilization highlight these differences, as shown in Exhibit 8.2.

Exhibit 8.2 Machine utilization at Conform

Machine	Week 1	Week 2
1	41.5 hours worked 37.5 hours available = 111 per cent	37.5 hours worked 37.5 hours available = 100 per cent
2	9.0 hours worked 37.5 hours available = 24 per cent	8.0 hours worked 37.5 hours available = 21 per cent
3	22.0 hours worked 37.5 hours available = 59 per cent	20.0 hours worked 37.5 hours available = 53 per cent
4	35.0 hours worked 37.5 hours available = 93 per cent	31.0 hours worked 37.5 hours available = 83 per cent
5	13.0 hours worked 37.5 hours available = 35 per cent	13.0 hours worked 37.5 hours available = 35 per cent
Total hours worked on the five machines	120.5	109.5

What do these calculations reveal?

- Higher than 100 per cent utilization figures signal to the company that the number of hours required is higher than planned and lower than 100 per cent signals lower than planned. Monitoring these figures over time will reveal whether or not this is a trend and allow adjustments accordingly.

- Capacity often varies. Differences in staff skill levels and types of machine mean that the staff or machines in question can provide different services or products. To provide an average utilization figure for these five machines for weeks 1 and 2 (in this instance 64 and 58 per cent respectively) would lack meaning.

- The 'hours worked' on each machine include both the time when a machine was being set up to make a product and the time when the machine was actually producing. Both these elements of work are classed as 'productive' but, while the time a machine is producing is called 'saleable productive time', set-ups are classed as 'non-saleable productive time'. This is discussed in more detail later.

Efficiency – operators

Whereas utilization compares the number of hours worked with the number available or planned, efficiency (also known as 'effective performance') measures the amount of work produced in the hours worked and compares this figure with the amount expected (known as the 'standard'). In a business where the products are the same (for example an automotive company), the calculation would be the number of cars produced in a day compared with the number expected. Where a company makes or provides several different services or products, comparisons are made by converting the latter into the hours of work they should have taken to complete and then comparing the total hours produced (that is, the number of units produced × the time per unit it should have taken to complete) with the total hours worked.

Exhibit 8.3 Calculating efficiency for machine operators at Conform

Product reference	# standard minutes to machine/complete	# produced Products	# produced Minutes
1612	10.0	14	140
4725	5.5	8	44
3408	25.0	3	75
0184	18.5	6	111
1229	36.0	4	144
4120	4.5	10	45
3678	12.0	30	360
2185	27.5	6	165
2766	3.0	25	75
Set-ups	15.0	9	135

Total minutes worked = 1294 = 21.6 hours

$$\text{Efficiency} = \frac{\text{\# hours of work produced}}{\text{\# hours worked}} = \frac{21.6}{24.5} = 88 \text{ per cent}$$

Notes 1 As two operators on day 1 of the week each worked one overtime hour, this made a total hours worked of 3 × 7.5 + 2.0 = 24.5 hours.
2 Set-ups or changeovers took 15 minutes. Work produced, therefore, included 1159 saleable productive and 135 non-saleable productive minutes as explained above. The issues around this are dealt with in more detail in Chapter 15.
3 Standard minutes (column 2 above) are explained more fully in Chapter 15 as are the issues and expectations around levels of efficiency.

In this example, the three operators on machining each worked 7.5 hours on day 1 of week 1, with two operators also each working one hour of overtime. If during this day they made the products listed in Exhibit 8.3, then their overall efficiency would be calculated as shown at the foot of the table. (Normally, this calculation would be made for a whole week. Taking a single day keeps the example short yet still illustrates the principles and calculations involved.)

Example 2 – John Michael

John Michael is a hairdresser in the centre of town. It employs seven part- and full-time staff and has seven hairdressing chairs that are used at different times during a week in line with expected demand, as shown in Exhibit 8.4. The working pattern illustrated reflects the mix of full-time (chairs 1 to 4) and part-time staff (chairs 5 to 7), while opening hours reflect expected demand levels each day. Exhibit 8.4 shows that the four full-time staff work five days each week and take a different day off as arranged. The three part-time staff work at pre-arranged times, as shown.

Exhibit 8.4 Salon opening and hairdressing hours

Day	# opening hours	# hours available per chair							Total hours
		1	2	3	4	5	6	7	
Monday	8	–	8	8	8	–	–	–	24
Tuesday	8	8	8	8	–	4	–	–	28
Wednesday	8	8	–	8	8	–	4	4	32
Thursday	8	8	8	–	8	4	4	–	32
Friday	10	10	10	10	10	8	8	8	64
Saturday	10	10	10	10	10	10	10	10	70

Utilization – facilities

As the facilities are the same, calculating overall utilization is a more appropriate statement than calculating the utilization of each chair. However, as service provision needs to match demand levels during each day, then planned capacity will be at different levels to reflect this. For John Michael, whereas on Monday to Thursday the salon opens for eight hours, on Friday and Saturday the planned capacity (that is, salon opening) is ten hours. During a week the daily utilization calculations need to reflect this, as shown in Exhibit 8.5.

Exhibit 8.5 Daily facilities utilization levels at John Michael

Day	Utilization (%)
Mon	43
Tue	50
Wed	57
Thu	57
Fri	91
Sat	100

Note   Utilization on Monday $= \dfrac{\text{Hours used}}{\text{Hours available}} = \dfrac{24}{56} = 43$ per cent

Hours available = 7 chairs x 8 hours (the opening hours of the salon)

Utilization – hairdressers

Similar calculations assessing the utilization of each hairdresser during each day would also be appropriate. In John Michael's case, the schedule for a hairdresser was based on 15-minute booking slots, with longer jobs being allocated more than one 15-minute slot. A simple check on the number of slots not filled during each day gave the owner an adequate statement on the utilization of each hairdresser.

Efficiency – hairdressers

The efficiency of the seven hairdressers may be calculated in two ways. The first would be based on standard times for each type of service – alternatives such as trim, restyling, shampoo and wash, highlighting and other forms of hair colouring would take different lengths of time. Calculations of efficiency would be similar to those completed in Exhibit 8.3.

A second method is available where businesses are not complicated and the services provided are similar to one another or will tend to average out over a given period. This uses a simpler, broadbrush calculation such as the revenue generated by each hairdresser per hour worked. With prices reflecting, in part, the time involved and each hairdresser undertaking a similar mix of work, then a 'revenue per hour worked' calculation would give a rule of thumb assessment of efficiency. It would be easy to calculate and yet provide a check on the level of efficiency achieved. In fact, the owner of the John Michael salon used this measure as follows, with net hours equalling attendance hours less non-booked time by clients:

$$\frac{\text{Revenue generated}}{\text{Net hours worked}} = \text{Revenue per hour worked}$$

Factors affecting the definition of capacity

So far we have looked at capacity decisions and definitions without introducing factors that affect their definition. This section now introduces these:

- make-or-buy decisions
- the range of services and products
- the service delivery system and process design
- the chosen service delivery system or manufacturing process.

Make-or-buy decision[3]

Theoretically, every item, process or service currently purchased from an outside supplier is a candidate for in-house provision and vice versa. In reality, however, the choice is not so extensive, as often buying from an outside supplier is the only option. Nevertheless, when alternatives are available, the make-or-buy decision needs to be considered at both the strategic and tactical levels. Apart from the level of capacity required, several other issues must be considered and these are now discussed.

Longer term competitiveness needing operations support

In the pursuit of short-term financial improvements, some organizations decide to subcontract tasks traditionally completed within their own operations function. In some instances it makes sense, but there are issues to be checked before making such a change. For example, a decision to subcontract may be taken as a matter of expediency. Facing a difficult problem requiring managerial time and expertise to put right can often be the stimulus for subcontracting, without undertaking essential checks on the long-term impact. Similarly, some companies have painted themselves into the 'hollow corporation syndrome',[4] with the long-term consequence of an eroded operations base (both process and infrastructure) from which it will normally be more difficult to initiate change.[5]

Finally, companies may decide to subcontract parts of their business without carefully thinking through the long-term impact on customer retention. For example, Capital One, the US credit card company, has retained most aspects of its service delivery system in-house, including call centres. Its rationale is that this keeps it close to its customers, provides customer intelligence and clearly states the importance of customer service within its business.

Delaying investment decisions by initially subcontracting

Process investment to meet the needs of new markets brings with it added uncertainty. One way of reducing the level of uncertainty is initially to subcontract operations until market demand is more clearly defined. A company making household products, for example, used subcontract capability in the early stages of the life cycle of a new product range until it was able to ascertain the volumes involved. When the picture became clearer and volumes more certain, it could then choose from the following alternatives: allocate the new range to a part of its own manufacturing facility in keeping with forecast volumes; leave it with the existing supplier; or switch the contract to another supplier, again based on volume fit. In this way it was able to reduce the investment risk and increase the fit between processes and requirements.

Handling technology uplifts

Stepped changes in technology often result in an organization having to buy in that technology. Although initially there may be no alternative, it is essential that organizations consider future make-or-buy positions once the technologies are more available and internal provision becomes an option. It is, however, more usual for some organizations not to review these fundamental make-or-buy decisions when circumstances have changed.

Tactical issues

There are several tactical issues to be considered, including:

- the ease or difficulty of providing the internal technical or skill capability to meet service and product specifications
- the effect of make-or-buy decisions on overall lead times
- the degree of dependence that results between a subcontracted item, process or service and the final service or product into which it goes
- availability of suppliers over time to meet the volumes and specifications involved
- comparative costings need to incorporate checks that the internal data used in making these decisions do, in fact, reflect the true costs, the real impact on internal overhead cost structures with volume changes and likely future actions by suppliers
- decisions to make in-house result in increased aggregate volumes and consequently contribute to spreading overhead costs and help to balance demand and capacity over time
- the protection of service, product and process ideas
- avoiding subjective decisions concerning beliefs about internal capabilities and cost structure costings that have not been checked.

Services and products – range and specifications

The role of operations is to provide the services and products a company sells. Determining the range, degree of change and extent of available options is, therefore, fundamental to establishing the capabilities and capacity required. Likewise, agreeing the specification of services and products within the range will involve similar outcomes. The issues and details concerning service and product design have already been covered in Chapter 4.

Service delivery system and process design

Although the subject of earlier chapters, aspects of the service delivery system and process design have a major impact on the provision of capacity within the operations process. Some key issues are now discussed.

Use of customers

As mentioned earlier, because of the inherent producer/consumer interaction within a service delivery system, the customer becomes a potential source of capacity. The extent of that provision within different service delivery systems is an important decision in terms of the overall source of capacity provision, and this unique opportunity needs to form part of the process design. The benefits of this involvement include:

- it cuts costs
- it helps to provide capacity at points in the delivery system where all or part of the service is consumed. For example, in a self-service restaurant, the job of the waiter is provided partly by the customer. In turn, this requires decisions on key aspects such as the movement and flow of customers and the roles of both server and customer in the system design
- some customers prefer to be able to make their own choices. For example, self-service food shopping is now the norm and salad bar provision in a restaurant is often preferred by customers because of similarly increasing control over the level of choice exercised.

Customers have proved willing to take part in the service delivery system if it can be shown to be beneficial, supportive of their needs, convenient or enhances the sociable nature of the total process. Examples include self-service facilities of all kinds, direct telephone dialling, purchases by television, online shopping, investment brokerage services, other financial services (including cash machines) and travel arrangements. The impact upon the provision and type of capacity is considerable.

However, if involvement in all or part of the delivery system does not meet expectations, then customers fail to participate in or do not complete their perceived involvement. For example, supermarket shopping trolleys (an integral part of the self-service provision) are often left abandoned after use because of the long distances involved in returning them to their designated areas. The resulting inconvenience and added costs have stimulated most large supermarket chains to introduce a deposit system, thus penalizing uncooperative shoppers.

Similarly, manufacturing companies need to recognize that what they sell invariably involves a service element (see Exhibit 1.6), and then determine a customer's potential role within this element. For example, a small company offering specialized material finishing capabilities experienced difficulties in keeping pace with demand. It recognized that one loss of capacity came from its earlier decision to deliver and collect items to and from customers. Not only was this time-consuming in itself but it invariably involved delays at customers' premises. A policy change requiring customers to deliver and collect enabled the company to improve its delivery turnround, with this being a major aspect of the total service and one that, for many customers, was an order-winner.

The perishable nature of service capacity

Service capacity is perishable. It cannot be put into inventory for use or sale in a future time period. A major task thus concerns adjusting capacity provision or influencing levels of demand in order to improve the trade-offs between the effective use of capacity and meeting the varying levels of customer demand. The alternative ways available are discussed later in the chapter.

Back office versus front office

Within a service business, a distinction needs to be made between the two basic parts of the process – the back office and front office. A fundamental distinction between these two parts of the system concerns customer interface. In the front office customers are present (for example in person or on the telephone) and the service system has to manage customers in the delivery of the service. In the back office, customers are not present in the system and the pressure to respond immediately is not there. Consequently, capacity requirements, the opportunity to spread demand and the potential to use technology will differ between these parts.

Back office

Because activities in the back office are decoupled from the customer, tasks can be delayed until cumulated volumes are sufficiently large to secure the advantages of size or their completion better fits the overall schedule. This not only increases the opportunity to manage demand fluctuations more efficiently but cumulated volumes (often from more than one location) also justify investment in technology. Being able to cumulate volumes facilitates the use of the latter, which not only improves productivity but also impacts capacity requirements.

Front office

This part of a process involves interfacing with customers and providing services to meet their requirements. Service provision and consumption are simultaneous. Capacity provision needs to meet demand not only in terms of the range of services provided but also to reflect the differing levels of demand during the day, week or longer time periods. When demand is greater than capacity, customers either wait or go elsewhere. Getting the balance right between capacity levels and queue lengths is an important decision affecting a business and ways of handling these trade-offs are discussed later in this chapter.

Ensuring adequate capacity at each stage of a delivery system

The importance of getting capacity right significantly impacts costs and customer support that, in turn, affects overall sales revenue and profit, as illustrated in Case examples 8.1 and 8.2. Where services or products require a single operation to complete them, the task of determining the necessary capacity is relatively easy. However, to provide a service or make a product often involves several steps and also differing amounts of time at each step. This makes determining the capacity required a more difficult task, as there are more stages and hence it is more complex.

Case example 1   **INCREASING RESTAURANT CAPACITY**

A restaurant experiencing high demand increased capacity in two ways. It added more tables in the existing dining areas and increased the speed of service in an attempt to improve throughput. Both provisions had a direct impact on customers' experience. Although the quality of the food and wine remained the same, customers' perception of the service specification on offer changed. Bookings fell, and sales and profit declined.

Case questions   1 What were the order-winners and qualifiers for this business?

2 Based on your answer to question 1, assess the company's decision. What alternative decisions could it have made about its shortage of capacity?

Case example 2   **DELL'S CUSTOMER SUPPORT CAPACITY**

Dell believes its place in the top five PC manufacturers, with sales in excess of £2 billion, is due, in large part, to customer loyalty. More than 80 per cent of its custom is repeat business. Key to sustaining this is the company's strong field support for customers. Direct selling to customers instead of through dealers not only means lower prices but also removes those personnel who traditionally supported a computer installation. To meet these needs Dell provides European sales and customer support through a telephone operation located close to Dublin. Highly trained multilingual staff offer 24-hour, seven-day support for Dell users across Europe, with similar arrangements in place for other regions of the world. Providing a hotline with continuous support is key for customers with computer problems and is considered to be an essential part of Dell's success.

http://www.dell.co.uk

Case question   What are the key dimensions of customer support that help make Dell a success? Why?

Breakeven analysis

The throughput speed of equipment will have a direct bearing on the amount of capacity required. The two dimensions involved when choosing equipment are set-up time (the length of time to prepare the equipment to process a service or product) and throughput speed (the time taken to actually process a service or product).

The relationship between set-up time and process time helps in the choice between options by using the breakeven concept:

$$\text{Breakeven} = \frac{\text{Additional setting-up time for a process}}{\text{Reduction in process time per service/product}}$$

Flexibility

The different dimensions of flexibility need to be recognized and reflected in capacity calculations. These include the ability to:

- produce a wider range of services and products
- respond to any seasonal demand factors
- meet shorter lead times
- cope with customer specification changes during the process.

Skills and mix

The introduction of technology into facets of the operations process will lead to changes in skill requirements and staff mix. This alters capacity requirements and so needs to be part of the decision process.

Chosen service delivery system or manufacturing process

The need for operations managers to understand the technology of the system or process used in providing services and products varies. However, it is essential for them to understand the business implications of the chosen delivery system or manufacturing process, several of which directly impact the definition, provision and management of capacity, as summarized in Exhibits 8.6 and 8.7.

The factors in service delivery systems that affect the nature of capacity and its management and provision have been highlighted earlier. They include the following:

- the nature of the service offering
  - non-repeat or repeat
  - the level of volume for a repeat service
  - the service/product mix
- what is being processed in the service delivery system – a customer, a customer surrogate (for example in car maintenance, the car is the surrogate for the customer) or information
- front- or back-office position in the delivery system
- single- or multi-step system.

With these factors in mind, Exhibit 8.6 provides an overview of how some of the key dimensions of capacity differ in relation to the non-repeat/repeat and low/high volume dimensions of services, while the accompanying narrative provides explanation and highlights some differences from the overview where other factors affect the outcomes.

Exhibit 8.6 Capacity-related implications of service delivery system choice

Capacity-related implications		Non-repeat services	Repeat services	
			Low volume	High volume
Capacity	basis for calculation	People	⟶	People/process
	scale of changes	Incremental	⟶	Stepped
	control	Difficult	⟶	Easy
Demand – level of definition		Low	⟶	High
Delivery system flexibility		Flexible	⟶	Inflexible
Dominant factor in measuring capacity utilization		People	⟶	People/process
Impact of	staff absence	High	⟶	Low
	equipment failure	Low	⟶	Significant

Non-repeat services are delivered by skilled staff and consequently capacity is based on the available working time of this key resource. As the services involved would be non-repeat, the definition of demand in terms of resource requirements would be low (it has not been provided before), making the provision and control of capacity difficult. The flexible nature of skilled staff, however, would facilitate the use of capacity in meeting the wide range of services on offer, the downside being the impact on capacity of losing key staff

Exhibit 8.7 Capacity-related implications of manufacturing process choice

Capacity-related implications		Typical characteristics of manufacturing process choice				
		Project	Jobbing	Batch	Line	Continuous processing
Capacity	basis for calculation	People	People	———————→	Process	Process
	scale	Small	Small	———————→	Large	Very large
	scale of changes	Incremental	Incremental	———————→	Stepped	New facility
	control	Difficult	Difficult	———————→	Easy	Easy
Demand – level of definition		Variable	Low	———————→	Established	Established
Process flexibility		Flexible	Flexible	———————→	Inflexible	Very inflexible
Set-ups or change-overs	number	Many	Many	———————→	Unlikely	Unlikely
	expense	Variable	Inexpensive	———————→	Expensive	Very expensive
Dominant factor in measuring capacity utilization		People	People	———————→	Process	Process
Bottlenecks	number	Few	Few	Often several	None	None
	position and nature	Random and movable	Random and movable	Fixed in the short and medium term	Not relevant	Not relevant
Impact of breakdowns		Variable	Little	———————→	Significant	Enormous

through absence in the short term and staff leaving in the longer term. The transitional nature of these dimensions as the service delivery system shifts to that for high volume repeat service is illustrated by the arrows in Exhibit 8.6. Calculating capacity in a fast-food restaurant is a combination of staff and processes, whereas capacity in cash machine services is predominantly to do with the number (and location) of ATMS. Adding capacity is often stepped in nature (for example adding a new outlet). In either case, the failure of the equipment involved in the system will have a significant impact on a company's ability to deliver services as it is central to their provision.

The implications for the management and provision of capacity overviewed in Exhibit 8.7 reflect the nature of the manufacturing process involved.

Project and jobbing

In both project and jobbing, the firms involved would typically be relatively small in size, skilled staff would be central to the process of making the products while offering a flexible response in terms of the range of products the manufacturing process could handle. Changing from one product to another would be an integral part of the manufacturing process and would not involve long expensive changes.

Line and continuous processing

Moving towards line and continuous processing brings with it a shift to the other end of each of these dimensions. Typically companies would be large in size, with processes and not people making the products involved. Demand here would be well defined as product knowledge would be well established and how much capacity was required would be easy to calculate. Capacity changes, on the other hand, would be large scale in nature. Having been designed to make a given product range, changing the process rarely, if ever, occurs except at the end of a product's life cycle. As the process is designed to run as a balanced line, bottlenecks are not a factor. The impact of breakdowns, on the other hand, would be significant as the process itself is stopped – in project and jobbing the skilled staff would simply switch to alternative tasks.

Batch

As shown in Exhibit 8.7, for most factors, as the arrows depict, batch is a transition between the two extremes of process choice. The exception is bottlenecks, and why this is so is now explained. A bottleneck occurs where the capacity in one stage of a process is less than the capacity in the other parts of the process. To help visualize this think of a wine bottle and the difference in size between the neck and the body. In multi-step batch processes there are often differences in demand and capacity ratios at each stage (the neck and body factor). Invariably some of these will show bottleneck capacity characteristics, a factor that in the short and medium term will not change.

Issues in determining levels of capacity

Once created, plant and equipment capacity is usually an irreversible investment decision, and, once created, staff capacity is an expensive decision to change. As a result, growth and its associated decisions present a challenging task. Not only are all these dimensions difficult in themselves but they also involve the interrelated aspects of market position and competitors' decisions on the size and timing of their capacity changes.

The process of deciding on capacity levels is complex. Organizations are faced with a number of important decisions, such as:

- Anticipating the end of growth
- Avoiding overcapacity
- Choosing to plan ahead of growth or to plan to follow growth – the lead or follow demand capacity alternatives
- What action to take in a situation of overcapacity – divest or diversify?

Similar dilemmas are also involved in downsizing. The timing and extent concern not only questions of cost but also the impact on sales and market share. As with capacity investment, downsizing decisions, once made, are costly to reverse.

To help manage capacity companies consider a range of demand/capacity issues and these are now discussed.

Demand-related issues

An organization focuses its planning efforts towards meeting the requirements of its customers. To do this it needs to manage demand. This involves identifying the nature and size of demand and determining how it is best going to meet it. One characteristic of demand that further complicates this provision and makes managing it more challenging is that it is never the same twice over. Some of these variations are, however, more predictable than others, as explained below.

Predictable variations

Although demand levels will vary, very often there are characteristics of sales from which patterns can be identified, enabling fluctuations to be more easily predicted. For example:

- Seasonality – the seasonal nature of many services and products is well recognized. Defined as variation that repeats itself at fixed intervals, seasonal patterns are caused by many factors including the weather (for example holiday bookings and sales of air conditioners and ice cream) and time of the year (for example the demand for air travel, types of clothing, gardening equipment, fireworks, training courses and tax processing).

- Peaks – whereas seasonality of demand occurs over a year, predictable variations in demand also occur at shorter intervals. To distinguish the two, the latter are normally known as peaks, and, as with seasonality of demand, these are caused by recurring factors that can be identified. For example, working hours affect traffic volumes; the day of the week will affect demand, for example the emergency unit in a hospital will be busier than usual late on a Saturday night; time of the day will affect the level of demand for sandwiches; and a firm's policies such as billing patterns and the push to meet sales targets will be reflected in the activity levels during a month.

- One-off demands – some services and products are subject to a predictable one-off peak in demand. This needs to be successfully managed to ensure potential sales are maximized. For example, the launch of JK Rowling's book *Harry Potter and the Order of the Phoenix* in 2003 and the film launch of the final part of the *Lord of the Rings* trilogy required appropriate demand planning as would the opening night at the Cannes Film Festival.

Unpredictable variations

Other demand characteristics are less predictable but still need to be managed. For example, to protect against 'no shows', airlines overbook on flights. The same policy is also adopted by hotel operators, particularly those in locations where the unpredictability of bookings or the frequency of late cancellations brings uncertainty in the pattern of demand and the resulting loss of revenue from having turned business away.

Capacity-related issues

As with demand, there are issues in the provision of capacity that increase the difficulty of this management task. Again, some of these are more predictable than others, as explained below.

Predictable aspects of capacity

The demands placed on capacity will vary to reflect the mix of services and products and the sales levels involved. For this reason there are bottlenecks in the process where capacity is less than the demand placed on it. However, bottlenecks are short- to medium-term phenomena and so are predictable in terms of their position and extent. Knowing where they are is essential as this enables a business to manage capacity within this constraint, while directing attention and resources to increasing capacity in these parts of a process.

Unpredictable aspects of capacity

As with demand, some aspects of capacity are less predictable and these introduce problems of a more ad hoc nature:

- Absenteeism – people stay away from work for a number of reasons. Estimates place the direct and indirect costs for UK businesses as high as £16 billion and absence rates on average are about 3.5 per cent. The short-term impact of this adds difficulty to the effective management of capacity. Ways of attempting to cope with this have centred on recognizing absenteeism as a management problem and attempting to reduce it to manageable levels. Lewisham Borough Council in the greater London area was affected by absentee levels averaging 17 days a year for each employee. Better monitoring helped bring this down to less than 11 days per year in just 24 months. Others argue that unpaid sick leave encourages employees to believe that no one loses when they are away. Paying for sickness, including the penalty of taking away this benefit for abuse of the system, is part of why Nissan believes it has achieved absenteeism levels of less than 2 per cent at its plant in Washington in the northeast of England.

- Short-term demand changes – short-term demand variations can often result in a temporary shortage of capacity, with the difficulties this presents in managing demand.

Successfully managing these capacity and demand issues is often central to the successful growth of a business, as Case example 8.3 illustrates.

Case example 3   PREDICTING CAPACITY AT PRET A MANGER

Lunch time food for workers in major towns and cities is big business, but being able to find fresh and tasty sandwiches and other snacks was never easy, until the advent of Pret A Manger. The founders of the chain of sandwich shops recognized an unfilled need to provide high-quality, freshly made food in a market where demand for good food was growing. Initially targeting central London, Pret A Manger (meaning ready to eat) has now been successfully launched in other major cities in the UK, for example Birmingham. Its sandwiches and cakes are all made to a high specification and genuinely are ready to eat, ready wrapped and freshly made. Made at each location, many lunch time favourites do not appear on the outlet shelves until an hour or so before time. The fresh ingredients are kept properly chilled until they are ready to be used as sandwich fillings. Coffee is made from the finest Arabica beans that are freshly ground in line with each customer's request. Unsold sandwiches are distributed to the homeless free of charge – last year this totalled over 14,000 leftover sandwiches.

http://www.pret.com

Case question	How do you think Pret A Manger copes with the predictable and unpredictable aspects of demand and capacity when determining staffing levels at its outlets?

Planning and managing capacity

The purpose of the first section of this chapter has been to introduce key definitions, provide an overall review of capacity and illustrate the purpose and outcomes of its provision. The rest of the chapter addresses the task of planning and managing capacity. It will address the longer range tasks of resource planning and rough-cut planning, with short-term operations control and scheduling being discussed in Chapter 10.

Capacity management is an essential responsibility of the operations function. The objective is to match the level of capacity to the level of demand, both in terms of quantity (how much) and capability (the skill mix to meet the service or product specification). Simple though it sounds, meeting this basic requirement is a challenging task and concerns issues of:

- **uncertainty** – forecasting demand is inherently uncertain
- **timescales** – day-to-day scheduling through to long-term capacity planning

- **alternatives** – choosing from the different ways of providing capacity to meet demand
- **execution** – fulfilling the plan.

The optimum approach to planning and managing capacity is to separate the task into its major elements and position these in terms of the time phases in which they need to occur. Exhibit 8.8 is a simplified schematic of these tasks, showing their position in each phase of the planning and control system.[6] The level of planning and control detail involved will reflect the complexity of the services and products provided. As you will no doubt appreciate, managing a sandwich bar will be less complex than managing a large hotel, as would a small assembly shop compared with a large pharmaceutical plant making

Exhibit 8.8   Operations planning and control systems

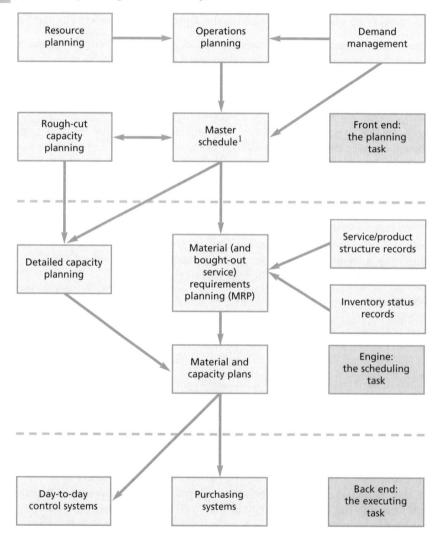

Note   1   Referred to in manufacturing planning and control systems as the 'master production schedule' or MPS.

Source   Adapted from Vollman, TE, Berry, WL, Whybark, DC and Jacobs, R *Manufacturing Planning and Control Systems for Supply Chain Management* (5th edn), McGraw-Hill/Irwin, Burr Ridge, IL (2004).

chemical formulations and a wide range of pack sizes and alternatives. In essence, though, the tasks are the same, as explained below:

- Planning – front-end planning provides key communication links between top management and operations. It helps form the basis for translating strategic objectives and future market needs into operations plans and resources and is essential in determining what can be achieved, the investments and decisions to be made and the timescales involved. It is in this phase where companies look forward and decide on the 'game plan' for the future. How far forward will depend upon the investments and timescales involved and these will be discussed in detail in the next section.

- Scheduling – the scheduling phase is the 'engine' of the system. It involves determining capacity several weeks, months and sometimes up to one year ahead. It details how demand will be met from available facilities and ensures that the capacity and material requirements are in place.

- Execution – the 'back-end' phase of the system concerns executing day-to-day operations by determining and monitoring material and capacity requirements to ensure that customer demand is met and resources are used efficiently.

The dimensions of both scheduling and execution are fully discussed in Chapter 10.

Exhibit 8.8 depicts several facets of the 'front-end planning task'. All are considered to be long term with regard to the timescales involved. In turn, these can be further split on the basis of time into:

- Resource planning – a strategic business issue generally involves looking five or more years ahead. It aims to provide for the long-term capacity requirements and resource allocations to meet the future organizational objectives by planning for capacity changes in line with major shifts in existing services and products and to meet plans for new services, products, technologies and markets.

- Rough-cut capacity planning (also referred to as aggregate planning) – used to plan for periods one to two years ahead. It details how demand will be met from available facilities that, in principle, are considered to be at a fixed level.

The timescales given here are arbitrary. For some businesses (for example oil exploration) the resource planning horizon could be greater than five years while for others, the long-term horizon could be two or less.

Resource planning

Anticipating future demand in terms of its size (associated volumes) and nature (the service/product mix) is an essential strategic decision. It needs to address three critical dimensions:

- **amount** – how much is required
- **timing** – when the capacity is needed
- **location** – where the capacity should be located.

What makes long-term capacity decisions difficult are the timescales involved and the fact that the above are not stand-alone questions. All three impinge on one another. For example, determining size is not just a question of total requirement but will need to address issues concerning units of capacity, their location and when they need to be available. Consequently, these elements of long-term operations planning need to be considered as an integrated whole.

As Exhibit 8.8 shows, resource planning is the first step in capacity planning. It is the most highly aggregated and has the longest capacity planning horizon. It typically involves taking a two–five-year time frame and converting monthly and annual data from the operations plan into statements of aggregate resources such as total staff hours, office space and support equipment in a service organization and staff hours, floor space and machine or process hours in a manufacturing firm. This level of planning potentially involves new capital investments such as buildings, warehousing and equipment that often have lead times of months or years.

As Exhibit 8.8 indicates, the operations planning task takes demand and resource planning information that details what is required and what is available and then highlights possible constraints in terms of lead times and levels of investment. These issues are large in size, complex in nature and concern the critical capacity issues of amount, timing and location. These and other aspects that need to be taken into account in the resouce planning task are now discussed.

General issues

Competition

As markets become more global and countries increasingly build up their own national capability to deliver services and make products, recognizing and incorporating these trends into long-term plans become more essential. In a world where demand is not growing as quickly as supply, overcapacity results. The impact on traditional industries such as steel, shipbuilding and automobiles is well reported. But, the same is happening in newer industries and segments of the service sector. Since the late 1980s there has been overcapacity in the semiconductor industry. The passenger airline industry is in a similar position. Over 90 per cent of airline passengers in the USA buy their tickets at a discount, paying on average about 35 per cent of the full fare. Although partly a response to deregulation, it is largely a reflection of the overcapacity in the industry. Since the early 1990s, similar patterns have been emerging in the European passenger airline industry. Setting future capacity levels, therefore, needs to recognize the potential actions of competitors and possible new entrants and the result these will have on overall capacity within a given market.

Developing countries

The need for developing countries to increase the size of their wealth-creating sectors is fundamental to their own longer term national prosperity. The resulting demand by governments to build local facilities increasingly affects the factors of location, size and timing in the capacity decisions of internationally based companies.

Technology

Changes in service, product, process and other technologies not only impact directly on levels of demand and capacity but also offer the opportunity to reposition capacity. The development of information technology allows companies to reposition the workplace of individual people (for example home versus office) and also to outsource a range of business processes, from basic call centres to the complex back-office operations of merchant banks. For example, the support unit answering a customer query can be located anywhere in the world to reflect issues of cost and time of the day. Lower cost countries in Europe (for example Ireland) are increasingly being used as support unit locations. Similarly, as offices close for the day in Europe, calls are initially transferred to the east coast of the USA and then progressively westwards to be handled by staff working during their normal hours.

Being able to send data via satellite has enabled information-based service companies to relocate relevant processing capacity to anywhere in the world. Newspapers are often composed in one location but printed in two or more sites close to their respective markets. The gains are not only the reduction in transport costs but also the speed of transfer that enables printing to be delayed until the very last moment. Similarly, companies involved in data processing are beaming the tasks to lower cost centres in countries such as India and South Africa without incurring the long lead times that previously would have made such decisions impractical.

A final example is healthcare. In most developed countries the post-war period saw a growth in hospitals that reflected the impact of the baby boom and people's expectations about health provision. Government-owned facilities were the largest healthcare provider and subsidies continued to be found to support existing capacity. Since the mid-1980s, dramatic improvements in medical technology and procedures have made the length of in-hospital stays shorter. On the other hand, advances in medicine have resulted in a wider range of treatments and replacements that have increased 'demand'. Managing these opposing trends adds to the complexity of the resource planning task.

Amount of capacity

Deciding on the amount of capacity needs to incorporate forecasts of demand, make versus buy decisions and how much capacity a company intends to hold in relation to anticipated demand. The factors involved in these complex decisions are now discussed.

Forecasting demand for services and products

One prerequisite for capacity planning is a statement of demand. Organizations need to forecast demand in order to anticipate future capacity requirements as well as the other resources in a business (for example buildings and facilities). But demand forecasting is difficult and no matter which method is used, it will not (by definition) be accurate. Despite this inaccuracy, it is essential to forecast demand, for the alternative is to have no forecast at all. Next, it is necessary to recognize the capacity planning horizon of different businesses. These will differ depending upon lead times. Where capacity is staff-based (for example in a manufacturing company using a jobbing process and in most service businesses), the relevant time horizon will normally be shorter than where investment in processes and equipment is involved. Manufacturing examples illustrating the dimension of long lead times readily come to mind, for instance new vehicle assembly and petrochemical plants. Also, service industries with a similar dependency on equipment will experience longer lead times, for example most elements of the transport industry.

Thus forecasting demand for services and products is critical in planning capacity. Without the scheduled passenger projections illustrated in Exhibit 8.9, for instance, plans for aircraft production and purchase would probably be nowhere near the actual requirement for this period.

Space precludes a detailed discussion of the options for demand forecasting but there are a number of books recommended at the end of this chapter.[7]

While demand forecasts are often completed elsewhere in a business, it is necessary for those involved in capacity planning to understand the forecasting procedures used, the assumptions made and the implications for the operations function. To help appreciate

Exhibit 8.9   Air traffic growth – scheduled passengers (2003–2007)

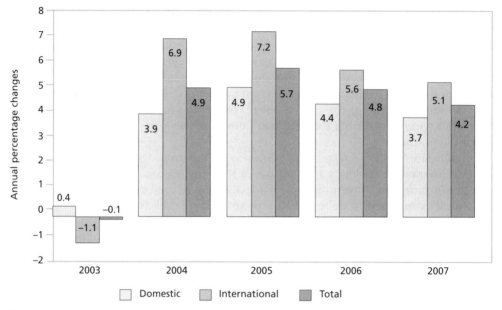

Source IATA

Exhibit 8.10   Global airline industry – operating profit as % of operating revenues (1970–2004)

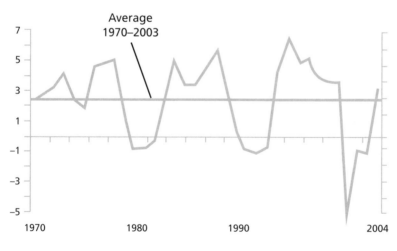

Source IATA

these issues, some of the features involved are now described. What follows is a short review of the dimensions to be taken into account when planning capacity within the air travel industry as a way of illustrating what may be involved. It is not, of course, intended to be comprehensive, merely illustrative.

The level of growth depicted in Exhibit 8.9 is significant. Couple this with aircraft replacement requirements in terms of investment costs, lead times and known aircraft developments (for example Boeing and European Airbus products) then the time frames are uncertain yet crucial. Put this within a framework of airline profitability trends on international scheduled services as given in Exhibit 8.10 and you will see that the need not only to plan capacity but also to be accurate in terms of amount and timing is critical to a company's overall financial success.

Within this scenario there are also current trends to be assessed in terms of the impact of deregulation on increased competition, customers who will become more demanding (through familiarity and being offered greater choice) and the need to achieve adequate returns on investment. The impact upon capacity forecasts and provision and the role of operations within the process are and will remain significant. The long-term capacity issues, including airports (size and location), aircraft (number and type), operations and support services, are significant in themselves and fundamental in nature.

Operations issues in forecasting

A key operations issue in forecasting concerns accuracy. The more general the statement and the longer the time period covered by the forecast, the more accurate it will be. The annual forecast for all services or products sold is likely to be more accurate than the weekly or monthly total for each item in the range. But, at some point, projections have to be translated into the actual services and products to be provided and made. Establishing assumptions, forcing clarification and moving from the general to the specific in terms of mix, volumes and other key operational differences is an essential operations task to manage future capacity requirements.

The choice of forecasting method

The inherent difficulties of forecasting have led to many forecasting models being developed in the past 50 years, and different models are based on different sets of assumptions. Understanding these assumptions, particularly those that may have an impact on operations, is an essential first step. Key factors to clarify so as to better understand forecast outcomes and signal aspects that need to be revisited at appropriate times within the long-term planning process include the following:

- The accuracy level of predictions sought and achieved and the trade-offs involved.
- The extent to which a model assumes that past behavioural patterns and relationships will continue in the future. A continuous check on presumed levels of stability between the past and future has to be embodied in the forecasting procedure in order to evaluate this feature of a model.
- Establishing the appropriate forecasting horizon that reflects the capacity lead time currently experienced.
- The need to establish a match between the selected forecasting model and the data patterns that are present in a particular business. The most common patterns are described as being constant, trend, seasonal and cyclical. A business needs to ascertain its own data patterns to ensure that the model chosen reflects them appropriately.

Make versus buy

The question of determining the make versus buy policy has already been signalled as a key step in the process of determining capacity. The issues and dimensions involved are discussed in detail in Chapter 13 and this section serves solely to restate its fundamental role in these decisions.

Size of operations units

How large to build an operations unit is bound up with many issues and the decision is made for a variety of reasons. The principal factor concerns scale – the size of operations units. The economies of scale argument is based on the premise that large units yield lower costs, as fixed costs are spread over more services or products. In some sectors (for example petrochemical plants) there is a minimum size below which it is difficult to justify the necessary process investment. Scale economies are truly present in these situations. Whereas some companies follow the economies of scale principle, others limit the size of units in order to avoid what they consider to be the disadvantages of large scale, including remoteness, poor motivational climate for staff, increased complexity and the difficulties of managing a larger organization. For these reasons, some businesses put an upper limit on size after which a new unit would be built. Other factors include:

- **Catchment area** – in some industries and particularly in the service sector, units are built to serve a certain catchment area. Demand outside this area will be met by building another facility. Examples include retail chains, banks and restaurants.

- **Distribution costs** – products have different distribution cost-to-item-value ratios. Those companies where distribution costs are high in relation to the product value will tend to build more plants than where the ratio is low.

- **Innovation levels** – many companies wish to encourage innovation and tend to operate smaller units in order to avoid the bureaucracy and centralized control that comes with size but which usually militates against innovative behaviour.

The critical nature of scale and how this may need to be reassessed over time is illustrated in Case example 8.4.

Case example 4   WAL-MART USES SCALE TO COMPETE IN THE US FOOD MARKET

Most of Wal-Mart's new stores are up to 200,000 square feet, the size of two (American) football fields, and too big to be built anywhere other than on the edge of towns. But in 2003, Wal-Mart opened its first Neighbourhood Market store in Rogers, Arkansas – the size, less than 40,000 square feet. The strategy is to limit store size and so allow the company to find sites in built-up urban areas allowing it to compete head-to-head with traditional supermarkets that dominate the cities. From its small beginnings in food sales in 1983, Wal-Mart became the biggest seller of food in the US by 2001. Its estimated $55 billion sales in 2004 outstrip those of Kruger, the #1 market chain.

Wal-Mart's first foray into food was not, however, a success. Inspired by retail giants such as Carrefour and Le Clerc's in France, Wal-Mart built large, 260,000 square foot supermarkets. But these proved to be too big for customers to handle and profits were low. Instead, it decided to move forward with its supercentres by adding groceries to its traditional discount stores which are no bigger than 200,000 square feet. By 2003 it had 1250 supercentres (rising to an estimated 2000 in 2006) which, with Sam's Club, accounts for 25 per cent of the US grocery market.

Since 1998, Wal-Mart has been tinkering with the smaller store formats. The Neighbourhood Market store offers about a fifth (24,000 against 120,000) of the product items found in a supercentre including a full assortment of food, health, beauty and household products. It includes a chicken rotisserie and home-made tortilla stand but lacks the extensive salad bars, delicatessens and butcher and fishmonger counters that competing supermarkets offer. Meat and fish arrive prepacked, ready for the shelf. There are also convenient extras – a drive-through pharmacy, a half-hour photo processing service and a self-serve coffee bar by the entrance. In addition, half the checkouts are self-scanning so reducing queue lengths and staff costs.

Wal-Mart is harnessing the same buying power and supply chain efficiency that enables it to offer food at prices some 10–15 per cent cheaper than its competitors. Its aim appears to be to provide convenience without the premiums that typically go with smaller size.   **http://www.walmart.com**

Case questions   1   How is Wal-Mart using scale to compete in the US food market?

2   Why is Wal-Mart pursuing its Neighbourhood Market store strategy?

Timing of capacity

As levels of demand change over time, when to increase or decrease capacity is a key business issue for both long-term (five or more years ahead) and medium-term (up to two years ahead) planning horizons. This section deals with the former; the medium-term responses to this and other relevant aspects of capacity will be discussed in the section 'Rough-cut capacity planning'.

Businesses need to base capacity on demand forecasts. Using assumptions of average demand, an organization can choose to provide adequate capacity to meet peaks, meet average demand patterns or maximize its utilization of capacity. The choice will reflect the requirements of, and chosen responses in, the different markets in which it competes.

The essential question of timing is whether to lead or follow anticipated demand. How these alternatives work in practice are now described.

Proactive strategy

A proactive strategy concerns building capacity in advance of forecast levels of demand. This approach maintains a positive capacity cushion by aiming always to have capacity in excess of demand, while limiting the size of the excesses at any time.

Certain industries always adopt a proactive strategy to capacity provision by planning to ensure that customers' demands can always be met. Utility companies such as gas and electricity aim for this level of provision. Hospital emergency units have similar objectives. In the case of the former, long-term decisions on capacity are essential given the timescales involved. Examples in recent years where a sector failed to plan sufficiently far ahead to ensure that demand levels are met include water utilities in several Western countries. Increasing demand, changing weather patterns and the long timescales in provision have led to a growing shortage of water at certain times of each year.

Reactive strategy

A reactive strategy concerns building capacity to follow demand. This results in a negative capacity cushion where there is insufficient capacity to meet demand. As the gap grows, investments in additional capacity are made, with companies managing the gap in the meantime.

Many companies prefer to allow demand to grow and then invest in capacity in line with known demand. The reason is that follower strategies are less risky and many companies prefer to manage the problems of excess demand rather than being in a position of having too much capacity and the problems this brings.

Combination strategy

A combination strategy is a mixed approach. Initially, capacity is allowed to move into a negative cushion position. Then capacity investments are made that match, or more often exceed, current demand levels and so create a positive capacity cushion. Demand continues to grow and the cycle is repeated.

Strategic positioning

The decision when to build capacity may be driven by considerations of strategic positioning. Developments within the European Union (EU), for example, triggered decisions by many international companies to build manufacturing facilities or take over existing businesses in order to meet the EU criteria on imported goods. The growth in Japanese investments in Europe provides an example of this. Similarly, the decision to 'be in on the ground floor' has led to organizations entering countries and regions with high growth economies. For example, companies from a diverse range of sectors from investment banks to automobiles and financial services to pharmaceuticals have made growth in Asia their top priority from the beginning of the 1990s. What drives the timing of these capacity decisions is primarily gaining position and helping to influence and shape developments rather than short-term profit.

Location

Where to position new or develop existing facilities is a key decision facing organizations. For companies involved in worldwide markets, the positioning of facilities concerns regional and country-level decisions as well as the more local concerns of where to locate within a given region. The significance of these decisions was highlighted in the last chapter where the issues involved in making location decisions at these different levels was addressed in full. Such considerations will need to be part of the decision and management of capacity, particularly where political pressure or incentives such as tax breaks and investment are significant factors in the overall scenario.

Support guarantees

Developments in IT and its application in tasks such as data processing have increased the level of dependence on technology to the point where support guarantees in terms of backup IT provision are a part of both internal and external customer requirements. Data processing and printing centres, for example, are now required to supply guarantees of client support in circumstances where loss of capacity due, for example, to fire would otherwise lead to having no operations capability. To avoid providing additional, off-site capacity (with its attendant high investment and low return outcomes) for this purpose, companies agree reciprocal deals with other organizations (often competitors) that have similar facilities. By 'spread agreements' involving as many as four or five companies, major catastrophes can be overcome while keeping underutilized investment to a minimum.

Rough-cut capacity planning

Rough-cut capacity planning (also referred to as aggregate planning) for periods of between one and two years[8] ahead is used within the overall framework of the long-term plan. It consists of establishing feasible medium-term plans to meet agreed output levels in situations where capacity is considered to be relatively fixed. As the name 'rough-cut' implies, this step in the planning process is designed to look ahead and resolve, in broad terms, the approach to follow to best provide sufficient capacity to meet forecast levels of demand and reflect the needs of customers. It examines the effects of the proposed master schedule (see Exhibit 8.8) on key areas of capacity (for example skilled staff categories and equipment), to assess any capacity changes that would need to be made, how feasible those would be to accomplish and the stages that need to be taken to meet the timescales involved. It also incorporates decisions about ways of managing demand and capacity in order to help in this essential task. It does this by adjusting demand and capacity variables within the control of the organization in order to help fine-tune the capacity plan. Alternative approaches are discussed in some detail later in this chapter.

As shown in Exhibit 8.8, the master schedule (referred to in manufacturing planning and control systems language as the master production schedule or MPS) takes statements of demand (both forecast sales and known orders) and translates them into operations requirements. The rough-cut capacity plan takes these requirements and checks them against the capacity available from existing known resources. This activity sets the overall planned level of output from period to period.

Although small adjustments to sales patterns can be accommodated from one sales period to another, it is necessary to develop rough-cut capacity plans in order to cope with an overloading or underloading of facilities in the longer term. In this way, an orderly and systematic adjustment of capacity can be made to meet any significant changes in aggregate demand and sales mix while facilitating the achievement of delivery commitments to customers and internal operating efficiency targets.

As sales orders are received, detailed schedules of the services and products to be provided are developed and the plans adjusted upwards or downwards to accommodate the actual as against forecast sales position. It is at this stage that the short-term operations control activities of scheduling and execution (see Exhibit 8.8) take over. Thus, rough-cut planning helps to control medium-term changes while allowing the short-term fine-tuning of the system to remain within manageable proportions.

Steps in rough-cut capacity planning

Exhibit 8.8 shows the position of the rough-cut planning step within the front-end planning phase. This section gives a more detailed explanation of what is involved, with the final section providing details of some of the ways in which the plan is achieved.

1 Develop the master schedule. Sales forecasts and known orders for each service or product within each time period are translated into statements of what operations needs to provide. Initial forecasts will be adjusted by the known trends in actual sales, thereby hardening the information on future requirements.

2 Make-or-buy decision. The make-or-buy decisions based on both the strategic and tactical perspectives will be under review. Changes in these decisions must be measured in capacity terms, initially through the rough-cut capacity plans and, where major shifts occur, against resource plans.

3 Select common measures of aggregate demand. The next step is to aggregate demand for all services and products into statements of exact or similar capacity groups. For single service or product organizations this is typically not difficult. For the brewer, it could be gallons of beer; the doctor, patient visits; a coal mine, tonnes of coal. For multi-

service or multi-product organizations, great care has to be used in arriving at appropriate measures.

4   Develop rough-cut capacity plans. Rough-cut capacity plans need to be developed to achieve agreed corporate goals. Primary objectives include meeting demand at lowest cost and supporting other relevant order-winners and qualifiers. It is also essential to agree secondary objectives, such as providing continuity of employment, as they form part of the basis on which these decisions may have to be made.

5   Select the planning horizon. For each business, it is necessary to select an appropriate planning horizon for the rough-cut capacity plan. While this will cover several time periods, the plans will typically be considered on a month-by-month basis due to the interrelated nature of the operations decisions that need to be made from one month to the next. Decisions made in one time period will often limit the decisions that can be made in the next. In addition, many operations decisions are, in effect, part of a set of decisions that need to form a consistent whole. Decisions that ignore future consequences will often prove costly.

6   Achieving the rough-cut capacity plan. This step involves choosing between a range of options to best achieve the plan. These concern taking steps to adjust demand patterns and ways of providing appropriate capacity. The next section discusses these in detail.

7   Select the rough-cut capacity plan. The final step is to select the most suitable rough-cut capacity plan to meet the corporate objectives determined earlier in the procedure.

Achieving the rough-cut capacity plan

The pattern of demand for services and products will vary over time and within a given period. Capacity to meet these variations will need to be provided as part of the rough-cut plan in order to reflect the timescales involved and the implications of the available options for a business.

However, before outlining the alternative ways to achieve the plan, it will be helpful to discuss the difficulty underlying this task, that is, that the nature of demand and capacity are markedly different. The rate and mix uncertainties of demand are in stark contrast to the relatively fixed nature of capacity. It is, therefore, not possible to provide services or make products in one time period that exactly match the pattern of demand in the same period, without using some combination of inventory, order backlog/queues or underused capacity ('order backlog' is also called 'forward load'). Often, companies choose a combination of options that may, in turn, be different in different time periods. Two of these (inventory and order backlog/queues) are now discussed in more detail.

These two prime ways of adjusting the imbalance that occurs between demand and capacity work as follows:

● One option is to allow the length of the order backlog or queue to increase or decrease as demand fluctuates.

● The other is to allow the level of inventory similarly to go up or down in line with changing demand patterns.

These alternatives are explained in Exhibits 8.11 and 8.12 respectively, with 8.13 illustrating a combination of the two approaches.

The second basic issue concerns which capacity plan a business decides to adopt. The alternative approaches are:

Exhibit 8.11 Handling demand/capacity differences by order backlog/queue

Demand/capacity differences held
in order backlog or queues

Capacity

Companies working on a make-to-order basis will use the length of their order backlogs or queues as a mechanism for coping with variable demand patterns. Where demand exceeds capacity, the order backlog will lengthen and vice versa. If demand continues to grow, raising capacity will need to be considered in terms of lengthening lead times and customer requirements.

Companies using this approach will normally be handling special and low volume standard services and products. However, some high volume businesses (for example Western car companies) also manage demand and capacity in this way.

Exhibit 8.12 Handling demand/capacity differences by finished goods and work-in-progress inventory

Demand/capacity differences met
by work-in-progress inventory

Capacity

Demand/capacity differences met
by finished goods inventory

Companies working on a make-to-stock or assemble-to-order basis will use finished goods or work-in-progress inventory levels respectively as a mechanism for coping with variable demand patterns. Where demand is greater than capacity, one or both forms of inventory will increase and vice versa.

Companies using this approach will be those handling higher volume services and products where future demand is more predictable and products are made in anticipation of customer sales. In service companies, decisions to make ahead of demand will invariably concern the product content of the sale, for example publishers printing books and restaurants part-preparing menu items.

Exhibit 8.13 Handling demand/capacity differences by order backlog/queues and finished goods inventory

| 2 | 1 | Capacity | 3 |

Demand/capacity
differences held,
in part, in order
backlog/queues

Demand/capacity
differences met,
in part, by finished
goods inventory

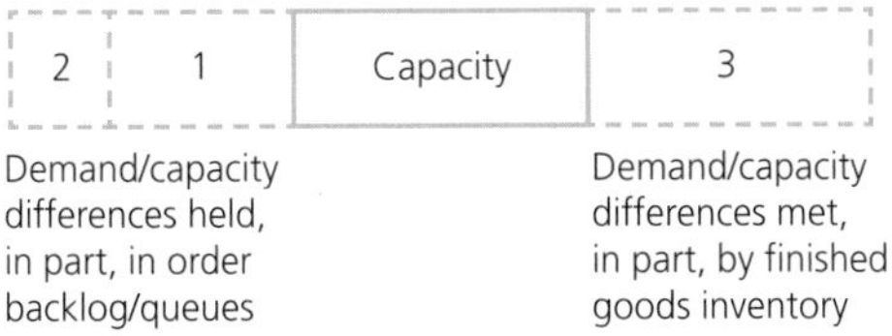

Companies making standard products can also use a mixed approach to handle demand/capacity differences. In the illustration above, the company allows order backlog/queues to grow to the equivalent of four weeks of sales (position 1). At this point a production order equivalent to 12 weeks of sales is initiated. During the process lead time, two further weeks of order backlog/queues accumulate (position 2). When the order quantity is completed in production, the six weeks of backlog orders are met and the balance creates finished goods inventory to meet future sales (position 3).

Companies using this approach will be typically those making low/medium volume standard products.

- level capacity
- chase demand
- mixed plan

and these are now described.

Level capacity plans

In a level capacity plan, operations capacity is set at the same level throughout the planning period, irrespective of the pattern of forecast demand. In this way, companies uncouple capacity and demand rates. Where companies choose to make to order or make to stock, alternative mechanisms are available to adjust demand/capacity imbalances as they occur.

- **In make-to-stock situations**, throughput levels can be smoothed by transferring capacity available in low demand periods to higher demand periods in the form of work-in-progress and finished goods inventory. This smoothing is used by companies to create stability in their capacity requirements, and has several attendant benefits, especially regarding people's continuity of employment. Exhibit 8.14 provides an illustration of this for a 12-month, rough-cut planning period. This principle of using inventory was illustrated in Exhibit 8.12, with Exhibit 8.11 offering an alternative approach by using order backlog/queue as part of the overall mechanism for handling the capacity/demand differences experienced by companies.
- **In make-to-order situations**, the level of order backlog/queue is the only adjusting mechanism to enable capacity levels to remain level (see Exhibit 8.11).

Exhibit 8.14 A level capacity plan and its effect on capacity and inventory for the rough-cut planning period

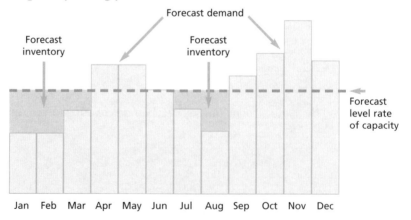

Chase demand capacity plans

The opposite of a level capacity plan is one designed to adjust capacity in line with anticipated changes in levels of demand. Known as a chase demand capacity plan, this involves changing capacity levels from one period to another by adjusting some combination of staff numbers, working hours and available equipment. This approach is more difficult to manage than a level capacity plan due to the increased complexity of the task. Changing

Exhibit 8.15 Chase demand capacity plans for a luxury Italian hotel

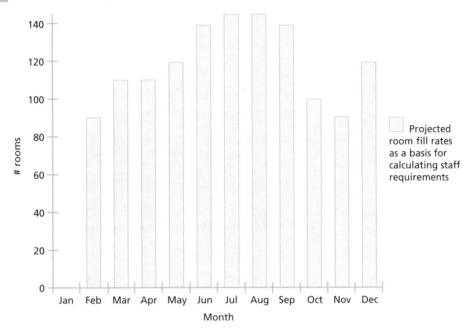

Projected room fill rates as a basis for calculating staff requirements

Note   The hotel has a total of 153 rooms.

variables, ensuring availability, training and retaining staff and the potential impact on quality conformance are some of the dimensions involved.

Manufacturing companies making standard products can take advantage of a level or mixed plan by using inventory as part of the means to manage imbalances, whereas service organizations and businesses making special products usually cannot. Because most services cannot be stored and special products, by definition, cannot be made ahead of demand, chase demand (see Exhibit 8.15) or order backlog (see Exhibit 8.11) are the only viable options open to these organizations.

The decisions, however, not only concern by how much to increase capacity but also need to embrace other issues such as:

● timing – when to increase capacity

● the extent to which a business is prepared to carry excess capacity as an alternative to the costs and concerns of repeatedly changing capacity

● the potential inability to meet required customer lead times due to lengthening order backlog positions.

Mixed capacity plan

The third option to handle capacity/demand differences is to choose a mixed capacity plan. Here, some inventory is accumulated to make effective use of existing capacity and some capacity changes are made to reflect changes in demand. For example, Exhibit 8.16 shows an increase in capacity during September to December. This has been based upon the introduction of a temporary evening shift (18.30–22.00hrs) to help reduce inventory holdings throughout the 12-month period.

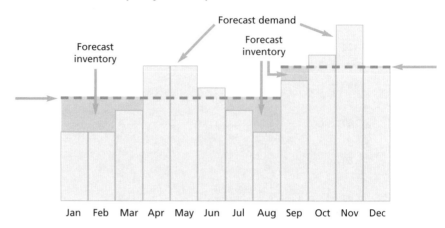

Exhibit 8.16 A mixed plan involving level capacity (for eight months of the year), inventory and an increase in capacity from September to December inclusive

Managing demand and capacity

So far we have discussed the concept and role of rough-cut capacity planning and the alternative approaches from which a business may choose. This section discusses the options for adjusting levels of demand and capacity within the overall plan. These will be within the control of an organization and are designed to help fine-tune the capacity plans so as to better meet the objectives of the business as well as the needs of the market.

Managing demand

Demand is inherently variable at all times and at all points on relevant timescales. That is the nature of market demand and the challenging task that operations needs to manage and discharge.

Within its overall chosen approach, however, an organization can select from alternatives to manage demand in order to better meet the needs of the business and its customers. These alternatives fall within a number of categories that are now discussed.

Changing the pattern of demand

One way of adjusting demand and capacity differences is to change the pattern of demand. Examples include:

- Altering price levels to differentiate, for example, between peak and off-peak periods. In this way, some customers are persuaded to choose periods where demand levels are normally lower in exchange for paying less. Lower, off-peak prices also attract customers who may not otherwise have purchased the service or product as well as those who switch from one alternative to another. For example, off-season holidays, matinee cinema and theatre prices, factory discounts for early- or late-season purchases, off-peak rail travel for otherwise road users and early-evening menu discounts at restaurants. The purpose of these pricing schemes is to help level demand through different time periods.

- Advertising can be used to stimulate demand. Often working hand in hand with price changes, the purpose is to stimulate demand in periods of otherwise low demand. As with pricing, the purpose is to change the pattern of demand and/or create new sales that otherwise would not have been made. Examples include extending the season for beach and ski resort holidays, increasing demand in the summer months for meat products by preparing food for weekend barbecues and stimulating demand throughout the year for products that have traditionally been purchased at festive or seasonal times, for example turkey sales other than to celebrate Thanksgiving and Christmas.

- Complementary services and products can be developed for counter-cyclic, seasonal trends. In this way demand for the complementary services and products will be in the periods of lower sales for the current services and products. Examples include the use of hotels in the winter for conferences, coach tour operators providing school bus services, fast-food restaurants offering breakfast menus and garden tractor and mower companies developing a range of blowing equipment to handle autumn leaves and winter snow.

Service and product design

Companies use a combination of materials, staff and process capacity to provide services or make products. In order to alter the shape and size of demand, companies are looking to redesign their service and product range in order to reduce the staff and process content, not only to lower direct costs but also to flatten capacity provision in peak demand periods. Buying in more work in the form of materials and subassemblies reduces demand on internal capacity, while getting the customer to provide more capacity within the system will have similar outcomes. For example, customers undertaking more of the front end (for example filling in forms to provide essential information or completing self-assessment tasks) or back end (for example self-assembly of knock-down products) of the service.

Scheduling

A third way is to develop elements of the scheduling procedure aimed specifically at modifying demand patterns. They include the following:

- Reservations and appointments are an effective way of helping to manage demand. In essence they are a mechanism to presell capacity within a service delivery system. When preferred slots are already taken, demand can be deflected into other available time slots within the system or to alternative systems within the same company. Many service delivery systems use this mechanism including hospitals, dental and other health practices, passenger airlines, hairdressing and beauty salons, hotels and restaurants.

- Fixed service schedules are often used by companies to enhance the effective use of capacity by forcing customers to adapt their requirements to the capacity schedule available. All forms of public transport use the fixed service schedules as one way to help manage capacity.

- Advertising, as described earlier, is a way to help change the pattern of demand. In addition it is used to change forecast demand into known orders by inducing (often through offering some kind of discount or complementary benefit) customers to make confirmed bookings at an early date. This helps facilitate the scheduling task by reducing the inherent level of demand uncertainty.

- Educating customers to work within scheduling system parameters also helps companies to alter the incoming shape of demand so that the inherent fit with capacity provision is enhanced.

Managing uncertainty

Demand is uncertain, even where companies have developed ways of moving some requirements from 'forecasts' to 'known' orders. One problem stems from the latent uncertainty
within reservation systems. To reduce this source of uncertainty companies use different
approaches. For example, in some service systems prepayment is coupled to pre-booking
which obviates the problem of lost sales. In other systems penalties are imposed that relate
to the number of days ahead of time a customer cancels. The passenger airline approach is
to offer a 'no change' deal through to a totally flexible ticket depending upon the level of
price discounting offered. Those passengers buying a non-discounted ticket have complete
freedom to change, while those with a discounted ticket receive no refund if they cancel.

Managing capacity

The other principal area where companies can manage the difference in demand and capacity is to consider different ways of managing capacity. These include the following.

Short-term capacity adjustments

These adjustments can be made in two ways – overtime and temporary staff. Although the
use of overtime is being reduced in many developed economies, the use of temporary labour
is increasing. The EU's aim is to limit the number of hours worked in any week to a
maximum of 48. In some countries (for example Germany and Japan) overtime levels are
nominal. In others the tradition of substantial overtime still remains, for example in the UK
overtime accounts for more than 10 per cent of hours worked. Within the EU, the UK
currently tops the hours worked list, with an average of 43.4 compared with Belgium at the
bottom of the list with an average 38.2 hours.

Temporary staff have long been used in many businesses as the preferred way of
handling marked changes in demand for which overtime working is not a sustainable
option. Traditionally, employment agencies principally provided staff to cover sickness,
holidays and known seasonal peaks. By the mid to late 1980s, as companies restructured to
cope with the new business climate and slimmed down in an effort to reduce overall costs,
they were left with a core of permanent staff that represented insufficient capacity to cope
with demand at peak times. Temporary and contract staff have increasingly been used to

Exhibit 8.17 Temporary staff market

World 2000			Europe 2000		
Region	Value (£bn)[1]	Share (%)	Country	Value (£bn)[1]	Share (%)
US	45.5	48	UK	17.6	49
Europe	35.7	38	France	8.0	22
Other	13.0	14	Netherlands	3.6	10
Total	94.2	100	Germany	2.9	8
			Belgium	1.4	4
			Switzerland	0.8	2
			Spain	0.5	2
			Other	0.9	3
			Total	35.7	100

Note   1 Invoiced sales to clients

Source CIETT.

provide the capacity shortfall on a need-to-have basis and this approach is proving to be an ideal way of providing capacity to meet predictable and random demand patterns that can be of a weekly, monthly or seasonal nature. In this way it helps companies to better control costs and respond quickly to fluctuations in demand. US companies have long since been high users of temporary staff compared to other nations, while in Europe the UK leads the way, as illustrated in Exhibit 8.17.

Flexible capacity

The last section dealt with ways of adjusting planned capacity levels. This section considers ways of being able to change capacity within the existing plan.

● **Flexible staff** provide the option of moving existing capacity within the system or process to reflect changes in demand, both those that are anticipated and those that arise unexpectedly. Training to increase each person's range of skills is fundamental to this option. Switching staff in line with forecast sales and known orders has been an integral part of manufacturing businesses for many years, but is more important than ever because of the increase in product options on offer and the shorter lead times required by customers.

  In service delivery systems this approach is also widely used. In fast-food restaurants, for example, staff switch from serving to cleaning tasks during periods of low demand and vice versa. Similarly, moving front-office staff to and from back-office tasks is increasingly used by financial service companies to provide better support for customers while managing overall staff capacity within agreed budgets.

● **Arranging different capacity levels within different phases of the same time periods** is also used to reshape capacity to reflect anticipated patterns of demand. Part-time staff, temporary staff, shift patterns and staggered working hours (including break times) are some of the more common ways organizations use.

Changing the form and nature of capacity

To meet the increasingly dynamic nature of markets and the varying patterns and fluctuations in demand that follow, companies have been changing the form and nature of capacity. Some of the more commonly used approaches are now discussed:

● **Annualized hours** entails calculating working time on an annual rather than weekly or monthly basis, with employees contracted to work, for example, 1748 hours per year rather than 38 hours per week. (This example comprises 52 weeks less 6 weeks of holidays × 38 hours per week.) The system gives companies more flexibility when scheduling work, allowing for longer hours at some periods and shorter hours at others. Overtime is not ruled out in these arrangements, but being able to match capacity to seasonal patterns of demand leads to marked reductions in overtime. Companies also point to lower levels of absenteeism. The use of annualized hours began to grow in Europe from the late 1970s, particularly in France and Germany. In the UK, recent estimates show that well over 10 per cent of all employees now work on this basis. Companies adopting this approach include BP Chemicals (Grangemouth), British Airways, Findus Foods (Newcastle), Bristol and West Building Society, television companies such as ITN, Yorkshire and HTV, Fisons Pharmaceuticals, Tesco Distribution, Matsushita Electric, Scottish Power, Manchester Airport and a number of national health trusts. Case example 8.5 provides BMW's approach.

Case example 5   FLEXIBLE WORKING AT BMW

One of BMW's key tasks when it took over the Mini car plant in Oxford (UK) was to increase productivity and bring levels of output per worker up to those of its factories in southern Germany. BMW estimated the gap at some 30 per cent and explained in discussions with local management and staff that the options were to close the gap or face significant job cuts. The changes sought concerned working practices that during the last decade had transformed BMW's shop floor into one of the world's most productive.

Among the important changes that BMW was looking to introduce was flexible working. In its own plants, BMW had dispensed with the standard eight-hour day and five-days-a-week shifts. Instead BMW staff work varied shift patterns (including a regular requirement to work on Saturday at no extra pay) that, on average, add up to four days a week. The shift patterns are very varied (about 250 models) to meet

different sets of needs. For instance, at one factory in rural Bavaria there is one model for a handful of workers who are also farmers that takes into account their need to leave early to tend their livestock.

The result is that BMW's expensive plants run longer and are not idle at the weekend, thereby cutting the actual costs per car by one-quarter compared to traditional work patterns. With machines and processes costing as much as $250 million, the savings are substantial.

Another element of flexible working that BMW is looking to introduce is the time accounting module. This allows the company to increase or decrease a person's hours (up to a maximum at any time of 200 hours) in line with demand and with workers later taking time off or working longer, again at no extra cost.

http://www.bmw.com

Case questions
1 Explain how these arrangements helped BMW become more competitive.
2 Give an example of when a company would use flexible working and the time accounting model.

- **Substituting capacity** by increasing the application of technology or use of customers in providing the service or product not only decreases costs but also helps to reduce the size of the task in terms of the provision and management of capacity in periods of changing levels of demand.

- **Subcontracting** similarly allows companies to spread the task of handling capacity/demand differences by requiring suppliers to manage part of the capacity implications resulting from changes in demand.

- **Sharing capacity** is a concept designed to spread the cost of expensive equipment or highly skilled staff resources that would normally be underutilized. For example, hospitals may agree to share expensive medical equipment. Similarly, smaller passenger and freight airlines reach agreement on sharing a range of facilities with other airlines from terminals to baggage handling equipment and ground personnel.

Case example 8.6 now provides a look at the different elements used by Lloyds TSB.

Case example 6   A JOB TO SUIT THE BUSINESS AND YOUR LIFESTYLE

Staff at Lloyds TSB (one of the major UK banks) are encouraged to work flexibly. Under the Work Options initiative staff no longer have to explain to their managers why they want to change their working hours: their case will be decided purely on whether it makes sense for the business. One outcome is that about 17,000 employees of Lloyds TSB work flexible or

reduced hours. From now on, the bank is adapting practices used successfully in the USA and the rest of Europe to allow staff to work differently. Under this new system employees choose from a menu of options: job sharing, reduced hours, a compressed working week (for example four longer days), variable starting and finishing times and working off site for one to three days a week. Staff can also propose alternative arrangements.

Applicants need to explain how they will fulfil their duties, how colleagues and customers will be affected, how the bank could benefit and how they propose to detect and handle any problems.

The approach was triggered after the merger of Lloyds and TSB in the mid-1990s, and an environment characterized by increasing competition (for example from supermarkets), the trend to 24-hour banking for which staff had to provide extended cover and the growing need to recruit and retain staff in a more competitive labour market. The new system aims to make flexible working a mainstream business practice, not an entitlement or a benefit. Past arrangements were recognized as being too dependent on individual relationships between employee and manager. The aim is to move these arrangements from the category of 'a favour' and to give everyone more control over when work was done, with the emphasis switching to output rather than the time spent at work. Employees need to think through how this will work for them and how they and their respective managers will review how well the process is working.

Part of the launch involved briefing managers on the new perspectives of work as well as the taboos of flexible working, for example that teleworking is impractical for managers. Working at home gives a greater opportunity to allocate more time to the activities of thinking and planning than is often available in the workplace. While each arrangement has to be supported by a business case, a change in attitude to work and work practices and the emphasis on the outputs and work contributions made will bring benefits to employees and the business alike.

http://www.lloydstsb.com

Case questions	1 How will flexible working help Lloyds TSB run its business better?
	2 What benefits do you see for employees?
	3 Make a business case for working a condensed week of four longer days.

Reflections

Managing operations capacity is both complex and challenging, due to the size of the task and the need for all facets of capacity to work well in themselves and together, in an environment where demand is increasingly dynamic and less predictable.

Exhibit 8.18 What it takes Delta to feed its passengers from Atlanta airport on one day

Aspects		Quantity
#	passengers	36,800
	flights	274
	trucks	60
	assembly lines	16
Kilograms	chicken	1,130
	pasta	535
	broccoli	23
	spinach	100
	tomatoes	140
	lettuce	1,120
	butter	235
	coffee	420
#	dinner rolls	18,500
	apples	5,800
Litres	olive oil	86
	wine	6,320

For example, the data in Exhibit 8.18 provide an illustration of the size and interrelated nature of capacity. This is what it takes Delta to feed one day's passengers from Atlanta airport. To assess the dimensions of internal and subcontract capacity and the coordination involved in this one aspect of running a passenger airline is a sizeable task in itself and well illustrates the forward-looking as well as the day-to-day nature of capacity management.

But all this is in an environment characterized by high levels of risk. As markets open up, capacity and location decisions, for instance, will have an impact on future market

Exhibit 8.19 Position in the late 1990s for four car plants in China

Company	Position
Peugeot	Halted production at its Guangdong plant, where demand has fallen far short of capacity
Citroën	Producing at a fraction of capacity at its $1.4 billion Wuhan plant
Volkswagen	New 150,000 unit plant in Changchun lost an estimated $100 million
Mercedes	Its $1 billion plant to make mini vans in Guangzhou is bogged down in negotiation. Many analysts think it unviable

position and opportunities. For example, several major car companies have built assembly plants to help position themselves early in relation to the potential market opportunities in China. China and India are two such examples where forecast GDP will exceed that of the US in 25 and 50 years respectively. As a consequence, companies in different sectors have sought to get an early foothold. All have found it tough, as Exhibit 8.19 shows. The same story is true for pharmaceutical companies, where concerns include new moves by the Chinese government to protect the local drug industry, fresh restrictions on foreigners' ability to sell drugs and serious problems experienced by foreign investors concerning the protection of intellectual property as patents are broken and substitute products are made locally. While some companies, such as Xian-Janssen and GlaxoSmithKline, have earned good profits, others are below target. With prescription and over-the-counter sales exceeding $5 billion, companies believe they cannot afford not to be present and are thus planning not only to stay, but to expand. Companies such as Bristol Myers Squibb, GlaxoSmithKline, Novo Nordisk, Pfizer and Pharmacia Upjohn are prepared to take the risk and gamble on the end game.

For any business, whether to increase or decrease capacity is typically a major decision. It comprises not only the level of permanency involved but also the issue of timing. A loss in market share always goes to a competitor. The competitor who adds capacity first does not necessarily make a profit. But the competitor that trails on the growth/capacity path will find great difficulty in regaining its future market share position, whether or not it decides to increase capacity at a later date. On the other hand, adding capacity that subsequently is underused is bound up with unnecessary costs and high exposure. There are few areas of decision making where the outcomes are under such an intense spotlight. Buying capacity that does not get used or having insufficient capacity to meet demand will always be viewed with a level of incredulity by those outside a company due to the fundamental nature of capacity provision in transacting business.

Within this scenario, therefore, one critical strategic dimension of capacity acquisition concerns whether to lead or follow demand. Most organizations opt for the latter, principally because it is less risky. The reason that companies select the 'follow' course of action is that the decision is easier to make rather than it being for reasons of strategy. Companies face uncertainty and to cope they need to increase their understanding of the issues involved. If not, they typically choose options that enable them to postpone the resolution of these dimensions. One outcome is that strategic decisions have then to be resolved at the tactical level. It is here where the yes/no choice will have to be taken. With regard to capacity it will typically lead to inefficiencies and higher costs on the one hand and an inability to support key order-winners and qualifiers such as delivery reliability and delivery speed, on the other. The examples given earlier concerning China reflect the size and nature of the dilemma. Furthermore, the dimensions underpinning these decisions are becoming more difficult to embrace as the timescales become shorter and the risks get bigger. As this chapter has highlighted, the issues impacting demand and capacity have an increasing measure of these characteristics. The dynamic nature of today's markets is matched by the developments in technology, the concept of work, the issue of where work needs to be undertaken, changes in organizational structures and repositioning in terms of the make/buy mix and their impact on capacity. The outcome serves only to reinforce the key decisions involved in the choice and management of capacity. A challenging task indeed!

Key Elements of Managing Capacity

Managing capacity is central to the basic business task of providing services and products in line with customer demand. As the elements of staff, delivery systems and processes contribute to operations capacity, its central role is further emphasized by the size and interrelated nature of capacity provision. Key elements of effectively managing capacity include:

- To determine the way capacity is most appropriately measured, given the nature of the business involved.

- Measuring output needs to distinguish between the dimensions of utilization (a comparison of actual hours worked to planned hours worked) and efficiency (a comparison of the work produced to the number of hours worked).

- The desired position is neither to have too much nor too little capacity. But, corporate decisions concerning make versus buy, service/product range, process design and the perishable nature of capacity (particularly in the service sector) are among the several variables that impact this issue.

- Within an environment where definitions of capacity are characterized by uncertainty, operations needs to reduce the difficulty of the planning and managing task in several ways including:
  - identifying those parts of total demand that can be predicted (for example seasonality and

  peaks) vis-à-vis the unpredictable variations in demand so reducing the uncertainty factor
  - influence demand to reduce the peaks and troughs that characterize demand profiles.

The remainder of the chapter addressed the long-term horizons of capacity provision and the ways to help when managing demand and capacity. Key points include:

- The approaches to resource planning (often five or more years ahead) and rough-cut planning that manages medium-term capacity (typically up to one or two years ahead) – Exhibit 8.8 provides an overview of these operations planning and control systems.

- The sections on resource and rough-cut planning also provided illustrations of alternative approaches that may be used. In resource planning, the aspects of amount, timing and location were central to the section. In rough-cut planning, the steps used to provide a plan were detailed together with alternative approaches to achieving the plan – level capacity, chase demand or a mixed plan.

- The final section in the chapter introduced alternative ways of managing demand (including changing demand patterns and scheduling) and managing capacity (for example short-term adjustments, forms of flexible capacity and changing its basic form).

Self-check

1 The two common denominators used in business to express, calculate and measure activities are:
   a Time and money ☐
   b People and money ☐
   c People and equipment ☐

2 In a business using a project or jobbing process, capacity is measured by the:
   a Number of staff hours ☐
   b Number of equipment hours ☐
   c Both a and b ☐

3 Efficiency is measured as:
   a Actual output compared to the level of output expected in the number of hours worked ☐
   b Expected level of output in the number of hours worked ☐
   c Actual number of hours worked compared with those planned to be worked ☐

4 Which of the following is **not** a factor affecting the definition of capacity:
   a The make-or-buy decision ☐
   b The service or product range and specification ☐
   c The level of market demand ☐

5 An example(s) of unpredictable aspect(s) of managing capacity is(are):
   a Absenteeism ☐
   b Short-term demand changes ☐
   c Both a and b ☐

6 Which of the following is true:
   a Cost structures and workforce availability are critical issues in location decisions ☐
   b The cost of changing to a more suitable location can always be justified ☐
   c It is still difficult to locate operations facilities in China and Eastern Europe ☐

7 The purpose of rough-cut capacity planning is to:
   a Determine how demand levels can be met in the short term ☐
   b Establish feasible medium-term plans to meet demand levels in situations where capacity is considered relatively fixed ☐
   c Establish medium-term plans to meet demand levels where capacity is considered relatively flexible ☐

8 Which of the following is a method(s) used to manage demand:
   a Annualized hours ☐
   b Fixed service schedules ☐
   c Both a and b ☐

9 Which of the following is a method(s) used to manage capacity:
   a Overtime ☐
   b Annualized hours ☐
   c Both a and b ☐

10 Most organizations choose to acquire capacity:
   a Before demand ☐
   b After demand ☐
   c In areas of highly skilled staff ☐

Study activities

Discussion questions

1 How do the capacity considerations in a hospital, wine bar and a company making lawn mowers differ?

2 Discuss the major differences between a call centre and a soft drinks company producing own-label products for major retailers with respect to:

   ● capacity provision
   ● facilities location.

3 Should an organization always attempt to match its capacity to its forecast and known demand patterns? Give two examples to illustrate your views.

4 Discuss the advantages and disadvantages of the following approaches for meeting demand:
- the build-up and depletion of finished goods inventory
- subcontract work
- using part-time workers.

5 Which approaches to capacity management would you favour using in an Italian ski resort hotel? Explain your choice.

6 Under what circumstances would it be best for a business to adopt a lead and when best a follow capacity provision policy? Give two examples for each alternative to illustrate your arguments.

7 What are your views on the business ethics of companies, such as hotels and airlines, that over-book their fixed capacity facilities knowing that sometimes they will have to turn away customers with a 'guaranteed reservation'? How do you think companies handle these times when more customers show than available capacity can accommodate?

8 Which approaches (order backlog/queues or work-in-progress/finished goods inventory or a mix of the two) would the following organizations use to help handle the rough-cut capacity plan issues discussed in the chapter:
- an architect's office?
- a high-quality, reproduction furniture manufacturer?
- a management consultancy company?

Assignment

1 A fully integrated oil company would be involved in the following major steps in the business process:
- searching for new oilfields
- drilling for oil
- building a new or extending an existing oil refinery
- managing an oil refinery
- delivering different fuel grades to petrol stations
- managing the sale of non-fuel goods at a petrol station.

What are the likely capacity planning time horizons for each of the above activities? Then, fit them into the long-, medium- and short-term time frames introduced in this chapter.

Exploring further

Atamturk, A and Hochbaum, DS 'Capacity acquisition, sub-contracting and lot-sizing', *Management Science*, **47**(8) (2001), pp. 1081–100.

Blackstone, JH *Capacity Management*, South-Western, Cincinatti (1989).

Buxey, G 'Production planning and scheduling for seasonal demand', *International Journal of Operations and Production Management*, **13**(7) (1993).

Dornier, S-P, Erast, R, Fender, M and Kouvelis, P *Global Operations and Logistics*, John Wiley & Sons, New York (1998).

Ferdows, K 'Making the most of foreign factories', *Fortune* March–April (1997), pp. 73–88.

Fisher, ML, Hammond, JH, Obermeyer, WR and Raman, A 'Making supply meet demand in an uncertain world', *Harvard Business Review*, **72** May–June (1994), pp. 83–93.

Fitzsimmons, JA and Fitzsimmons, MJ *Service Management, Service Development and Process Design*, McGraw-Hill, New York (2000).

Goldratt, EM *Theory of Constraints*, 2nd rev. edn, North River Press, Croton-on-Hudson (1990).

Harmon, RL *Reinventing the Factory II: Managing the World Class Factory*, Free Press, New York (1992).

Heskett, JL *Managing in the Service Economy*, Harvard Business School Press, Boston, MA (1986).

Katz, KL, Larson, BM and Larson, RC, 'Prescription for the waiting-in-line blues: entertain, enlighten and engage', *Sloan Management Review*, **32** winter (1991), pp. 44–53.

Klassen, RD and Whybark, DC 'Barriers to the management of international operations', *Journal of Operations Management*, **11** (1994), pp. 385–96.

Parasuraman, A, Berry, LL and Zeithami, VA 'Understanding customer expectations of service', *Sloan Management Review*, **32**(2) (1991), pp. 39–48.

Pullman, ME, Goodale, JC and Verma, R 'Service capacity design with an integrated utility-based method' in JA Fitzsimmons and MJ Fitzsimmons (eds) *New Service Development*, Sage, Thousand Oaks, CA (2000), pp. 111–37.

Radas, S and Shingan, SM 'Managing service demand: shifting and bundling', *Journal of Service Research*, **1** August (1998), pp. 47–64.

Senge, P *The Fifth Discipline, The Art and Practice of the Learning Organization*, Doubleday, New York (1990).

Vollman, TE, Berry, WL, Whybark, DC and Jacobs, R *Manufacturing Planning and Control Systems*, 5th edn, Irwin, Homewood, Il (2004).

Notes and references

1   Books that cover the subject of investment appraisal include Brealey, R and Myers, S *Principles of Corporate Finance*, 7th edn, McGraw-Hill, New York (2003); Luenberger, DG *Investment Science*, Oxford University Press, Oxford (1997); and Dixit, AK and Pindyck, RS *Investment under Uncertainty*, Princeton University Press, Princeton, NJ (1994).

2   In their article 'Coupling strategy to operating plans', *Harvard Business Review*, May/June (1977), JM Hobbs and DF Heany discuss problems concerning the gap between strategic plans and those prepared at the operating or functional level, and offer some practical steps to help improve this situation.

3   This issue is also discussed in Chapter 13 Managing the Supply Chain.

4   See, for example, 'The hollow corporation', Special Report, *Business Week*, 3 March 1986.

5   These strategic aspects of the issue are dealt with in some detail in Terry Hill, *Manufacturing Strategy: Text and Cases*, 2nd edn, Palgrave, Basingstoke – now Palgrave Macmillan (2000), Ch. 9.

6   The overview provided in Exhibit 8.8 will be used again as Exhibit 10.2. The decision to show the same illustration twice is to help provide continuity between the related topics in this chapter and those concerning scheduling and execution addressed in Chapter 10 on operations scheduling.

7   Books and articles that cover the subject of forecasting include: Fisher, ML, Hammond, JH, Obermeyer, WR et al. 'Making supply meet demand in an uncertain world', *Harvard Business Review*, **72** May–June (1994), pp. 83–93; Georgoff, DM and Murdick, RG 'Managers' guide to forecasting', *Harvard Business Review*, **64** January–February (1986), pp. 110–20; Makridakis, S, Wheelwright, SC and McGeeve, VE *Forecasting: Methods and Applications*, John Wiley, New York (1998); Sager, L and Cortese, A 'IBM: why good news isn't good enough', *Business Week*, 23 January, 1995, pp. 22–33; Willis, RE *A Guide to Forecasting for Planners and Managers*, Prentice-Hall, Englewood Cliffs, NJ (1987); and Wilson, JH and Keating, B *Business Forecasting*, 3rd edn, McGraw-Hill, Homewood, IL (1998).

8   As already highlighted. although the timescales for resource and rough-cut planning are classically referred to as two to five years and one to two years ahead respectively, for many organizations the need to plan so far ahead is not required as the lead times involved to change capacity are not that lengthy. While large facilities with capacity that takes a long time to change are characteristic of some sectors (for example oil refining and car plants), for many organizations one to two years may well be the furthest they need to look ahead without limiting options and opportunities.

book map

CUSTOMERS

OUTPUTS

PROCESSES

INPUTS

SUPPLIERS

Part

1
- 1 Managing Operations
- 2 Operations Strategy
- 3 Managing People

2
- 4 Designing and Developing Services & Products
- 5 Designing Service Delivery Systems
- 6 Designing Manufacturing Processes
- 7 Location and Layout

3
- 8 Managing Capacity
- 9 Technology Developments
- 10 Operations Scheduling and Execution
- 11 Managing Quality
- 12 Managing Inventory
- 13 Managing the Supply Chain
- 14 Process and Delivery System Reliability and Maintenance

4
- 15 Time and Productivity
- 16 Improving Operations

5
- Managing Operations in Practice: Long Case Studies

Chapter

Technology Developments

9

Outline of chapter

To provide an overview of the widespread developments in technology, this chapter summarizes the range of applications in the service and manufacturing sectors. In this way, the chapter provides context for other areas in the operations field, as well as illustrations of specific applications.

Why are technology developments important?

Executive overview

The last 50 years have witnessed significant developments in the systems used by companies in the provision of services and products. Many of these involve computer applications to the fundamental tasks within the operations process and have taken the form of hardware and software improvements and the essential links between the two.

Although several of these developments have been referred to elsewhere in the book, the purpose of this chapter is to provide an outline of the more important ones as a way of offering an overview of these changes, both in themselves and how they link to one another. In terms of layout, the chapter is divided into two parts. The initial sections are oriented towards service applications while developments in manufacturing are reviewed in the second half of the chapter, as shown below:

- **Technology applications in services** describe the general uses made in basic activities such as data processing, transmission, storage and presentation. In addition, this section illustrates specific uses in a wide range of service fields from education and healthcare to leisure and travel.

- **Technology applications in manufacturing** concern both the software (systems and procedures) and the hardware (products and processes) dimensions of a firm. These range from computer-aided design (CAD) through to a whole range of computer-aided manufacturing developments.

General technology applications in services

The application of automation in service businesses is part of the progression that has followed the growth of this sector. In a labour-intensive industry the opportunities to increase productivity through timely and appropriate investments are widespread. Some of these are of a general nature while others are specific to one or more types of service business.

Clerical, administrative and secretarial services support all types of business and are not unique to one sector. The application of microtechnology to the transmission of data and speech has introduced significant opportunities to improve the efficiency of all businesses. The basic tasks within this wide range of activities relate to:

- collecting, processing, analysing, storing and retrieving data
- transmitting spoken and written messages
- composing, preparing and distributing documents
- presenting, discussing and assimilating information
- coordinating activities within agreed timescales.

These activities have always formed the basic tasks within clerical, administrative and secretarial activities, but the application of technology to some of them has changed their nature, altered the role of those providing these services and enabled quicker and more accurate support to be available.

Collecting, processing, analysing, storing and retrieving data

Computers that store data in a way that facilitates access while reducing the time required at each step of the procedure have been used increasingly in all sectors. Although one principal benefit is the cost reductions involved, there are other significant advantages such as reduced space and faster retrieval. For many companies, the problem is paper. Before the widespread use of technology since the 1990s, it was estimated that over 1.3 trillion (million million) documents were created in the USA alone – enough to paper the Grand Canyon almost 110 times. About 95 per cent of company information is stored on paper – and it takes up space. With quick access required, this normally requires on-site storage which adds cost.

Technological developments in the form of document image processing (DIP) are transforming data processing, storing and retrieval. The theory of DIP is simple: information is stored and transmitted electronically. The advantages are significant. At Western Provident Association, the Taunton (UK)-based private medical insurance company, central filing took up 25 per cent of floor space while 25–35 per cent of all salary costs was dedicated to managing records. The introduction of DIP yielded significant benefits.

The combined use of CD-ROMs to store information and a pen-based computer to access it allows information to be stored, retrieved and transferred quickly and efficiently. For example, car insurance assessors have data on the most popular cars stored on a CD-ROM. When evaluating the damage to a car, a pen-based computer allows simple access by pointing to the parts of the car to be replaced, with all relevant information then being transferred and collated onto a relevant file for assessing the claim and agreeing the repair costs involved.

At the other end of the technology spectrum is bar coding. A bar code is a set of bars and spaces of various widths which are unique to an item. The information contained includes the key details necessary to recognize the item, together with information such as quantity, price, location and anything else relevant to its description and subsequent identification or retrieval. The information is stored on a computer and read on the item by an optical scanner. The use of bar codes is truly universal, although in the past it was restricted by the amount of information that could be squeezed onto a label; often as little as a single identification number. The advent of two-dimensional (2D) bar codes has increased a hundredfold the amount of information that can be stored and transmitted. This has opened the way to a simple but extensive support system in a whole range of applications. For example, NASA is using a 2D bar code system to improve its method of identifying spare parts in the space shuttle. This system enables NASA to bypass steps where a person would manually transfer serial numbers, thus reducing the risk of human error.

Transmitting spoken and written messages

The application of solid state electronics to telephone systems has enabled a range of developments to take place that have reduced the inconvenience of being unable to make contact with the person concerned, the task of redialling, the opportunity to redirect calls, hold discussions with several people at one time, to receive a signal when another call is waiting, and to leave and receive recorded messages. In addition, message exchange systems allow users to call their own numbers and receive any recorded message, thus facilitating communication between people on the move who do not have a high level of administrative support. But, as Mr James found out, it can't solve all problems (Exhibit 9.1).

Exhibit 9.1 Technology can't solve all your problems

© AMD Publishing

Further developments to speed communications and reduce the need to travel while providing essential contact with colleagues, customers and suppliers are provided by the growing and already widespread use of fax machines, email (see below) and video conferencing. The supercharged PCs accompanying these developments means that executives can converse while their PCs exchange data – the need for face-to-face meetings is declining.

At a lower technology level, managers use tape recording machines to dictate notes and reports, particularly when outside the office, which increases accuracy and saves time. Audio facilities also mean that the taped material can be transposed to a hard copy format with little error while decoupling the manager and support staff thus allowing each to work more effectively and efficiently.

Composing, preparing and distributing documents

Mailing lists can be stored on computer and, linked to a capability to prepare standard letters with customized changes, can offer personalized letters and mailing shots as a byproduct of the system.

The ability to transmit written documents using the telephone system in the form of facsimiles has been supplemented by DIP linked to email and internet systems. The DIP system converts images to electronic impulses while the receiving system converts the images back into an identical hard copy.

Developments to overcome some of the barriers to using PCs are being sought to facilitate their use still further. The first phase saw the introduction of software packages that recognize handwritten characters.[1] Using touch-sensitive screens, handwritten text then enters the PC and converts the manual to a typed format. These developments are considered evolutionary. The revolutionary step will be the voice recognition hurdle, for both comprehending voice commands and speech-to-typed format conversion. Developments are well on the way.[2]

Presenting, discussing and assimilating information

Technology is resulting in widespread changes to the way in which information is presented and assimilated. One fundamental development has been the use of CD-ROMs. Their use in general knowledge provision and as a data source for professional and leisure activities is widespread and continues to grow.

The convergence of the computer, broadcasting and publishing industries into the multimedia sector has led to changes in the role of newspapers and magazines, one which, some believe, will lead to their demise in the next decade. In the wake of these changes, some publishers are proactively generating new formats. For example, *Newsweek* has a quarterly, interactive CD-ROM video magazine. Other developments include computer services tied to magazines covering areas such as homes, gardens and car mechanics. Online electronic services are springing up everywhere and a growing number of proprietary online databases are available which subscribers can access. For example, British Telecom offers a range of services from a daily recipe to weather reports and the up-to-date position on selected sporting events, while in the USA there are more than 2000 commercial databases offering a range of professional services. These include stock price quotations, full texts of major foreign newspapers and local regulations and legal opinions to meet the needs of solicitors and lawyers. The facility to search for homes using a television programme and telephone systems to seek further detailed information including mortgage arrangements is also a growing feature of selling houses in the USA.

Specific technology applications

Besides the general technology applications described above, different levels of technology application have been taking place in several parts of the service sector. Some of these are specific to or predominantly developed for one part of the sector, while others have a more universal application. Driven principally by productivity gains, these developments have also allowed decisions to be made about the location of back-office and front-office tasks within a business's service delivery system. The main applications within parts of the service sector are described below.

Education

The introduction of automated equipment into the process of learning has provided a new range of options for those involved. For children it offers the opportunity to pace the speed of learning to their own capabilities while freeing a teacher to attend to individuals needing assistance. For adults, it presents similar opportunities, allowing them, for instance, to use the journey time constructively by listening to taped programmes. Furthermore, it enhances the learning process by extending the use of visual aids: a medium which is generally acknowledged to increase levels of knowledge retention. One example of this is the growing use of interactive videos. Optical discs are used to store sound, video images, text and graphics with which trainees interface, enabling them to control the pace of their learning, make choices by mouse pointer and get feedback. Advantages include higher levels of learning success, more flexible learning, a sharp reduction in learning time and lower training costs.

In some areas of learning, sounds can be prerecorded ensuring the highest quality reproduction. Language learning provides a classic example where the use of audio material can help in developing correct intonation and accent. In addition, recording the learner's own correct version of a particular item of learning (for example to improve spelling or increase a person's foreign language vocabulary) has been found to increase the progress of those with learning difficulties.

Finally, simulators now allow on-the-job training by creating virtual reality in a 3D format. Uses of this include the training of junior surgeons in the growing field of keyhole or laparoscopic surgery, the technique of inserting a camera and surgical instruments down tubes into the human abdominal cavity. Since its introduction in the mid-1980s, operations have been revolutionized and this technology is now widespread throughout the world. But this development requires surgeons to develop new skills. A 3D anatomical simulator enables junior surgeons to practise minimally invasive surgery in a real world.

Financial services

In the banking industry, in the back office, electronic funds transfer systems (EFTs) move monies electronically between different bank accounts. Direct payroll deposits and instant credit analysis are services made available through an EFT.

In the front office, ATMs enable customers to withdraw cash, make deposits and check their account balances without the help of bank employees. This not only improves the speed of service and reduces the administrative support within the back and front office but it also enables these basic services to be provided 24 hours a day throughout the year.

The use of credit card systems to replace cash and cheque-based payments is extensive and growing. This move towards a cashless society has been further enhanced by the introduction of electronic cash systems such as Mondex. These 'smart cards' have a microchip for storing electronic cash. A card's chip is loaded with money through special cash dispensers or by using telephone lines to access a bank account. The money is transferred between cards by special wallets and their use is ideal for services using pay machines and other developing technologies such as pay-per-view television.

Financial services are also using computer-based support to help automate several tasks. Trust administration and portfolio management are examples where automation is helping to improve the level of service while reducing administrative costs. The transfer of stock exchange dealings throughout the world's major finance cities was a well-publicized event in the late 1980s. This now enables share price quotations to be given on demand, has lengthened the period of stock dealings within a centre while in effect linking the markets to form the equivalent of a globally based activity.

Although the spending by banks on electronic-based services has grown at a compound annual rate of 150 per cent in recent years,[3] it has still not provided a clear lead over the non-banking players and could yet be eclipsed. The competition in some banking services from outside is growing and, for the most part, is technology-led. Retailers have long been competing in the field of credit. Now they are competing head-to-head in other financial services as fundamental as retail banking. Other threats to traditional banks are also coming from IT companies. As much of the work in the financial sector concerns transactions, transmission is a core activity that leads to technology-based competition.

Healthcare

Technology applications in the field of health are extensive. The types of application together with examples to illustrate the wide-ranging use of technology within this large and growing part of the service sector are outlined below:

- Diagnostic – including scanners, endoscopes, clinical test analyses, home diagnostic tests, fetal monitoring and electrocardiography. For example, at Kochi Hospital in Japan, computerization produces results of tests from the pathology department within a maximum of 26 minutes, while laboratory staffing costs have been cut by 50 per cent. More recent applications concern telemedicine. To provide the full range of specialist medical support on a local community basis is impractical. In the USA, for example, there are an estimated 35 million people who live in medically underserved areas. Using video conferencing, consultants are able to provide specialist advice for patients in remote areas. The benefits of these developments have also been extended to provide international links to help treat rare and complicated conditions. Case example 9.1 provides one illustration.

- Survival – for example intensive care and coronary care units.

- Illness management – including pacemakers and renal dialyses.

- Prevention and cure – such as computerized instruments to measure health risks, organ transplants and the use of probes and lasers in surgery. An example of the latter is stereolithography. By combining laser technology with medical tomography scans, precise 3D models of a patient's bone structure can be created, enabling surgeons to tackle operations that might otherwise be too risky to undertake. Also, the application of virtual reality systems is gaining acceptance in several areas of medicine, from helping the rehabilitation of people who have suffered traumatic brain injuries to reducing the stress levels of dental patients who wear a headset to watch a film or music video while undergoing treatment.[4]

- System management – ranging from hospital and medical records, access to biomedical data for research and teaching through to financial records. In El Camino Hospital near San Francisco a computerized operational care system enables doctors to access patients' medical records upon referral and write up the necessary orders even before admission. The results include shortening the average patient stay by a full day and an estimated saving on record-keeping time of eight hours per 34-bed ward per nursing shift.[5] In the UK's NHS, as elsewhere, the growing concern to reduce the cost of healthcare in an environment of finite financial resources has meant a long, hard look at efficiency. It now matters how much treatments cost and whether they are effective. The change in approach has been introduced under the banner of resource management that involves healthcare professionals in management decision making and captures relevant data to review existing activities, practices and approaches to help consider effective and efficient alternatives. The new systems collect data (for example how much resource a patient has cost during a given period) and enable these details to be reviewed as well as comparing costs for similar treatment, both within the same hospital and within hospitals in other parts of the country.[6] Information system improvements also mean that transactions (for example orders for blood tests) are now keyed in at source and with all associated data becoming instantly available from any terminal, including at a patient's GP practice, paperwork is minimized at all stages of the process.

The falling costs of telemedicine are increasing its use and availability. It concerns the transmission of medical data and images between medical centres. It makes specialists available to regions or countries that lack a particular expertise and improves services to remote areas. The system works by digesting and compressing images of patients' X-rays, magnetic resonance imaging (MRI) and computerized tomography (CT) scans. These are sent down telephone lines and in the course of a few minutes expert advice is provided. The advantage is that the system depends on ordinary telephone lines and so can support doctors and patients most likely to need this type of service support.

Video conferencing is also growing. Video connections save long round trips for patients while diagnosis of a wide range of medical problems can be completed in this way. Even psychiatric patients are interviewed using video links, according to the Department of Telemedicine at the University of Tromso, Norway.

Case question   What are the benefits of the use of telemedicine within the diagnostic phase of a healthcare service delivery system?

Hotel and catering

The use of automation within the hotel industry is increasing. Back-office applications now include food preparation, dishwashers, automatic laundry and ironing machines, and automatic clean-up, vacuum, washing and waxing machines. In the front office, investments are being made in automated reservation, message and morning-call systems as well as electronic key and lock systems.

In addition, a range of information-based systems are apparent in this growing part of the service industry. The applications relate to both the back and front office and are described as evolving through four stages:

- Clerical computer applications used for accounting, payroll and to maintain reservation records.

- Administrative computer applications, including food and beverage control, inventory control, guest histories, reservations and planned maintenance procedures.

- The provision of information to assist tactical decision making. This will enable managers to include in their decisions information on consumer tastes, tour operator schedules and link-ups, and money market fluctuations.

- Strategic decision making is the final phase where the computer is used to identify markets, plan services and products, schedule capital requirements, recommend manpower needs, allocate resources optimally to different business activities and suggest what kind of operations processes should be used in highly automated kitchens.

Leisure and travel

Whether it is as old as gambling or as recent as international business travel, technology is enhancing the delivery of a whole range of services in the leisure and travel industry:

- Gambling relies heavily on off-course betting outlets for a large part of its revenue. To help improve customer service, interactive touch-screen videos are being introduced in betting shops. These systems cover all sports for which betting is available and, using a touch-screen facility, selections are made, odds are advised and bets placed. The systems also provide background information to help selections such as form details, riders and trainers for race meetings.

● International business travel for the busy executive means long days and lost sleep. Any way, therefore, to reduce the overall length of a journey brings welcome relief and tangible benefits. Smart card technology at a number of airports in the USA and Canada has gone some way to bypassing one frustrating aspect of these journeys, waiting to be cleared at immigration. Known in the USA as Inspass and in Canada as Canpass, the cards allow those travellers enrolled in the schemes to check themselves through immigration and customs in a couple of minutes. The self-service system is built around fingerprint (Canpass) or hand geometry (Inspass) recognition and, when the two match, an automated gate swings open and the pass holder walks through. Have a look now at Case example 9.2 as an illustration of the range of developments in the travel sector.

Case example 2   SMART CARD TECHNOLOGY IN URBAN TRANSPORT

Smart card technology is starting to replace the traditional bus ticket in a growing number of urban transport systems around the world. Hong Kong introduced Octopus smart cards across all forms of public transport in the late 1990s. London Transport is doing the same with Oyster cards for both bus and underground travel.

Smart cards are the same size as a credit card, but their extra thickness contains a silicon chip that stores and processes information and an internal aerial that transmits data to a reader. This development allows the card to store much information such as details of fares, including discounts to encourage journeys at off-peak times, and to link overground and underground services. The cards do not need to be swiped, so the reading is quick and not subject to the faults that come with card wear and tear. For transport operators, records of journeys completed on the facilities of different providers can be made, allowing accurate revenue allocations, while the types of journeys that passengers make means services can be adjusted accordingly.

www.octopuscards.com; www.oystercard.com

| **Case question** | Using these examples and the one cited under 'International business travel' point above, what are the principal benefits of these developments in the respective service delivery systems? |

● Sound reproduction had its last major breakthrough in 1925 when modern speakers were launched. With the advent of compact discs in the 1980s, distortion has been virtually eliminated from audio recordings. The weakest link now became the sound speaker itself. That was until the recent development of hypersonic sound that allows big, boxy loudspeakers to be replaced by ones smaller than the palm of your hand. Existing electromechanical speakers use electrical signals to vibrate a thin diaphragm, creating sound waves in all directions. Using quartz crystals, hypersonic sound emits a pair of ultrasonic sounds that interact to create a sound which is better than that given by speakers costing thousands of dollars.

Restaurant and food services

Being tied to the kitchen sink has never had much appeal. The use of technology, however, is increasingly taking out some of the manual tasks while other applications are improving customer service. Automatic ovens, food processors, drink dispensing machines and disposal systems are illustrative of back-office applications. The increasing versatility of vending machines has offered improved service to the general public, while frozen food/microwave systems enable hot food choices at all times of the day and night.

At the point of sale in a restaurant, taking cash and giving change is slow and adds to queue lengths. Many companies providing in-house cafeterias and coffee bars, as well as other facilities such as golf clubs, have switched to swipe cards as the sole method of payment. Individuals top up their cards at cash pay-in stations and then pay by swiping their card at the till.

Transportation

No matter which way you travel the concerns are the same – safety, avoiding hold-ups and getting there on time. Technology applications to improve these dimensions within all forms of transportation have been high on the agenda over the last few decades. In parallel, the need to cut costs and improve several dimensions of customer service in more competitive markets has also driven the increased use of automation in all forms of transportation – air, rail, road, water and pipeline:

- Air – the increased use of computer-based control systems in modern aircraft covers all aspects of the workings of an aeroplane through to autopilot capability. On the ground, computer-based controls monitor the intricate traffic patterns and complex airline schedules. Meanwhile, support systems use many forms of automation and computer-based systems including reservations, check-in, baggage conveyancing and security surveillance.

- Rail – administrative tasks such as ticket sales, seat reservations and the entry and exit from stations have long been in place. On the track side, automated switching terminals, signalling and computerized rail car tracking systems form the core of the network.

- Road – the management and control of roads have included automated equipment in the form of traffic signals and motorway, tunnel and bridge toll systems for many years. Although government investment in roads has been high, the increasing congestion on city streets and many trunk roads and motorways has, in most developed economies, been a growing phenomenon in recent years. To help meet this, car systems to alert drivers to road congestion ahead have been introduced. The devices (increasingly being installed as a standard fitting in top-of-the-range cars) provide traffic congestion graphics and news information for an annual subscription. With the UK currently experiencing hold-ups twice a day and each trapping some 5000 motorists, it is estimated that being linked into systems can save users up to 2.5 hours a month.

  In a similar vein, car navigation systems that tell you not only where you are, but where to go and how to get there are gaining ground. Systems now include a synthesized voice for instructions. As costs lower, demand is taking off. In 2003 the car navigation market in Japan alone was estimated at over 2.5 million units. Not only of practical value to professionals in all sectors, taxi companies are installing them to help interpret passengers' less precise directions as well as giving them confidence that chosen routes are not unduly long.

- Water – to keep a ship afloat costs an estimated $20,000 a day. Faster turnarounds, therefore, are a major priority. The use of computers to manage and control ports and load and unload ships has been vital to their survival, as Case example 9.3 illustrates.

Case example 3   **FAST TURNAROUND TIMES AT SINGAPORE'S CONTAINER PORT**

Singapore is one of the world's busiest container ports. On average a vessel arrives and departs from the port every three minutes. At any one time, 700 ships are in port, 60,000 containers are in the dock compound and 6000 trucks enter or leave the port every 24 hours. Technology is vital to combat Singapore's land and labour shortage problems, keep costs down, improve port efficiency and handle the complex scheduling task of daily activity. An integrated computer system controls container movement from the freight forwarding agent to the hold of the ship. A database containing sailing times of vessels, length of delivery schedule en route and space availability is checked against a container booking, with details of content, weight of goods and ship required. Entry into the port is automated and vehicle clearance takes on average 45 seconds. Agents use transponders on the top of containers to register arrival. Cameras read the container numbers, the driver flashes his identification disc against a magnetic screen and, at the same time, the container is weighed. In less than a minute the driver receives a computer readout detailing where he should wait for a crane to unload his container. At the same time crane operators and dockside prime mover drivers receive computerized messages on where and when to pick up a container, on which ship to load it and the sequence in which the containers should be loaded. Retrieving containers from the store reverses the procedure. By 2005, it is estimated that annually Singapore will handle over 19 million TEU (twenty-foot equipment units) containers. One key to its growth is the investment in technology to provide a fast turnaround of ships. It can do this better than elsewhere, being able to turn around a ship carrying 1000 TEUs in less than 12 hours.

www.psa.com.sg; www.mpa.gov.sg

Case questions 1 Detail the service delivery system from agent to the container ship leaving Singapore.
2 Identify the technology applications in each part of the delivery system and explain the principal gains that have been made by these developments.

Wholesale/retail trade

Technology applications in the wholesale and retail sectors have long been in evidence. Security tagging to deter shoplifting is one of the early examples and has been singularly successful in reducing losses of this kind. It is now widely used but maybe not as far as the approach illustrated in Exhibit 9.2! More recent technology applications, however, concern the recording, retrieval and use of information on point of sale activity. Bar coding and smart tags have widespread applications in the wholesale and retail trade. The bar code system is a quick, low-cost operation that facilitates changes to variable data such as location and price by simply changing the information file for that product. A bar code can be printed directly onto a product or its packaging or can be printed onto a label for fixing at an appropriate stage in the manufacturing process.

At a supermarket checkout, the sales assistant (or customer self-scanning arrangement) uses an optical scanner to read the bar code on the product. The price is automatically recorded on the sales till while inventory records are updated.

Developments aimed at speeding up the retrieval of data are known as smart tags. These are radio frequency transponders containing silicon chips. For distributors, this will enable them to communicate via satellite to a stock-keeping tag attached to a container of goods anywhere in the world. This will trigger a communicating link to tags on smaller trading units (for example boxes) and then to individual products. For wholesalers and retailers the same facility will apply, allowing an instanta-

Exhibit 9.2 Technology helps to deter shoplifting!

MAYBE THE EXPLODING SECURITY TAG IS A TRIFLE OVER THE TOP FOR A STOLEN PAIR OF SOCKS

ROGER BEALE

© Roger Beale

neous update on inventory at all locations. In addition, these will also be a major plus regarding shoplifting. Small enough to fit in the cap of a lipstick, the smart tags can be read in boxes and are used to trace stolen goods anywhere in the world.

Other applications relate to intelligent price tags on items such as food and clothing. The aim is to build into the tag the cooking and washing programmes so that when placed into the microwave or washing machine, the transmitter will do the rest.

Utilities and public services

Utilities and public services describe a diverse group of activities including electricity, gas, communications, refuse collection, armed forces, libraries, social security departments, hospitals, fire service, legal system, tax offices, customs and excise, and postal delivery services. In addition to the clerical, secretarial and other more general applications described earlier, automation takes many forms within this diverse sector. Examples include library lending services with electronic-based checking, disposing and recording procedures, military warning systems, computer-based missile systems, automatic incinerary facilities, electronic fighting equipment, heat-sensing devices and power generation stations.

Credit cards

Perhaps the most widely recognized technology application in the banking and finance world has been the use of credit cards to transact purchases. This has seen significant growth within developed economies over the last two decades, to the point where, in 2003, Visa alone handled sales of goods and services of $3 trillion around the world. The widespread use of credit card transactions has replaced the branch as the prime link between customers and their bank, and the impact on the shape of banking will increase as this trend grows. Further developments of integrated computer chips will add more functions to a card while reducing the need for branches. Furthermore, such chip developments will lead to cards that will provide customers with information on when, where and how the card was used. A personal terminal or chip reader attached to a home PC would enable a customer to download information on recent transactions. Surfing the internet, shopping via virtual reality, selecting goods and paying for them with a credit card would be possible from home at any time.

Account management

Recording, storing and accessing documents and other relevant information on customers as part of the essential task of managing accounts is time-consuming and costly. Document image processing (DIP) and work flow automation are increasingly being used. In these IT applications, all information is screened in or entered as word processing files. This allows the storing and accessing of documents on screens instead of paper files. Original documents (other than, for example, property deeds in the case of mortgages) are no longer kept. Other benefits include automatic customer listings to help in the task of managing and improving control from accounts exceeding agreed overdraft limits to handling arrears, signalling higher than normal transactions and highlighting further sales opportunities with selected customer groups.

Cash transactions

Despite the widespread use of ATMs, handling cash transactions costs banks and other financial institutions billions of pounds a year. To meet this basic need yet reduce the cost of its provision has led to the development and introduction of electronic cash systems. The potential for reducing costs is very high. Worldwide cash transactions exceed $8 trillion and of these 22 per cent (or some $1.8 trillion) involve purchases of less than $10. To meet this requirement in a more cost-effective way, cash cards have been introduced. These are plastic cards with a microchip for storing electronic cash. The card's chip is loaded with money through special cash dispensers by using telephone lines to access a bank account, modified ATMs or cash-to-card terminals. The intention is for these cards to displace currency, especially coins, in low-value cash transactions for goods and services such as newspapers, car parking, pay phones, vending machines, pay-per-view TV and other developing technologies.

Before moving on to the next section, review Case example 9.4 as one example of an IT service application.

Case example 4   FASTER PROCESSING OF INSURANCE CLAIMS

A medium-sized insurance company handling 15,000 claims and issuing 300,000 policies a year introduced DIP and work flow automation. The results have been speedier claims handling, a halving of paper and telephone costs and an expansion in the business without moving to bigger offices.

All documents and records are now stored on the system, from incoming correspondence, diagrams and photographs to brief details of telephone calls. Once scanned in, original documents are kept for seven days simply as a precaution. The only documents kept longer are those that might be needed in court.

Now, when staff log in each day, the system lists the tasks due on specific claims. They can review the entire history of a claim, while daily reminders to undertake the priority tasks means that claims are handled much more quickly. The result is lower costs and faster processing of applications and claims.

Case question   From the information above, outline the service delivery system for the insurance company and highlight at which point the technology developments listed have been applied.

Technology applications in manufacturing systems and procedures

The application of technology within the manufacturing sector has been in progress for centuries. With the Industrial Revolution, developments quickened and have further accelerated since the 1950s. The nature of these changes reflects the technologies on hand and the widespread use of computers. Information technology has not only continued the pace of change but also widened its scope. Some of the key applications in systems and procedures are described first and then in process and product technologies.

Computer-aided design (CAD)

CAD concerns the use of computerized processes in designing and testing new products or modifications to existing products. In this way CAD is a generic phrase covering technology applications in several phases of the design process.

Computers were first used to mechanize the drawing phase. The similarity of tasks and the repetition of the basic elements of drawing made this activity an ideal place to start. Since then, developments include interactive graphics with full 3D capabilities and, with

Exhibit 9.3   Graphics work station for a CAD system

the advent of microcomputer architectures and large data storage facilities, an increasing use in design for both engineering analysis and automated drawings.

The central hardware of any CAD system is the graphics work station, as shown in Exhibit 9.3. This is supported by a range of software that includes design, drawing and engineering analysis applications.

Available as 2D and 3D systems, CAD software fulfils the physical production of drawings that would be based on corporate standards established within the database.

With 3D systems, wire frame or solid modelling systems are available, with spin-off advantages in marketing, training and other general purposes. The advantages include:

- improves response time to customers' initial and modified requirements
- reduces costs for creating and maintaining drawings
- supports the need for simplification, the use of standard components, and forms an integral and important part of value engineering/value analysis initiatives
- eliminates the more mundane facets of the drawing task
- facilitates adherence to corporate norms and procedures
- provides accurate and easily accessible records to support future requirements.

Engineering analysis

In the past, product development was a lengthy and often expensive phase in the design process. Designers, having to cope with the unknown, reduced uncertainty with a combination of modelling, analysis, prototype building and the overspecification of component and material requirements in order to address the range of possibilities at this early stage. Modifications also typically led to a lengthy and often expensive phase within the total design process.

The development of engineering analysis software has led to cost and lead time reductions as it is now possible to undertake 'what if' studies as an integral part of the procedure. This relates to fundamental questions of form, fit and function and involves assessments on aspects such as strength, stress, material content and weight. To provide a further link between the customer and the sale, Caterpillar, the American construction machinery and heavy equipment maker, has introduced a software package with extensive colour graphics and 'exploded' shots to give customers a close-up of the working parts of the equipment that they buy.

With an increasing need to respond quickly to consumer demand changes, the key advantages derived from CAD concern reductions in cost and response time. In fact, in many organizations it is the latter that can often be the more relevant gain and which should be given equal weight when evaluating investments in this area of a business.

Rapid prototyping

Rapid prototyping takes a CAD file, converts it to hundreds of layers and builds a prototype from these. The result is shorter lead times of up to 80 per cent. For example, Logitech, the computer mouse producer, used rapid prototyping to produce a mouse in 10 days for a meeting with IBM, one of its major customers.[7]

Laser measurement

Developments in laser measurement have increased the level of precision achieved by processes to the extent that the need for subsequent processing has been significantly decreased. Known as 'micromachining', the equipment works accurately down to 10 nm (10 millionths of a millimetre) using diamond tips no bigger than the point of a knife. The result on cycle times is significant. For example, the parabolic antenna on the radio telescope near Zermatt in Switzerland has a span of 3 m and would typically take several weeks of polishing to attain the desired degree of precision. Using a laser-based milling machine, one segment of the antenna was completed to specification in a few hours.

Computer-aided manufacturing (CAM)

CAM concerns the application of computerized processes to help integrate the production of parts through computer-controlled automatic processes. These computerized processes relate to both individual stages within the total design or manufacturing process and the link between the stages themselves. These developed applications are described while recognizing that the link between the parts will typically offer a greater set of benefits.

Computer-integrated manufacturing (CIM)

CIM refers to the total interpretation of design, engineering, manufacturing and the planning and control procedures used within an organization through the application of complex systems. In many continuous processing industries this level of integration has already been achieved because of the nature of the product and process involved. CIM seeks to move the manufacture of discrete parts (rather than homogeneous parts as in, say, oil refining) towards this level of integration.

Typically, investments in computer applications are one-off, designed in isolation and resulting in 'islands' of automation. The need to link these is an essential step in order to reduce the resulting problems and harness the potential benefits of interfacing these with each other and within a total system. CIM involves the interpretation of the various piecemeal applications into a coherent whole.

In the early 1960s some experts predicted that most manufacturing would be computer integrated by the 1990s, often referred to as the 'factory of the future'. That forecast has not been met and even in the first decade of the new millennium that reality is still a long way off. CIM is an industry-driven technology, with each sector conditioned by its own particular needs, experiences and circumstances. For all sectors, however, adapting computerized technology takes time, investment and a commitment by everyone. It often involves fundamental changes to existing systems, controls and skill requirements. The levels of financial investment and the time-consuming nature of these decisions bring their own levels of risk and often result in a cautious approach being taken. One outcome is that the integrating role potential provided by CIM is often the feature that is overlooked, being perceived as less essential, a fact that reduces the potential gain from investments, while contributing to the existing reluctance to invest and a tendency for caution.

Look now at Case example 9.5 that reviews an application in the printing industry.

Case example 5   TECHNOLOGY DEVELOPMENTS IN THE PRINTING INDUSTRY

Since the early days of printing, the technology used to transfer ideas, information and images to paper has been fundamental to the advances made throughout the last few centuries. From the woodblock printing developed by the Chinese to the movable type pioneered in Europe by Johann Gutenberg and William Caxton, the printed word has been at the centre of education, culture and entertainment.

The advent and use of computing power is bringing about changes as significant as those in earlier times. Now that sound, text and pictures can be handled digitally, printing companies are changing the very way they work. One area of development is in the pre-press activity from design creation to the scanning of images, the manipulation of text and pictures before they are put onto film and the page creation ready for printing. Software enables sophisticated artwork to be completed, leading to on-demand colour printing and, with the introduction of new printing technology, shorter runs are now economical. Also, the digital format allows the information to be changed as necessary or customized to target markets. The outcome is short-run, short lead time colour printing and, as the investment costs fall, the offering is becoming widespread.

Case questions

1 What are the advantages of these developments to the customer?

2 What do you think might be the concerns of printers with these technology changes?

Product and process technology applications

Whereas the last section dealt with the software dimension (system and procedure applications), this part of the overview looks at technology applied to products and processes, the hardware dimension of technology applications.

Automation is nothing new. Improvements in manufacturing based on increasing levels of automation (from the use of gravity to sophisticated robotics) have been a feature of engineering activity and have underpinned many of the substantial productivity improvements made since the Industrial Revolution.[8] Thus, the use of appropriate forms and degrees of automation is, and always has been, a critical feature when designing a process.

What is new, however, is the fusion of computing with control and machine technologies to produce systems that are both highly productive and flexible. Some of the different forms in which machines or other mechanisms can do the work conventionally performed by people are now described.

Transfer mechanisms

The introduction of transfer mechanisms into processes has developed from traditional, power-driven conveyor and gravity roller concepts into a range of machines that transfer a product from step to step at each end of which operations are performed automatically. Where such investments are made, it will move the manufacturing process into the hybrid referred to as a transfer line.

Mechanization

Varying forms of mechanized aid have been developed and designed into processes. These involve power-driven fastening devices with magazine feeds, quick locating and grasping devices for machines, strip feeders into stamping or punching machines, vibrating/rotating hoppers to feed components into automated machines, automated welding and jointing, assembly of products, automated product finishing, testing and materials handling including the use of automated guided vehicles (AGVs). All replace human effort either in part or in whole. Normally, they are specially designed to provide one or a few operations at the most.

Numerical control (NC)

The use of computers has led to a number of major improvements within the field of automation and the move towards the complete, automatic control of a process. Exhibit 9.4 shows three levels of automation culminating in the integration of a large number of machines or processes.

Exhibit 9.4 Different levels of automation and the corresponding machine configuration

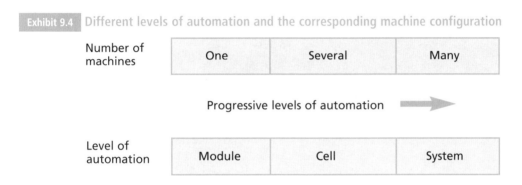

The move towards the automatic control of a process has been provided in the form of a series of coded instructions, and because mathematical information is the base used, the concept is called numerical control (NC). An NC machine refers to the operation of machine tools from numerical data stored on paper or magnetic tape, tabulating cards, computer storage or direct information.

It was first developed in the 1950s by the Massachusetts Institute of Technology (MIT) whose work was sponsored by the US Air Force to improve the manufacture of jet aircraft. The principal objectives were cost reduction and the repeatability of work requiring very close tolerances. The original NC machines used cards or punched tape with semi-skilled staff to load and unload a machine.

Recent NC machines no longer receive their instructions from a punched tape or card but from a computer. A system that has a computer controlling more than one machine tool is known as direct numerical control (DNC). The NC machine tools are linked to a common computer memory with access to all data being provided on request. Computer numerical control (CNC) systems, on the other hand, use a minicomputer to perform NC operations stored in the computer memory. This minicomputer may be used as a terminal to accept information from another computer source or by direct input. For example, dial control may be used to input dimensions for each workpiece.

An NC program is a means of machine control that initially (and most importantly) defines the relative position of the tool to the workpiece. The list of instructions that forms the program establishes feeds and speeds and normally includes adaptive control to sense operational variables such as torque, heat, vibration, material condition, tool wear or breakage and other machining conditions, and then adjusts the speeds and feeds accordingly.

Exhibit 9.5   Variable vanes cell – Rolls-Royce Inchinnan (Scotland) plant

© Rolls-Royce plc

A further development from the NC concept is the machining centre. This has a magazine storage for more than 100 tools on a permanent or semi-permanent basis that can be selected and used as programmed. Centres can start and stop machines, select and return tools to the magazine, insert them into a spindle, index the table and then mill, drill, bore, ream, tap and contour (with some operations being completed at the same time) in line with the programmed requirement.

In all the NC developments one important feature is their link to the CAD engineering database referred to earlier. The transfer of the design and processing information into the CAM procedure will further enhance the growing advantages of NC applications.

Within the context of Exhibit 9.4, an NC-based machine would be an example of a module. On the other hand, a cell would typically contain a small number of NC-based machines often with some level of automated loading and unloading. In some instances, the machines are in a semicircular arrangement to facilitate the materials handling function (Exhibit 9.5).

Coordinating measuring machines (CMMs)

Automating to reduce costs is one facet of the drive to increase competitiveness, but an equally important part of this automation initiative concerns quality conformance. NC-based equipment offers an important step in this direction. Also, direct applications to improve the level and reduce the costs of quality control are increasing and one estimate suggests that by the start of the new millennium more than 50 per cent of inspection systems in manufacturing had vision capabilities – see Exhibit 9.6. Cameras are currently used to check joints and welds and take measurements, and where accurate manufacture is essential then CMMs are available.

CMMs are computer-controlled machines that can be programmed to go through a routine set of measurements for solid objects. Using a probe at the end of an arm that registers when it touches an object's surface, the machine switches to the next dimensional check and thus, by following a programmed path, can undertake the measurement of complicated parts machined to close tolerances.[9]

Companies have developed ways to use CMMs in flexible manufacturing system (FMS) cells and link them to CAD systems to generate CMM programs as a byproduct of the computer-based design system.

Exhibit 9.6   Inline measurement on the body framework of the BMW 5 Series – BMW's Dingolfing plant

© BMW AG

Flexible manufacturing system (FMS)

An FMS links the work of a number of cells and/or individual modules (see Exhibit 9.4). It is a larger version of a cell and hence will typically require some form of automated transport to link the parts of the system together. These often include a combination of AGVs and conveyors (see Exhibit 9.7).

The first FMS was developed in the 1960s by Molins, but it was not until the advent of inexpensive and powerful programmable control in the early 1980s that the growth in applications took place. As with other forms of NC-based applications, the gains inherent in these developments come from linking different operations with built-in tool change capability supported by automated workpiece transfer. Thus, aspects of the manufacturing task such as production scheduling are now completed within the module, cell or system before the workpiece is transferred to the next stage.

On the other hand, FMS installations are expensive and complex systems that require

Exhibit 9.7   Layout of a flexible manufacturing system

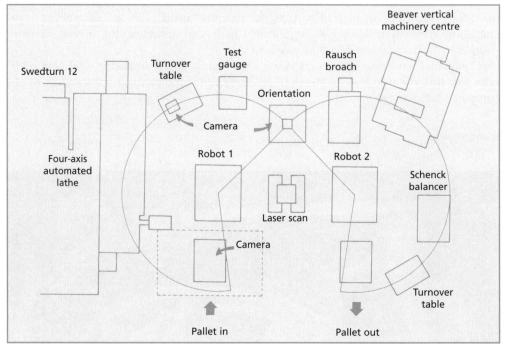

Source Open University (UK).

adequate utilization levels and appropriate manufacturing infrastructure provision and developments in order to be successful.

Two factors that affect the sophistication level of these system applications are the difficulties that suppliers experience in working at the forefront of technology, and determining customer requirements. The result is a shift away from complex, multi-machine systems to simpler alternatives.

Robotics

Robots are machines that can perform human-type operations. They are a form of programmable automation designed to undertake highly repetitive tasks. Initial applications were often to undertake heavy, dangerous or unpleasant work where the financial benefits for such investments were of secondary importance.

Robots do as they are told and, as yet, are not sufficiently intelligent to make judgements. The absence of sensory data, adequate control mechanisms and sophisticated programs incorporating artificial intelligence have limited the principal use of robots to repetitive tasks such as welding, paint spraying, palletizing, the loading/unloading of machines and assembly-related operations – see Exhibits 9.8 and 9.9 for examples of typical applications.

Improvements in the areas of path control, sensing devices and manipulative dexterity are increasing the opportunities for robot applications. However, as shown in Exhibit 9.10, the number and growth rate of applications differ from one country to the next.

Exhibit 9.8 Spot welding robots – Mini production, Oxford plant, BMW Group

© BMW AG

Exhibit 9.9 Robots at work – Land Rover, paint shop 21

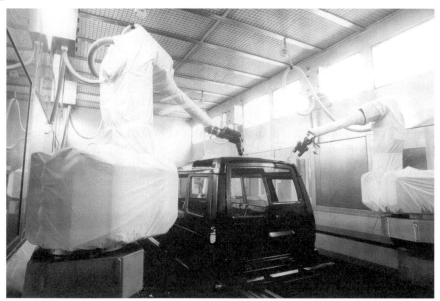

Source Land Rover, Solihull, UK.

Exhibit 9.10 Comparative data for selected countries – robot densities and market size in 1997 and 2002

Country	Total robot stock		Robot density[1]	
	1997	2002	1997	2002
Australia	2,416	3,310	23	33
Czech Republic	525	1,025	4	8
Denmark	824	1,553	18	43
Finland	1,633	3,023	40	68
France	15,632	24,277	43	67
Germany	66,817	105,217	86	135
Italy	28,386	46,881	68	109
Japan	412,961	350,169	330	308
Korea	30,199	44,265	81	128
Poland	401	644	1	3
Singapore	3,299	5,346	n/a	n/a
Spain	6,944	18,352	29	66
Sweden	4,986	6,846	71	91
Russian Federation	7,000	5,000	n/a	n/a
United Kingdom	9,958	13,651	24	36
United States	77,108	103,515	35	58

Note   1 Robot density is the number of robots per 10,000 persons employed in the manufacturing industry.

Source United Nations/Economic Commission for Europe (UN/ECE) World Robotics (1998 and 2003).

A computer-controlled robot system has three major components (see Exhibit 9.11):

- the mechanical structure (linkage or manipulator)
- an actuating or drive system to power the manipulation
- a control system.

The degree of sophistication within a system can be defined as being at two levels. In level 1 robots the system cannot be modified. Thus, all aspects of the task must be explicitly specified in advance. On the other hand, level 2 robots are systems that can be modified based on adaptive feedback and a control process that senses the external environment through some type of transducer. The result is a robot that can perform some tasks without having to specify explicitly all aspects in advance. Thus, in Exhibit 9.12 the ability to transport and manipulate an object falls within level 1 robotics, a factor that is reflected in the major areas of application (for example material handling, machine loading, spraying and welding). The ability to use external sensing for feedback control relates to level 2 robotics and allows applications in the areas of machining (involving tool positioning), assembly and inspection tasks especially where visual information is used to identify the part, determine its location and have the robot move into position and grip the part appropriately.

As expected, level 1 robots are more limited in their application, but nonetheless have many uses within manufacturing. By building in attachments to provide the equivalent of the manual function, the use of robots has shown a marked increase in the last 20 years. Many versions exist and some of the principal types of hand application are given in Exhibit 9.13.

Exhibit 9.11 Major components of a robot system

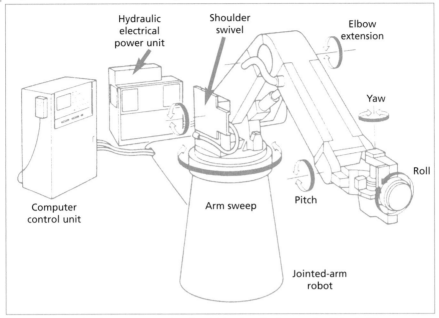

Source Dooner, M and Hughes, J *Structure and Design of Manufacturing Systems*, Open University (UK).

Exhibit 9.12 Major categories of robot applications in manufacturing

Major application area	Examples within the area	Capabilities required to perform application		
		Transport	Manipulation	Sensing
Material handling	Parts handling	✓		
	Palletizing	✓		
	Transporting	✓		
	Heat treatment	✓		
Machine loading	Die cast machines	✓	✓	
	Automatic presses	✓	✓	
	NC milling machines	✓	✓	
	Lathes	✓	✓	
Spraying	Spray painting		✓	
	Resin application		✓	
Welding	Spot welding		✓	
	Arc welding		✓	
Machining	Drilling		✓	✓
	Deburring		✓	✓
	Grinding		✓	✓
	Routing		✓	✓
	Cutting		✓	✓
	Forming		✓	✓
Assembly	Mating parts		✓	✓
	Acquiring parts		✓	✓
Inspection	Position control			✓
	Tolerance checks			✓

Exhibit 9.13 Some principal types of hand applications for level 1 robots

Hand types	Built-in applications
Magnetic	Photocell detectors
Vacuum	Television cameras for inspection
Spray gun	Microswitch sensors
Welding gun	
Hook(s) for heavy objects	
Extra-long finger(s)	

As future sales need to be justified on investment grounds, several things must happen:

- Continued reduction in robot prices, including the development of fixed price kits of parts for add-on conveyors and feeders to allow appropriate configurations to meet new needs at low costs.

- Improved robot simulation, with easier built-in, off-line programming. This enables a user to reprogramme a robot for a new application without taking it out of commission.

- The need for suppliers to abandon systems work. The ideal would be for suppliers to sell the equipment in modular form and so allow a company to organize the application to meet its own requirements without the added costs associated with current levels of systems support.

As labour costs continue to rise at a faster rate than the costs of robots, and as the flexibility of robots is improved and simplified, then the viability of robotic applications will continue to increase, as shown in Case example 9.6.

Case example 6   **ROBOTS ARE TAKING OVER THE ELECTRONICS INDUSTRY**

Robots are taking on more varied roles in the electronics industry and for a range of reasons. While the classic advantage is to reduce cost, practical considerations such as quality conformance are increasingly key issues. For instance, a semiconductor plant today needs to be 1000 times cleaner than an operating theatre in a hospital, which leads to the growing use of vacuum working by the chip makers and the need for robot not human inputs.

In disc drive assembly, robots are used widely because the intricacy of the work and rising quality standards pose problems for manual workers. In printed circuit board manufacturing, quality conformance and cost reduction are driving companies to automate, particularly those competing with low-wage regions of the world.

Not all the tasks performed by robots in the electronics industry are difficult. In semiconductor manufacture, robots carry out undemanding tasks such as loading and unloading silicon wafers from the various processes but in an environment where human presence is undesirable – a slight brush of an eyebrow would create a cloud of dust sufficient to close down the production lines. As a result, every semiconductor maker uses robots.

The same is true elsewhere. The most automated disc drive factory is Matsushita Kotobuki Electronics' (MKE) facility in Japan. The manufacturing arm of Quantum, MKE daily makes 50,000 disc drives using 400 people and 150 robots.

panasonic.co.jp/mke/en

Case questions
1. What are the advantages and disadvantages facing electronic product manufacturers in the use of robots?
2. While MKE uses many robots, Seagate (Quantum's main competitor) has facilities in Taiwan and Singapore where it produces about the same number of disc drives each day with a workforce of 25,000 and robots only where absolutely essential. Why?

Automated warehousing

The application of computers in warehousing has been undertaken for many years, with the number of fully automated warehouses in the UK alone estimated at over 200. It is based on an automatic storage and retrieval system using stacker cranes under computer control. The system identifies each arriving pallet using bar code technology; the operators need only key in the details and the system does the rest. For example, Frigoscandia's fully automated cold storage distribution warehouse in Bristol was built with 5600 spaces, uses stacker cranes fitted with microprocessors that are controlled by the warehouse's supervisory computer. The computer also operates a stock control system and uses critical path analysis to minimize crane movements. Case example 9.7 explains cross-docking warehouse systems.

Automated warehouses in a production set-up are based on principles similar to those in distribution, although often linked to the AGV system used in the plant. Thus, an AGV will deliver goods for storage to a load station from where a stacker crane will automatically pick up and transfer them to a given location. All instructions come from a warehousing control system that, in turn, is linked to its counterpart in manufacturing. The benefits include reduced labour costs, the elimination of paperwork, improved utilization of floor space, highly accurate inventory records, reduced damage and controlled inventory turnover.

Case example 7   CROSS-DOCKING WAREHOUSE SYSTEMS

The classic vision of a warehouse is a large building with aisles, racks and busy forklift trucks that speed around retrieving goods in what, overall, is a slow delivery system. The problem with traditional warehouse designs is time, while supply chain management is all about cutting delays out of the system. The latest warehouse developments, however, use technology to speed up the process. Typical of these developments is a cross-docking system that uses software to reduce the amount of time a product sits in a warehouse down to a minimum of six hours and a maximum of two days. The principle behind this is simple – the system takes data and positions goods in line with known customer call-offs. What is needed first is placed close to the loading bays ahead of time.

Unigate, a large UK food company, uses cross-docking software to keep close surveillance on food requirements in order to ship food quickly from regional depots into stores to replenish stock.

The US-based **Penske** truck leasing company uses a cross-docking system based on hand-held computers (known as personal digital assistants, or PDAs) that register stock as it arrives and departs and during the whole of its journey thanks to satellite tracking. This increased visibility helps reduce storage and its associated costs and cuts down lead times. Part of this is achieved by advising truck drivers of a cargo's destination while they are on the move. So confident is Penske that it agrees to a $12,000-a-minute penalty clause with some clients.

Whirlpool, the US white goods giant, has outsourced its logistics to Penske. The operation has eight regional centres with 60 cross-docking facilities behind them. With $300 million in finished goods inventory, the system gives Whirlpool the visibility it needs re inventory rotation, what to make and from which regional centre it's best to serve a customer with a given product. In peak times, such as the summer months, when the demand for refrigerators is high, customers need reassurance that orders will be on time. To help in this Whirlpool has taken this one stage further – a website through which customers can access the software system. This provides real-time tracking information linked to each customer order, so customers can check where in the delivery system their products are.

www.penske.com; www.whirlpool.com

Case questions
1 What benefits does the cross-docking system bring?
2 Using Whirlpool as an example, list the gains to the company and its customers of these technology developments.

Reinforced ceramics

In terms of industrial applications, the desirable characteristics inherent in ceramics – hardness, chemical stability and heat resistance – are nullified, to a large extent, by a lack of toughness. Ancient urns do not corrode as they lie under the sea or are buried on land, but break. One result has been that the use of ceramics has been passed over even where metal alternatives are in short supply and more costly.

Developments from the late 1980s have successfully combined ceramic with aluminium. This has led to a reinforced material that provides greater strength and a lighter alternative, critical in the aerospace and automotive industries. For example, avionic chassis for US military aircraft are now moulded as a single piece and weigh only one-third of the aluminium alternative. Also, the improved strength/weight ratio allows smaller parts than before to be moulded.

Semisolid metals

Semisolid metal (SSM) casting works on the principle that alloys move gradually from a liquid to a solid state over a range of temperatures. Within that range is a semisolid state with a consistency similar to that of butter. With SSM casting, a semisolid slug or bar of alloy is squeezed into a die or mould and cooled in the desired shape. The resulting castings are free of gas bubbles and so can be heat treated or welded and used in applications hitherto restricted to premium casting or forged components. Also, the SSM process involves lower heat levels than those used in liquid die casting which leads to less shrinkage, faster cycle times and shorter cooling times. The outcome is cost (closer tolerances result in less post-casting machining) and process time gains. All in all, cost reductions of 10–50 per cent are realized depending upon component complexity.

Reflections

Computer-based applications have underpinned many of the recent developments in manufacturing and service systems. The intention is to incorporate operations technology with management/business technology. Operations technology is concerned with the process that provides services or makes products. Management and business technologies deal mainly with the flow of information essential to the effective planning, control and management of the conversion process. Their increasing integration is helping to bring about vital coordination within organizations and the benefits that accrue.

It is essential, however, to recognize the key features underpinning these initiatives and ensure that they characterize the nature of the activities within an organization. These include:

● The need for the initiatives to be business- and not technology-led. System developments are not an end in themselves. Both the stimulus for and the specification of these initiatives must be to meet the needs of a business. Business objectives, as translated through an appropriate operations strategy, need to provide the parameters in which the technology developments should take place. Although providing a humorous slant, Exhibit 9.14 does highlight a tendency that those providing technology options can be in love with technology for its own sake.

● The initiatives should be multidisciplinary in nature. The opportunities offered by systems improvements and the mix of hardware and software developments require an integrated response best provided by a multidisciplinary approach. A combination of line executives and relevant specialists ensures that not only are the technical knowledge inputs provided but also that rigorous testing takes place in terms of the complex nature of reality. Unless solutions embody the application/evaluation loop (see Exhibit 1.12), then the constraints and needs of reality will not be adequately recognized. Furthermore, it is essential that the proposals form a coherent whole in order to avoid the serious limitations and potential inadequacies of piecemeal developments.

Exhibit 9.14 Neil's in love with technology!

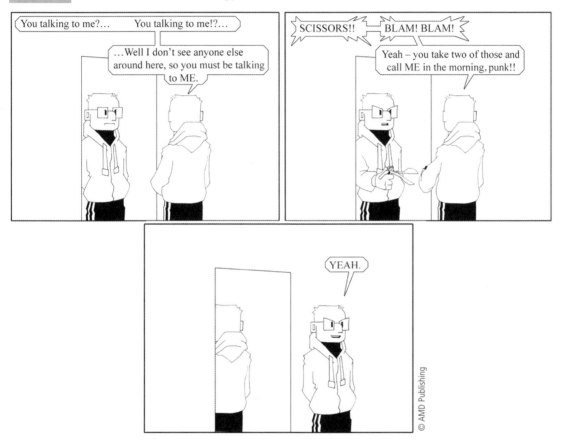

© AMD Publishing

- **The initiatives should be action- and change-oriented.** The success of systems development needs to be measured by the resolution of problems or realization of opportunities. Implementation should be made on a continuous basis and the practicality of improvements needs to form the ultimate test. A report, no matter how comprehensive, is not a measure of success. Action and change need to be the sole goals of these initiatives.

It is most important that organizations place systems improvements within the context of their business needs (see Case example 9.8). Major changes have too often been specialist-led and panacea-driven.[10] Organizations need to develop business-based strategies that can then provide the direction for developments. As emphasized in Chapter 2, investments in the operations function are both large and fixed by nature. It is essential, therefore, that a business understands what it is buying to ensure that the opportunity for systems development is maximized.

Case example 8   THE PRODUCTIVITY PARADOX IN INFORMATION WORK

Bill Gates, the founder and chairman of Microsoft, spends some 20 per cent of his time with customers. In late 2001, on a visit to Detroit to meet with executives from the US auto industry, he was berated by the top executives he met for including instant messaging in his company's software. They felt that rather than enhancing productivity, the technology was actually detrimental, because employees were spending more time sending messages to friends than working. And this was not the only productivity-related complaint.

Microsoft's response was to meet with other IT providers to talk through the productivity issues in the industry and how IT-related productivity could be evaluated and how best practice could be shared. It transpired that several other providers such as Cisco and Xerox were equally concerned about the same issues. The outcome was the setting up in 2003 of a Centre for Information Work Productivity at MIT, with the objective of conducting research on how to measure and improve the productivity of information work.

As Robert Solow, the Nobel economics laureate, pointed out in 1987: 'You can see the computer age everywhere but in the productivity statistics.' It is now called the 'productivity paradox'. In the growth years of the 1990s, when the IT industry was booming, it didn't matter so much. But the slowdown and contraction in the industry since 2000 has brought a new urgency to address the problem and demonstrate to customers that IT is beneficial and there is proof to support the claims. Many companies invest heavily in IT and fail to generate the expected returns. Productivity is fundamental to living standards and corporate profitability. IT's role in this is what the research is setting out to prove.

www.microsoft.com
www.mitsloan.mit.edu

Case questions   1   Why are users of IT questioning their investments?
2   Why does the IT industry need to demonstrate the links between IT investment and productivity improvements?

Key Elements of Technology Developments

- Operations concerns managing the business and not techncal dimensions of the task. Its role then is to use technology to support an organization's markets and customers while using the expertise of specialists to provide, develop and maintain the technologies involved.

- While engineering was the principal technology development in the period from the Industrial Revolution up to the mid-nineteenth century, IT has increasingly added to the technological thrust and contribution since that time.

- This chapter has described some of the key developments in both the service and manufacturing sectors. These are wide-ranging in their applications and provide all or some elements of cost reduction, reduced lead times, the ability to meet a wider range of services and products, and ensure higher levels of quality conformance.

- Managing the interface between these developments and their use within an organization is a key operations management task.

- Bringing many of them together in this chapter enables them to be handled in a comprehensive way and avoids the need to detour into technical explanations elsewhere in the book. I trust you found the illustrations a fascinating and absorbing look into the extensive and varied range of technology applications.

Self-check

1 Businesses in the service sector tend to be:
a Labour-intensive ☐
b Machine-intensive ☐
c Both a and b ☐

2 Which of the following is **not** an example of a general technology application:
a Storing data ☐
b Diagnostics ☐
c Transmitting spoken messages ☐

3 In hotel and catering businesses, technology applications can be used in:
a The front office ☐
b The back office ☐
c Both a and b ☐

4 Technology applications in manufacturing concern:
a Software dimensions of a business in terms of systems and procedures ☐
b Hardware dimensions of a business such as products and processes ☐
c Both a and b ☐

5 Which of the following is **not** an advantage of a 3D design system:
a Reduces costs for creating and maintaining drawings ☐
b Reduces training time for new staff ☐
c Supports the need for simplification and the use of standard components ☐

6 Engineering analysis software is used to assist:
a The level of precision achieved by processes ☐
b Machinery selection ☐
c Product development ☐

7 Which of the following is **not** a reason for the low level of adoption of computer integrated manufacturing (CIM):
a Level of financial investment required ☐
b Its potential role is overlooked ☐
c Its use is not applicable to many businesses ☐

8 Numerical control is used to:
a Operate machines through a series of coded instructions ☐
b Count the number of products manufactured ☐
c Improve product quality conformance ☐

9 Flexible manufacturing systems are used to:
a Link the work of a number of cells and/or individual machines ☐
b Enable machines to cope with demand fluctuations ☐
c Improve product quality conformance ☐

10 When choosing technology developments, it is most important that they are:
a Placed in the context of their business need ☐
b Specialist-led ☐
c Panacea-driven ☐

Study activities

Discussion questions

1 Visualize a holiday abroad. Assuming that you are flying to your destination, travel by car to the airport and use the long-stay car parking facilities, identify the technology applications from when you leave home to boarding the aircraft.

2 When you next go to the supermarket, identify the technology applications that are used in the store. What are the gains involved?

3 In June 1989, the *Daily Mirror* was the first tabloid newspaper to use a bar code. Broadsheets resisted longer, partly because the inclusion of a code cut into valuable front page editorial space. The last paper to fall into line was the *Financial Times* which printed a bar code in the bottom left-hand corner of the front page from late 1991. The universal use of bar codes in newspapers was brought about in part by increasing pressure from retailers to print bar codes – the campaign even included a threat not to stock newspapers without codes. Why did retailers put so much pressure on the newspaper companies to include a bar code on the front page? What are the potential advantages and disadvantages for newspaper companies to make this move?

4 In what circumstances will robots have the advantage over using people and vice versa?

5 The sales ordering process for a wine merchant is a core activity. Complex pricing structures (with up to 80 prices – 40 for both a bottle and a case), varying outlets from retail to warehouse and up to 5000 product lines, reflecting the types of product, vintages and bottle sizes, have to be handled by the systems in place. Identify the key dimensions of the operations task described above and where technology applications would be usefully applied.

6 Are pan-European mobile telephones a business necessity? Give three examples where their use would be essential in operations.

7 Farmers are using US navigational satellites in orbit 12,000 miles above the earth to beam down data on each field. How would this help operations to meet the basic tasks of improving grain and crop yields in increasingly price-sensitive markets?

8 What will be the impact of new information technologies on the operations managers' role?

9 Crime across Europe is becoming more sophisticated. Too often when police move in to arrest drug dealers or terrorists they find drugs or arms and radio scanners but no bad guys. What technology developments do you think are being introduced to improve police operations within countries and across Europe?

Assignments

1 Review a large supermarket, high street bank and library. For each complete the following:
   ● list the technology applications in use
   ● identify where in the delivery system these appear
   ● give the reasons/benefits for each technology application.

2 Choose two service delivery systems that you currently use and explain why these are suitable applications of technology. Now identify two further service delivery systems where technology applications are not in place but where applications could be suitably made. Explain which applications you would use for each of the delivery systems and give your reasons.

Exploring further

Del Sol, P and Ghemewat, P 'Strategic valuation of investment under competition', *Interfaces*, **29**(6) (1999) pp. 42–56.

Simons, V Jr, Wicker, CJ, Garrity, MK and Kraus, ME 'Process design in a downsizing service operation', *Journal of Operations Management*, **17**(9) (1999) pp. 271–88.

Stading, G, Flores, B and Olson, D 'Understanding managerial preferences in selecting equipment', *Journal of Operations Management*, **19**(1) (2001) pp. 23–37.

Swamidass, PM *Innovations in Competitive Manufacturing*, Kluwer, Dordrecht, NL (2000).

Thomke, S 'Enlightened experiment: the new imperative for innovation', *Harvard Business Review*, February (2001) pp. 67–75.

Notes and references

1 Forenski, T 'Coming up with the write stuff', *Financial Times,* 25 October 1994, p. 13.

2 Booth, SA 'Super-charged desktop PCs', *World Traveller*, April 1996, pp. 25–8.

3 Houlder, V 'High street dinosaurs wake up', *Financial Times,* 29 January 1996, p. 11.

4 Cole, C 'Seeing is relieving', *Financial Times,* 22 February 1996, p. 18.

5 'Computers streamline care in hospitals', *Sunday Times,* 7 May 1989, p. F5.

6 Gooding, C 'Recovering well after surgery', *Financial Times,* 23 January 1992, p. 16.

7 Baxter, A 'Making it quickly into metal', *Financial Times*, 15 July 1993, p. 18.

8 Chapter 16 provides basic approaches to improving operations and thus overlaps the applications referred to in these sections.

9 BS6808 *Co-ordinate Measuring Machines* gives users the measurements they should take, the directions of travel to use and the readings at the probe tip they should obtain if they follow the guidance.

10 Discussed in more detail in Terry Hill, *Manufacturing Strategy; Text and Cases*, 2nd edn, Macmillan, Basingstoke – now Palgrave Macmillan (2000).

book map

CUSTOMERS

OUTPUTS

PROCESSES

INPUTS

SUPPLIERS

Part

1
- 1 Managing Operations
- 2 Operations Strategy
- 3 Managing People

2
- 4 Designing and Developing Services & Products
- 5 Designing Service Delivery Systems
- 6 Designing Manufacturing Processes
- 7 Location and Layout

3
- 8 Managing Capacity
- 9 Technology Developments
- 10 Operations Scheduling and Execution
- 11 Managing Quality
- 12 Managing Inventory
- 13 Managing the Supply Chain

4
- 14 Process and Delivery System Reliability and Maintenance
- 15 Time and Productivity
- 16 Improving Operations

5
- Managing Operations in Practice: Long Case Studies

Operations Scheduling and Execution

Outline of chapter

Providing the services and products sold to customers is the very essence of the operations task. Scheduling the staff and other resources to meet these requirements, in an environment of fluctuating demand and growing expectations of customers, is at the heart of this provision.

Why are operations scheduling and execution important?

Executive overview

This chapter is concerned with the short-term control, scheduling and execution tasks and the systems appropriate to each choice of process and type of business. In summary, the chapter deals with the following topics:

- **Overview and interface** – these short, initial sections overview the aspects of operations planning and control and detail the interface between these phases.

- **Operations control – basic tasks** – the factors that influence the design of appropriate systems precede a detailed explanation of the basic tasks involved in operations control, loading, sequencing and scheduling.

- **Operations scheduling systems** – bar charts and network analysis are explained in detail with examples.

- **Material requirements planning (MRPI)** is then explained in detail with examples to illustrate how it works.

- **Manufacturing resources planning (MRPII)** is introduced and how it evolved from MRPI is explained.

- **Just-in-time (JIT)** is discussed and a detailed explanation of this control system is provided, together with the philosophy underpinning this approach and the prerequisites for its successful implementation. In addition, the extended use of JIT as a philosophy or general approach to help manage the operations function is discussed.

- **Optimized production technology (OPT)** is explained and how it fits into and supplements control systems is reviewed along with the extended use of the theory of constraints within operations.

- **Enterprise resource planning (ERP)** is outlined and its link into and extension of MRPII is discussed. Examples of successful and failed applications are provided as part of the general discussion on its use within businesses.

- **Reflections** looks at how the various scheduling systems fit the different service delivery systems and manufacturing processes, together with a review of relevant control statements and reports as a byproduct of operations control systems.

Introduction

The task of a business is to sell its goods and services and then provide them through its operations function. To do this, it invests in the primary facilities of buildings, processes, people, systems and procedures. The challenge confronting most organizations is how best to meet both the needs of their markets and the performance targets (for example output and efficiency) that a business places on its operations function. On the one hand, they are the basis of sales revenue, while on the other they underpin the cost structure and very success of the organization itself.

One cause of this tension arises from differences in the nature of the two activities. While markets are inherently unstable, the operations function needs to be kept as stable as possible in order to achieve the levels of performance (for example those regarding utilization, output and costs) essential to the success of a business. To cope with these differences, organizations invest in a number of ways to cushion the operations delivery systems from the instability of their markets (see Exhibit 10.1). One such investment is in appropriate operations control systems, the subject of this chapter.

Exhibit 10.1 Cushioning the operations delivery systems from the instability of the market

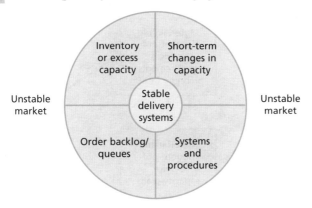

To provide services and goods, organizations invest in the necessary processes. However, investments concern not just process hardware, but include any change to the operations system that helps improve an organization's ability to meet customer requirements. Thus, as illustrated by Exhibit 10.1, investments to cushion the demands that an unstable market places on the desired stability of the operations delivery systems take several forms. Long-term capacity planning was discussed in Chapter 8. Inventory is the subject of Chapter 12. This chapter concerns operations control – the scheduling and execution phases outlined in Exhibit 10.2. Note that Exhibit 10.2 is, in fact, Exhibit 8.8, reintroduced here to give an overall picture of the planning and control systems.

In total the planning, scheduling and execution tasks cover an extensive set of procedures to help reflect forecast and actual demand in terms of capacity and capability. Such procedures cover a wide planning horizon that spans the strategic through to the tactical decision-making levels. These dimensions of planning and control were first introduced in Chapter 8 and are repeated here to reinforce the links between these key phases:

- **Long-term operations planning** is a corporate strategic issue looking (depending on the business) up to five or more years ahead and is dealt with in Chapter 8. It aims to provide the capacity requirements necessary to meet the sales forecasts that underpin an organization's long-term objectives, by planning for capacity changes in line with major shifts in existing services and products, and to meet plans for new services, products, technologies and markets.

Exhibit 10.2 Operations planning and control systems

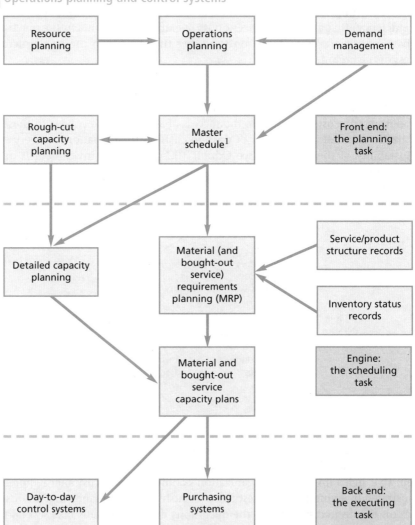

Note   1   Referred to in manufacturing planning and control systems as the 'master production schedule' or MPS.

Source   Adapted from Vollman, TE, Berry, WL, Whybark, DC and Jacobs, R *Manufacturing Planning and Control Systems for Supply Chain Management*, 5th edn, McGraw-Hill/Irwin, Burr Ridge, IL (2004).

- **Medium-term or rough-cut planning** is for periods up to two years ahead (again depending on the business) and details how demand will be met from available facilities which, in principle, are considered to be at a fixed level. This is also covered in Chapter 8.
- **Short-term operations control, scheduling and execution** is responsible for scheduling and executing the short-term, day-to-day operations activities to ensure that customer demands are met and resources used effectively. This is covered in this chapter.

Exhibit 10.3 provides a simple overview of the key steps in operations planning and control and relates back to Exhibit 8.8 (shown again here as Exhibit 10.2) when we discussed capacity. It represents the essence and sequence of the tasks that organizations need to undertake in order to calculate (if orders are known ahead of time) or assess (if

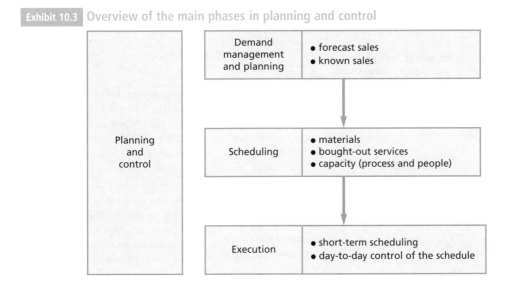

Exhibit 10.3 Overview of the main phases in planning and control

orders are not known and have to be forecast) demand, translate these calculations or assessments into material and capacity plans and schedules, and then develop ways to execute requirements on a short-term, day-to-day basis.

Operations planning and control – the interface

Before looking at the operations control tasks in more detail, it will be useful to explain the interface between the planning and control phases of a system. Exhibits 10.3 and 10.4 show that planning and control systems are designed to take a forward look at demand requirements and identify the implications for and constraints imposed by the availability of materials, bought-out services and capacity. This broad picture alerts a company to problem areas in the future and to recognize the decisions that need to be addressed, the investments (if any) that need to be made and the timescales involved. It is then able to plan for future sales levels accordingly, as the lead times for adjusting capacity, purchasing materials and bought-out services are within the time frame of the forward-looking review.

As the time for completing an order draws closer, handling these same dimensions and requirements moves the plan to the scheduling and execution phase. Part of this phase is again to review demand, capacity, material and bought-out service requirements but at a more detailed level (see Exhibit 10.4). This results in material, bought-out service and capacity plans over the short term that take the form of detailed schedules in terms of process allocations, staffing levels, material and bought-out service purchases and deliveries. This creates the operations response to meeting customer demand, with the day-to-day control and purchasing systems in place to help manage and execute the task.

Exhibit 10.2 shows the pivotal role of the master schedule within an operations planning and control system. Its key task is to take actual or forecast orders and translate these into demand statements for operations – process capacity, staff levels and material and bought-out service requirements. At the long-term and rough-cut planning stages, it provides information in a form that operations needs to assess capacity and identify any investments to reflect anticipated changes in volumes or service/product mix. In the same way, the master schedule provides operations information that not only enables the scheduling task to be

Exhibit 10.4 Aspects of the demand and capacity review by phase in the operations planning and control system

Aspects of demand and capacity reviews	Phase in the system		
	Planning	Scheduling	Execution
Timescales[1]	Although the length of time will be business-specific, it will always be long relative to the other phases of planning and control in a business	The scheduling task may be up to several weeks ahead (some car plants, for instance, fix the master schedule up to six weeks ahead), but the execution phase will typically concern one or two weeks at most	
Role	To provide a forward look and identify problem areas relating to the timescales of the review	To establish and agree the actual orders to be completed and the detailed plans involved. In service companies where demand is met on a daily basis (for example retail outlets, restaurants and hospital emergency units), patterns of past demand (for example time of the year and day of the week) will be reviewed to help identify anticipated customer requirements	
Nature	Broadbrush picture and long planning horizons	Detailed reviews identifying capacity and material, bought-out service provision from one or two weeks ahead down to an hour-by-hour level in some sectors (for example staff schedules in call centres are typically determined on a half-hourly basis)	

Note   1   This dimension is always specific to a business. Building a large manufacturing plant compared to buying and refurbishing an existing retail outlet will often be years compared to months, weeks or even days.

completed but, in turn, feeds into the day-to-day control and purchasing procedures that underpin the execution phase of a system. So a planning and control system starts off as a broadbrush statement of known or anticipated demand and capacity and results in a detailed schedule of staffing lists, process allocations and purchase orders for a day or sometimes as little as a half-hour period. Case example 10.1 illustrates decentralized demand planning.

Case example 1   DEMAND PLANNING AT MK ELECTRIC

MK Electric manufactures and distributes wiring devices, circuit protection and cable management systems. It services most of its distributors' and retail customers' ex-stock from a central warehouse that, in turn, is supplied by manufacturing facilities. The latter hold no stock. All marketing, sales and sales order processing were carried out centrally.

In the past, forecasts used to pass through a central manufacturing planning group that scheduled material deliveries to the factories and agreed production schedules. When reviewing the increasingly poor on-time performance of the business (only 30 per cent of the top 200 lines were delivered within

the 10-day target and another 30 per cent took over 30 days to fulfil), the company found that:

- product promotion and sales incentive programmes were not included as part of the sales forecasts

- operations was principally measured on its productivity and efficiency performance, targets which it tried to meet while trying to match sales patterns and short-term customer demands and schedule changes

- sales knew nothing of operations plans and offered ex-stock delivery even when there was no inventory in the warehouse.

One key problem in all of this was demand planning. To improve the accuracy of this key phase in the procedure, organizational and systems changes were introduced. Central planning was disbanded and replaced by teams comprising marketing, sales and operations. The teams had responsibility for demand planning with direct access to sales and marketing and used historical data, information on current sales levels and knowledge of promotional activity to improve the accuracy and timing of the essential forecasts of demands.

www.mkelectric.co.uk

Case questions

1 What were the principal weaknesses of MK Electric's original approach to demand planning?

2 What factors did MK Electric change in this procedure, and why?

Operations control – scheduling and execution

Operations control concerns meeting the short-term, specific demands placed on the process or delivery system. It comprises the scheduling and execution phases of the control task. Within the context of long-term and rough-cut planning, demand needs to be translated into operations requirements, both in terms of the capacity (the staff and processes to complete the tasks) and materials/bought-out items to complete the services and products required. Its principal activities are to create the instructions and plans to undertake the tasks necessary to meet customer orders and ensure that all the requirements to provide the services or make the products are available as and when needed.

Not all companies require the same operations control system. Factors that influence the choice and design of the system include:

- Service/product complexity – the complexity of the service or product directly impacts the choice and design of the scheduling system. Service businesses offering a limited and narrow range often provide a service within the delivery system as a single transaction. Neither the customer nor information is thus required to be processed at a second stage, which simplifies the scheduling task. At the other extreme, scheduling a range of multi-step services or products completed in different parts of the total delivery system will result in the need for a more complex scheduling system.

- Special vs standard services and products – bound up with the last point, another factor that affects the nature and type of operations control systems is whether a service or product is a special (non-repeat) or a standard (repeat). In the case of the latter, the steps to complete the task are known. This creates the opportunity to develop a system to manage scheduling and execution. Where services and products are specials, the control system is less detailed and relies on the skilled staff who provide the offerings to undertake the day-to-day scheduling tasks.

- Choice of service delivery system or manufacturing process – linked to the last two points is the choice of process. This reflects the nature of a business in terms of volumes, order sizes and markets, and the operations scheduling system will reflect these differences, as will be illustrated later.

- Internal span of process – the extent to which a company makes or provides internally the parts that comprise the services or products it sells will directly affect the complexity of the operations scheduling task. The more it purchases from outside, the simpler the task of scheduling the steps of the internal process. Similarly, the more it purchases from outside, the greater the orientation of the execution phase towards purchasing and supplier management.

- Decisions on demand and capacity reconciliation – the decisions taken by a business regarding the management of demand and capacity will directly affect the complexity of the scheduling task. The more demand and capacity are managed, the easier the scheduling task and its execution.

Operations control – basic tasks

An operations control system comprises three distinct but integrated activities designed to manage and execute requirements:

- loading – determining the capacity and volumes at each stage in a process. This step will include assigning tasks to staff groups or work centres
- sequencing – deciding on the order in which jobs will be completed at each stage in the process
- scheduling – involves allocating a start and finish time to each actual or forecast order.

These three activities are described in more detail before we move on to describe the types of operations control systems in use.

Loading

Loading concerns determining the capacity and volumes at each stage in a process and assigning jobs/tasks to a part of the process (for example person or work centre). As explained in Chapter 8, for planning purposes capacity plans need to be based on the net amount available. Staff only work for a given period, while processes, although theoretically available 24/7, are often not intended to run continuously. In addition, the normal scheduled time needs to be adjusted for necessary, known reductions such as set-up times, personal and relaxation time for staff and maintenance, as well as an allowance for unknown reductions such as breakdowns, absenteeism and training.

Within this task there are two principal approaches to loading operations – finite and infinite loading:

- Finite loading allocates work to an agreed upper limit. Examples where this applies include appointment systems for dentists, restaurants, hospital outpatient departments and hairdressers. Booking passengers onto scheduled airline flights falls into this category, but provides an example of how an operations control system also handles uncertainty. In this instance, airlines will overbook flights as a way of coping with passengers who have confirmed tickets but fail to turn up for the flight. As 'no-shows', as they are called, are not penalized, airlines overbook flights. The overbooking of a flight to take account of the anticipated no-shows can be as high as 15 per cent. The rationale for this overbooking decision is to avoid less than full flights in times of high demand. The downside is handling the occasions when flights are overbooked and 'dead heading' has to be implemented. As airlines deliberately overbook, the known outcomes include those times when more passengers turn up for a flight with confirmed reservations than there are seats. How to handle this is then built into the operations control procedures.
- Infinite loading places no limits on accepting customers' orders. Examples include acci-

dent and emergency care units in hospitals, fast-food restaurants and banks. In these businesses, customers accept that at busy times queues will be longer. But the operations system responds to situations by developing a capacity provision that can adjust its level up or down in line with fluctuating changes in demand. For example, in banks additional teller positions open as queues lengthen and close as queues shorten. Also, in times of major accidents, off-duty hospital staff are asked to report to work to meet the resulting higher levels of patient treatment and care.

Sequencing

When orders are received or customers arrive, the decision on which jobs to be completed at each stage of the process or which customers to serve first needs to be made. This activity is termed 'sequencing'. Prioritizing rules are often used to help in making such decisions, and include:

- Customer due date – typically customers' required delivery (or due) dates form the basis of the operations schedule. Where customers' requirements are processed as and when they are received (for example in a fast-food restaurant, bank, post office or retail outlet), then the 'schedule' reflects a customer's position in the queue. In businesses where customers order ahead of time, the sequencing within the operations control system reflects the relevant due date.

- Customer priority ranking – operations will sometimes alter the position of an order or customer in the schedule due to the importance attached to the customer involved, for example the relative value (£s) of business a customer places with the company. Other factors that may lead to a change in schedule position include remedying a service failure or faulty product.

- Minimizing set-ups – in some manufacturing processes, sequencing the order in which products are made has a significant impact on loss of saleable productive time through set-ups. In injection moulding, the length of time needed to change from one colour of plastic to another will vary depending upon the two colours involved. Thus, when sequencing colour changes, many companies move progressively from light (for example white and yellow) to dark (for example dark blue and black) colours for this reason. Similarly, the time to change the setting on a machine will vary by product sequence. In order to minimize total lost saleable productive time due to set-ups, decisions on the operations schedule will reflect these factors.

- First in, first out (FIFO) – some businesses schedule customer requirements in exactly the order in which they enter the service or production system. The examples given under 'Customer due date' apply here. Other examples include mail order companies, driving licence and passport applications and most high customer contact service systems where booking ahead of time is not a feasible option. Passenger air terminals use a FIFO system for checking in passengers. However, British Airways (BA) uses a mixed system for handling business class travellers at Terminal 4 of London's Heathrow Airport. Recognizing that business travellers are often short of time when arriving for flights, BA staff check the flight times of each business class passenger entering the check-in queue. If, in their opinion, passengers would be pressed for time if processed by normal check-in procedures and existing queues, BA staff reroute them through two check-in desks designated for such passengers. In that way, the system has been designed to provide a supplementary subsystem to bypass the normal service delivery provision so that the needs of all passengers can be met.

In a similar way, an accident and emergency unit in a hospital will treat patients in line with the seriousness of their condition and then on a FIFO basis. Medical staff assess the seriousness of a patient's condition into life threatening, serious but not life threatening, and routine. Within these categories, a decision on priorities may still be made, with the FIFO principle then being used within these bands.

Scheduling

A schedule is a detailed timetable allocating a start and finish date to each order while taking into account the sequence in which they will be completed. An integral part of this concerns the short-term capacity and materials management tasks. The scheduling and execution of the orders in a system are thus concerned with determining when to start jobs in order to meet delivery requirements and manage and control these orders through the process.

In some businesses, such as rapid-response service operations where customers arrive in an unplanned way, the scheduling of orders is linked to the arrival of customers within the service delivery system. Here, the key short-term control tasks concern material and bought-out services purchasing and capacity planning. The detailed scheduling task is an inherent part of the system with the server/customer interfacing in stimulus/response mode. Even so, the task of matching short-term capacity with uncertain patterns of demand creates a difficult task that companies alleviate by reshaping demand and varying capacity (see Chapter 8).

Many businesses are, however, faced with a more demanding scheduling task due to service/product complexity, choice of process, internal span of process and decisions of demand and capacity reconciliation.

Operations scheduling – systems

The remainder of this chapter describes the systems used to schedule and manage operations. As services and products differ, in terms such as complexity (the number of steps involved to provide a service or make a product), the one-off or repetitive nature of demand and the range offered, the system will differ to reflect the task on hand. The simpler the task, the simpler the scheduling system. In fact, in some businesses the level of system-based scheduling will be low. Here, whereas capacity and materials will be scheduled against expected levels of demand, hour-by-hour control will be exercised on an as-needed basis. Take, for example, a café on a main street that has a limited number of seats inside but space for more on the pavement, and also offers a takeaway service. The fresh food requirements will reflect the day of the week and time of the year. Staffing will be scheduled in line with each hour of a day and decisions taken regarding the preparation of some food (for example salads and sandwich fillings) in pre-peak time periods. Staff training to handle the various tasks (for example fresh coffee maker, toaster and hot foods) will facilitate staff flexibility during busy times. Then, within these dimensions, decisions on who does what will be handled by a combination of allocating principal tasks to staff supplemented by an ad hoc reallocation depending upon the level of demand during the day. Attempting to schedule in a more detailed way would be inappropriate, as being able to forecast daily demand would depend on factors such as the weather, level of passing trade and pattern of regular demand in a service business where demand needs to be met as quickly as possible and queue lengths kept short.

In other businesses, the level of operations scheduling will be more detailed as the system is more manageable, in that customer orders are not of the short duration demand profile described above. Even so, some scheduling systems are simpler than others but adequate to meet the control requirements of the operations system involved. We will start off by describing the easier systems, such as bar charts and network analysis and then move on to ones that meet the needs of more complex operations tasks, for example MRPI and JIT.

Bar charts

One of the simplest methods of operations control is a bar chart. In essence, this method shows the elements of capacity (for example staff or process) on the vertical axis and represents time as a bar on the horizontal axis – see Exhibit 10.5. Selecting the appropriate dimension of time (for example hours, days or weeks) will reflect the nature of the operations system to be scheduled. Exhibit 10.5 uses weeks as this best suited these scheduling needs. Often in professional companies there would also be a calendar running horizontally to show the schedule against actual dates as an aid, in this instance, in scheduling consultant availability against start times for new assignments. Finally, a description of the task (in the example provided by Exhibit 10.5, this is the name of the client) is added to the chart.

Exhibit 10.5 Bar chart representing assignment allocations

Consultant	Time (weeks)							
	1	2	3	4	5	6	7	8
Jim Brooks	Carr Group			Russell Taylor (London)				
Eve Williams	MDH & Partners (Birmingham)							
Anne Watts	Müller GmbH (Düsseldorf)							
John Burrows	Carroll Services (Dublin)							
Charlie Daniels	Carr Group			Russell Taylor (London)				
Bill Johnson	SM Associates (Brussels)							

Bar charts are also used to schedule and control more complex operations systems, particularly where choices can be made. Exhibit 10.5 represents an overview of consultant allocations to clients. Within each assignment, the various elements would be covered by the team of consultants allocated to that job. The lead consultant would typically control the allocation of tasks to other staff to reflect skills and experience, individual loadings and completion times. Exhibit 10.6 shows a bar chart to represent this. You will see from this that it covers some of the tasks identified at the start of the assignment. Other tasks will be identified as the assignment continues and these will be introduced into the schedule of work, allocated a team member(s) and a start and finish date. Typically, a weekly review would check progress against the schedule. The bar chart would then be updated in terms of the work completed, with any revisions to the schedule being incorporated at the review meeting.

Some services and products comprise several steps, each completed by a different part of the delivery or process system. Again bar charts are used to schedule these jobs through the system to meet the required delivery dates. A bar chart identifies and helps to resolve potential capacity problems, provides short-term control over the progress of work and allows a

Exhibit 10.6 Bar chart for scheduling initial tasks

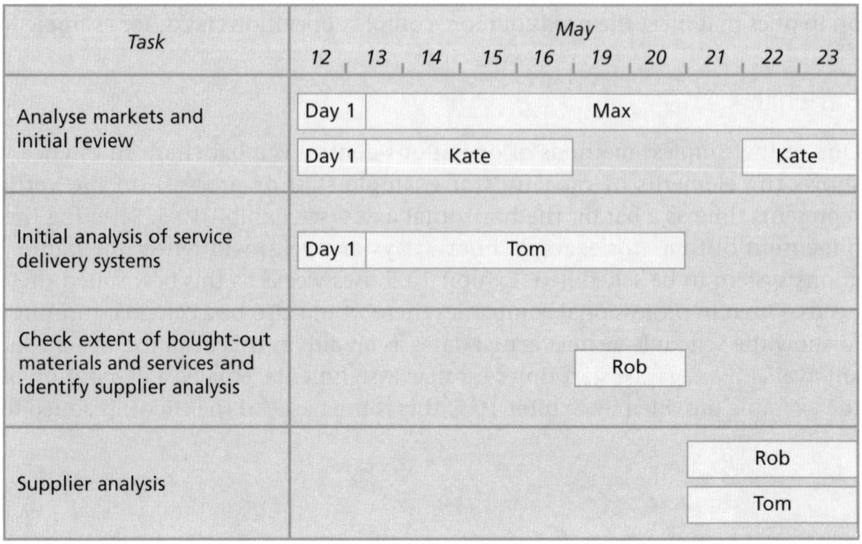

Task	May 12	13	14	15	16	19	20	21	22	23
Analyse markets and initial review	Day 1				Max					
	Day 1		Kate						Kate	
Initial analysis of service delivery systems	Day 1			Tom						
Check extent of bought-out materials and services and identify supplier analysis							Rob			
Supplier analysis									Rob	
									Tom	

business to assess whether or not operations is able to take on additional sales orders within existing capacity levels and delivery timescales. Exhibit 10.7 provides part of a schedule showing jobs loaded on different processes within the sequence necessary to complete the task. Here the products comprise a number of steps that, in turn, need to be completed on different processes. The resulting task is more complex and includes the need to determine priorities between jobs that require the same process.

Exhibits 10.5 to 10.7 show the use of bar charts to manage scheduling requirements of differing complexity in terms of variety and detail. The use of IT-based systems would typically be used to manage such schedules. In many businesses, the demands on and requirements of operations control lead to other systems being used to meet these more difficult control tasks. The sections that follow describe these.

Exhibit 10.7 Bar chart showing orders against machine processes

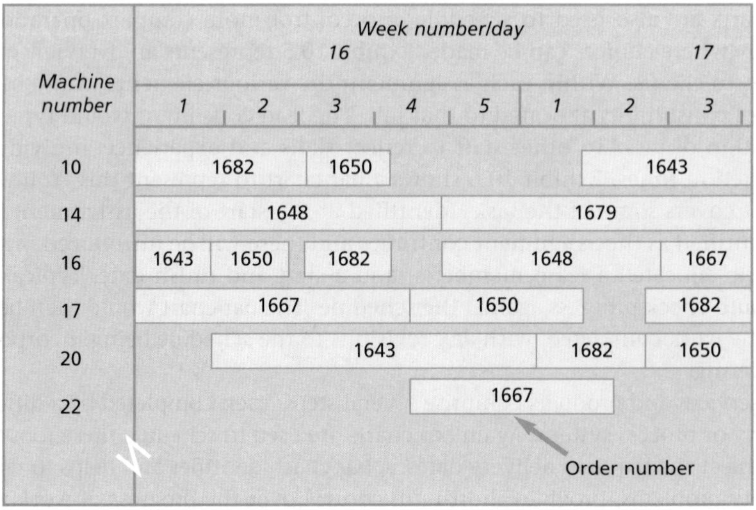

Machine number	Week number/day 16						17			
	1	2	3	4	5	1	2	3
10	1682		1650				1643		
14	1648				1679				
16	1643	1650	1682	1648			1667		
17	1667			1650			1682		
20	1643				1682		1650	
22	1667							

Order number

Network analysis

Businesses involved in providing services that can only be undertaken at a client's premises, or making products of such size or construction that they cannot be transported after completion, will often use a project process to undertake the work involved (see Chapters 5 and 6). If a project contains only a few activities, a bar chart or even an informal scheduling approach can be adopted. However, most projects are complex and involve many interrelated activities, necessitating the development of a formal plan and the use of IT-based systems. The one-off or infrequent nature of these tasks militates against the use of the more traditional scheduling and progressing methods described later. As a result, control systems under the heading 'network analysis' were developed, the principles of which are now explained.

General aspects of network analysis

The first task in network analysis is to determine the level of detail on which the activities to complete the task will be based. Often in large projects an overall network will be developed to provide a control system to overview the whole task, with subnetworks provided to give control at a more detailed level. When this has been agreed, the activities that have to be completed will be listed.

In a network, the task to be completed is stated as a series of 'activities', all of which have to be completed for the task to be finished. The key is to draw the network so that the activities are shown in the order in which they have to occur. To do this it is necessary to establish, for each activity, the other activity or activities that have to be completed before it can start. This is called 'dependency'. One or more activities will, however, be independent of any other activity being completed before they can start. These are obviously the ones that are completed at the beginning (although in complex networks some independent activities may not be started at the beginning, as explained later). When these independent activities have been completed (an 'event'), then any activities that can only start when these are complete can now commence and so on. In this way the network is developed. Those activities that follow others are said to be 'sequential', while those that can be completed at the same time as others (that is, they are independent of one another) are said to be 'parallel'. The language and symbols used in constructing networks are provided in Exhibit 10.8.

Exhibit 10.8 The principal building blocks used to construct networks

Type	Description	Symbol
Activity	Activities are tasks that have a time duration. At the start and finish of each activity there will be, in network language, an event	⟶
Event	Events occur instantaneously and state that the preceding activity (or activities) is (are) now complete and other activities that depend on its (their) completion can now start. As it is instantaneous, it has no time duration	◯
Dummy activity	Dummy activities are used in two ways: ● an aid to drawing a network, as will be shown later ● a way of extending the dependency of one or more activities to other activities	- - - -▸

Scheduling by network analysis

When constructing a network the steps to use are as follows:

- **Planning** – establish all the activities or steps to be completed, determine the dependency between these activities and draw the network.
- **Scheduling** – apply to a network any limiting factors such as time, cost and the availability of materials, bought-out services, equipment and staff. These factors will often necessitate the redrawing of parts of a network to accommodate the constraints they impose.
- **Controlling** – obtain feedback during a project to ensure adherence to the plan, and update the plan in the light of any changes.

These three steps are now explained in greater detail.

Planning

The first task when constructing a network is to establish and list all the activities necessary to complete a project and at the level of detail already agreed, although Mr James and Gianni appear unaware of this – see Exhibit 10.9. Following this, it is necessary to determine the level of dependency. The final task is to draw the network. Several examples that result from the completion of these tasks are provided later. The symbols used throughout were explained in Exhibit 10.8, and the following general guidelines will prove useful when setting about the task of drawing a network:

- all activities start and end with an event
- an activity is a time-consuming task
- an event is instantaneous; its occurrence means that all activities entering that event sign have now been completed and, therefore, all activities leaving that event sign can now be started
- any number of activities can go into and out of an event
- activities, wherever possible, should go from left to right
- activities occurring on the same path are sequential and thus directly dependent upon each other

Exhibit 10.9 Mr James and Gianni have been working out the brief for a new project

- activities on different paths are parallel activities; they are independent of other sets of parallel activities and can, therefore, take place at the same time
- dummy activities are not time-consuming (the time involved is already registered with the original activity), hence their name. They are used in two ways:
  - as an aid to drawing a network. As such they form part of the set of conventions to be followed. One of these conventions is that two or more activities cannot leave one event sign and enter the next event sign. In order to accommodate such situations, dummy activities are used (see Exhibits 10.10 and 10.11)
  - to extend the dependency of one or more activities to other activities (see Exhibit 10.13).

Exhibit 10.10 Introducing the use of a dummy activity

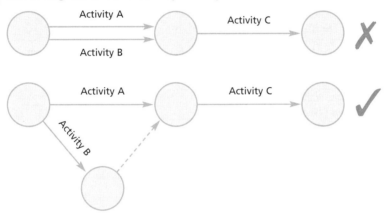

Exhibit 10.11 Network representing the task at the top of the next page

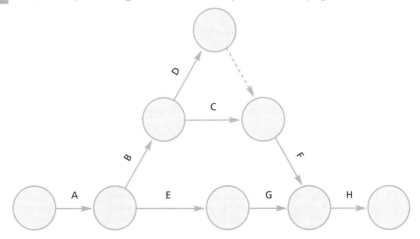

Notes   Activities A, E, G and H are examples of sequential activities.
Activities B, C, D and F are parallel to activities E and G.

To explain, the adjacent boxed example lists the activities to be undertaken to complete a task and indicates those activities on which an activity is dependent. Therefore, Activity B cannot start until Activity A has been completed and so on. The resulting network is shown as Exhibit 10.11. It starts with Activity A as this is the only activity that does not depend upon any other activity before it can start. Then the rest of the activities are built into the network to represent the statement of the task.

Activity	Activities on which it is dependent
A	–
B	A
C	A
D	B
E	B
F	C, D
G	E
H	F, G

Scheduling

The next step is to schedule the network. This involves applying limiting factors such as time and cost to the network. In the example presented as Exhibits 10.12 and 10.13, the activities are given for the production of an educational cassette, with the number of days it takes to complete each activity. All the tasks, unless specified, are completed by the consultant running the business. Note

Exhibit 10.12 The activities involved in preparing an educational cassette

Activity	Duration (working days)
1 Client briefing	4
2 Write draft 1	7
3 Await client approval of draft 1	5
4 Write draft 2	6
5 Await client approval of draft 2	5
6 Create the production script (PS)	3
7 Await client approval of the PS	2
8 Produce the cassette tape of the PS	5
9 Book studios	1
10 Confirm studio booking	1
11 Send script to the actors	1
12 Actors prepare the scripts	2
13 Complete artwork roughs	1
14 Await client approval of artwork roughs	5
15 Send artwork roughs to artist	1
16 Fine artwork and typesetting by artist	10
17 Check fine artwork and photocopy	2
18 Send copy of artwork to three printers	1
19 Await quotations of printers re artwork	3
20 Accept printer's quotation	1
21 Send artwork and confirmation to the printer	1
22 Artwork printed	10
23 Send artwork prints and cassette tapes to a duplicating house	1
24 Tapes duplicated and matched to artwork prints	10
25 Deliver to client	1

Notes 1 The consultant engaged in this work was able to vary his working week by working the odd Saturday or Sunday in order to meet any necessary deadlines, but this is to be regarded as the exception rather than the rule. However, for the purpose of this task, any parallel activities requiring the consultant's time should be regarded as not being able to be completed at the same time. All times are given in whole days even though some activities may only take a few minutes.
      2 The numbering of the activities is for reference purposes only.
      3 The earliest the studios can be booked is following Activity 3.
      4 Once Activity 6 is complete, Activities 10 and 11 can start.
      5 Artwork roughs can be completed after Activity 3 is complete.

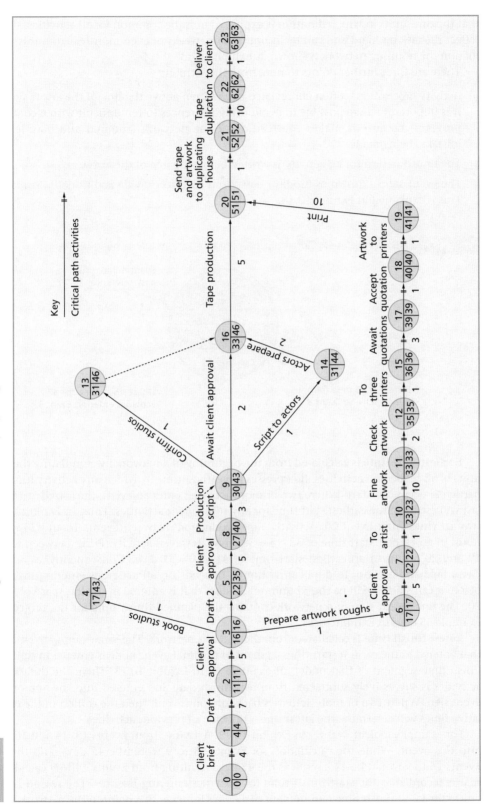

Exhibit 10.13 Network for the activities given in Exhibit 10.12 for preparing an educational cassette

that the time units in which duration is expressed must be common for all activities, should reflect the task on hand and can be in hours, days, weeks or even months. From this information the resulting network is shown as Exhibit 10.13.

There are three further points to note from this exhibit:

● Activity descriptions, often abbreviated, are written above the line of the arrow symbol. It is important where possible to avoid using references (often difficult with a computer program) because it makes the reading of the network laboured and may lead to mistakes being made.

● The time duration for an activity is written below the line of the arrow.

● The event signs (known as 'nodes') have been used to provide additional information. This is explained in Exhibit 10.14.[1]

Exhibit 10.14 Explanation of the information contained in an event node

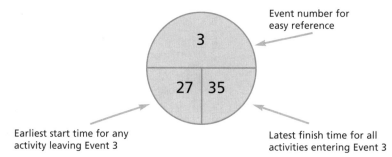

Event number for
easy reference

Earliest start time for any
activity leaving Event 3

Latest finish time for all
activities entering Event 3

Earliest start time is calculated from the beginning of a network by cumulating the time units of all sequential activities. It expresses the earliest time by which any activity leaving a particular event can start. Where two or more activities enter an event, the activity to finish last will establish the earliest start time for any subsequent activities. Thus, in Exhibit 10.13, two activities enter Event 20. Activity 'Tape production' between Events 16 and 20 would result in an earliest start time of 33 + 5 = 38 days. However, activity 'Print' between Events 19 and 20 results in an earliest start time of 41 + 10 = 51 days. Consequently, as activity 'Send tape and artwork to duplicating house' depends on all activities entering Event 20 before it can start, it will be the 51 and not 38 days that is entered in the left space of Event 20. The final event sign of a network contains the planned finish time for the project, for example 63 days in Exhibit 10.13.

Latest finish time is calculated from the end of a network. The same cumulative time as that entered in the earliest start time segment of the final event node is entered in the latest finish time segment of that node, for example 63 in Exhibit 10.13. Then, the duration of activities is successively subtracted from this finish date and entered into the appropriate event sign. Where two or more activities back into one event, then the earliest of the cumulative times will determine the latest finish time for all previous activities.

For example, look at Event 9 in Exhibit 10.13. Activities from Events 13, 14 and 16 back into this event. While the calculation for Events 13 to 9 would be 45 days, and that for Events 16 to 9 would be 44 days, it is the 43 days resulting from Events 14 to 9 calculation that is recorded as the start/finish time for activities entering Event 9. The reason is that unless the latest finish time requirement of 43 days is met at this point in the network, additional time to that planned will be added to the sequence of activities starting with the one between Events 9 and 14.

Critical path analysis – of essential interest in scheduling is the minimum length of time it will take to complete a project. This is determined by critical path analysis, which finds the longest path through a network and this represents the critical path. Each task on the critical path, moreover, is called a 'critical activity' because delays to any of these activities will increase the overall length of a project. The critical nature of these tasks is also shown by the fact that the earliest start and latest finish times recorded in the series of events on the critical path are the same. For these activities there is no flexibility; if the start of any activity is delayed, the project will be delayed. The critical path is then marked in one of several ways, see Exhibit 10.13 for example.

When activities do not fall on the critical path, some delay will have no effect on the completion time for a project. The extent of the delay before the overall time is affected is the difference between the earliest start time and the latest finish time less the activity duration. This is known as 'total float' or 'slack'[2] and is usually entered on the network diagram as part of the information necessary for the controlling phase of a project.

Controlling

A network is a control mechanism. Information on the tasks completed and delays anticipated or incurred needs to be fed back so that a network can be updated. Knowledge of these changes and the impact they have on a project as a whole are essential for three important reasons:

- It is a prerequisite for effective control.

- Throughout the life of a project, decisions need to be made on the best course of action to take in the light of changing circumstances. Networks readily help managers to appreciate the impact of delays. In turn, this allows them to consider, in advance, the action to take with knowledge of the impact on aspects such as cost and completion dates, rather than taking decisions in a crisis situation with insufficient time to evaluate alternative courses of action.

- Out-of-date networks soon fall into disrepute and managers stop using them.

The details discussed so far form the basis for network analysis and have introduced the concepts of scheduling the limiting factors and the task of controlling a project as it progresses. It is not intended here to go into further detail. But there are some important points of which an operations manager should be aware:

- The examples provided are intentionally simple. Network analysis is normally used for complex tasks consisting of many interrelated activities.

- For one-off projects used to plan and control the provision of non-repeat services and products, an essential element is to determine realistic details of activities and associated timescales. Without these, the wherewithal to create effective management and control will not be provided – a detail that Mr James sees fit to ignore (see Exhibit 10.15).

- Although one-off projects are the most frequent type of tasks for which network analysis is used, it is also applied to tasks that will be repeated. Its purpose in these situations is to establish the best way to complete the interrelated activities involved, which is then used on future occasions. The production of an educational cassette is an example of this application (see Exhibits 10.12 and 10.13).

- In complex project applications, there are usually several sets of constraints that need to

Exhibit 10.15 Mr James doesn't want to hear that the project due date is unrealistic

be accounted for within a network. This chapter refers to the use of critical path analysis (CPA). However, there are many more applications that provide for the more sophisticated requirements of complex one-off projects. These include PERT (programme evaluation review techniques), resource levelling and precedence diagrams.[3]

● An important safeguard to incorporate into any network is the concept of target or key dates. These are established at the end of different phases within a project and at which times reviews take place. In addition to being an integral part of the control phase, it helps prevent float or slack from one phase in a project being used up at an earlier stage. If this is not carefully controlled, projects can use up float prematurely and create a situation in which the end phases have little or no float, hence several critical paths emerge with sets of activities becoming unnecessarily critical.

Material requirements planning (MRPI) and JIT

The two most widely used forms of operations control to help manage more complex operations systems are material requirements planning (MRPI)[4] and just-in-time (JIT) planning and control. Both MRPI and JIT have extended definitions and roles that will be explained at the end of the relevant section. The purpose here is to introduce these two major systems before explaining them in full within their own separate sections that follow later.

Operations control systems start with a statement of demand. In businesses where demand is for special (that is, non-repeat) services and products, the nature of the control system will reflect this significant factor. In non-repeat businesses, the operations control and scheduling task will be undertaken by the person responsible for meeting a customer's requirements. This person may often use a bar chart or network to schedule the tasks involved – for example see Exhibit 10.6.

Where a business provides standard (that is, repeat) services and products (and also where a business sells technically complex services and products with many steps and stages), it needs to use scheduling systems that can handle the control requirements involved. Two of the more widely used systems in such circumstances are MRPI and JIT.

The key dimension to managing and controlling operations where the services and products are standard (as well as complex specials as explained earlier) is to recognize the principle of independent and dependent demand:

- **Independent demand** describes services and products for which the pattern of demand does not directly relate to the use of any other item. Examples include finished goods and services.

- **Dependent demand** describes services and products for which the pattern of demand is directly linked to the use of other items, for example parts that go into products. Thus, such items do not need to be forecast but can be calculated.

In a fast-food restaurant, daily demand for each type of burger, fries and other items on the menu would be classed as being independent. The demand for burgers, buns, other ingredients and packaging would be classed as dependent. Similarly, the oil and packaging for fries would have a dependent pattern of demand and, as with all such items, do not need to be forecast as they can be calculated.

With these principles now in place let us turn our attention to MRPI and JIT.

Material requirements planning (MRPI)

The role of an operations system is to translate demand into statements of capacity (staff and/or process) and material and bought-out service requirements in terms of how much and when. For services and products that have an independent pattern of demand, the statement of demand for these will be the starting point for the control system. In make-to-order businesses, the requirements for services and products, (that is, customer orders) will have been received beforehand. In make-to-stock businesses, the statement of demand may comprise both known orders and forecast requirements or solely the latter.

MRPI is a system that determines the final services and products (in terms of which ones and how many) that a company will provide during a future period and then specifies the necessary inputs to meet that demand. MRPI is then used to manage the material and capacity needs where demand for items is dependent. For example, the demand for engines, wheels, body panels and other parts that go into a vehicle assembly is linked to the demand for vehicles. To determine the number of engines, wheels, body panels and other parts we have first to determine the number of vehicles to be built in different time periods and then calculate the requirements for all dependent items.

The advent of low-cost computing enabled the widespread use of MRPI systems in the planning and control of different processes and conditions. The systems that went before were typically characterized by confusion and disorder supported by expediting and involving constantly changing priorities. By comparison MRPI offered a well-ordered system reducing the need to reschedule frequently.

Before the advent of MRPI, most operations control systems relied on models (such as order point) for managing materials inventory (see Chapter 12) for items with an independent and dependent pattern of demand. These systems frequently resulted in situations where there was simultaneously too much inventory of some items and too little inventory of others. The reason for this was that the earlier systems:

- failed to take advantage of the fact that demand for dependent items can be calculated and does not, therefore, have to be forecast
- looked to the past to determine how much to order and when; they assumed that the future would be like the past and used this information to generate forecasts for items that, in turn, drove operations schedules
- were based on replenishing inventory depleted by past schedules and not to meet the needs of current and future demand.

To remedy these deficiencies, MRPI was developed. The first task, as always, is to determine the future demand for all independent items. For each final service or product, an MRPI system contains a recipe (or 'bill of materials' in systems language) of the inputs necessary to make one unit. It then simply multiplies the number of finished services or products by the recipe. This results in a statement of the gross requirements to meet forecast demand. Any existing inventory of dependent items will then reduce the final requirement to give a net requirement figure.

What makes MRPI attractive is that it is straightforward, makes sense and is practical to use. Reality brings issues of uncertainty (for example suppliers meeting agreed delivery dates and actual internal capacity matching the plan) but the fundamental logic offers many advantages over past approaches. Having set the context in which MRPI was developed, let us now look at MRPI in more detail.

Overview of the MRPI system

MRPI starts with a statement of demand for independent items. This is determined from known and/or forecast orders modified by any existing inventories, and forms what is known as the 'master schedule' (see Exhibit 10.2), normally for one or more time periods. This then becomes the input into MRPI which, by means of a parts explosion, calculates the requirements for all dependent items by generating statements of the materials, services, components and subassemblies necessary to complete these. It is known as a 'push' system (as opposed to a 'pull' system, such as JIT, described in the next section), in that statements of requirements are made in line with agreed delivery dates and these are stimulated at the start of the process in line with relevant schedules. In this way, the necessary materials, components and subassemblies are pushed into the process. In order to keep inventory as low as possible and the associated inventory control task as simple as possible, the dates on which orders are due (referred to as 'due dates') are checked to ensure that materials are available. Materials are then 'pushed' through the process to meet due date requirements. The advent of low-cost computing offered companies the opportunity to plan and control complex operations processes in an orderly way by using MRPI principles. As explained earlier, MRPI relies on the fact that the demands for all materials, components and subassemblies are dependent upon the demand for finished services or products. For such items only one forecast is necessary. This must be made at the highest level (that is, where the item has an independent demand pattern) from which all other demand is then calculated. The principle on which this operations control information system is based is one of planned requirement, hence its name. Requirements for all dependent items are thus calculated based on the known and/or forecast demand for the independent services and products in which they are used.

Elements of an MRPI system

Developing a master schedule (the front-end planning task highlighted in Exhibit 10.2) needs to be completed no matter what type of control system is chosen to manage the operations scheduling task. Whether a company selects, for instance, JIT or MRPI, the phase concerning long-term planning and the translation of demand into a commitment by the company to make or provide an agreed mix of services or products has to be completed. Without a statement of what to provide or make (a master schedule), operations cannot function. How a business then schedules and executes the operations control task will depend upon which system it chooses and the basis of that choice should reflect its own business needs and characteristics.

An MRPI system takes the master schedule information and translates it into relevant operations tasks, as shown in Exhibit 10.2. It is a general model of a control system depicting MRPI as the scheduling function on which it is based and provides details of the inputs and outputs of the system. As shown in this outline, the MRPI system consists of several elements – the inputs, the computer software that carries out the calculations and the output reports. The general model depicted here may differ in terms of the content and descriptions used, depending upon the organization and the services or products in question, but it is important to appreciate the purpose of these elements in order to understand the basis on which MRPI is structured. At the top of the outline is the master schedule highlighting the key role that it plays within a planning and control system, and this is where we will start.

Master schedule

The master schedule is a management commitment to provide or produce certain quantities of services or products in particular time periods. To do this it takes statements of demand (both forecast sales and known orders) and tests them against statements of capacity and resources (rough-cut capacity plans and short-term elements of capacity) for the same period(s). The result is an anticipated schedule of finished services and products. As such, it is a statement of operations output and not of market demand. That is, the master schedule is not a forecast and should not be confused with such. Sales forecasts are a major input into the master scheduling function. However, by taking into account capacity limitations as well as the desire to utilize capacity fully, the master schedule will optimize these requirements when forming its statement of what is to be provided or produced. In this way the system highlights problems and the master schedule resets levels to match capacity, so forming an important and core communication link between sales and operations. It is a schedule and thus states requirements in terms of service or product specifications (for example part numbers or service/product descriptions) for which bills of materials (or recipes) exist. The detailed schedule produced drives the MRPI system that, in turn, drives the operations and purchasing records and procedures.

The master schedule thereby has a key role in the control system that leads to an agreement between marketing and operations on what to provide or produce and the financial implications that derive from these decisions. To perform this task well, accurate information is essential. This requirement includes inventory records, the quantity and timing of current operations schedules, outstanding purchase orders, up-to-date bills of materials that reflect changes and clear information about existing customer requirements, current orders and sales forecasts.

A master schedule is created for each item using known customer orders, sales forecasts and a knowledge of operations capacity. It is likely that the schedule will contain a major

Exhibit 10.16 Master schedule for a service or product at a point in time

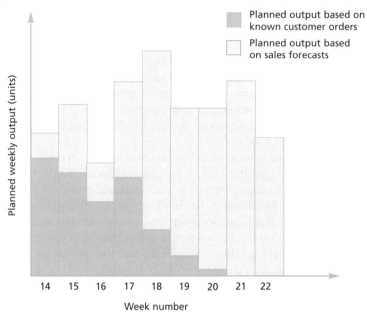

proportion of firm customer orders in the more immediate time periods and will be based mostly on forecasts in the later periods of the planning horizon, as shown in Exhibit 10.16. The length of the planning horizon is determined by calculating the operations lead time for an item (materials lead time plus process lead time) and adding a period of time to allow the purchasing function visibility over the future so that price and delivery advantages can be secured (see Exhibit 10.17).

Exhibit 10.17 Elements of the planning horizon

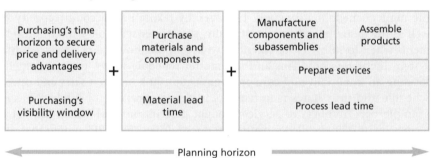

For many companies, the resulting planning horizon will be several months. It would, therefore, be impractical not to allow changes to the master schedule, particularly for time periods well into the future. One method of controlling changes to the master schedule is to split the planning horizon into time zones, each of which has different rules concerning acceptable levels of change (see Exhibit 10.18).

As shown in Exhibit 10.2, the master schedule forms part of the 'front end' of a planning and control system, whereas MRPI is at the centre (the 'engine' phase) of a system. Its primary purpose is to take the period-by-period demand statements for the specific services

Exhibit 10.18 Rules concerning the level of change allowed to the master schedule at different times on the planning horizon

Future time periods

Current period ➝

Emergency only	Alter sequence of services and products already scheduled	Alter the quantities of services and products	Any change allowed within known capacity and resource constraints

Level of change allowed to the master schedule

and products that are contained in the master schedule and calculate a time-phased set of subassembly, components, material and capacity requirements to meet these. An MRPI package completes these calculations at each level and so converts the master schedule of independent demand statements of finished services and products into planned orders for dependent demand parts. To do this it requires bills of materials information (including any specification change data) for relevant services and products, together with 'inventory status data' in order to make any necessary adjustments. In this way it provides the link between the front end of a business (demand forecasts and known customer orders) and the tasks to be completed by operations. Now let us move on to explaining two of the elements within an MRPI system; service/product structure records and inventory status records.

Service/product structure records

Service/product structure records provide information on materials and components (the bill of materials) and how each service or product is made (known as the 'routing file'). The bill of materials is a file or set of files that contains the 'recipe' or formula for each finished service or product (see Exhibits 10.19 and 10.20). The recipe consists of information regarding the services, materials, components and subassemblies that make up each finished service and product and is held on what is often known as a 'service/product structure file'. In addition, a parts master file contains all the standard information about each item, including part number, description, unit of measure, process lead time, materials lead time, purchase order quantities, buffer stockholding and inventory data.

Depending upon the complexity of the service/product structure, there will be a number of levels within a bill of materials. The end item itself is termed level 0. The components (subassemblies, parts and materials) that together make the end item will be listed in the parts explosion and designated level 1. Any level 1 components that themselves have a components list will, in turn, be exploded as level 2 and so on. This calculation would be completed for all components across all services and products. The requirements for each component would be accumulated plus any independent demand for a component (for example spare parts) and these would be added together (that is, treated by the system as one order quantity) to provide delivery plans. Using delivery lead times, a release schedule for each order to meet final assembly is then determined.

It is frequently an advantage to identify a component requirement with the higher level part or end items for which it is to be used. This is known as 'pegging' and provides a partial listing that identifies, at a desired level of detail, where requirements come from and are to be used. This is helpful when rescheduling.

The routing file provides information on the preferred sequence of operations to be undertaken to complete the components, subassemblies or service. It will also specify

Exhibit 10.19 Photographs of an EIW 20 mm gland as detailed in Exhibit 10.20

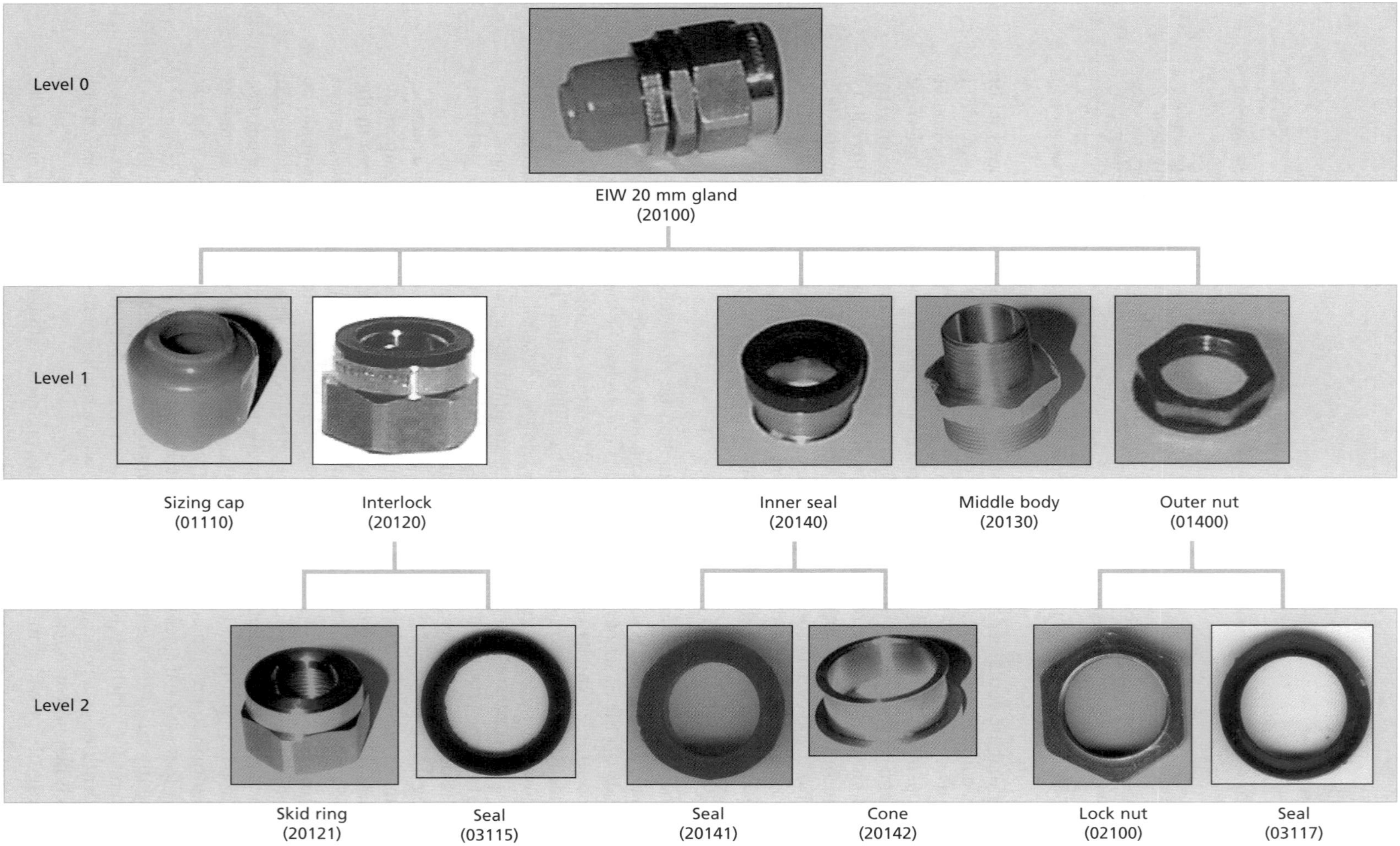

Level 0

Level 1

EIW 20 mm gland
(20100)

Sizing cap
(01110)

Interlock
(20120)

Inner seal
(20140)

Middle body
(20130)

Outer nut
(01400)

Level 2

Skid ring
(20121)

Seal
(03115)

Seal
(20141)

Cone
(20142)

Lock nut
(02100)

Seal
(03117)

Source Remora Electrical Limited, Sheffield (UK).

Exhibit 10.20 The bill of materials for an EIW 20 mm gland

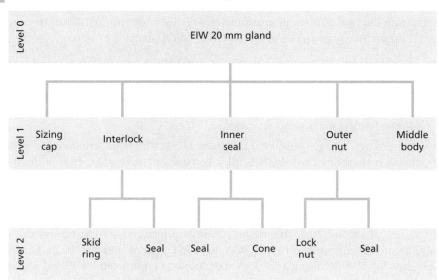

other possible routings. These would be suboptimal to the preferred routing and only used when necessary.

Inventory status records

The inventory status file records all transactions and inventory balances. The transactions are mainly receipts and issues. Adjustments to recorded balances will also be made as a result of inspection reports identifying rejects and physical inventory checks revealing balances different from that on file. As the required degree of control varies, the level of detail at which inventory records are kept will also vary. Where greater control is required, part-processed items (that is, work-in-progress (WIP) inventory) may be reordered at different stages within the total process. This enables relevant components and subassemblies to be monitored from one predetermined stage in the process to the next.

The main requirements of inventory status information are accuracy and timeliness. They are critical to the running of an MRPI system and their absence would undermine the very usefulness of the output reports that form the basis of the operations and purchasing plans.

For organizations with a range of services and products, MRPI is practical only with some form of data processing. Without this aid it would normally be too difficult to recalculate requirements for complex assemblies with each change in the schedule. MRPI provides a control and information system to help coordinate operations decisions concerning finished goods, material/component and WIP inventory levels and the scheduling and rescheduling of materials and components through operations to final assembly and inspection. It does this by time-phasing requirements by quantity, based on a due date planning system for higher level items. The independent/dependent demand principle is at work here. Higher level item (that is, final services or products) demand is calculated using known and/or forecast orders. The due dates for these are also recorded in the system and recorded by the master schedule. Dependent items, the materials, components and subassemblies necessary to meet these higher level items, both in terms of quantity and delivery (or due) dates, are then calculated (referred to as time-phased requirements). Any changes in terms of quantities or due dates are fed into the system and the time-phased requirements are recalculated. Accurate service/product structures and inventory records are a key requirement of the system.

There are two approaches to recalculating MRPI plans:

- **Regeneration** – previous plans are discarded and a new master schedule is calculated at the beginning of each time period. Each time the master schedule of forecast requirements for the independent items is exploded into the gross requirements for dependent items. Available inventories are then deducted and net requirements form the new planned orders for dependent items.

- **Net change** – here, only changes from the last master schedule are exploded down through the bill of materials until a component is reached that is unaffected by the change.

A working example of the MRPI system

As shown in Exhibit 10.2, the master schedule, inventory status and service/product structure records comprise the inputs into an MRPI system. Exhibit 10.21 shows the master schedule for EIW 20 mm gland. This schedule was completed for Period 7 (hence the firm programme in that period) with a forward look for Periods 8 and 9.

Exhibit 10.21 Master schedule for EIW 20 mm gland

Product – EIW 20 mm gland

Period	7	8	9
Forecast sales	5500	6000	7000
Forecast end of period inventory	1250	1400	1500
	6750	7400	8500
Opening inventory	1140	1250	1400
	5610	6150	7100
Firm programme	6000[1]		

Note 1 Any known orders for delivery in Period 7 would be noted and taken into account when determining the 'firm programme' quantity. If (say) an export order for 1500 EIW had been received in Period 7, the 'firm programme' quantity would probably be adjusted upwards to take account of this. The reason is to ensure that the forecast end of period stock of 1250 units would be achieved at the end of Period 7.

This schedule is then exploded by the bill of materials for EIW and the firm requirements are netted down by existing levels of relevant components and subassemblies (see Exhibit 10.22). This shows the gross and net requirements for EIW 20 mm gland. To help you follow the calculations completed in Exhibit 10.22, notes on the columns are now provided:

- **Inventory** – the current inventory holding (# units).
- **Scheduled receipts** – the quantity (# units) of an item already scheduled to be received during Period 7. This could be from a supplier (for example as with cone) or a subassembly made internally but currently in WIP waiting to be completed (for example as with outer nut and inner seal, see Exhibit 10.20).
- **Gross requirements** – the quantity required without taking account of any inventory.
- **Net requirements** – the quantity required when inventory and scheduled receipts are taken into account.

So now let's look at Exhibit 10.22 and see how the figures are derived. First, the net

Exhibit 10.22 Gross and net requirements for EIW 20 mm gland for Period 7

Part		Inventory	Scheduled receipts	Requirements	
Description	Number			Gross	Net
EIW (20 mm)	20100	1,140	–	–	6,000
Sizing cap	01110	3,500	5,000	6,000	–
Interlock	20120	700	–	6,000	5,300
Skid ring	20121	300	1,000	5,300	4,000
Seal	03115	600	1,000	5,300	3,700
Middle body	20130	1,500	–	6,000	4,500
Inner seal	20140	1,250	–	6,000	4,750
Seal	20141	–	2,500	4,750	2,250
Cone	20142	–	2,000	4,750	2,750
Outer nut	01400	5,000	10,000	6,000	–
Lock nut	02100	6,400	–	6,000	–
Seal	03117	12,900	–	6,000	–

Note   Part numbers 01110, 01400, 02100 and 03117, as the above quantities suggest, are common to other products. Hence the larger 'inventory holding' and 'scheduled receipt' quantities recorded here. Therefore, the MRPI system would aggregate the demand for these parts from all revelant products and undertake a similar calculation to that above to determine total requirements.

requirement for 6000 EIW 20 mm glands. Exhibit 10.21 shows that the calculation to arrive at a 'firm programme' of 6000 EIW 20 mm glands includes deducting the opening inventory figure, hence this is the net requirement. For all other parts, the net requirement is similarly calculated by deducting any existing inventory and scheduled receipts in the period from the gross requirement. Thus, the net requirement for Interlock 20120 is 6000 less 700 in inventory = 5300. In the same way, as Skid ring 20121 is part of Interlock 20120, the net requirement of the latter (namely, 5300) less the opening inventory (300) and scheduled receipts (1000) of the former gives a net requirement of 4000, and so on. Here again, reread the footnote to Exhibit 10.22 regarding common parts.

A key element of the MRPI system is the gross to net explosion. This is the procedure for translating product requirements into component part requirements while taking existing inventories and scheduled receipts into account. Only the requirements net of any inventory or scheduled receipts are considered, as shown in Exhibit 10.22. Thus, the gross to net relationship is not only the basis for calculating appropriate quantities but also the communication link between part numbers.

Outputs from MRPI

Looking back at Exhibit 10.2 you will see the principal outputs from an MRPI system. They comprise different levels of reports and executive instructions to make or purchase items. The initial outputs concern material and capacity statements and planned order releases for made in-house or purchased services or parts. As shown by the headings used in Exhibit 10.2, the initial MRPI outputs are plans and not committed actions. As plans are easier to change, it is important not to convert plans into actions any earlier than necessary. Eventually, the plans become actions covering purchase orders, operations orders and reschedule notices.

Evolution of manufacturing resources planning (MRPII)

MRPII has evolved to encompass not only the planning and control of operations and materials but also other areas of a company. This approach is intended to provide a planning and monitoring system for all the resources of a business including operations, marketing, finance and technical support. The organizational needs that stimulated this development include:

- **The need for integration** – in today's dynamic business environment, integrating different parts of a business brings major gains. The integration of these various parts ensures that all aspects of a business are taken into account when reaching an effective corporate decision. One principal facet of MRPII is an integrated system with one database used by the whole business according to individual functional requirements. This allows the resources controlled by individual functions (for example inventory and capacity in operations and cash flow controlled by accounting and finance) to form part of the corporate decision-making process. A single database reduces inconsistencies, facilitates updating and allows multifunctional perspectives to be taken into account.

- **Time-based-competition** – increasingly, important order-winners in many markets include delivery speed and the need for shorter lead times. More sophisticated IT systems provide timely and essential data to managers to help support customers' changing demands and respond more quickly to decisions and enquiries in a more informed manner.

- **National and international communications** – many companies currently support their markets using a national and international provision. Data embracing the whole supply chain enable operations executives to better coordinate worldwide operations and purchasing activities. Satellite-based communications displaying real-time information from around the world enables operations to respond to changes and react quickly even in widely dispersed systems and operations locations.

Powerful computer-based systems with large storage capabilities enable expanded MRPII systems to support the wide-ranging needs of companies in terms of real-time data and comprehensive reviews. Information on corporate activities and resources is updated continuously and this has led to decisions being made on the basis of the business as a whole, with current information providing an up-to-date picture.

JIT control system

An alternative approach to the operations control task that originated in the Japanese automobile industry and has since gained much support in other industrial countries and types of businesses is known as the just-in-time (JIT) system. Whereas MRPI is a plan–push system, JIT is demand–pull (see Exhibit 10.23).

The JIT operations system is relatively simple, requires little use of computers and in some sectors can offer far tighter levels of control than computer-based alternatives. The idea is to produce and deliver goods and services just-in-time to be sold, subassemblies just-in-time to be assembled into finished goods, parts just-in-time to go into subassemblies, and purchased materials just-in-time to be transformed into parts.[5] The purpose is for all materials to be in active use within the total process. In this way materials are always a productive element within the operations system which avoids incurring costs without corresponding benefits. Thus, the JIT system is based upon the concept of producing small quantities just-in-time as opposed to many alternative philosophies that are based on making inventory to optimize process capacity utilization or 'just in case' it is required.

Exhibit 10.23 The direction of orders and flow of the operations process in an MRPI and JIT system

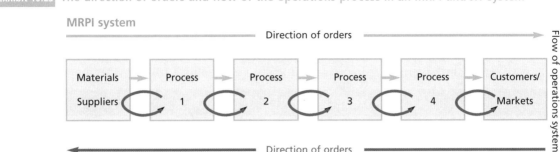

MRPI system

Direction of orders →

Flow of operations system

Direction of orders

JIT system

With the continued spread of JIT systems, many varieties or hybrids of this approach continue to be developed, some of which purport to being something they are not, mainly because those involved have not recognized the concepts on which JIT is based. Consequently, companies have introduced apparent JIT initiatives without understanding, examining and explaining the often significant modifications necessitated by these alternatives if they are to work. In some instances the concept has been so changed that the potential advantages of JIT throughout the supply chain are not forthcoming.[6]

JIT control systems are based on the principle that each part of the total operation (suppliers as well as a company's internal processes) delivers to the next stage the exact quantity needed for the following period's requirements. The period involved varies. In some instances the quantities equate to one day's requirement and in others deliveries may be made several times each day. This means that each stage in the process receives sufficient parts from the previous stage just-in-time to enable it to complete a given quantity. In turn, it meets the exact requirements of the subsequent stage in the process, again on a JIT basis. The more deliveries during a day, the less inventory in the operations process. The number of deliveries is typically not the same between all stages. Factors such as length of set-up time, the physical size of the parts and, in the case of suppliers, the distance involved will affect this decision. However, the procedure used to call for an order quantity is similar. Parts, components or materials are delivered from one stage in a process to the next in agreed quantities and in a designated container, together with a card or document relating to that part. When a container of parts, components or materials is taken to be used, the card (the most well-known system is *kanban*, which means card in Japanese) or similar signal is sent to the previous stage in the operations system. This signal now authorizes that part of the system to make an agreed order quantity. In turn it uses materials, components and subassemblies and this triggers its own signal to the previous part of the process and so on. In this way, all parts of operations supply the next stage just-in-time.

For suppliers the frequency of deliveries is bound up with the distance between locations and the physical size and value (£s) of the parts involved. Normally, the longer the distance, the greater the physical size and lower the value (£s) of a part, the less frequent the deliveries. To facilitate increasing the number of deliveries and hence reducing inventory, suppliers are encouraged to build smaller facilities close to a plant. For example, Johnson Controls, the Milwaukee-based international manufacturer with automobile sector sales alone of $17.1 billion in 2003, has 260 plants mainly in North America and Europe serving all the major car companies including Fiat, Ford, GM, Honda, Mazda, Mitsubishi, Nissan, Peugeot Renault, Toyota and Volkswagen. Although the seat plant is off site, it is typically connected to the car plant by an overhead conveyor system that transports the seats directly onto the assembly line to exactly match the build programme. Similarly, several suppliers to the Nissan car plant in Washington (UK) are just a few minutes away. To keep inventory as low as possible, deliveries are made every two hours throughout the day. To ensure delivery times are met, Nissan has agreed three different routes for suppliers' vehicles to take. These need to be used in a preferred order thus providing alternatives in cases of difficulty. Case example 10.2 provides more detail.

Case example 2   JIT SYSTEM DEVELOPMENTS AT NISSAN

Nissan's JIT system developments include synchronizing supplier deliveries with its own car assembly programme. One such link is between Nissan and Sommer Albert, a French-owned carpet and trim manufacturer that has a satellite plant 3 km away from the car factory. As each car starts its journey through Nissan's manufacturing system, a special coding tag triggers a message to Sommer that specifies which of the 120 variations of carpet and trim is needed for that particular vehicle, a factor that reflects colour, right- or left-hand drive, engine size and option selection. At Sommer the correct requirement is selected (including carpet, parcel shelves and boot linings), trimmed and finished before being stacked in sequence and loaded onto a vehicle in reusable carriers. On arrival (and that can be as many as 120 times a day) the driver takes the sets straight to the assembly line.

www.nissanmotors.com

Case questions	1 Why is a car plant particularly suited to JIT scheduling systems?
	2 What developments in this example have been important in making the system work?
	3 What advantages and disadvantages would be inherent in these arrangements?

To allow these exact deliveries to be met, end-users need to fix their own output programmes which cannot be altered within the agreed lead times of suppliers. Only with this certainty of requirements can a JIT control system be introduced and maintained where inventory is kept to a minimum at all stages of a supply chain.

The main features of JIT systems and some prerequisites for its introduction are now summarized:[7]

- It reverses the flow of information concerning parts and materials so that each stage calls off requirements from the previous stage as needed.
- Work-in-progress (WIP) inventory is kept to a minimum.
- Bottlenecks need to be eliminated and process downtimes reduced to a minimum. As WIP is now minimized, the cushion of inventory between the stages is no longer provided. Process uncertainty, therefore, has to be kept to a minimum.
- Changeover or set-up times need to be reduced so that smaller order sizes become practical. For example, the set-up time for a hood and fender stamping operation was estimated by Toyota for typical parts as follows: USA 6 hours, Sweden and Germany 4 hours and Toyota's time 0.2 hour.
- As a result of the last point, the operations system can handle smaller quantities on a more frequent basis as the relationship between set-up time and run length is maintained.[8]

The concept is very appealing. However, there are several prerequisites if it is to be achieved:

- It is most suited to high volume, low variety and repetitive operations situations.
- It must be end-user driven. The business making the final services and products must take responsibility for instigating this development and liaise with its suppliers accordingly.
- Operations schedules must be firm. The desired state in JIT is for no excess material in the system. Consequently, scheduled quantities cannot be increased (there is no material) or decreased (unnecessary inventory is the byproduct).

- Suppliers must be geographically close to customers thereby enabling regular deliveries to be made. Where the geographical distance is long, frequent deliveries of small quantities are not feasible. Larger amounts at longer intervals will be the alternative and inventory will result.

Key factors for this system to work effectively are stable schedules (that is, call-offs are fixed and cannot be changed inside the agreed material lead times of a supplier's supplier) and developing close relationships with suppliers. In many companies, however, the impact of the inherent instability of markets and a lack of close liaison with suppliers are more typically the operations situations that control systems have to handle. Customers desiring the benefits of JIT sometimes introduce or demand a JIT materials or parts provision and yet are unable to keep suppliers' schedules stable. The outcome is that suppliers hold inventory, with all its attendant costs, as a practical way of meeting the short lead time demands of customers.

Achieving JIT

JIT advantages include the pursuit of zero inventories. The gains associated with inventory reduction are typically large and comprise two major elements: the reduction in inventory itself and the cost of managing the inventory and other aspects of operations associated with materials control. Reduced inventory has implications for cash, space, insurance costs, loss through damage and obsolescence and so on. No inventory also means no control requirements and the attendant overhead costs of managing materials. In fact, these latter gains often outweigh the former.

One key difference between MRPI and JIT is the switch from using order quantities as the basis for loading onto the control system to one using throughput rates. In so doing, JIT replaces the time-based principle of MRPI (that is, loading is in line with due dates) with a rate-based one (that is, loading is in line with throughput rates that trigger the system to replenish the next stage in the process). To achieve this switch, several changes need to be made, including physical, employee and control system changes.

Physical changes

The several physical changes that need to become an inherent part of the process include:

- **High volume, low variety demand** needs to underpin operations. This justifies the investment and allows the creation of a series of processes that are as near to the coupled nature of a line process as possible. The fact that JIT was first developed in the automobile industry was not by chance. These conditions provide many of the prerequisites (especially high volume) necessary for JIT control systems. Ways to increase necessary volumes include simplifying products in terms of width of range and using standardized parts and the use of mix mode assembly to allow more products to be made on a process.

- **Set-up reduction** to allow order quantities to be reduced. In a line process there are no set-ups. Where processes need to be reset when a different product is to be made, reducing the time it takes allows smaller order quantities to be made.[8] This is necessary to enable quantities of components, subassemblies and final assemblies to be made in line with demand rather than needing to reflect the length of time it takes to reset a process.

- **Layouts** are changed so that the flow of products consistently follows the preferred routing (see Exhibit 10.24).

- **Operations arrangements** are often based on autonomous cells, each responsible for its own tasks and the supply to and from adjacent cells.

- **Balanced flow of materials** throughout the processes.

- **Preventive maintenance programmes** (see Chapter 14) normally support JIT initiatives to help remove causes of uncertainty and waste especially where inventory holdings are minimal.

- **Standard containers** to hold predetermined quantities are used to fix material levels and as partial substitutes for a control system and paper-based procedures.

- **Improved quality conformance** through the process. This would be based on the use of statistical control techniques (see Chapter 11) and results in lower costs and the elimination of stoppages and inventory to cover process uncertainties.

Exhibit 10.24 Simplified operations unit controlled by a JIT system

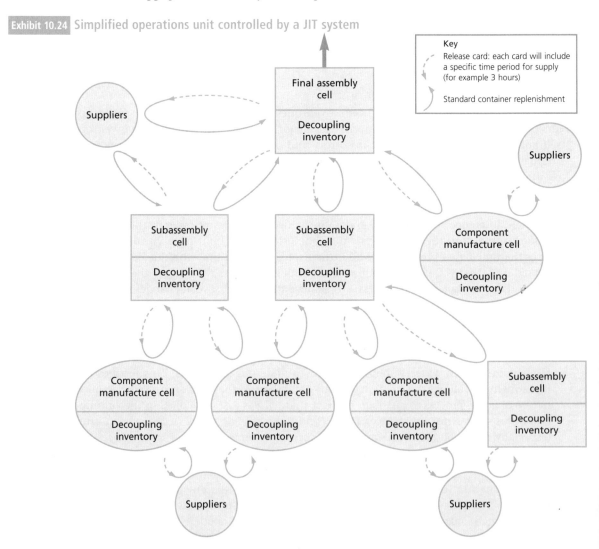

Employee involvement

The role of staff in the process is also radically changed in the following ways:

- **Broader, day-to-day role in terms of job content.** This includes cross-training regarding the tasks in a cell and often involves indirect work such as improving operations and scheduling being part of the tasks in a cell. This not only improves the quality of the task but also means that when there is no active work to complete (in JIT the authority to make an order quantity must be received before work can commence), staff can undertake control and evaluating tasks that are now forms of 'legitimate' work. However, in more traditional systems, when there is no scheduled work to do, then the choice is between making inventory and recording 'excess' labour hours.

- **Responsibility for quality conformance.** As part of the last point, employees assume responsibility for the quality conformance checks completed during the process (see Chapter 11). This includes authority to stop the process if a quality defect is discovered.

- **Continuous improvement.** The increased involvement of workers is also designed for them to use their knowledge to improve the system as part of the drive for continuous improvement. Exhibit 10.25 offers an amusing comment on this issue.

Exhibit 10.25 JIT brings a change in attitudes, or else (smiles)!

© Roger Beale

Control system changes

JIT impacts all areas of scheduling but principally within the operations and purchasing systems. These have already been overviewed and now a more detailed description of a JIT control system is provided.

The objective of a JIT system is to ensure that all materials in the process are active. In order to do this, steady schedules need to be supported by shorter set-up times so that appropriate quantities of parts can be delivered to each stage of the process. To enhance the basic quantity factor, standard containers designed to hold agreed quantities are introduced. Lastly, a card-type system (*kanban* was mentioned earlier – other systems have their own signal, for example 'action plate' at Nissan and 'DOPS' at Honda) forms the basis of all transactions. This document is the authority to produce, and only on receipt of it can work be started. Exhibit 10.24 provides an outline chart illustrating materials flow in a simplified manufacturing business. The last module in this illustration is the final assembly cell which makes the end product. In a demand–pull material flow system, final assembly will withdraw a standard container of work from a small quantity of decoupling inventory (see Chapter 12). Part of this transaction includes sending the release card to the previous, appropriate cell. In turn, this latter cell is now authorized to make a standard quantity of components or subassemblies. To do this it withdraws, from its own small quantity of decoupling inventory, a standard container of components or subassemblies. As part of this transaction, this cell also releases a card to its material supplier, as illustrated in Exhibit 10.24, and so on.

By striving continuously to reduce set-ups and work-in-progress inventory, the operations system is simplified in control terms, requires less inventory material to support transactions and has fewer interprocess dependencies. As a result, inventory levels continue to decline and the basis of control is simplified still further.

However, given the unstable nature of the marketplace, to achieve the high level of stability necessary to underpin a JIT system, the 'operations delivery system' has to be effectively cushioned – see Exhibit 10.1. This is achieved in three principal ways:

- **Schedules are fixed** – so that what is to be produced cannot be changed within the lead time it takes to make alterations to material purchases. This factor relates to one of the prerequisites listed earlier that such systems need to be end-user driven.

- **Finished goods inventory** is held. Thus, when demand is lower than output, inventory will be created to sell in a later period (known as capacity-related inventory – see Chapter 12). Exhibit 10.26 shows the inventory holding at a Mitsubishi outlet in California. The finished goods inventory at the time totalled 284 2-cwt vans of standard design over a given range of colours.

- **Adopt a make-to-order approach** which means that products are only made on receipt of an order and will result in an order backlog or forward load preceding the delivery system. Now the system works on known orders and material is scheduled accordingly. Most European car makers produce on a make-to-order basis and hence are able to use JIT control systems.

From these general requirements it can be deduced that JIT applications are suitable for the regular schedules of repetitive manufacturing and not for the irregular work demands associated with one-off, low volume batch processes providing the needs of markets with uncertain and intermittent demands. These issues need to be addressed when considering

Exhibit 10.26 Finished goods inventory at a Mitsubishi outlet in California

which control system best reflects the characteristics of a particular business. It is equally important to recognize that a company may require more than one type of operations control system to meet the needs of its different markets.

Finally, there are a number of prerequisites to be met at the operating level in order to support the conceptual base of a JIT system. These include:

- **Level schedules** – schedules must be level. That is, within a given period, daily workloads need to be equal.

- **Frozen schedules** – schedules must be frozen over a time period. To do this a company should be able to use the final assembly schedule as the master schedule. This, in turn, necessitates getting the cumulative process lead times sufficiently short to eliminate the need for parts holdings at an intermediate level.

- **Fixed routings** – routings must be fixed to allow schedules for parts to follow closely the final assembly schedule. As process times are fixed, all schedules can work in tandem with one another.

- **Frequent set-ups** – a large number of set-ups will be completed each day to support the basis of making only as required. Consequently, set-ups must be very short.

- **Order quantities** – order quantities for parts must be small and fixed in size.

- **Quality conformance** – quality levels must be high to reduce rework and increase the certainty of the output level of a process.

- **Process breakdowns** – processes must function. This requires diligent preventive maintenance to reduce breakdowns.

- **Labour utilization** – the principle of labour utilization should not be the basis on which schedules are determined. This requires that those involved are trained to cope with a wide range of tasks (including indirect work) in order to provide the necessary flexibility to meet both a wide range and times when output is not required.

- **Employee involvement** – employees must participate in making improvements in order to monitor the existing system to ensure that quality conformance levels are maintained in the short term and achieve continuous improvements in the future. The goal is, therefore, correct rather than hurried work.

JIT – a philosophy of operations management

The introduction and development of JIT within businesses often comprise a set of approaches that are integral to the success of its role as an operations scheduling system. This overall approach is referred to by some advocates of JIT as a philosophy in that it provides a set of steps, approaches and techniques to help manage operations.

In the management of operations, many of these techniques are now in general use as stand-alone approaches and form part of several other areas of development such as total productive maintenance and continuous improvement which are dealt with in Chapters 14 and 16 respectively. The set that typically forms an integrated part of JIT is now briefly reviewed.

Asset emphasis: inventory versus process

One driving force for many businesses in the past was the high utilization of fixed assets. Prior to the mid-1960s when, in most sectors, world capacity was less than world demand, high utilization of fixed assets (such as processes) was the way for a business to maximize its output and profit. This view continued to be held even in sectors where the imbalance between capacity and demand had been reversed. JIT challenged this view by trading off the objective of high utilization of processes for lower levels of inventory, as shown in Exhibit 10.27.

Exhibit 10.27 The different orientation of traditional and JIT approaches

Aspects		Traditional approach	JIT approach
Focus		Make so as to keep processes and staff working. Objective is high utilization	Make only when needed. Objective is low inventory
Use of inventory[1]	cycle	Large order quantities to reduce the impact of ups on net available capacity	Make as little as possible – reduce set-ups or leave processes pre-set until the next order quantity arrives
	decoupling	Allow processes to make to and draw from WIP[2] inventory. This decouples the dependency of processes and allows them to operate independently of one another	Minimize inventory between processes. This increases their mutual dependency and the need for cooperation and procedures to coordinate throughput
	overall	Make inventory just in case it is needed	Make inventory just at the time it is required
Operations emphasis		Process throughput speeds. Inventory facilitates high process utilization and high efficiency objectives	Set-up reductions or hold excess capacity to allow small order quantities to be scheduled and low inventory levels to be maintained

Notes　1　These types of inventory are explained in Chapter 12.
　　　　2　WIP = work-in-progress.

The advantages of material scheduled on a JIT basis are not restricted to those associated with the investment and cash benefits inherent in lower inventory. There are additional and sizeable gains concerning an easier scheduling task, simpler and less expensive systems and controls and lower overhead costs to manage the material system. The downside is that, as products are only made on an as-required and JIT basis, spare process capacity typically exists throughout the system.

Improvement through exposing problems

The JIT approach is designed to deliberately expose problems and use this as a vehicle for improvement. Exhibit 10.28 illustrates a classic example. This shows how excessive inventory (in the form of water depth) allows the delivery system (in the form of a ship) to operate with a whole range of problems going undetected. It creates a situation where management is unaware of the type and size of the inefficiencies that exist in the operations system and the improvements that need to take place. By reducing inventory (water) levels, the problems (depicted in Exhibit 10.28 as rocks) are exposed, the ship will now founder

Exhibit 10.28 Excess inventory covers over problems that are consequently not exposed and dealt with

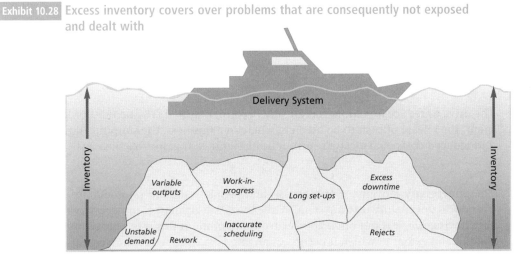

(management is alerted to issues) and the areas for improvement are highlighted. In more traditional approaches, problems are viewed as being a sign of inefficient management, are not deliberately sought and often are covered over (for example the role and origin of excess inventory as depicted in Exhibit 10.28). The opportunity to identify areas for improvement is thereby lost.

Incorporating indirect activities into the remit of direct staff

In traditional organizational approaches, direct staff are employed to undertake direct work. Thus, direct staff only provide services or make products. The results of this traditional philosophy include:

- In circumstances where there is no demand for a service or product, operations managers either have to make inventory or record direct staff as an excess cost (that is, not working). Most corporate performance measures make the latter less preferable than the former.

- The experience and capability of direct staff is limited to providing services or making products. The involvement of direct staff in indirect activities such as scheduling, quantity conformance and improvement is not an integral part of their role, and consequently is not provided for as part of their job nor seen as part of their contribution to a business.

One element of the JIT philosophy is to increase the involvement of staff, particularly in areas such as first-line maintenance, day-to-day scheduling, quality conformance and the drive for continuous improvement. (These aspects are dealt with in more detail in relevant chapters.) This is supported by appropriate training and by incorporating indirect tasks into the role of direct staff, with the new mix of work being reflected in the time allocations and expectations concerning performance and output of those involved. This approach not only secures the contribution of all staff in areas such as continuous improvement but also eliminates the 'make inventory' or 'no work' scenario. If there is no direct work on hand, staff now have legitimate indirect tasks to undertake.

Eliminating waste

Waste is any activity that does not add value. One of the cornerstones of the JIT philosophy is to identify and reduce or, where possible, eliminate waste that occurs throughout the operations system. Examples of waste include the following.

Inventory

The drive to reduce inventory has already been highlighted. The benefits of lower invest- ment, the release of cash to be used elsewhere in a business, the simplification of systems and reduced costs of associated control bring significant gains to a business.

Movement

The unnecessary movement of materials and people results in unproductive activity and introduces uncertainty into a system. While the waste element of unnecessary movement is easy to visualize, it is not often appreciated how common this is in operations systems and the size and extent to which it occurs. Changing layouts to reduce movement and improv- ing systems and procedures to eliminate the need to check, ask questions or fetch necessary materials that should have been on hand are common improvements that result in signifi- cant gains.

Lead times

One byproduct of waste is that operations lead times are extended. Unnecessary movement has already been highlighted. Other causes include:

- **Waiting time** – material in the operations system that is not being worked on results in delay and additional lead time. See the throughput efficiency index calculation given at the end of this chapter.
- **Set-ups** – long changeover times increase lead times.
- **Process failures** – equipment breakdowns introduce delays and lengthen lead times.

Set-up reduction

The relationship between set-up time and the length of time the order quantity takes to complete is often a core issue in operations. The ratio between these two activities and the non-saleable and saleable productive time respectively that results is carefully monitored, particularly where capacity is in short supply. To make products as required and on a JIT basis implies making smaller quantities on a more frequent basis. Reducing set-up times allows this to happen while keeping the ratio between these two productive time elements at an acceptable level. A one-hour changeover to make an order quantity equivalent to six hours of processing time offers the same ratio as a 10-minute changeover and an order quan- tity taking one hour.

Set-up reduction underpins the opportunity for smaller quantities to be made more often. Alternatively, excess process capacity offers the same opportunity to make small order quantities in that processes can remain unchanged as they are not required to make alter- native products or changeovers can be completed at times when a process is not being used.

Optimized production technology (OPT)

Much attention has been given in the last decade to a proprietary system called optimized production technology (OPT). The development comprises two parts. The first is the conceptual base of the system and the second is the software package (OPT/SERVE) which supports the system itself.

OPT's main impact concerns scheduling. In essence (although OPT does possess other inherent contributions) it is a sophisticated control system based on finite loading procedures that concentrate on a subset of work centres. The finite loading of the bottleneck processes within operations is at the heart of this system and the software package uses an algorithm developed by Eliyahu Goldratt to accomplish the finite loading.

In essence OPT addresses the following issue. To achieve the most profit from a given set of resources, it is necessary to maximize the flow through and not the utilization of those resources. Throughput is limited by processes with inherent capacity constraints. These are known as 'bottlenecks'. Thus, it is necessary to control the inputs into the operations process (that is, the amount of work scheduled into operations) in line with these constraints. The level of throughput that bottleneck processes can handle will determine the amount that can be completed and made available to sell. Companies, particularly in the past, often follow a policy of maximizing the utilization of all available resources. Where this policy is adopted, the result is that a business will generate part-completed work at some stages in the process that cannot be worked on at other stages (that is, the bottleneck processes) because of a lack of capacity. The result is WIP inventory.

Loading in line with the available capacity at bottleneck (or scarce resource) processes enables companies to maximize the flow of work to achieve maximum saleable output. Leading on from this, OPT prioritizes attention on increasing capacity at these bottlenecks by improvements such as set-up reduction and improved process yields. Creating more capacity at these processes leads to increased saleable output and greater profits.

In line with these central features, the OPT literature highlights other points to reinforce the logic and provide direction on the action to follow. These include the following:

- The aim of a company should be to balance flow and not capacity. Reducing bottlenecks will increase total flow through the system thus releasing the potential capacity of other non-bottleneck processes.

- As a consequence of the above, an hour lost at a bottleneck is an hour lost for ever, but an hour saved at a non-bottleneck is of no consequence. Thus, reducing set-ups at a bottleneck increases capacity and throughput, while additional set-ups at a non-bottleneck do not affect output but do minimize WIP inventory.

- The transfer order quantity may not, and often should not, be equal to the order quantity being processed. This recognizes the fact that a company needs to determine order quantities at a bottleneck process with a view to both reducing the number of set-ups and hence increasing available capacity (the concept of cycle inventory – see Chapter 12) and then reducing the order quantity it transfers to the next process in line with demand rather than to maximize the utilization of subsequent processes. Thus, the process order quantity should be recognized to be variable not fixed.

- When determining schedules, capacity issues and priorities need to be considered at the same time and not separately.

Theory of constraints

The principles underlying the OPT philosophy have universal applicability. Consequently they can be used to enhance many existing control systems as well as providing useful insights into the more effective management of the operations function both in manufacturing and service companies. To this end, the general use of the concepts introduced in the last section on OPT is encapsulated in the term 'theory of constraints', where a constraint is anything that limits an organization's ability to improve. Constraints can be physical (for example process capacity or resource availability) or non-physical (for example procedures or systems) in nature. It is the effective management of these constraints that makes this approach such a useful tool in managing a range of functions. The six-step process below can help managers get the most out of an organization's resources:

1   Identify a system's constraints, whether physical or non-physical.

2   Ascertain those that affect the overall throughput of that part of the organization (the idea of bottlenecks and non-bottleneck processes described earlier).

3   Decide how best to get the most possible within the limits imposed by the current constraint.

4   Avoid keeping non-constraint resources busy as this produces unneeded work that sits in the form of WIP or part-completed tasks.

5   Evaluate a system's constraints and take actions to reduce the effects of these constraints such as reducing existing capacity losses, increasing available capacity and offloading demand or parts of demand to another part of the operations system. It is important here to make everyone aware of these constraints and their effects in order to focus attention on the problem and solutions.

6   Where constraints are relaxed in Step 5, go back to Step 1.

Enterprise resource planning (ERP)

ERP systems are designed to provide the information backbone to cope with the complexities of modern business and the global nature of today's markets. They provide a seamless integration of all the information that was previously dispersed through a company and turn it into a tool that managers can use. This includes information from the supply chain, customers, human resources, finance and accounting and management reporting (see Exhibit 10.29).

In the late 1970s, the Germany company SAP (Systeme, Anwendungen und Produkte in Datenverarbeitung or Systems, Applications and Products in Data Processing) released an

Exhibit 10.29 ERP system

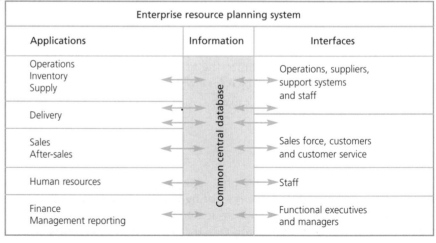

early version of ERP software referred to as 'R/2'. However, it was in 1994 when SAP released R/3, the next generation of software, which also marked a shift in the technology platform from mainframe to the increasingly popular UNIX-based client-server architecture, that businesses began investing in ERP systems. Since then sales by providers such as SAP, Oracle, PeopleSoft and JD Edwards[9] have grown significantly, with SAP alone accounting for sales of over $6 billion in 2002 involving more than 36,000 software installations in 15,000 companies across 120 countries.[10]

Benefits from introducing ERP[11]

There are several reasons for companies implementing ERP, and three of these are discussed.

To provide a common systems platform

ERP can trace its origins back to the material requirements planning (MRPI) systems that gave control of operations processes. MRPI became MRPII with the addition of more supply chain activities, such as distribution and other related activities in a business. These developments then broadened into ERP to take in financial control, human resource management and the international and diverse activities and locations that characterize today's companies.

Companies collect, generate and store vast quantities of data but in most instances this is undertaken by separate computer systems that cannot talk to one another. Each of these so-called 'legacy' systems provides invaluable support for the individual functions, business units, regions, factories or offices for which they were developed. The source of this disconnection is simple – IT developments have been undertaken in businesses over many years. The initial choice would have reflected specific sets of needs and, while the decision was sound in itself, it was taken, understandably, to meet the requirements on hand. This piecemeal growth of IT accepted the inherent lack of system interfacing, and the need to start again with a common system postponed until some later, often unspecified, time. The growing internationalization of business and the flurry of takeovers and mergers in the past 20 years has heightened the size of the incompatibility problem.

The developments in IT and the obvious impact that e-business is producing has brought to the fore the need to introduce systems using a common database. ERP fulfills such a need.

Process improvements

Multiple systems made a firm's underlying information platforms highly inefficient, expensive to maintain and update and unreliable. An integral part of introducing an ERP system is the opportunity to improve processes such as logistics and scheduling, by standardizing and re-engineering their business activities, both to take out costs and enable them to respond to market challenges.

Data visibility

The highly integrated nature of ERP systems increases data visibility with an end-to-end view of the supply chain. This leads to more informed decision making and the potential for more consistent and better decisions. The online, real-time transaction characteristic of ERP systems provides current as opposed to historical data, thereby improving a firm's response to customer needs and use of its internal resources.

Phases of an ERP implementation

The five phases of an ERP implementation are discussed below.

Selection and design

In this planning phase, firms have to address two fundamental design decisions. An ERP system is a generic solution with built-in assumptions about an organization's way of working and its transfer and use of data. First, the firm must decide on the level of system customization desired and the impact on lead times and cost. Second, the firm must recognize that it will need to adapt the way it works to fit in with the enterprise system logic. ERP, due to its all-embracing nature, will impose its own way of working on a company's strategy, culture and structure. Thus, the underlying systems logic will have to be accommodated by an organization.

Implementation

The need to plan for 'going live' is critical, as implementation is highly disruptive. All change brings problems, and ERP involves both implementing the new system and the new processes at the same time. Consequently, 'going live' introduces major organizational change.

Stabilization

This phase involves firms cleaning up their data and processes which typically includes more fundamental decisions on aspects such as service/product range, level of customization and standardization of parts and subassemblies. How long this phase takes depends on the size of the organization and the length and extent of the 'cleaning-up' process. But, typically, it is 4–12 months and sometimes much longer.

Continuous improvement

This stage concerns addressing the potential benefits that the new system and the increased data visibility bring. Process redesign, ways of leveraging the system and its opportunities and developing different ways of cooperating throughout the organization are at the forefront of the drive for continuous improvement. It also typically involves further developments to the system by improving its functionality through new modules or bolt-on additions.

Transformation

In this phase, organizations have moved to a different way of working which encompasses changing organizational boundaries, improved business processes, better customer responsiveness and more coordinated decision making, particularly at the strategy level.

How ERP works

So, how would an ERP-based system work? Let's say that a Milan-based sales team for a USA-based software house prepares a quotation for a customer. With an ERP system, basic information about the customer's requirements would be entered and a formal contract, in Italian, would be produced, specifying the product and service configuration, range of applications and locations involved, lead times concerning pre-application review, development phase and installation, post-development support, training and price. After contract discussions, any modifications would be made on the system and quotations would be updated as required. When the customer accepts the quotation, the order is recorded in the system, credit checks are made and all aspects of the delivery system are advised. Feedback on lead times is provided, capacity allocations are verified and recorded, schedules are revised, materials are ordered and the whole operations system is brought up to date and into line. The benefits that user companies enjoy are wide-ranging. Examples include:

- Autodesk, a leading US maker of CAD software, reduced delivery lead times from a two-week average to 24 hours for 98 per cent of orders.

- IBM's Storage Systems reduced the time to reprice all its products from 5 days to 5 minutes, the time to deliver a replacement part from 22 to 3 days and the time to complete a credit check from 20 minutes to 3 seconds.

- Fujitsu Microelectronics reduced order fill time from 18 to 1.5 days and halved the time to close its financial records to 4 days.

- Owens Corning replaced its total of 211 existing systems with an ERP system. This coordinates order management, financial reporting and its diverse, worldwide supply chain. It is now able to track finished goods inventory daily in all parts of its delivery systems and has cut spare parts inventory by some 50 per cent.

However, as with all applications, success is bound up with fitting the system to the business needs, including its strategic positioning. Two areas of concern are noted by companies, which reflect the size of ERP undertakings.[12]

- Failed or out-of-control applications – the cost of ERP projects in larger organizations runs from $50 million to over $500 million. The issue, however, is not just the investment costs but the fundamental nature of such sizeable developments. Fox Meyer Drug, a US pharmaceutical company, alleges that its ERP system installation helped drive it into bankruptcy. Mobil Europe spent hundreds of millions of dollars on its ERP system only to abandon it when it merged with Esso/Exxon. Dow Chemicals spent seven years and $0.5 billion implementing a mainframe ERP system, then decided to start all over on a client-server application. Case example 10.3 outlines Dell's experience.

- ERP systems: standard versus customized offering – clearly ERP systems offer substantial benefits. However, with past IT systems, organizations would first decide on what the business needed and choose a software package that would support these needs. They often rewrote large portions of the software to provide a better fit. With the size (investment and timescale) of ERP systems, the sequence is reversed. The business often needs to be modified to fit the system. ERP systems will enable a company to operate more efficiently. In some instances, however, the system's assumptions will run counter to a company's best interests. For example, a company, by developing a system that enabled it to shorten lead times by circumventing formal procedures, had increased sales that also attracted a premium price. If, after installing an ERP system, it had to follow less flexible procedures, its source of competitive advantage may be at risk.

Case example 3   IT SYSTEMS CHANGES AT DELL

Dell spent two years implementing SAP's R/3 to run its manufacturing operations, then found that its ERP system did not fit its new decentralized management structure. SAP was found to be 'too monolithic' to be altered for its changing organizational needs when its business model changed from a world-wide focus to a regional focus.

Some time later, Dell chose an i2 Technologies system to manage raw materials, an Oracle system for order management and a Glovia system for manufacturing. Putting in a piece at a time has worked for Dell.   **www.dell.co.uk**

| **Case questions** | 1 What appeared to be the principal reasons why the SAP R/3 application failed at Dell? |
| | 2 Why is the later IT systems approach working? |

In more general terms, the adoption of the same ERP system by companies in the same business sector also raises concerns. How similar can a company's information flows and processes be to those of its competitors before its source of differentiation is undermined? Similarly, for companies competing in price-sensitive markets, ERP system investments raise similar but different strategic issues. With the cost of ERP applications being so high, the eventual savings need to be rigorously assessed and weighed carefully against the investments involved. In some instances, companies may find that not going down the ERP system route may offer a cost advantage over competitors that do.

Just having good data does not mean that a business will improve. To gain the most out of ERP systems companies need to recognize the full business implications. Organizations may have good reasons to change. They may have struggled for years with incompatible information systems and may see ERP as a quick fix. However, before moving forward organizations need to address some key questions:

- How might an ERP system strengthen our competitive position?
- What will the system's effect be on our organization and structure?
- Do we need to extend the system across all functions, across all regions or only implement certain modules and reflect differences in need with differences in approach?

Because of the ERP system's profound implications for a business, any developments must be assessed in terms of meeting the needs of the business and the way the organization works. There is no one right answer. For instance, take Monsanto and Hewlett-Packard. After studying the data requirements of each business unit, Monsanto managers placed a high priority on achieving the greatest possible degree of commonality across the whole company even though they knew it would be difficult to achieve and that to standardize fully on more than 85 per cent of the data used would not be possible. At Hewlett-Packard, a company with a strong tradition of business unit autonomy, applications specific to each part of the business were developed. With little sharing of resources, the estimated investment was over $1 billion, but autonomy, a recognized corporate strength, was preserved.

Reflections

Operations strategy has been highlighted throughout in terms of its role to support a company's markets by meeting the requirements of relevant order-winners and qualifiers. One key part of this support is provided by the operations control system and its essential role in the effective and efficient provision of services and products.

Operations control links market demands with the necessary capacity and materials requirement, and contributes to the flow and control of services and products through the system. This part of operations will impact key dimensions in many markets such as delivery speed and delivery reliability. Selecting how best to provide this function is, therefore, a core operations management task. Alternative systems have been explained in the previous sections. Approaches to fulfilling this essential task are, however, characterized by a number of challenges.

Lack of integration

It is essential that the services and products, the delivery and processes systems for providing them and the system(s) to control them are developed as integrated parts of the one task. Controls are, however, often developed independently of other key dimensions of operations. The inherent weakness of inadequate systems can be reduced by adaptation and good management. But they will continue to be inadequate where these developments have not been integrated into the other functions of operations that impact key issues such as delivery reliability and delivery speed.

One scheduling system to support diverse needs

Many organizations implement a single scheduling system to meet the diverse needs of their various markets. A preference for single solutions, a desire to keep investment and running costs as low as possible and a failure to recognize that different processes and business needs require different scheduling systems (see Exhibits 10.30 and 10.31) are some of the reasons why this frequently happens. One result is that the control system deliverables do not match and support the wide range of needs, demands and characteristics of a typical business.

Exhibit 10.30 Operations scheduling systems and service delivery system type

Operations scheduling system	Service delivery system type		
	Non-repeat	Repeat Low volume	High volume
Networks			
Bar charts			
MRPI			
JIT			
OPT			

Exhibit 10.31 Operations scheduling systems and manufacturing process type

Operations scheduling system	Manufacturing process type				
	Project	Jobbing	Batch	Line	Continuing processing
Networks					
Bar charts					
MRPI					
JIT					
OPT					

Suboptimal applications

Attracted by the benefits associated with alternatives, companies implement scheduling systems without ensuring that they fit their needs or that the prerequisites for their introduction are in place. JIT scheduling systems provide a classic example of this. Whereas in

Japan, companies only apply JIT to control operations with certain characteristics, the allure of the benefits of JIT has led to suboptimal applications by Western companies:

● Japanese view – the term 'just-in-time' is used very strictly in Japanese companies and recognizes that its use is ideally related to supporting markets characterized by stable volumes and where the product mix is known well in advance. Delivering JIT means planning in plenty of time.[13] Furthermore, when Japanese managers refer to the approach embodied in the term 'just-in-time', they prefer to speak of the JIT philosophy embodied in the Toyota production system that spawned the development of the JIT system.

● Western view – although displaying the appropriate characteristics of high volume and stable product mix, Western companies have introduced JIT control systems without creating the environment for this to be developed in its optimum form. Two of the more critical dimensions essential to the introduction of a JIT system which Western companies often fail to provide are:
  – Not fixing forward schedules. As a consequence, the end-user, while requiring JIT response from suppliers, still retains the 'right' to change call-offs within material lead times. The only option for a supplier to meet such schedule changes in terms of quantity and/or delivery date is to hold inventory, thus undermining the underlying principle of minimizing inventory throughout a supply chain.
  – Overlooking the technical and people changes necessary to bring about WIP inventory reductions. This is often because of the greater corporate influence exerted by accountants relative to that exerted by operations.

Selecting the most appropriate approach

All too often, companies seek solutions rather than concentrating on understanding situations and problems, with the result that companies introduce systems inappropriately or in a form that fails to reflect the needs and characteristics of their business:

● OPT – companies often introduce OPT as a systems solution to a capacity problem. A better alternative is to recognize constraints as issues of capacity and flow and address them as such rather than tackling them with a computer program. Increasing capacity, re-engineering and rerouting services or products are alternatives to the IT approach advocated by OPT. Invariably, the operations-based solutions are simpler, quicker to bring about and less expensive to implement and maintain. Selecting OPT is often presented as an off-the-shelf solution that does not require an understanding of the issues and alternatives involved.

● Companies introduce approaches unaware that often modifying the system variables will better reflect the characteristics of their operations system and supply chain. For example, lead times on fixing schedules need to reflect a company's own reality. Japanese car companies vary considerably on the length of notice given to suppliers and the confirmation intervals during the period from the forecast projections several months ahead through to the finalized schedule. There are no fixed intervals. Details reflect the reality that suppliers can provide.

● The control task itself is characterized by and needs to reflect and embrace several major factors including:
  – The complexity of the link between services/products and delivery/processes systems in terms of dimensions such as total volumes, customer order size, service/product range, complexity of the task, whether the service/product is repeated (a standard) or

not (a special) and the delivery system or process chosen to complete the tasks involved.

- The level of certainty in demand forecasts, capacity provision, service/product supply and prior knowledge of the task.
- The organizational decision on how to cope with the imbalance between demand and capacity and the amount and timing of the approaches (for example inventory and excess capacity) taken.
- The overriding organizational style, level of development in the delivery system and the degree of maintenance or development of the control system over time.

Providing relevant control statements and reports

Finally, the system needs to provide relevant control statements and reports to help operations executives manage the function and assess how well it is supporting customers and meeting the internal, efficiency needs of the business. Typical statements and reports include the following:

- Delivery performance
  - Percentage of orders (by line item) delivered on time or within the timescale targets set by the business, including the number of instances when queues exceeded target lengths in retail-type outlets.
  - Percentage of times customers' requested lead times are agreed – the dimension of delivery speed.
  - Number and nature of customer complaints.
  - Throughput efficiency index calculation to assess delays in the delivery system:

    $$\frac{\text{Total process lead time}}{\text{Actual time to complete}}$$

  - Order backlog/forward load assessment to review the demand and capacity situation within the process at a point in time and shown as a trend:

    $$\frac{\text{Average \# orders waiting to be processed}}{\text{Average \# orders processed in the period}}$$

- Efficiency Measures around utilization and efficiency are provided in Chapter 8 (on capacity) and Chapter 15 (on productivity) respectively. In addition, variance reports need to be prepared to show actual staff, material and total costs incurred compared to budgets, so identifying areas for review.
- Quality conformance The various measures of quality conformance are outlined in Chapter 11.
- Inventory Checking inventory levels using the causal analysis approach is explained in Chapter 12.

These measures, supplemented by additional reports reflecting other key issues within a business, need to form an essential byproduct of an operations control system. The scheduling of services and products provides inherent information that is relevant to many key aspects of operations. Capturing these as an integral part of the control system is critical in itself and also provides essential insights into how well the delivery system is meeting the demands of the business and the needs of its markets, thereby reinforcing the essential role of the control system within operations.

Key Elements of Operations Scheduling and Execution

- In many markets, meeting the on-time delivery needs of customers is a prerequisite for getting and staying on a customer's short list, and providing this qualifier is a key operations management task.

- While the need is the same in all organizations, the way to schedule operations to meet this requirement differs from business to business and needs to reflect those dimensions that alter the control task and the control system design. These include the complexity of the service or product, whether the services and products are specials or standards, the choice of process to provide the services or products, how much of the process is undertaken in-house and the extent to which an organization manages the demand and capacity interface.

- A control system comprises three distinct but integrated activities:
  - loading – determining the capacity and volumes at each step in a delivery system or process and the assignment of tasks within a system to work centres or task groups
  - sequencing – deciding on the order in which jobs will be completed at each stage in the process or delivery system
  - scheduling – the task of allocating a start and finish date to each order.

- The main section of the chapter introduced the alternative scheduling systems that are available, explained these in detail and illustrated their use with examples. If you recall these were:
  - Bar charts – recording capacity (for example process or staff) against a timescale. Exhibits 10.5–10.7 illustrated some of their applications.
  - Network analysis – organizations often use this method to plan, schedule and control complex, one-off tasks. The simple example in Exhibit 10.11 is then followed by the more complex task in Exhibit 10.12.
  - MRPI and JIT – two of the most widely used systems to schedule standard products and

services are MRPI and JIT. Referred to as a push and pull system respectively, these two systems, and how they differ, are explained in detail (for example refer to Exhibits 10.23, 10.24 and 10.27).

- All operations control systems start with a statement of demand. Known and/or forecast sales are translated into statements of demand which in scheduling language is referred to as a master schedule. A glance back at Exhibit 10.2 confirms the pivotal position of the master schedule and its linking role between the planning and scheduling phases of a system.

- One other key reminder at this time is the principle of independent and dependent demand. Whereas assessing demand levels by known and/or forecast orders is the fundamental task for independent demand items, requirements for dependent items can be calculated as they are directly related to the pattern of demand of the independent items to which they relate.

- Once the master schedule for a service or product is established, the scheduling task of determining material requirements and process/staff capacities can be completed. These, in turn, provide the inputs for the day-to-day execution of the plan. Detailing the MRPI and JIT systems then completed this section.

- Next came OPT and its finite scheduling role in refining existing control systems was explained. The final section addresses the developments in ERP systems, outlining benefits and concerns and highlighting the key dimensions to ensure successful applications.

- The conclusions provided an overview of the various systems described throughout the chapter, related these one to the other in Exhibits 10.30 and 10.31 and highlighted some key concerns when selecting, developing and maintaining the systems that form the basis of the operations control and scheduling task.

Self-check

1 Which of the following is **not** a way to cushion the operations core from the instability of the market:
  a Inventory or excess capacity ☐
  b Long-term changes in capacity ☐
  c Order backlog/forward load ☐

2 The role of reviewing demand and capacity in the planning phase of a system is to:
  a Provide a forward look and identify problem areas ☐
  b Establish and agree the actual orders to be completed and detailed plans involved ☐
  c Both a and b ☐

3 Operations control concerns meeting the:
  a Short-term demands placed on the process or delivery system ☐
  b Long-term demands placed on the process or delivery system ☐
  c Forecasting future resource requirements ☐

4 Which of the following is **not** a factor that influences the choice and design of the operations control system:
  a The complexity of the service or product ☐
  b The choice of delivery system or process ☐
  c The nature of the competition in the market ☐

5 Scheduling is:
  a The decision on which jobs are to be completed at each stage of the process ☐
  b A detailed timetable allocating a start and finish date to each order ☐

  c Determining the capacity at each stage of the process ☐

6 Which of the following is **not** a system used to schedule and manage operations:
  a Statistical process control ☐
  b Network analysis ☐
  c Enterprise resource planning ☐

7 The most widely used form(s) of operations control to manage more complex operations systems is:
  a Material requirements planning (MRPI) ☐
  b Just-in-time (JIT) ☐
  c Both a and b ☐

8 Which of the following is **not** a prerequisite to implementing JIT:
  a It must be end-user driven ☐
  b Operations schedules must be flexible ☐
  c It is most suited to situations of high volume, low variety and repetitive operations ☐

9 Waste is any activity that:
  a Does not add value ☐
  b Does add value ☐
  c Both a and b ☐

10 Optimized production technology is most suited to which manufacturing process type:
  a Jobbing ☐
  b Batch ☐
  c Line ☐

Study activities

Discussion questions

1 Give an example of a business that would use a push and one that would use a pull operations control system. Explain your choice and briefly describe how the system would work.

2 What is the difference between independent and dependent demand? Give two manufacturing and two service examples to illustrate your answer.

3 Under what conditions should a company refuse a customer order that it is technically able to provide?

4 Your local dry cleaner always specifies a two-day lead time, no matter what items of clothing you take in to be cleaned. Suggest reasons why the outlet is able to do this and how it works.

5 Describe a service application where the principles of the theory of constraints can apply.

6 In operations, priorities manifest themselves in a conflict between meeting customers' lead times and due dates, and the productivity and efficiency goals of the operations system staff. Discuss and provide examples to illustrate your points.

Assignments

1 Each week nurses are assigned to different parts of a hospital. The table below shows the estimated number of nurses required in one department.

Period	Mon	Tue	Wed	Thu	Fri	Sat	Sun
0600–1000	15	15	15	15	15	10	8
1000–1400	18	15	18	15	18	10	8
1400–1800	15	15	15	15	15	10	8
1800–2200	10	10	10	10	10	6	4
2200–0200	5	5	5	5	5	3	3
0200–0600	3	3	3	3	3	3	3

Agreements with the nurses' union require that staff work a continuous eight-hour shift for five consecutive days followed by two days' rest.

(a) How many full-time nurses are needed to meet the staff levels detailed above?

(b) How many hours of overstaffing exist when you compare the number of staff called for in question (a) to the minimum levels given in the table?

(c) How many full-time nurses would be needed to meet the above schedule if the five consecutive days rule was relaxed so that the two days off in each seven-day week could be taken at any time including as single days?

2 A small business consultancy company has three specialists in one area of its work. Furthermore, each of these three is further specialized to undertake certain phases of an assignment. Jim Brown handles phase 1, Anne Dewar phase 2 and Jean Holden undertakes phase 3.

Details of the work to complete each of these assignments together with agreed completion dates is given below. In all cases, the phases need to be completed in the order 1, 2 and 3.

Client	Phase			Agreed completion
	1	2	3	(# days[1])
McCanley	10	16	8	49
Williams	3	9	16	46
Beattie	12	10	10	45

Note 1 Calculated from day 1 as the start date.

The three consultants can complete other, non-fee-paying work during the period.

Using day 1 as the start date, draw a bar chart to schedule the above tasks in order to meet the agreed completion dates and release each consultant as early as possible to take on other fee-paying work when their part of these three jobs has been completed.

3 A piece of equipment requires the following times to manufacture.

Activity	# days	Activity	# days
1 Purchasing	15	5 Assembly	7
2 Fabrication	5	6 Controls	6
3 Hydraulics	5	7 Test	3
4 Electronics	18	8 Packaging	1

Each of the activities must be completed sequentially except that fabrication can be started 10 days after purchasing begins and the hydraulics and electronics steps can be completed in parallel. Draw a bar chart for this job.

If the hydraulics and electronics steps could also be started 10 days after purchasing begins, draw a network for this job and calculate the critical path.

Exploring further

Ames, BC and Hlavacek, JD *Market-Driven Management,* McGraw-Hill/Irwin, Chicago (1997).

Bennett, D and Forrester, P *Market-focused Production Systems,* Prentice Hall, Hemel Hempstead (1993).

Curran, T, Keller, G and Ladd, A *Business Blueprints: Understanding SAP's R3 Reference Model*, Prentice Hall, Upper Saddle River, NJ (1998).

Davenport, TH *Working Knowledge: How Organizations Manage What They Know*, Harvard Business School Press (1997).

Davenport, TH 'Putting the enterprise into the enterprise system', *Harvard Business Review,* July/August (1998).

Dillon, JE and Kontogiorgis, S 'US airways optimizes the scheduling of reserve flight crews', *Interfaces* **29**(5) (1999) pp. 123–31.

Goldratt, EM *Critical Chain,* North River Press, Great Barrington, MA (1997).

Goldratt, EM and Cox, J *The Goal,* North River Press, Croton-on-Hudson, NY (1984).

Haksever, C, Render, B and Russell, R *Service Management and Operations*, 2nd edn, Prentice Hall, Upper Saddle River, NJ (2000).

Hammer, M and Champy, J *Reengineering the Corporation*, Harper Business, New York (1993).

Hill, T *Manufacturing Strategy: Text and Cases,* Macmillan, Basingstoke – now Palgrave Macmillan (2000).

Information Systems Audit and Control Foundation 'Cobit Management Guidelines' (2000).

Kolisch, R 'Resource allocation capabilities of commercial project management software packages', *Interfaces* **29**(4) (1999) pp. 19–31.

Krupp, JAG 'Some thoughts on implementing pull systems', *Production and Inventory Management Journal* 4th quarter (1999) pp. 35–9.

Lewis, JP *Mastering Project Management,* McGraw-Hill, New York (1998).

Lesant, D, Voudouris, C and Azarmi, N 'Dynamic workforce scheduling for British Telecommunications plc', *Interfaces* **30**(1) (2000) pp. 45–56.

Malhotra, MK and Ritzman, LP 'Scheduling flexibility in the service sector: a postal case study', *Production and Operations Management* **3** spring (1994) pp. 100–17.

McDowell, SW 'Just-in-time project management', *HE Solutions* April (2001) pp. 30–3.

Metters, R and Vargus, V 'Yield management for the non-profit sector', *Journal of Service Management* **1** February (1999) pp. 215–26.

Pinedo, M and Chao, X *Operations Scheduling with Applications in Manufacturing and Services,* McGraw-Hill/Irwin, New York (1999).

Ptak, CA and Schragenheim, E *ERP Tools, Techniques and Applications for Integrating the Supply Chain,* CRC Press, Boca Raton, FL (1999).

Vollman, TE, Berry WL, Whybark, DC and Jacobs, R *Manufacturing Planning and Control Systems for Supply Chain Management*, 5th edn, McGraw-Hill/Irwin, Burr Ridge, IL (2004).

Wainwright, M 'Myth vs reality: ERP uptake high among the blue chips', *Convergence* **3**(2), (2002).

Wallace, TF and Krezmar, MK *ERP: Making it Happen*, John Wiley & Sons, New York (2001).

Womack, JP and Jones, DT *Lean Thinking,* Simon & Schuster, New York (1996).

Notes and references

1 In more complex networks, the event node often contains more information.

2 Strictly speaking, 'float' and 'slack' are not the same, and in complex networks it may be important to distinguish between them. In many instances, though, this would not be a worthwhile exercise.

3 The following references treat network analysis in depth and provide more detailed information and analyses often used in the control of complex projects: Baker, BM 'Cost/time trade-off analysis for the critical path method', *Journal of Operational Research Society* **48**(12) (1997) pp. 1241–4; Duncan, WR *A Guide to the Project*

Management Body of Knowledge Project Management Institute Publications, Upper Darby, PA (1996); Herroslaw, W and Lens, R 'On the merits and pitfalls of critical chain scheduling', *Journal of Operations Management* **19** (2001) pp. 559–77; Burke, R *Project Management and Control*, 2nd edn, John Wiley, Chichester (1993); Meredith, JR and Mantel, S *Project Management: A Managerial Approach*, 3rd edn, John Wiley, New York (1995); Lockyer, K and Gordon, J *Project Management and Project Network Techniques*, 6th edn, Pitman, London (1996); Maylor, H *Project Management*, 2nd edn, Prentice Hall, New York (1999).

4   The system entitled 'materials requirement planning' has been extended into a system known as manufacturing resource planning. When the scheduling activities in materials requirement planning have been completed and tied in with purchasing, accounting, sales, engineering and the other relevant functional areas, the result is known as manufacturing resource planning. As both have the same initials their abbreviated forms are referred to as MRPI and MRPII respectively. MRPII is covered in a later section.

5   One of the earliest statements providing this definition comes from Schonenberger, RJ *Japanese Manufacturing Techniques: Nine Hidden Lessons in Simplicity*, New York, Free Press (1982), p. 16.

6   An example is where end-users require suppliers to provide materials and components just-in-time but do not fix their own schedules correspondingly. They demand JIT supply which can only be met by suppliers holding inventory. However, the JIT system is designed to reduce inventory in all parts of a supply chain. For this to happen, end-users need to play their part by creating the conditions where this can happen. Fixing their own schedules within material lead times is part of the necessary conditions. Without this prerequisite, when end-users change their requirements, suppliers in such situations can only meet JIT supply by holding inventory.

7   For further information and details on JIT systems refer to Harrison, A *Just-in-Time Manufacturing in Perspective,* Prentice Hall, London (1992) and relevant chapters in Vollman, TE, Berry, WL, Whybark, DC and Jacobs, R *Manufacturing Planning and Control Systems for Supply Chain Management*, 5th edn, McGraw-Hill/Irwin, Burr Ridge, IL (2004).

8   If a 30-minute set-up is reduced to 10 minutes, the order quantities to be loaded can be reduced to one-third while maintaining the ratio between length of set-up and length of run time.

9   Estimated sales and market share for leading ERP providers in 2000.

Company	Sales ($m)	Market share (%)
SAP	5939	30
Oracle	2870	15
PeopleSoft	1736	9
JD Edwards	980	5
Geac	901	5
Others	7228	36

Source The Report on Enterprise Management, AMR Research Inc. (2001).

10   Austin, RD, Cotteleer, MJ and Escalle, CX *Enterprise Resource Planning: Technology Note,* Harvard Business School (2001).

11   Also see Ross, JW and Vitale, MR 'The ERP revolution: Surviving vs thriving' *Information Systems Frontiers* **2**(2) (2001) pp. 234–41; Turnick, PA 'ERP: promise or pipe dream?' *Transport and Distribution* **40**(1), 1999; Chen, IJ 'Planning for ERP systems: Analysis and future trends' *Business Process Management Journal* **7**(8) (2001).

12   Also see Meneges, J 'ERP fails to improve bottom line says Forrester' *Computing Canada* **25**(45) (1999).

13   A thoughtful review of JIT systems is provided by Roy Westbrook in his article 'Time to forget just-in-time? Observation on a visit to Japan', *International Journal of Operations and Production Management* **8**(4) (1988), pp. 5–21.

book map

CUSTOMERS

OUTPUTS

PROCESSES

INPUTS

SUPPLIERS

Part

1

- 1 Managing Operations
- 2 Operations Strategy
- 3 Managing People

2

- 4 Designing and Developing Services & Products
- 5 Designing Service Delivery Systems
- 6 Designing Manufacturing Processes
- 7 Location and Layout
- 8 Managing Capacity
- 9 Technology Developments
- 10 Operations Scheduling and Execution
- 11 Managing Quality

3

- 12 Managing Inventory
- 13 Managing the Supply Chain
- 14 Process and Delivery System Reliability and Maintenance

4

- 15 Time and Productivity
- 16 Improving Operations

5

- Managing Operations in Practice: Long Case Studies

Managing Quality

Outline of chapter

Right first time is the #1 priority for most customers. Managing and developing delivery systems to meet these expectations is, therefore, central to retaining, and the basis for growing, market share.

Why is managing quality important?

Executive overview

The quality of the services and products provided by a business is an important concern to an organization and its customers. While the cost of quality calamities can be high in themselves, customer confidence in the level of quality will have a significant impact on a company's overall prosperity in terms of future levels of demand and the long-term success of the business. To ensure that quality levels meet market requirements, issues concerning quality need to be resolved at the corporate level and be seen to form an integral part of an organization's objectives, strategies and tactics. This is not easy to achieve, but unless addressed at the top it will, as in many organizations, be decided lower down in a business due to the day-to-day need at the operational level to achieve output levels, efficiency and other yardsticks, and meet delivery promises.

In view of the fundamental importance of meeting quality requirements in a business environment where customers' expectations regarding the quality of the products and services they purchase have changed noticeably in the last 20 years, the need to manage quality is increasingly critical to the overall success of any business. This chapter covers the issues and aspects of quality for which operations is responsible. In particular, it addresses the following topics:

- **What is quality and why is it important?** The opening section of the chapter clarifies definitions and positions the importance of quality within the context of the overall business.

- **Quality conformance** concerns the consistent meeting of product and service specifications and the key role of operations in achieving this.

- **Quality principles** help summarize the key facets of managing and controlling quality.

- **Quality philosophies** – the principal contributors to the improved management of quality are discussed in detail to provide the foundation and context for the more detailed sections of the chapter.

- **Tools and techniques** – this section outlines the main tools and techniques used to help analyse causes and provide ways to improve the management of quality.

- **The operations process: quality management in practice** – where to undertake quality reviews and the approaches to be used are explained; covers purchasing, operations process and output reviews.

- **Six-sigma quality** – the goal of reducing the level of defects to 3.4 per million transactions is being embraced by companies as part of the way to maintain and grow share in the competitive markets of the new millennium.

- **Formalizing the search for quality** – the need to set and meet national and international standards has seen the development of government and non-government-sponsored initiatives to help formalize the search for quality. The ISO 9000 series, Malcolm Baldrige Award and the European Quality Award are discussed.

- **Total quality management** – the concepts and approaches underpinning total quality management are explained and its role in fulfilling the quality mandate is discussed.

What is quality and why is it important?

Meeting, or better still exceeding, customers' expectations is an essential task for a business. The growing awareness of the importance of the dimension of quality performance was stimulated in the 1970s and 80s by the improvements made and sustained in Japanese companies and the impact that the resulting improvements had in terms of their increased sales and market share. The quality movement that followed accelerated the introduction of a range of philosophies, approaches, tools and techniques.

Part of this increased awareness also led to the word 'quality' being used to reflect a wide range of dimensions. A first step for us, therefore, is to clarify the meaning of quality for operations and define the dimensions to be addressed later in the chapter.

What is quality? What an offering comprises (the specification) needs to take into account what customers want and expect and what a company decides it wishes to offer. In this way companies position themselves in different markets and seek to attract customers whose wants and expectations match the specification a company offers.

The quality task for operations is to consistently meet the agreed specification of the services and products an organization offers:

- Service/product specification – the issues around services/product mix and design were covered in Chapters 1 and 4 respectively. Determining customers' needs and embodying these in the design specifications of the range of services and products on offer is the first step in meeting the quality requirements and managing their provision.

- Quality conformance – consistently meeting the service and product specification is referred to in operations as 'quality conformance'. For a customer, quality provision, therefore, combines the two elements of the specification itself (what a service or product comprises) and its consistent provision – see Exhibit 11.1. This exhibit highlights the interrelated nature of the quality offering. The link between these elements always needs to be tested and the level of fit assessed as an ongoing part of managing the quality offering. Gaps between the different elements need to be monitored and managed.

Furthermore, these decisions need to be made proactively as the outcomes determine the markets in which a company wishes to compete and, by definition, those in which it does not wish to compete. The phrase 'a customer is always right', therefore, only relates to a company's chosen markets and the sets of customer needs and expectations that comprise them. Continuously monitoring existing and potential customers' needs and expectations, competitors' offerings and potential changes to existing service and product specifications

Exhibit 11.1 The quality offering

is an essential part of managing quality. Finally, rigorously assessing how well operations consistently provides what is offered completes the quality offering provision cycle.

Why is quality important? What a company sells, customers' needs and expectations and the consistent provision of the service and product specifications on offer represent the essence of any business. The importance of consistently meeting the service or product specification is that it will influence whether customers repurchase in the future and, in turn, customer retention levels significantly affect the growth and success of an enterprise. Recognizing the interrelated nature of these parts of the task and ensuring that the essential dialogue and feedback are sustained alerts a company to what it is doing well, where it needs to improve and the actions it needs to take. The importance of continuously reviewing the quality offering (see Exhibit 11.1) is shown in Case examples 11.1, 11.2 and 11.3.

Case example 1   GUARANTEED REFUNDS AT HAMPTON INNS

The US-based Hampton Inns chain decided to offer guaranteed refunds to any customers dissatisfied with their stays for any reason. Guest surveys showed that the policy was pretty persuasive and the cost/benefit calculations revealed that additional sales revenues ($) brought in by the programme were almost 11 times that of the refunds paid out. An added bonus for the company was higher staff morale. With all staff being empowered to grant refunds, job satisfaction rose, while staff turnover fell from 117 to 50 per cent in a three-year period. The refund programme also helped to identify the aspects of service that most annoyed guests. One of the biggest in the Embassy Suites' part of the company's hotel chain was a lack of irons and ironing boards and the delay involved between request and provision. The company estimated that providing an iron and ironing board in every Embassy Suite room would cost less than $0.5 million, and would eliminate the service staff costs incurred in taking irons and boards from room to room.

www.hamptoninn.com

Case example 2   NO-FRILLS BAR CODE PRINTERS

Zebra Technologies Corporation, a US maker of bar code printers, had earned a reputation as a manufacturer of high-quality, top-of-the-line printers. The company saw sales potential at the lower end of this market, but had two concerns. First, it might affect its top drawer image while, second, it might cannibalize its existing product line. Its solution was to introduce a basic, no-frills version at a 25 per cent lower selling price. It was slower, could not print on different types of materials and, most importantly, could not be upgraded. The result – total sales went up by almost 50 per cent and, as margins on the new product matched those on the original line, so did profits.

www.zebra.com

Case example 3   SERVICE QUALITY AT UPS

United Parcel Services (UPS) had always assumed that on-time delivery was the paramount concern of its customers. UPS's definition of service quality centred almost exclusively on meeting its delivery promise, for example all next-day packages had to be delivered by 10.30 the following morning. So too did operations priorities and measures – elevator times and the delay in customers answering their doorbells were measured and included in schedules. UPS even shaved the corners off delivery van seats to help reduce time. In addition, surveys confirmed customers' satisfaction with its reliable delivery performance. The problem was that UPS did not ask customers what they wanted. When questions were broadened to address needs and expectations, the biggest surprise to UPS management was that customers wanted more contact with drivers. If they had more time to chat, customers could get some practical advice on shipping. The result – the company now encourages its drivers to visit customers along with sales staff and allows drivers thirty minutes each day to spend at their discretion to strengthen customer ties and bring in new sales. The programme costs UPS over $4 million in drivers' time but additional sales are many times higher.

www.ups.com

Case questions

1 Review these three cases and identify the elements of the quality offering that the companies changed or improved.
2 What benefits did these companies and their customers receive and what disadvantages or costs were involved?

Specifying the service or product

While the specification of the services or products a company provides has a direct bearing on operations, the prime responsibility for this task lies with other functions. In a service company it is often the sales and marketing function that is responsible for reviewing existing and proposing new service offerings. In a manufacturing firm this responsibility typically rests with the research and development or engineering function – points covered earlier in Chapter 4.

The need, however, for operations to be involved in these decisions is essential. Not only will operations contribute to the format of the service or product itself but its involvement will ensure that any constraints in terms of lead times and investments are recognized and the fit between alternative technical and business dimensions (see Exhibit 11.2) and operations is checked and evaluated.

Exhibit 11.2 The technical and business specifications of a service or product offering

Service or product	
Technical specification	The technical dimensions of a service or product
Business specification	The order-winners and qualifiers within relevant markets

Quality conformance

Quality conformance means providing services and products to specification and constitutes the quality-related task of operations. Most offerings combine elements of both services and products and a specification needs to be provided for all aspects. But what can happen is that whereas the predominant element of an offering is recognized and specified, the supporting service or product element receives insufficient attention and is inadequately defined. Companies are now more alert to these issues and, as the support elements often can be significant factors to ensure repeat business, the total offering needs to be defined, specified and the actual performance measured.

The steps involved in the quality conformance procedure are outlined below. As services and products constitute a number of characteristics, each characteristic will need defining and controlling as part of meeting the total specification.

Quality characteristics – definition

The first step is to determine the characteristics that make up the service or product to be provided. Many of these characteristics will form part of the specification at the design stage. These explicit characteristics are invariably the core of what is provided. But the total package also includes implicit services (for example level of attention and recognition of regular customers by restaurant staff) and supporting structural facilities (for example the quality of the table linen, plates, glasses and cutlery in a restaurant).

Quality characteristics – measurement and control

The characteristics that make up the specification need to be defined, wherever possible, in such a way that the dimensions can be measured and controlled. This involves taking a general quality characteristic and breaking it down into its constituent elements. For the restaurant example above, appearance would be a dimension within all facets of the service delivery system. But appearance, as such, is difficult to measure. To enable measurement and

Exhibit 11.3 Redefining a general quality characteristic into constituent elements

Dimension	Some elements of 'appearance' in the service delivery system of a restaurant
Explicit service	• Minimizing delays at different stages in the service delivery system, for example greeting guests, taking pre-dinner drinks orders, offering menus and taking orders for dinner in a timely manner • Food ingredients, for example freshness by food type, and size of portions • Food presentation, such as layout on a plate, spacing and colour combinations
Implicit service	Regular guests: • Identified by name • Staff advised ahead of time • Table preferences noted and allocated
Supporting structural facilities	• Table spacings • Table layout • Glassware and cutlery checked and polished with a dry cloth

control to be undertaken, 'appearance' would need to be separated into elements that, in themselves, could be more easily measured – see Exhibit 11.3.

The characteristics that describe quality fall into two groups:

- **Variables** can be measured on a numerical scale, such as weight, length and time. Examples of variable measurements are the dimensions of parts and components or the length of time to serve a customer.

- **Attributes** are measured by using the qualitative conditions of a process. These can be based on judgement or checks without detailed measurement. For example, pass/fail such as a go/no-go gauge that indicates that an item has failed to meet the specification without taking an exact measurement.

From the quality characteristics that can be measured, those to be measured are then selected and a standard is set, against which actual performance is checked. What is deemed acceptable has to be agreed in terms of level and frequency, for example customer queues should be no longer than three minutes, 95 per cent of the time.

When setting quality levels, the decisions that have to be made are:

- where in the operations process to check conformance to agreed quality standards
- how to undertake the checks.

Where to check

Within the operations process there are a number of possible points where quality checks could be made. The scope is wide, as outlined in Exhibit 11.4. Where to check needs to relate to each operations situation, reflect cost and take into account any technical considerations:

- Cost considerations fall into two sets. The first is the cost of checking or inspecting and the second is the cost of allowing errors (service) or defective items (product) to pass on through a process or correcting them. The optimal number and location of these inspec-

Exhibit 11.4 The broad stages in the operations process where quality conformance checks can be made

The service delivery system

Supply chain	Receiving	Operations	Service and delivery completed
Purchased items and services Vendor rating	Quality checks on purchased items and services	Process to provide the service and requiring several quality activities	Inspect level and quality of intended provision — Service consumed by customer

The process in a manufacturing company

Supply chain	Receiving	Operations	Finished items	Installation
Purchased items Vendor rating	Incoming quality inspection	Conversion and assembly processes involving several quality activities	Test and inspection of finished items	On-site installation and test

tion points is achieved when the total of these two sets of costs is at a minimum. Assessing these costs, especially the latter, is not easy and tends to be largely a matter of judgement. When making this choice, factors include identifying points before relatively high-cost parts of a process are started or where error correction would subsequently become substantially more expensive or not cost-effective at all.

- **Technical considerations** include making checks before any stages in a delivery system where one of the following conditions might apply:
  - previous defects or problems might afterwards be concealed
  - where checking is difficult
  - after which rectification or recovery is expensive
  - where functional responsibility changes
  - the point where the provision and consumption of the service take place.

How to check

Having decided where to check, the next step is how many services or products to check. If we wished to guarantee that the quality level was being attained, the first reaction may be to say 'let's check everything'. In theory this should ensure that no substandard service or product is allowed to proceed through a process. But, in reality, this approach has some major limitations:

- it is expensive
- it adds tasks and therefore lead times are increased
- when people are involved in the checking or monitoring it leads to errors
- deterioration may result from excessive handling.

Identify causes of below-standard quality and seek improvements

The checks made to ensure that the specification is being consistently met will record instances of below-standard quality conformance and identify causes. By recording quality failures, the more common reasons will form the basis for prioritizing improvements. A proactive response by operations managers typifies the current approach to controlling quality. Failure is seen as a guide to process improvement rather than a negative criticism of the delivery system. This more enlightened response captures the benefits that can come from failure and uses it as a signpost to correct faults and thereby improve quality.

Before moving on to the next section, take a look at Case examples 11.4, 11.5 and 11.6 which illustrate the very nature of quality conformance.

Case example 4   REGAINING CONSUMER CONFIDENCE AT JOHNSON & JOHNSON

In 1982, Johnson & Johnson, the US healthcare products group, faced a dilemma. An extortionist contaminated capsules of its Tylenol painkiller with cyanide. Seven people died. While the US government pondered what to do and before the media had time to put the company on the defensive, Johnson & Johnson recalled all Tylenol products at a cost of $100 million and the loss of short-term sales. But it emerged with consumer confidence enhanced and quickly regained its leadership of the painkiller market.

www.jnj.com

Case example 5 MARLBORO BRAND

In 1995, Philip Morris recalled all its Marlboro cigarettes from the US market because a batch of filters had become contaminated with a chemical that caused coughing and sneezing. Philip Morris went to great lengths to ensure a total recall, including full-page newspaper advertisements and a free inquiry service. The recall cost $200 million and was believed to contribute to the increase in Marlboro's market share that followed.

www.philipmorrisinternational.com/pages/eng/

Case example 6 TARNISHED REPUTATIONS AT COCA-COLA AND PERRIER

In 1999 Coca-Cola finally admitted that products going into some European markets (particularly Belgium) had been tainted by two separate incidents – the accidental injection of 'defective' carbon dioxide gas into some cola and the contamination of the outside of cans by a fungicide used to treat wooden shipping pallets. But the admission only came after several days of Coca-Cola assuring consumers that its products were safe, during which time dozens of children were hospitalized following complaints of stomach cramps, dizziness and vomiting. Coca-Cola's plan was a partial withdrawal of its products. This was met by the governments of Belgium and Luxembourg banning the sale of all Coca-Cola products, and some major supermarkets (for example Carrefour in France) unilaterally removing all Coca-Cola products from their shelves to avoid confusion. Coca-Cola also earned the hostility of the media, with one paper portraying its trademark polar bear doubled up in pain and another renaming the company 'Coca-Colic'. Coca-Cola's response was similar to that of Perrier, the French producer of sparkling water. In 1990, Perrier reacted slowly and grudgingly when traces of benzene were found in its products. At first reluctant to act, it was eventually forced to recall every bottle at a cost of $200 million and suffered a tarnished reputation and loss of market share.

www.cocacola.com; www.perrier.com

Case questions

1 Describe the reaction of these four companies to the quality conformance problems they faced.

2 Was quality conformance an order-winner or qualifier in these four companies and how did it affect their markets?

3 What role would operations have in each situation? Give details to explain your points.

Quality principles

It will help at this point to summarize the key principles in managing and controlling quality. This reflects the issues covered so far and also links into the next parts of the chapter. This first section lists four key principles in quality management and highlights the benefits of consistently meeting customers' needs. The sections that follow then cover philosophies, tools and techniques and implementation.

1 Meet customer requirements

Consistently meeting customer requirements is at the core of quality conformance. Requirements originate with the customer, result in an understanding and agreement on the specification and necessitate the consistent meeting of these needs. At the same time, companies also have requirements that suppliers must fulfil if the quality offering is to be met. In that way quality is a three-dimensional proposal – a company, its suppliers and its customers.

2 Error-free work

Error-free work sets the standard for how often a customer's requirements are met – the need to consistently meet the service or product specification. There is only one standard for which to aim – right first time and every time. This does not mean that errors will not occur. What it does mean is that adopting an attitude that errors are OK is not acceptable.

This approach to quality requires that the question 'why?' is always asked when an error occurs. The cause needs to be identified and changes made to keep the error from happening again.

3 Manage by prevention

An organization has to decide whether to adopt a reactive or proactive approach to managing quality. In the former, the emphasis is on detection, with the aim of preventing faulty work from being passed onto subsequent processes, so minimizing the costs of rectification, scrap, returned or rejected services or products, reimbursement, compensation and, most importantly, lost business.

The alternative is a proactive approach aimed at preventing errors in the first place by allocating resources to provide services and products right first time. To manage by prevention means that a rigorous approach to meeting quality standards must be built into the delivery system. It cannot be inspected in or repaired in. Emphasis on prevention will result in more consistently meeting customer requirements. Identifying what could go wrong and why leads to preventive action and backup plans.

4 Measuring the cost of quality

Measuring the cost of quality aims to reduce the cost of doing business by eliminating errors. The costs involve detecting and correcting errors on the one hand and preventing errors on the other. For most companies, the largest costs are associated with detection and correction. Doing things right the first time and every time reduces overall costs. Measuring quality costs prioritizes improvements and tracks progress.

Investing resources in identifying causes and preventing errors will reduce overall costs. However, in time these prevention costs also need to be reduced. Analysing and assessing how the measurement, detection, correction and prevention are undertaken with the aim of reducing costs becomes, in itself, a key task in managing quality. Case example 11.7 highlights some quality issues in the passenger airline industry.

Case example 7   ON-TIME FLIGHTS

The performance of airlines in terms of being on time is a key measure in terms of meeting customer needs and expectations. The level of success is continuously monitored by the relevant overseeing organizations (for example the Association of European Airlines and the US Department of Transport) who provide data on this key measure on a regular basis. Study the statistics for 12 US carriers in February 2004, shown opposite,. before answering the questions.

www.transtats.bts.gov

Case questions   1 Why is this level of detail collected by the Bureau of Transportation Statistics?

2 What reasons can you suggest for the different level of on-time flights for the 12 carriers?

Airline	# flights	Percentage of flights							
		On time	Air carrier delay	Weather delay	National aviation system delay	Security delay	Aircraft late	Cancelled	Diverted
Alaska Airlines	12,481	78.6	5.3	0.2	5.7	0.3	7.5	2.0	0.4
American Airlines	57,000	75.0	4.6	1.9	10.2	0.0	6.1	2.1	0.2
American Eagle	35,762	74.4	4.9	0.8	9.0	0.0	8.4	2.5	0.1
Continental Airlines	23,741	79.9	2.8	0.2	13.3	0.2	3.2	0.4	0.1
Continental Express	27,795	80.4	3.0	0.3	11.8	0.1	4.0	0.4	0.1
Delta Airlines	54,423	70.9	5.3	0.5	14.5	0.0	6.7	2.0	0.1
Hawaiian Airlines	3,743	89.6	4.2	0.4	0.1	0.2	4.4	0.9	0.2
JetBlue Airlines	6,726	88.2	2.8	0.1	5.4	0.2	3.0	0.1	0.2
Northwest Airlines	39,750	77.4	5.5	0.8	11.9	0.1	2.6	1.5	0.1
Southwest Airlines	77,190	82.2	3.6	0.3	3.4	0.1	9.0	1.2	0.2
United Airlines	42,675	81.9	3.4	0.2	9.4	–	4.3	0.7	0.1
US Airways	32,019	83.8	3.3	0.2	6.7	–	5.0	1.2	0.1
Total[1]	553,876	77.5	4.8	1.1	9.0	0.1	5.7	1.7	0.1

Note   1 Total is for 19 airlines from which the above 12 have been selected.

Source Bureau of Transportation Statistics (US Department of Transport).

Quality philosophies

During the 1980s concerns about competitiveness stimulated many companies to a new interest in quality. The growth in market share achieved by Japanese and Southeast Asian companies leading up to and during this period was impressive and much of the gain was on the back of a markedly superior quality performance.

The principal quality contributors at this time were Deming, Juran and Crosby. All were active consultants and writers in the field, with many years of practical, business-based experience. At the time of their impact in the West, Deming and Crosby were in their eighties and Juran was in his sixties. Each had a distinct orientation, although they all argued the same salient points. Deming saw quality as a management responsibility that required fundamental change and a long-term (three to five years) time frame. Juran centred much of his argument on the cost of quality and used data to shock management into action. Finally, Crosby looked to make an impact in a few months and, in that way, stir management into action. Now let us look at those three world-renowned contributors on quality in more detail.

W Edwards Deming

Deming is widely credited with leading the Japanese quality revolution. He exposed Japanese managers from the 1950s onwards to the fundamental concept of variance reduction through the introduction of tools and techniques such as statistical process control (SPC) which will be dealt with later in the chapter. He envisaged quality as an organization-wide activity rather than a technical task for quality specialists.

His early life was with the US Department of Agriculture as a mathematical physicist, during which time he was exposed to the theories and practices of statistical science and statistical control. Deming visited Japan in 1946 as a representative of the economic and scientific section of the US Department of War. With its manufacturing base destroyed by the US Air Force, Japanese managers listened intently on how to rebuild their manufacturing processes based on quality systems. Beginning in 1950, thousands of Japanese managers attended Deming's courses on statistical process control.

Recognizing Deming's important effect on the performance of manufacturing firms, the Japanese government created the Deming Prize in 1951. This annual award is given to a company or individual for active contributions to the development of quality management tools or the spread and implementation of quality improvement programmes.

Deming summarizes his views on what management must do to improve quality in his 14 points for management[1] which are given below:

1 Create constancy of purpose towards improvement of service and product
His call is to managers at all levels in an organization to promote a clear vision of the firm, its customers, its methods of delivering value and the role of quality in that provision. He stresses the need for managers to change from a preoccupation with the short term and to build for the longer term and focus on efforts to reduce unnecessary variance in a system.

2 Adopt the new philosophy
Mistakes, defects, rejects, shoddy materials, inadequate training, ineffective supervision and poorly motivated managers are unacceptable. Putting procedures and systems right is essential. To survive and grow requires managers to accept the need for continuous change and innovation.

3 Cease dependence on mass inspection
Planning 100 per cent inspection, Deming argues, is planning for defects and a recognition that the process cannot consistently meet specified requirements. Such an approach comes too late and is ineffective and costly. The orientation of effort needs to be on process improvement to eliminate errors and rejects.

4 End the practice of awarding business on the basis of the price tag alone
Price has no meaning without a measure of the quality being produced. The focus must change from the lowest initial cost of material purchased to the lowest total cost. Management must establish new guidelines, and long-term relationships with fewer suppliers need to replace short-term, multisourced approaches. Working together will lead to the lowest total cost position.

5 Improve constantly and for ever the system of production and service provision
Waste must be reduced in every part of the system by never-ending improvement. This will not come, however, by measuring defects but by measuring the process. Quality needs to be built in at every stage, starting with design and then increasing uniformity in the process to reduce variation and waste. Putting out fires is not a form of process improvement. Using data, adjusting the process and observing the effects is the way to improve.

6 Institute training
Training must be reconstructed and centred clearly on the concepts of acceptable work and then management needs to remove any inhibitors to achieving good work.

7 Adopt and institute leadership

The job of management is not supervision but leadership and should concentrate on improving the quality of the service and product.

8 Drive out fear

Fear of speaking out inhibits people from taking sensible actions. The results are costly. People must be encouraged to ask questions, report problems, express ideas and come up with solutions.

9 Break down barriers between staff areas

People in research, design, sales, procurement and incoming materials need to know the problems encountered with various materials and service specifications in operations. Each function must change from optimizing its own contribution and replace it with a team-based approach for corporate advantage.

10 Eliminate slogans, posters and exhortations

Exhorting people through slogans and posters is superficial and fails to bring the long-term benefits of sustained improvement. Posters and slogans never helped anyone to do a better job. Instead, management should ensure that people have the right tools and training to do the task and improve the process.

11 Eliminate work standards and numerical quotas

Quotas focus on quantity not quality. Over time, attempts to meet reasonable quotas lead to complacency since workers achieve their goals and need do no more. As a result, the inherent room for improvement is lost. Quotas, therefore, distract from the drive to continuously improve.

12 Remove barriers that rob people of pride in their workmanship

Within operations systems there are inherent barriers and obstacles to good workmanship. Barriers that hinder pride in one's work must be removed, including not knowing what constitutes good work, supervisors motivated by quotas, below-standard materials and out-of-line processes.

13 Encourage education and self-improvement for everyone

Continual training keeps people up to date with new developments, design and process changes, new tools and systems and innovative techniques. Because quality and productivity improvements reduce staffing levels, people must be trained and retrained. All training must include basic statistical techniques.

14 Take action to accomplish the transformation

To accomplish these steps, top management needs to create a structure to drive forward the other 13 points on a continuous basis. Top management's actions communicate the true importance of quality throughout the firm and they need to lead by example. Managers, and not staff lower down an organization, are the key to achieving continuous improvement.

Deming used his 14 points for management to highlight and underscore the central role of managers in bringing about essential improvements in quality conformance levels and productivity. He sees managers, and not staff lower down an organization, as the real obstacle, pointing out that 85 per cent of quality problems could be traced to management actions and failures. He also recognizes that implementing these 14 points would put a strain on managers' skills and determination. As a first step, therefore, he advocates that companies should address the five 'deadly diseases', as he calls them:[2]

1 Lack of constancy of purpose. Once a company commits to quality improvement it

cannot permit any variation in the message. Quality conformance has to be judged by absolute and not relative standards. It is better to protect the investments in a business by working consistently towards process, service and product improvements.

2   Emphasis on short-term profits. The pursuit of short-term profits defeats the constancy of purpose. It encourages short-term thinking and short-term actions and sacrifices long-term growth.

3   Performance evaluations and annual reviews. Most organization have systems by which a manager's performance is rated annually. These nourish short-term performance, rivalry and politics and militate against long-term improvements. What is basically wrong with this approach is that it does not focus on leadership to help people.

4   Mobility of management. In many organizations managers are moved to other roles or other parts of the same overall business every two or three years. It is put forward as a way to broaden and develop and invariably, in turn, becomes a clear signal that a person is on the promotion ladder. Lack of regular movement, on the other hand, is interpreted as a failure signal. The downside of this common approach is a lack of tenure and an understandable lack of commitment to long-term improvement. In fact, there is a strong argument that if managers are not going to be there to see through their developments, it is better for them not to undertake major improvement programmes in the first place.

5   Running a company on visible figures alone (counting the money). While visible figures are important, it is essential to take account of other factors when assessing performance. Maximizing figures to reflect good performance emphasizes the short-term and also underpins several of Deming's other 'diseases'.

Deming's belief that an uncompetitive business was due to the 'failure of top management to manage'[3] is central to his argument and the changes he advocates on how to manage. Quality and productivity are not to be traded off against each other. Rather, improved productivity needs to be recognized as a byproduct of improved quality and of doing a job right the first time. Management must take the lead in changing the systems and processes that generate current problems. The changes needed are often fundamental and corporate-wide. For example, to ensure consistent quality of incoming materials and purchased items means developing long-term relationships with vendors and working with them to maintain and improve quality. Similarly, management have to set aside the 'low price' brief for buyers and train its own staff in statistical control techniques to create data as part of assessing quality and identifying improvements. This typifies the long-term and fundamental nature of the changes that Deming advocates have to be made.

Joseph M Juran

Juran defines quality as 'fitness for use'. That is, users should be able to expect that a service or product would provide what they needed or wanted to do with it. His work on quality spanned over 30 years and included 12 books.[4] His contribution to the ideas and approaches on quality management[5] centres on five themes that are now explained:

1   Quality of design reflects the suitability of a design concept and specification for its intended use.

2   Quality conformance reflects how well an actual service or product achieves the intentions of its design.

3   Availability relates to the absence of problems that could affect a service or product's use. Reliability and the ease of maintenance and repair affect the availability factor.

4   Safety concerns the threat of harm to a user.

5   Field use represents the condition of a service or product when it reaches a customer and depends on aspects such as packaging, storage, field support and maintenance.

To achieve fitness for use, Juran developed a comprehensive approach to quality that spans a service or product's entire life – design, vendor relations, process development, operations control, test, distribution, customer relations and field service. All aspects must be carefully analysed to include the impact of each part or component on the elements comprising fitness for use and leading to solutions to those dimensions most critical to the performance and safety of a service or product. A whole range of statistical methods are used in this analysis and for setting realistic improvement targets and quantifiable goals.

Cost of quality

Juran's analytical methods led to improvement targets with built-in tracking to monitor the implementation programme. However, these statements were in the language of operations, such as defect rates and so on. Recognizing that executives would not be interested in these dimensions of a business problem, Juran developed the concept of the cost of quality (COQ). This approach relates quality to the common denominator of money, the language of top management. It states quality in terms of the costs associated with defective services or products – the costs of making, finding, repairing or avoiding errors or defects. To help focus attention further, all costs are allocated to four categories:[6]

1   Internal failure costs that result from the detection of quality failures before shipment to customers. These include scrap, rework, reinspection, yield losses and disposal.

2   External failure costs that arise from finding defects after despatch to a customer, such as complaint adjustments, the return of materials, warranty claims, handling complaints, field service support and repairs.

3   Appraisal costs associated with assessing the condition of services, products and materials. These include incoming inspection, service/product and delivery system/process checks, quality assurance/control, staff and support costs and the purchase and maintenance of test equipment.

4   Prevention costs that result from activities to prevent defects including quality planning, new service and product reviews, process control, data collection and analysis, reporting and improvement activities.

In most companies, internal and external failure costs account for 50–80 per cent of COQ. Juran argued that when these are converted into money, top management usually sits up and takes notice. COQ not only provides cost-based information but also improvement targets for quality programmes. With guidelines for investment and an assessment of the benefits involved, companies launch quality programmes until additional investments do not provide acceptable returns.

Quality habit

Juran's ultimate goal for a quality programme is for the company as a whole to be totally involved and committed to a process of continuous improvement. Slogans, posters and exhortations would not result in the necessary level of change. As with Deming, Juran identifies management action as the key to bringing about such a fundamental shift. An unwavering focus on the need for better quality should develop into a quality habit that is based on objective results and the lessons to be learned from the process and outcomes of these activities and tasks. To help a company develop this quality habit, Juran advocates a four-stage process:

1 **Goals** – establish specific goals for the organization
2 **Plans** – detail plans for reaching these goals
3 **Responsibilities** – assign clear responsibilities for undertaking these plans and achieving the set goals
4 **Rewards** – base rewards on results.

Quality offensive

To achieve and maintain a successful quality management programme, Juran proposes a three-stage offensive for improving quality.

1 Breakthrough projects

In the early stages of a quality improvement programme, when failure costs greatly exceed the sum of appraisal and prevention costs, there will be many significant opportunities for breakthrough projects aimed at chronic problems (see Exhibit 11.5). The approach needs to be based on a COQ Pareto analysis, gaining management's support for the programme of change and underpinning the activity with the goals, plans, responsibilities and rewards sequence introduced in the last section. Juran claims that as over 80 per cent of quality problems are under the jurisdiction of management, the approach is to involve relevant staff throughout, identify the key people to successfully implement proposals and use appropriate authority to overcome resistance to change in order to bring about and sustain improvements.

Exhibit 11.5 Juran's sporadic and chronic quality problems

Source Adapted from JM Juran and FM Gryna *Quality Planning and Analysis*, New York, McGraw-Hill (1993), p. 10.

2 Control sequence

After successive breakthrough projects, a company reaches the optimum level of quality, the bottom level of the COQ curve, as shown in Exhibit 11.6.

An organization must then introduce an ongoing control sequence to maintain its gains. As Exhibit 11.5 illustrates, after improvements a new 'zone of quality control' is reached. This involves choosing new objectives, defining the control measures to use, setting standards, measuring performance and introducing a reporting system. Current underperformance created by introducing new standards identifies gaps and leads to action programmes to close the gap.[7] This control sequence is also used to handle sporadic problems (see Exhibit 11.5).

Juran's approach encompasses vendor selection and review through to customer service. Its comprehensive nature and the rigour associated with the breakthrough and control phases described here led Juran to advocate the need for quality control engineers, and for this function to be involved in all phases of a programme.

Exhibit 11.6 Minimizing the costs of quality

	Improvement projects zone	Reappraisal zone	High appraisal costs zone
Total quality cost curve		Optimum	
Zone	Improvement projects zone	Reappraisal zone	High appraisal costs zone
Costs	Failure >70 per cent	Failure ~50 per cent	Failure <40 per cent
	Prevention <10 per cent	Prevention ~10 per cent	Appraisal >50 per cent
Action	Find breakthrough projects and pursue	If profitable projects not available, shift emphasis to control	Analyse cost per defect and adjust action. Check accuracy of standards. Audit decisions

Source Adapted from JM Juran and FM Gryna *Quality Planning and Analysis*, New York, McGraw-Hill (1993), p. 26.

3 Annual quality programme

Juran's approach uses the annual quality programme as the principal vehicle to involve top management. This gives objectives for management, reinforces the quality habit and ensures that complacency does not set in.

Breakthrough project sequence

Introduced in the last section, breakthrough projects identify actions directed towards achieving major leaps in quality levels. To facilitate this Juran advocates a sequence of steps to be followed, the effective application of which absolutely requires prior management acceptance of the responsibility for improvements. The steps involved are:[8]

1 **Proof of need.** The first step is recognizing that a fault in the current process needs an immediate response. This proof of need is underscored by demonstrating that the costs of not changing exceed the costs of the change itself. Using costs introduces a simple but powerful denominator that is readily understood by all and needs no further explanation.

2   Project identification. To concentrate improvement efforts, specific projects are used to focus attention and become catalysts for change. Breakthroughs start with project identification and with people working on proven needs and clear problems. Careful choice helps to concentrate on projects with large and highly visible pay-offs.

3   Organizing for improvement. The successful completion of projects needs infrastructure in place at two levels – a steering group and a diagnostic group. The former comprises staff from several departments and defines the programme, suggests problem causes, lends authority to the activity, helps overcome any resistance to change and implements the improvements. The diagnostic group is made up of quality professionals and line managers, with the task of allocating resources, analysing problems, identifying improvement, setting out a programme of change and agreeing a timetable for implementation. To undertake this step successfully, the following phases need to be completed:

- **Analysis.** The diagnostic group studies symptoms, develops hypotheses, tests alternatives and identifies a problem's true causes. In so doing it separates defects into those that are within an operator's and those that are in management's control. To be in an operator's control, a problem has to meet three criteria – operators know what they are supposed to do, have the data to understand what they are actually doing and are able to regulate their own performance. Using past and current data and conducting experiments lead to solutions.
- **Overcoming resistance to change.** An essential element of any change programme is to identify the key people involved. Including them from an early stage and preparing them for the technical and cultural aspects of change is an essential step.
- **Implementing and maintaining the changes.** Overviewing the cost of the problem, looking at alternative solutions and associated costs/benefits, reviewing the steps to be taken and highlighting the changes involved need to be presented to all those involved in appreciating, implementing and maintaining the programme. The final challenge is to maintain the changes and prevent any return to old procedures, processes and habits. Consolidating improvements is a key task and will be enhanced by establishing new standards, increased training, developing new control systems with reliable warning signals, employing statistical techniques and feedback loops and introducing relevant performance measures.

Philip B Crosby

Crosby addresses his message to top management, proposing that quality management provides a viable strategy for corporate survival and growth. Furthermore, Crosby denies that a firm has to make large investments to improve quality. He asserts that a quality management programme would lead to such a level of savings that it would pay for itself; ultimately, 'quality is free'.[9]

The goal of quality improvement is zero defects, to be achieved through prevention rather than after-the-fact inspection. The key to quality improvement, he believed, was to change top management's thinking. Management needed to establish a higher standard of performance and communicate these expectations throughout all levels of the company. Zero defects is possible, but needs to be a management standard and not simply a motivational programme for employees. To help managers understand the size of their quality problems, Crosby provides the following ideas and approaches.

Cost of quality

In most companies, Crosby estimates that the cost of quality is 15–20 per cent of sales. Identifying the size of the problem arrests management's attention, illustrates the opportunities for profitable improvement and thereby gains corporate support for a quality programme.

Absolutes for quality management

Crosby identifies the fundamental elements of an effective quality management system and called the following four laws 'the absolutes for quality management':

1 Quality is conformance to requirements, not goodness. Crosby required only one definition of quality – when the services or goods meet or exceed customers' expectations. Management must ensure that everyone understands these requirements and then provide the tools and systems to allow this to happen.

2 Quality management is based on prevention. Successful quality management begins with an analysis and evaluation of current processes. The analysis needs to use essential statistical tools to identify all the opportunities where quality problems could disrupt a process. The elimination of these opportunities then leads to the prevention of quality problems.

3 Zero defects is the performance standard. Effective quality management sets a goal of zero defects. Such an aim creates a corporate environment that accepts no errors and promotes systems and procedures designed to eliminate defects.

4 The price of non-conformance. To make quality a corporate issue, the cost of failing to meet conformance to requirements needs to be measured and expressed in money terms, the language of top management. The high cost of quality motivates top management to become involved with subsequent improvement programmes. The investments in training, improved service/product and process design, and better supplier relations are, in turn, the price of conformance.

Quality management maturity grid and 14-point programme

To help identify a company's position on the dimension of quality management, Crosby introduced a 'maturity grid' for corporate self-assessment. It identifies five states of quality awareness, as summarized in Exhibit 11.7. For each of the five stages, Crosby also examined the status of the quality function, the problem-solving procedures used, the reported versus actual costs of quality and the actions taken.

Once companies had positioned themselves on the maturity grid, they could introduce Crosby's 14-point programme for quality improvement:

1 Management commitment. Managers must be convinced of the importance of quality and demonstrate a clear commitment to improvement throughout the organization by aligning actions, policies and priorities to improving quality.

2 Quality improvement team. The quality improvement programme needs to be supported by a multifunctional team that reports directly to top management. Its role should include establishing quality-oriented policies, involvement in educational activities and coordinating and supervising changes in corporate culture.

3 Quality measurement. Quality measures need to be introduced that are meaningful and relate specifically to areas needing improvement. They need to relate to all functions and address key dimensions.

4 Cost of quality evaluation. The programme collates the price of both non-conformance and conformance. This forms part of the essential guide to prioritizing action in line with different opportunities for improving quality.

Exhibit 11.7 Crosby's quality management maturity grid

Categories of quality

Categories of quality		1 Uncertainty	2 Awakening	3 Enlightenment	4 Wisdom	5 Certainty
				Stages		
Management understanding and attitude		Fails to recognize quality as a corporate issue	Supports quality management in theory but does not allocate resources	Embraces quality management and actively supports it	Participates personally and provides leadership in quality activities	Recognizes quality as necessary for corporate survival and growth
The organizational status of the quality function		Quality limited to the operations and technical functions and largely comprises inspection and checking activities	Quality leader appointed but otherwise activities remain similar to those in Stage 1	Quality function reports to top management and its leader actively involved in company management	Quality manager is a top management appointment and activities reoriented to prevention	Quality manager is on the board of directors. Prevention now the main activity and zero defects the management goal
Approach to handling problems		Fire-fighting approach. Symptoms, not causes, addressed	Teams established to resolve problems but still short term in nature	Problems resolved in an orderly fashion and involves corrective action	Problems identified at an early stage and preventive action taken	Problems are prevented at the design and development stage
Cost of quality as percentage of sales	reported	Unknown	5 per cent	8 per cent	6 per cent	2–3 per cent
	actual	0–40 per cent	18 per cent	12 per cent	8 per cent	2–3 per cent
Quality improvement actions		No organized activities	Actions based on exhortation and short term in nature	Implements the 14-step programme	Continues the 14-step programme	Quality improvement is a regular ongoing activity
Overview of corporate position on quality management		'We don't know why we have problems'	'Do we always have to have quality problems?'	'Management's commitment and quality improvement programme is resolving our quality problems'	'We routinely prevent quality problems from occurring'	'We no longer have quality problems, we know why, and we aim to do better'

Source Adapted from PB Crosby, *Quality is Free*, New York, McGraw-Hill (1979), pp. 32–3.

5 Quality awareness needs to be promoted and coordinated throughout the company. Raising awareness among employees of the need for quality conformance and the cost of non-conformance is essential.

6 Corrective action. Opportunities and ideas for action are brought to the supervisory level and resolved there if possible. The team takes any remaining problems to higher levels for action.

7 Zero-defects planning. Managers need to plan the move from corrective action to achieving the goal of zero defects.

8 Employee education. Early in the quality programme all staff need to be trained in the principles of quality management and relevant tools and techniques.

9 Zero-defects day. Crosby recommends scheduling a particular date as zero-defects day. This signals a company's new standard of zero defects and the start of its move towards this new goal.

10 Goal setting. To achieve zero defects, a company needs to turn commitment into action by setting goals that represent progress towards this target. Not only do these guide action but they also guide performance measurement and evaluation.

11 Error cause removal. A quality programme should encourage staff to identify and report any problems that prevent them from producing error-free work. Everyone should take responsibility for identifying and correcting problems and preventing them recurring.

12 Recognition. A programme should include public, non-financial appreciation for all those whose actions have helped achieve or exceed a firm's quality goals and objectives.

13 Quality councils. Crosby recommends forming a quality council comprising quality professionals and team leaders who should meet regularly to share experiences, problems and ideas.

14 Do it all over again. To highlight the never-ending process of quality improvements, the final step returns the programme to the beginning to start the process again. This renews a company's commitment to quality and will bring a new round of quality improvement opportunities and gains.

Quality vaccine

To help make quality management an integral part of an organization's activities, Crosby introduced the concept of the quality vaccine – see Exhibit 11.8. This idea describes a corporate quality state that improves the overall health of a firm by addressing and correcting many of its problems. Corporate integrity represents the honest commitment to improve performance and satisfy customers in the most effective way. The concept embodies a firm's policy commitment to offer services and products that are right first time, every time. Communications represent the flow of information through the whole supply chain, emphasizing the need for regular exchanges of information on quality problems, performance, progress and related issues. The

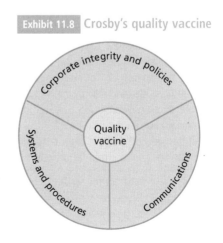

Exhibit 11.8 Crosby's quality vaccine

final element is the systems and procedures designed to maintain the new quality management environment.

Tools and techniques – general issues

The key to good quality lies in good management, a point central to the views of all the main contributors to improving quality. Management has the responsibility and has to give the lead in changing the systems and processes that create quality problems. A key part of this provision is to train everyone how to use the tools and techniques to enable the quality offering to be consistently met. Sound quality management relies heavily on contributions from empowered staff and, in turn, this requires access to appropriate tools.

The tools and techniques used in quality management are based on analysis and statistical approaches to measure and improve the level of quality in a company's processes and delivery systems. These tools indicate how well operations is consistently meeting the agreed specification of its services and products and, in turn, identify the source of any problems. Take a look at Case examples 11.8 and 11.9 as illustrations.

Case example 8   MOTIVATION AND SUPPORT ARE NOT ENOUGH TO DO YOUR JOB

Bill Conway (Nashua Corporation) was addressing some top management visitors from Ford. He started the meeting with a challenge. 'Suppose I ask two of you successful vice-presidents at Ford to enter a contest. The winner will win a trip around the world for his whole family. I know that both of you are totally motivated and dedicated by virtue of your exalted positions at Ford. The contest is to see who can drive a nail into this wall. One of you will get a hammer, the other nothing but management encouragement. Who do you think will win?' The answer was obvious. Motivation and management support and encouragement are important, but employees having the correct tools is essential.[10]   **www.nashua.com**

Case example 9   ANSTRUTHER FISH BAR'S SECRET BATTER RECIPE

The Anstruther Fish Bar, a modest fish and chip shop in a quiet Scottish fishing town in Fife, was sold in 2004 for £1.6 million. The reason for such a high price premium for what is a modest building facing Anstruther's harbour is the thousands of customers it attracts, with queues up to 1.5 hours at busy times. The owner Ian Whyte decided to sell up the family business, purchased in the late 1990s for £200,000, and retire. The eightfold price increase reflects the size of the business built up over the last few years, with upwards of 2000 customers a day and daily takings exceeding £10,000. This success is a result of the care taken by the proprietors in all aspects of the shop's service delivery system, from the preparation of food to clean floors .

The secret of the perfect fish supper is the consistency of the batter and the quality of the fish, factors that may be obvious but require considerable skill to judge. 'The way to build good trade,' reflected Ian, 'is to give customers what they want and guarantee consistency – give customers the same quality they had last time.'

The quality of haddock, for example, can vary considerably depending on the time of year, with fish caught in early spring, the spawning season, being much thinner than later in the year. In early summer, on the other hand, haddock typically feed on herring and land eels which make the fillets more oily. To counter such changes, subtle alterations to the batter recipe are made to retain the consistency of the fish quality when fried. The batter mixture developed by Mr Whyte consists of flour, spring water, vinegar and baking powder, although the quantities remain a closely guarded secret! The result is a very light batter coating that literally drops off when the fish fillet is broken.

Case questions	1 What are the similarities between the two examples?
	2 Review the service delivery in the Anstruther Fish Bar and identify the key aspects that help to guarantee quality.
	3 Which aspects of Deming, Juran and Crosby's approaches does the fish bar highlight?

In general, these tools and techniques fall into those used in the design phase and those used in the service delivery system or manufacturing process phase:

- **Design tools** help staff to develop new services and products that incorporate the needs and expectations of customers into the specification while reducing or preventing quality problems inherent in the design itself. Similar tools and techniques are used in the design of the delivery system or process to reduce or prevent problems in the way services or products are provided.

- **Process tools** enable staff to assess the conditions and capabilities of existing delivery systems or processes in relation to meeting set standards. These help detect problems that require intervention to regain any lost control within a delivery system or process.

To apply design and process tools and techniques, data are required. In general, the tools help staff to draw pictures of the process. These highlight trends or provide indicators of actual or potential quality problems. Process conditions can be measured using variable or attribute data.

Variable data measure quantifiable process conditions. They can be counted and allow absolute or comparative positions to be established. Exhibit 11.9 illustrates the point. A receiving department checks incoming products by taking a sample of 40 from each delivery. If there are four or less (≤10 per cent) defects, the delivery is accepted. With five or more defects, the whole delivery is rejected. By this method, 12 of the 15 deliveries in Quarter 1 (see Exhibit 11.9) were accepted and three were returned to the supplier – an acceptance rate of 80 per cent. In this example, the number of defects provides variable data because it can be arranged in ways to allow comparisons to be made. For example, the early part of Quarter 1 showed a high percentage of rejects compared to the latter part. Furthermore, when deliveries were rejected, the percentage of defects was relatively high, between 15 and 25.

In contrast, **attribute data** measure qualitative conditions of a process such as the accept/reject decision in Exhibit 11.9. Comparisons using attribute data provide limited insights. For example, without column 2 in the exhibit, the differences in the number of rejects for each delivery would not be available: a delivery has been rejected with in excess of 10 per cent rejects.

Variable and attribute measures are, however, linked and from the simple example in Exhibit 11.9, it can be seen that knowing what data will provide the insights required is essential when designing process controls.

Exhibit 11.9 Data on 15 deliveries in Quarter 1

Delivery date	# defects per batch of 40 units	Decision: accept (✓) or reject (✗)
3 Jan	6	✗
6 Jan	2	✓
11 Jan	10	✗
24 Jan	4	✓
3 Feb	7	✗
17 Feb	0	✓
19 Feb	3	✓
28 Feb	3	✓
3 Mar	2	✓
6 Mar	2	✓
12 Mar	1	✓
18 Mar	1	✓
24 Mar	3	✓
26 Mar	4	✓
30 Mar	4	✓

Process tools and techniques[11]

This section describes the tools and techniques available to undertake quality checks. As you will see, some of them have been introduced and described in other chapters and are, therefore, only included here by a brief statement with appropriate references.

Companies use these tools and techniques to evaluate how well delivery systems and processes consistently meet the service and product specifications and hence the expectation of their customers, identify problems and their most likely causes and assess the effect of corrective actions. These tools and techniques provide different and complementary analyses, so using a combination of these gives greater insight and more information by which to manage and control quality.

Pareto principle

The size and importance of problems, causes or other aspects of quality will vary and often the relationship between their relative frequency will reflect what is known as the Pareto principle or 80/20 rule (explained in more detail in Chapter 12). The 80/20 rule indicates that, say, 80 per cent of the total quality problems identified would be the result of 20 per cent of the total number of causes.

In managing quality, a Pareto analysis would begin by listing the quality problems identified and recording the number of times these occurred. Additional information such as the costs (for example rectification or reject) associated with each problem would also be kept. Over a given period data would be collected and the number of occurrences or total costs involved would be identified for each problem. Placing the highest (either number of occurrences or total costs depending on which dimension was perceived to be the more relevant) at the top of the list, the second highest next and so on (see Exhibit 11.10) gives a Pareto listing. A Pareto analysis thus highlights where a company should start its improvement efforts. Beginning with those at the top will bring a higher return than starting lower down the list.

Exhibit 11.10 Pareto analysis of reasons for flight departure

Problem	Percentage of incidences	Cumulative percentage
Accepting late passengers	39	39
Waiting for tug pushback	24	63
Waiting for fuelling	14	77
Late weight and balance sheet	9	86
Cabin cleaners take longer than scheduled	8	94
Waiting for food services	4	98
Other	2	100

Checklists

A checklist is a simple, widely used tool to collect data in a form that records the size and other dimensions of quality (and other) problems. Exhibit 11.11 provides an example for a retail outlet. A number of problems were chosen to be reviewed and by using the five-bar gate method of recording, each occurrence was logged and totals calculated. You will also see from this list that the 80/20 rule applies here as two of the five problems account for 71 per cent of the total problem occurrences. (This also illustrates that the phrase 80/20 is one indicating relative size and not exactness.) Looking at these in more depth would be the place to start.

Exhibit 11.11 Checklist of frequency of problems at a retail outlet

Problem	Frequency	Total	Percentage of total
Shelf display differs from bar code record	1111 1111 1111 1	16	14
No goods on shelf	1111 1111 1111 1111 1111 1111 1111	34	29
Goods out of stock	1111 1111	10	8
Length of checkout queue exceeds target	1111 1111 1111 1111 1111 1111 1111 1111 1111 1111	49	42
Items returned faulty	1111 111	8	7
Total		117	100

Cause and effect diagrams

Also known as fishbone (due to their shape) or Ishikawa charts (named after the person who developed this tool),[12] cause and effect diagrams (discussed in Chapter 16) identify potential causes and help to direct problem-solving and data-collection efforts towards the most likely causes of observed defects.

These diagrams are built up from a problem statement through to detailed causes using the following steps:

- Problem statement. Analysis of the symptoms and causes yields the problem statement. This becomes the label for the root effect arrow, as shown in Exhibit 11.12.
- Major causes. The second step is to identify major categories of causes. These are then drawn at an angle to the root effect arrow. For example, 'airport' and 'personnel' in Exhibit 11.12.
- Detailed causes. The next step is to list all the detailed causes within each of the major categories. For example, 'weather' and 'other air traffic control delays' under the major cause 'other' in Exhibit 11.12.
- Principal causes. The final step is to identify the principal causes within the list of detailed causes as a guide as to where to look first. For example, Exhibit 11.12 indicates these with an asterisk.

Sumitomo Electric has developed the use of cause and effect diagrams by adding the following refinements:

- For each cause, two coloured cards are introduced. One records details of facts and the other details of ideas.
- Any number of 'fact' cards are placed on the left of each cause. These contain data and issues relating to a particular cause.
- In the same way, any number of 'ideas' cards are placed on the right of each cause and these contain suggestions for improvements.
- All 'fact' cards are first reviewed as part of the problem clarification stage before moving onto 'ideas' cards that address potential improvements.
- All cards are initialled by the contributor allowing for explanation, questions and greater clarity.

Exhibit 11.12 Cause and effect diagram used to ascertain the cause of flight delays

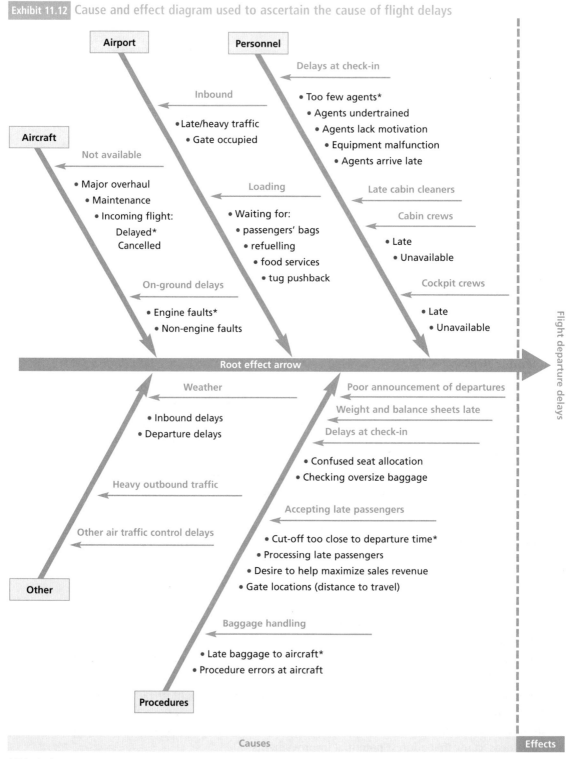

* Principal causes

Process mapping

One key process tool for improving quality is to record the existing system or process. Charting the sequence of steps and clarifying what goes on at each step is an important analysis to make. As this is covered extensively in Chapter 16, further explanation is not provided here. By turning to this chapter, however, you will be able to review the different types of process maps and charts available and which ones are used where.

Scatter diagrams

Collecting data is one step, identifying why a variable happens turns data into information from which insights result. One way of doing this is to construct a scatter diagram. This tool illustrates graphically the relationship between two variables. It reveals relationships between pairs of variables (known as a bivariate relationship), such as the number of errors per day and the length of an operator's experience or the number of training days received. Exhibit 11.13 is a scatter diagram illustrating the relationship between the percentage of defects and the length of a production run. It shows that as the run length increases, the percentage of rejects decreases and this decline follows a consistent pattern.

Exhibit 11.13 Scatter diagram

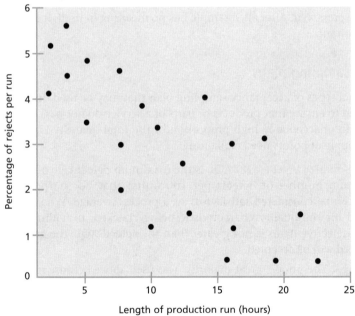

Sampling

To ensure that the level of quality is consistently met, 100 per cent inspection should, in theory, ensure that below-quality services or products are not allowed to proceed through the process. Technology developments, particularly in high volume manufacturing processes, have enabled this to be undertaken as an integral part of the system. For example, checking the weight of, or liquid level in, a container provides a simple pass/reject mechanism ensuring that a pack contains the required amount. However, where inspection is undertaken by people, there are in practice major limitations. Checking becomes monotonous and errors creep in, it is costly, it takes longer and where testing would make a product unusable (for example lighting fireworks to see if they work), sampling is a practical alternative.

Where 100 per cent inspection is not an integral part of the operations process, the limitations above give rise to the concept of acceptance sampling. Most acceptance checking or inspection procedures are based on the principles of statistical inference, by which conclusions are drawn about the characteristics of a large quantity of services or products by careful inspection of a small sample from the total. Any acceptance sampling plan may lead to a wrong judgement. This is known as sampling risk and is covered later.

There has been much written about the subject of sampling and the methods are so well refined that it is not necessary to understand the mathematical principles involved. Also, tables are available to show the inferences that can be drawn from the different sampling procedures and outcomes. Should you wish to review these aspects in more detail, suggested readings are included at the end of the chapter.[13]

When using the concept of sampling, the following principles must apply:

- The sample has to be either truly random or stratified (that is, the samples are chosen so as to be representative of what the operations system produces over the time period involved).
- The sample size needs to relate to the size of the total quantity involved to ensure that what is checked is sufficiently representative of the whole.
- The identity of the total quantity from which the sample has been taken should, where possible, be preserved. After all, a sample has no meaning in itself; it is the total quantity that is important.

Acceptance sampling plans

There are several types of acceptance sampling plan that may be used. In each instance, the plan is designed to ensure that products or parts of a service do not pass to the next stage in the process if an unacceptably high proportion of the total quantity is outside the quality limit. First a couple of points need explaining:

- Acceptable quality level (AQL) AQL is the maximum percentage of defective items (or the maximum number of defects per 100 units) that, for purposes of acceptance sampling, can be considered satisfactory as a process average. When a value of AQL is determined for the quality characteristic being checked, providing that the average number of defective items is not greater than the agreed AQL, the great majority of the lots inspected will be accepted.
- Sampling risk The phrase 'great majority' was used above because no sampling scheme is perfect. There will be the risk that an unacceptable batch will satisfy the AQL and, therefore, be accepted (known as the consumer's risk) and, similarly, that an acceptable batch fails to meet the AQL and, therefore, is rejected (known as the producer's risk). The way to reduce this risk is to take a larger sample, with 100 per cent sample plans being the upper limit where, theoretically, no risk is taken.

A sampling scheme contains a range of sampling plans and procedures and the results of inspecting one or more samples are used to assess the quality of a total quantity and help determine whether or not to accept it. Each sampling plan states the sample size to be taken in relation to each different total quantity size and the decision criteria to be used for accepting or rejecting it. The sample sizes are based on the mathematical theory of probability and will not be covered here. Earlier, the limitations surrounding a 100 per cent inspection procedure were discussed. While the concept of sampling holds true in most situations, there are times when 100 per cent inspection is necessary, for example where safety is of the utmost importance.

Single sampling plan

This plan is essentially a go/no-go procedure. The sampling size related to the total quantity is determined and the acceptable quality level is applied. Only if the number of errors (services) or defective items (products) meets the AQL criteria is the total quantity accepted.

Double sampling plan

A double sampling plan introduces another option to the single plan above. The example shown in Exhibit 11.14 requires a sample of 100 to be taken from a total quantity of a known size. If on the first sample of 100 the number of errors or defects is two or less, the whole batch is accepted on the first sample. Conversely, if the number of errors or defective items is seven or more, the whole batch is rejected on the first sample. If, however, the number of errors or defective items is between three and six, a second sample of 100 is taken. If the cumulative number of errors or defective items from both samples of 100 is seven or less, accept it, if eight or more, reject it.

Exhibit 11.14 Double sampling plan

| Sample | | Number of errors or defective items | |
#	Size	Acceptable quality level	Unacceptable quality level
1st	100	≤2	≤7
2nd	100	≤7	≤8

Multiple sampling plan

The principle of the double sampling plan can be extended into a multiple sampling plan. This too uses not only the AQL concept but also the unacceptable quality level (UQL) concept. This latter relates to the percentage defective level at which the total quantity would be rejected. As in the case of double sampling plans, there is a yes, no and don't know

Exhibit 11.15 Multiple sampling plan

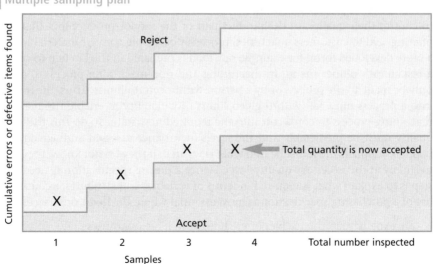

situation. A first sample is taken which is usually smaller than in a single sampling plan. If the number of errors or defective items is between the accept and reject areas, further samples are taken until the cumulative results of the multiple samples fall into either the accept or reject category, as illustrated in Exhibit 11.15.

Sequential sampling plan

A sequential sampling plan is similar to a multiple plan. The sample size is one, with the results normally plotted on a graph. The sampling is repeated until the graph contains sufficient information on which to reach a decision.

Normal, tightened and reduced inspection

Normal inspection is defined as that used where there is no reason to think that the quality of a service or product differs from that specified. Inspection is tightened or reduced when the results of normal inspection indicate that the quality of the total quantity is worse or better than specified.

The operations process – managing quality in practice

Having explained the important, general aspects of managing quality, this section looks at the major stages in the operations process and the types of quality checks to apply and tools to use. Several of the techniques explained earlier (for example, the Pareto principle, checklists, cause and effect diagrams, process mapping and scatter diagrams) will be used as part of a general approach to managing quality in practice. This section identifies the more quality-specific tools, while recognizing that the more general techniques invariably form part of the overall approach used to manage quality.

Earlier in the chapter the question 'where to inspect?' was introduced. This section now reviews in more detail the issues of where to check and some of the principal tools used at each stage.

Supply chain

The ever higher percentage of total costs that purchased items constitutes increases the need to control their quality. In the product part of the service/product mix that constitutes the offering sold to customers, machines, processes or people convert material from one form to a more developed form, for example raw food is prepared in the kitchen to create an item on a restaurant's dinner menu. In machining and non-machining processes, adjustments can only be made to the process or by a person within certain limits. Thus, the material being fed into a process must fall within given limits of variability to enable the machining or non-machining process to convert it into the required new state. To do this the level of material quality must be predictable and the levels of variance assessed and agreed. But for this to happen, suppliers must first be told what is wanted. If they do not know, they will not be able to supply at the necessary quality level. Hence a precise specification is needed, and the first step is to explain what is required in terms of variables and attributes, as outlined earlier. The use of a purchasing specification is most essential where the items or services:

● are expensive in themselves or are bought in large quantities

- relate to the essential attribute (service) or essential function (product) to be provided by what is sold
- will cause difficulties and expense in the process if they are below the service or product specification.

To help maintain desired quality levels it is necessary to buy services or materials from reliable suppliers. While it is essential to recognize that there are other important considerations, such as cost and delivery reliability, that will form part of this choice, these are not discussed in this section.

The quality of purchased components and materials is rooted in the delivery systems and processes of suppliers. A company will not receive the required level of quality if the methods used by its suppliers are not capable of consistently meeting the agreed specification. It is, therefore, important that an evaluation of procedures is established, particularly for those suppliers that provide services or materials critical to the process and end-product or service. This will usually contain three distinct phases:

- **Vendor appraisal** that is completed before placing an order and is designed to assess the ability of a supplier to deliver services and goods at the required level of quality.
- **Supplier evaluation** which is designed to vet a supplier's control of quality when an order has been given, and the services and goods supplied.
- **Supplier rating** which monitors the actual performance of a supplier.

Checking purchased items and services

Where the maintenance of quality levels is critical to the service or end-product, organizations typically insist on monitoring a supplier's processes and quality control procedures. A classic example of this is the aviation industry. Civil and military aircraft companies have developed sophisticated quality assurance procedures to meet the high safety requirements of many of their components and equipment purchases. Tracking the origin of materials and evaluating and monitoring suppliers' processes forms part of their supplier controls. Similar checks are increasingly being introduced in the service sector. For example, companies purchasing consultancy services will interview the consultants themselves as part of the selection process. In the same way, companies contracting out the supply of executive education will interview those providing direction and also require to see first hand the teaching faculty in a classroom or other learning environment as part of their decision-making procedure. However, most organizations limit themselves to checking services or items once they have been purchased. Understandably, as items become more complex, so do the inspection procedures. In many instances these checks may be no more than a quantity count as, for example, with office supplies. Yet even where an organization wishes to check the characteristics of a service or products, it will not usually inspect each one: the costs of doing so are just too high. Thus, the inspection procedure agreed with a supplier has to include not only what is intended to be the quality level but also how it is to be judged and measured and the level of imperfection that is acceptable (see earlier in the chapter). Where some level of imperfection is permitted, then sampling is the basis on which to proceed.

Consequently, the principle of acceptance sampling will be applied in such situations. The design of any sampling plan is a trade-off between sampling cost and risk. To help in this choice, a useful way of depicting the relationship is provided by plotting an operating characteristic (OC) curve (see Exhibit 11.16). Each OC curve is associated with a particular sampling plan and it shows how well a plan discriminates between acceptable and non-acceptable deliveries. Exhibit 11.16 explains how a particular acceptance plan operates, but

Exhibit 11.16 General relationships of an OC curve

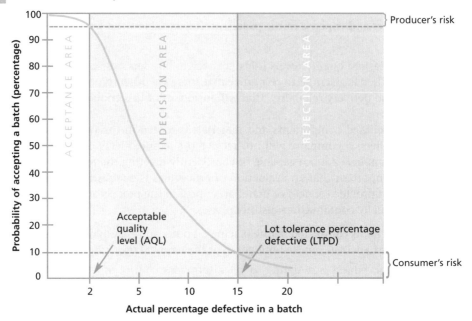

as each acceptance plan relates to a particular situation, then each OC curve will usually be uniquely designed, offering different choices between sample size and the acceptable number of defects – see Exhibit 11.17.

Now let's go back and look at Exhibit 11.16 in more detail. Here the OC curve must meet the following conditions:

Acceptable quality level (AQL)	2%
Lot tolerance percentage defective (LTPD)	15%
Producer's risk	5%
Consumer's risk	10%

Let us remind ourselves of what these factors mean:

- AQL is the desired quality level at which the probability of acceptance would be high.

- LTPD is the rejection quality level at which the probability of acceptance would be low.

- Producer's and consumer's risk are the probabilities of good order quantities (at AQL) being rejected or substandard order quantities (at LTPD) being accepted.

A curve that passes through the two specified points AQL and LTPD can be found by trial and error or by using tables.[13] This example shows the power of the plan to discriminate between acceptable and non-acceptable deliveries and also the extent of the risk of accepting bad deliveries and rejecting good ones. The question now is, 'How can managers modify acceptance plans in order to minimize this risk?' The most obvious way is to increase the sample size. Exhibit 11.17 shows the effect of this and the larger discriminatory power of the sample size, as shown by comparing sample plans 1 and 2 against two deliveries, delivery A with 1 per cent actual defects and delivery B with 5 per cent actual defects. It can be

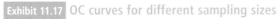

Exhibit 11.17 OC curves for different sampling sizes

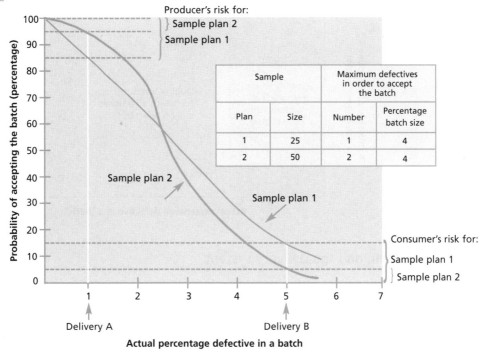

seen clearly from the figure that sample plan 2 reduces both the consumer's risk and producer's risk. As it is consumers who are most concerned about the degree of acceptable risk inherent in the application of sampling plans to incoming inspection, it is they who not only set the AQL but also the steepness of the OC curve. As illustrated in Exhibit 11.17, this is related to the sample size, for although the maximum percentage allowable for acceptance was the same, at 4 per cent of the sample, the increase in sample size resulted in a steeper curve. Exhibit 11.17 also illustrates the probabilities of accepting a delivery if sample plan 1 or 2 were adopted. Where the actual percentage defective in a batch was only 1 per cent (as in delivery A), the probability of accepting the batch increases; where the actual percentage defective in a batch was 5 per cent (as in delivery B), then the probability of accepting this batch decreases.

An OC curve, therefore, is a graph showing what any particular sampling plan will be expected to do in terms of accepting or rejecting deliveries. Although any sampling plan can be used without understanding its operating characteristics, it makes sense that the quality assurance function of any organization should be able to compare one sampling plan with another to help establish appropriate quality controls. As the selected AQL is the dividing line between good and bad deliveries, the ideal system would be one in which all order quantities whose quality was better than the AQL were accepted, and all whose quality was worse, rejected. This, of course, is only possible with 100 per cent inspection (see Exhibit 11.18). Sampling, being the alternative to this method, will not provide this level of discrimination and means that the vertical line shown in Exhibit 11.18 will have to run at a slope, as shown in Exhibits 11.16 and 11.17. Which OC curve to choose balances risk and cost. The closer the OC curve fits the slope of the curve in Exhibit 11.18, the lower the risk but the nearer to 100 per cent inspection and the costs associated with this form of checking.

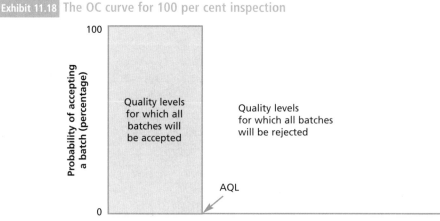

Exhibit 11.18 The OC curve for 100 per cent inspection

Processing and the delivery system

The way a process or person performs is independent of the service or product. To manage and control quality, therefore, it is necessary to know what the process will do, is likely to do or, better still, what it is doing. Furthermore, delivery systems and manufacturing processes do not provide or make identical but merely similar services or products. Variability is inherent in a process or delivery system and the need to appreciate this is an important first step in managing process quality.

In process control, information is received on what is happening in a process or delivery system and so distinguishes between those quality changes resulting from the natural variations of the system itself (referred to as 'assignable causes') and those resulting from some new, persistent influences on the process (referred to as 'random causes'). This distinction is fundamental to controlling process quality and allows corrective action to be taken only where it is required. To do this effectively, it is necessary to:

● use the knowledge of what has been happening in the process
● differentiate between assignable and random changes in the level of quality being attained
● determine the causes of any random changes and rectify them.

Case example 11.10 provides one illustration of the insights gained by knowing more about the system or process.

Case example 10 **CUSTOMER SATISFACTION AT THE ROYAL BANK OF SCOTLAND**

As the financial services sector becomes more competitive, companies are analysing what they need to do to maintain and grow share in a market characterized by overcapacity. Take the Royal Bank of Scotland (RBS) which made a surprising discovery when it decided to measure how much customer satisfaction dictated future buying intentions. It divided its customers into three categories:

● those with a problem that was not resolved
● those with a problem that had been efficiently dealt with
● those whose experience with the bank had been problem-free.

Predictably, those still dissatisfied were the ones least likely to buy any more of the bank's services. But, the surprise was that those customers with settled grievances were the most likely to buy RBS products in the future. In approximate terms the percentage of customers who will purchase from the same supplier shows 40 per cent for the dissatisfied group, 60 per cent for the problem-free group and 80 per cent for the settled grievances group.

This picture is broadly consistent across most similar studies: keeping customers happy is not simply a wise move to help retain existing business but a way of increasing future revenues from the same sources. **www.rbs.co.uk**

Case questions 1 Why do you think the 40:60:80 ratio described in the case consistently reflects customer attitudes re future purchases?

2 How should companies manage this aspect of service quality to best reflect customers' responses to getting things right?

Control charts

While acceptance sampling of a completed order quantity is an important part of managing quality, other forms of control are necessary to help prevent worsening levels of quality conformance going undetected until after the services or products have been completed.

To measure what is going on requires checks to be made at points in a delivery system or process. Where and how to complete these checks can vary as follows:

- **Where** – at predetermined points in a delivery system or process or 'patrol' checks involving routine or random visits to several stages in a system.

- **By whom** – undertaken by independent quality control staff or by those responsible for providing the service or making the product being monitored.

Except where 100 per cent checking of products is built into a manufacturing process, decisions on the 'where' and 'by whom' checks will need to be taken. The dimensions affecting where to check were covered earlier. The recognition that controlling quality works best where the person responsible for providing a service or making a product is also responsible for meeting the specification needs to be reflected in these decisions. In this way, managing quality is based on the principle that the person responsible for a process also has to measure the process, monitor quality movements and rectify the delivery system or process as needed.

One effective way to measure quality is using control charts that record outputs from the process while it is taking place. For the most part they can be used to control both variables and attributes of repetitive processes.

- Control charts for variables – typically, the delivery system or process mean or average is established and acceptable levels of deviation agreed. These have two sets of limits: warning (or upper and lower control) limits which form the band of usual variation, and action limits which form the band of unusual variation – see Exhibit 11.19.

- Control charts for attributes – as attribute measures of quality are obtained by an acceptable or unacceptable classification, an exact measure of the delivery system or process is not taken. Consequently, to control attributes through the use of control charts, sampling is used, as shown in Exhibit 11.20. The control chart measures the number of defectives in a sample that, when plotted, show any variation in the process (the warning and action limits) for which corrective action needs to be taken.

- Cumulative sum charts – a control chart is a clear way of presenting data. However, it is based on checking specific observations independently from one another. Cumulative

Exhibit 11.19 Control chart for variables

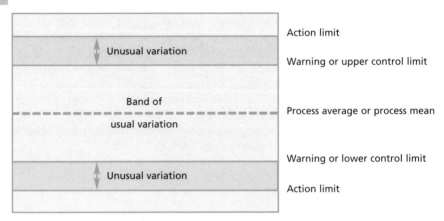

sum (cu sum) charts, on the other hand, take into account past data and, by incorporating these into the chart, allow trends to be more clearly shown than in control charts.

A cu sum chart is devised by establishing a reference value for the process that is usually the process mean. An actual reading is made and is subtracted from the reference value. This result is then plotted. The next reading is similarly calculated but is added to the previous result and then plotted. In this way, slight changes in a delivery system or process can be detected, for if the mean value increases, there will be a rise in the cu sum level. Similarly, a downward slope will mean a decrease in cu sum, while a horizontal graph will show stability in the data and, therefore, the process.

Exhibit 11.20 Control chart for attributes

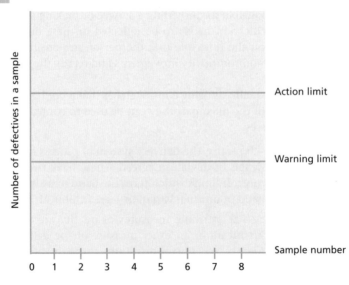

Statistical process control

The increasing competitive pressure to provide higher quality services or produce higher quality products has brought about changes in attitudes and expectations. Coupled with these changes has been a greater use of statistically based tools to create data as the basis for analysing problems and identifying causes. The use of statistical process control (SPC), incorporated within the responsibilities of those completing the task, is increasingly being employed to help achieve these necessary and significant improvements. Only through monitoring the process or delivery system on a continuous basis (for example using charts similar to Exhibits 11.19, 11.20 and 11.21) can quality levels be systematically improved by checking the outputs from a process or system and making any necessary adjustments on an ongoing basis.

Exhibit 11.21 Control charts in a call centre

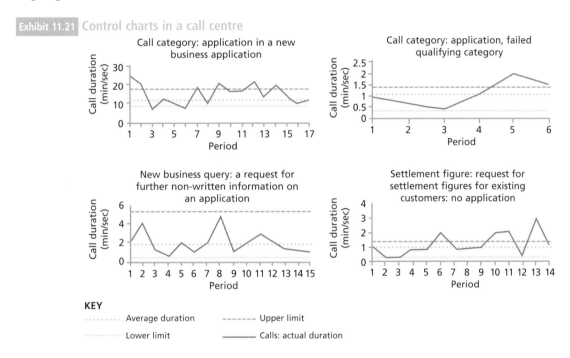

KEY

.... Average duration   ------- Upper limit

_____ Lower limit   ━━━━ Calls: actual duration

It is important to recognize that the purpose is not to achieve a position where all sample points are within limits and close to the average. If this prevails, it is usually a sign that the proactive use of this approach has not been recognized. The Shewhart rule for a process in control is to have two-thirds of the points within the limits and one-third of the points outside the limits.[12] The purpose of SPC includes the need to change the control chart limits in such a way as to achieve the Shewhart result. The next step is to improve the delivery system or process, thereby bringing all the points within the new limits, and then begin the cycle again, with the overriding aim of continuously reducing variability by systematically improving process capability. Remember, the purpose is to reduce variability and thereby improve quality.

Building the responsibility for quality conformance back into the job of the person responsible for providing the service or making the product and supporting these responsibilities with appropriate training and top management's active and continued support are essential to achieving and maintaining quality improvements. As emphasized earlier, quality is not free but the return on investment is most attractive!

Outputs

The final stage concerns the control of quality at the end of a system or process, including delivery and installation where appropriate. In make-to-stock situations, inspecting finished items will usually form an integral part of the system. For products of high value there will usually be a 100 per cent inspection of certain functional aspects of an item. As with ongoing inspection, the first step will be to prepare a specification based on appropriate variables and attributes and then detail the inspection procedures to be followed. With less expensive items, a sampling plan is more appropriate and would be based on the same factors as those discussed earlier under purchased services and items.

In make-to-order organizations, decisions similar to those described in the last paragraph will prevail. In addition, with high-value items or in the case of large organizations, including governments, strict procedures concerning quality checks will form part of a contract and will be undertaken by the customer. From the viewpoint of customers, you are now a supplier and the tools and procedures discussed in the section under 'Supply chain' will form part of their approach.

Six-sigma quality

The drive to improve existing levels of quality conformance has been encapsulated in the mandate of six-sigma quality. In the late 1980s Motorola's Semiconductor Products Division laid down for itself the six-sigma challenge: that is, 3.4 defects per million transactions or virtually error-free output. It set the goal of achieving ±six-sigma capability in all phases of the business including product design, manufacturing, sales and services. Most companies currently fall well short of that. Typical processes generate about 35,000 defects per million, which sounds (and is) a lot but is consistent with the defect levels of most successful companies – in statistical terms this constitutes three and a half sigma (see Exhibit 11.22). Other companies are also recognizing the competitive advantages of setting quality conformance goals that will change the rules of the game. They include 3M that makes a wide range of products from dental fillings to Scotchguard tape, Sun Microsystems, a manufacturer of servers and software, Carlson Companies whose businesses include the Radisson hotel chain and Home Depot, the US retailer.

Exhibit 11.22 Specification limit and corresponding percentage good quality and # defects per million

Specification limit	# defects per million	Percentage good quality
±one sigma	691,000	31.00
±two sigma	308,700	69.13
±three sigma	66,810	93.32
±three and a half sigma	35,900	96.41
±four sigma	6,210	99.37
±five sigma	233	99.98
±six sigma	3.4	99.99

Issues concerning continuous improvement are covered in Chapter 16 which also includes a section on benchmarking – the approach of setting best-in-class corporate goals – and the idea of changing the rules of the game.

Take a look now at Case examples 11.11 and 11.12 that provide illustrations of organizations' use of a six-sigma approach.

Case example 11 GENERAL ELECTRIC'S SIX-SIGMA QUALITY GOAL

General Electric set itself a corporate 'goal of becoming a six-sigma quality company, which means one that produces virtually defect-free products, services and transactions'. Three- to four-sigma quality is typically 10–15 per cent of revenues. In GE's case, with over $80 billion in revenues, that amounts to some $8–12 billion annually, mostly in scrap, reworking of parts and rectifying mistakes in transactions. So the financial rationale for embarking on this quality journey is clear.

But beyond the pure financials, there are even more important rewards that will come with dramatically improved quality. Among them is the unlimited growth from selling services and products universally recognized by customers as being on a completely different plane of quality from those of competitors. It recognized that six sigma would be an exciting journey and the most difficult and invigorating stretch goal that GE had ever undertaken. The magnitude of the challenge of going from 35,000 defects per million to fewer than 4 defects was huge. It would require the company to reduce defect rates 10,000-fold – about 84 per cent for five consecutive years. But GE wanted to make its quality so special, so valuable to its customers, so important to their success that GE's services and products become their only real value choice.

www.ge.com

Case questions
1 What will be the key tasks for GE to reach its goal?
2 How will this change the competitive factors in its markets and what strategic advantages will result?

Case example 12 AIRLINE INDUSTRY'S SAFETY RECORD

While the year 2001 will be remembered by the September 11 hijacking, it is ironic that in this year there were fewer fatal airline accidents than at any time in the last 50–60 years – 18 crashes against the previous best of 20 in 1998. The number of fatal crashes since the late 1940s high of 50 has decreased year on year (see below), with an annual average in the 1990s of 24.3. But the size of the aircraft has grown, increasing the likelihood that more people die in a single crash.

But flying is safe – in fact it is now put at 100 times safer than it was 60 years ago, with the risk of dying in a jet crash put at 1 in 3 million. In 1998, for example, 1008 people died in air crashes out of a total of 1.3 billion passengers carried on the 18 million flights completed by the world's airlines.

A study in the 1990s found flying to be 22 times safer than travelling by car. In the US, for example, some 21,000 people died on the roads in a typical six-month period, roughly the same as for all commercial jet fatalities worldwide since the start of the jet age. Even so, there are many who have a fear of flying and with the intangible terrorist factor on top, the airline industry is struggling to overcome this aspect of its image with the public at large.

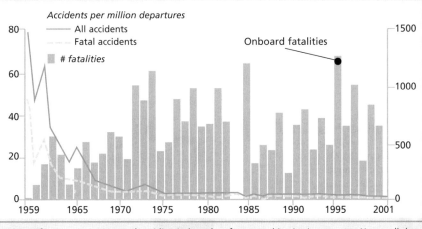

Case questions
1 Assess the airline industry's safety record in six-sigma terms. How well does it perform?
2 For which category of passenger would an airline's safety record be a qualifier and for which category an order-winner?
3 Why are people afraid of flying and yet travel all the time by car?
4 Many travellers are choosing European rather than US airlines for transatlantic travel. Why?

Formalizing the search for quality

To meet the increasing importance of consistent quality conformance in today's markets, companies have highlighted the dimension of quality management within their own organizations. As quality conformance levels in one organization are affected by the ability of its suppliers to meet the specification of the services and products they deliver, knowing how well suppliers are able to conform consistently to these standards is a key element of managing quality.

To this end, many large organizations (for example international companies and governments) have, for a long time, set up their own system of approving suppliers. These approval procedures assess potential suppliers as a whole and their operations function's ability to meet the volume and specification requirements in particular. The growing awareness of the need to improve quality has led directly to the introduction and use of national and international programmes that formalize systems for evaluating the capability of any organization consistently to design, provide and deliver services and products to specification. ISO 9000, the Malcolm Baldrige National Quality Award and the European Quality Award are three widely used programmes to help formalize the search for quality, which are now reviewed.

ISO 9000

Established in 1947, the International Organization for Standardization (ISO) is a non-government body to which over 100 countries subscribe. Its role is to secure international agreements on key topics and publish these as international standards.

The ISO 9000 series is a set of worldwide standards that detail the requirements for an organization's quality management systems. The series, adopted in 1987, defines internationally accepted standards for business quality. They provide a framework that governs the activities and procedures for managing quality that customers expect of a supplier to demonstrate the effective control of its processes. Most countries have their own equivalent, if not identical, standards,[14] but accept ISO 9000 as the internationally recognized and accepted certification. As of 2003 there were in excess of 400,000 certifications awarded to firms in 158 countries.

ISO 9000 comprises five documents that list a whole range of standards that have to be met to gain certification.[15] Third-party assessment of a company's quality standards is

Exhibit 11.23 ISO 9000 certification – what it isn't!

© AMD Publishing

undertaken and, following registration, is audited regularly. ISO 9000 certification thus assures customers that a company has designed processes and is managing them to assure delivery of services and products to specification. But, as the cartoon in Exhibit 11.23 is intended to highlight, certification is not a cosmetic exercise.

An overview of the ISO 9000 series of standards is now provided:

- **ISO 9000** 'Guide to selection and use' details how to use the other standards in the series and is essential to the correct interpretation and application of them. It also has three subset documents (ISO 9000–2, 9000–3 and 9000–4) that give, among other things, guidelines to the use of ISO 9001, 9002 and 9003.

- **ISO 9001** specifies design/development, operations, installation and servicing. It has 20 clauses covering the following:

management responsibilities	inspection, measuring and test equipment
quality system	inspection and test status
contract review	control of non-conforming product
design control	corrective action
document control	handling, storage, packaging and delivery
purchasing	quality records
purchaser supplied material	internal quality audit
product identification and traceability	training
process control	after-sales servicing
inspection and testing	statistical techniques

- **ISO 9002** covers circumstances where an organization is responsible for assuring the service or product quality during the course of provision or installation only. This part has 18 of the 20 clauses above excluding 'design control' and 'after-sales servicing'.

- **ISO 9003** contains specifications for final inspection and test. It is used when conformance to specified requirements can be assured solely at final inspection and test and contains 12 elements of those listed above under ISO 9001.

- **ISO 9004**, as ISO 9000, is a guide to good quality management practice. It gives more detail than ISO 9001, 9002 and 9003, contains references to a number of quality aspects (for example quality risks, costs and product service liability) that are not covered to the same level as in ISO 9001, 9002 and 9003 and places considerable emphasis on the satisfaction of customer needs and requirements. As with ISO 9000, it has three subset documents (ISO 9004–2, 9004–3 and 9004–4) that give guidance and comprehensive overviews for establishing and implementing a quality system for services, the application of quality management for processed materials and for implementing continuous quality management within an organization respectively.

Malcolm Baldrige National Quality Award

The Malcolm Baldrige National Quality Award was a response by the USA to the competitive challenges facing businesses in the early 1980s. A US government mandate for a national study on productivity led, in part, to a recommendation by the National Advisory Council for Quality and the American Productivity and Quality Center that the US government should sponsor a national quality award. This was established in 1987 and renamed after Malcolm Baldrige (the secretary of commerce at the time who was a strong advocate of this step) following his accidental death in July of that year.

The Baldrige Award, as it is now referred to, seeks to recognize and encourage quality and productivity improvements by:

- stimulating companies to attain excellence in quality
- recognizing outstanding companies and helping disseminate experience and best practice regarding quality and its impact on corporate performance
- establishing guidelines for organizations on the assessment and management of quality
- gathering information on how to manage for superior quality by changing corporate cultures and practices.

Exhibit 11.24 Baldrige Award – 2004 criteria for performance excellence

Categories and items	Points	Value
1 LEADERSHIP		
● organizational leadership	70	
● social responsibility	50	120
2 STRATEGIC PLANNING		
● strategy development	40	
● strategy deployment	45	85
3 CUSTOMER AND MARKET FOCUS		
● customer and market knowledge	40	
● customer relationships and satisfaction	45	85
4 MEASUREMENT, ANALYSIS AND KNOWLEDGE MANAGEMENT		
● measurement and analysis of organizational performance	45	
● information and knowledge management	45	90
5 HUMAN RESOURCE FOCUS		
● work systems	35	
● employee learning and motivation	25	
● employee well-being and satisfaction	25	85
6 PROCESS MANAGEMENT		
● value creation processes	50	
● support processes	35	85
7 BUSINESS RESULTS		
● customer-focused results	75	
● product and service results	75	
● financial and market results	75	
● human resource results	75	
● organizational effectiveness results	75	
● governance and social responsibility results	75	450
TOTAL POINTS		1000

Source www.baldrige.nist.gov.

The award is administered annually by the National Institute of Standards and Technology, and the process involves an independent review by outsiders, on-site visits and judges' reviews. The award examination defines seven categories against which an applicant's performance is evaluated. Exhibit 11.24 lists the categories, items and assigned weights for 2004 and shows the emphasis placed on business results which account for 450 of the 1000 total points awarded. The scoring system reflects three different aspects:

- Approach – appropriateness of methods
  – effectiveness of methods
  – evidence of innovation
- Deployment – use of the approach by all work units
- Results – current performance
  – demonstration of sustained performance.

The three applicant groups are service, manufacturing and small business (less than 500 staff) and up to two winners in each group can be nominated each year. Past winners include Motorola, Xerox, Federal Express, Ritz-Carlton Hotels, AT&T, Cadillac and Texas Instruments.

European Quality Award (EQA)

In 1988, 14 leading West European companies formed the European Foundation for Quality Management (EFQM) and by the year 2000 it had over 850 members. One of EFQM's core objectives is to recognize quality achievement and to this end it launched the European Quality Award (EQA) in 1992. Each year participating companies initially apply for their own national award and the top firms from each country go into the EQA competition. The scoring system reflects the 'approach', 'development' and 'results' aspects as outlined under the section on the Baldrige Award. The EQA also has categories and a total of 1000 points are awarded, with weight reflecting the levels of importance and emphasis, as shown in Exhibit 11.25.

Exhibit 11.25 European Quality Award: categories and weights (2004)

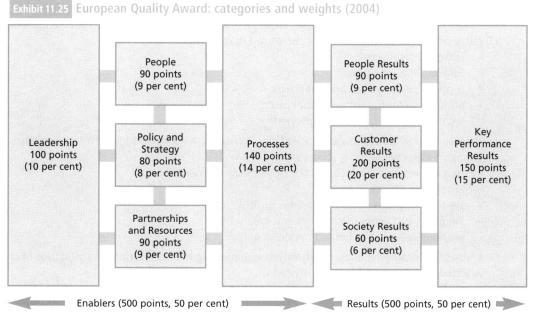

Source www.efqm.org/model_awards/eqa/intro.asp.

The nine elements shown in Exhibit 11.25 are defined by the EFQM as follows:

- Leadership: how the behaviour and actions of the executive team and all other leaders inspire, support and promote a culture of total quality management (TQM). Evidence is needed of how leaders:
  - visibly demonstrate their commitment to a culture of TQM
  - support improvement and involvement by providing appropriate resources and assistance
  - are involved with customers, suppliers and other external organizations
  - recognize and appreciate people's efforts and achievements.
- Policy and strategy: how an organization formulates, deploys, reviews its policy and strategy and turns them into plans and actions. Evidence is needed of how policy and strategy are:
  - based on information that is relevant and comprehensive
  - developed
  - communicated and implemented
  - regularly updated and improved.
- People: how an organization realizes the full potential of its people. Evidence is needed of how people:
  - resources are planned and improved
  - capabilities are sustained and developed
  - agree targets and continuously review performance
  - are involved, empowered and recognized
  - and the organization have an effective dialogue
  - are cared for.
- Partnerships and resources: how an organization manages resources effectively and efficiently. Evidence is needed of the sound management of:
  - financial resources
  - information resources
  - supplier relationships and materials
  - buildings, equipment and other assets
  - technology and intellectual property.
- Processes: how an organization identifies, manages, reviews and improves its processes. Evidence is needed of how processes:
  - that are key to the success of the business are identified
  - are systematically managed
  - are reviewed and targets are set for improvement
  - are improved using innovation and creativity
  - are changed and the benefits evaluated.
- Customer results: what an organization is achieving in relation to the satisfaction of its external customers. Evidence is needed of:
  - customers' perceptions of the organization's services, products and customer relationships
  - additional measures relating to the satisfaction of the organization's customers.
- People results: what an organization is achieving in relation to the satisfaction of its people. Evidence is needed of:
  - the people's perception of the organization
  - additional measures relating to people satisfaction.

- Society results: what an organization is achieving in satisfying the needs and expectations of the local, national and international community at large (as appropriate). This includes the perception of the organization's approach to quality of life, the environment and the preservation of global resources, and the organization's own internal measures of effectiveness. It will include its relations with authorities and bodies that affect and regulate its business. Evidence is needed of:
  - society's perception of the organization
  - additional measures of the organization's impact on society.

- Key performance results: what an organization is achieving in relation to its planned business objectives and in satisfying the needs and expectations of everyone with a financial interest or stake in the organization. Evidence is needed of:
  - financial measures of the organization's performance
  - additional measures of the organization's performance.

Total quality management (TQM)

The evolution of quality management stimulated, at least in part, by the impact of the demand by customers for higher quality conformance levels and the increasing competitiveness in world markets has resulted in the need to address quality management in all aspects of a business, including customers and suppliers. This development is known as total quality management (TQM).

TQM requires that the principles of quality management are applied in all aspects of and at every level in an organization. It is a company-wide approach to quality management with improvements being undertaken on a continuous basis by everyone. It thereby embraces the collection of management theories, approaches, tools and practices that help an organization to reap greater profits by increasing service and product quality and decreasing costs. It requires a broadening of outlooks and skills, an innovative approach to improvement, a more sophisticated application of quality management tools and approaches and an increased emphasis on people and their involvement. The process extends to suppliers and customers and the activities will include a marked orientation towards customers and their needs.

You will see by these statements that TQM is a philosophy and set of guiding principles for managing an organization, and, as such, embodies several key elements that are now summarized:

- Commitment and leadership from the top: as with many approaches, the belief and commitment by those at the top of an organization coupled with the leadership to make these changes happen are critical to the success of a TQM initiative. Without the allocation of resources and time, and a clear statement of the priority that needs to be given to this initiative, TQM will not succeed.

- Planning and executing the programme: TQM represents a major shift in approach, and changes of this nature and magnitude need to be well planned and their execution carefully managed. Features include:
  - integrated into the rest of a business
  - part of the long-term execution of strategy within an organization
  - linking functions and ensuring that cooperation is improved
  - quality dimensions are built into service and product design as well as delivery systems and processes

- move to a proactive approach to quality management in all aspects of a business
- quality dimensions need to be part of the way performance is measured.

● **Using tools and approaches:** to support and develop a process of continuous quality improvement, an organization will need to use a selection of quality management tools and approaches. Their use is designed to identify problems, facilitate improvements, implement solutions and sustain the new ways of working.

● **Education and training:** to achieve the last requirement, organizations need to provide the necessary levels of education and training for all concerned. These need to cover a general awareness of quality management concepts, skills and attitudes that address the philosophy of continuous improvement and the changes in personal, functional and organizational behaviour involved. A formal programme of education and training needs to be arranged on a timely and regular basis to help people improve their approach and contribution to improvement initiatives. Such programmes introduce new approaches to resolving problems and new attitudes to change. They need to be recognized as an investment in people that increases their ability and helps them fulfil their overall role, together with an associated range of short- and longer term benefits in terms of greater efficiency, higher levels of market support and sales revenue growth.

● **Involvement and teamwork:** one key to the successful introduction and maintenance of TQM within an organization is the involvement of people and increased cooperation through greater teamwork. Managers need to release the capabilities and skills of those working in their areas and also empower people to seek and make improvements in their own areas of responsibility. People have to be encouraged to undertake initiatives, especially given the managerial approaches that typified organizations in the past. Involvement is also further enhanced by teamwork, because without it, it is difficult to gain the commitment and participation of people throughout an organization.

● **Measurement and feedback:** there is a need to provide positive feedback and recognize and reward achievement. People must not only see the results of their actions and endeavours but also see that their improvements really count and their contributions are recognized by the organization. This requires regular feedback and constant support. For TQM to be successful, the results of improvements need to be proactively and extensively communicated to all involved.

   Part of this communication needs to include results against key internal and external targets, including internal and external benchmarking. This enables true measures to be made and will, in turn, identify gaps and help develop new improvement programmes.

● **Culture changes:** for many organizations, TQM is a marked style change from past approaches. Underpinning the success of these initiatives, therefore, is a need to change attitudes, behaviour and working practices throughout an organization. Key areas include:
- responsibility for one's own quality
- improvement as being an integral part of everyone's job
- the whole organization and those working in it need to be focused towards meeting the needs of customers
- suppliers and customers need to be part of the improvement process
- mistakes should not be seen as reasons for criticism, but as opportunities to correct processes thereby eliminating error situations in the future.

How 3M are approaching the drive to achieve six-sigma quality is outlined in Case example 11.13.

Case example 13 COMMITTING TO QUALITY IMPROVEMENT

It is difficult to argue against the idea that companies should strive to improve quality. While the approaches come in different flavours, the essential ingredients show more similarities than differences and at the core are the relentless improvements in business processes. This constitutes a sizeable commitment. For example, when Jim McNerney left GE to take the top job at 3M in 2001, one of his first moves was to launch a corporate-wide six-sigma quality initiative. Early on 3M selected 500 up-and-coming managers to work on quality programmes full time for two years. It also provided a week's training on six sigma for each of its 28,000 salaried staff.

But companies need to recognize that this is a long haul and need to address all aspects and levels of an organization. As Joseph Juran pointed out, it took Japanese companies more than 30 years to transform their collective reputation

for poor product quality, and that in his experience a company would take at least six years to achieve a position of quality leadership within its sector and with ten years more the norm. And, Jim McNerney agrees. For him it is about addressing the DNA of the company that constitutes a 10–15-year commitment.

One outcome of these reflections therefore implies that a quality initiative will outlive the executive teams that introduce it. For this reason, companies should avoid top management-led programmes that aim to change the whole company at once. 'It is a fallacy of programmatic change,' reflects Harvard professor Mike Beer, 'you don't change a large company all at once. You have to go unit by unit and get real buy-in from the organization.'

www.3m.com

Case questions
1 How do these examples fit the reflections on introducing TQM?
2 Analyse Jim McNerney's approach at 3M in the context of your answer to question 1 and comment.

Reflections

The evolution of quality management has, to some extent, come full circle. In pre-Industrial Revolution times, skilled craftsmen were responsible for both undertaking tasks and ensuring that they were completed to specification. The Industrial Revolution saw the advent of high volume requirements and with it the separation of the making or providing task from the responsibility for quality – ensuring that specifications were met. One outcome was that inspection was performed by non-producers and completed after the work was finished. However, since the 1970s systems for monitoring and managing quality have evolved rapidly, as illustrated by Exhibit 11.26. Since this time simple inspection activities were first replaced or supplemented by quality control, then enhanced by quality assurance developments, with many organizations now working towards TQM that returns the responsibility for quality conformance to those who have the task of providing the service or product. While TQM embraces other key dimensions such as involvement with suppliers and customers, the progression described in Exhibit 11.26 concerns core responsibilities and attitudes towards the key competitive dimension of meeting service or product specifications. In this way, TQM signals the need for the mutual cooperation of everyone in an organization and associated business processes such as suppliers to meet customers' needs and expectations.

What drives these developments is more than the efficient management of a company's business processes. It is also the requirements of today's markets and the expectation of today's customers. Companies who early on proactively improved quality also succeeded in gaining market advantage by changing the role of quality conformance from a qualifier to an order-winner. This was notably so with emerging Japanese companies in several manu-

Exhibit 11.26 The evolution in managing quality

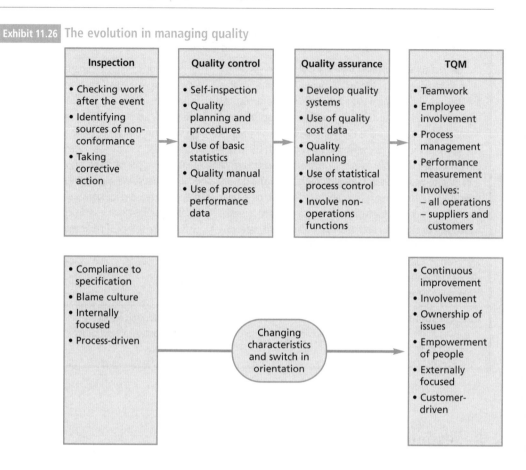

facturing sectors from automobiles through to televisions and office equipment. Disadvantaged by these significantly higher quality conformance levels, European and US companies were forced to address the quality gap to prevent further loss of market share and as a matter of commercial necessity. The result is that by the turn of the last century, quality's competitive role had reverted to that of a qualifier but involving much more exacting standards of conformance. The role of quality conformance within the set of competitive dimensions that relate to the markets of most organizations is now clearly recognized. And the response of operations to the provision of this key requirement has appropriately raised the profile of and changed attitudes to the key task of managing quality throughout organizations.

But the need for quality improvement to be applied at all levels and address all aspects of organizations has become an increasingly high-profile requirement.[16] After the scandals at WorldCom, Enron, Tyco, Parmalat and the rest, the need to apply the same level of rigour to corporate governance as is now the expectation in operations has become sharply apparent. To reflect such changing needs, the Malcolm Baldrige Award criteria for 2004 now specifically include 'Governance and social responsibility results' (see Exhibit 11.24). In theory there is no reason (while there is much sense) why quality approaches should not be applied to corporate boards in terms of independent directors, governance, accounting compliance or executive compensation. Those companies that take this next step may well be the ones that prosper and succeed in today's competitive environment or at least the ones that do not fall into disrepute and destruction.[17]

Key Elements of Managing Quality

- The quality of its services and products is fundamental to the success of organizations. Operations is responsible for quality conformance and how best to manage this aspect of quality was addressed in this chapter.

- The specification on offer reconciles customers' needs and expectations with that which a company sells and provides. The interrelated nature of these dimensions constitutes the quality offering as depicted in Exhibit 11.1.

- How to undertake these tasks in terms of defining the quality characteristics and their measurement and control, where to check, how to check and the need to identify causes of below-standard quality levels and seek improvements was explained in detail.

- As part of providing the background of and context for the topic of managing quality, a number of quality principles were introduced and explained. These were:
  - meet customer requirements – the core of quality conformance
  - error-free work – only one standard to aim for – to be right first time, every time
  - manage by prevention – adopting a proactive approach to managing quality leads to prevention rather than the detection of faulty work
  - measure by the cost of quality – the key measure is the cost of doing business – doing things right the first time reduces costs in the task of meeting customers' needs and expectations.

- A review of the principal quality philosophies and approaches was the topic of the next section and a detailed summary of the work of Deming, Juran and Crosby and their contributions to this field was provided.

- Next came a section covering general issues and the specific tools and techniques used including the Pareto principle or the 80/20 rule, the use of checklists, cause and effect diagrams, process mapping, scatter diagrams, sampling and acceptance sampling plans.

- With the background issues in place and an introduction about where and what to do, the task of managing quality in practice was addressed. This began by looking at the purchasing function and the appropriate checks and approaches to be used to control the quality of purchased items and services. This section introduced the aspect of OC curves and their use with different sample sizes.

- Then followed a look at how to measure quality in the processing and service delivery system stages of operations. Control charts were introduced and their use with regard to variables and attributes was explained.

- The concept of statistical process control was then addressed and an example of its use in a call centre formed part of the review.

- The final part in this section concerned the control of quality at the end of a process, including delivery and installation where appropriate. Here, the nature of the items would influence how quality was controlled, for example whereas high-value items may attract 100 per cent checks, inspecting less expensive items would more typically be completed by a sampling plan.

- The growing awareness of the need to improve quality has led to the introduction and use of national and international programmes that formalize systems for evaluating the capability of an organization to consistently design, provide and deliver services and products to specification. The three most widely used programmes (ISO 9000, the Malcolm Baldrige National Quality Award and the European Quality Award) were explained in detail.

- To conclude the chapter, the evolution that has taken place in managing quality and the change in orientation that parallels these developments is summarized.

Self-check

1 From an operations perspective, quality concerns:
   a Determining customers' needs and embodying these in the design specifications of services and products ☐
   b Consistently meeting service and product design specifications ☐
   c Both a and b ☐

2 The first step in the quality conformance procedure is to:
   a Identify causes of below-standard quality ☐
   b Define the quality characteristics ☐
   c Measure and control the quality characteristics ☐

3 Which of the following is **not** a consideration when setting quality levels:
   a Where in the operations process to check conformance to the quality standards ☐
   b Which variables to check ☐
   c How to undertake the check(s) ☐

4 Measure by the cost of quality means:
   a Managing the cost of checking quality characteristics ☐
   b Reducing the cost of doing business by eliminating errors ☐
   c Managing the cost of implementing quality systems and procedures ☐

5 Deming's quality philosophy focuses on:
   a The cost of quality and used data to shock management into action ☐
   b Making an impact in a few months and, in that way, stir management into action ☐
   c Quality as a management responsibility that required fundamental change and a long-term time frame ☐

6 A point central to the views of all the main contributors on improving quality is:
   a The key to good quality lies in good management ☐
   b The concept of the quality vaccine ☐
   c Slogans, posters and exhortations ☐

7 In general, quality tools and techniques can be categorized as
   a Design tools ☐
   b Process tools ☐
   c Either a or b ☐

8 Which of the following is **not** an example of a quality tool or technique:
   a Network analysis ☐
   b Cause and effect diagrams ☐
   c Process mapping ☐

9 Which of the following is **not** an example of a quality award:
   a Six sigma ☐
   b ISO 9000 ☐
   c Malcolm Baldrige ☐

10 Implementing total quality management (TQM) in a business requires the following culture change:
   a Improvement is the responsibility of the quality department ☐
   b Mistakes should be criticized and corrected ☐
   c Suppliers and customers need to be part of the improvement process ☐

Study activities

Discussion questions

1 The table below lists data concerning the errors in an account management function in the financial services sector.

Error type	Frequency in last period	Estimated costs involved (£s)
A	40	12,500
B	4	2,800
C	33	36,000
D	56	15,500
E	22	7,500
F	12	5,750
G	16	23,000
H	28	116,000

Prepare two Pareto lists – the first based on frequency and the second on estimated costs.

Comment on these rankings.

2 Discuss the advantages and disadvantages of staff recording their own performance data in the form of a control chart and analysing the outcomes for the delivery system for which they are responsible.

3 Explain what is meant by acceptance sampling. Give an illustration for each of the sampling plans included in this chapter.

4 The evolution in how best to manage quality has been described as follows:

Product reliability → Process reliability → People reliability → Total quality management

Discuss.

5 What are the advantages and disadvantages of 100 per cent inspection?

Assignments

1 Draw a fishbone diagram to represent why your car might be two hours later than the promised completion time at an auto service centre.

2 To assess part of its service delivery system, a fast-food chain undertakes regular checks on certain elements of the system. One such check at an outlet revealed the control data below.

Draw a control chart for each of these four aspects. What are your comments on what you found?

Aspects	Product freshness (minutes)	Queue length (# customers)	Time to serve (# minutes)	Cleanliness Floor (# items)	Cleanliness # tables not cleaned
Upper control limit	7.0	8.0	3.0	10	6
Average	3.0	4.0	2.0	5	4
Lower control limit	1.0	2.0	0.5	0	0
Sample #					
1	6.5	3.0	1.5	8	3
2	4.5	7.0	3.0	6	5
3	5.0	6.0	3.0	2	1
4	3.5	2.0	1.5	4	5
5	2.0	8.0	1.5	3	4
6	6.0	5.0	2.0	7	6
7	3.0	6.0	3.5	9	3
8	2.5	10.0	1.5	12	8
9	6.0	4.0	1.0	2	1
10	6.5	3.0	2.5	4	0
11	5.5	2.0	2.5	6	2
12	1.5	9.0	3.5	8	4

Notes
- Product freshness – length of time (to the nearest half-minute) since any of the next to be used main item products were made. Any product made eight or more minutes before is discarded.
- Queue length – number of customers waiting: assessment above was made on all customer queue lengths in the service delivery system.
- Time to serve – worst and best times in a ten-minute period for a selected server to serve a customer (to the nearest half-minute).
- Cleanliness – floor: number of items (for example food, packaging and cutlery) on the floor; tables: number of free tables that have not been wiped down since the last customers left.

3 An operations manager records the daily output and number of rejects on a bag-making line that runs for a single eight-hour shift with occasional overtime on a Saturday. The data for the last 40 days are given below.

(a) What tools would you use to manage this process?
(b) What does the data analysis tell you?
(c) What management action should be taken?

Day #	Day	Output	Rejects	Day #	Day	Output	Rejects
		(# bags)				(# bags)	
1	Mon	2040	24	21	Wed	2440	36
2	Tue	2210	28	22	Thu	2290	30
3	Wed	2090	34	23	Fri	2180	26
4	Thu	2235	20	24	Sat	2260	31
5	Fri	2050	14	25	Mon	2095	37
6	Sat	2240	32	26	Tue	2080	19
7	Mon	2080	39	27	Wed	2290	22
8	Tue	2280	34	28	Thu	2260	38
9	Wed	2260	30	29	Fri	2125	41
10	Thu	2260	41	30	Sat	–	–
11	Fri	2150	38	31	Mon	2235	37
12	Sat	2290	18	32	Tue	2140	38
13	Mon	1970	29	33	Wed	1985	24
14	Tue	2285	41	34	Thu	2195	31
15	Wed	2265	26	35	Fri	2180	37
16	Thu	2160	32	36	Sat	–	–
17	Fri	2165	37	37	Mon	2165	41
18	Sat	2365	20	38	Tue	2265	37
19	Mon	2100	26	39	Wed	2280	44
20	Tue	2190	24	40	Thu	2165	39

4 Casual Elegance is a mail order business in clothes for the younger businessperson. From time to time customers complained about errors in their orders – wrong style, wrong size and so on. The company wishes to keep order errors to less than 2 per cent. To check how well the system was working, a sample of 50 orders was taken several times over a representative period. The results are shown opposite.

(a) What type of control chart is appropriate for checking the process capability of the ordering operation?
(b) Construct a control chart using these data. What observations can you make about the process?

# orders					
#	OK	problem	#	OK	problem
1	50	0	11	47	3
2	47	3	12	50	0
3	49	1	13	45	5
4	48	2	14	48	2
5	48	2	15	47	3
6	46	4	16	46	4
7	50	0	17	48	2
8	50	0	18	50	0
9	49	1	19	50	0
10	48	2	20	49	1

Exploring further

Bank, J *The Essence of Total Quality Management*, Prentice Hall, London (1992).

Bounds, G, Yorks, L, Adams, M and Ramsey, G *Beyond Quality Management: Towards the Emerging Paradigm*, McGraw-Hill, New York (1994).

Breem, M, Jud, R and Pareja, PE *An Introduction to ISO 9000*, Society of Manufacturing Engineers, Reference Publication Division, Dearborn, MI (1993).

Britz, G, Emerling, D, Hare, L, Hoerl, R and Shade, J 'How to teach others to apply statistical thinking', *Quality Progress* June (1997), pp. 67–79.

Brown, SA *Total Quality Service*, Prentice Hall, Scarborough, Canada (1992).

Chase, RB and Stewart, DM 'Make your service fail-safe', *Sloan Management Review* spring (1994), pp. 35–44.

Costin, H *Strategies for Quality Improvement*, 2nd edn, Dryden Press, Ft Worth, TX (1999).

Crosby, PB *Let's Talk Quality*, McGraw-Hill, New York (1989).

Dale, BG (ed.) *Managing Quality*, 2nd edn, Prentice Hall, Hemel Hempstead (1992).

Dean, JW Jr and Evans, JR *Total Quality: Management, Organization and Strategy*, West, Minneapolis/St Paul, MN (1994).

Dunkerley, D and Wong, WS (eds) *Global Perspectives on Quality in Higher Education*, Ashgate, Aldershot (2001).

Evans, JR and Lindsay, WM *The Management and Control of Quality*, 5th edn, South-Western/Cincinnati, OH (2002).

Foster, TA *Managing Quality*, Prentice Hall, Upper Saddle River, NJ (2001).

Garvin, D *Managing Quality*, Free Press, New York (1988).

Harvey, J 'Service quality: a tutorial', *Journal of Operations Management* **16**(5) (1998), pp. 583–97.

Heskett, JL, Jones, TO, Loveman, GW, Sasser, WE Jr and Schleringer, LA 'Putting the service–profit chain to work', *Harvard Business Review* March–April (1994), pp. 164–74.

Ho, SKM *Operations and Quality Management*, International Thomson Business Press, London (1999).

Huw, TO, Tavakoli, M and Malek, M (eds) *Quality in Health Care*, Ashgate, Aldershot (2001).

Imai, M *Kaizen: The Key to Japan's Competitive Success*, Random House, New York (1986).

Jones, TO and Sasser, WE Jr 'Why satisfied customers defect', *Harvard Business Review* November–December (1995), pp. 88–99.

Kehoe, DF *The Fundamentals of Quality Management*, Chapman & Hall, London (1996).

Lim, D *Quality Assurance in Higher Education: A Study of Developing Countries*, Ashgate, Aldershot (2001).

Logothetis, N *Managing for Total Quality*, Prentice Hall, London (1992).

Montgomery, DC *Introduction to Statistical Control*, 2nd edn, John Wiley & Sons, New York (1991).

Oakland, JS *Total Quality Management: Text and Cases*, 2nd edn, Butterworth-Heinemann, Oxford (2000).

Oakland, JS *Statistical Process Control*, 4th edn, Butterworth-Heinemann, Oxford (1999).

Pande, S, Neuman, RP and Cavanagh, RR *The Six-Sigma Way*, McGraw-Hill, New York (2000).

Paton, JM 'Service quality: Disney-style', *Quality Digest* January (1997), pp. 24–9.

Porter, LJ, Oakland, JS and Gadd, KW *Evaluating the Operation of the European Quality Award Model for Self-assessment*, CIMA Publishing, London (1998).

Prahalad, CK and Krishnan, MS 'The new meaning of quality in the information age' *Harvard Business Review* September–October (1999), pp. 109–18.

Ran, H '15 years and still going…', *Quality Progress* July (1995), pp. 57–9.

Reichfield, FF and Sasser, WE Jr 'Zero defections: quality comes to services', *Harvard Business Review* September–October (1990), pp. 105–11.

Reinartz, W and Kumar, V 'The mismanagement of customer loyalty', *Harvard Business Review* July (2002), pp. 4–12.

Seddon, J *In Pursuit of Quality: The Case Against ISO 9000*, Oak Tree Press, Dublin (1997).

Slater, R *Jack Welch and the GE Way*, McGraw-Hill, New York (1999).

Stahl, MJ *Management – Total Quality in a Global Environment*, Blackwell, Cambridge, MA (1995).

Teboul, J *Managing Quality Dynamics*, Prentice Hall, London (1991).

Zeithanil, VA, Paraswamann, A and Berry, LL *Delivering Quality Service: Balancing Customer Perceptions and Expectations*, Free Press, New York (1990).

Notes and references

1   These 14 points are explained fully in W Edwards Deming's book *Out of the Crisis*, Cambridge University Press, Cambridge (1986).

2   Ibid., Chapter 3, pp. 97–148.

3   W Edwards Deming, *Quality Productivity and Competitive Position*, Center for Advanced Engineering Study, Massachusetts Institute of Technology, Cambridge, MA (1982), p. i.

4   Also see the following articles written by Juran that provide an overview of his thinking, approach and concepts: 'Japanese and Western quality: a contrast', *Quality Assurance* **5**(1) (1979), pp. 12–17; 'Product quality – a prescription for the West: Part I: Training and improvement programmes', *Management Review* June (1981), pp. 9–14 and 'Part II: Upper management leadership and employee relations', *Management Review*, July (1981), pp. 57–61.

5   Artemis March, 'A note on quality: the views of Deming, Juran and Crosby', in *Readings in Total Quality Management*, Harry Costin (ed.), Harcourt Brace, New York (1994), p. 143.

6   Refer to Joseph M Juran and Frank M Gryna, Jr *Quality Planning and Analysis*, 3rd edn, McGraw-Hill, New York (1993), pp. 16–19. Also see Juran, JM *Juran's Quality Handbook*, McGraw-Hill, New York (1999).

7   The description of this control sequence is based on Joseph M Juran *Managerial Breakthroughs*, McGraw-Hill, New York (1964), pp. 183–7.

8   This summary is adapted from Juran and Gryna, op. cit., pp. 47–52.

9   This assertion was captured in Crosby's book *Quality is Free*, McGraw-Hill, New York (1979).

10 Taken from Keri R Bhote *Strategic Supplier Management: A Blueprint for Revitalizing the Manufacturing–Supplier Partnership*, American Management Association, New York (1989), p. 168.

11 Chapters 5 and 6 covered process design and introduced tools and techniques to improve the provision of quality conformance in the delivery system. A glance back at this will be useful here.

12 Ishikawa, K *Guide to Quality Control*, Quality Resources, New York (1985), pp. 18–29.

13 For details on sampling, see Dodge, HF and Romig, GH *Sampling Inspection Tables – Single and Double Sampling*, 2nd edn, John Wiley & Sons, London (1959); Duncan, AJ *Quality Control and Industrial Statistics*, Irwin, Burr Ridge (1974); Ledolter, J and Burrill, CW *Statistical Quality Centre*, John Wiley & Sons, New York (1999); Montgomery, DC *Introduction to Statistical Control*, 2nd edn, John Wiley & Sons, London (1991); Owen, M *SPC and Business Improvements*, IFS (1993); Schneider, H, Pruett, J and Legrange, L 'Uses of process capability indices in the supplier certification process', *Quality Engineering* **8**(2) (1995/96), pp. 225–35. In the UK, the British Standards Institute provide a range of suitable sampling plans, with explanations on how to use them. They include OC curves, AQLs, single, double and multiple sampling plans and cover both attributes and variables – see BS 600 (1991, 1993, 1994 and 1996) and BS 6002 (1993 and 1994).

14 For example,

- Australia AS3900
- Belgium   NBN X50
- Denmark DS/EN 29000
- Germany DIN ISO 9000
- Malaysia MS 985
- Netherlands NEN 9000
- South Africa SABS 0157
- Sweden   SS-ISO 9000
- UK   BS 5750

15 See Rabbit, JT and Bergh, PA *The ISO 9000 Book*, Quality Resources, White Plains, NY (1993) for a detailed review.

16 For example, see Oakland, JS *Total Organisational Excellence*, Butterworth Heinemann, Oxford (2001).

17 London, S 'When quality is not quite enough', *Financial Times* (London), 15 July 2002, p. 9.

book map

Part	
1	
2	
3	
4	
5	

CUSTOMERS

SUPPLIERS

OUTPUTS

INPUTS

PROCESSES

1 Managing Operations

2 Operations Strategy

3 Managing People

4 Designing and Developing Services & Products

5 Designing Service Delivery Systems

6 Designing Manufacturing Processes

7 Location and Layout

8 Managing Capacity

9 Technology Developments

10 Operations Scheduling and Execution

11 Managing Quality

12 Managing Inventory

13 Managing the Supply Chain

14 Process and Delivery System Reliability and Maintenance

15 Time and Productivity

16 Improving Operations

Managing Operations in Practice: Long Case Studies

Managing Inventory

Outline of chapter

Inventory in its various forms helps in the design of delivery systems in meeting short customer lead times. Meeting these needs while keeping inventory levels to a minimum is part of the task of effectively managing operations.

Why is managing inventory important?

Executive overview

The reasons why inventory management and control is a key operations task are that it is large (£s), helps operations to run smoothly and efficiently and affects the supply of services and goods to customers.

In Chapter 8 we dealt with capacity, the capability to provide services and make products. This chapter is on inventory. It concerns managing and controlling the materials that go into the services and products at different points in the conversion process. As Exhibit 1.1 illustrated, these include the inputs (materials, components and services) into the conversion process, the part-finished items (products, customers or information) in a process (called work-in-progress inventory) and the outputs (finished items) from a process to be sold or supplied to customers (see Exhibit 12.1). These relationships are also clearly illustrated in the overview at the start of this chapter which shows inventory in the three phases of operations – inputs, operations process and outputs. You will see from both this executive overview and Exhibit 12.1 the presence of inventory throughout operations.

Exhibit 12.1 Flow of materials and position and types of inventory

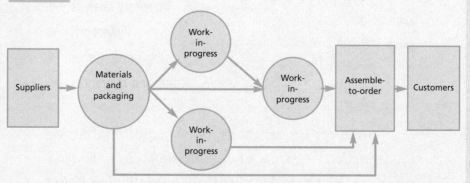

Flow of materials in a fast-food restaurant, showing the position and types of inventory

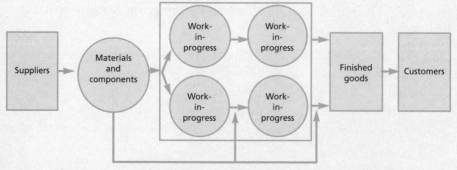

Flow of materials in a manufacturing company, showing the position and types of inventory

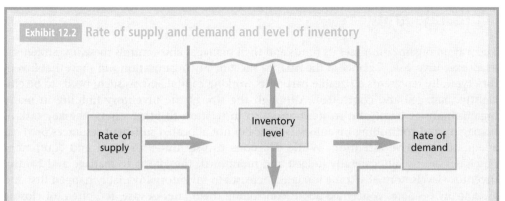

Exhibit 12.2 Rate of supply and demand and level of inventory

As the flow of materials into and through the process differs from the pattern and rate of customer demand, inventory will form or be held to cushion the operations delivery system from these changes. How much inventory there is will depend upon the relative rates of demand and supply, as illustrated in Exhibit 12.2 which depicts the relationship between the rate of supply, rate of demand and the level of inventory, using the analogy of a water tank. In this example, the rate of inflow and outflow of water will directly affect the level of inventory in the tank which depicts the conversion process. Why inventory is kept, the level of inventory involved and its management and control are dealt with in this chapter, which covers the following sections:

- **Corporate attitudes** – inventory, although typically sizeable in balance sheet terms, tends not to be a priority task within a business.

- **Role, types and functions of inventory** – the forms and functions of inventory are explained and the division between corporate and operations inventory is defined as part of the way to effectively manage this important asset.

- **Managing and controlling inventory** – these aspects of inventory are separated into general and specific issues. The general issues highlight the different functional attitudes to inventory, the impact of inventory on profit levels, inventory cost structures and corporate issues around service levels, lead times and supplier relations. The specific issues cover the independent/dependent demand principle, the Pareto principle, the use of economic order quantities and how reorder levels are calculated and used.

- **Inventory decisions** – the key questions to be addressed in managing inventory are what and how much to hold and to order. The approaches to follow and concepts to use in answering these key questions are explained in detail.

- **Inventory systems and analysis** – this section explains the different systems to manage inventory and goes on to give a detailed review of analysing inventory by cause and using this as the basis for reducing levels.

Corporate attitudes

The way an organization uses its funds and then manages and controls these investments is a key executive task. A glance at the balance sheet of any organization will show that inventory typically represents a sizeable part of its working capital and, as such, needs to be efficiently managed and controlled. Although the size of the inventory holding in many organizations is significant in itself and also in relation to other assets, the key task of managing and controlling inventory is typically not allocated sufficient resources or given adequate executive attention. While decisions to use funds for plant and equipment purchases are usually carefully judged and monitored, the efforts to manage and control inventory levels normally come too late. Increases in inventory invariably happen first and a company becomes concerned about controlling them later. A case, too often, of closing the stable door after the horse has bolted.

Although investments in equipment/processes and inventory are both sizeable, typically the former is better managed than the latter. There are several reasons for this, including the following:

- Inventory is an inherent part of a company's operations. When output exceeds sales, purchases exceed output or purchases exceed sales, inventory increases or vice versa. Thus changes to the level of inventory are a consequence of a company's day-to-day activities, but are usually not specifically addressed each time these events take place. With equipment purchases, the investment is a one-off event and invariably made following a conscious decision to address a particular proposal to buy an item of equipment. Control in this instance is easier to effect.

- Inventory all looks the same and there are normally large but acceptable quantities of it; more of the same is not easy to detect. However, new equipment, no matter how small, draws attention, questions and thereby control.

- The control of inventory investment needs to be ongoing. Plant investment on the other hand is a one-off decision and over a period is often not so demanding of management's time.

- Inventory control is often not seen as a senior executive task. It has no qualities or characteristics that give it inherent attraction or bring it to the attention of top management. It is not dynamic. It is a task of day-to-day detail seen by most as mundane. The content, issues and discussions on inventory all appear to be the same. As a consequence, it is not normally an agenda item for a management meeting (unless the horse has bolted), whereas fixed asset investment usually is.

- Companies fail to distinguish between records and control. Consequently, the inventory information provided is typically in the form of a record – a statement of the past, often for historical, financial purposes. However, companies mistakenly interpret this as control data, whereas it merely expresses the value of inventory in a format required for financial statements. One outcome is that ongoing controls necessitated by the size of this asset are not developed, often contributing to unnecessarily high levels of inventory.

Inventory – role, types and functions

What is the role of inventory and why do organizations hold it? Before answering this question, let's first discuss what we mean by inventory. In the context of this chapter it concerns those services or materials that directly or indirectly form part of the ongoing task of delivering the services or making the products that an organization provides or sells. It comprises the inputs, services or materials used, any part-finished items (services or products) and those items that are complete and held awaiting their sale. On the other hand, it does not comprise the equipment or fixtures and fittings (for example the tables, chairs, tablecloths, napkins, cutlery, plates, dishes and glasses in a restaurant) needed to provide services or make products. These are the fixed assets of a business and do not form a direct part of what it sells.

Perhaps the easiest way to explain and illustrate these differences is to ask you to reflect on the inventory you keep and why you keep it. You hold stocks of food and other items which you use as part of day-to-day living. In addition, you have other assets such as cooking equipment and clothes which are used and reused as part of your everyday routines. The former is used and replenished while the latter items are purchased and consumed (that is, the function they provide is used) over a much longer period. This chapter concerns the management and control of a company's equivalent of the stocks of food and other consumables you keep. And, just like you, they need to make decisions about which items to hold, how much of each item (that is, inventory) to carry, when to replenish stocks and how much to buy at any one time.

Before addressing the question of the management and control of inventory, let us first consider its role, the types of inventory and the functions they provide.

General role of inventory

The underlying purpose of inventory is to uncouple the various phases of a service delivery system or manufacturing process and thereby allow each to work independently of the other parts. Hence, keeping food in the kitchen allows you to prepare a meal without first having to shop. However, in reality there are many other issues and dimensions involved. For example, you may only need fresh milk for your breakfast coffee but you have to buy milk in larger quantities as prescribed by the retail store from which you buy it. Similarly, you may buy a larger box of food or more than the one item that you need for a meal as the direct result of a price deal offered by the food store. These dimensions of inventory management will be addressed later, but need to be recognized early on.

Types of inventory

There are two principal categories of inventory: process-related and support. **Process-related inventory** comprises items directly used in providing the services and making the products sold by an organization. Thus, the wheels, subassemblies, windscreens, engines and other parts that go into a motor vehicle are examples of process-related inventory. The ingredients to bake bread and pastries would similarly form part of the process-related inventory for a bakery as would the foodstuffs to prepare meals in a restaurant. All items going into the services or products, from raw materials through to packaging, fall within this category.

Support inventory comprises items that are not an integral part of the service or product produced but are essential to the overall running of any organization. For instance, maintenance and office supplies are examples in the car assembly and bakery examples. Cleaning materials for kitchen utensils, ovens and the like are examples for the restaurant.

Generally, organizations with activities centred on products or manufacturing processes have more inventory and need to develop more controls and systems than organizations where the service/product mix is oriented more to the service end of the service/product continuum described earlier in Exhibit 1.6. This is because the fewer process-related materials that are involved, the less inventory there will be in the system to control. For example, in a bank most services are consumed as they are generated and the process material content is negligible. In fact, the forms and other paperwork used in a bank's delivery system are examples of support inventory. While in all organizations the control of support inventories is an important task, more emphasis will normally be given to process-related inventories because of their greater importance to the business, as they are an integral part of the service and product and also represent a much higher investment. And this is so in both service and manufacturing organizations. Where the service or product sold is less labour-intensive, inventory management will be more important. Retail shops, for instance, have substantial inventories essential to their business. Similarly, hospitals will carry large amounts of inventory from plasma and drugs to supplies of linen and foodstuffs.

Finally, within process-related inventory, there are three categories, consisting of raw materials and components, work-in-progress and finished goods. How they link to the stages in the process and a brief explanation of each is given in Exhibit 12.3. These categories provide an essential insight into the management and control of inventory and will feature throughout the rest of the chapter.

Exhibit 12.3 Process stage and types of inventory

Process stage		Inventory type	
		Process-related	Support
Inputs	Raw materials	Inputs into the process or delivery system used to provide the service or make the the product. These include raw materials, services, bought-out parts and componen	Supplies that are not central to thes services or products provided. They include maintenance and office supplies and consumables such as cleaning materials
In-process	Work-in-progress	Partly completed items in the process waiting to go into the next stage. These include subassemblies and partly prepared items such as foodstuffs awaiting cooking	
Outputs	Finished goods	Outputs of the process. Inventory in its finished form waiting to be sold. These include items to be sold in a retail store, baked bread and pastries in a bakery and manufactured items to go to an end-user in the service or manufacturing sectors	

Functions of inventory

Why does an organization invest so much in inventory? Why does it exist and what is the return? Earlier, the underlying purpose of inventory was identified as one of uncoupling various phases of the service delivery system or manufacturing process. This is a common, overall function, but there are also important advantages that relate more to one type of inventory than another. Using the three categories explained above, some of the principal reasons are outlined in Exhibit 12.4. Note how they differ from one inventory category to another.

As you read the detail in Exhibit 12.4 you will notice that some advantages relate to operations issues while others relate to the business as a whole. To help identify these different

Exhibit 12.4 Role of different types of inventory

Raw materials and bought-out parts inventory allows an organization to:

- cater for the variability of supply
- take advantage of quantity discounts or market prices
- provide holdings of parts that could in future be in short supply due, for instance, to anticipated supply problems
- form an investment when price increases are anticipated
- reduce overall lead times

Work-in-progress inventory helps maintain the independence of stages in the process by uncoupling the steps involved. This leads to:

- orders being easier to schedule
- stabilizing the different output rates at each part of a process
- reducing the total delivery lead time to supply customer demands
- facilitating higher utilization of plant, processes and labour

Finished goods inventory enables an organization to:

- provide fast, off-the-shelf delivery
- achieve a steady delivery of goods to customers in the face of intermittent production or supply
- cope with fluctuations in demand, particularly in the case of seasonal products
- provide an insurance against equipment or process breakdowns and, in some instances, against suppliers' strikes

functions, it is helpful to categorize them into two broad types of inventory, each of which comprises a number of subfunctions. These two types are known as **corporate** and **operations inventory**. While the latter directly helps operations to undertake its basic tasks, the former comprises inventory that is held to provide advantages for other parts of an organization. These two categories and their assorted subcategories are useful ways to help in managing and controlling inventory and will be used in some of the sections later in the chapter. They identify the basic function being provided by clusters of inventory and so help to evaluate the impact on inventory levels of actions taken and decisions made within a business and the specific roles that different types of inventory provide.

Corporate inventory

Corporate inventory is that inventory which does not provide an operations function. The types of corporate inventory are numerous and reflect the nature of the organization involved. One dimension of corporate inventory is, however, a common feature – typically it accounts for 20–25 per cent of the total. Examples include:

- sales inventory to support customer agreements
- sales inventory owing to actual sales being lower than forecast sales
- corporate safety inventory due to the uncertainty of supply (for example in anticipation of national or international strikes)
- purchasing inventory incurred to take advantage of quantity discounts
- marketing inventory to support a service or product launch
- inventory to reduce lead times as a strategic response to market needs; this can be held at the raw material, work-in-progress, finished goods stages or all three.

Operations inventory in manufacturing processes

Regardless of whether the operations inventory under review is at the raw material, work-in-progress or finished goods stage, it may be further described as one or more of decoupling, cycle, pipeline, capacity-related or buffer inventory. Each of these fulfils a specific function. Exhibits 12.5 and 12.6 illustrate the inventory functions and how they relate to both the category of inventory and the particular choice of manufacturing process. An explanation is now provided of these five types of operations inventory (and the two related exhibits) within manufacturing processes.

Exhibit 12.5 Inventory functions related to categories of inventory in manufacturing

Inventory function	Inventory category		
	Raw materials	Work-in-progress	Finished goods
Decoupling		✓✓✓[1]	
Cycle		✓✓✓	
Pipeline		✓✓✓	✓
Capacity-related		✓✓	✓✓✓
Buffer[2]	✓✓	✓✓	✓✓✓

Notes 1 ✓ = Degree of function typically provided.
2 Concerns variation in supply or demand around the average, essentially to cover instances where supply delays or actual levels of demand are above average. However, where inventory is held for reasons such as uncertainty of supply, it should be identified under a relevant category within corporate inventory.

Exhibit 12.6 Inventory functions related to manufacturing processes of jobbing, batch and line

Inventory function		Type of manufacturing process		
		Jobbing	Batch	Line
Decoupling			✓✓✓	
Cycle			✓✓✓	
Pipeline		✓✓	✓✓	
Capacity-related	– work-in-progress		✓	
	– finished goods		✓✓	✓✓✓
Buffer	– raw materials		✓	✓✓
	– finished goods		✓✓	✓✓✓

Decoupling inventory

Decoupling inventory separates one process from another. Thus, a product is worked on at one stage and from there it goes into work-in-progress from which the next stage in the process draws the work as and when required. Decoupling inventory is predominately found in batch manufacturing processes which allow processes to work independently of one another, thereby facilitating scheduling and enhancing the level of efficient working of each stage. The emphasis is on the material waiting for the next manufacturing process so that the process itself can work most efficiently. The principle is, therefore, that the material waits for the process. In jobbing there is no decoupling inventory as the skilled person will progress a job on a continuous basis. Similarly, in a line process there is no need for decoupling inventory as the line itself is a set of coupled processes. An apparent exception to this is where inventory is used to decouple the dependency of one part of a process from the preceding part by providing an inventory which can be used in the case of machine break-downs or yield uncertainty. When such inventory is held, it is not due to the line process itself, a factor which is illustrated by the absence of a tick in Exhibit 12.6. Thus, where this exists, it should be recognized as corporate inventory under the category 'process or yield uncertainty'.

In the same way, inventory typically decouples steps in the total supply chain, for example between producer, warehouse, distribution centre and retailer.

Cycle inventory

Cycle inventory relates to the decision to make a quantity of products (referred to as an 'order quantity' or 'lot batch size') that reflects dimensions such as the time to complete a set-up compared to the order quantity processed or size of customer demand. The rationale behind using cycle inventory in the operations system is to reduce the number of set-ups and thereby increase the amount of capacity that can be used to make saleable output. In jobbing there is little need for this function as the skilled person will set up for each job individually and is often making an order quantity of one. Similarly, cycle inventory is a function which a line process does not require as it is continually set up to manufacture an agreed range of products and processes one at a time. As shown in Exhibits 12.5 and 12.6, cycle inventory is a feature of batch processes where set-up or make-ready tasks are an inherent feature of this choice. The principle here is that by processing two or more products at a time, the costs of setting up a manufacturing process are spread, thereby reducing the set-up costs per unit.

Pipeline inventory

Pipeline inventory (also referred to as 'transit inventory') concerns the inventory that exists as a result of companies deciding to subcontract one or more operations to an outside supplier at some time during the total manufacturing process. This subcontracting decision can be partway through the operations process or at the distribution stage. Examples during the process include a manufacturer having the finishing processes (for example plating and painting) completed by a subcontractor.

In both jobbing and batch many companies decide to subcontract a particular operation during the process and, in so doing, create pipeline inventory in support of that decision. Decisions to subcontract despatch at the end of the operations process will typically incur pipeline inventory holding as part of making this decision. A decision to subcontract one operation within line processing would be unfeasible and therefore does not happen.

Capacity-related inventory

Capacity-related inventory transfers work from one time period to the next in the form of inventory, and provides one way of stabilizing operations capacity in an environment of fluctuating sales levels. For example, the seasonal demand for fireworks to celebrate national festivals and the high demand for toys and gifts at peak periods such as Christmas are also accommodated, in part, by capacity-related inventory. The other way to cope with anticipated sales is to plan operations in line with sales forecasts. This, however, often leads to situations of peak capacity requirements involving overtime, recruitment of additional staff, the use of temporary part or full-time staff or the holding of spare process capacity.

Buffer inventory

Buffer inventory relates to the fact that average demand, by definition, varies around the average. In order to cope with those situations where demand exceeds the average, businesses hold buffer inventory. The function of this inventory holding is to help cushion the manufacturing process (see Exhibit 10.1) against unpredictable variations in demand levels or supply availability. The higher the delivery on-time performance level set by a business or the lower the level of stockout risk it is willing to endure, the higher the size of buffer inventory it must carry. However, inventory held that exceeds buffer levels falls into the category of corporate inventory.

Operations inventory in service delivery systems

This section reviews the use of inventory in service delivery systems and follows the same format as the last section by reviewing the five functions provided by operations inventory. As the roles and rationale are the same in service delivery systems as those in manufacturing processes, this part of the discussion will not be repeated. First let's clarify what constitutes inventory in a service company. A delivery system can involve the processing of:

● customers or customer surrogates (a car being serviced is a surrogate for the customer)

● information

● materials that go into the product element of the service/product offering provided.

Consequently, inventory of all or any of these may be found in a service delivery system and the functions provided will be similar in nature to material inventory in a manufacturing process. While inventory in the form of customers or information does not have a direct cost or investment dimension, it will impact the ability of operations to meet certain order-winners or qualifiers such as delivery speed and delivery reliability. The sections that follow illustrate how the five functions of operations inventory form part of the service delivery systems of different organizations. The use of inventory differs depending upon the service/product mix and also whether information or customers are processed within the delivery system (see Exhibit 12.7).

Exhibit 12.7 Inventory functions in relation to different service delivery systems

Inventory function	Type of service delivery system		
	Non-repeat	Single-step repeat	Multi-step repeat
Decoupling			✓✓✓
Cycle		✓✓	✓✓✓
Pipeline	✓✓		✓✓
Capacity-related		✓✓	✓✓
Buffer	✓	✓	✓✓

Decoupling inventory

Decoupling inventory in a service delivery system allows steps in the system to work independently of one another and thereby facilitates the efficient use of resources (staff or equipment). For these reasons, decoupling inventory is typically found in multi-step delivery systems. The emphasis is on the information or customers waiting for the next step in the system to be available. Thus, a patient in a hospital waits at each step in the delivery system (for example the hospital consultants or X-ray facility) before being processed at that step. Similarly, in a garage handling bodywork repairs, cars will often have to wait for the next stage to become available (for example one of the spray booths).

Cycle inventory

Cycle inventory relates to a decision to hold back information or customers and then process a large quantity or number at the one time. In most delivery systems, information and customers are processed singly but there are examples where an organization clusters two or more together before starting the next step. Examples of cycle inventory being used include information processing in back-office processing such as cheque clearance and the preparation of personal or business bank statements, and customer clustering during a conducted tour of a museum or art gallery where some customers wait until the group is sufficiently large for that stage in the system to begin.

Pipeline inventory

Pipeline inventory within services is used to provide the same role as in manufacturing. Examples of pipeline inventory used during a service delivery system include a dentist subcontracting the manufacture of a crown for a patient's tooth and a doctor having blood samples analysed off site. In both instances, the completion of the service for a customer is put on hold awaiting the subcontracted dimension of the total service to be completed.

Capacity-related inventory

Capacity-related inventory is where a city centre sandwich bar will prepare the fillings and garnish for its products (or the finished items themselves) in the hours before its peak demand periods around lunch time. Fast-food outlets and restaurants do the same, using work-in-process (part-finished) and finished goods inventory to transfer staff capacity in low demand periods to be sold in high demand periods. In the same way, by changing a service delivery system from one based on making to order (MTO) to one based on assembly to order (ATO) or making to stock (MTS), lead times are reduced and service delivery times are now in line with customer expectations.

Buffer inventory

Buffer inventory, where products are involved and demand is uncertain, is when companies will increase inventory levels of some items to avoid being out of stock should demand substantially exceed forecasts.

Managing and controlling inventory – general issues

This and the next section concern some general and specific issues regarding the management and control of inventory. Their purpose is to provide essential context in which these tasks have to be implemented and set the scene for the sections that follow.

With regard to general issues, one factor influencing the size of the inventory investment is the pressure applied by the various functions within a business, each of which will have a different view of what is a desirable inventory level (see Exhibit 12.8). The result is a conflict of views over where the company's funds should or should not be invested, and these are outlined below.

Exhibit 12.8 General preferences of three key functions towards the level of holding by type of inventory

Type of inventory	General preference by function		
	Finance/ accounting	Operations	Sales
Raw materials	Low	High	Indifferent
Work-in-progress	Low	High	Indifferent
Finished goods	Low	Indifferent	High

Inventory and its impact on profit levels

So far this chapter has looked at inventory as a part of working capital. However, it is not just in this form that pressure is applied to inventory levels. Consider the situation facing managers where a company is going through a period of reduced sales. It is difficult to shed costs quickly in the short term by reducing either variable or fixed costs. Such a course of action would normally be expensive. On the other hand, if all the overhead costs are carried by a level of throughput set in line with the current, lower sales activity, the profits for that period would be considerably reduced. Instead, management often decides to carry over some of the costs from the current to a future period. It does this either by using spare capacity to make products for stock or undertaking work (for instance research work or the development of current or new services) for which there are no sales but for which it is anticipated there will be sales in the future. In this way, a proportion of the costs from one time period can legitimately be absorbed into the inventory value of that period and carried forward to a future period when the work-in-progress or finished goods inventory is sold. Thus costs incurred in one time period are transferred to a future time period in the form of inventory, as the value of the inventory includes the associated direct and overhead costs involved.

One result of this action is that profits will not fall as much as they would otherwise have done and the value of the company will be held more in check. With an upturn in sales, the inventory will be sold and the associated costs of the inventory incurred earlier will be recovered.

If the upturn in sales does not come about, then a company will often be reluctant to sell the excess inventory at a low price in order to recover at least some of the investment. Such action would usually lead to further reduced profits and a further reduction in the value of the company. This aspect of inventory can, therefore, frequently result in organizations operating with too much inventory and yet being reluctant to remedy the situation.

Inventory cost structures

The management of this sizeable asset is, in part, to provide the roles of inventory on the one hand, while controlling the cost of inventory on the other. One important prerequisite to undertake this task is understanding the make-up and structure of the associated costs of the inventory investment. These are:

- **Item costs** concern the cost of buying or producing the individual items held in inventory. Volume often reflects on the cost of an item, as quantity discounts can be secured for purchased items and services and non-variable costs such as overheads can be spread over more items if a greater number of items were produced.

- Ordering and set-up costs relate to the ordering and provision of a given quantity. Any costs associated with arranging and providing services or products fall into this category. They include order preparation and placement, monitoring the order, transport, receiving and invoice reconciliation and payment.

- Carrying costs concern the costs of holding inventory. These include the cost of the inventory investment itself, the storage costs including space and insurance, and the costs of deterioration, obsolescence and losses that occur during the period in which the inventory is held awaiting its use in the process or sale to a customer.

- Stockout costs reflect the economic consequences of running out of stock. This concerns the lost profit on a particular sale and any loss of customer goodwill occasioned by the late or non-delivery of a service or product.

Corporate issues

At the corporate level in organizations, there are a number of key decisions that affect the competitive stance of a business which, in turn, impact inventory requirements. These include:

- Service levels are statements concerning the targets set by a business with regard to meeting the demand and expectations of its customers. Those concerning shorter lead times and service or product range support will have a direct impact on the levels of inventory to be maintained. The impact on inventory of agreed targets must be recognized and assessed as part of a company's review of its competitive positioning and the role that inventory investment makes in meeting these targets.

- Lead times are directly affected by decisions concerning whether a company:
  - makes to order (MTO)
  - assembles to order (ATO)
  - makes to stock (MTS).

  Progressively, lead times are reduced as companies move from MTO to MTS, with an increasingly larger part of the service or product being undertaken before a sale is made. Part or all of the task is made ahead of the sale, thereby reducing the lead time required to fulfil a customer order.

- Supplier relations concern the level of cooperation between customers and their suppliers. This entails not only accurate and timely information with regard to demand schedules but also a mutual understanding of the services and products and the processes involved in both organizations. As suppliers are part of the total supply chain, customers need proactively to involve them in order to helps reduce materials in the system. These issues are addressed in detail in Chapter 13 which covers managing the supply chain.

Managing and controlling inventory – specific issues

This section looks at the more specific issues relating to several aspects of managing and controlling inventory. Introducing them in this way allows you to understand the issues involved, so when the approaches to managing and controlling inventory are reviewed these can be referred to as needed.

The independent/dependent demand principle

The starting point for the management and control of inventory is customer demand. Companies translate their forecasts of demand into statements of operations requirements, for example the capacity and materials needed. In completing this task, companies use the principle of dependent/independent demand.

Dependent demand items are the components or materials used in a process to provide a service or make a product. They are, therefore, dependent on the number of final services or products sold. Hence, an automobile company will need five wheel rims and tyres for each vehicle it makes. The quantity of these and other parts directly relates to the number of automobiles made. The wheel rims, tyres and other components and materials are classed as dependent and can be calculated on the number of automobiles scheduled to be made. Similarly, a fast-food restaurant would calculate the number of fillings, buns, frozen French fries and other items based on its forecast of each type of meal to be sold. Items for which demand is linked to the use of other items are, therefore, said to have a dependent pattern of demand.

Independent demand items, on the other hand, are the final services provided or products made. They are independent because they are neither a function of nor are they linked to the demand pattern of other items. Thus, the demand for automobiles and meals would be classed as having an independent pattern of demand.

The choice of inventory management system reflects whether an item has a dependent or independent pattern of demand, as will be explained later. The key difference here is that with independent demand items, the number of services or products is either known (that is, orders have already been received) or has to be forecast. With dependent demand items, the number can be calculated.

Pareto analysis[1]

The size and importance of items will vary and often the relationship between the relative value or importance of a range of items will typically reflect what is known as the 80/20 rule. A review of inventory will typically show support for this principle. The 80/20[2] rule concerns the phenomenon that, for example, with regard to inventory, 80 per cent of the inventory value will be held by 20 per cent of the items in stock. Given this relationship, most of the effort in managing inventory should be concentrated in the areas of high value – the number of items to manage is reduced but most of the inventory value is under control.

Where to direct this major effort is easily derived from a Pareto analysis based on the annual requirement value of each item. For each item of inventory two facts are needed: unit value and annual usage. The product of these two figures is known as the annual requirement value (ARV).

The inventory items are placed in order, with the largest ARV first, then the next largest and so on. Exhibit 12.9 lists a representative sample of 30 items in order of decreasing ARV. Such a list would be typical in many organizations. Because of the wide range of ARVs, it would not make sense to spread the effort of inventory control equally over each part. Pareto's 'vital few' and 'trivial many' idea, or the 80/20 rule, applies here, as illustrated by Exhibit 12.10.

From this summary it can be seen that 74 per cent of the total ARV is accounted for by as little as 23 per cent of the total items held in inventory. This approach to inventory control is further extended into an ABC analysis. Here, the high ARV items are classed as A items, the middle range as B items and the low ARV as C items (Exhibit 12.11). Once this has been accomplished (bearing in mind that the ARV for an item may change over time and so,

Exhibit 12.9 A representative sample of inventory items in order of decreasing ARV

Part number	Unit value (£)	Annual usage (units)	Annual requirement value (£) Actual	Cumulative
303-07	58.50	6,000	351,000	351,000
650-27	2.46	80,000	196,800	547,800
541-21	210.00	500	105,000	652,800
260-81	164.11	450	73,850	726,850
712-22	2.39	25,000	59,750	786,400
054-09	5.86	10,000	58,600	845,000
097-54	136.36	300	40,908	885,908
440-18	17.30	2,000	34,600	920,508
440-01	337.35	100	33,735	954,243
308-31	136.20	200	27,240	981,483
016-01	12.89	2,000	25,780	1,007,263
305-04	45.30	475	21,518	1,028,781
155-29	38.02	500	19,010	1,047,791
542-93	62.91	300	18,837	1,066,664
582-34	32.08	500	16,040	1,082,704
323-34	71.30	200	14,260	1,096,964
412-27	23.01	600	13,806	1,110,770
540-80	24.76	500	12,380	1,123,150
137-29	12.31	1,000	12,310	1,135,460
401-53	30.64	400	12,256	1,147,716
418-51	168.86	65	10,976	1,158,692
418-50	168.80	65	10,972	1,169,664
390-02	17.47	500	8,735	1,178,399
037-41	24.05	200	4,810	1,183,209
402-50	22.00	600	4,400	1,187,609
900-01	41.64	100	4,164	1,191,773
543-61	15.10	200	3,020	1,194,793
900-11	46.80	50	2,340	1,197,133
003-54	11.41	200	2,282	1,199,415
691-30	0.41	5,000	2,050	1,201,465

Exhibit 12.10 Summary of items in Exhibit 12.9

Percentage of total items	Percentage of total ARV
23	74
44[1]	21
33	5[1]
Total 100	100

Note   1 Figures have been rounded up.

Exhibit 12.11 Pareto curve and ABC analysis for items in Exhibit 12.9

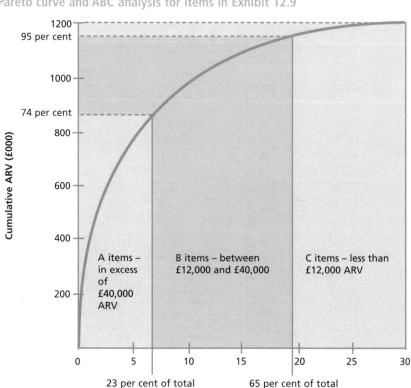

therefore, would its classification), the approach used to control items in each of these categories will differ to reflect the varying levels of inventory value.

It stands to reason that A items should be controlled and checked, and requirements calculated in order to keep inventory levels in line with forecast usage. It is worth the administrative and management costs involved. C items would be managed with less control and effort, as explained later in the chapter. B items fall in the middle ground and the level of control and attention to be assigned would need to be considered individually.

Economic order quantity and economic batch quantity/economic lot size

One of the fundamental decisions in inventory management concerns how much to order, in the context of what quantity will result in the lowest total cost. The order quantity decision, therefore, needs to relate the various costs involved in placing an order and carrying the inventory to the quantity that is ordered. The economic order quantity (EOQ) and economic batch quantity (EBQ)/economic lot size (ELS) models address the question of how much to order to minimize the total cost of holding inventory. The formulas for each are given below:

$$EOQ = \sqrt{\frac{2zC_s}{cC}} \quad \text{for instantaneous replenishment}$$

or

$$EBQ/ELS = \sqrt{\frac{2zC_s}{cC} \times \frac{p}{p-d}} \quad \text{for replenishment at rate } p$$

where z = total annual usage, C_s = cost of placing an order, c = unit cost of the item, C = carrying cost rate per year, p = production provisioning rate (units) per day and d = demand rate (units) per day.

However, it is important to note that these models make the following simplifying assumptions:

- the rate of demand is constant
- costs remain fixed
- operations capacity and inventory holdings are unlimited.

Despite the fact that these assumptions are fundamental to the basis of the models and would seemingly restrict their use, they provide useful guidelines for ordering decisions even in operating conditions that depart significantly from these assumptions.[3] Mr James, however, proves to be the exception (see Exhibit 12.12).

Reorder levels

A key question to be addressed by inventory systems is when and how much to order. In some situations the decision is in response to another event. For example, ordering dependent items is typically linked to the decision on the number of independent items to provide. The same goes for companies working on a make-to-order basis as explained earlier. Here, the customer order triggers the other decisions.

In other situations, companies need to deal with the question 'When should an order to replenish inventory be placed?' Assuming that a company does not wish to run out of inventory, the level at which it must reorder is calculated by multiplying the time it takes to get an order into the company from an outside supplier (the lead time) by the number of units of this particular item used during the same period. Thus, if the delivery lead time for an item is one week and the weekly usage is 100 units, the reorder level (ROL) is $1 \times 100 = 100$ units. Ideally, the time to place an order is such that the last item of inventory is used as delivery of the next order for this item is made.

But the rate of usage will vary with demand, and may often vary considerably. In calculating the ROL, the average figures used are based upon historical data. However, the pattern of demand will vary around the average and it is the incidence of above-average usage that will result in a stockout. To avoid this, it will be necessary to carry inventory to cater for the above-average demand during a lead time. This extra quantity is called buffer inventory, as explained earlier. Hence, the ROL calculation can now be modified as follows:

ROL = average usage in a lead time + buffer inventory

So far we have discussed stock levels without stating what they mean. As the example below illustrates, physical stock levels need to be adjusted for both allocations and stock on order.

Item 746B		
Actual physical stock	125	the actual number of items in stock
Less allocated stock	38	items needed to fulfill any existing orders
Available stock	87	physical less allocated stock
Plus stock on order	100	the quantity on any outstanding orders
	187	

ROLs are normally based on available stock figures. Stock allocations are ignored in these calculations where they relate to time periods in the future such that they will not affect inventory levels within the material lead time. Similarly, stock on order is taken into account when defining available stock with regard to future allocations and purchase order decisions.

Inventory decisions

Inventory comprises the process-related (that is, materials and components, work-in-progress and finished items) and corporate categories introduced earlier. For both these categories decisions on inventory concern:

- what items to hold in stock
- how much to hold and how much and when to order.

The answer to these questions will relate to the general and specific issues covered in the last two sections as well as other agreements with customers and suppliers and any internal decisions made within a business. One of the most fundamental factors affecting the decisions to be made, systems to use and approaches to follow is the independent/dependent demand principle explained in the last section. This factor is reflected in the following sections that address the above questions.

What items to hold in stock

Companies will decide to complete services or make products ahead of time for a number of reasons. Known orders or scheduled call-offs against customer contracts will often be made or provided in advance to ensure that due dates are met. Similarly, inventory to meet future demand peaks, known seasonality patterns or to level out operations capacity requirements over a period are practical inventory responses used by companies to manage these different circumstances. The factors affecting the decision as to what items to hold in stock are now discussed.

Make-to-order, assemble-to-order or make-to-stock

A major factor influencing the decision of what to hold in stock is whether a company selects a make-to-order, assemble-to-order or make-to-stock response to meeting customer needs:

- Make-to-order (MTO) businesses are usually involved in the provision of special (that is, will not be repeated)[4] services and products. In addition, some companies decide to meet demand for standard (that is, repeat) items only on an MTO basis. Either way, an MTO response means that inventory will not be held either as part-finished or finished items. What may be held in stock are the materials and components that form all or part of an item.

- Assemble-to-order (ATO) businesses are those that part-finish an item beforehand and then complete it on receipt of an order. The stage of part-completion reflects the associated value of inventory and process lead time reduction that results. Fast-food restaurants prepare beforehand the individual items in the range (for example French fries and different types of burgers) and then assemble to order customers' requirements. Similarly, top restaurants part-prepare some food (for example desserts and vegetables) ahead of time.

- Make-to-stock (MTS) business are those that complete or purchase items ahead of demand and then meet orders from finished goods inventory. Examples include all retail outlets and manufacturers making finished goods. Others such as newspaper shops can only sell this way – if a newspaper is not available on the day, the sale is simply lost.

80/20 rule

As explained earlier, the 'vital few' and 'trivial many' phenomenon is a characteristic of inventory. Based on this, companies often decide to hold inventory of low annual requirement value items based on the principle of setting purchasing costs against inventory holding costs.

As part of these decisions, the 80/20 rule will often be employed to help guide a company as it attempts to balance the level of inventory investment with the level of support for its markets and customers and/or the costs in operations as it adjusts capacity to meet varying levels of demand. Corporate issues such as agreements with customers to hold certain items in stock will also influence this decision.

Independent/dependent demand items

Decisions to hold items in stock are affected by whether or not they fall within the independent or dependent demand categories. As explained earlier, the former are end items and are more open to choice concerning whether or not to hold them in stock. However, as the usage for dependent items is linked directly to the demand for independent items, there is no requirement to hold inventory for these until the decision is made to provide relevant independent items. Decisions to otherwise hold inventory for dependent items will be for reasons such as safety (to guard against uncertainty of supply), buffer (to reflect the variance within suppliers' delivery time), as well as economic order quantity benefits, purchasing discounts, reduced transaction costs and so on. Holding dependent demand item inventory to gain lower costs and improve a company's ability to support its markets and customers makes for sound management practice.

Corporate inventory

Companies often hold inventory for non-operations reasons. Classic categories include customer agreement and corporate safety stock:

- *Customer agreement inventory* is where a company agrees to hold a given level of inventory at all times in anticipation of a customer order or call-off. This may be provided on a consignment stock[5] basis and held on a customer's own premises.

● *Corporate safety stock* is held due to the uncertainty of supply, for example to guard against national or international strikes or in anticipation of a general national, regional or world shortage.

Illustrations of corporate decisions on inventory that reflect the nature of a company's business or to meet market needs are now provided. First though take a look at Case examples 12.1, 12.2 and 12.3 to reflect on what has been covered so far.

Case example 1   HOLDING INVENTORY IN RETAIL OUTLETS

Retail outlets need to hold inventory in order to sell products and display the extent and nature of a range of goods. Where the purchase price is low or a lack of stock will lead to a lost sale (for example a newsagent or food store), the policy will be to hold inventory in line with forecast sales and will reflect demand fluctuations. Where the items are of high value (for example a suite of furniture, china dinner service or set of cut-glass wine glasses), examples of the range (typically those that sell the most), supported by fabric choices, catalogues and the like, will be the basis for what is held in stock.

Case example 2   PRE-PREPARED FOOD IN RESTAURANTS

Restaurants hold the basic food and other ingredients in stock and part- or fully prepare food in line with the menu and anticipated sales of the various menu options. The extent to which materials are part-prepared will reflect the level of choice provided and the speed of service offered or expected by customers.

Case example 3   BALANCING INVENTORY APPROACHES

A company selling a range of household items used two approaches to holding inventory of its products. Category 1 products were made in anticipation of sales and on a make-to-stock basis. Orders for a category 2 product were allowed to go into arrears and then a quantity of a product would be made that covered:

(a) outstanding sales orders
(b) sales orders received during the process time to make the order quantity

(c) inventory to cover a given number of weeks of future sales.

When the quantity was made, outstanding orders in (a) and (b) would be met. Future sales would be met from the finished goods inventory that remained. Eventually the company would go into an outstanding order position for its category 2 products and the procedure outlined above would be repeated.

Case questions   1   What is the role of inventory in these three illustrations?
                      2   Explain in detail how inventory would be used in each delivery system.

How much stock to hold, and how much and when to order materials

The three issues of how much stock to hold and how much and when to order materials are an integral set of decisions and so are addressed together. The factors that affect these questions include some of those discussed in the previous section as well as others that are specific to these key questions.

Demand forecasts and scheduling horizons

Key factors in answering these three questions are demand forecasts and the scheduling horizons determined by a business. In part this will reflect the nature of a company's markets as explained earlier.

Make-to-order – special services and products

Companies providing special services and products will use customer orders already received (known as order backlog or forward load) together with forecast sales profiles to estimate capacity and determine material requirements. How much and when to order the necessary materials will be in line with the size and start dates of the orders on hand. In some instances, particularly where expensive materials are involved, customers, as part of the contract, will provide materials on a 'free issue' basis (that is, a customer buys the materials and has them delivered to the supplier). Companies will often stock some non-specific materials that are in general use for a number of services and products and replenish these in line with the forward orders that a business has on hand. For materials that are specific to an order, companies will normally purchase quantities in line with customer order requirements. An exception to this is where minimum order quantities are imposed by a supplier and these exceed the materials required to meet a specific customer order. In such instances the minimum order quantity will need to be purchased. Companies should then build the total cost of this minimum order quantity into their price calculations for an order and hold the balance in stock where there is a possibility of future use. Balances so held should be recorded as having a zero value, thereby ensuring that any gain is only registered when it happens. (This is based on sound accounting practice. However, although the book value of such inventory is zero, the physical items are in stock and will need to be managed and controlled in the normal way.)

Standard services and products

Where companies supply standard services and products, decisions on how much stock to hold and how much and when to order materials are influenced by a number of factors, of which demand forecasts, make-to-order or make-to-stock decisions and operations scheduling horizons are key.

Companies providing standard services and products can do so using a make-to-order or make-to-stock approach. Using make-to-order as the basis for scheduling means that companies provide services and products only in line with actual customer orders or contract call-offs and thereby the timing and quantity of materials required are known and built into the scheduling procedure. This becomes the essential mechanism for managing and controlling inventory.

Companies choosing to provide services and products on a make-to-stock basis convert sales forecasts of demand into statements of operations requirements, as explained in Chapter 10. These operations requirements are then converted into schedules and material call-offs, identifying materials and when they are needed. In this way, the scheduling system ties in the aspects of capacity and material requirements to forecast demand and arranges the timing of these to meet future sales.

To help in managing these decisions, companies use a number of approaches to help control the different categories of inventory. These approaches are now discussed.

Reorder point

Companies use the principle of reorder levels as the basis for deciding how much stock to hold and when to reorder. This system can be used for finished items as well as for raw material and component inventory holdings.

The logic of an order point system is to trigger the reorder of a part or item every time the inventory level of that part or item falls to a predetermined level. As illustrated by

Exhibit 12.13 Control of an individual part through an order point system

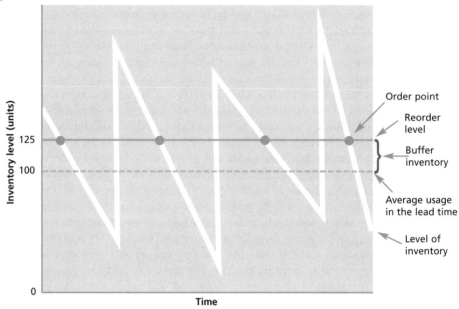

Exhibit 12.13, the timing and quantity of the reorder take into account the usage in the lead time plus the agreed buffer inventory to take account of above-average usage. The reorder level is the sum of the average usage in the lead time ($1 \times 100 = 100$ units) plus the extra inventory to cater for the above-average demand during a lead time (estimated here as 25

Exhibit 12.14 Above-average demand above the reorder level followed by below-average demand

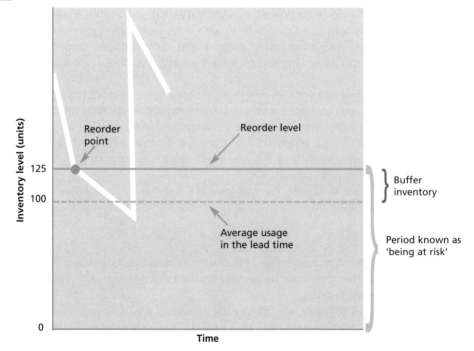

units). The three cycles in this example show different levels of usage during the lead time, although the pattern of usage has been simplified (it would not normally be so regular) and the actual lead times are shown as being more consistent than experienced in reality.

However, this illustration shows the importance of recognizing that only usage patterns after the reorder level is reached are of consequence in terms of stockouts, and so the period following an order point is known as 'being at risk'. Let us explain this important point more fully. Demand patterns above a reorder point will only result in inventory falling to this level either more quickly or more slowly than average depending upon whether actual demand is higher or lower respectively. As far as potential stockouts are concerned, demand patterns above the reorder point are not a factor. However, above-average demand patterns experienced after a reorder point has been reached influence whether or not stockouts occur. Above-average demand will result in a stockout if the amount of buffer inventory is insufficient to cover the level of actual demand experienced. Hence the term 'being at risk'. Exhibits 12.14 and 12.15 illustrate these points. In Exhibit 12.14, above-average demand is followed by a period of below-average demand, whereas in Exhibit 12.15 the reverse demand patterns are shown and their impact on inventory levels and stockouts is illustrated.

Finally, a reminder that the illustrations of the reorder point model have been kept simple without invalidating the principles involved. In all three examples, material lead times have been assumed constant and usage patterns have been shown as being regular. In practice these factors (and especially usage patterns) will typically vary during a period.

Exhibit 12.15 Below-average demand above the reorder level followed by above-average demand

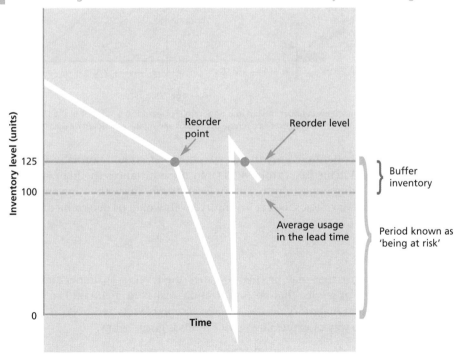

Buffer inventory

The function of buffer inventory is to provide a safeguard against periods of above-average demand and thereby avoid or reduce the number of stockouts. Where there is sufficient information, buffer inventories can be calculated using basic statistics. The first step would be to calculate average usage for an item and the standard deviation of usage around that average. For example, assume that an item has an average weekly usage of 100 and is normally distributed with a standard deviation of 12 units. By applying normal distribution curve theory (see Exhibit 12.16), the individual weekly usage would be within two standard deviations either side of the average for 95 per cent of the time (the mathematical explanation is not given here, but for those interested it will normally be available in any textbook on inventory control). Of the 5 per cent of the time that usage does not fall within two standard deviations, half can be expected to be less than average and half to be more than average. Now, the organization is concerned only with instances where usage is above average, therefore it can expect that only for 2.5 per cent of the time would usage exceed the average plus two standard deviations. That is $100 + 2(12) = 124$. In this situation, if the reorder level was set at 124, a stockout would not be expected more than 2.5 per cent of the time or one time in 40 occasions.

Exhibit 12.16 Normal distribution curve

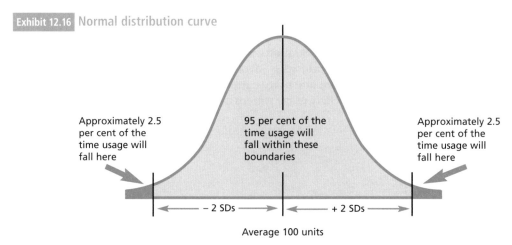

Average 100 units

The shaded areas under the left and right tails represent the 5 per cent of the time when actual usage would exceed average usage plus and minus 2 standard deviations (SDs)

Calculating buffer inventory in this way, however, should normally apply only to A and possibly some B items (see Exhibit 12.11). In these instances the high annual requirement value and resulting impact on inventory levels would make the time and cost worthwhile. For other B and all C items, buffer inventory levels would be determined using much cruder methods.

Service levels

A further measure that may be used to gauge the level of customer support is the service level. The level of service that an organization wishes to maintain can be established and the level of buffer inventory needed to yield acceptable service levels can be calculated. One commonly used way of expressing service levels is given below:

$$\text{Service level (percentage)} = \frac{\text{\# customers served without delay}}{\text{Total orders received}} \times 100$$

To approach this requirement from the opposite perspective, companies can determine the risk of a stockout they are prepared to accept. This is also known as the 'protection level' and is the equivalent of $100 \times (1 - \text{probability of a stockout})$. Protection levels can thus be established and the level of buffer inventory to provide these levels can be calculated.

Economic order and economic batch quantities

The economic order quantity (EOQ) and economic batch quantity (EBQ) or economic lot size (ELS) models were explained earlier. They are, as their titles suggest, directed towards helping to determine the quantity that would give the lowest total cost outcome. Although these models are built on a number of simplified assumptions, they are useful in providing guidelines on how much to order or provide.

Some companies use different criteria for arriving at the order quantity to be processed. For example, a company making high specification reproduction furniture limited its order quantity to that which equated to no more than two days of work for their staff. To this company, limiting the amount of time on the same piece of furniture would support job interest and help ensure that conformance to the very high specification demands of its product range would best be met.

Consignment stock

As explained earlier, consignment stock describes inventory held at a customer's premises that is not paid for until it is used. Suppliers typically retain the responsibility for checking inventory levels and replenishing stock as needed. In these instances, how much to hold on a customer's site and when to replenish are based on actual usage and agreed minimum stock levels.

Corporate inventory

Many of these latter approaches are often directly influenced by corporate decisions on a range of issues. Those classified as 'customer agreement' and 'safety' stock have already been explained. Other illustrations of corporate inventory include purchase-discount inventory (that held at above-normal levels to acquire the price discounts on offer) and marketing inventory (that held at above-normal levels to support a marketing initiative, for example promotions).

Inventory systems

The models and approaches described so far to help control inventory have simplified the size of the problem. Coping with thousands of stock items, supplied by many different suppliers and supporting the needs of numerous customers, results in a complex and dynamic operations task. To cope with this level of complexity, operations managers need to do several basic tasks:

- recognize that the level of control to be provided reflects the ARV of an item
- select and develop a control system in line with other existing systems (for example operations scheduling) and the nature of the item itself (for example dependent versus independent items)
- undertake checks on current inventory levels to verify the system, test how well it is working and identify changes in working practices, customer demands and other business issues and how they impact on inventory. Regular stocktaking is an integral part of managing inventory and helps check on the current position, sometimes with interesting results, as in Exhibit 12.17.

Companies use a variety of systems to help manage and control inventory. Which to use

Exhibit 12.17 One value of regular stocktaking

© AMD Publishing

will reflect the nature of their business and take into account several background issues discussed earlier and listed below:

- **Operations scheduling systems** interface with the control of inventory. The translation of customer orders into operations requirements has already been mentioned and Chapter 10 addresses these issues in detail. The aspect of inventory control is an integral part of the material schedules that form part of the operations control system. High volume, make-to-stock or make-to-order businesses (for example motor vehicles) typically use JIT systems that dictate material call-offs and help control and maintain low levels of inventory. Where companies adopt a make-to-order policy for the scheduling of standard services and products, actual customer orders and call-offs will trigger the operations schedule that, in turn, activates the demand for materials. For those companies using a make-to-stock approach for scheduling operations, they will use one of the systems described in the section entitled 'Operations inventory control'.

- **Dependent demand items** are, by and large, calculated in line with requirements for independent demand items as described earlier. This approach is typically supplemented for low ARV items by simple systems which are low cost to manage and control and designed to ensure no stockouts. These are explained in the section entitled 'Operations inventory control'.

- **The 80/20 rule** should determine the level of control that companies provide. The selection of appropriate systems for low ARV items is concerned with keeping the management and control costs low while ensuring that stockouts are avoided. Calculating and ordering small quantities of these items would not make sense. For high ARV items the reverse is true.

Corporate inventory control

In most companies some 20–25 per cent of inventory is held for corporate rather than operations reasons. Several categories of these were given earlier. The control of this inventory is specific to its provision. Based on the value involved, companies will need to evaluate the investment in terms of its size and return (what advantages and functions the inventory provides). Each category will need to be assessed item by item (see the later section 'Causal analysis').

Operations inventory control

Operations inventory typically accounts for 75–80 per cent of the total. This inventory exists for operations reasons and provides a number of the functions described earlier. The systems used to control operations inventory are now discussed. Several of the aspects and issues introduced earlier in the chapter are included, which enables us to refer to them without going into detail.

Continuous review systems

In a continuous review system, the inventory position is monitored after each transaction (that is, continuously). When the inventory drops to a predetermined level (or reorder point), a fixed quantity is placed on order. Since the order quantity is fixed, the time between orders will vary in line with the different levels of demand. The continuous review system is also referred to as a 'fixed order quantity system' (or Q system for short). Exhibit 12.13 provides an example using this principle and shows the following characteristics:

- a fixed quantity (that incorporates the economic order quantity principle) is purchased
- the material lead time (the time between an order being placed and its delivery) is deemed to be the same
- the gap between purchase orders will vary in line with the different levels of demand.

The calculation of the reorder level is the average quantity used in the lead time plus buffer inventory to cover the likelihood and extent of above-average usage. Another factor to be taken into account in this calculation is any variation in material lead times. If these vary, any above-average length of lead times would need to be factored into the reorder level calculation.

Periodic review systems

While the virtue of the continuous review system is that it can make use of economic order quantities, monitoring and checking inventory levels continuously (even when using suitable, computer-based systems) is time-consuming and expensive. An alternative and similar approach is the periodic review system, also known as 'fixed order period system' (or P system for short). In a periodic review system, the stock position is reviewed at fixed intervals and a reorder quantity is placed that constitutes the difference between the actual and target inventory level. The target level is set to cover demand until the next periodic review plus the delivery lead time. As usage varies so the amount ordered will vary and hence one disadvantage of this system is that the economic order quantity principle cannot be used.

Using P and Q systems in practice

Both P and Q systems together with modified versions of them are widely used for the management of independent demand items. The choice between the two is not an easy one and will be made on the basis of management practices as well as costs. Conditions that favour the use of one system as opposed to the other include the following:

- **Timing of replacement inventory** – when orders must be placed or material delivered at specified intervals, a P system should be used. Weekly deliveries of items to a retail store would be an example of this condition.
- **Multiple item shipments** from the same supplier would follow a P system in order to

secure the gains of consolidating items into a single shipment and the resulting reduction in delivery and paperwork costs.

● Inexpensive items not maintained on inventory records should use a P system. Low-value items such as fasteners (for example nuts, washers and bolts) could be stocked in bins and periodically checked and replenished to a given target quantity. No records of use or receipts of inventory would be made, in keeping with the low-cost management needs of such items.

● Expensive items are best managed using a Q system that helps keep inventory to a minimum. To safeguard against stockouts, P systems require higher buffer stocks which makes them less suited to expensive items. The increase in costs associated with Q systems, and the management of higher ARV items, is justified by the greater control provided and associated lower inventory levels that result.

In practice, hybrid systems are developed with a mixture of P and Q inventory rules. One such hybrid is the optimal replenishment system. Here inventory is checked both on a quantity and time basis. Either of these factors will highlight the inventory items for review, but an order is placed only if the inventory level has reached the point where the economic order quantity would be required.

Supplementary systems and approaches

In addition to the systems described above, companies use a number of supplementary systems and approaches to manage different inventory requirements. Three of the more common requirements are now explained: managing low ARV items, seasonal demand and limited shelf-life items.

Managing low ARV items. The costs involved in managing and controlling inventory can be high. For low ARV independent and dependent items, we need systems that ensure no stockouts but are not costly to maintain. Two of the more commonly used systems that provide this low-cost requirement are now described:

● **Single-bin systems** involve filling up a shelf, bin or tank periodically. Examples are shelves in retail outlets, small-part bins in repair shops and fuel tanks in petrol or gas stations. These are examples of P systems. Individual records of receipts and usage would normally not be made. Control is provided by checking expected usage levels over a period compared to the level of purchases made during this time.

● **Two-bin systems** comprise inventory held in two bins. The one in current use is open and the second is sealed. When the first container is empty, the second is opened and this act triggers a replacement order. This is a Q system, with the quantity in the second container equal to the reorder level. As with single-bin systems, records of individual transactions are not kept, with control provided by periodic checks similar to those described for single-bin systems.

Seasonal demand. Demand patterns for many businesses have a seasonal element. As explained in Chapter 8, some companies alter capacity to meet these changing requirements. Where companies can make products in one period to sell in the next, meeting seasonal demand by using capacity-related inventory is an alternative to changing capacity levels. While the downside of using inventory is the investment and cost involved, advantages include maintaining a stable and experienced workforce and avoiding the costs of training and lower productivity levels associated with temporary staff.

Where companies use capacity-related inventory as one way to balance fluctuating demand levels, it is important for them to establish the different ratios between the staff content (# hours used) of inventory and its overall value. Calculating the ratio between inventory value and standard hour content will enable a company to elect to produce for stock those items with the most favourable ratios. In this way it will be able to absorb 'spare capacity' for the lowest inventory value increases. Exhibit 12.18 provides an example of this approach. Representative items from a company show the inventory value (column 3) and also the number of standard hours required to make the item (column 4). Dividing the inventory value by the standard hours to make an item gives the value of inventory made per standard hour used (column 5). In low-demand periods companies can then absorb the overcapacity in operations but restrict increases in inventory value. Let us look at Exhibit 12.18 to see how it works. While item E180 has a unit inventory value of £25.80, in effect it uses 6.3 standard staff hours to produce each item. Consequently its inventory/staff ratio is only £4.10/hour. On the other hand, E150 and WD162 both have unit values less than E180 at £13.50 and £18.65 respectively. However, their inventory/staff ratios are significantly higher than that for E180 at £19.30/hour and £23.30/hour respectively. Thus, using this calculation as one factor in planning inventory at times when capacity is greater than sales will enable companies to keep inventory increases to a minimum while effectively using the capacity on hand.

Exhibit 12.18 Inventory/staff hour ratios

Products		Inventory value (£s)	Staff content (standard hours)	Inventory made per standard staff hour used	Product rankings – to minimize inventory value (£) increases per standard hour of staff used	
Reference	Inventory	Per unit		£ p	WIP/ finished items	Overall
WB674		66.05	13.2	5.00	2	3
WA321		35.50	2.6	13.70	8	13
WC193		32.85	3.2	10.30	5	10
WB280		21.15	4.1	5.20	3	4
WB055	work-in-	19.00	1.4	13.60	7	12
WD162	progress	18.65	0.8	23.30	10	18
WD610		6.35	0.4	15.90	9	16
WB405		4.25	0.9	4.70	1	2
WE350		3.54	0.4	8.90	4	8
WC184		1.15	0.1	11.50	6	11
G163		150.10	10.1	14.90	7	15
D114		122.50	8.0	14.20	6	14
A195		93.75	3.2	29.30	9	19
B680		65.00	12.5	5.20	2	4
B008	finished	33.60	5.5	6.10	3	6
D710	items	28.00	2.9	9.70	5	9
E180		25.80	6.3	4.10	1	1
E150		13.50	0.7	19.30	8	17
B160		11.50	1.3	8.80	4	7
D109		6.75	0.2	33.75	10	20

Limited shelf-life items. Some products have a limited life. This could be due to the shelf life of the item itself or products that are linked to major events, for example companies designing and making products for the Olympic Games in Athens in 2004.

Inventory analysis

Inventory is an integral part of business activity. It is an asset that helps companies in the provision and sale of services and goods. Recognizing that an organization needs inventory and that this investment is costly, the more pertinent question concerns 'Is the amount of inventory necessary?'

We have already reviewed the systems and procedures from which companies choose to best meet their inventory management needs. As with all systems, these will have to be developed and improved to provide sound controls and ensure that the inventory levels are kept to a minimum, while providing the benefits and functions inherent in these investments.

To evaluate how well systems are working and highlight aspects that need to be checked, companies should also analyse inventory as part of this review process. In many businesses the recording and valuation of stock lead to statements which separate total inventory into the categories of raw materials and components, work-in-progress and finished goods. Typically this is done once or twice a year, in line with the need for the accounting function to prepare a profit and loss account and balance sheet. While this analysis meets these requirements, it provides little information useful to managing the task of evaluating inventory. The insights on inventory provided by the categories raw materials/components, work-in-progress and finished goods concern the state and position of material within the system. In other words, material has not been processed (raw materials and components), the processing of material is now complete (finished goods) or the material is somewhere between these two positions (work-in-progress). But, while this is adequate as a basis for assessing the value of inventory, it fails to provide the key insight to help manage and assess inventory levels, that is, why is it there? To provide this insight, companies need to undertake a review of inventory to determine why it is there, or what caused the inventory.

Causal analysis

It is not necessary to undertake this task at the same time for all the inventory held. Parts can be reviewed at different times and the first step is to select a portion of the inventory holding for review. Inventory is then reviewed, asking the question, why is it there? The answers are then categorized into:

- one of the many categories of corporate inventory that exist
- one of the five functions of operations inventory explained earlier.

In addition, the position of the inventory in the operations process is recorded. Position here identifies the stage through which it was last processed and the stage it is waiting to enter. Where inventory is recognized as providing more than one category or function, the value of the holding is split equally between the categories or functions provided and recorded as separate entries.

In this way a picture of inventory is developed that shows clusters of inventory by category or function and stage in the operations process. Large clusters are then checked to see why they exist. This allows the rules and procedures involved to be reviewed and modified where it is considered that such changes would still meet the relevant corporate or operations needs but would reduce the amount of inventory involved. This approach is based on the recognition that changing the rules that allow inventory to be made will reduce the level of stock entering the system, thereby lower inventory holdings.

Let us consider Case examples 12.4 and 12.5, one involving corporate and the other operations inventory.

Case example 4 REDUCING THE LEVEL OF CUSTOMER SUPPORT INVENTORY

Corporate inventory – support inventory for a customer was found to be running at the equivalent of three weeks of sales. This was due to an agreement with the customer to hold finished goods inventory at a given level. On reviewing the current position it was found that weekly sales of this item to the customer had reduced but the inventory holding had not been recalculated. Whereas the original agreement was to hold two weeks of sales, the inventory equivalent had not been recalculated to reflect this lower sales position. Discussions with the customer also included revising the agreement. The overall result was that the level of customer support inventory was reduced to one week of sales at current levels.

Case example 5 REDUCING THE LEVEL OF OPERATIONS INVENTORY

Operations inventory – a review of inventory highlighted a large cluster of inventory awaiting to enter a given process. The resulting analysis led to the purchase of an additional process, as it was found that there was insufficient capacity at this stage. The alternatives to handling this bottleneck were considered, but as the process investment costs were low, it was decided that purchasing additional equipment was the most effective solution.

Case question   1   How did causal analysis help the companies in the two examples?

Reflections

Inventory is a significant asset in most organizations. Its effective management, therefore, is a key task within the auspices of operations. But controlling inventory is far from easy and represents a challenging task. It involves a complex set of decisions due to the many forms inventory takes and the many functions it provides. In addition, inventories are the result of functional policies within an organization as well as the short- and long-term decisions in purchasing, operations and sales. There is, therefore, a need for the corporate perspectives of inventory to be exercised at the highest level as well as the detailed control systems and procedures to be used lower down in an organization. Furthermore, the all-embracing and interrelated nature of this investment necessitates that its provision and control are shared by all concerned.

The challenging task facing operations is to ensure that the amount of inventory held is necessary in terms of the functions provided. Often, particularly in the past, the level held included quantities and types which brought questionable gains. This chapter has detailed the ways in which inventory can be effectively managed and controlled. All facets provide part of the answer. As Oliver Wight's parody on John Godfrey Saxe's poem 'The blind man and the elephant' illustrates, choosing the combination that meets the needs of a situation is a key management decision:

> It was six men of management
> To learning much inclined
> Who discoursed on production control
> And the answers they did find –

From experience, and the lessons
That reward an inquiring mind.

'Order to mins and maximums',
The first was heard to say,
'You'll have neither too much nor too little
When production's controlled this way.'

'But the answer lies in the forecast',
Said the second in line,
'Just anticipate your sales,
And everything will be fine.'

'I doubt it' said the third one,
'You've forgotten the EOQ.
With balanced setups and inventories,
What problems can ensue?'

The fourth one said: 'Use order points
To get the desired control.
When you order materials soon enough,
You'll never be "in the hole"'.

'But you really need a computer.'
Said the fifth – 'PC's a dream
With loads run from last week's payroll cards
And exception reports by the ream.'

Said the sixth, 'Materials management
Is a concept to which I'm devoted –
Instead of learning production control,
I've escaped by getting promoted.'

So study each book and seminar,
Attend every one you can, sir!
You'll find a thousand experts –
Each with PART of the answer![6]

Key Elements of Managing Inventory

- Inventory is not only sizeable in asset terms but is also complex to manage and control.

- Companies wish to keep the investment as low as possible, yet inventory is an integral part of a company's activities and central to the workings of its processes and delivery systems, so must be efficiently managed and controlled.

- One overriding principle is that of distinguishing between independent and dependent demand items. As usage rates of the latter are linked to the levels of demand of the former, requirements for dependent demand items can be calculated and scheduled in line with demand for the independent items to which they relate.

- This principle of calculating requirements for dependent demand items is central to managing and controlling this type of inventory. However, it may make more sense for a company to hold inventory of some of these dependent demand items at a level that is not tied to a calculated rate of requirement. Reasons for severing this link are to do with issues of overall cost. For items that have a low unit cost (for example C items), it may lower total unit cost (price per unit plus related inventory costs) to buy in quantities that exceed demand patterns. Buying or making in large quantities will almost always lower the actual cost per unit and such items lend themselves to the use of systems such as two-bin type controls that are simple to operate and inexpensive to manage.

● The approaches to managing and controlling independent items need to reflect the several issues and dimensions that were introduced and discussed throughout the chapter. Foremost will be the choice of whether to provide services or make products on a make-to-order, assemble-to-order and make-to-stock basis.

● In make-to-order businesses, material and work-in-progress inventory will reflect the delivery dates of customer orders for the services and products provided. When finished, items will go straight to customers.

● Where items are part-made and then assembled or finished in line with customer orders and where items are made-to-stock, what and how much is made and when and how much to order need to take into account issues such as the 80/20 rule, corporate inventory commitments, reorder point, buffer inventory requirements and economic order quantities.

● The key throughout is fitting the decisions to the characteristics and requirements of an organization. Knowing the alternatives that can be used and incorporating relevant dimensions into the decision-making process should always form the basis of the management and control outcomes.

Self-check

1 The level of inventory in an organization reflects:
   a The rate of supply
   b The rate of demand
   c Both a and b

2 The underlying purpose of inventory is to:
   a Uncouple the various phases of a service delivery system or manufacturing process
   b Provide overall support for a service delivery system or manufacturing process
   c Neither of these

3 Corporate inventory is:
   a Strategic inventory to support operations
   b All forms of non-operations inventory
   c Neither of these

4 The general preferences of the finance/accounting, operations and sales functions to the level of finished goods inventory held is:
   a Low, indifferent and high, respectively
   b Indifferent, indifferent and high, respectively
   c Low, high and high, respectively

5 Using the independent/dependent demand principle means:
   a Demand for services or products with a dependent demand is forecast
   b Demand for services or products with an independent demand is calculated
   c Neither of these

6 The Pareto principle is:
   a Used to reduce inventory
   b Another name for the 80/20 rule
   c Used in calculating economic order quantities

7 Annual requirement value (ARV) is:
   a Calculated by multiplying the forecast demand for a service or product by its unit value
   b Calculated by multiplying the annual usage of a service or product by its unit value
   c Neither of these

8 If a company decided to hold additional inventory to safeguard the business from

uncertainty of overseas supply, this additional inventory would be classed as:

a Buffer inventory ☐
b Corporate inventory ☐
c Both a and b ☐

9 Special services and products can only be:

a Made to order ☐
b Assembled to order ☐

c Made to stock ☐

10 Consignment stock is:

a The quantity of a product assigned to inventory ☐
b Another name for capacity-related inventory ☐
c Inventory held on a customer's premises that is not paid for until it is used ☐

Study activities

Discussion questions

1 How does inventory contribute to the value-adding activities of a firm? When should inventory be considered a symptom of waste?

2 What types of material inventory would you find in the following businesses?
- a retail pharmacist
- a petrol station
- a coffee bar
- a stone and gravel extraction company

3 What activities add to the cost of inventory and which functions are responsible for incurring them?

4 What aspects of the delivery system in service companies need to accommodate their inability to convert capacity into inventory?

5 How realistic are the assumptions of the EOQ model? Why is this model still being used in both textbooks and businesses?

6 Describe the difference between independent and dependent demand and give two examples of each for a pizza restaurant.

7 Explain the ABC classification system and detail its advantages.

8 Referring back to Chapter 10, how does JIT influence inventory holdings?

9 Textet Computing sells software through the internet. With each purchase, the company includes a computer manual and currently it is rethinking whether it should outsource the preparation of these manuals or continue to make them in-house. Below are the cost estimates for the options:

Outsourced – total cost of £0.50p per manual
Make in-house – variable cost per manual £0.30p
– annual fixed costs of £7500

(a) Which alternative has the lower total cost if annual demand is 30,000 copies?
(b) At what annual volume do these alternatives have the same cost?
(c) Textet Computing estimates that its sales of software next year will increase to 55,000 units. The outside supplier will drop the price per manual to £0.43p on these volumes. At what quantity are the cost of making in-house and the cost of outsourcing at £0.43p equal?

10 In making reservations for services, a common approach where demand is uncertain is to 'overbook' to avoid the cost of no shows.
(a) Using a passenger airline and a good quality restaurant, discuss the pros and cons of this approach.
(b) How ethical is this practice?

11 Some top restaurants part-prepare some food (for example desserts and vegetables) ahead of time. How is this both an example of assemble-to-order and the use of capacity-related inventory?

Assignments

1 Choose one service and one manufacturing company and extract the following information from their latest balance sheet:
- inventory or stock

- each category of fixed assets
- total fixed assets

Compare your findings to the observations made in the early part of this chapter.

2 What difficulties are, in general, forced on service organizations as a result of their inability to inventory their capacity?

3 How do organizations attempt to manage the difficulties identified in Question 2? Illustrate your answer using the following businesses:
- sandwich bar
- passenger airline
- bank
- call centre

Following your analysis, compare and contrast the approaches you identified.

Exploring further

Abernathy, FH, Dunlop, JT, Hammond, JH and Well, D 'Control your inventory in a world of lean retailing', *Harvard Business Review*, **78**(6) (2000) pp. 169–76.

Arnold, D 'Seven rules of international distribution', *Harvard Business Review*, **78**(6) (2000) pp. 131–37.

Bernard, P *Integrated Inventory Management*, Oliver Wight Manufacturing Services, Wiley, Chichester (1999).

Bowers, MR and Agarwal, A 'Lower in-process inventories and better on-time performance at Tanner Companies Inc.', *Interfaces* **25**(4) (1995) pp. 30–43.

Coleman, BJ 'Determining the correct service level target', *Production and Inventory Management Journal* **41**(1) (2000) pp. 19–23.

Donath, R, Mazel, J and Dubin, C *The Ioma Handbook of Logistics and Inventory*, Wiley, Chichester (2002).

Flores, BE and Whybark, DC 'Implementing multiple criteria ABC analysis', *Journal of Operations Management* **7**(1–2) (1987) pp. 79–85.

Noblitt, JM 'The economic order quantity model: panacea or plague?', *APICS – The Performance Advantage*, February (2001) pp. 53–7.

Reid, RA 'The ABC method in hospital inventory management: a practical approach', *Production and Inventory Management Journal* 4th quarter (1987) pp. 67–70.

Vollman, TE, Berry, WL, Whybark, DC and Jacobs, R *Manufacturing Planning and Control Systems*, 5th edn, Irwin/McGraw-Hill, Burr Ridge, IL (2004).

Wild, T *Best Practices in Inventory Management*, Butterworth Heinemann, Oxford (2002).

Notes and references

1 In 1906, Vilfredo Pareto observed that a few items in any group contribute the significant proportion of the entire group. At the time he was concerned that a few people in a country earned most of the income. The law of the significant few can be applied in many areas, including inventory. See Pareto, V *Manual of Political Economy*, Kelley Augustus, Fairfield, NJ (1969).

2 The 80/20 relationship implied in the rule is only intended as an indication of the size of the actual figures involved, as shown in Exhibit 12.10.

3 The limitations of the EOQ model are further discussed in Schönenberger, RJ and Knod, EM *Operations Management and Continuous Improvement*, 5th edn, Irwin, Burr Ridge, IL (1994).

4 Special services and products are ones that will not be repeated or the time gap between one order and the next is so long that investments (including inventory holding) will not be made.

5 Consignment stock is inventory held at a customer's site but not invoiced until used. The customer houses and manages the physical inventory but the responsibility for replenishing what is used remains with the supplier.

6 Plossl, GW and Wight, OW *Production and Inventory Control: Principles and Techniques,* Prentice Hall, Englewood Cliffs, NJ (1967), p. 190.

book map

Part

1
- 1 Managing Operations
- 2 Operations Strategy
- 3 Managing People

2

PROCESSES

INPUTS — **SUPPLIERS**

OUTPUTS

CUSTOMERS

- 4 Designing and Developing Services & Products
- 5 Designing Service Delivery Systems
- 6 Designing Manufacturing Processes
- 7 Location and Layout
- 8 Managing Capacity
- 9 Technology Developments
- 10 Operations Scheduling and Execution
- 11 Managing Quality

3
- 12 Managing Inventory
- 13 Managing the Supply Chain

4
- 14 Process and Delivery System Reliability and Maintenance
- 15 Time and Productivity
- 16 Improving Operations

5
- Managing Operations in Practice: Long Case Studies

Managing the Supply Chain

Outline of chapter

Whether elements of a supply chain are internal or external to an organization, operations needs to manage and coordinate the parts in order to provide services and products while meeting the order-winners and qualifiers within relevant markets.

Why is managing the supply chain important?

Executive overview

Companies rarely, if ever, own the resources and activities to provide a service or make a product from start to finish, including delivery to customers. Consequently, what to provide or make internally and what to buy are key operations management decisions. Furthermore, whether a company makes or buys an element of the eventual service or product it sells, it needs to manage effectively the internal and external phases of the supply chain, both in terms of parts and as an integrated whole.

Increasingly, businesses must recognize that they are at the centre of networks of materials and information flows. These flows extend from the customer interface through operations to the building of relationships with suppliers. The operations role, however, is not just the integration and management of the parts of the supply chain but also the constant reviewing and alignment of these closely linked networks to better meet the changing needs of its markets and help achieve the sales revenue and profit goals of the organization. This chapter addresses these tasks and in particular covers the following:

- The question, what is a supply chain? is addressed to provide clarity for you regarding the aspects covered in the chapter.

- Managing the supply chain and what is entailed is overviewed and the synchronization of the business dimensions involved is explained.

- To make or buy and the reasons for making these choices are discussed in detail. This section also explains why these decisions are often made in practice, together with a comprehensive review of the advantages and disadvantages of these alternatives.

- The decision to buy also requires the choice between domestic or offshore sourcing options. This section addresses the key issues to be taken into account when addressing this issue.

- Other options to making or buying are introduced, including joint ventures and non-equity-based collaborative arrangements.

- The section on managing the supply chain gives a detailed review of the issues involved such as the impact of globalization, the need to incorporate uncertainty and different types of supplier relationship developments.

- The origin and evolution of supply chains introduce the section on developing supply chains. This section also highlights the changes that need to be embraced by managers to secure these important developments. These include effective consumer response, the increasing use of IT, the impact of e-commerce and strategic partnering.

- Within supply chain management developments sits the role of e-procurement

> that extends electronic applications into the wide range of indirect goods and services bought by staff at all levels in an organization.
>
> - The section on process tools to help in managing supply chains highlights sourcing as a core task and how to develop the supplier base including supplier selection.
>
> - Distribution and transportation systems reviews the alternatives of rail, road, air freight, water and pipelines.

What is a supply chain?

If you reflect on any purchase that you make, there will be a series of steps between the origin of the service or product in question and your use or consumption of it. The series of steps involved are known as supply chains. Organizations will undertake some of these steps themselves while buying in earlier steps in the form of materials and services and contracting other organizations to undertake the later stages, for example distribution to the end-user in a retail outlet. Exhibit 13.1 provides an overview of a supply chain for a sandwich bar and a company making consumer products. As you can imagine, there will be a varying number of tiers of suppliers and customers, depending on the complexity of the service or product, and a varying number of suppliers and customers in each tier, reflecting not only the complexity factor but also how much of a service or product was provided in the internal operations phase and how much was bought in from outside. This constitutes the make-or-buy decision, a factor discussed in a later section.

Most of the book is concerned with managing the internal operations process that transforms inputs into outputs (see Exhibit 1.1 and the examples given in Exhibit 1.2), while this chapter concerns managing those parts of a supply chain at each end of the internal operations process.

Supply chain management

The challenges of managing the supply chain are considerable. It requires a shift away from traditional functional organizational models towards managing a set of integrated processes that encompass several key facets of a business, as illustrated in Exhibit 13.2.

Developments need to be made based on a vision of the entire supply chain that, in turn, must reflect a company's markets as well as the efficient organization and management of all parts of the chain itself. By developing integrated supply chains, companies are able to respond to the opportunities and competitive pressures that increasingly characterize the markets in which they compete. In essence this involves:

- collaboration throughout the supply chain by exchanging information to ensure end-users' needs are met
- moving more from a supply chain to a demand chain
- competing as a supply chain rather than as an individual organization.

Exhibit 13.1 Supply chain for a high street sandwich bar and a manufacturer of consumer goods

SUPPLY CHAIN FOR A SANDWICH BAR

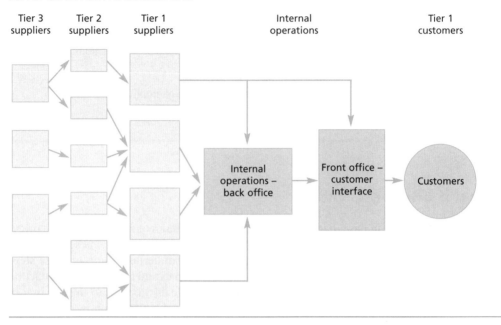

SUPPLY CHAIN FOR A MANUFACTURER OF CONSUMER GOODS

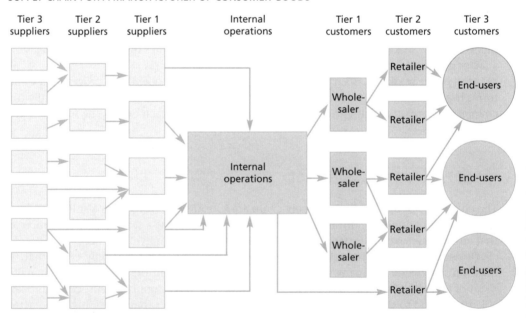

Note   The above diagrams are not to scale and the number of customers and suppliers are illustrative.

However, before proceeding any further on the issues that are central to the effective management of supply chains, we need first to look at the reasons for choosing whether to make or buy.

Exhibit 13.2 Managing the supply chain and synchronizing the business dimensions involved

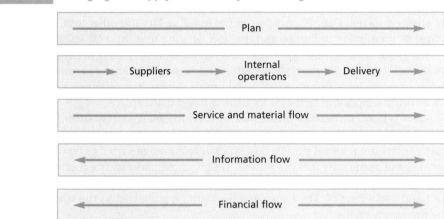

Exhibit 13.2 Managing the supply chain and synchronizing the business dimensions involved

The make-or-buy decision

Although in theory every service or product can be provided internally or bought from outside, in reality the choice is far more restricted. In many instances, organizations have no alternative other than to outsource materials, components, products or services because they lack the in-house technical capability or because of the unjustifiably high levels of investment that would be involved. This section discusses the factors to be considered when deciding whether to make or buy and provides examples to illustrate decisions.

Retaining the core technologies of the business

Most companies choose to keep in-house those processes that represent the core elements of their business. For example, companies that make their own products will invariably retain in-house the assembly-onward end of the production process. Similarly, many service firms wish to retain the process that constitutes the ultimate link with customers. For example, in the late 1990s NatWest Bank considered whether or not to subcontract the service processing end of the retail and corporate banking sectors (for example voucher and cheque processing and account management). In the past these back-office activities had always been an integral part of the in-house banking service, but now options to subcontract were available. In the end, NatWest decided to retain these activities in-house, because they provided a direct link with its customers – an essential element of the banking service. Similarly, Fidelity, one of the world's largest fundraisers, regards most of its administrative systems as part of its core business. Consequently, it has invested in systems technology for decades and will continue to do so.

Strategy considerations

Make-or-buy decisions need to be made within the strategic context of a business. The order-winners and qualifiers (for example price, delivery reliability, delivery speed and quality conformance) that relate to a company's markets and are affected by make-or-buy decisions need to be reflected in such decisions and their outcomes. For example, Dell Computer Corporation developed the capability to assemble PCs quickly in response to customers' orders, but found that this potentially competitive dimension was constrained by component suppliers' long lead times. However, other companies, alert to key market-related issues, incorporate these issues into their make-or-buy and sourcing decisions. For example, Lego, the privately owned Danish manufacturer of building kits and other toys, has for years concentrated its production in Europe and the USA, arguing that this best satisfies its design and quality conformance requirements. And Lego is not alone in basing decisions on strategic rather than cost factors, for example Benetton's decision not to source garments in Southeast Asia but to retain local suppliers that would meet the fast response needs of its supply chain was a critical supporting factor for its fashion-based marketplace.

A key factor is how current and future positions on the make-or-buy continuum impact the ability of operations to support those market criteria for which it is responsible. Similarly, issues concerning relevant process and product technologies need to be considered.

Whether or not a company makes in-house, supply chain performance regarding relevant order-winners and qualifiers will directly impact a company's ability to retain customers, grow share and make money. The issues involved will be addressed in the later section on managing the supply chain.

Impact of service, product and process technologies on span of process

The earlier sections highlighted situations where companies retained relevant service, product or process technologies. In cases where there is a significant increase in a related service or product technology, the very opposite can happen. Where a company applies new technology developments to its existing services or products or to the introduction of new, if similar, services or products into its current range, it may find itself without the in-house capability to meet all the new and more complex technology requirements. The result is that it buys in the technology in the form of components or materials for products and the expertise in the form of customer or information processing for services.

For example, the drive in the US for fund managers to improve their trade settlements from T+3 (trade date plus 3 days) to T+1 by 2005 presents big IT upgrades, resulting in a flurry of outsourcing deals. Similarly, the spate of mergers and acquisitions in the financial services sector in the late 1990s resulted in outmoded, mismatching technologies. The need to integrate these disparate, legacy IT systems has led to companies outsourcing these systems. For example, Pimco, the US fund manager, and UK-based Scottish Widows Investment Partners use an outsourcing platform from State Street, a US provider.

Service and product volumes

Companies faced with sets of demands for services and products that have different volume levels may consider buying out one set of demands for which it may not wish to develop the in-house process. Examples of this include a manufacturer of engine parts for agricultural and diesel trucks. When the low volume spares demand in a product's life cycle was reached, the company increasingly outsourced the components involved. Similarly, an upmarket ladies' clothes outlet undertakes internally any minor garment change for a customer, whereas more complex modifications are sourced from outside specialists.

The globalization of world trade

Trade barriers across much of the world have declined sharply. It is estimated, for example, that the average tariff by 1998 stood at 6 per cent or just over one-sixth of the level in 1960. This has made global manufacturing more commercially feasible. One outcome is the reduced need for many overseas plants. Markets that previously demanded local production facilities because of high tariff levels can now be supplied by imports. A good example of this is the Australian automotive sector. In the eighteen years to 2005, tariffs on imported cars dropped from 57.5 to 10 per cent, while imported cars rose from 15 to about 70 per cent of the market.[1] Domestic car plants (for example Nissan) have already started to close.

The reality of make-or-buy decisions

The previous sections identified some of the principal reasons that may form the basis of make-or-buy decisions. In reality, many companies approach this critical task and base the strategic decision involved on reasons that are less rational and seldom sound. The more common of these are now discussed.

History – continuing yesterday's decisions

Make-or-buy decisions taken at one moment in time are often not reconsidered at a later date. Inertia, a reluctance to add additional executive tasks and avoiding possible short-term problems militate against taking appropriate reviews. Once made, make-or-buy decisions often remain unchallenged.

The dominance of cost and technology arguments

The format used to address the question whether to make or buy is typically centred on the issues of technology and cost. The initial consideration is whether or not a company has the technical capability to deliver part of or the whole service or make a component or product. Where the necessary competence is not already in-house, the automatic response is often to buy from outside.

Where process technology is not a barrier, the next consideration is the cost of provision. While a most important dimension in itself, a make-or-buy decision taken without considering the requirements of markets and corresponding order-winners and qualifiers, such as delivery speed, quality conformance, ability to ramp up and delivery on time, will lead to inappropriate conclusions and have a potentially damaging impact on a firm's short-term, let alone long-term, strategic position. Organizations addressing such decisions need to embrace a range of issues and often arrive at different conclusions, as Case example 13.1 illustrates.

Case example 1   STRATEGIC OUTSOURCING DECISIONS

When an organization decides to deal with some of its customers by telephone, fax or email rather than face to face or by post, one of the first questions it needs to address is should we do it ourselves or get someone else to do it for us?

Why should companies want to hand over something as important as customer relations to outsiders? And, if they do, where, in turn, would the outsourced facility best be located?

The dominant reason for outsourcing is cost. Companies specializing in outsourced call centre provision cumulate greater volumes and also find it easier to ramp staff capacity levels up and down. It is no surprise that the areas chosen by companies within their own countries are in places where wages are relatively low and alternative work is difficult to come by. In the US they tend to be in a group of midwestern states running from Arizona and New Mexico to Utah and the Dakotas. In Europe the choice is based on similar criteria, with companies often also using the proximity to large groups of university students as a factor in where best to site their centres. But for many companies the preferred choice is in a developing country such as the Philippines, Costa Rica or India.

Despite being more expensive, some companies prefer to set up and run their own call centres. Capital One, the US credit card company, outsources only a few specialized parts of its service, such as revenue collection from customers who have fallen a long way behind in payments. The reason is that Capital One sees managing its customers as a competitive advantage.

Delta also provide another exception to the rule. The US airline decided to build its European customer reservation centre in London. Labour costs are high and competition for staff is fierce but Delta believes that the advantage of access to staff speaking a wide range of languages makes it worthwhile.

www.capitalone.com; www.delta.com

Case questions
1 Why are most companies subcontracting call centre facilities?
2 What reasons would make a company elect to set up and manage its own call centre?

Advantages and disadvantages of making and buying

The previous sections introduced some of the important perspectives, issues and context concerning make-or-buy decisions. These next sections outline the benefits of making or delivering internally and also the advantages and disadvantages of outsourcing.

Benefits of vertical integration or providing or making more in-house

All make-or-buy decisions bring a mix of internal or external benefits and costs. In particular, decisions on vertical integration (or making or providing more in-house) offer a company a number of inherent competitive advantages that are linked to increased knowledge of markets and technology, improved control over its environment and increased opportunity to support the characteristics of its markets. These include:

- Improved market intelligence – this increases a company's ability to forecast more accurately trends concerning key aspects of a business from demand patterns to cost changes.

- More readily available technological innovations and options – this enables companies to share technology initiatives, increases opportunities for collaboration and facilitates the transfer of experience within the one organization or between groups of companies.

- Increased control over relevant aspects of a firm's competitive environment – these opportunities can take the form of backward integration to reduce dependency on suppliers and forward integration to help gain market penetration or acceptance.

- The provision of low-cost opportunities – this is accomplished by generating internal demand and thereby contributing to high volume requirements and their associated low-cost potential. Japanese companies such as Fijitsu, Hitachi, Mitsubishi, NEC and Toshiba have progressively outcompeted their competitors (particularly their US rivals) partly through the high level of integration that characterizes their businesses. The highly integrated Japanese semiconductor manufacturers are able to make their products at substantially lower costs than their competitors elsewhere in the world. One key reason for this is the high volume base created by internal corporate demand. These giant Japanese zaibatsus make semiconductors along with everything else. The result is that Japan currently has 50 per cent of the world semiconductor market.

Benefits of outsourcing

On the flip side of this key decision are the benefits to be gained from outsourcing. These primarily concern cash, costs and technology and include the following:

- Freed resources – buy decisions reduce or more often eliminate the associated resources necessary to provide the service, component, subassembly, final assembly or technical capability involved. One result is that resources are freed, making funds available to be used elsewhere in a business.

- Reduced operating costs – with less being made internally, the process technology requirements and associated support are reduced, together with the management and control tasks that accompany operations.

- Easier to control costs – with buy decisions, the dimension of cost control is simplified to one of a supplier's unit price. Although contract negotiations demand their own set of skills, the task of cost control for the services, materials, components, subassemblies or assemblies involved is, in itself, simplified.

- Superior design – suppliers can often provide superior designs or improved specification of services than organizations can using their own internal resources. Examples include car radio specialists and bakers supplying rolls and croissants to restaurants.

- Market perception of sound design – purchasing from suppliers renowned for providing high specification items can lead customers into attributing a similar view of high specification levels to a company's own services and products. For example, microcomputer users purchase small manufacturers' products in part based on the knowledge that they are assembled using components from the world's best suppliers such as Intel and Sony.

- Access to capacity – meeting demand surges or known peaks in demand within certain markets is often made easier by being able to access suppliers' capacity. Within limits, companies can use suppliers' operations processes and other elements of their supply chains as alternatives to holding excess capacity, increasing capacity in the short term through overtime working and carrying inventory.

- Up-to-date technology – where a supplier's specialist capacities are accompanied by high volumes, investment in more recent technologies and operations capabilities is justified. Conversely, suppliers' customers will also reduce the risk of having underused technical investments and being exposed to the likelihood of out-of-date technologies.

- Access to world-class capabilities – purchasing from selected vendors creates the opportunity to source from potentially world-class capabilities. It gives access to the technologies and expertise that make up a supplier's business.

- Increased focus on own core tasks – the reverse side of the last point, it allows a company to increase its attention, in terms of development time and investment, on its own primary business and associated core tasks.

Disadvantages of outsourcing

To some extent the disadvantages of outsourcing are the inverse of the benefits discussed in the last section and include:

- Loss of control – outsourcing brings with it the possibility of losing control of key capabilities. For example, dimensions such as quality conformance, delivery speed and delivery reliability are now, in part, within the processes and systems of suppliers. An underlying fear is losing control by being locked into a deal over the provision of activities that are going wrong and need putting right.

- Increased vulnerability – the loss of control factor may, at the extreme, lead to a company becoming commercially vulnerable through supplier failure. As single sourcing is the desired norm in some sectors (for example the motor industry; see Case example 10.2), in order to reduce investment and maximize the gains from cooperation, or is the only practical option (for example the provision of back-office and middle-office activities in the financial services sector), then companies may become vulnerable.

Case example 2   LAND ROVER'S SINGLE SOURCING POLICY

When UPF-Thompson, the sole supplier of chassis frames for Land Rover's Discovery model, which accounts for about a third of the company's sales revenue, went bankrupt, critics pointed to the fact that Land Rover should never have relied on a single source for such a crucial component. KPMG, the receivers brought in to run the troubled supplier, poured fat on the fire by demanding that Land Rover should pay off UPF's debt of £50 million to guarantee a 12-month supply of chassis. In early 2002, Land Rover won a High Court injunction to guarantee supply until May that year.

For Land Rover and most of the motor industry, single sourcing is now accepted as normal. In fact, more than 90 per cent of Land Rover's components are bought from single suppliers. The single most important reason is to reduce invest-

ment in tooling and equipment – the Land Rover chassis frame alone amounted to £12 million. Moreover, the security of dual sourcing is apparent, not real. The principles of lean manufacturing, favoured by companies, governments, industry bodies, consultants and academics, mean that idling reserve capacity is kept to a minimum. So even if one supplier goes down, others can't pick up the volume.

Land Rover and KPMG came to a compromise but the increased risk of being vulnerable to supplier failure is in the air and, with 900 supply contracts (with more than 500 in the UK) to handle, Land Rover, as with many companies, is more exposed than it was a decade ago.

www.landrover.com
www.kpmg.com

Case questions   1   Comment on KPMG's role in this dispute with Land Rover.

2   What would you advise Land Rover to do in general about its single sourcing policy?

- **Intellectual property** – outsourcing increases the risk of key intellectual property and ideas being exposed to outside organizations. Although patents can be used to protect ideas and developments, the potential risk remains.

- **Reversibility** – the decision to subcontract is invariably irreversible. This is partly due to a reluctance to reconsider and then change direction on previous outsourcing decisions, coupled with the stepped nature of such a change in terms of buying in technical capability and expertise from a zero base.

- **New management skills** – managing a supply chain requires different, and often more demanding, skills than those needed to handle the in-house operations process. Often, and particularly in the past, purchasing and related functions within a business have been allocated Cinderella status, with corresponding levels of resource and management talent. Integrating the essential links within a supply network requires skills of a high order to secure the essential contribution of meeting the needs of a firm's markets.

Domestic vs offshore sourcing options and strategic fit

Companies across all sectors are taking advantage of lower priced goods and services offered by offshore suppliers. The advantage of lower labour costs means that they are able to undercut domestic competitors. But, outsourcing decisions include an offshore as well as a domestic option. So, what are the trade-offs involved in this choice, particularly regarding strategic fit?

Recent research on retail companies in North America and the UK and the sourcing of goods from both domestic and overseas suppliers highlighted many of the trade-offs involved.[2] As the results in Exhibits 13.3 and 13.4 show, not only does the domestic vs offshore alternative differ but so does the offshore region involved. The trade-off between high discounts and low latitude for change is clearly evident for Central American and Asian suppliers versus alternatives. As the whole supply chain needs to support the needs of a company's chosen market, both the external and internal phases of the chain need to support the relevant order-winners and qualifiers of these markets, the concept of strategic fit.

Exhibit 13.3 Sourcing location, percentage of goods purchased and discounts available

Retailer	Percentage of goods purchased over 12 months by location						
	Asia	Africa	Central America	Europe	North America	UK	Other
North America	20	3	24	1	52	0	0
Average discount (%) available	20–30	10–15	20–25	5–10	0	–	–
UK	36	2	0	24	3	34	1
Average discount (%) available	25–35	15–20	–	10–15	1–5	0	5–10

Source Based on Lowson, RH 'Offshore sourcing: an optimal operational strategy?', *Business Horizons*, November–December (2001), pp. 61–6.

Exhibit 13.4 Suppliers' latitude for volume or mix change before and during the sales season, by geographical region[2]

Relative to start of the sales season	Sourcing region	Supplier latitude for change once order is placed					
		Order volume change (%)			Order mix change (%)		
		None	Some	Substantial	None	Some	Substantial
Before	Asia	66	22	12	70	19	11
	Africa	58	19	23	62	20	18
	Central America	41	38	21	46	34	20
	Europe	29	43	28	37	38	25
	North America	16	49	35	21	49	30
	UK	9	52	39	21	46	33
	Other	34	40	26	30	37	33
After	Asia	70	21	9	86	12	2
	Africa	66	16	18	73	8	19
	Central America	52	33	15	63	30	7
	Europe	35	38	27	41	35	24
	North America	39	33	28	47	29	24
	UK	19	46	35	28	39	33
	Other	32	42	26	39	37	24

Source Based on Lowson, RH 'Offshore sourcing: an optimal operational strategy?', *Business Horizons*, November–December (2001), pp. 61–6.

Case example 3   **CREATING A POSITIVE RETAILER EXPERIENCE AT FENDER INTERNATIONAL**

Fender International, the US-based manufacturer of world-famous electric guitars such as the Stratocaster, Telecaster and precision base, set an objective to double market share in Europe, the Middle East and Africa. Part of its strategy to achieve this was to commit to a 'positive retailer experience', which included a condition that when a retailer took a guitar out of its box it must be playable. Whereas this requirement was already being met in the USA, the distribution networks and multi-carrier deliveries to 22 countries in Europe and a further 10 in the Middle East and Africa seemed an insurmountable obstacle. Discussions between Fender International and UPS Worldwide Logistics overcame all that. Operations are now centred in the UPS European Distribution Centre at Roer-

mond in the Netherlands, where Fender guitars are received from manufacturing sites around the world and then tuned up by professional and amateur musicians prior to final distribution. All guitars, from standard models to some of the most expensive and elite guitars in the world, are now inspected by players before being sent to customers. UPS also handles the return of damaged guitars for repair and the central facility manages inventory for the whole region. This has led to lower inventories in the whole supply chain, shorter distribution lead times and enabled Fender to get closer to distributors, retailers and customers. One unexpected outcome is that many distributors are ordering products that they never ordered before.

www.fender.com

Case questions   1   What was the significance for Fender International of the guitar tuning provision offered by UPS?
2   Why do you think distributors are now ordering products that they never ordered before?

Alternatives to the make-or-buy option

The discussion so far has implied that the choices on offer to companies must involve an ownership or non-ownership option – either organizations invest in operations capabilities or they outsource their requirements. However, where greater control is considered necessary, companies should include the following alternatives in their list of options: joint ventures, co-sourcing and non-equity-based collaboration.

Joint ventures

Companies often have to exploit opportunities, particularly in areas such as applied technology and research. Where two or more organizations have similar needs and can benefit from combining, a joint venture is a sensible alternative.

Joint ventures are separate entities sponsored by two or more actively involved organizations. Because joint ventures draw on the strengths of their owners, they have the potential to tap into the synergy in such a relationship and the improved competitive abilities that should accrue. Since the late 1970s, the number of joint ventures has increased substantially, particularly in the communication systems, IT and service sectors. As Exhibit 13.5 shows, most companies see joint ventures as a viable alternative and one that, in most businesses, will increase.

Joint ventures should not be seen or used as a convenient means of hiding weaknesses. If used prudently, such ventures can create internal strengths. They can be resource-aggregating and resource-sharing mechanisms, allowing sponsoring firms to concentrate resources where they possess the greatest strengths. Exhibit 13.6 provides a list of reasons for forming joint ventures that have been classified into operational and strategic advantages. As you will see, joint ventures not only share investment but can provide direction and help create fresh opportunities.

Exhibit 13.5 Responses to the question 'Are joint ventures a viable alternative?'

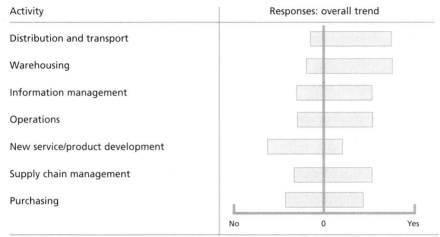

Activity	Responses: overall trend
Distribution and transport	
Warehousing	
Information management	
Operations	
New service/product development	
Supply chain management	
Purchasing	

No   0   Yes

Source PricewaterhouseCoopers 'Shaping the value chain for outstanding performance: meeting the challenge of global supply chains' (1998), p. 6.

Exhibit 13.6 Reasons for forming joint ventures

	Advantages

Strategic	● Strengthen current strategic position:
	  – pioneer developments into new segments
	  – rationalize existing segments
	
	● Pre-empt competitors:
	  – facilitate access to new markets and customers
	  – support market share growth
	  – gain access to global markets
	
	● Augment current strategic position:
	  – create and develop synergies
	  – technology and skill transfers
	
	● Widen service/product range

Operational	● Share investment and risk
	
	● Process capacity sharing:
	  – increased utilization
	  – avoids process/skill duplication
	
	● Share facilities in other parts of the supply chain, for example distribution channels and outlets
	
	● Increase technological know-how by:
	  – facilitating information exchange
	  – potentially creating critical mass in areas such as research and development
	  – broadening expertise, for example in IT systems
	
	● Help retain key staff:
	  – increased job scope
	  – improved job opportunities

Source Developed from Harrigan, KR 'Managing joint ventures – Part I', *Management Review*, February (1987), p. 29.

Co-sourcing

Similar to a joint venture, co-sourcing (also referred to as an industry utility) is where a company brings in one or more competitors together with a specialist outsourcing company. In 2002, one of the largest deals saw Barclays and Lloyds TSB (the UK's third and fourth largest banks respectively) pool their cheque processing into a new company controlled by Unisys, the US consultancy. The new company, in which the two banks each have a 24.5 per cent stake, expects £500 million of revenues during the next 10 years and will compete for business with other banks. Most banks are reluctant to outsource due to concerns of handing their skills to rivals or specialist companies that would sell them to rivals. But banks have been forced to respond to global competition and co-sourcing is one alternative.

Non-equity-based collaboration

Companies unwilling or unable to cope with joint venture arrangements can resort to an appropriate form of non-equity-based collaboration to meet their needs. These collaborations provide the means of establishing cooperative working arrangements that need a long-term base if the collaboration is to yield meaningful and useful results. Such arrangements include:

- Research and development consortia to enhance innovation and exploit results.
- Cross-marketing arrangements to provide opportunities such as widening service or product offerings and sharing distribution channels.
- Cross-operations agreements to share capacity especially in peak demand times, provide vertical integration opportunities and transfer technical know-how in areas such as IT systems.
- Joint purchasing activities to enhance buying power.
- Joint provision of other support facilities including staff and executive development and recruitment.

Managing the supply chain

The make-or-buy decision is not only critical in itself but it also governs the nature of the supply chain and the resulting management tasks. Whether a company makes or buys, the need to effectively manage the whole supply chain has increasingly been recognized as a key executive role and one that directly impacts a company's ability to compete in its chosen markets.

The concept of a totally integrated supply chain – from material producer through to end-customer – is bringing great changes to the way businesses operate. Increasingly, a company no longer competes as an individual organization, but rather as a supply chain. To bring this about companies need a supply chain that is managed as an integrated whole to secure maximum support for the competitive factors in their markets and is underpinned by responsive and adaptive systems and procedures. In turn, this requires meaningful collaboration and fuller relationships to provide the essential basis for cooperation and joint developments. As Case example 13.4 illustrates, this may lead to a fundamental rethink of an organization's objectives, structure and style.

Case example 4   CHIQUITA RELOCATES FROM CINCINNATI TO COSTA RICA

In 2004, Chiquita, the global food company, moved its main division's purchasing team from the US to Costa Rica in order to forge closer links with its fruit-growing producers. Chiquita Fresh (one of the world's largest banana producers) transferred its 20-strong procurement team from Ohio, plus several staff from the US head office in Cincinnati, to San José, one of its seven Latin American export locations. As well as procurement skills, buyers must also speak Spanish and understand local cultures.

The move was part of a wider initiative to integrate

procurement, which had previously been seen as a support function, within the wider supply chain operation. The relocation provided the opportunity for procurement specialists to provide direct, on-the-spot support to the people who buy fresh fruit for its world markets – more than half of Chiquita's products are sold in Europe.

The company is also stepping up its corporate social responsibility policy by getting its materials and services suppliers to adhere to its own code of conduct in all future contracts.

www.chiquita.com

Case questions   1 Why did Chiquita move its main division's purchasing team to Costa Rica?
2 What opportunities did the relocation offer?

Supply chain management issues

In the 1980s, companies turned their attention to fixing their operations problems, but few addressed total supply chain costs and other dimensions such as lead times. By the early 1990s, firms started to realize the need to shift emphasis. With shortening service and product life cycles, more customer choice and reducing lead times set within the context of growing world competition, it became essential to review the supply chain as a whole, identify opportunities and manage these improvements. As most companies expect outsourcing

Exhibit 13.7 Outsourcing in the supply chain continues to grow

KEY:
Now
Within 5 years

Source Based on PricewaterhouseCoopers 'Shaping the value chain for outstanding performance: meeting the challenge of global supply chains' (1998), p. 6.

to increase in future years (see Exhibit 13.7), the need to manage the supply chain effectively has to be high on the corporate agenda. Whether you make or buy, the responsibility for managing the whole chain can no longer be ignored. Some of the key management issues involved are now discussed – not quite Mr James' idea! (see Exhibit 13.8).

Exhibit 13.8 Why Mr James wants to outsource the customer service call centre!

Globalization

With trade barriers easing, markets opening up and technology developments facilitating access to markets, the globalization of business activity has accelerated. Two key issues result from this – a widening choice of suppliers and the need to manage the global supply chain that emerges.

The growing manufacturing base of regions and countries such as Eastern Europe, China and other parts of Southeast Asia, Mexico and South America has received high exposure. Similarly, the growing IT capability of countries such as India and the availability of satellite communications allows the outsourcing of data processing and computer programming even where meeting short lead times is essential.

There is an increasing emphasis on global capability. In order to take full advantage of this opportunity, companies need to manage the processes and interfaces involved. It is essential to avoid the scenario of gaining advantage in one phase of a supply chain and losing the benefits in the next. Key to this is globalizing total customer relations from design through logistics to the end-user.

Incorporating uncertainty

Today's markets are characterized by shortening service and product life cycles and stiffening requirements for all aspects of customer service. Against this background, large companies are characterized by complexity, as shown by the different markets they serve, the ever-widening service or product range provided and the multiple suppliers of services, materials and parts.

The real management problem within this complex network is, however, the uncertainty that characterizes it. But many companies still treat this task as if it were predictable. The planning and scheduling systems inadequately incorporate demand uncertainty. They are designed as if certainty rather than uncertainty was the reality with which they had to cope, and, as today is increasingly less predictable than in the past, this leads to situations of unnecessary inventory and high obsolescence. To illustrate, data on the percentage of markdowns within US department and speciality stores is given in Exhibit 13.9. The levels since 1970 have risen dramatically.

Exhibit 13.9 Rising level of markdowns in the retail sector

Year	US department store markdowns as a percentage of dollar sales
1970	8
1989	17
1997	20

Source Financial and operating results of department and speciality stores, National Retail Federation (USA).

Furthermore, all this is in the context, on the one hand, of IT developments such as electronic point-of-sale (EPOS) scanners that provide up-to-the-minute data on customer buying patterns and, on the other hand, manufacturing improvements concerning the production of smaller order sizes; while the drive to meet customer requirements has typically widened service/product ranges dramatically, even in industries that traditionally have not been considered fashion-driven. For example, the annual number of new product introductions in the US food industry rose from some 2000 in 1980 to over 20,000 in the late 1990s.

But new service or product introductions have two adverse side effects:

- Average life cycles are reduced which shortens the relative duration of the more stable phase of demand in relation to the less certain initial and end phases.

- Total demand is spread over more stock-keeping units (SKUs), leading to increased difficulty in forecasting sales for a larger number of items. (Stock-keeping unit is the phrase used for all services and products that have a different code number in a company's system.)

Overall the result is growing unpredictability that increases the need to manage each phase of the supply chain and the interface between them. As highlighted earlier, Dell Computer Corporation, having shortened its own assembly lead times in response to the delivery speed requirements of its customers, found itself constrained by the long lead time of its component suppliers.

Types of supplier relationships

The relationship between customers and suppliers is influenced by the level of dependency of one with the other – see Exhibit 13.10.

Part of the make-or-buy decision is how best to structure relationships with suppliers. Customers can position themselves in a number of ways within the constraints of dimensions such as the 'dependency factor'. Characteristics of these different types of supplier relationships are now reviewed.[3] Which one a company should choose needs to reflect the characteristics of the services, materials or components involved and the marketplace in which a company operates:

- Trawling the market – here suppliers are held at arm's length, with a growing amount of business completed using computerized interaction. For example, General Electric (GE) in the USA is increasingly purchasing more components over the internet where it posts details of

Exhibit 13.10 Customer/supplier dependence

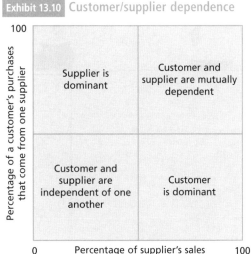

parts electronically and prequalified vendors then quote for the contract. Within these internet auctions there is little face-to-face interaction and the key order-winner is price. Delivery on time and quality conformance are qualifiers and form part of the listing prerequisites. Gains also include reduced processing costs, for example GE quotes a 90 per cent reduction using this method of purchasing compared to traditional paperwork procedures. This approach is appropriate for commodities rather than value-added purchases critical to resaleable goods and services. In fact, this phase may well entail placing a significant amount of business with competitors.

- Ongoing relationships – these involve establishing medium-term contracts with suppliers, developing relations in terms of information sharing and require sound management by customers.

- Partnerships – involve long-term contracts characterized by the extensive sharing of information and increased trust. For example, since 1988 the average contract length between US auto makers and their suppliers has more than doubled.

- Strategic alliances – the trend in sourcing is towards strategic alliances that are characterized by the increased depth and breadth of the whole customer/supplier relationship. A prerequisite of more cooperative relationships is a dramatic reduction in the supplier base and a recognition by customers that their costs, quality conformance levels and lead times are partly within the processes of their suppliers. For example, Xerox has reduced its suppliers from over 5000 to about 400, while Chrysler has saved more than $0.5 billion from supplier-generated ideas.

Exhibit 13.11 Mr James wants to introduce strategic alliances so he can threaten suppliers more formally

Strategic alliances are marked by long timescales, extensive sharing of information, increased trust, joint development of services, products and processes and the intent to work together over an extended period (not quite Mr James' interpretation – see Exhibit 13.11). Boeing has strategic alliances with GE, Rolls-Royce and Pratt & Whitney, partly to reduce the financial risk of new aeroplane programmes and partly to cope with the complex technical interfaces between engines and airframes that have to be designed in conjunction with each other. Case example 13.5 also shows the advantage of a strategic alliance.

● **Backward integration** – the final step is to change from relationship to ownership. This leads to the full sharing of information and the transfer of goals and culture.

Case example 5 FEDEX AND KINKO JOINED FORCES TO SPEED DELIVERY

Companies can use the internet to bypass existing layers of the supply chain or engage new participants in the provision of a service or product. Take, for example, FedEx and Kinko (the US-based visual communication and document copying service company). They created a new document delivery flow path that bypassed FedEx's own air-transport fleet. Both companies could receive documents electronically from customers and immediately route them to printers close to the intended recipients. Same-day delivery was provided which cost far less than the traditional two- or even three-day deliveries. Following this alliance, FedEx acquired Kinko.

www.fedex.com

Case questions   1 What did FedEx and Kinko 'bring to the table' in this strategic alliance?
  2 What benefits did the individual companies gain from these new arrangements?

Developing the supply chain

The goal of supply chain management is to link the market, distribution channel, operations process and supplier base such that customers' needs are better met at lower costs. As highlighted earlier, while many companies began fixing their operations problems from the early to mid-1980s, few addressed the total cost of ownership. By the early 1990s, progressive companies had begun to realize the need to refocus from 'fixing' manufacturing to addressing how to better manage the supply chain, a fact confirmed by a 1996 European-based survey. This identified that 88 per cent of the companies reviewed had been carrying out significant overhauls of supply chains and saw supply chain management as the focus for improvement in their overall performance.[4]

But we should have learned from history that little ever changes. In 1929 Ralph Borsodi observed that in the '50 years between 1870 and 1920 the cost of distributing necessities and luxuries had nearly trebled, while production costs had come down by one fifth... what we are saving in production we are losing in distribution'.[5] The same scenario exists today.

Phase 1 – the origin of supply chains

The origin of organizations in the twenty-first century is rooted in functional management and control, resulting in fragmented supply chains, with an emphasis on vertical rather than horizontal processes, as illustrated in Exhibit 13.12. For most companies, developing a supply chain is a multiphased task as explained in the next sections.

Exhibit 13.12 Phase 1 – fragmented supply chains

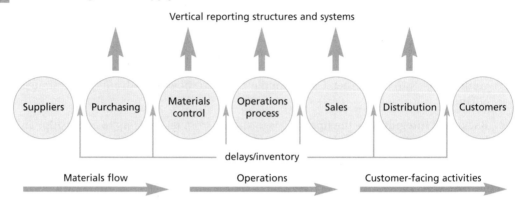

Phase 2 – integrating activities within a business

Phase 2 – integrating activities within a business

The first development phase is to integrate the steps within the internal supply chain, as illustrated in Exhibit 13.13. This internal coordination emphasizes the horizontal nature of the processes inherent in the basic tasks of procurement through to finished goods provision, forges cooperation between the steps to create an integrated whole and the opportunity to reduce costs and delays and improve responsiveness to customer needs.

Exhibit 13.13 Phase 2 – integrating supply chain activities within a business

Phase 3 – coordinating activities between businesses

The next step is to coordinate activities between businesses. As shown in Exhibit 13.14, this stage involves recognizing additional facets within the supply chain (for example tier 1 and tier 2 suppliers and stages in the distribution channel) in order to ensure that these form part of the collaborative development between supply chain partners.

Exhibit 13.14 Phase 3 – coordinating activities between businesses

Phase 4 – synchronizing the planning and execution of activities across the supply chain

The final phase is to synchronize the planning and execution of activities across the supply chain (see Exhibit 13.15). This requires partnership and strategic alliance arrangements that will include the transfer and access of data between businesses from design through to order fulfilment, call-offs and delivery schedules. Traditional roles and responsibilities will change dramatically, with suppliers at times taking responsibility for design through to the internal supply chain deciding how much and when to ship goods to customers – refer back to Exhibit 13.2.

Exhibit 13.15 Phase 4 – real-time planning and execution of activities across the supply chain

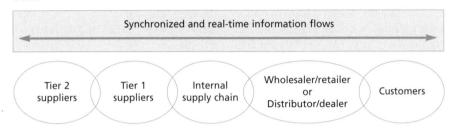

The principles underlying these changes have their origins in the recognition that the whole and not solely the internal phase of a supply chain is the basis for today's competition. Given the extent and nature of the support for markets that is provided by operations, aligning the supply chain provision with the requirements of agreed markets needs to be a central feature of strategy implementation. Key issues that result include:

● Overcoming the barriers to integration – functions within organizations and organizations themselves create barriers to integration. Viewing the supply chain as a whole is a prerequisite for rethinking how best to provide market support through the entire supply chain and overcoming these inherent obstacles.

● Responding to short lead time – delivery speed is an order-winner or qualifier in many of today's markets. Customers are seeking to reduce lead times and the strategic support of suppliers has to match these quick response demands. To do this reliably requires developing lean logistics and managing the supply chain as an integrated whole. A study completed by Ernst & Young and the University of Tennessee in the late 1990s showed that with outsourcing, average order cycle times fell from 6.3 to 3.5 days.[6]

● Eliminating costs – an integrated approach lowers costs by reducing inventory, simplifying procedures, eliminating duplication and other non-value-added activities together with associated overheads. Viewing the supply chain as a whole enables processes and procedures to be structured, with the associated gains of reduced time and cost. In the same Ernst & Young and University of Tennessee study,[6] outsourcing in participating businesses led to average logistics costs and average logistic assets falling by 7.8 and 21.6 per cent respectively.

● Moving information, not inventory – non-integrated approaches have built-in delays comprising time and inventory. By moving information, delays are reduced and subsequent parts of the chain can match real-time needs rather than using inventory to provide against uncertainty and the unknown.

One parallel to lean supply chain management is provided by the revolutionary changes brought to high peak climbing by Reinhold Messner, as Case example 13.6 explains.

Case example 6   **THE DIRECT ALPINE APPROACH TO MOUNTAIN CLIMBING**

Reinhold Messner, the Italian climber, is one of the great sports heroes of Europe. His claim to fame is not so much that he has climbed all 14 of the world's highest peaks, but that he introduced a totally new way of climbing – the direct alpine approach – which uses little equipment and no oxygen support to reach the top.

Conventional mountaineering strategy is based on massive support, including extra oxygen, thought essential for climbs over 25,000 feet. Men such as Sir Edmund Hillary and Chris Bonington relied on hundreds of guides who carried food,

oxygen and supplies; a 1963 American expedition to climb Everest included 900 porters carrying 300 tonnes of equipment.

Messner argues that under this strategy, the slowest man sets the pace. His goal is speed of execution. Although assisted by guides up the base of the mountain, Messner makes the final assault by himself, or with one other person, in a single day. When Hillary and Tenzing first climbed Mt Everest in 1953, they took 7 weeks. On 22 May 2004, Pemba Dorji Sherpa took 5 hr 10 min using the direct alpine approach![7]

www.reinhold-messner.de

Case questions   1 Review the stages in the supply chain represented in Exhibit 13.12 with that of the conventional mountaineering strategy described above. What similarities can you draw?

2 Repeat the analysis for Exhibit 13.15 and Messner's approach to mountaineering.

Aspects of change

Underpinning the developments set out in the last section are a number of changes that need to be secured if the desired supply chain management improvements are to be realized. The most important of these changes are now outlined.

Effective consumer response

There is more to supply chain management than hard-nosed procurement and tight controls over inventory levels. While effectively managing the supply chain concerns eliminating delays and reducing resources along the way, the orientation of such improvements needs to be towards more effective consumer response, where market requirements, and not traditional dimensions such as cost reduction, underpin priorities and direction.

The result fosters closer relations with fewer suppliers. The greatest challenge is working both the internal and external dimensions of the chain in line with the needs of agreed markets. The key to making this happen is attitude and information, the topics of the next two sections.

Changes in attitude

Relationships with suppliers have a history where cooperation was not the way in which customers behaved. Absolute control over aspects such as design and scheduling, pitting suppliers against each other and ruling by threat and fear are being abandoned in favour of long-term relationships, often with single suppliers. Companies are also bringing suppliers on board much earlier in the design process, seeking technical help and contributions and even inviting suppliers to help in identifying future services and products. An illustration of the type of change taking place is provided in Case example 13.7.

To underpin these changes customers are reviewing the way they handle suppliers and the level of cooperation involved. The trend towards greater cooperation goes hand in hand with a more proactive style, as illustrated in Exhibit 13.16.

Case example 7 JAPANESE COMPANIES' APPROACH TO SUPPLIERS

Viewed in the past merely as purchasing, supply chain management is now recognized as a strategic part of operations that stretches from suppliers to end-customers. Suppliers are no longer transient providers selected solely on the basis of lowest cost but partners contributing to the continuous improvement of the supply chain that delivers value to customers. While Japanese buyer–supplier relationships vary from firm to firm and sector to sector, companies as diverse as Toyota, Canon and Nintendo display certain common aspects in their different approaches to suppliers.[8] Once selected,

component suppliers are retained during the life cycle of the specific model. Staff from the buyer will typically train supplier's staff on their operations and quality procedures and other aspects of the organization.

Finally, the buyer firm will evaluate the supplier organization to test the viability of a long-term relationship by ensuring the robustness of the whole organization.

www.toyota.com; www.canon.com; www.nintendo.com

Case questions
1 Review the common aspects in the Japanese companies' approach to suppliers.
2 How do these illustrate the 'change in attitude' highlighted above?

Exhibit 13.16 Phases in changing customer attitudes to suppliers

Threat and fear	Traditional stance. Perceptions based upon: • customer dominates the relationship with suppliers • suppliers respond to demands • customers pitted against each other • constant threat of purchases being given to other suppliers • supplier's ongoing fear of losing a contract
Reward	First steps towards cooperation and moving from a reactive to a proactive stance. Characterized by elements such as: • fewer suppliers • long-term contracts • customer is proactive in building a relationship with suppliers
Collaborate	Progressive move towards fuller and more cooperative relationships, the pace of which is set predominately by the customer. Evolution through a series of steps such as: • customer identifies improvements that a supplier can make • customer provides support and resources (for example technical capability) to undertake improvements • customer gives actual help to improve suppliers' capabilities, including training a supplier's staff • customer starts to take into account the processes of its suppliers when designing services and products to help them improve their support • customer focuses attention on tier 2 suppliers as a source of improving tier 1 suppliers' support (see Exhibit 13.14)
Integrate and synchronize	The final step is to integrate activities achieving benefits typically associated with ownership – the concept of virtual ownership. Based upon mutual respect and trust, these include suppliers' access to real-time information, with customers harmonizing their suppliers' work and synchronizing their support. These changes range from: • access to design-related information and responsibility for service/product design • suppliers' responsibility for deciding when and how much to ship

Increasing use of IT

Since the early 1960s four major stepped changes in IT developments have transformed the way that companies have conducted business, and each wave of technology has radically altered the supply chain that links suppliers through to end-users.

Phase 1 – mainframes

The initial phase of IT application was based on mainframe computers. This began in the early 1960s and continued to be the dominant technology for the next decade. Business applications included material requirements planning and manufacturing resource planning (MRPI and MRPII respectively). These enabled companies to standardize and systemize the day-to-day tasks in operations and parts of the supply chain. As a result, companies developed functional expertise supported by systems design based on the tasks of relevant functions.

Phase 2 – PCs

The second phase was based on PCs that began in the 1970s and continued well into the 1980s. PC applications like word processors, spreadsheets and presentation software facilitated communication across functional boundaries. PCs also resulted in the power of computing being in the hands of employees, and businesses built on this opportunity by focusing on the development of cross-functional processes that brought both functional and overall business benefits.

Phase 3 – network computing

The third phase of computer-based IT applications is based on network computing. Starting in the mid-1980s it continues to have a dominant influence on how companies are managed and business is conducted. Network computing, customer/supplier applications, electronic data interchange (EDI), electronic point-of-sale (EPOS) response and other forms of electronic mail are reducing the costs of handling information and transactions, speeding up information exchange that allows real-time systems and responses to be developed and leveraging the efficiencies of functional expertise (phase 1) and cross-functional business processes (phase 2). IT applications help improve businesses in a range of ways, as illustrated by Case examples 13.8 and 13.9.

Case example 8   **ELECTRONIC SERVICE ALERTS AT CATERPILLAR**

Caterpillar, the giant US earth-moving equipment manufacturer, has developed electronically based systems that identify ahead of time when equipment needs servicing. An electronic message is relayed to the Caterpillar centre. The local dealer is alerted as well as the necessary parts to complete the servicing requirement being sent. Dealers agree appropriate dates with customers and the specified work is then completed.

www.caterpillar.com

Case example 9   **STOCKHOLDING AND INVENTORY AT GAP**

GAP, the US-based apparel company, is currently achieving 14 inventory turns a year while also being able to change the stockholding in all its outlets 13 times per year and on the same day. The data requirements and real-time systems that underpin these arrangements include accurate inventory data, electronic point of sale (EPOS) facilities and synchronized logistics.

www.gap.com

Case question   Explain how IT developments have enabled Caterpillar and GAP to change their business model.

Phase 4 – e-commerce

The fourth phase is e-commerce based on the internet and world wide web. Providing a universal infrastructure, the internet facilitates the interchange of information between businesses, not only by reinforcing existing trends of cooperation but also helping companies to consider their supply chains as a whole and taking on the role of managing and orchestrating process priorities and performance. By fostering better communication and interchange of information between companies, this phase enables fully integrated processes between businesses, not only customers to suppliers but also between suppliers.

One of the lasting effects of these technology applications is that they have facilitated the breakdown of barriers from cross-individuals to cross-corporations – see Exhibit 13.17.

Exhibit 13.17 The evolving role of IT in managing supply chains

Phase	Aspects of change
1 Cross-individuals	Broke down barriers between functional experts themselves and between these and the executives responsible for managing core parts of a business, particularly operations
2 Cross-functional	Facilitated links between functions by requiring and helping the interchange between different parts of the same business
3 Cross-businesses	Impact on the way companies conduct business by removing barriers within an organization and between parts of the immediate supply chain
4 Cross-corporate	Continued the cross-corporate changes by facilitating cooperation of businesses within a supply chain including tier 2 suppliers

The rapid growth of e-commerce has, however, brought with it some concerns that originate from both the delivery system that underpins the system and the speed of its use within commercial activities and transactions:

- **Fraud** – the Fraud Advisory Panel (the UK government's Serious Fraud Office) estimates that fraud could be costing £5 billion a year and is likely to increase. US data from the National Consumers' League supported this trend. Its reports showed that incidents of internet fraud in 1996 were 689 and by 1999 these had increased to 10,660 at a value of $3.2 million. The rise has continued, with 37,183 incidents with a corresponding value of $20.5 million by 2003.

  While Exhibit 13.18 depicts the humorous side of fraud (but no doubt equally concerning if you were the parent!), the implications are suitably highlighted.

- **Vulnerability** – the level and nature of vulnerable outcomes inherent in the growing use of the internet are being highlighted in a series of incidents through-

Exhibit 13.18 One type of internet fraud

© Roger Beale

Exhibit 13.19 A vulnerable side of the internet

© Roger Beale

out the world from bomb-making to arranging and managing gang violence. Exhibit 13.19 provides a humorous exposition of the trend and possible outcomes.

- Focusing on non-value-added activities – increasingly companies have focused attention on minimizing non-value-added activities while providing information and communication tools that allow employees to focus on the value-added and strategic activities within a business. As firms reduce non-value-added activity, they redirect those newly released resources to the value-added and strategic dimensions of their business. For example, companies are increasingly using electronic intranet catalogues that enable office staff (the actual consumer) to order non-operations goods (for example office supplies and computer software) directly from agreed suppliers. Not only does this break down barriers but also eliminates non-value-added activities such as data re-entry and checking, thus allowing more time for purchasing staff to focus on their value-added activities such as developing supplier relations and contract negotiations.

E-commerce presents some businesses with promising new opportunities, while posing a significant threat to those that ignore it. Many sectors have seen the increasing and competitive impact of the internet. For those ready to adapt to the new technology, it represents an opportunity to rethink all aspects of order fulfilment, from order entry to distribution, as shown in Case example 13.10.

Case example 10 SUPPLY CHAIN INTEGRATION AT DELL

One company that is building on its current history of excellent supply chain management is Dell Computer Corporation. Dell uses supply chain management to continuously improve its direct model that is underpinned by sound supply chain integration as follows:

- Dell purchases components on a JIT basis, thus benefiting from the latest (that is, lowest) component prices.

- Dell only makes to order – no resources are committed until a customer order is received.

- By holding little inventory Dell is able to respond to component developments quickly and without incurring inventory losses through obsolescence.

- Short component lead times also allow Dell to meet the delivery speed characteristics of its market with minimum inventory investment.

Dell continues to develop and improve the capabilities of its supply chain in several ways. Now the Dell website is generating daily revenues of more than $20 million, an increase from about $8 million at the start of 1998. The website makes online ordering quick and convenient by allowing customers to specify the product features they want and instantly quoting a price.

In the corporate sales market Dell has also created 'Premier Pages'. These are websites dedicated to corporate clients that can be accessed by a client's authorized employees to research, configure and price PCs before purchase. Each website page holds client-specific data such as preferred configurations and prices. This development increases order accuracy and simplifies Dell's order entry processes. The cost of buying PCs is greatly reduced. For example, the Ford Motor Company estimates that Premier Pages saves it up to $2 million annually. **www.dell.com**

Case questions

1 Explain how Dell integrates its supply chain.

2 How does the Dell website feature in these integrative developments?

3 How is the Ford Motor Company able to save up to $2 million annually by using Dell's Premier Pages?

Strategic partnering

The need to be more competitive has led to a major drive to partner with other companies in the supply chain. Customer/supplier relations continue to undergo major changes where the goal is to synchronize activities to the point where virtual integration is achieved (see Exhibit 13.16). The extent to which this can be secured is not only constrained by the parties involved but also by the stage in a sector's evolution. For example, in the early days of the computing industry the major players had no option but to build the infrastructure necessary to produce all the components and parts a computer needed. As the industry grew, more specialized companies developed to produce specific components. This allowed new entrants a choice. As Michael Dell (founder of Dell) explained:

> As a new start-up, Dell couldn't afford to create every piece of the value chain. But more to the point, why should we want to? We concluded we'd be better off leveraging the investments others have made and focusing on delivering solutions and systems to customers... It's a pretty simple strategy, but at the time it went against the dominant 'engineering-centric' view of the industry. The IBMs, Compaqs and HPs subscribed to a 'we-have-to-develop-everything' view of the world. If you weren't doing component assembly you weren't a real computer company.[9]

Strategic partnering is based on a conscious decision that sees its ultimate goal as virtual integration. This seeks to incorporate other parts of the supply chain as if they are part of one's own business – a long way from the not uncommon stance of outsourcing parts of a business that were, in fact, problem areas that a company could not fix.

On the delivery end of the chain, companies work with their customers to better understand their needs. In some partnerships, retail stores are sharing EPOS data to help suppliers better meet market trends and changes. On the sourcing end of the chain, suppliers are delivering more frequently, keeping consignment stock in a customer's warehouse (and only invoicing on use) and managing the replenishment cycle to reflect usage, while helping to optimize their own schedules. While the customer frees up resources, the supplier has longer term customer commitment, a barrier from competition that reduces sales and marketing effort and provides firm data on which to plan and schedule operations and its own suppliers. One illustration of increased partnering is provided in Case example 13.11.

Case example 11 SYNCHRONIZING THE SUPPLY CHAIN AT CALYX AND COROLLA

Calyx and Corolla, a US-based company, pioneered the delivery of fresh cut flowers direct to customers from the growers. Using Federal Express (FedEx), customers' orders are relayed to one of only 25 suppliers (the flower growers) who assemble the chosen bouquet from one of 150 SKUs. Within the supply chain FedEx visits all suppliers to train their staff on the best ways to pack the flower arrangements and ensure that the delivery phase of the chain synchronizes with the work schedules and product availability of individual growers. Direct supply results in the flowers lasting nine to ten days longer than competitors' product offerings. For Calyx and Corolla, this not only results in a no-inventory arrangement but the delivery speed and quality conformance advantages allow the company to price its products at a 60 per cent premium. Sales revenues in the period 1992–98 grew from $10 million to $25 million when the company was acquired by the Vermont Teddy Bear Company.

www.calyxandcorolla.com

ir.vtbearcompany.com

Case questions
1 How has Calyx and Corolla synchronized its supply chain?
2 What advantages has the company gained from these developments?

E-procurement

Within these supply chain management developments is the role of e-procurement. While supply chain management addresses the core activities within a business, e-procurement extends electronic applications into the wide range of indirect goods and services that are bought by staff at all levels in an organization. As with the purchase of direct services and goods in the past, the procurement of indirect services and products has received little attention, while the size of spend is sizeable. For example, in the UK government, procurement accounts for some 4.5 per cent of the country's GDP. Similarly, at the corporate level, it is estimated that companies can spend up to 15–20 per cent of sales revenue on indirect services and products.

While the IT investment required to move to e-procurement systems has to be made, the change is more cultural than technological. Many organizations have already taken on board electronic catalogues but the necessary cultural changes do not stop there. Online procurement is not a new tool for the purchasing function but a new way of working for the whole organization. With e-purchasing everyone in the organization is now empowered to buy online. For this transition to take place, a leap of faith is required. Gone is the system based on forms, counter-forms and authorizations. This is replaced by checks and controls embodied in the software. It is not a case of computerizing the old manual process but of re-engineering the system itself. Now repetitive ordering can be devolved through the organization in a controlled manner.

As illustrated in Exhibit 13.20, electronic catalogues are at the heart of this development. These can be managed by the purchasing company or a third party such as British Telecommunications Group and Commerce One, a US-based provider. Goods are purchased by anyone in the organization by completing an electronic purchasing application. The system checks the specification, searches, visualizes the requirements, offers checks on price and

Exhibit 13.20 E-procurement system

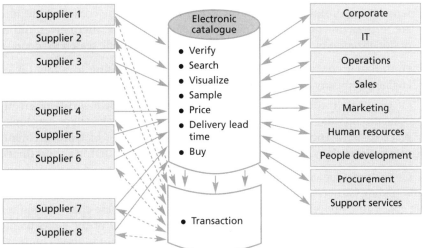

delivery dates and then places the order. Progress of an order is then monitored electronically. The electronic catalogue is updated by supplier information and the growing needs of the organization. Estimates suggest that companies can save up to 11 per cent of indirect purchasing costs by introducing e-purchasing systems for dealing with the procurement of indirect services and products.

Online procurement has arrived and the challenge for companies is how to turn its potential to best organizational advantage. The principal benefits awaiting these developments include:

1 Increase in contract compliance – typically this benefit comprises the largest element of the e-procurement development, bringing with it:
   ● increased use of preferred suppliers
   ● reduced off-contract spending
   ● reduced processing errors.

2 Leveraging the purchasing spend – e-procurement brings together the disparate purchasing transactions that characterize most organizations' traditional approach to purchasing indirect services and products. In so doing it allows companies to improve the potential leverage of these purchases through:
   ● providing greater oversight of the purchasing spending
   ● recording details of the actual spend by supplier and service/product category
   ● allowing full purchasing power to be leveraged when negotiating discounts, with more goods ultimately purchased at lower prices.

3 Lower processing costs – the business, staff and system costs involved in procurement will be reduced as a result of several factors including:
   ● faster processing times
   ● lower number of fax/telephone calls
   ● reduced error rates.

Cisco Systems, for example, has reduced the cost of procurement from an average of $130 to $40 per order – its target is to lower the cost even further to $25 per order.

4   Increased involvement of people – being able to purchase online takes delays out of the procurement process. The result is that staff feel more involved, with an increased sense of responsibility for their own sphere of work. The controls built into the system are further enhanced by an individual's ability to seek alternatives and the increased personalization of the system, both of which enhance the search for good value.

5   Optimizing corporate tax savings – locating purchasing in a low tax economy can enable a company to attribute cost savings (that is, profit) there.

6   Offers a sure route to an early e-business success – the low risk nature of these developments in what are non-business critical systems make these developments a good place to start. Furthermore, the measurable objectives of e-procurement investment proposals result in a clear and persuasive business case offering a short financial payback.

Online procurement offers the opportunity to break down departmental and intercompany trading barriers that opens the way to reducing costs and time in the purchase of indirect goods and services. The organization-wide nature of these changes requires a top-down process in order for an organization to grasp the potential of the e-procurement opportunity. While the technology base of these developments is not in itself complex, the cultural change within the organization should not be underestimated.

Process tools within supply chain management

So far we have addressed the important issues concerning whether to make or buy and managing and developing the supply chain that results. This section now looks at some of the key tools used in managing the supply chain and addresses the key areas of suppliers and logistics.

Sourcing

Within the context of managing the supply chain, relations with suppliers will be critical and will raise some compelling managerial issues that need to be addressed and resolved. As emphasized throughout this chapter, managing operations entails the key component of the supply chain and a recognition that operations has to reach beyond its own capabilities and resources and look to suppliers to help add value to customers. Good suppliers are more than providers of goods and services, they need to be recognized as an invaluable resource, making a direct contribution to an organization's success. Looking at supply chains creates the appropriate context for this to happen. Making it happen requires the necessary systems to be in place and appropriate action to be taken. The key elements involved are now discussed.

Developing the supplier base

An appropriate and adequate supplier base, like other functions within a company, is an essential resource. The trend towards fewer suppliers changes the emphasis to one where evaluation and selection are key dimensions in providing adequate supplier resources, while using significantly fewer suppliers (for example Xerox reduced its supply base by over 90 per cent) allows the potential gains of smaller numbers to be realized.

This dimension of sourcing starts with a knowledge base of potential suppliers with current evaluations on performance. Sources of supplier information include:

- **In-house supplier information files** concerning material and service range, delivery reliability performance, quality conformance record, ability to handle long-term growth as well as short-term demand uplifts and an evaluation of the technical and managerial capabilities of key areas and executives.

- **Supplier catalogues** – a catalogue library helps promote general background information and highlight potential sources of relevant services and materials.

- **Trade registers, directories and journals** – registers (for example Kompass Publications) provide not only technical but other important, general background on potential suppliers, while trade journals give current information on suppliers that are specific to the technical areas that a journal covers.

- **Trade exhibitions** – provide opportunities to discuss general and specific sourcing dimensions with potential suppliers while assessing their technical and professional offerings.

- **Professional colleagues** – purchasing executives often use their professional colleagues whose judgement they respect to suggest and assess possible suppliers based on their own experience.

Supplier selection – internal review mechanisms

While supply chain executives have the ultimate responsibility for supplier selection, companies approach this task in a number of ways. These include giving the task to the supply management team alone, using cross-functional teams and putting together commodity teams to source and manage a group of similar services or products. Cross-functional and commodity teams typically consist of buyers, process or systems specialists and schedulers. The difference between these two is that while commodity teams tend to manage ongoing arrangements that cover a given range of services and products, cross-functional teams are often put together at specific times and tend to handle specific tasks.

Supplier selection – evaluation

From the long list of potential suppliers, companies need to evaluate prospective providers. This evaluation process should include:

- a check on the overall viability of the potential supplier organization, particularly regarding its financial condition including credit ratings and resources to grow in the future

- a review of technical know-how to assess the ability of a supplier to meet the service or product specifications, and its potential for matching or contributing to future technical changes

- an assessment of managerial capabilities and attitudes towards undertaking self-initiated developments and improvements, the desire to meet customer needs and willingness to move towards partnership arrangements over time

- an evaluation of operations to help assess a supplier's technical capability, the company's current capacity to support anticipated levels of demand and any plans to meet future growth

- a check on how well a supplier currently meets the relevant order-winners and qualifiers of its customers' markets will help provide valuable insights into its ability to support your own markets.

Supplier selection – process

When companies have established a shortlist of potential suppliers, the next step is to decide which of these will be selected. The preliminary survey stage would have already checked on the points raised in the last section. Selecting which suppliers to work with now moves to a more in-depth phase where the dimensions covered in the last section are checked in the following ways.

Site visits

By visiting the facilities of potential suppliers, the sourcing team can obtain first-hand information regarding the adequacy of key dimensions such as technical capabilities, operations capacity and management's technical know-how, attitude and orientation. Specific aspects to check include:

- attitude and stability of the top and middle management teams
- level of process, equipment and system investment
- competence of the technical and operations management teams
- morale of staff at all levels
- willingness of a potential supplier to work with the buying organization and its top management's goals regarding the eventual level of customer/supplier relations
- current major customers
- internal measures used by the potential supplier to evaluate its own performance, appropriateness of the measures chosen and its actual performance over the past few months.

In addition, the degree of professionalism demonstrated by a potential supplier's team in handling the visit and the level of internal staff involved will help in assessing the overall calibre of the company's executives and the importance attached to the visit.

Checking specific capabilities

During this process, checks also need to be made to assess whether a potential supplier is able or, more importantly, has had experience in providing the capabilities that are specific to a customer's needs. These include:

- **Quality conformance** – ISO 9000 registration and records, together with any similar registrations with other customers
- **JIT capability** – experience in providing JIT schedules for customers
- **Short-term capacity increases** – the extent to which a potential supplier is able to increase capacity in the short term and an assessment of the approach to be adopted and a check on how feasible this support would be
- **Inventory support** – an evaluation of potential consignment inventory and customer-specific inventory arrangements that could be accommodated
- **Future growth** – the potential of a supplier to increase capacity to match anticipated growth in future demand and a check on the approach that would be followed and, where possible, an illustration of similar past or current support for other customers
- **Technical support** – the extent to which a potential supplier could liaise in the future on the technical aspects of the purchased items and services

● **Partnering** – an attitude and feasibility check on how developments towards partnering in the future may evolve.

Selecting the supplier

In many instances, one prospective supplier is so obviously superior to the others on the shortlist that selection is a simple decision. In other instances, however, the choice is not so clear-cut and here a weighting system can help in the decision process. Using such a weighting system calls for three tasks:

● agreeing the selection criteria

● weighting each criteria to reflect the level of importance in the selection process

● rating each potential supplier on all the selection criteria.

Exhibit 13.21 provides an example of this approach. Here, four potential suppliers have been evaluated, with company C coming out on top. Other points to note in this illustration include the range of factors reviewed and the weightings allocated to each category. In

Exhibit 13.21 The weighted-factor rating approach to supplier selection

Factors		Weights	Potential suppliers			
			A	B	C	D
Order-winners and qualifiers	● delivery on time	60	50	60	60	50
	● delivery speed	80	40	40	70	50
	● quality conformance	40	40	35	35	35
	● price	30	30	30	20	30
	● after-sales technical support	40	30	30	35	30
	Subtotal	250	190	195	220	195
Operations	● current capacity	20	20	20	20	20
	● ability to increase capacity in the short term	10	0	0	10	5
	● meet long-term growth requirements	50	30	40	45	40
	Subtotal	80	50	60	75	65
Technical	● level of technical staff provision	50	40	45	45	40
	● staff technical know-how	30	25	25	30	25
	● future contributions to developing products and services	20	10	10	15	15
	Subtotal	100	75	80	90	90
Corporate	● managerial and financial standing of the organization	70	50	50	60	60
	Subtotal	70	50	50	60	60
Totals		500	365	385	445	410

this instance, the importance of the market-related dimensions (the order-winners and qualifiers) is obvious and they have been heavily weighted to reflect the key contribution of suppliers within the strategic role of operations. However, the factors and the weightings would need to reflect the particular requirements of specific supplier evaluations. Consequently, both the factors used and the weights awarded would change accordingly.

Maintaining the supplier base

These last sections have addressed the tasks involved in developing the supplier base by selecting suppliers to meet the needs of a business. Another important dimension of sourcing concerns maintaining the existing supplier list. In many ways the procedures and checks used in supplier selection will form the basis of the evaluation process for existing suppliers. The critical difference between the two procedures is the ongoing relationship with a supplier, the first-hand knowledge of a supplier's performance and the opportunity to measure a supplier over time, thus replacing estimates and opinions with hard data and facts.

What should be measured and evaluated will be similar to that provided in Exhibit 13.21, while again needing to reflect the importance of the different aspects of supply. The ongoing relationship that exists, however, provides an opportunity to change the style and method of evaluation rather than what is measured. Key changes include:

- Agree with the supplier the performance measures, with an explanation of why and how they will be used.

- Both customer and supplier need to keep records of performance and meet regularly to discuss trends and improvement opportunities. Keeping separate records will reveal any discrepancies, thereby allowing these differences to be identified and corrected, while the need for both parties to record performance keeps these dimensions at the top of their respective corporate agendas.

- Regular meetings should not only cover current levels of performance but also provide an opportunity to inform each other of known or possible changes that could affect customer requirements or supplier performance.

Distribution and transportation systems

Distribution is a key element in the management of a supply chain. For some companies, distribution and transportation costs can be as high as 20 per cent of total costs. For service companies involved in the distribution of retail items such as catalogue sales, the percentage of total costs can be even higher. In one year, LL Bean (the US-based merchant) despatches 11 million packages or an average of 650,000 each week. At peak times, the company fills a 40-foot trailer every 20 minutes.

Distribution and transportation costs depend largely on where a company is located, relative to its customers, and the means of transportation selected, which reflects issues of lead time, volume and, for some businesses, the physical nature of the product. For example, oil and gas are typically transported using pipelines, due to the physical nature of the product and the volumes involved between one part of the supply chain and the next. Thus, oil from oil well and oilfield to refinery will be piped, as will gas from extraction site to processing and distribution network. However, oil products such as petrol and diesel will be taken to petrol or gas stations by road tanker.

Exhibit 13.22 A comparison of transportation systems

Price per tonne/mile[1]		Pipeline and water	Rail			Road	Air	
	Low						→	High
Speed, door to door		Water	Rail	Road		Air	Pipeline	
	Slow						→	Fast
Percentage of total goods moved		Rail	Road		Pipeline	Water	Air	
	High						→	Low

Note   1   Price per tonne/mile = one tonne of freight carried one mile.

The five principal commercial modes of transportation are rail, road (trucking), water, air and pipeline. The options have different pricing structures and speed factors and the typical mix in a developed economy is shown in Exhibit 13.22. Note, however, that some of these relative positions would change if the distance travelled was lengthened or shortened.

Rail

Railways are best suited for transporting low-value, high-density, bulk products such as raw materials over long distances. Examples include coal, minerals and ores. Although fast between points, the total lead time for rail transportation is significantly lengthened by the before and after phases of the rail travel itself.

Road

Providing flexible point-to-point service and delivering small loads over short to long distances makes road transport the most popular way of moving freight. In more developed economies, road haulage systems are extensive and the service provided is typically fast, reliable and less prone to damage than some alternatives. The growing use of articulated vehicles (in which the trailer detaches from the front pulling unit) and containers allows vehicle loading to be completed while the front pulling unit (and high investment part of a truck) can be used elsewhere.

With greater emphasis being placed on reducing inventory in a supply chain, the need for orders to be delivered on time and without damage is becoming essential. Carriers are now a critical link in supply chains and the need to match the short lead time, delivery reliability and quality conformance requirements are paramount.

Airfreight

Recently the number of airfreight carriers that carry relatively small packages (for example UPS, Federal Express and DHL) has been increasing. Using both passenger and airfreight flights, goods travelling by air is the fastest growing transportation segment. The types of product shipped by airfreight tend to be lightweight or small. Examples include medical supplies, electronic components, perishable products such as flowers, fruit and vegetables, and documents.

The advantages of airfreight are speed and reliability. It is an efficient and economical way to transport high-value, lightweight products, important documents or skilled people over long distances, particularly where the destination is overseas. However, air transport is so much more expensive than alternatives that it is cost-prohibitive for most products. Furthermore, the collecting, handling, loading, unloading and delivery adds to the point-to-point overall time, making it not much quicker than road haulage for distances up to 500 miles.

Water

Carrying goods by water is one of the oldest means of freight transportation. Inland the system of waterways may include rivers, canals and lakes. In addition, there is coastline and sea travel across the world's oceans.

As Exhibit 13.22 indicated, while water transportation costs are low, it is also the slowest form of shipping goods. In addition, inland water transportation is tied to a fixed system of river and coastal ports that serve as terminals and distribution points. It is particularly suited to moving heavy bulk items such as raw materials, ores, grain, chemical, mineral and petroleum products. For international shipping, water is the only option for transporting these latter types of product, as airfreight is unable to handle them.

Transocean shipping companies have developed intermodal transport systems in order to reduce overall point-to-point delivery times and lower handling costs. They combine trucks, railroads and ships, with container systems being at the heart of these developments. Here, standardized containers are packed at the point of origin, loaded onto trucks, reloaded either onto rail flat cars or directly onto a container ship, with the process in reverse at the other end of the journey. And throughout the journey the goods never leave the container.

Pipelines

Pipelines are used to transport liquids or gases from one point to another. For example, crude oil and natural gas are piped from an oilfield to refineries (for example there are over 150,000 miles of crude oil pipelines in the USA) and petroleum products such as petrol and diesel from refineries to tank farms. For example, ExxonMobil has pipelines taking aviation fuel to Heathrow Airport from its refinery at Farley near Southampton on the south coast of England.

Other uses include carrying water (probably the most common use) and slurry products (for example products that have been pulverized and transformed into liquid form such as kaolin (china clay) and coal). Once the latter products arrive at their destination the water is then removed leaving the solid material. Although characterized by high initial investment, pipelines are economical because they carry materials over terrain with which other forms of transportation could not cope (for example the transAlaska and North Sea oil pipelines) and, once in place, they have a long life and are low cost to operate.

E-commerce

Although introduced in relevant sections earlier in the chapter, the impact of e-commerce demands additional coverage particularly within the context of supply chain management.

The spread of electronic commerce (e-commerce), both B2C (business-to-consumer) and B2B (business-to-business – often referred to as e-business) creates the potential for building more efficient and effective supply chains. Other constraints (such as capacity, material supply, material lead times and inventory) apart, the opportunity to improve the way companies do business has been dramatic. At the very least it speeds up transactions, cuts costs and promotes interbusiness cooperation, fostering a recognition that suppliers are part of a company's strategic resource. At its most potent, e-commerce allows companies to provide or make services and products to order rather than against a sales forecast, while also increasing the extent to which customers can configure what they buy. But to deliver the commitment requires control over the supply chain to ensure that fulfilment matches promise. A stark example of this was provided by the high-profile problems that Amazon.com and other online providers had in failing to meet the Christmas 1999 levels of demand.

Thus, e-commerce transforms a supply chain into a demand chain, in which the core activity of the system is not to fill a warehouse, but to deliver to a customer. The well-known exponent of this approach is Dell and earlier examples have already illustrated this. Dell builds all its products on a make-to-order (MTO) basis, with about $20 million of business a day transacted on the internet. MTO in the Dell sense changes the place in the supply chain where inventory is held. In MTO mode, operations needs to be prepared for every eventuality which requires excellent partnerships with suppliers based on sharing information and the ability to meet short lead times. There can be no interfunctional or interbusiness silos. The intermediaries in a supply chain not only need to exchange information, but increasingly move to interworking mode. Having such links and working practices in place makes it possible to enhance customer support. On the one hand, customers can track the progress of their orders in their suppliers' systems and, on the other hand, suppliers can proactively anticipate delivery requirements without waiting for an order. In addition, suppliers can also gain access to other suppliers in the chain, allowing them to track the entire process.

Putting internet-based information in front of consumers is transforming the supply chain in the pharmaceuticals industry. In the USA, unlike Europe, companies are allowed to advertise their products. Drug information via the web is a fast and effective way of communicating details of approved products. Patients can find out about new treatments quickly and become more proactive in the treatment phase of illness. For example, GlaxoSmithKline's new treatment for diabetes, Avandia, outsold rival products in its first six months on the market.

Establishing close supplier links can also help boost sales. For the UK supermarket Sainsbury's, special promotions account for about 10 per cent of sales revenue. But planning promotions is difficult, particularly if it concerns perishable goods. To help overcome these problems, Sainsbury's built a web-based supply chain, planning and collaboration system, which allows suppliers and buyers to work through every detail of a product promotion in advance and track its success in real time.

Companies are also changing emphasis regarding IT supply chain investments from cost cutting to sales revenue growth – see Exhibit 13.23. The above-mentioned Dell and GlaxoSmithKline examples illustrate this. Similarly, Chrysler recognized that car-purchasing decisions were perceived by many consumers to be tedious. As a result, it now has an online system for customer purchases, with sales estimated at $15 billion.

Exhibit 13.23 Main goal of IT investment

Period	Goal (% total)	
	cost-cutting	sales revenue growth
1991–92	69	31
1996–97	37	63
2001–02	20	80

Source *The Economist* survey of electronic commerce.

As sales revenue growth adds value to a business, current e-commerce developments are reflecting this potential core contribution. Whereas currently e-commerce typically allows customers to order from a specified range of services and goods, increasingly customers will be asked 'What is your need?' The requirement for supply chains to be able to cope with exceptions is the next phase of development. To do this the supply chain will move from a passive to a more dynamic mode, responding to customer demands, advising if it has the capability to meet the requirement, at what price and in what lead time. The impact that such developments will have on the supply chain will require fresh approaches to how services and products are managed in operations.

Reflections

Organizations and traditional management approaches can stand in the way of an integrated supply chain. Many companies still operate with structures that typically lead to optimizing the functional dimensions of performance. Within this format there are only functional links between key parts of a supply chain and, with the absence of an integrating mechanism, functions work and plan separately and in line with their respective priorities. At best, these priorities may be inconsistent, while at worst they may be incompatible. The result is reduced internal cooperation diluting an organization's ability to meet customer requirements. Furthermore, similar problems can arise between a company and its suppliers on the one hand and with its customers on the other.

The extended enterprise

The conflicts described above can be overcome, first, by internal supply chain cooperation and liaison and, second, by extending these developments to suppliers and customers, thus forming an integrated supply chain. Known as the 'extended enterprise', here planning is shared and execution processes are integrated. Where this is achieved, the supply chain now begins to truly encompass the business from tier 2 and tier 1 suppliers to tier 1 and tier 2 customers.

The transfer of a service or product from one stage in a business to the next or from one business to another business comprises the internal and external phases of a supply chain respectively. A supply chain is integrated when all the steps are coordinated through practices such as collaborative planning and vendor-managed inventory to manage costs and inventory levels while maintaining customers' on-time and lead time delivery requirements.

These approaches signal a critical change in organizations as they now begin to see and manage business processes as they truly are – chains of activities performed by different organizations.

Embracing technical developments

An earlier section emphasized the need to recognize technology development opportunities. The ability to move information across a supply chain through IT systems gives a new perspective to the dimension of integration. Similarly, at the point of customer interface, e-commerce provides the opportunity not only to change the EPOS procedure but also increase sales. Empowering customers leads to more sales for a number or reasons, including:

- Companies are able to sell additional services by giving customers and potential customers more information about the services or products on offer.
- Eliminating steps helps conclude a sale and reduce delivery lead times.
- Customers have more insight into what is on offer thus increasing choice.

Exhibit 13.24 Some unforeseen consequences of e-commerce

© Roger Beale

- Increased choice and introducing new ideas and opportunities leads to more sales as customers buy more – one dimension of which is shown in Exhibit 13.24.

Competing at the level of supply chains

Earlier sections emphasized the need for organizations to recognize that firms increasingly compete at the level of the supply chain. For example, the delivery problems that Boeing, then the world's number one aircraft maker, experienced in the late 1990s not only resulted in lost revenue but also in customers turning to competitors. To build a large passenger jet such as a 747, 767, 777 or A340 you need about 6 million parts – complex in itself. But, in addition, between 1992 and 1999 Boeing had increased production from 228 to 620 aircraft per year while reducing delivery lead times from 36 to 8–12 months. During this period, however, Boeing failed to ensure that suppliers could handle these critical changes in activity. The result was insufficient parts to meet the aircraft build programme. While its sales were booming, the company had failed to develop its supplier base to meet the new task and fell well behind on its delivery schedule. While not the only reason, this supply chain management failure contributed to European Airbus taking over the #1 spot from Boeing at the beginning of 2004.

Managing the supply chain for competitive advantage

Markets evolve and what is important to customers needs to be identified and then form the basis of functional strategies. Recent research[10] confirms the trend away from price to other operations factors. The increasingly important role of the supply chain in the dimensions of delivery performance is clearly shown in Exhibit 13.25.

Exhibit 13.25 How companies rank market drivers as potential order-winners and qualifiers

Potential for order-winners and qualifiers
(percentage of companies)

Source PricewaterhouseCoopers 'Shaping the value chain for outstanding performance: meeting the challenge of
global supply chains' (1998), p. 6.

Overviewing the trend towards increased outsourcing

Since Kodak blazed a trail in the late 1980s by procuring its IT support and services from an outside provider, in terms of the wholesale transfer of assets and employees to a third-party supplier under a long-term agreement, outsourcing has been on a roll. The range of services (and providers), other than the more classic functional candidates such as logistics and call centre management, is increasing and adding to the flow, as the following examples illustrate:

- Xerox – customer financing, revenue collection and billing to GE Capital
- Cable & Wireless – HR processes to e-Peopleserve, a joint venture between Accenture, the management consultancy company, and BT, the telecommunications group
- Amazon relies on publishers for product development, Visa and Mastercard for revenue collection and UPS for logistics
- BP agreed a $600 million five-year deal with Exult to contract out the administration of its human resources across the world
- Bank of America – human resources processes with Exult
- Dell, Cisco and Wal-Mart have all outsourced manufacturing and logistics
- Royal National Institute for the Blind – a six-year deal with Arval PHH for vehicle fleet management.

Whether outsourcing or collaboration is the chosen way forward, the resulting supply chains are more complex and have, in fact, evolved into supply networks. But the main ingredient of a supply network is not technology but trust, in that whereas the former is not a barrier, the latter is. For it to work all suppliers must have all the information they need.

Thus, it is now essential for companies to share information previously regarded as confidential. While larger companies still use EDI systems, smaller suppliers are being brought in via internet portals and web-based technology. Once the supply chain has been upgraded into a supply network, dramatic time and cost reductions become possible. The need to rethink corporate norms in the context of outsourcing does not stop with the sharing of information. Other corporate values will also come under scrutiny, for example:

- Where companies outsource services and goods from less developed regions of the world, their approach to corporate social responsibility will often come in for critical review. One example is Nike, where allegations of its subcontractors using child labour were the subject of a BBC documentary in 2000 and the ongoing subject of the press ever since.[11] For Nike the result has been much self-analysis, increased monitoring of subcontractors and the reallocation of work in an attempt to ensure that child labour is no longer used.

- Where companies develop the long-term supplier relations that go hand in hand with supply chain management developments, one test of the new depths of these joint working arrangements is their response in times of reduced sales. For example, Toyota's commitment to its suppliers is underlined by the fact that no supplier has closed down in the last decade even though Toyota's total production has dropped 25 per cent since the early 1990s. Western companies, as part of developing more effective and more responsive supply chains, are moving into closer collaborative relationships and agreements than in the past.

With global GDP estimated in the order of $30 trillion and the cost of loading, unloading, sorting, reloading and transporting goods some 12 per cent (or about $3.5 trillion) of this total, the opportunities for savings provide an overwhelming case for supply chain development. But the spirit and practice of customer–supplier relations needs to fundamentally change, as illustrated in Exhibit 13.26. While the potential benefits are considerable, the necessary time and investment need to be recognized by top management as a corporate priority and demonstrated by commitment throughout the organization.

Exhibit 13.26 Changing nature of customer–supplier practices

Dimension		Customer–supplier practice	
		Traditional	New millennium
Strategic role		Price, price and price	Help meet end-customer needs
Customer orientation		Make	Buy
Suppliers	number	Many	Few
	length of relationship	One-night stand	Long-term partner
	customers' role	Reactive	Proactive
	basis of relationship	Threat and fear	Collaboration
	selection	Functional level	Board level
Customer support	training	None	Ongoing
	technical help	Little and reactive	Ongoing and proactive

Key Elements of Managing the Supply Chain

- To effectively manage a supply chain requires a shift away from traditional functional organizational models towards managing a set of integrated processes that encompass the key facets of a business. Examples to illustrate the nature of these integrated processes are provided in Exhibits 13.1 and 13.2.

- Fundamental to the size and scope of supply chains is the make-or-buy decision. Whether to make or buy is tied up with a range of factors from core technology and strategy considerations through to the greater opportunities brought by the globalization of world trade. The challenge is for companies to continuously review this decision as the factors influencing the outcomes change.

- The benefits of providing or making more in-house vis-à-vis the advantages and disadvantages of outsourcing are discussed, including a review of the domestic vs offshore sourcing options.

- The task of effectively managing the supply chain that results is an important priority within operations and its impact on the business as a whole is increasingly and appropriately a high-profile and corporate-wide task.

- The alternatives to the make-or-buy option, such as joint ventures and non-equity-based collaboration, complete the introductory phase of this chapter. The orientation then switches to supply chain management issues and developments. These sections detail the original evolution of supply chains (in particular, refer back to Exhibits 13.12 to 13.15) before outlining the key aspects of change. These include effective consumer response, changes and attitude to supplier relations (see Exhibit 13.16) and the increasing use of IT.

- The next section addresses the areas of sourcing, supplier base development, supplier selection and evaluation and how to maintain the supplier base followed by a detailed review of alternative distribution and transportation systems and comparisons between rail, road, airfreight, water and pipeline alternatives.

- The final section on e-commerce builds on the earlier IT section. Its inclusion here is to highlight the dramatic impact those developments are having and will continue to have on supply chain management, not only in B2C but also in B2B dealings.

Self-check

1 A supply chain is:
   a The steps between the origin of the service or product in question and its consumption or use ☐
   b The steps in the process or delivery system managed by suppliers ☐
   c The steps in the process or delivery system directly managed by an organization ☐

2 Outsourcing comprises:
   a Overseas suppliers ☐
   b Domestic suppliers ☐
   c Both a and b ☐

3 Types of supplier relationships include:
   a Trawling the market ☐
   b Partnerships ☐
   c Both a and b ☐

4 Which of these typically has the highest price per tonne/mile
- a Water ☐
- b Road ☐
- c Rail ☐

5 Most goods are moved by:
- a Pipeline ☐
- b Rail ☐
- c Road ☐

6 The benefits of outsourcing include:
- a Increased focus on core tasks ☐
- b Freed resources ☐
- c Both a and b ☐

7 The disadvantages of outsourcing include:
- a More control ☐
- b Difficult to change the decision once made ☐
- c Less vulnerable ☐

8 An alternative to outsourcing is:
- a Co-sourcing ☐
- b Joint ventures ☐
- c Both a and b ☐

9 Non-equity collaboration is:
- a A form of outsourcing ☐
- b A type of joint venture ☐
- c An alternative to outsourcing ☐

10 Developing integrated supply chains involves:
- a Moving more from being a supply chain to a demand chain ☐
- b Competing as a supply chain rather than as an individual organization ☐
- c Both a and b ☐

Study activities

Discussion questions

1 What factors should be taken into account when taking make-or-buy decisions? Illustrate your answer with examples from a service and a manufacturing organization.

2 Under what circumstances would you consider that each of the following would be advantageous to a company:
- single sourcing
- multisourcing

Use a service and a manufacturing organization to illustrate your views.

3 Given the increasing importance of environmental concerns, how would a company incorporate these issues into the make-or-buy process? Give two examples to illustrate your views.

4 How will e-commerce continue to impact the supply chain?

5 Using the website of an online supplier such as Amazon.com, detail the delivery system involved and list the benefits to the consumer.

6 List two firms that you think have achieved competitive advantage through vertical integration. Explain why and give illustrations to support your views.

7 What benefits do suppliers receive from developing closer ties with major customers?

8 A major company decides to move to a more collaborative stance with a supplier. What would be the first key changes it would need to take? What possible initial responses might be made by the supplier?

9 Give two examples (with reasons) for both a service and manufacturing company where outsourcing a service:
- makes sense
- does not make sense

10 What type of call centre service providers lend themselves and do not lend themselves to overseas provision?

11 What benefits would a company derive from introducing e-procurement? What are the obstacles you would expect to hinder this development?

Assignments

1 Exhibit 13.21 lists five order-winners and qualifiers as part of an example to illustrate an approach to supplier selection. What practical measures could be used to check a supplier's performance against these five criteria? Illustrate your answer by selecting a supplier to a large supermarket and a clothing manufacturer.

2 What criteria do you think the owner of each of the following independent outlets would use to evaluate and select key suppliers?
● restaurant
● stationer
● coffee shop

Now visit an independent outlet of each of these and ask the owners how they evaluate and select key suppliers. Compare the results and explain any significant differences.

3 Select a service and manufacturing company and give two examples where it would be best to use a multisourced supply and two examples where it would be best to use a single-sourced supply.

Exploring further

Amese, F, Dragoste, L, Nollet, J and Ponce, S 'Issues on partnering: evidences from subcontracting in aeronautics', *Technovation*, **21**, (2001), pp. 559–69.

Arnold, D 'Seven rules of international distribution, *Harvard Business Review,* November– December, (2000), pp. 131–7.

Bhote, KR *Strategic Supply Chain Management*, American Management Association, New York (1989).

Burt, DN and Pinkerton, RL *Strategic Proactive Purchasing*, American Management Association, New York (1996).

Child, J and Faulkner, D *Strategies for Cooperation: Managing Alliances, Networks and Joint Ventures*, Oxford University Press, Oxford (1998).

Croom, SR 'The impact of web-based procurement on the management of operating resources supply', *Journal of Supply Chain Management*, **36**(1) (2000), pp. 4–13.

Gattorna, JL (ed.) *Strategic Supply Chain Management*, Gower, Aldershot (1998).

Gattorna, JL and Walters, DW *Managing the Supply Chain: A Strategic Perspective*, Macmillan – now Palgrave Macmillan, Basingstoke (1996).

Groncutt, J and Griseri, P *Mastering e-Business*, Palgrave Macmillan, Basingstoke (2004).

Guide, Jr, V and Daniel, R 'Supply chain management for recoverable manufacturing systems', *Interfaces*, **30**(3) (2000), pp. 125–42.

Hammer, M 'The superefficient company', *Harvard Business Review*, September (2001), pp. 82–91.

Handfield, RB and Krause, DR 'Avoiding the pitfalls in supplier development', *Sloan Management Review*, **41**(2) (2000), pp. 37–50.

Harvey, M 'Innovation and competition in UK supermarkets', *Supply Chain Management*, **5**(1) (2000), pp. 15–21.

Lamming, R *Beyond Partnership: Strategies for Innovation and Lean Supply*, Prentice Hall, London (1993).

Lancioni, RA, Smith, MF and Oliva, TA 'The role of the internet in supply chain management', *Industrial Marketing Management*, **29**(1) (2000), pp. 45–56.

Liker, JR and Wu Y-C 'Japanese automakers, US suppliers and supply chain superiority', *Sloan Management Review*, **42**(1) (2000), pp. 81–93.

Narasimhan, R and Das, A 'Manufacturing agility and supply chain management practices', *Production and Inventory Management Journal*, first quarter (1999), pp. 4–10.

Norman, PM 'Are your secrets safe? Knowledge protection in strategic alliances', *Business Horizons*, November–December, (2001), pp. 51–60.

Rowley, J *E-business Principles and Practice,* Palgrave Macmillan, Basingstoke (2002).

Smeltzer, LR and Carr, A 'Reverse auctions in industrial marketing and buying', *Business Horizons*, March–April (2002), pp. 47–52.

Stuart, FI and McCutcheon, R 'The manager's guide to supply chain management', *Business Horizons*, March–April (2000), pp. 35–44.

Yoshino, MY and Rangan, VS *Strategic Alliances: An Entrepreneurial Approach to Globalization*, Harvard Business School Press, Boston (1995).

Notes and references

1 Tait, N 'Handling the sourcing secision: lowest cost is not always the answer', *Financial Times*, 15 October 1997, p. 13.

2 Lowson, RH 'Offshore sourcing: an optimal operational strategy?', *Business Horizons*, November–December (2001), pp. 61–6.

3 Tait, N (1997) op. cit., p. 13.

4 Economist Intelligence Unit and KPMG Management Consultants' Report 'Supply chain management: Europe's new competitive battleground', 1996.

5 Borsodi, R *The Distribution Age*, D Appleton & Co (1929).

6 As reported in Allen, E 'One-stop shop is no cure-all', *Financial Times*, 17 June, 1999, p. 16.

7 Bleeke, JA 'Peak strategies', *McKinsey Quarterly*, spring (1989).

8 These are discussed extensively by Nishiguchi, T and Brookfield, J, 'The evolution of Japanese subcontracting', *Sloan Management Review*, **39**(1) (1997), pp. 89–101.

9 Margretta, J 'The power of virtual integration: an interview with Dell Computer's Michael Dell', *Harvard Business Review*, March–April (1998), p. 74.

10 PricewaterhouseCoopers (1998) op. cit., p. 4.

11 For example, see Skapinker, M, 'Why Nike has broken into a sweat', an article in a feature on corporate social responsibility, *Financial Times*, 7 March, 2002, p. 13.

book map

Part

1

- 1 Managing Operations
- 2 Operations Strategy
- 3 Managing People

2

- 4 Designing and Developing Services & Products
- 5 Designing Service Delivery Systems
- 6 Designing Manufacturing Processes
- 7 Location and Layout
- 8 Managing Capacity
- 9 Technology Developments
- 10 Operations Scheduling and Execution
- 11 Managing Quality

3

- 12 Managing Inventory
- 13 Managing the Supply Chain

4

- 14 Process and Delivery System Reliability and Maintenance
- 15 Time and Productivity
- 16 Improving Operations

5

- Managing Operations in Practice: Long Case Studies

Process and Delivery System Reliability and Maintenance

Outline of chapter

The managed maintenance of processes not only affects capacity but also impinges on the predictability of a delivery system. Where lead times are short and delivery reliability is a key competitive driver, a system to meet schedules and customers' expectations is a key factor.

Why is process and delivery system reliability and maintenance important?

Executive overview

As part of the need to lower costs, reduce lead times and improve the availability and format of information, investments in processes and systems will continue to be made and are likely to increase in the future. Rapid advances in technology, many of which were highlighted in Chapter 9, have led to more opportunities to invest in the hardware and software parts of the operations process. The technology dependence, however, is changing, with the increasing use of electronics (for example microchips) in both the working and control of process equipment and IT-based systems applications. This pattern of investment has led to a growing need in most organizations to recognize the continued importance of and reconsider their approach to the management of the maintenance function. This chapter outlines the important maintenance decisions and illustrates the types of controls and tasks that managers should address, as part of the overall operations function. In particular, it covers the following sections:

- **Process reliability and checking for failure** introduces process reliability and outlines ways of assessing and measuring failures, how to establish both the rate of failure and level of process reliability as well as ways to calculate mean time between failures and process availability measures. It concludes with an introduction on how to identify levels of failure, approaches to failure analysis and ways to improve a system.

- **Maintenance and terotechnology** explains the broader concept of terotechnology and positions maintenance of the delivery system within this context.

- **Maintenance** highlights the increasing investment by businesses in equipment and technology and the subsequent key role of maintenance within operations.

- **Types of maintenance** explains the alternative approaches to maintenance, how they differ and the need to match type with requirement in order to ensure best fit.

- **Planned maintenance** is discussed in more detail due to the fundamental role provided by this approach.

- **Other policy issues** are listed and discussed. These range from the options of outsourcing maintenance provision to systems and controls and the style of management to be considered.

- **Total productive maintenance** is described in detail and the reasons why this approach is increasingly being adopted are explained.

- **Energy management** introduces this key area and explains how the effective management of these costs contribute to the overall business.

> ● **Managing maintenance** outlines some of the developments to help assess and manage this function.

Process reliability – making a system fail-safe

The concept of integrating fail-safe mechanisms into a process in order to reduce failures is increasingly being used in service and manufacturing systems. The introduction of *poka-yoke* (*poka* meaning inadvertent errors and *yoke* from *yokeru* meaning to prevent) as part of the operations improvement methods used by Japanese companies emphasized these developments and highlighted the benefits to be gained. The principle underpinning these approaches stems from the fact that people and processes can make errors. Consequently, if situations in which errors take place can be eliminated, this is often the best way to reduce failures. Making a system foolproof by introducing mechanisms that counterbalance potential failures with a signal of some kind is the basis of *poka-yoke* developments.

Examples of *poka-yoke* devices are now provided to illustrate the principles and highlight how they work. You will see from these that they are designed into the service delivery system or manufacturing process itself with the purpose of fail-saifing staff or customers as they interface with the system.

Service delivery system and process illustrations:

- cut-out switches to prevent spillage, for example on self-serve fuel pumps
- in-process gauges on filling lines to check the quantity in each pack by weighing or measuring the fill levels in each container
- limit switches on machines that allow the process to start only if the part to be processed is the correct one
- positional gauges that check that a part is correctly positioned before allowing a process to begin.

Staff-related illustrations:

- hospitals use different size tubes to dispense (say) blood and food, thereby eliminating mistakes
- automatic dispensing machines that ensure that correct quantity of a product (for example soft drink) is delivered
- bar code readers at supermarket checkouts reduce pricing errors
- in hospital operating theatres, instruments in preformed trays are used to allow a count back at the end of an operation to eliminate potential errors
- the outline of tools in a machine shop allows tool placings to be identified and highlight tools not replaced at the end of a job
- multi-stack filing cabinets that only allow one drawer to be open at a time. This prevents serious accidents where cabinets may tip forward if two or more drawers were open simultaneously.

Customer-related illustrations:

- the days of the week are stamped on capsule packs to enable a person to double-check their routine
- similarly, colour coding of tablet dispensers helps elderly patients particularly to avoid mistakes in self-administering their drug treatments
- the main light switch in aircraft toilets is triggered by the door closure thus avoiding embarrassing situations
- beepers on telephones are used to signal that a handset has been replaced correctly and, therefore, that batteries will be charged
- similarly, telephone handsets not replaced correctly will emit a loud signal to draw the user's attention to this fact
- go/no-go bag checks are used by airlines to allow passengers to self-check the size of the hand luggage they wish to take on board.

Process reliability – checking for failure

Reducing or even eliminating process failure is high on the agenda of most businesses as they strive to improve the reliability of their processes. For some organizations process failure is critical, even life-threatening, as in the failure of aircraft in flight or prolonged power cuts to emergency and intensive care units in hospitals.

While there is always the possibility of a process failing, it is essential to recognize that:

- Some failures are not as critical as others, and this factor needs to be reflected in the time and effort allocated to managing a system or process.
- Managing failure is a key part of the operations task – that failure will occur is a given. What is important is to manage and control failure in line with the consequences that such failure brings.

Assessing and measuring failure

Failure is a function of time. For the most part, the longer the life of a product or piece of equipment, the more likely it is to fail. However, this is not always so. Products often reflect three stages where the likelihood of failure differs: where this occurs the phenomenon is known as the bathtub curve (see Exhibit 14.1). However, surveys show that less than 10 per cent of all equipment has a bathtub profile. Electronic equipment has an infant mortality profile, but only 50 per cent of all equipment has a pattern of failure that is uniform and linear, a fact that makes the statistical calculation of the time of failure unreliable. Because of this, planning maintenance becomes a key factor in reducing failure and maintaining the reliability of a process or system.

Similarly, delivery systems based on human capabilities, as in many service systems, often show patterns of deterioration that are more to do with staff complacency and lack of management interest and control than other factors. The pattern and level of failure in these types of service delivery system would tend not to be uniform and consequently the reliability of the process would need to be monitored in a planned way so as to check for potential deterioration.

Exhibit 14.1 The bathtub curve

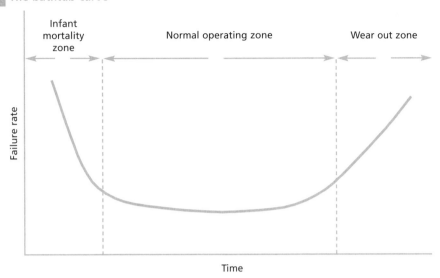

The principal ways of measuring failure are now explained:

- Rate of failure – as the name implies, failure rate is the number of failures that occur in a given period or as a percentage of the total number of services provided or products produced. For example, a banking system could be measured by the number of errors in a period, while a mail order company may check the number of errors as a percentage of the total orders received:

$$\text{Failure rate} = \frac{\text{number of failures} \times 100}{\text{total produced or service transactions completed}}$$

$$\text{Failure rate} = \frac{\text{number of failures}}{\text{operating time}} \times 100$$

- Process reliability – the reliability of a delivery system or process is a measure of how well it performs. Where a system has two or more stages, the reliability of each step will affect the overall reliability of the process. For example, a mail order process involves three steps and the processes involved and the current reliability of each step is given below:

Steps	Reliability
1 Customer order checked	
– Accurate and goods requested are available	
– Order amended where goods not available	0.980
2 Items picked and collated	0.935
3 Items packed and sent to mail routing	0.990

If any of these steps is completed incorrectly, the order will not be delivered correctly or within guaranteed timescales. Thus, the reliability of the total system is:

Reliability of the system = $0.980 \times 0.935 \times 0.990$

$= 0.907$

You will see from this example that the reliability of the system at 0.907 is markedly less than any of the individual parts of the process. Hence, the more interdependent steps in a process, the lower the reliability of the total system.

● **Mean time between failures** – an alternative way to measure the failure of a system is the mean time between failures (MTBF) which is calculated as follows:

$$MTBF = \frac{operating\ hours}{number\ of\ failures}$$

Thus, if an ATM at a bank averages three failures every two weeks, the MTBF would be:

$$MTBF = \frac{21\ days \times 24\ hours}{3} = 168\ hours$$

● **Process availability** – a process is not available to work if it has either failed or is being repaired following failures. To calculate process availability, you need to know the MTBF for a process and also the mean time to repair (MTTR), which is the average time taken to repair the process or equipment from the time it fails to the time it is again in use.

In the last example, the bank was reviewing alternative ways to increase the availability of ATMs. Currently, the MTTR was 7.5 hours, which made the availability:

$$Availability\ of\ an\ ATM = \frac{168}{168 + 7.5} = 0.957$$

Option 1 to increase availability was to reduce the interval of regular servicing which would increase the MTBF to 194 hours. Option 2 was to improve the speed of response time in the existing repair contract, thus lowering the MTTR to 5.0 hours. To determine the better option, both options need to be assessed, as follows:

Option 1 $Availability = \dfrac{194}{194 + 7.5} = 0.963$

Option 2 $Availability = \dfrac{168}{168 + 5.0} = 0.971$

Option 2, therefore, will improve availability more than option 1.

Identifying levels of failure

There are two ways to proactively check the delivery system to identify failures that have occurred and need attention.

The first is by in-process checks which ascertain whether the process is maintaining the required level of quality conformance. These can be undertaken in a number of ways, which include checking how well a service is progressing (for example verifying with customers in a restaurant that the food and service are of an acceptable standard at each stage during a meal) or undertaking point-of-departure interviews with customers as they leave the service delivery system. In manufacturing, checks using control and statistical process control (SPC) charts help monitor processes.

The second method is by overall checks which ask customers to discuss aspects of a delivery system at times other than when they are in the process itself. For example, complaint cards, feedback sheets and questionnaires can be mailed to solicit views about the services and products provided; focus groups of customers brought together to discuss specific services and products or the delivery system in general are often used to gain insights into where failures have occurred or may occur; similarly, telephone surveys are used to identify all aspects of services, products and delivery systems including points where failures may occur or have occurred in the past.

Analysing failures

One important activity in the quest for establishing process reliability levels is analysing failures. At one end of the spectrum are large-scale accidents or disasters such as airline crashes and major oil tanker spills. At the other end of the spectrum is the systematic analysis of complaints by companies as part of their way of ascertaining failures and identifying their source.

One way to undertake these checks is failure mode, effect and criticality analysis (FMECA). This approach analyses potential system failures in the light of the probability of occurrence and their likely impact on the successful operation of the system. The three elements of FMECA are:

- **Failure mode analysis** – a study of the system to determine how likely it is that a failure will occur.
- **Failure effect analysis** – a review of possible failures and their likely effects.
- **Failure criticality analysis** – a check on the potential failures in a system and the consequences of these in terms of affecting the service or product quality conformance levels and the impact on delivery reliability or delivery speed performance and system breakdowns.

Each potential cause of failure is assessed and quantified in terms of these three perspectives and the outcomes are prioritized. Corrective action then follows to reduce or eliminate potential failures. The main steps in the FMECA procedure are:

- list all parts of the system under review
- identify all possible ways in which each part of the system could fail, known as the failure modes
- for each failure mode, ascertain the causes and also the effect on the current system
- rate the probability of each cause in a given period, the seriousness of an occurrence and the possibility of detecting failure on a scale of 1 to 10
- calculate the criticality index by multiplying together the three ratings and use this to rank failures by level of importance
- identify corrective action to reduce the criticality of factors.

Maintenance and terotechnology

The necessary importance of reviewing physical assets in terms of investment and cost has led to the concept of 'terotechnology', defined in BS3811 (1993) as:

> A combination of management, financial, engineering, building and other practices applied to physical assets in pursuit of economic life cycle costs.[1] Its practice is concerned with the specification and design for reliability and maintainability of plant, machinery, equipment, buildings and structures, with their installation, commissioning, operation, maintenance, modification and replacement and with feedback of information on design, performance and costs.[2]

Although there is little that is new about each of these activities and ideas, terotechnology highlights the need to focus attention on the gains to be made by coordinating their interrelated functions. How these important aspects relate to one another needs to be understood. The introduction of terotechnology (from the Greek *terein* meaning to care for plus technology) is designed to concentrate awareness on this important concept and help promote and apply it appropriately throughout an organization.

Whereas maintenance is the largest aspect of terotechnology, on which the rest of this chapter concentrates, many activities at earlier stages of the business cycle, such as design and purchasing, can significantly affect maintenance costs and effectiveness. For example, the coordination necessary to identify that a modified design may lead to reductions in maintenance costs is typical of the gains to be made from reviewing activities on a wider perspective.

Maintenance – the concept

In most developed countries, gross national product continues to increase markedly faster than population growth. In all sectors this is largely the result of replacing manual operations by technological innovation. One result of this trend is a need for companies to become increasingly equipment conscious and build this dimension into the way in which they manage operations. This will contribute to improving many key aspects of a business. These include avoiding unnecessary equipment investment, ensuring the maximum use of existing equipment, enhancing the throughput and usage rates of processes, reducing the costs of energy and limiting the environmental side effects through innovations in equipment and improving the way they are used.

These tasks are solely or partly provided by sound maintenance practices. Current costs of this provision are high and typically far outweigh the purchase of new equipment. A recent survey revealed that the UK spent £14 billion annually on maintaining equipment worth £80 billion, while spending on new equipment was only £4.3 billion. With maintenance typically adding some 8–12 per cent to operations costs, it is not surprising that improving the practice and management of this function has become a major factor in the drive to improve aspects such as increasing productivity, reducing costs, improving on-time delivery performance and shortening lead times. To secure these opportunities, companies need to manage and coordinate their maintenance activities both in terms of the efficiency (internal) and effectiveness (needs of the market) dimensions. The direct costs of spares and staff and the indirect costs of unplanned equipment failure, secondary damage, unplanned overtime, output loss and excess spare parts offer significant saving opportunities. In addition, good maintenance practice needs to emphasize the role of equipment reliability within the wider corporate context. Several of the order-winners and qualifiers relevant to a company's agreed markets are based in part on the reliability of its systems and processes. The increase use of just-in-time agreements also makes it essential to ensure that all equipment is available when needed and called for within the operations plan.

Maintenance – the task

All physical facilities are susceptible to failure through breakdown, deterioration in performance through age and use and obsolescence due to improvements in technology. Reducing the likelihood of these features occurring involves considerable expenditure. If the sole objective was to reduce instances of failure, deterioration or obsolescence, eventually the investment and expense involved would exceed the actual costs of allowing the status quo to exist. Achieving a balance has to be addressed and determined. Each situation will be different, with some systems and processes requiring more sophisticated maintenance support than others.

The starting point for a sound maintenance programme, therefore, is to have a clear understanding of what maintenance tasks have to be undertaken. Only then is it possible to specify the staff needed to do the work, the spare parts necessary to support it and the systems required to manage and control the programme.

The maintenance function encompasses a wide range of responsibilities in different organizations.[3] Although the prime task usually concerns keeping the operations process in good working order, there are other important responsibilities that fall within its total function (see Exhibit 14.2). The list given in the exhibit is not exhaustive but is typical of the set of tasks frequently placed under the control of this function, if only as a matter of convenience.

Exhibit 14.2 Typical maintenance activities

Area of responsibility		Typical activities
Buildings and structures		To provide extensions, modifications and repairs to all buildings and structures, including grounds
Support function provision		To arrange the re-layout, modification and non-equipment provision and repair in office and administrative functions
Utilities		To maintain and provide supplies of all utilities including power, light, gas, water, steam, heating, air conditioning, pollution, sewage, refuse disposal and general housekeeping
Plant and equipment	repair	To maintain (including re-layout) all items of plant equipment in the operations process and the support functions
	essential work	To design, manufacture and install equipment as part of major modifications. To manufacture auxiliary equipment (for example tools and jigs) for new and existing equipment
Safety		To ensure that the necessary safety requirements are met, including the provision of mechanisms to reduce the chance of accidents

Although maintenance involves the range of responsibilities referred to in Exhibit 14.2, the rest of the chapter will concentrate on those functions directly concerned with the operations process. At times other areas will be referred to, but it is not intended to comprehensively address the management issues involved in these. The four areas listed below are key considerations in the sound management of the maintenance function and will be discussed in detail in the following sections:

1 Determine which parts of the process are to be maintained.

2 Decide between the different types of maintenance that could be employed and agree when maintenance should take place.

3 Consider the various policies available to an organization, including repair or replacement, the use of internal or external personnel and a centralized or decentralized approach to maintenance provision.

4   Develop procedures, systems and performance measures to help manage and control these activities.

Which parts of a process to maintain

A prerequisite in determining the scope of activities to be provided is to list all items that need to be maintained. The list should include equipment in the process as well as other equipment, transport, building and structures in line with the range of activities set out in Exhibit 14.2. This list will comprise the physical asset register and provide details of each item including:

1   A unique reference number for identification, often coded to show location and function

2   Description – make, model, age and modifications

3   Location

4   Details of major components or parts (including any items common to other equipment) and inventory holdings

5   Comments upon the critical nature of the equipment to the process.

The maintenance task will vary depending upon the number and complex nature of the equipment involved. Take British Airways (BA) for example. It has about 300 aircraft. The fleet ranges from Boeing 747s, Boeing 767s, A320s and A319s flying international routes to turbo-props island-hopping on Scottish domestic services. To keep these flying while conforming to the exacting safety and service quality standards it sets, BA employs over 9000 engineering staff worldwide and annually spends some £600 million on engineering services and maintenance. The maintenance schedule dominates an aircraft's working life, as Case example 14.1 shows.

Case example 1   **AIRCRAFT MAINTENANCE REQUIREMENTS INFLUENCE FLIGHT PATTERNS**

An aircraft's early life is dominated by its engineering and maintenance requirements. Its flight pattern for months ahead is planned to ensure that it is back at base in line with its maintenance schedule. In practice, its flight programme is so well organized that only in exceptional circumstances does an aircraft even come close to the legally permitted limits on the number of flying hours between overhauls.

An aircraft's working life is punctuated by a rigid succession of maintenance schedules based on the number of hours it has flown. These checks are frequent and become progressively more thorough as the air miles mount. In brief, the schedule comprises:

● **pre-flight inspection** by ground engineers and flight crew before take-off

● **every day** a small engineering team carries out a more detailed inspection including electrics, tyre pressures, oil

and hydraulics as well as investigating and rectifying all small problems reported during the previous day's flying

● **every 150 flying hours** (about 2 weeks*) a series of scheduled checks are completed. Typically this is between scheduled flights and at night

● **every 1000 flying hours** (about 3 months*) a full 24-hour check is made

● **every 18 months** the regular maintenance is supplemented by a major overhaul (called an intermediate check in BA) which involves 120 engineers spending a week or more on the aircraft

● **after 24,000 flying hours** (about 4 to 5 years*) an extensive overhaul is completed (called a major check in BA). The aircraft is out of service for one month while a large team of engineers virtually dismantle the entire aircraft to carry out a rivet-by-rivet inspection of the entire airframe. Not only do engines and surfaces come off for inspection or replacement but also any necessary major structural work

is undertaken such as replacing main undercarriage units, renewing skin panels and replacing fuselage frames

* These figures are typical for a big jet flying on international routes.

Case question How does this case example illustrate points 1 and 2 in the 'sound management of the maintenance function' list provided earlier in the section 'Maintenance – the task'?

Different types of maintenance

A company may undertake its maintenance function in a number of ways. The most effective method will reflect the item concerned and its importance in the operations process. The mix will, therefore, vary from one facility to another and will depend upon the goals of the maintenance provision, the nature of the facility and the type and age of the processes involved. The essential provision, however, is to make them part of a coordinated approach by introducing the key element of planning. Approaches will typically include a mix of maintenance types to reflect the particular requirements and conditions of the tasks involved. These various types of maintenance are now described.

Reactive maintenance

Reactive maintenance repairs equipment as needed and undertakes emergency maintenance as required. The systematic identification of parts of the process that need, or may need, to be replaced or maintained is not a feature of this approach. This form of maintenance is also known as 'breakdown' maintenance which concerns repairs being carried out after failure. This approach may be a consequence of problems occurring even though other types of maintenance are in place to prevent unscheduled and unanticipated equipment failures.

However, some companies deliberately use reactive maintenance as part of their overall approach to carrying out the maintenance task. This is particularly so for equipment where this method has advantages (for example where the impact of breakdowns on other parts of the organization or on support for its markets is relatively small) or where there is a significant variation in the rate of deterioration which makes such equipment less responsive to the benefits of periodic inspection. There are also occasions when a machine will continue to be operated even though maintenance is known to be needed. This is described as 'run to failure' where, for instance, the value of production resulting from an extended manufacturing run may outweigh the maintenance costs incurred following failure.

However, the reactive approach can still be planned in nature. When breakdowns occur, maintenance teams are allocated to the problem and their role is to respond quickly and make the necessary decisions to minimize the effect of the breakdown on the delivery system. In many instances, temporary repairs may be made so that the process can function again as soon as possible. Permanent repairs would then be made at a later and more convenient time.

Preventive (or scheduled) maintenance

Preventive or scheduled maintenance is carried out at predetermined intervals or in line with prescribed criteria (for example equipment hours worked) and is intended to reduce the probability of failure or the performance degradation of an item. Its objective is to reduce the probability of breakdown by replacing worn components at set intervals. The replacement interval is usually based on the mean failure time of certain components. However, in critical areas such as aircraft maintenance, replacement and maintenance schedules are typically specified by a legal or government body. Planned activities can range from simple inspections and adjustments to full overhauls.

Condition-based (or predictive) maintenance

Condition-based maintenance concerns preventive maintenance initiated as a result of knowledge of the condition of an item that comes from routine or continuous monitoring.[4] It involves a procedure of systematic inspection (especially of key parts or those that are expensive either in themselves or to replace) and can be undertaken to identify instances where maintenance could be performed either earlier or later than the regular preventive maintenance schedule dictates.

This planned procedure also enables ongoing checks to be made on the effectiveness of a preventive maintenance schedule, enabling it to be fine-tuned where necessary and so reducing some of the disadvantages that would accrue from the original schedules.

Condition monitoring or predictive maintenance involves taking a set of measurements to indicate the operating condition of each process, machine or item of equipment. This 'wear out' profile then enables maintenance to be scheduled shortly before the failure is anticipated.[5] Over time, the profile changes and so constant monitoring needs to be completed to enable companies to ensure that the interval between maintenance activities is as long as possible without risking excessive failure.

Stand-by equipment

The provision of stand-by equipment for all or part of a process is another potential element of an appropriate maintenance plan. It will typically be used where the cost or risk of breakdown is extremely high. Thus, it offers an alternative to the cost of a high level of maintenance in order to reduce the impact of breakdowns. In addition, backup equipment can be an effective alternative where time constraints demand that planned maintenance is undertaken in normal working hours. However, it is less likely to be a viable alternative for core processes on account of the high investment involved. Its use is more likely to be as a cover for support services such as compressed air, water, other utilities and control units.

Stand-by equipment does not take the place of regular maintenance but serves as an insurance policy for equipment that can seriously disrupt the process or delivery system if it breaks down. However, if stand-by equipment is provided, it is important to ensure that it is fully operational. Where possible it is advisable to run the equipment at regular intervals.

If several pieces of equipment are identical, one stand-by unit can serve this function for all online processes and result in a substantially lower cost provision. Examples of this include generator and compressed air equipment to support the processes within a manufacturing plant.

Corrective maintenance

Corrective maintenance involves making improvements to existing equipment, in addition to its general upkeep through other types of maintenance, with the aim of eliminating problems at source. It is intended to change the design of the equipment in such a way that a failure no longer occurs, or, if it does, that the failure no longer matters.

Equipment upgrades

Upgrades can form part of an overall approach to maintaining equipment. This involves redressing or modifying equipment to achieve one or both of the following:

- to increase process reliability
- to facilitate maintenance and repairs.

Data from other maintenance activities will invariably provide key indicators on which to base an updating programme. These upgrades may also form part of a wider decision to enhance a process in terms of its technical capability and/or throughput speeds.

Planned maintenance

Different approaches to maintenance are needed for different equipment or even for different parts of the same equipment. For example, consider on-site vehicles used in the construction industry. Changing the engine oil and undertaking a general service at fixed intervals are forms of preventive or scheduled maintenance. Items such as brakes and tyres are checked for wear on a regular basis and changed before they become defective, a form of condition monitoring. Headlights are probably a run to failure item, whereas replacing pneumatic tyres is a form of equipment upgrade to reduce the high number of punctures, the problems these cause to work schedules and overall costs. The underlying concept underpinning these examples concerns determining which type of maintenance to use for each part of the task. Planned maintenance is the term used to describe this approach.

As the above example illustrates, while planned maintenance does not advocate one approach compared to another, it does emphasize the need to determine the maintenance provision so that it is organized and carried out in a conscious manner. Thus, while reactive maintenance and condition monitoring are two ends of the maintenance provision continuum, both can contribute appropriate planned responses as part of a company's overall approach to maintenance.

In developing a plan, important decisions need to be taken on the approach and extent of planned maintenance and mix of maintenance types to be used. Thus, decisions are based on conscious choices that need regular review in order to check the appropriateness of current approaches.

Planned maintenance programmes yield a range of benefits including:

- Reduced maintenance costs – plans can be made and material and spare parts ordered in line with the plan.
- Maintenance can be completed when it is convenient to the operations process thus keeping capacity losses to a minimum.
- Capacity losses are further reduced as maintenance tasks can be planned to minimize time lost during normal working hours.
- Minimum material and spare parts inventory can be achieved, with levels of inventory in line with planned requirements rather than in anticipation of possible breakdowns.
- Increased opportunity to use contract maintenance more effectively, as work of a similar

or specialized nature can be planned to be completed at the same time thus reducing the higher costs associated with one-off jobs.

● Reduction in maintenance overtime working following fewer emergency repairs with increased planning.

● Less disruption from emergency work.

● The need for stand-by equipment can be reviewed and the trade-off between the reduced incidence of emergency breakdown and the costs associated with stand-by equipment can be reassessed, as Neil finds out in Exhibit 14.3.

Exhibit 14.3 Neil and his so-called stand-by equipment

© AMD Publishing

A common misconception about planned maintenance is that it is a high-cost alternative. However, even setting aside the capacity gains associated with this approach, the actual maintenance costs are also typically lower compared to unplanned maintenance provision. Furthermore, a key management task is to continuously check the costs of providing the current planned maintenance programme and to seek lower cost alternatives. This is achieved by comparing current costs with those which would have been incurred if alternative mixes of the different types of maintenance had been chosen. This checking and rechecking leads to choosing different approaches to the various elements of the overall maintenance task as conditions and alternatives change.

One outcome of a research programme completed over a 30-year period led to the development of reliability-centred maintenance (RCM).[6] This helps refine approaches within a planned maintenance programme by establishing a sensible framework for making choices. It starts with the premise that failures are a cause for concern only because they have consequences. Sometimes these consequences only cost money to repair while others interfere with operations; in the most serious cases they can lead to environmental incidents or fatalities.

Clearly, the more serious the consequence of a failure, the more time and effort should be spent trying to prevent it occurring. RCM is a decision-making framework to help companies evaluate the failure consequences of the maintenance options from which they can choose. Examples of the benefits gained from an RCM programme are provided in Exhibit 14.4.

The key step in planned maintenance is to agree on what the company is trying to prevent when it undertakes such a programme and then assess the consequences of each

Exhibit 14.4	Benefits from using RCM

Source of benefit	Examples
Improved plant availability and reliability	• Automotive wheel plant trebled output per man per shift in a six-month period • Emergency shutdowns of a main boiler were eliminated for three years, with savings of over $11 million • Plant efficiency increased from 68 to 98 per cent in the first month
Environmental integrity	• At an effluent treatment plant, the time after every major start-up when environmental hazards could possibly occur was reduced from one hour to zero
Safety	• The aviation industry recorded a reduction in crashes per million take-offs caused by equipment failure from 40 in 1960 to 1 in 3 million in 2000
Increased efficiency	• Maintenance schedule completion rates improved from 50 to 100 per cent in a toffee-making plant • In a steel mill, all fixed interval overhauls were eliminated

failure. Depending upon the nature and severity of the consequences, the final step is to select the most appropriate type of maintenance to deal with each failure.

A planned maintenance programme identifies and agrees what needs to be maintained, the type of maintenance to be employed and the frequency and timing of the schedule. However, it is easy to let the schedule of planned maintenance work slip because of pressures from the operations function to continue to use a process or handle emergencies and other work of a high priority. Inevitably, if this slippage is not checked, the benefits of planning are lost and total costs will rise. It is essential to agree a sensible schedule and then adhere to it. However, a regular review of the programme content is necessary. This typically leads to decreasing or excluding some parts of the programme while introducing or increasing the frequency of others. RCM and other reviews will be the basis of such changes.

In establishing the maintenance programme, short- and longer term plans will be determined, with each task allocated throughout the period. A planned approach will not only ensure that all the items are included but also provide for a fairly even workload across the maintenance function both in the short and long term. This evenness will help reduce overtime working and purchasing and overall maintenance costs.

Other policy issues

In addition to decisions concerning the nature and extent of planned maintenance activities, there are other issues of policy that concern maintenance provision. These include decisions around the use of internal or external personnel, centralized or decentralized maintenance, group or individual replacement policies and replacement parts inventory.

Internal or external personnel

The decision whether to provide the necessary maintenance personnel or facilities internally or externally is based primarily on cost and technical know-how. Often a combination of the two will be the most suitable arrangement. When the needs are irregular or require high technical know-how, maintenance will usually be contracted to outside firms. For instance, organizations frequently contract out their maintenance requirements on lifts and computers, while for other specialist equipment, such as photocopying and telephones, maintenance forms part of the rental agreement. With supplies such as inks and lubricating oils,[7] there is a growing trend to have the supplier provide technical support as part of a contract. In the case of ink, suppliers often have their own staff on a customer's site as part of the deal. Such decisions are relatively straightforward.

The more difficult decisions on provision are associated with the mainstream maintenance tasks – the operations processes. Where the technical know-how is not available within an organization (for example when new equipment is purchased), often external maintenance services are initially used. However, an organization will normally wish to build up its internal skills because of the high downtime costs associated with such processes. It will do this through training courses supported by sound documentation, where possible, building self-diagnostic facilities into the equipment and the use of diagnostic tools and instruments to enhance visual checks (for example vibration monitoring equipment). In situations where the internal maintenance expertise is available, problems of demand peaks for these capabilities will be eased through planned maintenance and other forms of forward planning, and will be supplemented by overtime working or buying in expertise on an as-needed basis.

Centralized or decentralized maintenance

Maintenance may be organized on a centralized or decentralized basis. With centralization, all staff are in one location with work being allocated as the need arises. In a decentralized set-up, staff are located in different geographical areas, with responsibilities more or less confined to those areas. Advantages of centralization include:

- improved utilization of people (especially specialists) and equipment
- more able to balance maintenance capacity to fluctuating workload demands
- allows more centralized control (for example one manager, centralized systems and more control over capital work)
- better training and the employment of specialists can be justified.

Advantages of decentralization include:

- faster service, with travelling time reduced
- improved continuity from shift to shift
- greater knowledge of the particular processes
- improved supervision with reduced geographical area of working.

Group or individual replacement policies

Some components are increasingly prone to failure as they age. Sudden failure creates more difficulty than wear and tear. Therefore, where a large number of identical low-cost items fall into this category, a group replacement policy becomes feasible. At the other end of the scale, individual replacement applies to when a single item is replaced when it fails. Several types of policy are possible, for example to replace:

- only failed units as they fail
- only failed units periodically

- all units (both good and failed) periodically
- failed units as they fail and all units periodically.

Which method to use will be determined by the critical nature of the item. For instance, a policy of replacing all units (both good and failed) periodically may be feasible for certain light bulbs in a building but not for electronic components or relays in a critical part of the process. To help in making this decision, three zones in the operating life of an item need to be identified and then used to determine which policy should be followed (see Exhibit 14.1):

- *Infant mortality*, the initial failure period
- *Normal operating life*, if a component survives the initial failure period, the chances of failure tend to be low for a time
- *Wear out zone*, where the probability of failure rises sharply, peaks and then falls.

The shape of the curve for items will differ and must be discovered by analysis.

Replacement parts inventory

Replacement parts carry the same costs as those outlined in Chapter 12. On the other hand, the costs of failing to have a part available when needed can be considerable. As a first step, it is important to classify spare parts and tools as follows:

- Spare materials and parts:
  - *Critical parts* are essential to the process, in that shutdowns would occur if they were not available, long purchasing lead times and possible safety or pollution hazards if the part is not replaced quickly.
  - *Normal parts* are used frequently in maintaining a process.
- Equipment and tools:
  - Portable plant used by maintenance personnel in carrying out their tasks.

An analysis of spare materials and parts and equipment and tools will normally reveal a sizeable investment. However, a check needs to be made on the purpose and importance of these items and then an ABC analysis established to distinguish the level of control to be used for the various categories of parts. These steps will ensure that a distinction is made between those items that need to be held in stock and those that do not. Of those that do, the large cost items are to be controlled, as described in Chapter 12.

Computerized records

As part of the drive to reduce costs and improve the accuracy of records, computers are used in this function as elsewhere in organizations. Particular applications include asset registers and recording systems, such as for costs and spares.

Total productive maintenance

A coherent theme throughout several chapters has been the need to involve people in the development and implementation of key activities at all levels in an organization. The area of maintenance provision is no exception. At the core of total productive maintenance (TPM) is the need to involve people to help to improve equipment effectiveness and this feature will be discussed in more detail in a later section. The format, introduction and development of this approach need to be part of the policy decisions that make up a company's overall maintenance provision.

The Japanese Institute of Plant Maintenance defines TPM as a system of maintenance covering the entire life of equipment and involving everyone from the top to the bottom of an organization. The approaches to maintenance described earlier in the chapter were recognized as implying that they were principally, if not exclusively, the concern of the maintenance function. It was recognized that while an organization was concerned with prevention, it was more concerned with the productive output of the equipment or process. Hence the switch from the word 'preventive' to 'productive'. Furthermore, and as part of a wider move to increase employee involvement, it is also recognized that operators are in the best position to note the first signs of a problem and assigning them to complete some aspects of maintenance would not only reduce overall maintenance costs but also increase their overall involvement in the productive output of a unit. Hence the inclusion of the word 'total'.

TPM can only be built on a sound maintenance programme encompassing the issues and alternatives outlined earlier. It requires a planned approach to maintenance which will identify the type of maintenance to be used. The distinguishing principles that guide a TPM programme are:

- Staff must always strive to improve equipment effectiveness based on constant attention to detail and aimed at solving problems by identifying causes rather than just treating symptoms.

- Routine care needs to be carried out as part of the job. A literal translation of the Japanese term is 'parlour factory', suggesting that the working environment should be as clean and tidy as the home.

- Operators are recognized as being in the best position to monitor equipment performance. Their involvement in and responsibility for its continuous monitoring improves performance and increases their role in the checking and enhancement tasks within the overall maintenance function.

- Skill development is based on transferring suitable maintenance tasks to operators and using breakdowns and other problems as learning opportunities, thereby increasing operator understanding and ownership.

As with other employee involvement applications, the potential of a company's equipment is being released through the potential of its employees. In effect, TPM is uncovering the 'hidden factory' trapped behind process and equipment inefficiencies. However, given that business-wide TPM can take years to implement fully, it is important to recognize the four phases in a successful TPM application:

1 An awareness study, pilot programmes, plant clear-and-clean exercises and developing analytical techniques such as problem solving.

2 Bring all sections up to 'best practice' by using agreed approaches across all areas and at all times.

3 Raise overall performance by developing the capability of employees, equipment and processes. This requires employees to become increasingly proactive in searching for new ways to improve equipment effectiveness.

4 'Strive for zero losses'. Although unattainable in a practical sense, its purpose is to set targets as an essential facet of the improvement process.

The benefits of TPM are marked, as the results in Exhibit 14.5 testify. As with other employee involvement initiatives, time and staying with the task are prerequisites for securing large and sustainable gains, as Case examples 14.2 and 14.3 illustrate.

Exhibit 14.5 Benefits resulting from the introduction of TPM

| Company and product | Breakdowns per month reduced | | | Productivity | | OEE %[1] | | |
	From	To	Period (years)[2]	Current indexed on previous year[3]	Period (years)	Now	Before	Period (years)
Dynamic – book covers	18	3	5	125	2	75	55	3
Gunze – clothing	707	15	2	120	2.5	85	71	3
Sekisui – chemicals	200	10	4	150	4	100[4]	100[4]	4
Daikin – air conditioning	250	5	6	200	6	88	65	6
Toshiba – lighting	387	33	4	247	4	88	71	4

Notes 1 Overall equipment effectiveness, which is covered in detail in the final section of this chapter.
2 Length of time over which the improvements were gained.
3 Indexed figures have been based on the previous year's performance.
4 Data available only in this form.

Case example 2 INTRODUCING TPM

Hoechst Trespaphan's Swindon (UK) plant makes polypropylene film for labelling and packaging products for the food industry. The company restructured its plant into six units, each with a dedicated shift team, with all units supported by a separate maintenance team. Training and cross-skilling increased staff flexibility and helps keep all the processes running in a business where capacity is having difficulty matching demand.

At the time of these changes, the plant averaged 300 breakdowns per month, together with equipment deficiencies that affected quality conformance levels. The high level of automation in the plant included integrated process control so when one item of the plant fails the whole line stops. In addition, the planned preventive maintenance schedule required each line to stop one day in every 12 weeks. The outcome of all this was that the uptime level of the plant was only 78 per cent.

The introduction of TPM first examined bottleneck processes and set the basis for future improvements and activities, including eliminating set-up failures, increasing throughput speeds (for example the speed of the main film slitting machine was doubled), stopping leaks on feed pipework, the reintroduction of routine checks, finding the root cause of minor problems and the immediate implementation of low-cost improvements.

The plant is now zoned and shift teams select projects within their areas. Regular audits monitor progress, and improvements are significant. But TPM is a long journey. Overall equipment effectiveness (OEE) is now a principal measure, and while significant gains have been made, 69 per cent is a long way off the 85 per cent posted by world-class performers.

www.trespaphan.com

Case questions 1 What were the key steps in bringing about the improvements in this plant?
2 Why has OEE replaced process uptime as the principal measure used at Hoechst Trespaphan?

Case example 3   CULTURAL BENEFITS OF TPM AT FORTIES ALPHA

One hundred and twenty miles northeast of Aberdeen in Scotland, Forties Alpha is one of Apache's platforms extracting oil from the North Sea. At almost 30 years old, it is a declining asset. Around 1980 the oilfield was delivering its peak daily output of 150,000 barrels of oil, while today, with reserves falling and more and more water being dragged up with the oil from under the sea bed, Alpha's potential is down to around one-third its peak.

While full capacity is out of reach, equipment efficiency eroded production output in the mid-1990s to about 50 per cent of potential. At that time, improvement efforts were concentrated on controlling and improving the visible operational costs (people, maintenance, overheads and material) of the platform. What received little, if any, attention were the hidden costs of lost opportunities that continued to erode the platform's business performance. These hidden costs included water management cutbacks, unplanned shutdowns, restart losses, safety and technical integrity, water content in the product, poor work environment and a lack of staff flexibility. All were factors affecting overall efficiency.

The platform's five-shift complement of 75 technicians and supervisors went through a TPM training programme. The first project, to review the platform's system for disposing of the water dredged up with the oil, which reduces oil production, identified 143 improvements. When these were implemented, the throughput of the water disposal plant increased by 80,000 barrels a day, while one water treatment unit was able to handle 45,000 rather than the previous 20,000 barrels per day. The knock-on effect of this was that the platform's OEE rose from 29 to 63 per cent in the first six months of the TPM project. Asset care was more diligently carried out because the need for it was clearly understood.

These improvements were complemented by the cultural benefits that resulted – stronger teamwork, a proactive approach to maintenance, all-round increased knowledge of processes and procedures and the resolution of problems. Technical information, knowledge, routines and experiences were all shared. As a result, problems were resolved rather than given a quick fix. The impact on the business as a whole became the context in which problems, improvements and descriptions were reviewed.

www.apachecorp.com

Case questions
1 Why do companies such as Apache typically concentrate their efforts and measure their performance on operational costs such as people, maintenance, overheads and materials?
2 To what did the TPM programme switch the focus of the platform's attention?
3 What was the key to the success of the TPM initiative?

Energy management

A significant part of the maintenance task concerns energy management in terms of its storage, conversion, distribution and utilization. The increasing use of automation and IT systems within operations and other departments in a business is placing even greater emphasis on this function.

To successfully manage energy, the following tasks need to be addressed:

1 *Assessments and targets* – first undertake an audit to determine the actual amount of energy used in each part of an installation. Once completed, usage targets can be set within the different parts of a building or process. Perhaps Lloyd should repeat this step – see Exhibit 14.6.

2 *Energy use* – the second aspect concerns the level of efficiency at which energy is used. The drive in businesses to improve overall efficiency has led to increasing attention being given to overhead costs. In energy terms this concerns reviewing usage rate, reducing losses and the possibility of reclaiming and recovering certain forms of energy such as heat.

3   Energy management system – the final task concerns installing a system to manage and control each form of energy from electricity through to compressed air. The main components of these management systems include:

- sensors to monitor existing conditions, for example controls to measure inside and outside temperatures, lighting requirements and humidity levels
- direct digital controllers that activate or shut down the system depending upon the information received from the sensors
- a network to link the digital controllers
- supervisory terminals to inspect the information, including the automatic display of faults.

Energy management system investments in the USA now exceed £2 billion. While those in Europe are about half that level, the recognition that these investments concern not only cost savings but form an integral part of employee working conditions and a company's green agenda is increasing corporate awareness of the overall benefits to be gained.

Exhibit 14.6 Lloyd undertakes an energy audit

© AMD Publishing

Managing the maintenance function

The management task in maintenance is similar to that for other functions – the planning and control of work against realistic standards, both in terms of capacity and costs and measuring performance against these, as discussed below.

Measuring workloads

The next chapter outlines ways of measuring the capacity requirements and utilization levels in a function. One of these, group capacity assessment (GCA) is well suited to the task of determining maintenance capacity requirements compared with a function's current workload. It also enables management to monitor workload fluctuations and adjust capacity as required.

In addition to the GCA method of establishing times for maintenance tasks, the universal maintenance standards (UMS) scheme is also available. This is similar to analytical and comparative estimating as described in Chapter 15. In UMS, a large number (200–300) of benchmark jobs are chosen as being representative of the maintenance work involved. Each of these is directly observed and the method checked. An analysis is then completed for each element using methods time motion (MTM) values, and times for completing each element are then determined.[8]

From this analysis, a table of about 20–30 elements is constructed. All other work is then analysed, and, with the aid of the benchmark jobs, the elements of each job are matched to this table and time standards are then established.

Planning maintenance

By introducing a TPM approach, companies are able to separate maintenance tasks into time frames (daily through to annual tasks) and maintenance staff/operator allocations.

The first step, therefore, is listing all the maintenance work to be undertaken, the frequency of the schedule and to which category of staff it will be allocated. Maintenance calendars then need to be devised to cover the scheduled times that eventually result in annual, monthly, weekly and daily plans. From these, detailed schedules are drawn up for

Exhibit 14.7 Part of a maintenance plan for a zinc plating unit

Unit / Location	Maintenance Task	Period (weeks)	Total hours (# staff)	Parts Used	Costs (£s)	Assigned to	1	2	3	4	5	6	7	8	9	10	11	12	Remarks
Pump / Circulation pump	Over-haul	26	16 (2)	–	–	M		/							/				
Outer pump	Over-haul	52	100 (2)	–	–	M													
Valve	Replace sealing gasket	52	30 (4)	Sealing gasket	640	M	X								/				
–	Tighten	13	16 (2)	–	–	M&O		/			/			/			/		
Electricity supply / # 2	Replace roll	4/5	9 (2)	Roll	200	M	X	/	/	/	/	/	/	/	/	/	/	/	
Bearings																			

Key 1 M = maintenance. O = operations.
     2 / denotes plan. X denotes completed.

each item of equipment (see Exhibit 14.7), each department and each section within a department. These will, in turn, be translated into monthly and weekly calendars of work to facilitate ordering spares and balancing capacity over a period of time.

Measuring performance

A key factor in managing a maintenance function is to agree the key measures to help gauge and monitor performance. Below are some of the more important measures used.

Internal department performance measures

These should include:

- The level of effective performance by relating the hours of maintenance work produced to clocked hours in the department and expressed as a percentage. This shows the amount of work produced per hour.
- Actual tasks completed compared to the plan in terms of the hours of work involved. This helps to assess overall performance and checks the maintenance support for operations during a given period.
- Total hours of work by each type of maintenance as a percentage of the total maintenance hours. This measures the actual types of maintenance used to the level set in the plan and helps assess how well the function is managing its maintenance response.

Operations-related measures

These should include those that assess the cost of maintenance support overall and those that measure trends in the key areas of improvement. For example:

- Checking the number of maintenance hours worked with the number of direct hours worked in operations helps assess trends in the relative size of maintenance support. Comparing maintenance costs (including hours, materials and overheads) with the value of the services and products completed in the same period would provide a similar check.
- Relating the number of breakdowns, both in terms of occasions and time lost to the number of operations hours worked, would provide an insight into the success of reducing this element of maintenance. However, where a run to failure type of maintenance had been chosen, the incidence of breakdowns that occur as a result of adopting this policy should be shown separately and would not form part of the trend review.
- Safety-related measures such as the number of days lost through accidents help highlight this important aspect of work and the joint role of operations and maintenance in driving these incidents down to zero.

Overall measures

These help to set the maintenance contribution within the context of the overall business. For example:

- Overall equipment effectiveness (OEE) is one of the most widely used measures. How it is calculated and used is illustrated in Exhibit 14.8. This measure combines both maintenance and operations performance and can be calculated for individual items of equipment, a section or the business as a whole.

Exhibit 14.8 Overall equipment effectiveness (OEE)

Week	Availability %		Performance %		Quality %		OEE %
1	84	×	92	×	96	=	74
2	89	×	88	×	97	=	76
3	86	×	90	×	94	=	73
4	83	×	91	×	98	=	74
Average	86	×	90	×	96	=	74
Best of the best	89	×	92	×	98	=	80

Initial OEE figures for a typical company are in the 40–50 per cent range, while world-class performers post 85 per cent and above. Such potential offers much scope for improvement, with sizeable benefits for organizations that continue to manage their way to levels similar to those shown in Exhibit 14.5.

● Checking on the relative cost of maintenance is provided by expressing maintenance cost as a percentage of sales revenue. Although this will be affected by changes in the make-or-buy decision, adjusted trends help to provide a valuable, overall measure.

Reflections

For organizations to secure essential increases in productivity requires the combined efforts of all functions. The increased use of technology has resulted in the tasks of maintenance and making processes and systems reliable becoming major contributors to the effective activities of many businesses. Furthermore, the growing introduction of JIT scheduling arrangements and the increasing importance of delivery reliability and delivery speed places greater emphasis on equipment and processes being available in line with schedules and customer needs.

As a result, the role and activities within the maintenance function have changed to meet these new requirements. For example:

● To help reduce the growing cost of maintenance, organizations are considering the maintenance dimension much earlier in investment decisions, in recognition of the importance of post-installation costs as an essential factor within investment appraisal procedures.

● As part of the importance of meeting delivery performance targets (speed and on-time) while keeping inventories low, high and guaranteed levels of equipment availability are essential.

● Where equipment does fail, then process support becomes a vital role. Quick and effective response to process problems and breakdowns is an increasingly important task. On-site, well-trained staff are needed to support core processes, while those companies using control systems often supplement their own in-house capability by establishing computer links to outside specialists to help diagnose problems through the use of computer-based control systems.

The need to reduce costs has also led companies to reduce total manning levels within maintenance and to compensate for the loss of skill areas by more staff training and changes in working practices through teamwork approaches based on multiskilling principles and the increased use of operators to take on appropriate routine maintenance tasks – the concept of TPM.

As part of this development, companies involve the maintenance function in the later stages of installation and throughout the commissioning phase of equipment as the first stage of training and to provide the opportunity to identify possible modifications to help simplify process support in the future.

All organizations will continue to invest in technology at an increasing rate in order to reduce costs and improve response times in terms of data provision, control and decision making. It is important for organizations to recognize the consequences of this. Operations managers need to bring top management's attention to these important perspectives before the technology decisions are made. Furthermore, with investment and growth, the need for supporting specialists will also increase. It is essential, therefore, that the management of the company's physical resources is at the appropriate level and the controls to ensure that this is so are installed and developed.

Key Elements of Process and Delivery System Reliability and Maintenance

The reliability of the delivery system is a key factor in operations as it impacts both the internal and external (or market-related) tasks in managing this function:

- Internal tasks include cost targets, assessment of capacity which, in part, will need to take into account the reliability of the process, and inventory management that similarly will need to reflect the level of uncertainty of a process in terms of the level of inventory it will carry.

- For market-related tasks such as on-time and fast delivery, process reliability will be a key factor.

- The first section of the chapter addressed the issues around process reliability and introduced ways of checking for failure. The methods of assessing failure discussed included rate of failure, process reliability and process availability measures.

- This section also covered how to identify levels of failure and analysing failures as a way of improving process reliability.

- The final part of this section introduced ways to improve process reliability by introducing fail-safe mechanisms as an integral part of systems design.

- The remainder of the chapter then addressed ways to maintain processes and the management tasks involved.

- The opening sections clarified meanings and terms and identified the different types of maintenance – reactive, preventive, condition-based, use of stand-by equipment and corrective maintenance before leading to a major section on planned maintenance.

- The final part of the chapter highlighted the key issues in managing the maintenance function. The areas covered included measuring staff workloads, planning maintenance tasks and ways of assessing performance.

Self-check

1 The concept of integrating fail-safe mechanisms into a process in order to reduce failures is increasingly being used in:
- a Manufacturing processes ▪
- b Service delivery systems ▪
- c Both a and b ▪

2 An illustration of a customer-related fail-safe (or *poka-yoke*) device is:
- a Positional gauges that check that a part is correctly positioned before allowing a process to begin ▪
- b Beepers on telephones used to signal that a handset has been replaced correctly ▪
- c Bar code readers at supermarket checkouts to reduce pricing errors at the till ▪

3 When managing process failure, it is essential to recognize that:
- a Some failures are not as critical as others ▪
- b Managing failure is not an important part of the operations task ▪
- c All failures are as critical as each other ▪

4 Failure is a function of:
- a Time ▪
- b Quantity ▪
- c Value (£) ▪

5 The largest part of terotechnology relates to equipment re its:
- a Operation ▪
- b Maintenance ▪
- c Modification and replacement ▪

6 Which of the following is **not** a method of maintenance:
- a Preventive ▪
- b Reactive ▪
- c Productive ▪

7 The concept of planned maintenance involves:
- a Advocating one form of maintenance over another ▪
- b Moving away from activities such as condition-based maintenance ▪
- c Carrying out the maintenance provision in a conscious manner ▪

8 An advantage of decentralized maintenance is:
- a Improved utilization of the workforce (especially specialists) and equipment ▪
- b Faster service ▪
- c Better training and the employment of specialists can be justified ▪

9 At the core of total productive maintenance (TPM) is the need to:
- a Involve people to help to improve equipment effectiveness ▪
- b Have a central maintenance function ▪
- c Use highly skilled maintenance engineers to monitor the process ▪

10 The main components of an energy management system include:
- a Sensors and direct digital controllers ▪
- b Supervisory terminals ▪
- c Both a and b ▪

Study activities

Discussion questions

1 The radio alarm clock you recently purchased needs three elements to be working for it to provide the alarm in the morning. The reliability of these three elements are shown opposite.

Element	Reliability
Clock	0.96
Alarm switch	0.94
Radio	0.98

What is the probability that the alarm will ring in the morning?

2   A major European bank has 2378 ATMs. When an ATM has a machine or software failure, the system controlling an ATM would trigger an automatic call-out to NCR who are contracted to provide a backup maintenance service to the bank. Last year the total number of 'auto-calls' to NCR was 19,738. What was the average mean time between failures for an ATM?

In addition, there are several occasions during a year when ATMs run out of cash. This is particularly so when national holidays fall on a Monday or around major holiday periods such as Christmas and Easter. If these cash-outs are added to the auto-calls, the total for last year is now 22,115. What would be the mean time between failures now?

3   How does planned maintenance differ from the other types of maintenance outlined in the section entitled 'Different types of maintenance'. What are the underlying principles that distinguish planned maintenance?

4   A photocopying outlet has several machines, three of which are under heavy demand during most days. The mean time (operating hours) between failures (MTBF) and minimum time (hours) to repair (MTTR) for these machines are as follows.

Machine reference	MTBF	MTTR
3	80	4
5	100	2
8	75	4

What is the availability for each of these three machines?

Assignments

1   Identify three *poka-yoke* examples used in service delivery systems. Classify them into process, service and customer-based applications as described and illustrated in this chapter.

5   For the three machines in Question 4, the company would be able to change the maintenance and service contracts with the following outcomes.

Machine reference	Revised	
	MTBF	MTTR
3	95	3.5
5	130	2.0
8	85	3.0

If the cost to complete these improvements was similar one machine to another, which machine would you improve first.

6   Why is stand-by equipment usually not a sound part of providing maintenance? Give two examples where stand-by equipment would be an essential provision.

7   The photocopying machine in a solicitor's office has the following performance data during a six-week period.

Week	Availability %	Performance %	Quality %
1	80	90	93
2	74	88	96
3	82	92	97
4	83	91	92
5	76	87	94
6	78	89	93

Calculate the overall equipment effectiveness:

- for each week
- as a six-week average
- the best of the best in this period.

2   Analyse the maintenance work completed on your car in a 12-month period and classify each activity into its relevant category.

Exploring further

Alire, S, Greenwood, G, Gupta, A and Terwilliger, M 'Workforce – constrained preventive maintenance scheduling using evolution strategies', *Decision Science*, **31**(4) (2000) pp. 837–59.

Ambs, K, Cwilich, S, Mei Deng et al. 'Optimzing restoration capacity in the AT&T network', *Interfaces*, **30**(1) January–February (2000) pp. 26–44.

Chase, RB and Stewart, DM 'Make your service fail-safe', *Sloan Management Review*, **35**(3)
(1994).

Chen, F 'Continuous improvement for preventive maintenance, *Production and Inventory
Management Journal*, **38**(4) (1997) pp. 13–16.

Cua , K, McKone, KE and Schroeder, RG 'Relationship between implementation of TQM, JIT and
TPM, and manufacturing performance', *Journal of Operations Management*, **19**(6) (2001)
pp. 675–94.

Davis, R *Productivity Improvements Through TPM*, Prentice Hall, Hemel Hempstead (1995).

Dhillon, BS *Engineering Maintenance: A Modern Approach*, Technomic Publishing, Lancaster, PA
(2002).

Japan Institute (ed.) *Focused Equipment Improvement to TPM Teams*, Japan Institute of Plant
Maintenance, Tokyo (1997).

Mobley, K *Root Cause Failure Analysis*, Butterworth Heinemann, Oxford (1999).

Nakajima, S *Introduction to TPM; Total Productive Maintenance*, Productivity Press, Cambridge,
MA (1988).

Senju, S (ed.) *TQC and TPM*, Asian Productivity Organization, Tokyo (1992).

Smith, DJ *Reliability, Maintainability and Risk*, Butterworth Heinemann, Oxford (2000).

Takahashi, Y and Osada, T *TPM: Total Productive Maintenance,* Asia Productivity Organization,
Tokyo (1990).

Westerkamp, TA 'Plan for maintenance productivity', *IIE Solutions*, **33**(8) (2001) pp. 36–41.

Womack, JP, Jones, DT and Roos, D *The Machine that Changed the World*, Rawson Associates,
New York (1990).

Notes and references

1   Life cycle costs are defined as the total costs of an item throughout its life including initial, maintenance and support costs.

2   *Glossary of Terms used in Terotechnology*, BS3811 (British Standards Institution, 1993) No. 1101 and *Guide to Terotechnology*, BS3843 (British Standards Institution, 1992), Part 2.

3   The maintenance function is usually either an engineering or an operations management responsibility. This will depend on aspects such as the size of the organization and the nature of its products/services. Exhibit 1.3 illustrates this function as part of the operations task. In other organizations it may report to the V-P research and development or, more normally, to the V-P engineering.

4   Also see Holder, R 'Why condition-based monitoring offers solid bottom line results', *Works Management*, March (1996), pp. 18–19.

5   These issues are discussed in an article by Bates, A 'Effective strategies deliver plant reliability', *Works Management*, July (1996), pp. 45–9.

6   This approach is reviewed by Moubray, J 'Reliability centred maintenance: making a positive contribution to asset management strategy' in *A Guide to Best Practice Maintenance Management*, Part 1 Shell Oils, London (1996).

7   See, for example, Raynes, M 'Outsourcing: the way to solve your lubricating problems' in *A Guide to Best Practice Maintenance Management*, Part 2 Shell Oils, London (1996).

8   MTM is a widely used predetermined motion time standard. This form of measurement is covered in Chapter 15. Suffice it to say here that with MTM, predetermined times for operations are used that have been built up through research and analysis, and issued as tables.

Improving Operations

book map

Part

1
- 1 Managing Operations
- 2 Operations Strategy
- 3 Managing People

SUPPLIERS — INPUTS

CUSTOMERS — OUTPUTS

PROCESSES

2
- 4 Designing and Developing Services & Products
- 5 Designing Service Delivery Systems
- 6 Designing Manufacturing Processes
- 7 Location and Layout

3
- 8 Managing Capacity
- 9 Technology Developments
- 10 Operations Scheduling and Execution
- 11 Managing Quality
- 12 Managing Inventory
- 13 Managing the Supply Chain

4
- 14 Process and Delivery System Reliability and Maintenance
- 15 Time and Productivity
- 16 Improving Operations

5
- Managing Operations in Practice: Long Case Studies

Time and Productivity

Outline of chapter

To manage operations, the range of services and products provided by an organization are scheduled, using time as the common denominator. Similarly, the input/output ratio that comprises productivity is at the core of the drive for greater efficiency within organizations. The definition and composition of both time and productivity are, therefore, essential features of the task of managing operations.

Why are time and productivity important?

Executive overview

This chapter addresses two important dimensions that are central to managing operations:

- **Time** – measuring how long a job should take.

- **Productivity** – measuring the outputs from a system in relation to the inputs that go into their creation.

On reflection you will clearly recognize the link between these two aspects of operations, as the measurement of time will invariably form part of measuring the outputs and inputs (the numerator and denominator respectively) of the productivity calculation.

The layout of the chapter reflects the link between these two aspects by incorporating them in the same chapter and the separate perspectives involved by addressing each in its own section. First we will discuss the aspect of time, with the section on productivity coming later. An overview of the aspects covered in the chapter are:

- **Why time is the common denominator of operations management** with illustrations to highlight this issue.

- **Measuring the content of work** – measuring work sets out to answer the question, how long should a job take? This section overviews the approach to follow.

- **Approaches to measuring work content** – as jobs are different, the approach to measuring jobs will also differ. This section illustrates how the approaches to measuring short repetitive tasks, long non-repetitive tasks and techniques to measure capacity utilization and requirements differ, giving examples of each.

- **Productivity** – what it is and what, in general terms, it measures.

- **Productivity and efficiency** are compared to help distinguish between these two dimensions used in evaluating the improvement results.

- **Approaches to measuring productivity** are discussed and the difference between single-factor and multi-factor measures and the use of added value is explained.

- **Ways to improve productivity** are outlined and the link between these and the next chapter on the ways to improve performance in operations is established.

- **Service applications** – with the growing importance of the service sector in the more advanced economies, the need for and ways to secure productivity improvements in service businesses are discussed.

Time – the common denominator in managing operations

The two dimensions used by a business to control its activities are time and money. Time is the basis for tasks such as planning, estimating, costing and payment systems, and money is the basis for trading, accounting and financial reporting.

Whereas the money dimension is primarily explained through accounting and finance, it is through operations management that an understanding of the time dimension may be gained. It is essential, therefore, that operations managers fully understand how work may be measured and are able to choose the most appropriate method of measurement to meet a given requirement. This section explains these aspects of the task. Furthermore, operations managers must understand both the time and money dimensions in themselves and ensure that the translation from one to another is both accurate and appropriate. For, whereas operations is managed on a time base, the costs associated with services, products, customers and investments will be reported in terms of money.

This opening statement explains that operations uses time as the common denominator for assessing, controlling and managing many of its activities. The question is, why? To explain let us use three examples.

Example 1 – Conform

A glance back at Exhibit 8.3 shows that the nine products made on day 1 of that week all had different standard times. Therefore, to use the quantity of products made as the measure of how good a day was or as the basis for calculating capacity requirements would be of little value. Making 100 of product reference 2766 at 3.0 standard minutes each is not the same as making 100 of product reference 1229 at 36.0 standard minutes each.

Example 2 – Heath Motors

Heath Motors makes three small electric motors for a wide range of applications. As in Example 1, to use the quantity of products as the basis for calculating capacity requirements or to assess weekly performance would not provide a meaningful approach to these and other dimensions of operations, as Exhibits 15.1 and 15.2 illustrate.

Using quantity as the basis for assessing output, Exhibit 15.1 shows that week 2 appears to be a much better period than week 1. The factor missing from this assessment is how long it takes to make each different motor. When these data are introduced (see Exhibit 15.2), it can be seen that, in terms of hours, the output for weeks 1 and 2 is very similar.

Exhibit 15.1 Heath Motors – output in terms of units produced

Week	Electric motor type	Quantity produced	
		#	Total
1	HM 40	100	
	HM 60	100	440
	HM 80	240	
2	HM 40	480	
	HM 60	200	830
	HM 80	150	

Exhibit 15.2 Heath Motors – output in terms of hours produced

Week	Electric motor type	Quantity produced (#)	Time per product (hours)	Hours produced	
				#	Total
	HM 40	100	0.5	50	
1	HM 60	100	1.5	150	1160
	HM 80	240	4.0	960	
	HM 40	480	0.5	240	
2	HM 60	200	1.5	300	1140
	HM 80	150	4.0	600	

Example 3 – John Michael

For the owner of John Michael (see Exhibit 8.4) to determine how many hairdressers would be required or to assess the output of a day based upon the number of customers served would be misleading. The time taken will depend on whether a customer has a simple wash, cut and blow dry or a perm. Yet the factor of time needs to be included when calculating capacity, scheduling appointments, measuring performance and determining costs.

Measuring the content of work

The purpose of measuring the content of work is to establish the time for a qualified person to complete a specified job at a defined level of performance.[1] In other words, measuring work sets out to answer the question, 'How long should this job take to complete?' As the time dimension is the basis for managing most key operations activities, establishing times and knowing what the statements used to express time comprise are essential operations management tasks.

Before describing the approaches used to provide this information, it is useful to first understand the reasons for and objectives of measuring work, and these are summarized in Exhibit 15.3.

Exhibit 15.3 The reasons for and objectives of measuring work

With the continuous improvement approaches described in Chapter 16, measuring the content of work plays an essential role in tasks, such as to:

- eliminate ineffective time, with work content determining the extent of possible improvements
- allow comparisons of alternative methods to be made
- balance work members in a team
- determine an adequate workload for a person

As a basis for:

- planning and scheduling work
- estimating and costing
- staff and staff cost control
- payment and reward systems
- estimating future capacity requirements both in terms of staff and equipment
- establishing delivery promises

The simplest way to measure work is to time how long a task takes. However, the reality of work does not lend itself to such a simple method. In particular, there are three dimensions that can make a significant difference to the time it takes to complete a job. These are listed in Exhibit 15.4, together with the ways used to account for these factors.

Exhibit 15.4 Factors affecting the time to complete a task and approaches to overcoming these factors

Factors affecting the length of time to complete a job	Approaches used to account for these factors
Different methods may be used to complete a task	The time to complete a task is based on an agreed method. A revised method would require a new time
The time taken directly relates to the speed and effort of the person doing the task	Variations in speed and effort are accounted for when assessing how long it takes and adjustments are made to account for such differences. This is known as 'rating'
Some tasks are more strenuous or difficult than others and require more time for a person to rest and recover	All observed rest time is excluded from the initial assessment of how long a job takes. This 'net' time is later increased uniformly to include an allowance for rest and personal needs in line with the type of job being undertaken

The steps to measure the work content of jobs are explained below, with a brief explanation of what is involved:

1 Select, record and analyse the job: which jobs to measure are selected to help undertake a number of tasks including continuous improvement, capacity planning, scheduling work and establishing delivery lead times (see Exhibit 15.3). Recording what is involved in the work selected, agreeing the method to be used and analysing what the work entails are the next steps.

2 Measure the job and establish the time: there are a range of ways to measure jobs. The choice will depend on the level of accuracy required and the length of time a job takes, for example short, repetitive tasks will normally be expressed in minutes and parts of minutes. Long jobs such as undertaking a management consultancy contract and building an oil tanker will normally be expressed in weeks and parts of weeks.

3 Check that the measurement is accurate: before the times for a job can be used, it is essential to complete studies to check that the calculations have been correctly made so that their use will lead to sound decisions.

Approaches to measuring work content

This section provides more detail on the approaches to measuring the work content of a task. To reflect the fact that different approaches need to be used depending on the nature of the task, the section is in three parts, giving the approaches to measure short, repetitive tasks, long, non-repetitive tasks and capacity utilization, with Exhibit 15.8 providing a summary of which approach would be the best in a given situation.

Approaches to measure short, repetitive tasks

As a general rule, the techniques used to measure short, repetitive tasks will be chosen to provide accurate information expressed in minutes and parts of a minute. The reason for this is fundamental to the task itself; as it only takes a short time to complete but will be completed on numerous occasions, the time taken to complete the task needs to be measured accurately.

The techniques most commonly used to provide this level of accuracy are time study, predetermined motion time standards and synthetics. The first of these will be described in more detail and will include the procedure to establish a 'standard time'. This will provide a sound basis for understanding how to measure the content of work. The other two approaches will then be described in less detail.

Time study

As providing a more accurate time is needed for work that is of short duration and repetitive in nature, the job under review is broken down into elements, enabling the time involved for each element to be more accurately assessed. When undertaking this type of measurement, the elements of work are further identified as being either:

- **repetitive** – occurring regularly in every work cycle or once in a given number of cycles
- **occasional and contingency** – occurring irregularly and, although not directly part of the job on hand, are part of the general working conditions, for example discussing work with a supervisor.

When the job is being studied, there will typically be activities other than the work elements described above. These will be either periods of rest or tasks not directly to do with the job under review (for example undertaking work on another job). These are duly recorded but are set to one side. An allowance for rest is added later but the activities that are unrelated to the job being reviewed are simply excluded from the calculations.

To establish how long to do a job under time study, a trained person measures the time taken to complete each element observed, while at the same time assessing the speed and effectiveness with which the person undertaking the task is working. Often the recording part of this procedure is completed by videoing the work. This facilitates the person doing the job to become involved and the time element is easily and accurately established. Assessing the speed and effectiveness of a person is known as 'rating' and takes into account a person's speed of movement, dexterity and consistency of application. Rating is based on a numerical scale, of which there are three in use, 60–80, 0–133 and 0–100, each serving the same purpose.

The role of rating is to allow the observed times for elements to be adjusted up or down to reflect the speed at which a person is working. In that way times are established based on a common rate of working (for example, at 100 on the 0–100 scale).

So far we have identified that, in time study applications, a job is broken down into elements, each element is measured and the time taken to complete an element is then adjusted by the rate at which the person observed was working. The same elements of work are measured on several occasions (ideally at least three different people on three different occasions) to provide an average. This is known as the 'basic time' or 'normal time'. A basic time is calculated for each element of a job, to which a percentage is then added to cover occasionals and contingencies, plus an allowance for rest to reflect the need for relaxation and personal time and compensation for more strenuous or demanding work. The various elements are added together and the total is known as the 'standard time' to complete the job under review. To help you put this description together, the procedure described here has been summarized in Exhibit 15.5 and illustrated in Exhibit 15.6.

Exhibit 15.5 Steps to establish a standard time for a job

Step	Description
1	Select the task to be reviewed
2	To facilitate the accurate measurement of the task, it is broken down into the following elements: ● repetitive ● occasionals and contingencies These elements then become the basis on which the measurement is made
3	A person undertaking the task is observed and the time taken to complete the various elements is recorded. Often videoing is used to complete this step. Work not directly to do with the job under review is identified but excluded from the final calculations
4	At the same time that each element of a job is being measured, the rate the person undertakes these tasks is assessed
5	At the end of the study, the time recorded for each element of work is adjusted up or down to reflect the lower or higher rate compared to an agreed norm. On the 0–100 scale, this 'norm' is usually the rate of 100. The observed time adjusted for the recorded rating is known as the 'basic time' or 'normal time'
6	To the basic time is added an allowance for occasionals and contingencies (work to be done but not specific to any particular job) and rest. The result is called the 'standard time'
7	The respective elements are totalled together and this becomes the standard time for the job reviewed

Exhibit 15.6 Exhibit 15.5 details shown diagrammatically

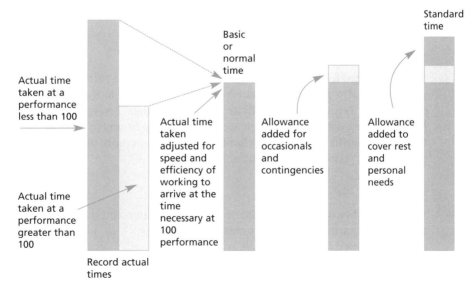

Predetermined motion time standards (PMTS)

The essence of time study is to time and rate the task by direct observation. However, from the genesis of time study, the concept of having predetermined times for operations was recognized. Several effective systems have been devised that replace observations by highly detailed method study in order to analyse and classify the motions used. Tables of predetermined times for each classified motion are drawn up, thus the total time for an operation can be calculated by adding together the predetermined times of its constituent parts. Later developments of PMTS systems provide higher level data that provide times for complete tasks (as opposed to the motions comprising a task) and this enables the time for a job to be calculated more quickly.

Synthetics

In the same way that PMTS systems provide predetermined times for basic operations, synthetic times can be built up from previous time studies carried out in an organization. In this way, times for completing part or all of a task can be calculated from numerous past studies, and used to build up the time to complete a range of similar work at a defined level of performance. Normally, these times would embody higher level data and cover much longer parts of a task than basic human movement, for example dust a chair, paint one running metre of window frame or make an outer carton.

Approaches to measure long, non-repetitive tasks

Many tasks have a long work cycle and will often occur infrequently. For such, time study and PMTS are not cost-effective ways of measurement. It is more appropriate to use one of the following forms of estimating.

Estimating

This form of measurement involves an 'assessment of the time required to carry out work, based on a knowledge and experience of similar types of work'.[2] This assessment is made on the total job without a breakdown into elements (Exhibit 15.7) and is thus dependent upon the knowledge and experience of the evaluator. In making an assessment, the evaluator will often use historical times in an informal way.

Analytical estimating

This is a refined form of estimating, in which 'the time to carry out elements (of a job) at a defined rate of working is estimated partially from knowledge and practical experience of the work concerned and partially from synthetic data'.[3] When using this technique, the work is broken down into suitable elements and the times for these are either estimated or taken from synthetic data (see Exhibit 15.7). Although more time-consuming to apply than estimating, it is normally more accurate.

Comparative estimating

This is a further development of estimating, in which the time taken for a task is evaluated by comparing the work involved with the work in a series of similar tasks. This method is based on the principle of using categories of work, where jobs are not given precise times but are placed in a time band (for example two to three hours – see Exhibit

Exhibit 15.7 Types of estimating to determine the time to be allocated to complete a task

Task	Estimating	Analytical estimating	Comparative estimating

Office cleaning	An estimate of the time it would take to empty all the waste bins, vacuum and dust the office under review would be made. This would be based on the estimator's own past experience of similar work	The tasks involved in cleaning the office under review would be broken down into smaller parts, for example:
		
		 Emptying 10 waste bins
		 Dusting 10 desks
		 Dusting 10 chairs
		 Dusting 20 filing cabinets
		 Dusting 50 metres of skirting board
		 Dusting 10 window ledges
		 Dusting 5 doors
		 Vacuuming 150 square metres of carpet with a high level of furniture congestion
		
		 The next step is to complete an estimate for each of these parts. The individual estimates would be added to give an overall time to complete the cleaning of this office. Again, the times should be based on the estimator's own past experience of similar work
			From past experience of cleaning offices, a number of job categories would be compiled by the estimator. These would be chosen to reflect the different time bands of the work undertaken, and one or more benchmark jobs would be selected as being representative of each band. When selected, each benchmark job would then be analysed in greater depth, and a detailed study would be completed to check that the time band to which each job had been allocated was appropriate. A full description of the individual tasks involved in each job would also be recorded and filed for later use:
			
			 Time band (hours) Benchmark job(s)
			
			 0.0–0.5 Partner's office, 8 Southall Gardens
			 0.5–1.0 Purchasing department, AB Imports,
			                        Floor 4, Bradley House
			 1.0–1.5 Drawing office, Markham,
			                        Roberts & Co.
			 1.5–2.0 General office, housing department,
			                        Bursley DC
			 2.0–3.0 Main open-plan office, British Energy,
			                        West Midlands
			 And so on.
			 All future jobs would then be compared to each benchmark job and, usually, the midpoint of the time band for the job to which it was most similar would be allocated and used in all the appropriate calculations

15.7), and the use of benchmark jobs on which comparisons are based. These latter jobs are chosen as being representative of a time band, and their times are based on a primary method of work measurement (for example time study). The use of benchmarks makes for a speedy evaluation by slotting tasks into broad bands of time.

Techniques to measure capacity utilization and requirements

In many work situations it is important both to measure the extent to which existing capacity is being used and to be able to monitor utilization in the future. The techniques available to produce this information are described here.

Activity sampling

Activity sampling involves making random observations over a representative period of time to provide information on:

- capacity utilization of the facilities or persons employed on a task or in an area
- the average time taken to complete a common task.

Applications of these techniques include operations areas with several pieces of equipment, warehousing and administrative or technical units. In each, an assessment of utilization or an average time taken can be established.

The overall time spent on a specified activity is deduced from a number of random observations. Owing to the limitations inherent in sampling, an error is introduced. The size of this error can be calculated statistically. For this purpose, a 95 per cent confidence limit is considered to give sufficient accuracy, and is built into the following formula:

$$N = \frac{4P(100-P)}{L^2}$$

where N = number of random observations, P = percentage occurrence of the particular activity being reviewed and L the level of accuracy required. For example, if, through observation or pilot study, a PC (or other piece of equipment) is estimated to be unused, say, 35 per cent of the time, the number of observations required to determine the actual percentage of time unused to an accuracy of ± 5 per cent, with 95 per cent confidence in the answer, would be:

$$N = \frac{4(35)(65)}{5^2} = 364$$

Conversely, it may be that a study has been completed, and the level of accuracy obtained at 95 per cent confidence limits needs to be ascertained. The following equation would be used:

$$L = 2 \times \sqrt{\frac{P(100-P)}{N}}$$

For example, if the percentage of time that warehouse staff were not working was 10.1 per cent of the time observed and the number of observations totalled 6500, the level of accuracy at 95 per cent confidence limit would be

$$L = 2 \times \sqrt{\frac{10.1(89.9)}{6500}} = 0.7$$

So, the warehouse staff were not working between 9.4 and 10.8 per cent of the time. If there were 20 staff observed, then the capacity needed to cope with present throughputs could be reduced by some 10 per cent.

So far the activity sampling study has revealed the percentage of time an activity has happened during the period of observation. To assess how long on average a task took, the percentage of time observed when staff were doing the task is first established in the way described here. A period of time (for example day or week) is then studied to determine on how many occasions the task was completed (for example orders dispatched, invoices processed or units produced). If, during an eight-hour day, four staff were employed 65 per cent of their time on dispatches and in that period completed 180 dispatches, the average dispatch time can be calculated as follows:

$$\frac{65 \text{ per cent} \times 4 \times 8 \text{ hours}}{180 \text{ dispatches}} = \frac{1248 \text{ minutes}}{180} = 6.9 \text{ minutes per dispatch}$$

Information provided in this way enables operations to establish the capacity required to handle the throughput observed during the period studied. Whether this is a normal load can be checked by comparing (say) the number of dispatches completed within the observed period with the number of dispatches completed in a reference period in the past. This reference period is chosen to represent a period of normal working over a given time (for example three months).

When capacity required to handle a normal workload has been established, monitoring throughput against capacity levels on a regular basis can be put into effect. This is achieved by comparing (say) the weekly net hours available (that is, total hours less rest and personal time) in a finished goods warehouse with the amount of work completed in the same period (for example the number of dispatches made, deliveries received, stock checks made and paperwork processed), the times for these activities having been established through activity sampling. Where work was not seen during the sample (for example tasks completed on a monthly basis only), estimates of the time taken to complete these tasks are established.

This comparison enables management to monitor any throughput changes and their effect on, in this instance, the warehouse and enables them to come to better decisions on whether to increase or decrease capacity on a temporary (through overtime or by making an internal transfer) or permanent (adding staff or natural wastage) basis.

Group capacity assessment (GCA)

Group capacity assessment (GCA) provides a basis for controlling staffing levels in indirect areas where more rigorous forms of work measurement are more difficult and expensive to apply. The first task is to establish times (that a trained person is expected to achieve on a day work basis without allowance for rest) for all the major tasks in a particular department. This is accomplished by using an appropriate form of work measurement, for example time study, synthetics, activity sampling or analytical estimating. Often a video recording is made (it is easy to do, reduces the levels of sensitivity that accompany observation and allows those videoed to be party to the calculations) and the number of completed work cycles counted in that period. An average time is then established.

While this information is being generated, the number of tasks completed in the department each day is being recorded. The average number of tasks completed in this period is calculated and extended by the time allowed. The number of people required (making due allowance for rest and personal needs) can then be established.

As in activity sampling, the capacity required is agreed, and changes are monitored in the future. This is done by totalling the number of tasks completed each day, extending these by the agreed time and calculating the total staff content of the work done that day. This is compared to the hours worked during that day, and an 'efficiency percentage' is calculated. These daily controls are monitored at departmental level, with weekly controls for each department being provided for the next level of management.

Clerical work improvement programme (CWIP)

Banks and other high volume service sectors (for example insurance and other parts of the financial sector) often monitor staff requirements through a programme similar to that described under GCA, but specific to their own organization. One example is the clerical work improvement programme (CWIP) that measures staff requirements for different administrative units and centres. Synthetic times are established for the range of activities undertaken. One common approach is to video the tasks and watch the tape to observe and calculate the times for elements of work. Standard times (an allowance being added to the observed time to cover occasionals, contingencies, rest and personal needs) are established and used to calculate times for existing and future jobs. Typically, all times are verified by observing the tasks being completed, where possible, at a number of locations.

The assessment of staff needs is primarily based on the number of transactions completed. Daily volumes are recorded (normally as an automatic byproduct of the system) and continuously reviewed over a 20-day period. Four-weekly reports would form the basis by which a company monitors capacity and helps to control costs.

Exhibit 15.8 provides a summary of some likely applications in the service sector of the approaches to measuring work that have been outlined.

Exhibit 15.8 Approaches to measuring work – some typical service applications

Approaches to measuring work	Some typical applications
Time study, PMTS and synthetics	Maintenance schedules (for example vehicles, aircraft and equipment) Cleaning services Secretarial and clerical tasks services and word processing Administrative functions
Estimating, analytical estimating and comparative estimating	Maintenance schedules Restaurants – back- and front-office operations Hotels – back- and front-office support services Consulting assignments Design services
Activity sampling	Warehousing and stores provision Equipment utilization Call centres Supermarkets – back- and front-office activities
GCA and CWIPs	Banking and financial services Administration Secretarial services and clerical tasks Warehousing and stores provision

Reflections

As time is the common denominator in managing many of the key tasks in operations, understanding the alternative approaches to measuring time and recognizing which alternative is the most appropriate to use is fundamental to an operations manager's role. Determining capacity requirements, setting realistic throughput targets and evaluating performance are core tasks. With typically 70–80 per cent of people and costs falling within the remit of operations, controlling and managing these large resources in line with budgets and customer needs is central to the overall success of a business.

Also, given the need to reduce costs and improve all dimensions of performance, evaluating and choosing alternatives is an essential part of securing the improvements necessary for the short- and long-term success of a business. Measuring time is a key facet of this task and provides essential dimensions of the need for continuous improvement in operations, the subject of Chapter 16.

Productivity

The prosperity of nations and organizations alike is recognized as being dependent upon their comparative productivity. At a national level, the relationship between the level of output per hour in the manufacturing sector from 1960 to 2000, the share of world trade in manufactured goods and the GDP per capita for seven more advanced economies is shown in Exhibits 15.9, 15.10, and 15.11 respectively. Productivity is a most useful comparative measure at a national, sector or individual business level to provide comparisons between relative performances and measure trends over time.

Exhibit 15.9 Trends in output per hour in manufacturing for selected countries 1960–2000 (1992=100)

Country	1960	1970	1980	1990	1995	1998	2000
Belgium	18	33	65	97	113	129	133
Canada	39	56	75	95	111	113	117
France	22	43	67	94	115	130	141
Germany	29	52	77	99	113	121	130
Italy	21	40	70	92	110	111	116
Japan	14	38	63	94	111	121	133
Netherlands	19	38	69	98	118	125	–
Norway	37	58	77	97	102	104	104
Sweden	27	52	73	95	122	140	150
United Kingdom	30	43	54	89	105	106	116
United States	53	62	71	97	114	127	145

Source *Monthly Labor Review*, Bureau of Labor Statistics, US Department of Labor, August 2001.

Exhibit 15.10 Share of world trade in manufactured goods for selected countries, 1980–2002

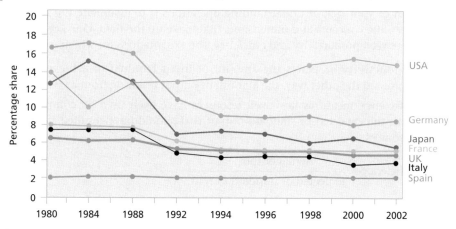

Source International trade statistics, World Trade Organization, 2003.

In general terms productivity expresses the relationship between the outputs from a system and the inputs which go into their creation, as shown below:

$$\text{Productivity} = \frac{\text{Output}}{\text{Input}}$$

An increase in productivity, therefore, can be secured by changing either or both the numerator or denominator of this simple equation. However, it follows that an increase in output itself does not necessarily mean an increase in productivity unless there has been a less than pro rata increase in inputs.

Exhibit 15.11 GDP per capita for selected countries 1983–2002

Year	Canada	Germany	France	UK	Italy	Japan
1983	87.3	89.0	81.8	70.2	75.7	73.1
1984	86.1	86.4	77.9	67.6	73.1	70.8
1985	86.8	85.9	76.4	67.8	72.8	71.7
1986	85.9	85.8	75.9	68.6	72.7	71.7
1987	86.5	85.2	75.8	70.0	73.2	72.8
1988	86.9	85.1	76.3	71.0	73.7	75.1
1989	85.3	85.4	77.3	70.6	73.8	77.0
1990	83.5	87.9	78.3	70.4	74.8	80.2
1991	82.0	80.3	79.9	70.2	76.9	83.8
1992	80.1	79.8	78.9	68.7	75.7	82.6
1993	79.8	77.2	76.8	69.2	74.4	81.3
1994	80.2	76.4	75.7	69.9	73.7	79.6
1995	80.5	76.4	75.8	70.7	74.6	79.6
1996	78.8	75.3	74.6	71.1	73.8	80.0
1997	78.8	73.1	74.4	72.1	72.1	78.8
1998	79.0	72.4	74.6	71.9	72.6	75.4
1999	79.9	70.8	73.4	70.7	70.6	72.8
2000	81.0	69.7	73.1	71.0	70.0	72.6
2001	84.3	72.0	77.3	75.5	72.4	75.1
2002	84.9	71.3	77.7	77.0	71.2	74.0

Source DTI.

Part of your task in understanding operations is to assimilate the technical differences between the concepts and dimensions that make up the field. One key difference concerns that between productivity and efficiency, the explanations for which follow:

● **productivity** measures the amount of input required to achieve a given output or, expressed the other way, the amount of output resulting from a given input

● **efficiency** measures how well resources have been used by comparing actual output with the expected or standard output that should have resulted from the use of these resources:

$$\text{Efficiency} = \frac{\text{Actual output}}{\text{Expected or standard output}}$$

Approaches to measuring productivity

Single-factor and multi-factor are the commonly used measures of productivity. As an example of single-factor measurement, staff productivity typically measures output per hour. Multi-factor productivity, on the other hand, includes not only labour but also other inputs such as processes, energy and materials. All productivity measures are exposed to a number of indirectly acquired sources of improvement. For example, technological change and the increasing skills base and know-how of people would, in themselves, typically lead to an increase in productivity in related areas but may not appear to be directly associated with the improvement. However, as a measure to reflect trends and compare performance, productivity is a simple and effective way of providing these insights.

Examples of single-factor, multi-factor and added value measures are now provided.

Exhibit 15.12 European Automotive Productivity Index, 2002: top five and bottom five

Manufacturer	Plant	Country	# Vehicles produced	# Vehicles per employee
1 Nissan	Sunderland	UK	296,489	95
2 Ford	Saarlouis	Germany	408,405	87
3 Toyota	Burnaston	UK	156,000	87
4 Fiat	Melfi	Italy	350,756	82
5 GM	Eisenach	Germany	137,272	77
5 PSA	Rennes	France	305,472	38
4 Volvo	Born	Netherlands	122,071	36
3 GM	Russelsheim	Germany	165,009	36
2 PSA	Suschaux	France	384,644	36
1 VW	Baden	Germany	258,600	32

Single-factor productivity measures

- **Staff productivity** is the most commonly used measure and relates output to hours worked. Its universal application derives from several factors including that it is easy to calculate and the like-for-like dimension of staff/labour, both within and between nations, sectors and businesses, as illustrated in Exhibits 15.9 and 15.12:

$$\text{Staff productivity} = \frac{\text{Output (£s)}}{\text{Hours worked}}$$

- **Process productivity** measures the value of the outputs produced in relation to the process time involved:

$$\text{Process productivity} = \frac{\text{Output (£s)}}{\text{Process time (hours)}}$$

Another means of evaluating process productivity is to compare the value of goods sold (£s) to the fixed asset investment in the processes under review.

Multi-factor productivity measures

The single-factor dimensions of staff/labour and process measures of productivity provide one view of a total picture and when using them, this needs to be borne in mind. However, by using a multi-factor measure of productivity, certain of these problems will be overcome.

Multi- (also called total) factor productivity includes not only staff/labour inputs but also some or all of the costs of capital, energy, materials and other purchased services:

$$\text{Multi-factor productivity} = \frac{\text{Output (£s)}}{\substack{\text{Costs (£s) of staff, capital, energy,} \\ \text{materials and other purchased services}}}$$

This measure provides an improved framework for assessing the whole of operations and gives a basis for analysing productivity changes due to substituting or improving one or more of the factors involved.

Added value

One useful refinement to measuring productivity is to relate factors to added value. The latter refers to the value added to a service or product by a business and is, therefore, the difference between sales revenue and all material and service costs incurred to make those sales. These costs include materials and components, stationery, subcontract and any other elements of material or staff costs purchased from outside a business (see Exhibit 15.13):

$$\text{Added value} = \frac{\text{Sales revenue minus materials and service}}{\text{costs purchased from outside a business}}$$

Thus, over the period being reviewed, the added value measures the wealth produced by a unit. The added value index (AVI) is also a useful overall measure because it relates the added value to total employment costs (for example salaries, pensions and other state contributions). It is calculated as follows and is often expressed as a percentage:

$$\text{Added value index} = \frac{\text{Total employment costs}}{\text{Added value}}$$

Exhibit 15.13 Added value in relation to bought-out materials/services and sales

Materials and outside services (£s)

ADDED   VALUE   Sales (£s)

The ratio is a valuable measure of operations management's performance because, unlike profit, it is less affected by factors outside a manager's control (for example inflation) and it focuses on a fundamental aspect of management's task, that of being responsible for employee productivity.

AVI measures operations by relating the current AVI against a previously agreed standard, with a lower figure indicating an improvement in this ratio. Added value reward schemes are also used by some organizations.

Ways to improve productivity

There are three levels at which productivity improvements can be made:

- **scientific**, involving research leading to new knowledge in, for example, materials, processes and IT chips
- **technical**, which comprises the adaptation or application of new scientific knowledge to replace existing ideas or introduce new ways to complete tasks
- **operational**, where the aim is to develop procedures that make the best use of technical developments.

In terms of productivity improvements, the activities at the scientific and technical levels provide the principal increases. However, they will also be more expensive to fund and take much longer to bring to fruition than activities at the operational level, where the investments are relatively inexpensive but yield quick, although less significant results (see Exhibit 15.14). Consequently, many organizations have pursued productivity improvements solely at the operational level. The methods adopted, however, vary. Some improvements come through experience, trial and error or ingenuity. Other ways of studying work have been developed that provide a systematic approach to investigating existing methods and developing and implementing improvements as ways to increase the productivity of existing resources. Chapter 16 introduces many of these approaches and provides examples of how and where they may be used.

Exhibit 15.14 Approaches to improving productivity and some of the trade-offs involved

Aspects	Approaches		
	Scientific	Technical	Operational
The cost of providing the necessary facilities and staff to complete these activities	High	⟶	Low
The potential for improving productivity	High	⟶	Low
The length of time to yield the productivity gains	Long	⟶	Short

Service applications

The growing importance of the service sector within more developed economies places increasing emphasis on the need to improve productivity in this sector. Past trends indicate that, even in the USA which is often regarded as having the most developed of all service sectors, productivity improvements lag behind. Exhibit 15.15 shows that whereas manufac-

Exhibit 15.15 Percentage changes in productivity for the total business (excluding farming) and the manufacturing sectors in the USA (1984–2003)

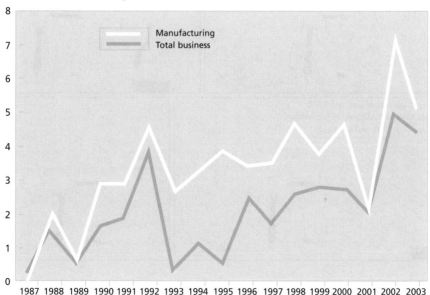

turing productivity has been increasing year on year since the mid-1980s, total business (excluding farming) productivity in the USA has been declining year on year, which suggests that service sector productivity has also been declining over the same period.

The need to improve and measure productivity in service businesses (and the white-collar/service dimension in goods-producing firms) is a significant and necessary task. As the service element of economies grows, productivity in this sector has an increasing bearing on the living standards of nations.

It is important, therefore, to accomplish this in an effective way. In so doing, organizations should remember to incorporate lessons from the past and recognize the expectations and abilities of the staff involved. Essential to the successful introduction and maintenance of approaches to measuring and improving productivity are the following:

●   Involve those concerned – the failure of companies to involve blue-collar workers in the past led to resentment and resistance at the time, an attitude which sometimes prevails even today. The success achieved by other nations (for example Japan) has, in part, been based upon appropriate high levels of involvement. Including people in the process needs to be undertaken as early as possible, particularly in service industries where procedures are less rigid and the outputs less tangible. Discussing the purpose of the measures and their ultimate use will allay fears, reduce resistance and match the expectations of incumbents concerning levels of responsibility and their role in the interpretation of the service and managing and improving the delivery system. Not quite the James approach (see Exhibit 15.16)!

Exhibit 15.16 One way to create productivity improvements by involvement

© AMD Publishing

- **Establish the purpose** – starting with the goals of the organization, measures should be developed to fit relevant targets. Congruency between measures and objectives ensures relevance of effort and consistency and coherence of purpose. In the service sector this linkage is normally inherently less defined than its goods-producing counterpart.

- **Determine appropriate measures** – be aware of using existing output/input ratios as this approach brings with it the potential problem of modifying, at a later date, a measure which is not fit for purpose. The approach should be to determine first the outputs, then the inputs and lastly the ratios. This will enable the different factors to be assessed independently of one another, then later assessed within the relevant measures. Defining each part separately simplifies the task.

- **Output measures** – by electing to define outputs first, the more difficult and important factor in the equation is addressed without introducing additional complexity. As output measures are often difficult to determine directly, surrogate measures are sometimes used. It is most important, therefore, to involve those concerned in such decisions to ensure that what a measure is intended to accomplish is understood and deemed suitable. This avoids unduly emphasizing non-critical factors which may distort what constitutes good performance. Group consensus not only reduces this possible outcome but also creates the opportunity to refine measures over time.

- **Input measures** – should be chosen to reflect the task. Choices between single-factor and multi-factor measures were discussed earlier and some illustrations are given in Exhibit 15.17. When choosing which inputs to use, the need to relate them to the output measures must also be appreciated. One aspect to consider here is the appropriate time base of the input(s) compared to the output(s) involved. Thus, clerical staff inputs may be measured in hours or days, whereas a research department would be more appropriately described by the numbers of people or salary bill.

Exhibit 15.17 Examples of single-factor and multi-factor productivity measures

Organization	Single-factor measure	Multi-factor measure
Law firm	$\dfrac{\# \text{ briefs filed}}{\text{Lawyer}}$	$\dfrac{\# \text{ briefs filed and court attendances undertaken}}{\text{Lawyer}}$
Bookshop	$\dfrac{\# \text{ customers served}}{\text{Full-time equivalent staff}}$	$\dfrac{\# \text{ customers served, deliveries handled and despatches sent}}{\text{Full-time equivalent staff}}$
University	$\dfrac{\# \text{ student contact hours}}{\text{Faculty member}}$	$\dfrac{\# \text{ student contact hours, research assistants supervised (hours) and administrative tasks (hours)}}{\text{Faculty member}}$
Consultancy firm	$\dfrac{\# \text{ consultancy days billed}}{\text{Total consultancy days available}}$	$\dfrac{\# \text{ consultancy days billed, training undertaken (days) and administrative tasks (days)}}{\text{Total consultant days available}}$
Engineering design firm	$\dfrac{\# \text{ design projects completed}}{\text{Engineering staff days}}$	$\dfrac{\# \text{ design projects completed, tenders submitted and site visits undertaken}}{\text{Engineering staff days}}$

- Ratios – the last step in defining the measures is to select the ratios. The multiples on hand will be many. Some factors to consider in general terms, as well as to do particularly with service applications, include:
  - Keep the number of measures small and focused. Avoid any measures that are not central to a review.
  - Select measures with the following characteristics:
    – data are readily available
    – reflected performance is understood by all concerned
    – some control is exercised by those being measured.
  - Measures for one function are compatible not only with other parts of an organization but also with the corporate measures in use.

- Revise – implementing a productivity measurement system is not a one-off project. In service industries particularly, changes in mix, the continuous reinterpretation of tasks, the application of technology and changes in organizational goals will bring about short- and long-term implications for a business and may change the best measures to evaluate performance and improvement. Periodic revision needs to be built into the system, in relation to productivity measurement in particular and as part of an ongoing, corporate review in general.

Case example 1   PRODUCTIVITY AT CONVERGYS

Convergys, one of the biggest US suppliers of outsourced customer services, has a number of call centres for customers across the country. In the South Jordan centre a team of 14 staff handle calls from customers of Direct TV, the satellite television company. These call centre staff have to handle 63 calls during a seven-hour shift. But this is a relaxed pace by US industry standards. A worker in a unionized call centre averages 73 per day while at non-unionized centres this can rise to 108 calls per day.

The modern call centre is not all about numbers, however. Companies are increasingly interested in the quality of service that callers receive. To cut costs they are looking for ways of creating different tiers of service, encouraging many callers to use automated services while saving human contact for high spending customers or those who might buy additional products and services.

www.convergys.com

Case questions
1 How is the number of calls handled per day a useful measure of productivity?
2 Why do you think the number of calls handled would vary by as much as almost 50 per cent in the figures quoted above?

Reflections

While factors such as national resources will play a major part in determining a country's level of wealth, the prosperity of a nation and the living standards enjoyed by its people are also bound up with productivity. The standard of living enjoyed today by many of the more advanced economies has its roots in the primary (mining and farming) and secondary (manufacturing) sectors' productivity gains over the last several decades. The improvements secured in these areas of the economies of many nations have been significant.

The increasing importance of service industries in the more developed economies has switched the spotlight onto the need to improve productivity in this sector. Only in this way will the improvements in national prosperity and individual living standards be sustained. Current overall performance, as shown in Exhibit 15.15, points to a current

Exhibit 15.18 Comparative prices for a three-minute international telephone call for selected countries (1994–2003)

Country	Price (US$) for a three-minute international call				Index 2003 (1994 = 100)
	1994	1997	2000	2003	
Australia	3.13	3.14	0.60	0.50	16
Canada	2.67	1.10	0.71	0.48	18
Denmark	3.70	2.56	1.11	0.71	19
France	2.91	1.27	0.62	0.28	10
Germany	3.49	2.18	0.61	0.33	9
Italy	4.28	1.87	1.00	0.78	18
Japan	6.98	3.57	1.70	1.48	21
Singapore	5.81	2.50	1.66	0.66	11
South Africa	6.43	3.23	1.86	1.12	17
Spain	4.50	1.96	1.03	0.69	15
Sweden	2.62	1.44	0.58	0.31	12
UK	1.90	0.98	0.95	0.94	49
USA	3.32	0.36	0.36	0.45	14

Note   1   US$ per three minutes in peak hours to USA (for USA to Europe).

Source The World Competitiveness Report 1994 and 2004.

failure to meet these expectations. In part this may be explained by a failure in some elements of the service sector to acknowledge this essential task. However, there are other parts where this need has been fully recognized. Often this goes hand in hand with the increasing move of services from a sheltered to a traded environment, a factor often enhanced by the progressive privatization in many countries of large service industries that had historically been developed and managed in the public or government domain. The results, as Exhibit 15.18 illustrates, can be as dramatic as many of the earlier gains in the primary and secondary sectors.

Exhibit 15.18 shows that all thirteen countries now provide a three-minute international telephone call at a significantly lower price than in 1994. In fact, while the average price for all these countries was $3.98 in the mid 1990s, it had fallen to $0.67 by 2003. Also, as the figures do not take into account inflation in the period, the reduction in prices are, in real terms, even more pronounced. Underpinning these significant decreases was a parallel improvement in productivity, driven by a combination of technology investment and continued improvements in all areas of telephone provision.

The need for and benefits that accrue from sustained productivity improvements are central to the continuing prosperity of nations, whatever their level of development. Bringing this about is a central feature of operations management and some of the ways and approaches that can be used are addressed in Chapter 16.

Key Elements of Time and Productivity

- The fundamental nature of time in managing operations is often overlooked or not fully recognized. Assumptions are typically made about the origins and appropriateness of this fundamental input into key operations activities such as cost data, capacity calculations and work schedules.

Functions in a business use the data and assume them to be accurate and a sound basis on which to undertake calculations and make decisions.

- The chapter started by illustrating why time needs to be an essential part of assessing, controlling and managing many of the activities within operations. Specific illustrations of the role of time in key activities were then provided.

- With an understanding of the essential role of time in so many aspects of operations management, the approaches to measuring the content of jobs were reviewed. At the start the need to recognize that the time taken would need to reflect the agreed method, take account of how effectively the work was completed and provide allowances for rest and personal needs was emphasized.

- Then followed a description of the principal approaches used and the types of work where they were most appropriate to determine the

question, how long should this job take to complete?

- The second major topic of the chapter addressed productivity. The national as well as corporate dimensions provided context and background before introducing the definitions of productivity, the difference between this measure and that of efficiency and the perspectives provided by added value calculations.

- The final section addressed the ways to improve productivity and the key role of service sector improvements in sustaining the productivity gains made in the primary and secondary sectors particularly during the last century.

Self-check

1 The common denominator for managing operations is:
   a Money ☐
   b Time ☐
   c Quantity (number of services or products) ☐

2 Which of the following is **not** a reason for measuring work:
   a Eliminate ineffective time ☐
   b Reduce inventory levels ☐
   c Balance work members in a team ☐

3 Appropriate methods for measuring work content vary depending on:
   a The length of the task ☐
   b The repetitive (or non-repetitive) nature of the task ☐
   c Both a and b ☐

4 Predetermined motion time standards (PMTS):
   a Allow times for jobs to be calculated more quickly ☐
   b Are mainly used for non-repetitive tasks ☐
   c Can be calculated before a new service/ product is introduced ☐

5 Which of the following is **not** a form of estimating for non-repetitive tasks:
   a Analytical estimating ☐
   b Comparative estimating ☐
   c Synthetics ☐

6 Activity sampling is used to provide information on:
   a Capacity utilization ☐
   b Time estimation ☐
   c Cost estimation ☐

7 Time studies would typically be used in which service business:
   a Administrative functions ☐
   b Consulting assignments ☐
   c Design services ☐

8 Productivity measures:
   a Output resulting from a given input ☐
   b Actual output against expected (or standard) output ☐
   c Actual input against expected (or planned) input ☐

9 Operational productivity improvements tend to involve:

a Long length of time to yield the productivity gains ☐

b High potential for improving productivity ☐

c Low cost of providing the necessary facilities and staff to complete these activities ☐

10 Which of the following is **not** essential to the successful introduction and maintenance of approaches to measuring and improving productivity:

a Involve those concerned ☐

b Determine appropriate measures ☐

c Use slogans and posters ☐

Study activities

Discussion questions

1 The owner of a photocopying outlet wishes to know how busy the receptionist is in the front office. The observations based on random sampling made so far are below.

Day	# times receptionist		Total # observations
	busy	no work	
1	20	4	24
2	14	3	17
3	28	5	33
4	16	2	18
5	32	8	40
8	25	6	31
9	18	4	22
10	30	9	39

If the owner wants an answer that has a 95 per cent confidence limit with an accuracy of ±4 per cent, how many observations are needed?

2 What is the difference between basic or normal time and the standard time for a job?

3 A worker assembled 15 units in 60 minutes during a time study. The analyst rated the worker at 90 on the 0–100 scale. The allowance for occasionals and contingencies, rest and personal time totals 18 per cent. At the standard rating of 100 calculate:

● basic or normal time for this assembly

● standard time for this assembly

4 The manager of Oils and Tyres wishes to establish a standard time for an oil change. Jim Beswick completed 32 oil changes over a period of time in a total of 260 minutes. Jim is the best mechanic at the outlet and was rated at 115 on the 0–100 scale. The rest allowance is 12.5 per cent. Calculate the standard time for an oil change.

5 Reflecting on questions 2 and 3 above, how does the process of rating normalize the eventual standard time?

6 What are the advantages and disadvantages of using output per staff hour as a measure of performance?

7 How does efficiency qualify productivity measures?

8 What are the advantages of using a video as opposed to a person to help calculate the length of time to complete a job?

9 Why does an operations manager need standard times?

10 Take a look at Exhibit 15.12 and answer the following questions.

(a) What do you think are some of the reasons for the significant differences in vehicles per employee in the 10 automobile plants?

(b) In the light of your first answer, do you still consider the productivity measure of vehicles per employee per year to be of value?

Assignments

1 As a small team complete a survey of both a fast-food and waitress-served restaurant using activity sampling procedures. What differences and similarities did you find? What surprised you most?

2 Review the following service organizations and suggest one single-factor and one multi-factor productivity measure for each:

- library
- sandwich bar
- food takeaway outlet
- wine bar
- dental surgery
- health clinic
- small retail outlet
- accountancy firm

Explain the reasons for your choice and review the limitations of the measures chosen.

Exploring further

Deo, BS and Strong, D 'Cost: the ultimate measure of productivity', *Industrial Management*, **42**(3) (2000) pp. 20–3.

Dewan, S and Kraemer, KL 'Information technology and productivity: evidence from country-level data', *Management Science*, **46**(4) (2000) pp. 548–62.

Ford, H *Today and Tomorrow*, Productivity Press, Cambridge, MA (1988).

Heskett, JL, Jones, TO, Loveman, GW, Sasser, WE Jr and Schlesinger, LA 'Putting the service–profit chain to work', *Harvard Business Review*, March–April (1994) pp. 164–74.

Meyers, FE *Time and Motion Study for Lean Manufacturing*, 2nd edn, Prentice Hall, Saddle River, NJ (1999).

Niebel, BW and Freivalds, A *Methods, Standards and Work Design*, McGraw-Hill/Irwin, New York (2003).

Ousnamer, M 'Time standards that make sense', *IIE Solutions*, December (2000) pp. 28–32.

US Bureau of Labor Statistics: http://stats.bls.gov/

Wrege, CD *Frederick W Taylor: The Father of Scientific Management: Myth and Reality*, Business One Irwin, Homewood, IL (1991).

Notes and references

1   Definitions of work measurement are provided in the British Standard 3138 (1992).

2   Ibid.

3   Ibid.

book map

CUSTOMERS

OUTPUTS

PROCESSES

INPUTS

SUPPLIERS

Part	
1	
2	
3	
4	
5	

1 Managing Operations

2 Operations Strategy

3 Managing People

4 Designing and Developing Services & Products

5 Designing Service Delivery Systems

6 Designing Manufacturing Processes

7 Location and Layout

8 Managing Capacity

9 Technology Developments

10 Operations Scheduling and Execution

11 Managing Quality

12 Managing Inventory

13 Managing the Supply Chain

14 Process and Delivery System Reliability and Maintenance

15 Time and Productivity

16 Improving Operations

Managing Operations in Practice: Long Case Studies

Improving Operations

Outline of chapter

The ongoing drive for improvement is a priority in most organizations. Given that the bulk of costs and investments resides in operations, its contribution to this corporate requirement is essential in itself and central for the continued sales growth and profit expectations within a business.

Why is improving operations important?

Executive overview

This chapter concerns the task of improving operations. It explains the different methods and approaches to help undertake this key activity and, in particular, covers the following:

- **Measuring performance** – what to measure, setting targets and standards (including benchmarking) and setting the improvement agenda.

- **Stepped versus incremental improvements** – identifying the difference and relative contributions made by undertaking improvements that are stepped (or large) in nature and those that comprise small, incremental gains. The link back to the levels of productivity improvements in the last chapter will also be established.

- **Continuous improvement** – the notion of undertaking improvements on a continuous basis will be discussed and the inherent merits of this approach will be explained.

- **Approaches to making improvements** – how to review tasks will be explained in detail and examples used to illustrate the different approaches that can be used.

- **Employee involvement** – whereas the last section reviewed the content of what to do, the aspect of how to undertake these reviews and the key dimension of involving those staff responsible for the aspects of work being examined is introduced. This aspect was explained in greater detail in Chapter 3 and also in Chapter 11 under the heading 'Total quality management (TQM)'.

Measuring performance

The maxim 'what gets measured gets done' is singularly true. The reason for this is simple. If data are collected to measure an aspect of operations performance, then how well that dimension is being achieved will be noted, monitored and reviewed. As a consequence, performance levels will be highlighted and the attention given to that aspect will result in time and resources being allocated to maintaining or improving that operations task.

When reviewing performance, a key step is selecting which aspects to measure and why. With this agreed, the next step is to set the standards to be met within agreed timescales. In this section we are concerned with what to measure and setting the standards. The rest of the chapter deals with how to bring about required improvements.

The ways to measure productivity were introduced in the last chapter. These comprised general reviews that give an overview and facilitate comparisons between the overall performance of nations, sectors and organizations. This section looks at the different measures that may be used, highlights the necessity to separate the strategic and internal dimensions of operations and introduces the role of benchmarking in setting standards and agreeing targets.

Strategic versus operational dimensions of performance

Chapter 2 emphasized the strategic dimension of operations and highlighted the need to recognize the external as well as the internal tasks of the operations function. Exhibit 16.1 lists some of the dimensions for which operations is solely or jointly responsible and is based on Exhibit 2.17. A glance at these shows a mix of the strategic and operational. However, the purpose of this list and subsequent narrative is not to identify when a dimension would be strategic rather than operational but to provide an overview of the range and nature of the measures that may be used to help evaluate the performance of the operations function. You will also note from the list that most are not new, they have been used by companies for many years. What is new is the importance attached to them. These measures truly drive the operations process, replacing the traditional cost accounting and variance reporting procedures of the past.

Exhibit 16.1 Operations tasks and some relevant performance measures

Dimension	Task	Performance measures
	for which operations may be solely or jointly responsible	
Price	Maintaining and/or reducing costs	• Staff cost per unit • Material yield • Unit overhead cost • Efficiency (also known as effective performance) • Experience curves
Quality conformance	Providing services or making products to specification	• Defects as a percentage of total service transactions completed or units made • Customer complaints – number and percentage of total sales • Warranty claims – number and value (£s) • Scrap levels – percentage of material costs and value (£s) • Customer satisfaction scores
Delivery speed	Matching customers' requested lead times	• Meeting customers' requested lead times – number agreed and as a percentage of total customers • Operations lead times – trends • Queue lengths – actual versus target during selected periods
Delivery reliability	Delivering orders on time	• Percentage of orders delivered on time – line item review • Orders part-delivered – number and percentage of total
Service/product range	Supporting the services or products on offer	• Stock-keeping units (SKUs) – number and trends • Inventory holding – value (£s) by each product or item • 80/20 review – sales value (£s) related to inventory held (£s) by service or product
New service or product introductions	Reducing the operations phase involved	• Rate of service or product introductions – number and trends • Lead times – actual and trends by service or product category
Demand spikes	Match demand with inventory and/or short-term capacity increases	• Monitor overtime and inventory costs • Measure effective performance in high demand periods against non-peak levels

Price

Monitoring and/or reducing costs is an integral part of operations whether or not price is an order-winner within a market. As up to 70 per cent of costs are typically incurred by operations, effective cost control is essential. That materials and overheads typically account for upwards of 80 per cent of total costs is reflected in the suggested measures. One measure listed in Exhibit 16.1 does, however, require some explanation.

Efficiency was introduced in Chapter 15. This measures actual service or product output with that expected, or 'standard output', as it is called. Using time as the common denominator, both the numerator and denominator are expressed in minutes, hours, days or even weeks, whichever is the most appropriate unit of measurement. Exhibit 16.2 is the result of extending the number of individual tasks completed (that is, the output of the staff) by the standard time to complete each task and comparing this total with the total hours worked in the distribution warehouse involved. It is typically (as here) expressed as a percentage. Reflecting back to Chapter 15, all tasks would be given a standard time, that is, the time in which a company would expect an average-skilled and trained person to be able to complete the task on hand. As the time would include an allowance for rest, one hour of work should result in the equivalent of one hour's worth of tasks. Hence the effective

Exhibit 16.2 Calculating the weekly efficiency for distribution warehouse staff

Task description	Standard minutes per task	# completed	
		tasks	standard minutes
Check customer order details (including labels), pick order and label each carton	6.5	892	5798.0
Load orders onto vehicle	40.0	21	840.0
Unload incoming vehicle and put away products	115.0	11	1265.0
Stock take one-third of locations (monthly)	210.0	–	–
General duties (sweeping and cleaning)	180.0	1	180.0
Meetings (including general information and continuous improvement reviews)	340.0	1	340.0
Total	–	–	8423.0

# hours worked	Normal	Overtime hours	Total
Sue Gibbons	35.0	1.5	36.5
Alec Carpenter	35.0	–	35.0
Jill Sawyer	35.0	1.5	36.5
Anne Roper	35.0	–	35.0
Total	140.0	3.0	143.0

$$\text{Efficiency} = \frac{\text{\# standard minutes produced}}{\text{\# hours worked} \times 60 \text{ minutes}} \times 100$$

$$= \frac{8423}{8580} \times 100 = 98.2$$

performance expectation would be 100 per cent. The example in Exhibit 16.2 is for a distribution warehouse with four staff each working 35 normal hours per week.

Experience curves

Evidence clearly shows that as experience accumulates, performance improves and experience curves are the quantification of this improvement.[1] The basic phenomenon of the experience curve is that the cost of providing a service or product falls in a regular and predictable way as the total quantity increases and Exhibit 16.3 provides a general illustration of this principle.

The price of a service or product typically declines after its initial introduction as it becomes more widely accepted and available. However, it is not so commonly recognized that cost also follows a remarkably consistent decline. The pattern is that costs (in constant £s) decline by a consistent percentage each time cumulative unit output is doubled. The sources of these improvements are not only the result of reduced staff costs due to learning

Exhibit 16.3 The experience curve principle showing cost/volume or price/volume relationships expressed on both a linear and log-log scale

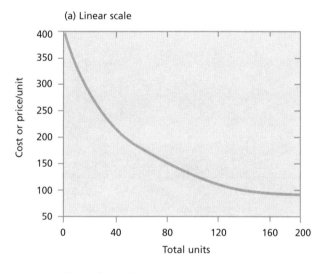

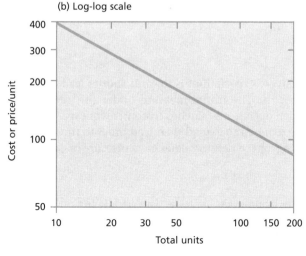

curve benefits. In fact, the real source of the experience curve effect comes from organizational improvements. The importance of calculating the extent to which the opportunity to reduce unit costs has been achieved is an important measure, particularly where markets are or will become price-sensitive. The characteristic decline in cost or price per unit was established by the Boston Consulting Group's (BCG) work in the 1960s and early 1970s as between 20 and 30 per cent for each doubling of cumulative output. Reflecting this rate of decline, experience curves are expressed in percentage terms; thus an 80 per cent experience curve slope means that each time output doubles, the cost or price per unit will be 80 per cent that of the previous output and so on. Exhibit 16.4 provides an example for a large voucher processing centre showing the consistent reduction in unit processing costs over a six-year period.

Exhibit 16.4 Experience curve over a six-year period – voucher processing centre

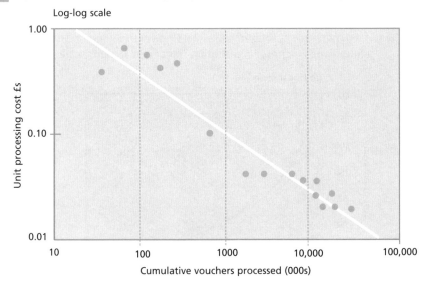

Quality conformance

Much was said on this issue in Chapter 11. The task in operations concerns providing a service or making a product to specification. The relevant measures suggested in Exhibit 16.1 are largely self-explanatory.

Delivery speed

The trend in customers' delivery expectations is towards shorter lead times. Operations task is to meet these requirements. The initial measure under this section in Exhibit 16.1 concerns the extent to which operations matches customer requests. This signals how often a company's customers are required to extend their lead times to those which the company can offer. Checks on meeting agreed delivery dates are a measure of delivery reliability.

Delivery reliability

Having agreed when services or products are to be delivered, being on time is the measure to test how well delivery dates are met. One key element of this measure is that only where all items on a customer's order are delivered by the agreed date should an order be considered as being on time, hence the 'line item review' element of the first measure. Mr James's approach is not what's intended (see Exhibit 16.5).

Exhibit 16.5 Mr James's way to make delivery performance look good

Service/product range

As markets become increasingly different, service/product ranges will tend to widen to reflect this trend. Developing a capability to cope with this dimension becomes part of the operations task. Measuring increases in service or product range should be supplemented by monitoring how operations meets this requirement, for example through holding inventory.

New service/product introductions

New services and products are the lifeblood of an organization. Reducing the time it takes to develop and introduce them is a key element in this core activity. Monitoring operations role in this total provision is an essential measure here.

Demand spikes

Demand is rarely predictable or uniform. For many businesses how and how well operations copes with supporting this is an important measure in assessing this dimension.

Benchmarking

Benchmarking, the practice of comparing business practices and performances between companies, has become widely adopted across all sectors. It provides a systematic way of identifying, measuring and setting improvement targets in key areas of performance against competitors, especially those recognized as market leaders.

Benchmarking is part of a continuing need to improve operations. Knowing both the competition's and your own performance is central to this approach, as Sun Tzu (a notable Chinese general) reflected in 500 BC: 'Know your enemy and know yourself and in a thousand battles never be in peril.'

Benchmarking is concerned with the search for best practice. It presents the 'what' rather than the 'how' (the subject of later sections in this chapter) and consequently companies are presented with targets not solutions. For benchmarking to be successfully implemented, some key elements need to be in place:

● Rigour – targets need to be set high enough and continually reviewed.

● Overcoming disbelief – initially, companies often need to convince themselves that they can do better and that the benchmark performances are achievable. The closed mind syndrome has been and still is a characteristic obstacle to change, as these quotations bear testimony:

'Everything that can be invented has' (Head of US Patent Office, 1889)
'There is a world market for fifteen computers' (IBM chairman, 1945)
'Japan is not likely to become a world leader in aerospace' (SBAC Report, 1989).

● Accountability – measuring performance and ensuring improvement requires everyone to become responsible for checking, identifying and implementing the changes necessary to bring this about.

● Manageable task – although the underlying aim of benchmarking is to set targets 'outside the box', it is essential to make the targets achievable. As an ongoing process, when targets are met, new ones are set. The need for companies to assess themselves against externally derived standards is at the heart of benchmarking. Identifying 'best-in-class exemplars' is a key step and examples often need to come from a number of company classifications, including:
  – internal: other parts of the same organization
  – direct competitors
  – companies in the same sector, but not direct competitors
  – latent competitors
  – companies outside the industry.

How companies have used different sources to provide targets is provided in the examples that follow:

● Rover Cars (UK) halved its test times after benchmarking against Honda

● Lucas Verity (USA) cut the number of shop-floor grades fourfold after a review against a German competitor

● British Rail (UK) reduced the time taken to clean a train to eight minutes after benchmarking British Airways

● GE Capital (USA) aims to achieve six-sigma quality (3.4 defects per million operations) in its financial services sector following IBM's lead

● McDonald's (USA) reduced the factory-based build time for constructing a restaurant from 18 to 10 days by adopting best practice methods in the management of construction projects, many of which came from the British Airports Authority. It has even managed to finish a restaurant in just 2 days.

Stepped versus incremental approaches to improvement

Improvements come in many forms. One key difference concerns the extent of the change and resulting improvement. The alternatives are referred to as 'stepped' and 'incremental', thereby signalling different approaches to bringing about different levels of change.

Stepped improvements result from major changes to existing practices and normally involve large investments. Incremental improvements, on the other hand, comprise smaller but more frequent steps. The philosophy here is to undertake small improvements on an ongoing basis, with the continuous nature rather than the size of improvements holding the key to achieving and sustaining change programmes over time.

Now take a look at Case examples 16.1–16.4 as a way to reflect on these alternative approaches.

Case example 1   SHEFFIELD CITY COUNCIL'S GEOGRAPHIC INFORMATION SYSTEM

Sheffield City Council (UK) introduced a new geographic information system. By inputting Ordnance Survey sheets and details from more than 1350 information maps on property holdings, road details, 'street furniture' (such as road signs, and traffic lights), it has significantly reduced the time to answer queries, for example one day instead of four weeks to undertake a land and property deed search and 30 seconds to give information on any property or parcel of land. Planning temporary diversions and modifying existing route options similarly takes minutes, while assessing the impact on school numbers by altering catchment areas can be reviewed and refined almost at will.   **www.sheffield.gov.uk**

Case example 2   REVOLUTIONIZING PRODUCTIVITY IN SOUTH AFRICAN GOLD MINING

Applying established methods of quarrying stone to underground mining has revolutionized productivity in South African gold fields. A synthetic-covered steel cable, studded with industrial diamonds, saws through the rock face, cutting away the ore in large chunks. At $290 a metre it is expensive. But it can operate 24 hours a day, requires less labour and minimizes the amount of waste rock mined by eliminating many of the 900,000 blasts the gold mines in South Africa currently make every day.

Case example 3   THE PERSONAL SHOPPING ASSISTANT AT METRO'S FUTURE STORE

In 2003 Metro, the German retailer, and 39 partners ranging from SAP and Intel to Coca-Cola and Procter & Gamble, unveiled Future Store, a converted 1970s supermarket in Rheinberg, Germany. A personal shopping assistant (PSA) is a personal computer that staff fit onto the store's trolleys as customers enter. The touch screen device is at the centre of Future Store's high-tech developments. Holders of Metro's loyalty cards swipe it and those who have prepared a shopping list on the store's website before setting off can call it up on the PSA's colour screen. Looking for items could not be easier – if in doubt the PSA search engine points to the desired item's location on a map of the store. As goods enter the trolley, the bar code is scanned, the item is added to the on-screen shopping list and the cumulative price is displayed. In addition, the PSA signals any special offers as you walk by. Fresh fruit and vegetable weighing and pricing has also been simplified. A built-in camera powered by IBM's 'Veggie Vision' software identifies the product and prints the necessary label. All this to make shopping easier and Metro's goods cheaper.
www.future-store.org

Case example 4   MINIMIZING COSTS AT MCDONALD'S

McDonald's fast-food chain is renowned for its lean operations to provide capacity, tight portion control and fast service. But the drive to reduce costs is not only limited to its core tasks. By analysing electricity costs on a half-hourly basis, reviewing this provision and proactively seeking alternative suppliers, McDonald's has cut £1.4 million from its £18 million electricity bill for England and Wales. A separate deal for Scotland has led to savings of more than 30 per cent.
www.mcdonalds.com

Case question   Review the four examples given here. How are the first three examples stepped and why is the McDonald's example classed as incremental?

Exhibit 16.6 Stepped versus incremental change programmes

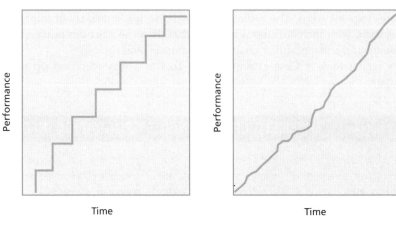

The pattern of improvement
resulting from stepped changes

The pattern of improvement
resulting from incremental changes

Exhibit 16.6 reviews the pattern of performance resulting from stepped and incremental change. The picture is self-evident and helps highlight the difference between the two approaches to securing improvements. However, for most companies, combining these two approaches makes most sense and will typically provide the best way to achieve and sustain improvement over time (see Case example 16.5).

To help evaluate which approach to use and when a combination of the two would be more suited to the needs of an organization, Exhibit 16.7 summarizes some of the key differences that would form part of the decision on which approach better suits the needs of a business.

Case example 5   **INTRODUCING LEAN OPERATIONS AT PORSCHE**

Porsche AG's sales fell from a 1986 high (including 30,000 in the USA alone) to less than 13,000 cars in 1993, pushing the small German car maker to the brink of collapse. As profits fell and losses mounted, the challenge was to transform a company steeped in laborious craftsmanship into an efficient and profitable competitor. The key has been a mix of stepped and incremental change. The workforce was reduced by 34 per cent by the new millennium. In addition, introducing lean operations methods also led to an inventory reduction of over 50 per cent and production time halved from over 120 to 60 hours. Mean-

while, in purchasing, the number of suppliers has been reduced from 900 to less than 300, while in design 36 per cent of parts in the latest version of the 911 are identical to those in the new Boxster.

The results from the all-time low have been dramatic. Sales since 1993 have increased year on year, with vehicles sold in 2003 reaching an all-time high of over 60,800. Similar levels of improvement have been made in terms of the number of vehicles/staff from 2.6 in 1994 to 6.2 vehicles in 2003.

www2.us.porsche.com

Case questions   1 How do the improvements at Porsche illustrate the continuous nature of its improvement drive?

2 Check on the Porsche website (www2.us.porsche.com) to see how well the company is currently doing.

Exhibit 16.7 Features of stepped and incremental approaches to improvement

Features	Stepped improvement	Incremental improvement
Level of investment	Large	Small
Basis of improvement	Technology	Systems and procedure reviews
Relative time frame	Long term	Short span
Nature of task	One-off, additional large project	Continuous, inherent part of day-to-day activity
Involvement	Few, led by specialists	Many, with all staff contributing
Maintaining the gains	Self-sustaining improvements are·inherent in the investment	High level of maintenance necessary to sustain gains and make future improvements

Continuous improvement

The last section highlighted different approaches to securing improvements. This section discusses the importance of fostering an approach to improvement that recognizes the necessity, as well as the sense, of implementing improvements on an ongoing basis. In this way, the drive towards improvement becomes a never-ending journey. Being better than the day before by encouraging everyone within an organization to identify and act on opportunities for improvement is at the centre of the continuous improvement philosophy.

Furthermore, the philosophy of continuous improvement highlights the fundamental nature of improvement. As illustrated in Exhibit 16.8, cost is the substance of a company's activities and the need to address all areas of cost within an organization is fundamental to the continuous improvement approach. Leaving no stone unturned and realizing that all improvements, no matter how small, are central to the philosophy driving continuous improvement throughout the whole of an organization.

Continuous improvement often goes hand in hand with incremental change. But it does not set any conditions on the size of improvements, thereby not ruling out stepped improvements as a byproduct of the activity. Stepped changes, however, while being identi-

Exhibit 16.8 The cost iceberg

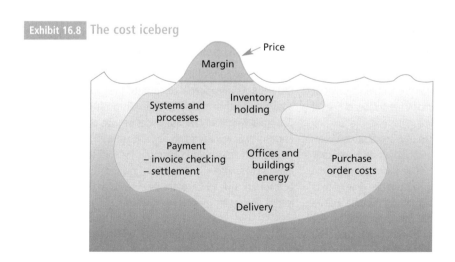

fied in the context of continuous improvement, would normally be handled in the way outlined in Exhibit 16.7.

Kaizen is a Japanese name for a formal system to promote continuous improvement. Masaaki Imai has described the approach in detail,[2] citing the system as an important basis for the success of many leading Japanese firms. He highlights, as fundamental to *kaizen*, the need for everyone in an organization to be involved in the philosophy and reality of continuous improvement. It begins with the notion that an organization can only ensure its long-term success when everyone actively seeks ways to identify and implement improvements as part of their approach to work. In this way, it keeps people thinking about the current processes, systems and structures. Understanding the system and procedures, continuously reflecting on how well they work and the source of the problems that occur help in spotting improvements and create an environment for ongoing developments as a byproduct of day-to-day activity.

The nature of continuous improvement highlighted by *kaizen* is explained by three guiding principles:

- Process reviews – the basic unit for analysing a system in *kaizen* is to review the processes involved. This analysis would review the whole supply chain from the design of a service or product through to its provision and delivery to a customer.

- Success comes from people – successful *kaizen* programmes rely on people's knowledge and insight of the systems and procedures involved and their ability to identify improvements. High levels of skill, employee participation and corporate support for implementing improvements are key factors in bringing success, as Case examples 16.6–16.8 illustrate.

- Constant need for change – a successful *kaizen* programme depends on everyone feeling the constant need for change and never accepting the current process, however good, as being adequate. Complacency is avoided. Feeling the need to improve, seeking out improvements and implementing the changes that result are the basis on which this approach is built – successful change programmes need to concentrate on outcomes and not the process.[3]

The contrast between more traditional approaches in organizations to an environment that encourages and recognizes the need and benefits of continuous improvement is provided by Case examples 16.6–16.8.

Case example 6   MEASURING PRODUCTIVITY AT IBM

In part of his study of the problems at IBM, Paul Carroll identified that in IBM's software development function, quality, at the time of the review, was measured by the number of lines of code written per day. The more lines, the more the function was deemed to be productive. When IBM and Microsoft combined to review certain programs, a Microsoft developer took an existing IBM code requiring 33,000 characters of space and rewrote it using only 200, thereby reducing the time to read into memory and process the code to $1/160$ of the time. From a professional viewpoint, such action was considered by IBM managers to be 'rude'. Other Microsoft developers then rewrote other parts of IBM's code to make them smaller and faster. IBM's managers' complaints then went further – according to their measurements, Microsoft had not been pulling its weight. In fact, using lines of code as the measure, Microsoft was actually doing 'negative work'.[4]

The encouragement in Microsoft for staff to identify and implement improvements was in marked contrast to the bureaucratic style which, at the time, pervaded the IBM organization. The results speak for themselves.

www.ibm.com; www.microsoft.com

Case example 7   **SAVING ENERGY AT VOLVO**

Volvo, the Swedish motor vehicle manufacturer, came up with a simple way to save energy that it is now applying across other parts of its business. Instead of using heat to dry newly painted engine blocks before they were assembled into motors, it now uses dry air. This represents a 90 per cent saving in energy consumption, from 650 to 70 kw an hour, with no adverse effects on quality. The fuel-saving idea was the work of five staff competing for the group's internal environmental prize.

www.volvo.com

Case example 8   **CUTTING COSTS AT RICOH**

At Ricoh's copier plant in Shenzhen, China, the 3500 staff are encouraged to come up with suggestions to cut costs. With each person averaging 1.26 suggestions a year, there are several ideas to consider each day. Soliciting suggestions from workers does not necessarily mean cutting-edge or high-tech solutions. For example, one Ricoh worker recently suggested narrowing the distance between two work stations from 120 to 90cm, the distance of one stride. It didn't amount to much but the cumulation of such ideas is essential when profit margins are down to below 2 per cent. Also, implementing changes helps motivate people and demonstrate the importance and relevance of their contributions.   **www.ricoh.com**

Case question   Use these examples to illustrate the three points guiding continuous improvement.

An approach to improvement: the Deming cycle

This section looks at ways to improve current systems and processes. Before looking at these, it is useful to place them within the context of an overall procedure, thus providing you with an overview as well as a way to help undertake the necessary analysis. One approach is the Deming cycle, also called the Deming wheel or the PDCA cycle (from the sequence plan/do/check/act, as shown in Exhibit 16.9). This series of linked activities is used to examine systems and processes and helps to identify opportunities for continuous improvement.[5]

Exhibit 16.9   The Deming cycle

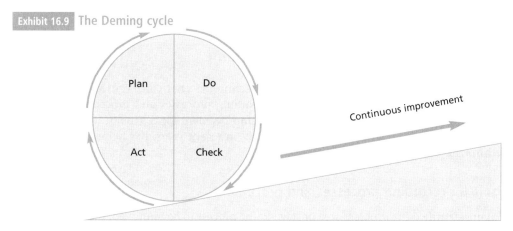

Plan

The start point is identifying a problem or selecting an aspect of the current system or process that can be improved. This step is critical, for where and on what the investment of time and money is spent will be the basis for the gains that follow. The work needs to be of lasting benefit and can be at different levels. On the one hand, the areas of improvement can be in line with the market-related priorities set within an organization. On the other hand, the improvements can relate to any areas where benefits can be secured. While the former are set within the strategic direction of an organization, the latter concern the equally important need of improving the efficiency of the internal activities of a company.

Having selected the areas for improvement, the way forward is to record all the relevant facts about the present work, examine these critically using a number of the tools and techniques discussed later in the chapter and then develop ways to improve the current system or process.

Do

Having formulated the plan, the next step is to implement it. By involving those with responsibility for the area of work being reviewed, acceptance of the improvements tends to be an integral part of the activity. Sometimes the outcomes will necessitate improving existing skills and the training requirements that go hand in hand with such changes also need to be identified and arranged.

Check

The principal activities of this step are to monitor and check the results of the improvements. They include ensuring that the improvements identified are in place and the anticipated gains are forthcoming. Performance measurement is an integral part of this step as this facilitates the checking and quantifies the improvement. Reasons for any shortfall are also examined.

Act

In the final stage, information is collected and reviewed and any necessary corrective action is taken. This step is also designed to ensure that the improvements made are maintained. Periodic checks both monitor the progress achieved and ensure that the system or process is now running as intended. Finally, this step allows adjustments to be made as part of the overall improvement initiative and in line with the continuous nature of the approach.

Tools and techniques for improvement

This section explains the various tools and techniques that can be used as part of the improvement process. There are tools for recording processes and procedures, those for identifying problems and those for generating improvement ideas. Finally, there is a section on business process re-engineering (BPR) which, in recent years, has helped companies to rethink the way they do business.

Tools for recording processes and procedures

Having identified the problem area or stage in the process to be improved, the next step is to record the systems and processes involved. There are a number of ways to chart the sequences and these provide different levels of detail and show different aspects of a task.

Recording of a delivery system or process can involve a range of approaches including outline process charts, information or material flow process charts, person flow process charts, multiple activity process charts, multiple activity bar charts, service maps and videoing and these are explained below. However, before this, Exhibits 16.10 and 16.11 detail the symbols used to complete process charts and service maps respectively.

Exhibit 16.10 Process chart symbols

Symbol	Activity	Used to represent	
		Material or information	Person doing the task
○	Operation	Materials, products or information are modified or acted upon during the operation	Person completes an operation or task. This may include preparation for the next activity
□	Inspection	Materials, products or information are checked and quality, quantity or accuracy is verified	Person checks and verifies for quality, quantity or accuracy at this stage in the process or procedure
⇨	Transport	Materials, products or information are moved to another location without being part of an operation or inspection	Person moves from one position to another as part of the process or procedure without being part of an operation or inspection
⊐	Delay	Temporary storage or filing of an item. Not recorded as 'in store' or filed and not requiring authorization for its withdrawal	Person unable to complete the next part of the task
▽	Storage	Controlled storage, governed by authorized receipt and issue; document filed and retained for future reference	Not used
◉	Combined activities	To show activities performed at the same time or a person completing two tasks at the same time	

Exhibit 16.11 Symbols used in drawing service maps

Symbol	Explanation
●●●●●● ●●●●●●●●●	*Line of visibility* used to divide the part of the operations visible to the customer (including telephone and written communication) from the rest of the service delivery system
△	*Fail points* – points in the process where there is a high level of service failure
➡ ⇨	*Service paths* – the optimal and 'when things go wrong' service paths are shown as follows: ● optimal service path ● path where things go wrong
⬠ P	*Problem* – indicates where problems occur in a process
⬡ D	*Dialogue* – indicates where customer interface with the delivery system takes place – the line of interaction

Outline process charts

The two principal activities in a procedure or process are operations (completing tasks) and checks or inspections. These charts give a valuable overview of the work being reviewed, with the minimum of recording effort, by showing the sequence of only the main operations and inspections involved. They are usually completed at the start of an investigation

Exhibit 16.12 Relationship of charting techniques

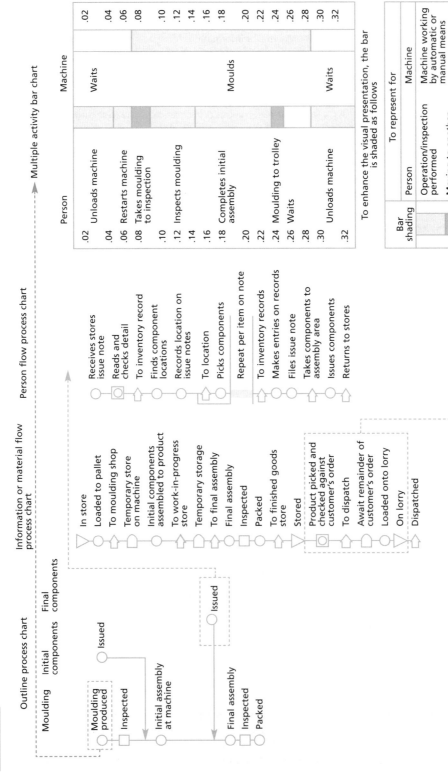

Multiple activity process chart

Dispatch supervisor

- Receives dispatch set
- Separates labels and advice note from set
- Puts sales office copy of invoice into tray
- Takes labels etc. to picker
- Gives labels etc. to picker
- Returns to desk
- To file tray
- Takes sales office copy of paperwork from file
- To dispatch area
- Checks items against paperwork
- Supervisor signs sales office copy
- Returns to desk
- Puts sales office copy into internal mail system
- To next task

Picker

- Receives labels etc.
- Walks to storage area with truck
- Locates goods
- Picks goods onto truck
- Repeats for each item required
- To dispatch
- Sticks labels to outer cartons
- Stacks all items and paperwork to await loading
- Repeat throughout the working day with other tasks
- Puts advice note into one carton and marks for customer's attention
- Loads orders onto lorry
- To next task

Goods

- Loaded onto truck
- To dispatch
- Labelled
- Stacked
- Checked against paperwork by supervisor
- Advice note put into one carton and marked for customer's attention
- Loaded onto lorry
- On lorry

Dispatch set and labels

- Received by supervisor
- Separated
- Labels etc. wait
- To packer
- Given to picker
- In picker's hand
- Files sales office copy
- Picked up by supervisor
- Taken to dispatch area
- Used to check against picker's items
- Signed by supervisor to authorize invoicing
- Returned to dispatch
- Put into internal mail system
- Await collection

into a system, department or function to help decide the further areas for study. Against each main operation and inspection, a brief description is shown together with the time taken, if available.

Information or material flow process charts

These record what happens to documents or materials in the process, system or procedure being studied. They amplify an outline process chart by showing all operations and inspections as well as the movement, delay and filing or storage of the documents or materials involved.

Person flow process charts

These show the movements of a person who has to go from place to place to carry out a task. As with information or material flow process charts, they show all the operations and inspections that take place together with any movements and delays.

Multiple activity process charts

These show the interrelated activities of persons, equipment, documents or materials, with the latter particularly relating to clerical and administrative activities. They record, on a common scale, all the activities completed in the task and how they relate to one another within the process or procedure.

Multiple activity bar charts

As with multiple activity process charts, these show the interrelated activities of persons, equipment, documents or materials but have a time dimension, using bar charts to show relevant lengths of time for each activity.

As the examples in Exhibit 16.12 show, the level of detail is significantly greater for some charts. For the operations manager, the most useful is often the outline process chart which gives an overview of the main activities. This can then be used to agree a work programme for future investigations and also provide a framework to guard against situations where a change in one part of a procedure or process will cause problems elsewhere.

Service maps

Service maps (also known as service blueprints) chart the movement of customers, information and tasks through the service process. While sometimes using some of the symbols explained in Exhibit 16.10, service maps predominantly use the symbols in Exhibit 16.11 to chart what happens. As mentioned in Chapter 5, a key analysis when completing a service map is to determine the line of visibility that separates front- and back-office activities and the line of interaction where the customer interfaces with the service delivery system.

Videoing

As an alternative to charting a process, videoing what happens and using the outcome as a basis for analysis is increasingly being preferred. Improvements in video recording equipment have not only simplified its use but also led to significant reductions in cost, both in terms of the initial investment and subsequent applications. Its advantages over methods of charting include:

- **Level of accuracy** – it provides a complete record of the activities that take place, especially where the task itself is complex.

- **Facilitates analysis** – the medium of a picture record facilitates subsequent analysis including an assessment of the skill and experience levels of those involved.

- **A visual record of events** can be reviewed by all concerned and on any number of subsequent occasions. In addition, it allows all concerned to participate in the examination of activities.

- **Acceptability** – by taking away the element of human interpretation and presenting a more neutral approach to the activities under review, those involved more readily accept the record of events (the camera shows it as it is) and acknowledge their participation in the procedure, leading to improved ways of working.

Tools for identifying problems

As explained in the last section, mapping provides an overview of a process to help understand what happens, where duplication occurs and where potential improvements exist. This section concerns tools and techniques to help identify what causes the problems experienced in a process or procedure.

Cause and effect diagrams

These were first introduced in Chapter 11 and are also known as fishbone diagrams (from their shape – see Exhibit 16.13) or Ishikawa charts after Kaoru Ishikawa who first developed this tool.[6] This approach provides a mechanism to help solve problems by identifying the causes and effects involved. The example in Exhibit 16.13 is the outcome of an investigation into a company's problem of being unable to supply products to specification and so consistently meet the requirements of the high-speed production lines of one of its customers. Excess processing waste was clearly identified, involving a minimum annual loss of over $40,000, in addition to the serious problem of failing to achieve acceptable levels of delivery reliability. The detailed and systematic analysis provided by the cause and effect diagram enabled the company to review the causes and identify several areas where improvements were needed and could be made.

Why-why reviews

These offer another way to identify the causes of problems. The approach is to start with the problem and ask why the problem occurred. The reasons are recorded. Then, the process is repeated by again asking of each reason the question 'why it had occurred?' These reasons in turn are recorded and so on.

Tools for generating improvement ideas

The charting/recording stage described in the last sections comprises a review of the process or system but also embodies the task of identifying improvements. Most people, because of their training and background, are good at analytical thinking. On the other hand, few are good at divergent or creative thinking, either on its own or in combination with analytical approaches. Barriers are consciously or unconsciously set up that prevent the growth of ideas. These restrictions have a number of sources:

Exhibit 16.13 An example of a cause and effect diagram

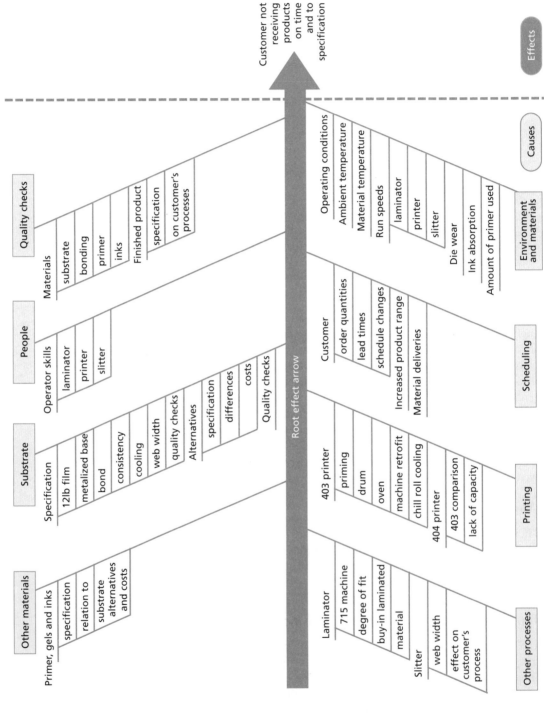

- self-imposed limits to possible solutions
- an inherent belief that there is one right answer
- fear of being wrong
- conformity to behaviour norms
- unwillingness to challenge the obvious.

Analytical approaches restrict imagination, and continuous evaluation puts the brake on ideas outside apparent norms or perceived boundaries. Creative thinking, on the other hand, is the process of linking ideas or things that were previously unrelated. By consciously suspending judgement and evaluating ideas at a later stage, the mind is given the opportunity to think laterally rather than being constrained within the vertical dimension associated with analytical approaches.

The stages involved in creative thinking are:

1 **Preparation** – collecting the known facts, defining the problem in different ways and restating/clarifying the problem

2 **Generation** – concerns the need to generate ideas, both in themselves and as a stimulus to creating other perspectives

3 **Incubation** – leaving the problem in the subconscious state as a way of creating new thoughts, the process of 'association'

4 **Insights** – linking ideas to possible solutions

5 **Evaluation** – analysing all the facts on which to base evaluations of the possible solutions.

Stages 1 and 5 are based on analytical approaches, whereas the other three are based on creative thinking. The key in this procedure is the deliberate separation of the phases involving the creation and evaluation of ideas. Completing stages 2, 3 and 4 is best done in groups, with the aim of creating quantity not quality of ideas. By creating large numbers of ideas, new ideas are sparked off. To help achieve this, the following rules apply:

- **Suspend judgement** – criticism of ideas is not permitted. Evaluation comes after the creative stage. Bringing these two phases together will lead to implied criticism and a reluctance to contribute. The key is to discourage self-evaluation from entering the process.
- **Freewheel** – wild ideas are deliberately fostered as they lead to better results.
- **Cross-fertilize** – at set stages, give participants the task of combining and improving on the ideas of others.

To help in the generation of ideas, a number of techniques may be used including:

- **Brainstorming** – 6–20 people take a problem and, working with the above rules, seek solutions. All ideas are written so as to remain visible throughout. Typically, stages 1–5 form the basis for using this technique.
- **Reverse brainstorming** – asks, of an idea being considered, 'In how many ways can this idea fail?'
- **Attribute listening** – lists the main attributes of the idea or object and examines how it can be changed.
- **Forced relationships** – list the ways in which ideas or objects can be combined.

These approaches generate what is referred to as 'effective surprise'. The eventual improvements are typically not of an 'off-the-map' nature but, in fact, have the quality of obvious-ness. The element of surprise is that, in retrospect, the solutions/improvements were obvious, in fact 'how else would it have been solved?' The role of creative thinking is to push down the self-imposed barriers to alternatives so that we can access alternatives.[7]

Business process re-engineering (BPR)

BPR helps companies to rethink the way they do business, and is a more radical approach to bringing about improvements.

In all but the smallest organizations, systems and procedures have always been carried out laboriously across a number of fragmented functions or specialist departments. These include service/product design, marketing, operations and accounting. Each has its own hierarchy and vertical communication and reporting system through which the require-ments pass on their way to the next stage that is performed by another part of the business. Ways of bridging these structures have been sought over the years, from permanent matri-ces through to project teams and task forces. Business re-engineering goes one step further. It transforms processes by reconfiguring them into ones that flow permanently across the relevant departments, with the tasks performed at the appropriate (often, organizationally, at a low) level. This involves delayering structures and breaking up existing functions and then reconstructing them around the redefined tasks and processes.

In essence, BPR seeks to develop processes that meet the needs of and provide the highest value for customers. Its aim is to achieve dramatic improvements in critical areas of performance and its radical nature stems from the approach it adopts to secure these. Underlying the BPR approach are two key dimensions:

- Operations should be organized around the total process that adds value to customers and not around the functions and activities that form the value-adding activity. In turn, a review of operations should similarly be based on the process rather than the functions providing the various parts.

- The analysis should begin, not with the existing process or procedure, but with the outputs from the process or procedure that customers want. The next step is to develop a process or system that delivers these outputs.

Since BPR was championed in the early 1990s,[8] it has been successfully used in many companies including Ford, IBM, Kodak, Bell Atlantic, Astra-Merck, Xerox and Taco Bell. However, like many of the tools and techniques advocated to help improve processes, BPR is

Exhibit 16.14 Mr James wants to start a BPR project

Exhibit 16.15 Re-engineering principles in practice

Purpose	Approach
Elimination	Remove a procedure or process
Compression	Remove time within a procedure, process or system
Integration	Re-engineer interfaces between successive steps in a procedure or process
Concurrency	Undertake procedures or operate processes in parallel rather than sequentially

not new. As early as the 1920s,[9] both Henry Ford and Alfred P. Sloan (General Motors) used this approach to make cars. What is new is the fact that companies are rethinking the approaches to bring about fundamental change and looking for ways of doing it.

Business process re-engineering (or more accurately described by some as 'core process redesign') advocates a fundamental rethink of the core processes from customer need or expectation through to the delivery process to bring this about – a more fundamental review than Mr James imagined (see Exhibit 16.14)! It begins with an impact statement which summarizes the costs and implications of maintaining the current process.

The process continues with a rethink of current procedures and embodies several key dimensions around the need to merge parts of a process or procedure, often in a fundamental way (see Exhibit 16.15). To achieve these improvements, some of the tactics employed include the following:

- the stages of generating, processing and using data should be embodied, wherever possible, in the same step of the procedure, employing the maxim – 'those who use the output of a process should perform the process'
- put the decision-making step where the work is performed and build controls into the process; merging the checking and action steps reduces overall control costs
- look to link geographically dispersed resources and seek the benefits of size by managing them as one centre even when they are located in different areas.

The benefits of a fundamental redesign of a company's core processes bring with them stepped changes in performance, as Case examples 16.9–16.13 illustrate. Such benefits are not, however, forthcoming without securing major changes in staff attitudes and corporate response. BPR entails major upheaval inside existing organizations that typically brings with it resistance built around internal politics, organizational status and human inertia.

Case example 9   REVIEWING THE ACCOUNTS FUNCTION AT THE FORD MOTOR COMPANY

Ford Motor Company reviewed its accounts payable function with the aim of reducing it from 500 to 400 staff. Ford was enthusiastic about its plan until it looked at Mazda, with an accounts payable staff of only five people. A review found that Ford's purchasing department placed an order and copied it to accounts payable. On receipt of the items or materials, goods inwards did the same. When the vendor invoiced, accounts payable had to find and reconcile the three documents. Checking, queries and investigations (in all, accounts payable had to match 14 data items) led to delays and the need for a lot of staff and cost. Now there is 'invoiceless processing' where checks are automatic. Also, if goods are received and there is no record, they are returned. As for invoices, customers are told not to send them – Ford pays on receipt of goods.

www.ford.com

Case example 10 REDUCING PROCESSING TIMES AT MUTUAL BENEFIT LIFE

Mutual Benefit Life handled customer applications through a series of linked but independent steps taking the paperwork from one department to the next:

- credit checks
- quotation
- rating
- underwriting
- document preparation.

Typical process times were 5–25 days, with delays, checking and rechecking throughout the procedure. A relook using linked databases swept aside job descriptions and made case managers responsible for an application from start to finish – no more file hand-offs, no more backtracking and no more delays between stages. Turnarounds can now be completed in as little as four hours and typically take 2–5 days. And this with 100 less staff and each core manager handling twice the number of applications as before.

Case example 11 RADICALLY IMPROVING PERFORMANCE AT TACO BELL

Taco Bell, the US fast-food chain with a Mexican menu, looked to improve its performance radically. At the time, each outlet had its own kitchen and prepared food on site. This took up space, reduced the customer seating area, increased overhead costs and lengthened service lead times. Starting with its customers, Taco Bell found that they did not want extensive facilities and children's play areas but placed great emphasis on good food served hot and fast at an affordable price. The conclusion reached was that outlets should switch from making food to retailing food. The 'K-Minus' system replaced existing kitchens with smaller food preparation areas where staff, in response to customers' orders, assembled the various menu items from food (for example meat, corn tortilla shells and beans) prepared centrally and delivered to the various outlets. In addition to savings on outlet running costs of $87 million, the re-engineered process brought additional benefits, including improved quality control, higher staff morale and lower staff turnover, in part, through eliminating the drudgery of food preparation and savings on outlet running costs.

www.tacobell.com

Case example 12 REDUCING TAKE-OFF COSTS AT JET BLUE AIRWAYS

In the cockpits of **Jet Blue Airways'** planes, pilots pull out sleek laptops and punch in relevant data from each phase of the take-off process, such as outside temperature, fuel load, number of passengers, baggage weight, number of bags in each bin and the length of the allocated runway. In a few seconds the system advises how much engine thrust they should apply. Using a laptop, besides being less error-prone, offers real savings. Having take-off calculations can slash as much as 5 per cent from the maintenance and operating costs of an aeroplane, worth millions of dollars over the life of a plane. Traditional paper charts offer generalized rules and manual calculations lead to generous safety margins being applied. Now pilots know exactly what their thrust settings and take-off speeds should be, which saves fuel, lightens engine wear and cuts down noise.

www.jetblueairways.com

Case example 13 IMPROVING PRODUCTIVITY AT WESTERN PROVIDENT ASSOCIATION

Western Provident Association (WPA), a UK-based health insurer, improved productivity by almost 50 per cent by introducing BPR. For example, processing an application previously involved seven staff and 28 days. It now involves one person and takes four days. This includes reviewing the medical history, setting up the policy and arranging the collection of insurance premiums. In the old system that took 28 days, a file was worked on for only 45 minutes. Like many companies opting for BPR, WPA combines image processing and work flow software to speed up re-engineered procedures. Image processing captures a complete image (including signatures and graphics) of a document on a computer. Work flow software automatically forwards the document image onto the relevant worker handling the next stage. Looking at targets that a business wants to reach (in WPA's case, shortening processing lead times and reducing costs), BPR then works backwards to achieve this.

www.wpa.org.uk

Case question   Using these five examples, identify the BPR-based changes made.

Employee involvement

To introduce and maintain an effective continuous improvement programme requires that employees are involved in all phases – agreeing the aims of the programme, delivering the results and implementing the ideas. The commitment of all concerned is fundamental and involvement is the way to ensure this happens. In fact, the very term 'continuous improvement' goes hand in hand with employee involvement. As emphasized elsewhere, using the capabilities and experience of everyone in an organization is an essential part of successfully developing and growing a business. The approaches used were covered extensively in Chapter 3. The purpose of this short section is to underscore the essential nature of this dimension of successfully managing an operations function, while Case example 16.14 reinforces the point.

Case example 14 IMPROVING WORK SYSTEMS AT UNIPART

Scattered around the plants and warehouses of Unipart, the UK manufacturing and logistics company, are wood-panelled rooms filled with computers. The rooms are training centres and form part of the company's commitment to improving the skills of its staff and underpin the drive for improvement. Inside the rooms (called 'faculties on the floor'), small groups meet to share ideas and experiences on how best to improve work systems and processes from the manufacture of exhaust systems to the distribution of products to customers.

Via the internet, computers link staff to one another throughout the company's many locations. The drive is to devise training and education that can be applied to today's problems and opportunities. The company also uses around 400 internal facilitators to organize training sessions for everyone, with coaching the predominant medium in the learning process. Passing on solutions and seeking ideas from others are key elements in Unipart's drive to continuously improve.

www.unipart.com

Case questions   1   What aspects of Unipart's approach illustrate the concept of continuous improvement?
2   How is employee involvement central to this initiative?

Reflections

Most of the approaches described in this chapter have been around for a long time and have comprised the content of books in the field of operations over the last 50 years. The significant change in recent years is a recognition in operations that the approaches adopted need to form part of an overall philosophy rather than a list of alternatives or independent initiatives. The outcome is a marked change in approach:

● While needing to foster improvement as an inherent part of everyone's job, companies need to monitor what is going on and establish priorities as ways of keeping the task manageable. A major European bank reviewed its change programme initiatives across the group and was startled with the outcome, which is summarized in Exhibit 16.16. With such large staff numbers involved, individual businesses had simply put some programmes on hold.

● The approaches chosen need to build on one another and form part of a coherent way to bring about change.

● Improvement does not end with implementation. The hallmark of successful improvement is the stress placed on the continuous nature of the task. The aim is to move closer all the time to an absolute ideal by making small beneficial changes throughout the process and infrastructure of the operations function.

Exhibit 16.16 Change programmes in selected sectors of a European bank

Sector		Change programmes	
		#	Equivalent staff days
Card services		13	7,000
Mortgage services		5	9,000
Banking services	corporate	4	16,100
	retail	22	25,000
Life products and investments		7	19,500
Insurance services		1	1,200

Many chapters of this book have addressed ways of achieving improvements. What follows is intended to reflect important features of this core activity, incomplete in itself, but designed to provide linkage, with more extensive coverage provided elsewhere.

Improved design

Costs, quality conformance and service/product range are an integral part of design. In fact, the ease with which operations can meet the requirements of these dimensions is inherent in the service/product design itself. Consequently, early involvement in the design procedure and designing for operations are key facets of the corporate improvement process. Approaches to improving design were addressed earlier in Chapter 4.

Eliminating waste

A key dimension of improvement is the elimination of waste. Excesses in all forms are unnecessary and costly and, on a global scale, the use of the earth's resources is now recognized as being unsustainable. F. Cho (Toyota Motor Company) provides a concise definition of waste as 'anything other than the minimum amount of equipment, materials, parts and workers which are absolutely essential'. The aim is to strive to achieve this ideal by introducing continuous improvement throughout a range of activities. Because services tend to be staff-intensive, many of the improvements concern changing the activities and roles of people. However, other key areas of waste reduction come from activities such as improving housekeeping and the immediate environment in general.

Improving staff productivity

Staff productivity gains go hand in hand with eliminating waste. The essential source of these gains does not, as is often thought, come from getting staff to work harder or faster. Instead it comes from eliminating waste and creating a work environment where staff work more of the time per se and more of the time on productive tasks.

Jidoka – quality at source

Introduced in the early 1950s by Taiichi Ohno, *jidoka* is based on the philosophy that all staff should be personally responsible for the services they provide or products they make.

In the car assembly plants, *jidoka* push buttons were introduced and all employees are authorized to stop the line for reasons of quality, safety or pace of the line. This overt mechanism facilitates the drive for quality at source – stopped production concentrates the mind on putting things right. The same levels of concern need to form part of the continuous improvement drive.

Process redesign

A continuous and rigorous re-examination of how services, products and information are delivered needs to be made. Of concern is not just cost – delivery speed, delivery on time and quality conformance are often of a higher priority in today's competitive markets.

Involving people

To support these approaches, companies need to involve people extensively, both within and outside the organization. Work needs to be restructured in terms of increased participation, involvement, responsibility/authority links and job interest. This leads to environments where continuous improvement can flourish as an integral part of the way an organization works.

Companies need to adhere to the principle of employing people for their heads as well as their hands. This has not always been the case, especially in the West. As Konosuke Matsushita explains:

> Your firms are built on the Taylor model; even worse, so are your heads. With your bosses doing the thinking, while the workers wield the screwdrivers, you are convinced deep down that this is the right way to run a business. For you, the essence of management is getting the ideas out of the heads of the bosses into the hands of labour.[10]

Although spoken in the mid-1980s, it remains a stark warning, as the executives of many organizations still do not recognize that their task is to create environments to get the ideas out of the heads of staff and into the hands of staff.

Similar differences in approach are to be found in supplier relations. Many US and European customers still manage their suppliers in terms of contract placement by threat and fear – the you-need-us-more-than-we-need-you syndrome. They fail to appreciate that win/lose situations are a poor base on which to build mutually beneficial relations. Suppliers need to be recognized as partners in terms of design, quality, cost and delivery improvements. As customers generally hold the power, they must initiate sound and mutually beneficial relations with suppliers. As a partnership, both sides need to contribute. Win/win situations need to be developed in order to compete successfully in today's global markets.

As the service sector becomes more important, it is essential that, in their quest for better performance, organizations not only recognize the benefits but also the opportunities to realize these by adopting a philosophy of continuous improvement. As product quality and manufacturing productivity were a central feature of the 1980s, service quality and productivity was a major theme of the 1990s and continues to be so in the new millennium. Attitudes to improvement, however, need to be developed. Without this core activity, many firms will, at best, underperform and, at worst, miss out altogether.

Key Elements of Improving Operations

- Reflecting the important strategic and short-term aspects of performance in the measures used within operations is an essential dimension in managing this function – 'what gets measured gets done'.

- To help provide context, Exhibit 16.1 overviews some of the relevant dimensions, tasks and performance measures that affect operations, followed by explanation and examples.

- How to improve operations and the key role of continuous improvement is then introduced,

highlighting alternative approaches including the Deming cycle and business process re-engineering.

- The tools and techniques used in the continuous drive for improvement follow, including those for mapping process sequence, identifying problems and generating ideas.

- The final short section reinforces the key role provided by employee involvement and also serves as a link to Chapter 3 which dealt specifi-cally with the core task of managing people.

Self-check

1 The first step of reviewing performance is to:
   a Set standards that have to be met ☐
   b Select which aspects to measure and determine why they should be measured ☐
   c Determine how to improve current performance levels ☐

2 An example of a measure that would maintain or reduce cost is:
   a Rate of new service or product introductions ☐
   b Operations lead times ☐
   c Efficiency ☐

3 Experience curves clearly show that as experience accumulates:
   a The cost of providing a service or product falls ☐
   b The rate of new service or product introductions decrease ☐
   c Operations lead times reduce ☐

4 Benchmarking, the practice of comparing business practices and performances between companies:
   a Is only applicable to the automotive industry ☐

   b Has become widely adopted across all business sectors ☐
   c Is not yet used in service businesses ☐

5 Stepped improvements tend to:
   a Involve a small level of investment ☐
   b Be over a relatively short time frame ☐
   c Involve few people, typically led by specialists ☐

6 Incremental improvements tend to:
   a Be based around technology changes ☐
   b Involve few people, typically led by specialists ☐
   c Be over a relatively short time frame ☐

7 In business process re-engineering (BPR), the analysis should start with:
   a The existing process ☐
   b A summary of costs and implications of maintaining the current process ☐
   c Both a and b ☐

8 Which of the following is a method for mapping process sequences:
   a Multiple activity bar charts ☐
   b Cause and effect diagrams ☐
   c Why-why reviews ☐

9 When generating improvement ideas, it is important to:

a Ignore wild ideas ☐

b Evaluate ideas as they are generated ☐

c Give participants the task of combining and improving on the ideas of others ☐

10 The hallmark of successful improvement is that:

a It ends once the ideas have been implemented ☐

b It only focuses on stepped improvement activities ☐

c It is continuous in its nature ☐

Study activities

Discussion questions

1 A retail outlet offering a range of high specification women's clothes wishes to develop relevant performance measures. Suggest those that you consider appropriate.

2 Explain the difference between stepped and incremental change programmes. What are the advantages and disadvantages of each?

3 Draw an outline process chart when arranging a holiday for which the hotels and flights are directly booked by you.

4 Why is the use of video gaining widespread use in the field of continuous improvement?

5 Company A achieves 85 per cent experience curve gains while Company B achieves gains of 80 per cent. Company A's first unit cost was £200 while Company B's was £240.

(a) How much will the 128th unit cost for each company?

(b) When will Company B's unit cost match that of Company A?

6 Why is there actual conflict between management and staff over productivity levels? What actions can operations managers take to resolve these differences?

Assignments

1 Develop a cause and effect or fishbone diagram to explain lengthy service at a restaurant.

2 Use the Deming cycle approach to suggest and implement improvements to the library lending delivery system.

Exploring further

Adler, PS, Goldoftas, B and Levine, DL 'Flexibility versus efficiency? A case study of model changeovers in the Toyota production system', *Organisation Science*, **10**(1) (1999).

Dixon, JR, Nanni, AJ and Vollman, TE *The New Performance Challenge: Measuring Operations for World Class Competition*, Dow Jones-Irwin, Homewood, IL (1990).

Feldman, CG *The Practical Guide to Business Process Re-engineering Using Idefo*, Dorset House Publishing, New York (1998).

Hall, RW, Johnson, HT and Turney, PBB *Measuring Up: Charting Pathways to Manufacturing Excellence*, Business One Irwin, Homewood, IL (1991).

Harrington, HJ, Esseling, EKC and Nimwegen, HV *Business Process Improvement Workbook:*

Documentation, Analysis, Design and Management of Business Process Improvements, McGraw-Hill, New York (1997).

Hobbs, DP *Lean Manufacturing Implementation*, J Ross Publishing/APICS, Boca Raton, Fl (2003).

Holland, M *When the Machine Stopped*, Harvard Business School Press, Boston, MA (1989).

Johansson, HJ, McHugh, P, Pendlebury, AJ and Wheeler, WA III *Business Process Reengineering: Breakpoint Strategies for Market Dominance*, John Wiley & Sons, Chichester (1993).

Kobayashi, I *Twenty Keys to Workplace Improvements*, Productivity Press, Portland (1995).

Konz, S and Johnson, S *Work Design: Industrial Ergonomics*, 5th edn, Holcomb Hathaway, Scottsdale, AZ (2000).

Lapre, MA and Van Wassenhove, LN 'Learning across lines: the secret to more efficient factories', *Harvard Business Review*, October (2002), pp. 107–11.

Melnyk, SA and Christensen, RT *Back to Basics: Your Guide to Manufacturing Excellence*, CRC Press LLC, Boca Raton, Fl (2000).

Pande, PS, Neumann, RP and Cavanagh, RR *The Six Sigma Way: How GE, Motorola and Other Top Companies are Honing their Performance*, McGraw-Hill, New York (2000).

Pande, PS, Neumann, RP and Cavanagh, RR *Six Sigma Way Team Field Book: An Implementation Guide for Project Improvement Teams*, McGraw-Hill, New York (2002).

Rohleder, TR and Silver, EA 'A tutorial on business process improvement', *Journal of Operations Management*, **15**(2) (1997) pp. 139–54.

Senge, PM *The Fifth Discipline: The Art and Practice of the Learning Organisation*, Random House, London (1990).

The Productivity Press Development Team *5S for Operators: 5 Pillars of the Visual Workplace*, Productivity Press, Portland (1996).

Thonike, S 'Enlightened experimentation: the new imperative for experimentation', *Harvard Business Review,* February (2001) pp. 67–75.

Womack, J, Jones, D and Roos, D *The Machine that Changed the World*, Macmillan, New York (1990).

Notes and references

1 The compilation of the experience curve is detailed in *Experience and Cost: Some Implications for Manufacturing Policy*, Harvard Business School paper 9-675-228 (1975). Also, see Ghemerant, P 'Building strategy on the experience curve', *Harvard Business Review*, March–April (1985), pp. 143–9.

2 Masaaki Imai *Kaizen: The Key to Japan's Competitive Success*, Random House, New York (1986).

3 Schaffer, RH and Thomson, HA in their article 'Successful change programs begin with results', *Harvard Business Review*, January–February (1992), pp. 80–9 emphasize the need to evaluate change programmes by an assessment of the true worth of their outcomes.

4 This example is taken from Carroll, P *Big Blues: the Unmaking of IBM*, Crown, New York (1995), p. 101.

5 Deming, WE *Out of the Crisis*, MIT Centre for Advanced Engineering Study, Cambridge, MA (1986), pp. 88–9.

6 Ishikawa, K *Guide to Quality Control*, Quality Resources, White Plains, NY (1985), pp. 18–29.

7 Also see Kelley, T and Littman, J *The Art of Innovation: Lessons in Creativity from IDEO, America's Leading Design Firm*, Doubleday/Currency Books, New York (2001) and Schrage, M *Serious Play: How the World's Best Companies Stimulate to Innovate*, Harvard Business School Press, Boston (1999).

8 In particular, Michael Hammer in his article 'Re-engineering work: don't automate, obliterate', *Harvard Business Review*, July-August (1990), pp. 104–12 and with Champy, P *Re-engineering the Corporation*, Harper Business, New York (1993). Also see Davenport, TH and Short, JE 'The new industrial engineering: information technology and business process redesign', *Sloan Management Review*, **31**(4) (1990), pp. 11–27.

9 See, for example Ford, H *Today and Tomorrow*, Productivity Press, Cambridge, MA (1988).

10 Matsushita, K 'Why the West will lose', *Industrial Participation,* spring (1985), p. 8.

Managing Operations in Practice: Long Case Studies

book map

CUSTOMERS

OUTPUTS

PROCESSES

INPUTS

SUPPLIERS

Part

1

1 Managing Operations

2 Operations Strategy

3 Managing People

2

4 Designing and Developing Services & Products

5 Designing Service Delivery Systems

6 Designing Manufacturing Processes

7 Location and Layout

3

8 Managing Capacity

9 Technology Developments

10 Operations Scheduling and Execution

11 Managing Quality

12 Managing Inventory

13 Managing the Supply Chain

4

14 Process and Delivery System Reliability and Maintenance

15 Time and Productivity

16 Improving Operations

5

Managing Operations in Practice: Long Case Studies

Ash Electrics

Ash Electrics plc is a manufacturer of door-bells, door chimes, switches, industrial alarms and a range of small transformers. Producing some five million units per year (from a 38 cm diameter bell to a replacement bulb in a lighted switch), the company sells to electric wholesalers throughout the UK and abroad. One of its important selling features is to meet home orders on a same-day-as-receipt basis while the dispatch of export orders only waits for the next appropriate shipping arrangements.

The range of manufacturing activities includes coil winding, simple cropping and punching and other operations such as bending, forming and crimping simple components for later assembly. The principal activity, however, is the assembly, test and packing of products from the necessary bought-out and made in-house components, mouldings and parts. In outline, the operations process is shown in Exhibit 1. To reduce operations costs and material inventory levels, the company has standardized many components in each of the products from fixing screws through to clips, bobbins, coils, lamps and multilingual instruction leaflets. Besides the metal bars or domes

which produce the sound, the principal material used is plastic. Plastic bases, front pieces and components are bought in from outside suppliers to meet demand forecasts for each final product.

The company works on 13 four-week periods and it forecasts for each product both sales and finished stock level for several periods ahead. When setting the production programme, any anticipated differences between actual and forecast sales will be taken into account so that the actual end-of-period finished goods inventory is as close as possible to the forecast level. These adjustments are made at the start of each period when firm production outputs are agreed.

Questions

1 What are the critical operations scheduling features?

2 What is the key operations scheduling task?

3 Outline the development of a suitable scheduling system for the business.

Exhibit 1 **Outline of the operations process**

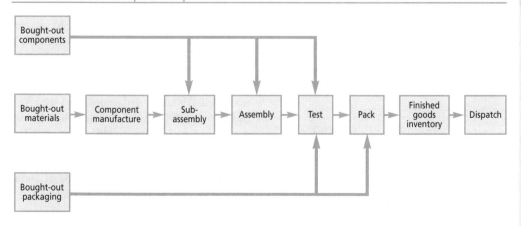

This case study was written by Terry Hill (University of Oxford). It is intended as the basis for class discussion and not as an example of good or bad management. © AMD Publishing.

Case study 2

Berwick Carpets

Berwick Carpets plc (BC) manufactures and sells tufted and woven carpets and carpet yarn. Although part of an international group of companies, it is managed as an independent business responsible for its own marketing, operations and investment requirements. It ranks about tenth in size in the industry, with current sales revenue of £150 milllion. In common with the rest of the carpet industry over the past 25 years, it has experienced a shift in the balance of sales towards tufted and away from woven carpets.

The manufacturing facilities consist of a spinning mill and both a tufted and woven carpet facility. While the spinning mill is on a separate site, the carpet manufacturing processes are in the same location as the sales and other functions of the business. The tufted and woven carpets, however, comprise two separate divisions, and this case study concerns the tufted carpet division (TCD).

The products

Unlike many UK carpet companies, BC has held its sales levels for tufted carpets over the past three years. It makes a range of carpet qualities and Exhibits 1 and 2 show these in three grades and the average operations costs of a typical product. The company's marketing strategy has been to provide products in

Exhibit 1 Grades of tufted carpet

Grade	Tufted carpets
1	Marble, Grenoble, Firenza, Barcarole, Casino
2	Maltese, Gazelle, Baroque, Barbary
3	Dalmatian, Royalty, Centurion, Lotus

Notes 1 Grade 3 is the highest quality of carpet.
2 Contract carpets are one-off carpets designed to customer specification and sold direct to the customer (for example hotels, house and office block builders and cinema chains). Invariably, they are made from non-standard colours, and often in material qualities not used on the standard range of carpets.
3 All non-contract carpets are sold to retail shops.
4 On contract carpets, one problem is judging the required yarn delivery to meet the order. Excess yarn is difficult to use while underproduction constitutes failure to meet a customer's contract.

Exhibit 2 Average operations costs for a typical product

Aspect	Percentage of total manufacturing costs
Direct labour	7
Direct materials	81
Operations overhead[1]	12
Total	100

Note 1 'Other' overhead is included at a later stage in the costing procedure.

the top segment of each of the grades shown in Exhibit 1. Hence, each of the grade 1 carpets is at the top of the grade 1 range, and so on. Details for sales up to the current year are given in Exhibit 3, together with forecasts for the end of next year, which have been based upon the upturn in actual sales in the second half of the current year and known orders in the first two months of next year.

Raw materials

Each carpet is offered in a range of colours and is made from either a spun polypropylene, nylon or spun woollen base. The colours offered and raw materials used are given in Exhibit 4. Both polypropylene and nylon are man-made, while wool is a natural fibre. Consequently, there is a relatively high incidence of faults in the spun woollen yarn deliveries. Without raw material inventory in the appropriate colour, faults in a yarn delivery would typically result in missing a customer's delivery promise. This problem is invariably so on contract carpets where the yarn colour(s) involved will be customer-specified. If faults go undetected and the yarn enters the process, the additional costs associated with substandard carpet and the further impact upon delivery delay can be considerable.

Raw material inventory is valued at about £600,000, with work-in-progress standing at a further £300,000.

This case study was written by Terry Hill (University of Oxford) and KHA Negal. It is intended as the basis for class discussion and not as an example of good or bad management. © AMD Publishing.

Exhibit 3 Past and forecast sales of tufted carpets

Grade	Carpet	Actual sales[1]			Next year's forecast[1]
		Current year −2	Current year −1	Current year	
1	Marble	1423	1321	1457	1400
	Grenoble	76	35	30	20
	Firenza	38	6	4	4
	Barcarole	24	4	2	4
	Casino	59	35	36	55
	Total	1620	1401	1529	1483
2	Maltese	42	46	45	50
	Gazelle	213	225	166	150
	Barbary	54	52	64	180
	Baroque	202	268	286	250
	Total	511	591	561	630
3	Dalmatian[2]	–	28	57	100
	Royalty	106	84	108	130
	Centurion	184	134	168	230
	Lotus[2]	–	–	16	100
	Contract	7	11	28	160
	Total	297	257	377	720
Total		2428	2249	2467	2833

Notes 1 All figures are in square metres (000).
       2 Dalmatian was introduced in current year −1 and Lotus will be introduced at the end of the current year.

Exhibit 4 Raw materials and colour range offered

Grade	Carpet	# colours	Raw material		
			Spun polypropylene	Nylon	Spun woollen
1	Marble	26	3		
	Grenoble	8	3		
	Firenza	(see note)		3	
	Barcarole	(see note)		3	
	Casino	(see note)		3	
2	Maltese	(see note)		3	
	Gazelle	15	3		
	Barbary	7			3
	Baroque	12	3		
3	Dalmatian	10	3		
	Royalty	(see note)		3	
	Centurion	20			3
	Lotus	(see note)		3	
	Contract	Unlimited	3	3	3
Material delivery lead times (weeks)			2	6	6

Note These are dyed on site in a day to meet a range of colours.

Production process

The process lead time (the time it takes a carpet to pass through all the production stages) is between two and five days. Each carpet goes through some of the common processes which are shown in Exhibit 5. Carpets can be delayed between one process and the next without affecting the quality of the carpet. All carpets are tufted (that is, the primary backing cloth for the carpet is fed underneath a needle carrying the yarn. At predetermined intervals, the needle passes through the backing cloth and a looper on the underside retains a loop of yarn beneath the cloth). After several other processes, the carpet has its secondary back, either jute cloth or latex foam, put on by the backing plant.

Exhibit 5 Production processes by carpet quality

Grade	Carpets	Production process							
		Tuft	Yarn dye and dry[1]	Repair[2]	Print[3]	Steam	Shear	Steam[4]	Back
1	Marble	✓					✓		✓
	Grenoble	✓					✓		✓
	Firenza	✓	✓		✓		✓		✓
	Barcarole	✓	✓		✓		✓		✓
	Casino	✓	✓		✓		✓		✓
2	Maltese	✓	✓				✓		✓
	Gazelle	✓					✓		✓
	Barbary	✓					✓		✓
	Baroque	✓					✓		✓
3	Dalmatian	✓		✓			✓		✓
	Royalty	✓	✓				✓		✓
	Centurion	✓		✓		✓	✓	✓	✓
	Lotus	✓	✓				✓		✓
	Contract[5]								

Notes 1 For nylon-based carpets only.
2 All carpets are inspected after tufting. If a repair is necessary, it is completed on the tufting machine except for Dalmatian and Centurion where any repairs are completed on a separate frame.
3 This printing process is to apply dye-resistant chemicals to these carpets.
4 Only the top-quality grade 3 carpets go through the steaming process before and after shearing.
5 Contract carpets go through different processes depending upon the raw material. Polypropylene is as for Gazelle, nylon as for Royalty and woollen as for Centurion.

Exhibit 6 Tufting machine average output

Tufting machine	Carpet type	Average weekly output (square metres)	Tufting machine	Carpet type	Average weekly output (square metres)
1	Dalmatian	5,500	6	Marble	15,000
	Contracts	3,000		Grenoble	20,000
2	Casino	10,000		Maltese	10,000
	Barcarole	10,000	7	Marble	15,000
	Firenza	10,000		Grenoble	20,000
3	Royalty	7,000		Maltese	10,000
4	Centurion	4,000	8	Gazelle	12,000
	Lotus	4,000	9	Grenoble	20,000
5	Baroque	10,000		Barbary	10,000
	Contracts	8,000			

Notes 1 Centurion outputs on machine 4 can vary between 3000 and 5000.
2 Contracts on machine 5 can vary between 6000 and 10,000.
3 Dalmatian on machine 1 can vary between 4000 and 7000.
4 Woollen contracts are completed only on machine 1 and both polypropylene and nylon on machine 5.
5 Not all tufting machines are run throughout a week. The output figures above express the potential, not actual, levels of output, as machines are run in line with sales demand.
6 The output figures above show alternative figures depending upon the carpet type. Hence machine 1 can produce either 5500 m²/week of Dalmatian or 3000 m²/week of contract carpet.
7 Carpet types can only be made on the machines shown above. In a very few instances it may be possible to make a carpet on another machine, but it would result in lower throughput figures and a significant increase in faults.

Spun woollen yarn deliveries

On deliveries of spun woollen yarn, the number of faults experienced on a delivery reduces the tufting process, because of delays involved, to about two-thirds of its standard output. It is estimated that for every square metre of yarn tufted there will be, on average, one yarn break due to faulty yarn.

In addition, because of the different yarns and the different carpet qualities involved, not all tufting machines can be used to make all carpets. Exhibit 6 shows the range of tufting machines, the average weekly potential output and the carpet types for which the machines can be used.

Dyeing and drying are processes only used on nylon yarn which is purchased as a natural shade. After tufting, nylon-based carpets are then dyed and dried, a process called 'piece dying'. The dye house currently works a 40-hour week and can produce in a single eight-hour shift sufficient dyed yarn to make 10,000 square metres of carpet.

The shearer crops the tip of each tuft as a cylinder lawn mower trims grass. The length of yarn removed by the cut can be adjusted on the machine. The pre- and post-steaming processes take place before and after the shearer. They are, however, only used for Centurion and its purpose is to ensure that the tuft is presented in a way to yield the best quality results. The shearing machine is currently utilized for about 65 per cent of its time.

The backing plant is currently running with two 12-hour shifts on a 24-hour basis over five days, with weekend overtime where necessary. The skills required for this job are difficult to find and consequently three eight-hour shifts are not feasible. Also, an agreement with the local trade union restricts the total hours which can be worked over a 12-month period. Average actual output from this process is some 45,000 square metres per week. This figure takes into account average maintenance, breakdowns and changeover times. The number of working weeks available in a year is 46 when account has been taken of annual shutdowns and public holidays.

Staff

Of the 220 direct staff employed at BC, 70–80 work on the production processes described in the case. In total, there are about 350 employees on this site. Exhibit 7 gives the breakdown of gross pay for a direct worker. Bonus payments are made in direct proportion to output and do not relate to hours worked. The payments made vary depending upon the weekly output and are shown in Exhibit 8. In the current pay discussions, the trade unions are requesting, among other things, a higher incentive payment for output. They argue that the current actual bonus earnings are reducing and that a productivity-linked payment increase through the incentive scheme would make sense all round.

Exhibit 7 **Composition of gross pay for a typical direct worker**

Payment	Percentage of total gross pay
Basic	75
Overtime	10
Bonus	15
Total	100

The future

BC's marketing strategy is to continue to produce the present range of carpets and also to start to increase sales in the contracts market. Currently, 50 per cent of all contract carpets are made of spun woollen yarn and it is expected that this composition of sales will remain the pattern for the future. If it does change, it is anticipated that it will show an increase in spun woollen yarns of up to 10 per cent.

Contracts is a very price-competitive market, but one where very large repeat orders may be earned by a successful supplier. BC sees this segment of the market as providing an important area of sales growth. BC's all-round success, however, has been built on its growing reputation as a manufacturer of

Exhibit 8 **Standard production hours for different carpets and bonus payments**

Grade	Carpet	Standard hours to produce 100 square metres
1	Marble	4.1
	Grenoble	3.0
	Firenza	5.1
	Barcarole	5.1
	Casino	5.1
2	Maltese	5.4
	Gazelle	4.5
	Barbary	6.8
	Baroque	4.9
3	Dalmatian	6.8
	Royalty	5.9
	Centurion	8.5
	Lotus	4.8
	Contract	Varies depending upon the yarn

Bonus payments

Weekly output (square metres)	Bonus payment per thousand square metres (£)
Up to 30,000	1.50
31,000–40,000	1.80
41,000–50,000	2.20
51,000 and over	2.50

quality carpets. It recognizes quite clearly that this is the basis for its current and future strategy in the marketplace.

Questions

1 Based on the forecast sales for next year, what advice would you offer Berwick Carpets about its tufted carpet manufacturing process capacity?

2 Review the present bonus system and comment upon the suggestions made in the case study about the present level of payments and the future proposed changes.

3 Briefly outline the important factors involved and the key tasks to be addressed by an operations scheduling system for the tufted carpet division.

British Airways

As the world changes so the service requirements of customers change. For British Airways (BA) the need to match and anticipate such changes has increased in recent years as the general overcapacity within the passenger airline industry has led to growing competition on many of its prime routes. Foremost of these are transatlantic flights that carry corporate and business executives to and from Europe and North America. By the late 1990s BA found itself losing first and business class passengers to rival airlines that were transferring capacity from Asia to transatlantic routes while reducing fares to increase sales and grow market share.

With the hangover effects of BA's problems in the late 1990s (such as the three-day cabin crew strike in 1997 and the problems associated with its decision to subcontract its in-flight catering facilities and provision) still around, profits had fallen sharply and BA's share price halved.

Meeting competition head-on is not new to BA. Its rise from being an airline not well regarded by most and making losses more times than it was in profit to becoming one of the most profitable airlines in the world was acknowledged as an example of sound business management. Central to this metamorphosis was orienting its staff and systems to customers and their needs partly built on the Putting People First initiative launched in the mid-1980s.

To keep ahead British Airways continued to consult passengers to help identify improvements to the service it offered. In the mid-1990s it unveiled a new and very different approach to in-flight service. Cabins were redesigned, and the passenger service offering was redesigned as well. Whereas previously the emphasis had been on an efficient but slightly homogeneous service, the pendulum had swung back the other way; now the emphasis was on customized, personalized service that attempted to cater to each passenger's individual needs.

At the heart of the changes was the concept of customer focus. In Club World (BA's business class), the change process began with a customer consultation exercise. The results were good – but not great. The service was perceived as being acceptable, and indeed comfortable within the limits of the space provided, but it was also seen as predictable. Rather than seeing this result as confirmation that the existing service offering was working, BA chose to see it as a sign that change was needed.

The first task was to redesign the environment, as far as possible, for greater passenger comfort (although, of course, without compromising safety). Exhibit 1 gives examples of some of the features introduced. From this it can be seen that the major focus was on seating arrangements. On the principle 'if you don't do it on the ground, why do it in the air?', designers sought for a seat design that would give the maximum possible comfort. The result was a cradle seat designed to give full-body support. Features of the new seat included lumbar supports that adjusted individually to fit passengers' preferences; a much wider footplate; a cushion that provided support behind the knees; an adjustable leg rest extension that again could be suited to the height of a passenger; and an adjustable headrest that included wings to support the head while passengers slept. Overall, the new design increased the pitch (the distance between one seat and that of the seat in front) from 40 to 50 inches while improving the level of recline to 140°.

Along with the physical design, there was a change in the manner and mode of service delivery. BA consulted cabin crews as well as passengers and found that both wanted a more personalized service. Cabin crew also found the previous service predictable and wanted to be able to offer a more 'spontaneous' service to passengers. Putting the wishes of both crew and passengers into effect, BA's Club World

This case study was written by Terry Hill (University of Oxford) and Alex Hill (University of Kingston). It is intended as the basis for class discussion and not as an example of good or bad management. © AMD Publishing.

Exhibit 1 **Examples of some of the features introduced within Club World (business class)**

Features	Detail
The seat	The first business class seat to fold into a six-foot completely flat bed, while a unique footstool makes the most of the generous legroom and allows customers to really stretch their legs out and relax. The ergonomically designed seat is fully electronic with integrated lumbar support and can adopt any recline position between fully upright and completely flat.
Lounge in the sky	There is a 'lounge in the sky' cabin environment and interior. Seats have been rearranged facing each other, with blinds that can be drawn to help maximize personal space and privacy. Fewer seats means 30 per cent more personal space.
Greater in-flight entertainment	A choice of up to 18 channels of films and 12 channels of CD-quality audio.
Dining	Features new classic white china, coloured glasswear and simpler, better quality food. Meanwhile, passengers flying out of major US east coast airports can eat from a hot or cold buffet prior to flying to maximize on-board sleep time. A 'raid the larder' service is also available, offering 'help yourself' treats and snacks.
Business amenities	In-seat laptop power points and telephones give customers the opportunity to work and stay in touch during their flight.
Two-piece hand baggage allowance	To suit the needs of business travellers, the hand baggage allowance has been doubled to two pieces, up to 18kg total, with more space in newly designed overhead and side bins. Wardrobe space has also been doubled.
Departure lounges	The unique 'terraces' concept is steadily being introduced at more departure lounges worldwide. The inspiration for terraces came from a recognition that customers want to use an airline lounge in different ways, at different times. They have discrete 'zones' including a Combiz Centre (communications business centre), World Wine Bar, Library; Larder, Cappuccino and Juice Bar, Sanctuary and Terrace.
Arrivals lounges	Arrivals lounges are available at London Heathrow, London Gatwick and Johannesburg to help customers refresh themselves after a long flight. Here they can take a shower, have their change of clothes pressed, get a bite to eat, make any urgent calls or simply relax before starting the day.

now concentrates on letting passengers, in effect, design their own service. For example, on overnight transatlantic flights, in order to allow customers to rest and get as much sleep as possible, passengers are offered both blankets and sheets to make them feel more as if they were tucked up in bed. While in the morning, unlike the old system where passengers were awakened and served breakfast at a standard time before landing, passengers wake in their own time. As and when they wake, cabin crew offer each a mug of coffee and a choice of croissants or other breakfast foods. Passengers can now wake up more or less in the fashion they are used to at home.

Breakfast was not the only meal to undergo change. Lunch and dinner have always been flexible, with passengers able to opt for just one or two of the three courses, but now another dimension has been added; passengers who feel hungry between meals can quite literally 'raid the larder'. Chocolate, fruit, biscuits and cheese are available on short flights, while on longer flights, pies, sandwiches and other snacks are ready for passengers who wish to

help themselves. Again, the aim is to create a comfortable atmosphere reminiscent of a passenger's own home. Being able to help themselves rather than waiting for meal times or asking for service improves the passenger's sense of being in control.

The changes in Club World in the mid-1990s were mirrored by design and service changes in first class. Here the designers sought ways to make better use of existing space. On 747s, for example, the number of first-class seats was reduced from 18 to 14. The regimented rows of seats were broken up to give greater privacy. Those on the edges of the cabin now sit alone, while those in the centre can sit side by side with a travelling companion, or be screened for greater privacy.

Not content with repositioning the seats, the designers went further. Each seat, which resembles a deep bucket chair, has a small 'visitor's seat' attached to the foot. In an atmosphere specifically designed to resemble a small sitting room, passengers can sit together and have a drink, chat or discuss business for as long as they like, then go back to their original seats. The 'visitor's seat' then converts into an extension to the main seat, and the whole ensemble can be converted easily into a horizontal bed, allowing passengers on overnight flights the chance of a real night's sleep.

The same flexibility is extended to food service in first class. Set meal times were abolished; an extensive menu is provided and passengers order and eat when they wish, after the fashion of a restaurant.

But in markets with overcapacity (as is the case with passenger airlines), the need to stay competitive and continue to anticipate or meet the needs of customers is ongoing. As a result BA is continuously trying to keep one step ahead of its rivals. To this end, BA made a whole series of changes starting in 1999 to reinforce its position and differentiate itself from its rivals on dimensions other than price.

BA's promise to its customers at this time recognized 'that simply getting through the airport and onto the plane is not always a hassle-free experience'. To this end BA declared its intent to make a customer's journey 'as smooth as possible, from check-in to aircraft seat and beyond'.

Underpinning these changes was BA's Putting People First Again programme, intended to link back to and build on developments in the mid-1980s. Launched in 1999, all BA's 62,000 staff underwent an intensive customer service course that involved staff from different parts of the company evaluating each other's attention to passengers.

In addition, BA also introduced more executive lounges (over 200 worldwide as shown in Exhibit 2) modelled on a Mediterranean style (called terraces), incorporating coffee, fruit juice and wine bars, together with a Combiz centre providing telephone, fax and plug-in laptop capability.

Other facilities were also made available. Showers are on hand for long-haul passengers to freshen up. On the return journey to London from the east coast of the USA, customers can now eat dinner (for first-class passengers this includes a waiter silver service provision) before they fly from Washington, JFK, Newark, Philadelphia, Detroit and Boston airports. Cutting out breakfast is also an option, thereby making even more time to sleep. Instead of eating before you land, breakfast (as well as a shower and clothes pressing service) is available in BA's arrivals lounges, which are open from 4 am to 7 pm, with a full English breakfast available until 12 noon.

But development did not stop there. In March 2000 BA introduced beds in business class – a quantum leap in comfort for the business traveller. With a click of a button the seat turns into a flat 1.83m bed. These are currently available on flights to and from London and New York (JFK and Newark), Hong Kong, San Francisco, Washington, Chicago, Johannesburg, Singapore (operating on to Melbourne and Sydney respectively), Los Angeles, Toronto, Capetown, Philadelphia, Madras, Islamabad, Sao Paulo (on to Rio de Janeiro), Bangkok, Peking, Mexico, Calcutta, Boston, Dhaka, Seattle, Miami, Montreal, Vancouver, Mumbai, Dubai, Cairo, Delhi, Lagos, Houston, Kuwait, Nairobi, Mauritius, Abuja, Abu Dhabi (on to Muscat), Riyadh and Bahrain (on to Doha). Finally, on arrival in London, fast-track immigration is provided for non-EU citizens so cutting out particularly long queues.

All these developments are an integral part of BA's overall strategy to concentrate on premium, high-yielding travellers and focus on point-to-point traffic rather than uneconomic routes that transfer passengers onto more lucrative long-haul flights.

Exhibit 2 **British Airways lounges by type and region**

Region	# lounges available by type		
	Departures		Arrivals
	First	Terraces	
UK and Ireland	2	30	2
US and Canada	15	40	–
Europe	–	57	–
Africa	–	10	1
Middle East	1	13	–
South Asia	2	6	–
Asia Pacific	2	8	–
Australasia	–	5	–
South America and Caribbean	2	11	–

Underpinning this plan has been BA's shift in its long-haul fleet to smaller aircraft. It has been replacing 747s with smaller 777s and shedding a few rows of backpackers (economy tickets sold to cut-price travellers) pushes up yields.

This strategy plays to BA's strengths. It already has a brand with which business executives identify. And, London Heathrow and London Gatwick are BA's backyard, with a 43 per cent share of available capacity between Heathrow, its main hub, and the USA. While some passengers may not care which airport they go through to and from the USA, most executives have some business in London. Flying directly to Heathrow and Gatwick with fast and frequent rail services to central London (four times an hour to and from Heathrow, dedicated rail track avoiding delays and a journey time of a little over 10 minutes) reduces total travel time before and after the flight.

As BA recognizes, its customers' time is a 'precious commodity'. Its aim is to demonstrate its intent to offer 'the highest service specification as well as helping to streamline the travel process of its customers'.

www.ba.com

Questions

1 How does BA compete in this particular market?

2 How well does the delivery system fit these market needs?

Caltrex Engineering (A)

Bob Murray, CEO of Caltrex Engineering, explained the reasons for the review:

> Sales, profit and cash targets are a high priority in terms of our corporate performance measures. Recent efforts, particularly with our existing large customers, and the contract with a new large customer in Germany have resulted in a sales growth which keeps us well on target for this year. The improvements in operations have lowered costs and the shedding of some low price work and the growth of higher margin sales will, in turn, ensure that our profit forecasts will be met. The third leg of these key measures is cash, and one critical facet of this concerns our inventory levels. Hence this review. As a first step we have undertaken a number of analyses to gain some insights into why the inventory levels are high and to help us consider the actions to take to reduce them.

Background

Caltrex Engineering manufactures seals for a wide range of applications in the aerospace, automotive and general industrial sectors. It is part of Lambrin Industries, a US-based group of companies which comprises a wide range of businesses including electronics, electrical engineering and mechanical equipment. Based in New Jersey, Lambrin currently has sales revenues of $16.5 billion.

Markets

Caltrex manufactures and sells a range of products customized to meet the specific needs of a wide range of customers. Mike Daley, vice-president of marketing, explained:

> As you would guess, the seals are specific to one application and the materials and shapes involved are typically specified by the customer concerned. Our business, however, is very much at the engineered end of the seals market involving expensive materials, high specification designs and with quality conformance an essential requirement. Orders for these customized products vary from sector to sector and within a sector. The principal sales patterns, however, are contracts with scheduled call-offs, orders placed on a regular basis (although the frequency will vary markedly) and those that allow little predictability. The latter include orders for most spares.

Mike went on to explain that this was a make-to-order business, in that products were only made in response to orders and scheduled call-offs. The main customer sectors were aerospace, automotive and industrial. Over the last year, operations had been split into two areas to reflect the differences in these markets. However, to provide some association with the past, areas retained the names aerospace and automotive whereas, in fact, sales in the aerospace unit comprised orders from automotive customers and vice versa.

Manufacturing

Process

All products go through the same set of processes. As Exhibit 1 shows, the materials from which seals are moulded are either further processed in the rubber mill or, in the case of the material used in injection moulding, are delivered directly from an outside supplier. At the blank preparation stage, the material is formed into smaller, pre-cut sizes, known as blanks. These vary in size depending upon the dimensions of the final seal. One blank is prepared for each seal irrespective of its size. Once prepared, blanks go straight to the moulding areas or are held in the blank stores awaiting call-off by a moulding area.

The seal is often moulded around a metal component to form the final product. In these instances, the metal components are made by outside suppliers to the exact specification of customers' drawings and despatched to Caltrex in line with agreed schedules.

This case study was written by Terry Hill (University of Oxford) and Alex Hill (University of Kingston). It is intended as the basis for class discussion and not as an example of good or bad management. © AMD Publishing.

Exhibit 1 **Operations process**

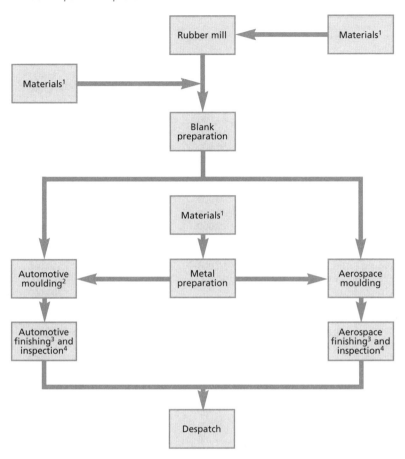

Notes 1 Materials indicate an outside supply.
       2 Automotive moulding includes general industrial sectors.
       3 Finishing can be either internal or external.
       4 All inspection is completed internally.

Following moulding, the seals are finished, which typically involves separating out the formed product from the rest of the blank. Whereas finishing for all aerospace parts is completed internally, automotive seals are finished by outworkers (trained staff who work at home, with products being delivered to and collected from them on a regular, often daily, basis). All finished parts are inspected internally and packed at this stage. Completed seals go to despatch to meet customer orders, or into finished goods inventory awaiting customer call-offs.

Planning and control

Production is planned one month ahead to meet customer orders scheduled for the following month (see Exhibit 2). To balance the trade-offs between the length of changeover times and the size of the

production runs (in terms of time taken), manufacturing order quantities (MOQs) are calculated and these become the length of a production run unless the actual customer requirement is greater (see Exhibit 2). As Sam Isaacs (vice-president of operations) explained:

> There are times, however, when production is scheduled for call-offs two months ahead. This is where it suits manufacturing to make in one period to meet sales in the next. Most of the time, though, we make in line with the following month's demand.

Inventory

Sam Isaacs continued:

> Performance targets are an important part of the way we are judged as a company, as well as individ-

Exhibit 2 Work-in-progress inventory, planned production, MOQ and other data for parts within the moulding, finishing and inspection areas for a representative sample of products

Part #	Position within the operations process		Moulding				Customer schedule (# units)		Last 12 months' sales (# units)
			cost per part (£s)	# units			planned call-offs		
	last	next		inventory at 31 May	planned production in June	MOQ	June	July	
00042	AU14	EF	0.09	258,300	250,000	50,000	250,000	250,000	1,750,000
05891	EF	AUIN	0.71	40,760	–	10,000	20,000	20,000	200,000
14567	AU4	IF	0.52	52,100	–	50,000	20,000	–	300,000
37148	AU6	IF	1.24	2,110	2,000	2,000	2,000	2,000	14,000
37215	EF	AUIN	0.10	100,160	100,000	50,000	100,000	100,000	850,000
38215	AU11	EF	0.13	199,550	200,000	50,000	200,000	200,000	2,000,000
40101	EF	AUIN	0.24	306,150	200,000	100,000	250,000	250,000	2,450,000
42156	EF	AUIN	0.37	81,670	60,000	20,000	40,000	100,000	650,000
42157	AU4	EF	0.24	39,240	40,000	10,000	40,000	40,000	500,000
44752	EF	AUIN	0.11	150,060	150,000	150,000	150,000	150,000	1,000,000
45210	AU8	IF	0.59	74,810	–	25,000	30,000	30,000	450,000
45273	AU12	IF	0.08	106,360	–	50,000	75,000	–	1,500,000
47213	IF	AUIN	0.72	21,090	–	20,000	6,000	6,000	120,000
47215	IF	AUIN	0.76	15,750	15,000	5,000	15,000	15,000	200,000
48001	AU14	IF	1.17	8,430	–	8,000	5,000	–	15,000
48153	IF	AUIN	1.02	15,620	5,000	5,000	10,000	10,000	60,000
52708	EF	AUIN	0.77	78,850	–	40,000	50,000	–	880,000
81400	AE5	IF	3.19	215	–	200	120	–	360
84206	IF	AEIN	2.21	645	–	600	600	–	1,800
84543	IF	AEIN	3.01	63	–	60	50	–	200
87210	AE4	IF	2.98	78	70	70	70	70	700
87214	IF	AEIN	1.98	670	–	600	400	–	4,000
87412	IF	AEIN	2.87	196	200	200	200	–	600
92143	MP	AU2	1.02	15,810	15,000	5,000	10,000	20,000	75,000
94153	MP	AE5	3.78	55	–	60	10	–	20
95123	MP	AU9	0.84	41,420	40,000	20,000	40,000	40,000	240,000
97214	MP	AU2	1.02	50,280	50,000	10,000	50,000	50,000	750,000
97841	MP	AE6	2.75	836	–	250	250	250	750

Key   MOQ = manufacturing order quantity.
       AU14 = automotive moulding machine 14, and so on.
       AE5 = aerospace moulding machine 5, and so on.
       EF = external finishing. All inventory where the next
            process is identified as EF has already been or is
            waiting to be despatched to an outworker.

IF   = internal finishing.
AUIN = automotive inspection.
AEIN = aerospace inspection.
MP   = metal preparation.

Exhibit 3 Review of inventory analysis

Exhibits 2 and 4 provide details of the work-in-progress inventory review completed in early June. A representative sample of part numbers was agreed for the inventory held in the following areas:

● Moulding, finishing and inspection areas   – Exhibit 2
● Blank preparation and blank stores   – Exhibit 4

As explained in the case narrative, Caltrex Engineering uses batch manufacturing processes. Each part has been separated into a number of operations (the preparation of the material, blank preparation, moulding and so on) through which each part is progressed in line with a route sheet. Although

customized, these are standard products in that they have been made before and are, therefore, a known product in which investment has been made (for example route sheets and moulds). Also, the blanks are made for one part and then the equipment is reset for the next part and so on. This format is similarly used in moulding, finishing and inspection.

Causal analysis

To undertake a causal analysis of the data given in Exhibits 2 and 4, you need to refer to the relevant sections in the accompanying text in Chapter 12.

uals. One area where we know we need to improve is working capital. For this reason, we have been reviewing and analysing our inventory holdings particularly in terms of work-in-progress and finished goods. The analyses given here have been confined to the automotive and aerospace markets, but similar analysis is now under way for industrial products. At the moment inventory levels are too high, especially given that we are a make-to-order business. As inventory is principally regarded as the responsibility of the operations function it is our task to identify and implement ways of reducing it. Exhibits 2 to 4 provide our initial review of work-in-progress inventory. The question is, however, what do we do from here?

Questions

1 Complete a causal analysis of the inventory data in Exhibits 2 and 4.

2 What does your analysis reveal?

Exhibit 4 **Inventory and other data for a representative sample of parts in the blank preparation area and blank stores**

Part #	Position within production process		cost per batch (£s)	Blank preparation			Moulding (# units)		
				# units			production planned in		last 12 months' sales
	present	next		inventory level at 31 May	planned production in June	MOQ	June	July	
70017	BS	AE8	0.81	155	–	600	–	–	450
71412	BS	AU7	0.65	15,720	–	15,000	15,000	–	60,000
72086	BS	AE8	0.92	275	–	1,500	–	–	3,400
72141	BS	AE22	1.24	110	–	100	40	–	80
72891	BS	AE12	1.42	1,065	1,500	500	1,000	1,500	10,000
73248	BS	AU9	0.72	8,140	–	4,000	8,000	–	16,000
74152	BS	AU4	0.89	4,020	–	2,000	4,000	–	8,000
74260	BS	AE6	0.76	915	–	800	700	–	700
75143	BS	AE4	1.08	430	–	500	100	–	200
75147	BS	AE8	0.81	75	–	500	–	–	425
76123	BS	AU1	0.54	10,090	10,000	10,000	8,000	8,000	130,000
77521	BS	AU5	0.82	8,110	20,000	20,000	–	12,000	50,000

Key   BS   = blank stores. Having been formed, parts go into blank stores awaiting allocation to the next process or go directly into the relevant moulding area. Typically, high volume part numbers fall into the latter category.
AE8 = aerospace moulding machine 8, and so on.
AU7 = automotive moulding machine 7, and so on.
MOQ = manufacturing order quantity.

Caltrex Engineering (B)

Exhibit 1 Finished goods inventory, planned production, MOQ and other data for a representative sample of parts

		Moulding				Customer schedule			
Part #	cost per part (£s)	inventory level at 31 May	production planned in		MOQ	planned call-offs		last 12 months' sales	agreed inventory level
			June	July		June	July		
					# units				
03521	4.66	596	–	–	260	–	–	25,650	–
06702	2.75	584	3,000	3,000	1,000	2,500	2,300	26,425	–
07444	6.20	120	–	–	120	80	–	160	–
07615	3.08	1,535	–	–	1,200	600	600	7,200	–
07616	4.56	1,207	–	–	140	200	200	5,500	–
07618	2.96	1,100	–	–	2,000	–	50	650	–
07778	3.14	5,085	4,000	4,000	2,000	4,000	3,500	40,000	5,000
08445	2.81	210	200	100	100	250	250	7,500	–
10094	4.73	5,901	–	–	2,500	–	–	8,700	–
11136	2.32	8,895	–	–	2,750	2,200	1,850	18,400	–
12136	2.12	5,063	–	–	–	2,600	1,550	12,150	–
12727	3.13	8,037	1,500	–	1,500	3,250	2,675	24,010	–
14460	4.75	180	300	300	300	346	346	7,460	–
19782	4.14	4,400	2,500	2,500	2,500	–	4,650	20,000	4,000
24711	5.12	153	–	–	200	–	–	2,650	–
24713	3.96	750	–	1,500	1,500	–	1,000	5,150	–
25303	2.68	425	–	–	–	–	–	480	–
28420	5.05	160	–	–	300	–	–	240	–
28423	3.24	7,308	1,750	–	1,000	4,500	2,600	29,400	–
28743	3.06	341	380	–	–	200	200	1,120	–
34226	2.47	27,500	30,000	20,000	10,000	24,000	22,500	328,500	25,000
37891	2.32	1,152	–	–	–	420	370	2,990	–
43071	3.86	4,567	5,250	3,500	1,750	4,270	4,350	49,500	4,000
48522	3.33	332	–	–	430	120	180	1,560	–
53062	3.10	2,000	1,000	1,000	1,000	2,000	2,000	44,500	–
56669	3.14	2,150	2,000	2,000	2,000	–	6,000	28,400	–
57375	2.56	39,910	48,000	48,000	6,000	46,500	47,000	290,900	45,000
57376	3.08	4,146	–	1,100	550	–	3,000	20,070	–
57554	3.54	31	–	–	150	–	–	40	–
59528	2.36	63,914	–	–	20,000	22,000	22,000	226,400	–
60123	4.52	28	60	60	60	40	60	480	–
64265	2.42	11,471	9,000	12,000	3,000	10,000	10,000	65,500	10,000
66446	4.86	1,519	1,650	1,650	550	1,500	1,500	9,650	1,500
69123	4.15	3,816	3,600	2,400	1,200	3,800	2,800	37,550	3,000
71685	2.96	12	420	–	–	70	70	450	–
72142	4.01	967	–	–	550	–	–	4,070	–
73712	3.51	2,598	–	–	1,500	1,000	1,000	15,000	–
82595	4.05	6,521	6,000	6,750	750	6,500	6,500	72,000	6,000
87431	4.56	284	160	–	160	135	140	1,780	–
96537	3.75	750	1,050	1,050	1,050	1,100	1,350	8,560	–

This case study was written by Terry Hill (University of Oxford) and Alex Hill (University of Kingston). It is intended as the basis for class discussion and not as an example of good or bad management. © AMD Publishing.

Exhibit 2 Comments on finished goods inventory

Part #	Comments
03521	Customer has cancelled call-offs in the last 3 months.
06702	Overproduction due to inaccurate scrap rate.
07444	To meet customer's future orders.
07615	To meet customer's future orders.
07616	Customer has reduced scheduled call-offs in the last month.
07618	Overplanned as a result of manufacturing order quantity.
07778	Customer agreement to hold a minimum of the equivalent of 1 month of sales in stock at all times, together with reduced call-offs in the last 3 months.
08445	Overproduction due to inaccurate scrap rate.
10094	Customer has cancelled call-offs in the last 3 months.
11136	To meet customer's future orders.
12136	Supplier's minimum order quantity.
12727	To meet customer's future orders.
14460	Overplanned as a result of manufacturing order quantity.
19782	Customer agreement to hold a minimum of the equivalent of 1 month of sales in stock at all times, together with reduced call-offs in the last 3 months.
24711	Overproduction due to inaccurate scrap rate.
24713	Overplanned as a result of manufacturing order quantity.
25303	Supplier's minimum order quantity.
28420	Overplanned as a result of manufacturing order quantity.
28423	To meet customer's future orders.
28743	Supplier's minimum order quantity.
34226	Customer agreement to hold a minimum of the equivalent of 1 month of sales in stock at all times, together with minimum batch sizes.

Part #	Comments
37891	Supplier's minimum order quantity.
43071	Customer agreement to hold a minimum of the equivalent of 1 month of sales in stock at all times, together with minimum batch sizes.
48522	Overproduction due to inaccurate scrap rate.
53062	To meet customer's future orders.
56669	To meet customer's future orders.
57375	Customer agreement to hold a minimum of the equivalent of 1 month of sales in stock at all times, together with minimum batch sizes.
57376	To meet customer's future orders.
57554	Overproduction due to inaccurate scrap rate.
59528	To meet customer's future orders.
60123	Overproduction due to inaccurate scrap rate.
64265	Customer agreement to hold a minimum of the equivalent of 2 months of sales in stock at all times, together with minimum batch sizes.
66446	Customer agreement to hold a minimum of the equivalent of 2 months of sales in stock at all times, plus a quantity of inventory to cover for inaccurate scrap rates.
69123	Customer agreement to hold a minimum of the equivalent of 1 month of sales in stock at all times.
71685	Supplier's minimum order quantity.
72142	Customer has cancelled call-offs in the last 3 months.
73712	Customer has reduced scheduled call-offs in the last 6 months.
82595	Customer agreement to hold a minimum of the equivalent of 1 month of sales in stock at all times, together with minimum batch sizes.
87431	To meet customer's future orders.
96537	Overplanned as a result of manufacturing order quantity.

Sam Isaacs, vice-president operations at Caltrex (see Case study 4, Caltrex Engineering (A)) explained:

> As in the previous case, we have completed an analysis of the finished goods inventory for the aerospace and automotive parts of our business. Data is now being collected for industrial products.

The data Sam refers to is given in Exhibits 1 and 2, with the latter providing information on the data in Exhibit 1.

'Again', reflected Sam 'the question is where do we go from here?'

Questions

1 Complete a causal analysis of the inventory data in Exhibit 1.

2 What does your analysis reveal?

Fabritex

The room bore all the hallmarks of a long meeting. The Fabritex management team relaxed in their chairs. Empty coffee cups patterned the boardroom table. Not for the first time Charles Franklin, the company CEO, reflected on the quality of the business-based discussions and the noticeable financial improvements over the last 18 months.

'Well I think we're agreed. Next year we'll target Pearlwear as one of our major areas for sales growth.' Charles glanced around and got the nods of approval he was anticipating.

'Good. However, before we finish for today, let us review the issues around how we will grow our share of the Pearlwear business.'

Charles looked towards his sales and marketing director. 'Perhaps you can start us off, John.'

Background

Fabritex is part of the Wardman Group which manufactures a range of textiles for a wide variety of fashion and industrial applications, as well as having interests in engineering, furniture and finishings. Because of intense competition from Southeast Asia, particularly on price, the UK textile industry had undergone major reorganization and much of the overcapacity in the sector had now been squeezed out.

Fabritex focuses on knitted fabrics for garment manufacturers, mainly for lingerie. These customers in turn sell either to major retailers or through independent outlets. Some of the garment manufacturers sell under their own brand name but many are making products to retailers' specifications to be sold under a retailer's own name.

Much of the development of new fabrics is done by manufacturers like Fabritex or even prompted by suggestions from raw material suppliers. Fabritex believes its strength lies in developing innovative fabrics that look good and perform well technically. Even when customers like a supplier's new fabric design, this does not guarantee that supplier all its business, particularly over the longer term. It is common for customers to show designs to their other suppliers, with the intention of dual or triple sourcing, a commercial practice accepted within the industry.

The life of a particular fabric can vary widely from a few months to several years. It all depends on the popularity of the material with the final consumer. As part of the fashion industry, the search for a new and different feel or look is a constant task, essential to a company's future growth and prosperity.

After a struggle in the early days to become profitable, Fabritex has increased profits to the point where it is above average for the Group. Sales at £45 million have grown rapidly in the last two years and similar growth levels are forecast over the next few years. The management team believes that the basic operations capability is in place which will underpin the continued sales growth. This view has the support of the Group but funds for investment are limited and Fabritex still has to demonstrate that it can outperform its competition rather than just hold its own.

Marketing

Fabritex regards its market as a number of distinct segments that reflect differences in product, geography and type of customer. Customers are described as 'branded', selling under their own product name, or 'non-branded'. Customers are also grouped by garment type and divided into lingerie and outerwear (see Exhibit 1) and they can appear in several segments. The product distinction relates to the way the fabric is knitted, either warp or weft.

Many segments have a degree of seasonality associated with the type of garment in which the fabric is used. If a garment is well received, repeat orders for fabrics may come

---

This case study was written by Terry Hill (University of Oxford) and R Lily. It is intended as the basis for class discussion and not as an example of good or bad management. © AMD Publishing.

Exhibit 1 Sales forecast by segment

Segment	Current year forecast (£m)		Next year forecast (£m)	
		Sub-total		Sub-total
UK lingerie warp knit				
Branded	12.3	15.9	15.9	19.5
Non-branded	3.6		3.6	
UK lingerie weft knit				
Branded	15.3	16.2	15.6	16.5
Non-branded	0.9		0.9	
Export lingerie warp knit				
Branded	5.4	5.4	6.3	6.3
Non-branded	0.0		0.0	
Export lingerie weft knit				
Branded	0.9	2.1	1.2	2.4
Non-branded	1.2		1.2	
UK outerwear				
Branded	0.9	4.2	0.9	4.2
Non-branded	3.3		3.3	
Export outerwear				
Branded	0.6	2.1	1.2	2.7
Non-branded	1.5		1.5	
Total		45.9		51.6

very quickly. Consequently, forward demand is not easy to predict, particularly for new fabrics.

Responding to Charles Franklin's request, John Watson (the sales and marketing director) pulled himself forward, shuffled through the pile of papers in front of him and began:

The segment in which we have chosen to grow is UK lingerie warp knit which currently generates £15.9 million sales, about 35 per cent of our total sales revenue. Within this segment Pearlwear sales total £4.2 million. As you are aware, Pearlwear is a premium company with an internationally recognized brand name with manufacturing plants in Europe and Southeast Asia. Pearlwear sales and its share of its markets are both growing. Where it places those additional sales and grows capacity is in part, as you would expect, related to the performance of its manufacturing plants. Initially we intend to grow our share with Pearlwear's UK factory, which we estimate to place purchase orders to the value of some £30 million, of which we have only £4.2 million, or 14 per cent. The opportunity to grow is, therefore, realistic.

The Pearlwear brand name is key in selling its products and that has implications for us. We have to remain competitive on price to avoid losing share but the name of the game is conformance quality.

If we have any significant problems with meeting the specification of our fabrics, then Pearlwear will take its business elsewhere.

So far our two companies have worked well together over a number of years and we appear to have a good understanding of its requirements. Also, the management team at Pearlwear's UK plant is committed to developing sound customer–supplier relations. And this is by no means a lip service statement. Pearlwear is keen to discuss problems and has, on a number of occasions, cooperated on changes that have affected the way both companies work. If we are proactive in those developments, we will undoubtedly be able to grow our share next year.

Pearlwear currently splits its business between three or four main suppliers. Some fabrics are allocated to only one company for the life of the fabric and some are ordered from two or more suppliers. Pearlwear seems to be happy with its current suppliers and overall share has not changed much, even though demand from the UK plant has increased significantly over the last five years. We continue, however, to be very much the minority supplier, taking about 14 per cent of Pearlwear's total business.

Where we are the sole supplier for a fabric, Pearlwear is absolutely dependent on us. The annual sales from these 'sole supplier' fabrics are £2.7 million and should grow by about 10 per cent next year. Responding to short lead times on sales orders is important but even more crucial is meeting our promises on delivery. Nothing gets Pearlwear more upset than having to reorganize its production schedules due to missing agreed delivery promises.

John paused for a sip of cold coffee and noticed the wry look from Mike Stewart, the operations director, after his last comment. Mike said:

We do recognize the delivery issue, John, but from an operations point of view the pattern of orders is very unpredictable. Some of these fabrics have regular orders. Demand for other fabrics keeps going over time but we never know when we will see the next order. This affects our response, for example on raw material inventory. And short runs do reduce our capacity due to changeover losses.

John Watson nodded and continued:

When Pearlwear sources a fabric from two or more suppliers, the company that wins the lion's share is usually the one that can supply to the shortest promise date for an initial order. Of course, thereafter a supplier must hit its delivery promises consistently. Failure to deliver on time can affect our share of jointly sourced products. Mike's point about a mix of regular and irregular orders applies to these fabrics as well, although probably to a lesser extent.

Price can also influence the volume split when a fabric is running regularly with joint suppliers. At the moment I estimate Pearlwear's total purchases of fabrics that are shared by two or more suppliers are £5.1 million per annum and we have 30 per cent of this. The spend should grow by 10 per cent next year.

The fabrics that are only sourced from one of our competitors constitute the biggest part of Pearlwear's annual purchases at £22.2 million. Some of these fabrics are reaching the end of their life cycle and I think purchases in this category will decline next year, perhaps to £20.4 million. If we are selective there may be opportunities on the higher volume fabrics to become a second supplier. The attraction to Pearlwear would be to gain more insurance on obtaining short delivery lead times. The usual reason we do not have a share is that we have not provided the design and performance characteristics of particular fabrics for which Pearlwear is looking. On occasions we believe we can but we have not been close enough to Pearlwear's designers to convince them that we have the technical know-how. Designers have their favourite suppliers, for whatever reason, so cultivating that relationship is important. So, the way forward is to carefully target some fabrics and get our technical people working closely with theirs.

Also, we may have to sweeten our move a bit on price to get them through the hassle of approving us. My initial assessment suggests that next year, if we really go for it, we could gain perhaps 7 per cent of the sales that currently go solely to one of our competitors. But it will mean allocating a special team in the technical department to this end.

Finally we need to consider new fabrics. Next year about £1.2 million of Pearlwear's purchases will come from fabrics currently under development. The value of these fabrics can grow substantially in later years if they include some real winners. To get our slice of this business (we should be looking at half), the criteria are the same as those we have just considered. First, the fabrics must look good and perform well. Second, if the designer is sympathetic to Fabritex and works with us on the development, clearly we have a better chance of supplying a production fabric. And on some, attractive prices can then help tip the balance.

John paused and looked round his colleagues.

If we can achieve all those objectives, we will take a quarter of the Pearlwear business in the UK lingerie warp knit segment. And that accounts for most of the growth required in our overall business forecast.

Charles Franklin thanked John for his clear overview of the position and asked him to circulate a statement to everyone. He then turned to his operations director:

Also, Mike, I would like you to tell us how we are performing against the operations issues raised. After that we can start to review the technical situation.

Operations

The basic manufacturing task is knitting the fabric and then dyeing it. There are two knitting processes known as warp and weft. They use different machine types, giving different fabric characteristics. The dyeing is done at another plant in the group located 12 miles away. Part of the dye plant is dedicated to Fabritex's requirements, with the remaining capacity being used to process fabric from other customers outside the Wardman Group.

A fabric is described by the specification that identifies the knitted fabric and the 'shade' that results from dyeing.

Knitting times for fabrics vary substantially. Some typical knitting times for Pearlwear orders are shown in Exhibit 2. The knitting machines require skilled staff support to complete a set-up on a fabric change. Set-up or changeover times for warp knitting average four hours. (A set-up or changeover is where the required quantity for one fabric is completed, the machine is stopped and then reset to make the next fabric. During this set-up or changeover, no saleable output is produced.) The knitting machines are manned over three shifts

Exhibit 2 Sample of knitting times for Pearlwear fabrics

Order #	Specification[1]	Quantity (metres)	Knitting time (hours)[2]
43651	PN503	250	140.8
43600	PN522	500	289.9
43360	PN523	200	96.4
44754	PN704	1200	578.3
43671	PN713	450	236.8
43900	SA12	1100	354.8
44826	SA9	400	190.5
44849	SK24	900	371.1
44852	SK28	400	142.9
46096	SK33	2600	298.9
44347	SK51	74	41.1
44784	TD468	700	53.5

Notes 1 The term 'specification' identifies the knitted fabric before dyeing.
      2 The knitting time includes an allowance for set-up.

covering 24 hours per day, five days per week. Over-time at weekends is commonly worked to supplement capacity.

Knitted fabric is called greige and is held in store until the required batch size for dyeing has been reached. No two knitting machines produce exactly the same fabric so dye batches unique to a knitting machine are usually accumulated before dyeing is commenced. The dyeing process determines the shade of a fabric. Setting up the process consists of loading the greige onto beams, which is done off-line, and loading the beams onto the machine which only takes about 20 minutes. Some colour sequences require the dyeing machine to be cleaned before use which takes another two hours. Typical dye times are seven hours for white and nine hours for coloured shades but about 10 per cent of dyed fabrics are unsatisfactory and have to be redyed. These times include an overall allowance for cleaning where necessary. The dye plant works a basic 24 hours per day for four days per week. Four dyeing units are used solely for Fabritex work.

The dyed fabric is shipped back to the knitting plant where it is inspected and finished before delivery to the customer. On average this takes about six days. For new or difficult fabrics the customer may require a sample of the fabric before approval is given for delivery.

Fabrics are normally made to order. On receipt of a customer enquiry a promise date is given based on knowledge of the fabric, raw material availability and current knitting loads. The scheduling system is based on actual times for completing past orders. When a customer places an order, it is scheduled on the system. Losses in the knitting and dyeing processes can be high and unpredictable, and the volume of the final fabric is unlikely to match exactly the order quantity.

Some key customers place orders for greige stock prior to orders for final fabrics. Marketing is also allowed to place orders for greige stock to cover special situations agreed by the management team. An example would be in anticipation of a large order where the required knitting capacity would mean an unacceptably long lead time to the customer. If marketing misread the situation, Fabritex can end up with unwanted greige stock to be gradually disposed of at lower prices.

The way forward

Charles Franklin was determined to give his team a strong lead at what he saw as a crucial stage in Fabritex's development.

I have a lot of confidence in the group of people sitting round this table and in the people out there working for us. We have done well in recent years in growing the business. Now is the time to be ambitious. Now is the time to build on our success and deliver a further big increase in sales revenue. We can show the Wardman Group that Fabritex is the place in which to invest for the future. Pearlwear is a major customer and represents a big opportunity. Our two companies have developed together over a number of years. We know the people in Pearlwear and the way they like to do business.

Competition for the Pearlwear business is and will continue to be tough. But it is time we moved from being a minority supplier. Our target must be to secure half the Pearlwear business. We have to do this by improving our communications at all levels and by fast and reliable response to their orders. We currently have the manufacturing capacity to respond. This way we can drive the sales revenue from the current £4m to something close to £15m.

Following the meeting Mike Stewart set about collecting some information for his operations analysis which is given in Exhibits 3 to 6.

Exhibit 3 Sample of Pearlwear orders showing required delivery times

Order #	Specification	Shade	Quantity (metres)	Order value (£s)	Date order received		Customer required delivery	
					Week #	Day #	Week #	Day #
42322	SK28	Black 1	424	1823	10	3	15	2
43360	PN523	Beige	200	736	16	4	33	1
43600	PN522	White 0	500	2600	13	2	18	3
43651	PN503	Beige 4	250	920	2	2	7	4
43671	PN713	Beige 4	450	1665	21	2	29	4
43893	PN522	White 0	600	3120	19	3	25	1
43900	SA12	White 0	1100	5280	7	4	16	1
43904	SK28	Black 1	600	2844	4	3	15	3
43906	SK28	Champagne 73	400	1896	18	1	29	1
43924	SA9	White 0	330	1584	10	1	13	1
43985	PN704	White 0	700	2499	4	4	8	1
44207	PN522	White 0	1600	8320	25	4	33	4
44212	SA12	Black 1	300	1482	16	4	23	2
44213	SK24	White 0	800	3680	22	3	27	4
44214	SK24	Black 1	750	3555	22	2	31	2
44224	SA9	Black 1	300	1482	36	3	42	1
44347	SK51	Beige 4	74	204	16	4	21	3
44354	SK33	White 0	555	1487	15	3	28	1
44643	SK51	White 0	778	2085	15	4	22	1
44649	SK51	White 0	178	477	33	3	38	2
44650	SK51	White 0	709	1900	23	2	30	1
44662	SK33	White 0	709	1900	14	3	20	4
44663	SK33	White 0	140	375	28	3	32	1
44674	SK51	White 0	555	1487	33	1	37	3
44687	SK51	White 0	1993	5341	18	3	23	4
44754	PN704	White 0	1200	4284	13	2	23	1
44755	PN704	Black 1	100	368	18	2	28	1
44784	TD468	White 0	700	5054	22	3	24	4
44825	SA12	White 0	1000	4800	19	1	22	4
44826	SA9	Champagne 73	400	1976	23	1	34	1
44827	SA9	Black 1	500	2470	30	4	34	2
44832	SA12	Black 1	400	1976	34	3	38	1
44849	SK24	White 0	900	4140	14	4	20	2
44852	SK28	Champagne 73	400	1720	28	4	34	2
44935	SA12	Champagne 73	500	2470	31	5	35	3
44952	SK33	White 0	1993	5341	5	4	16	1
44976	SA12	Champagne 73	300	1482	32	5	40	1
45060	TD468	Black 1	150	1116	35	1	39	1
45074	SA9	Champagne 73	150	741	17	1	23	3
45075	SK24	Black 1	200	948	19	1	21	3
45175	SK24	White 0	400	1840	34	4	41	1
46096	SK33	White 0	2600	6968	8	4	19	1
2611	SK51	White 0	2400	6432	22	2	27	1
2612	SK51	White 0	2400	6432	13	1	19	2
2613	SK51	White 0	2400	6432	20	4	28	2
2614	SK51	White 0	2800	7504	29	4	38	4
2669	SK33	White 0	1400	3752	15	2	19	4
42302/1	SK24	Black 1	500	2370	13	2	18	4
43231/1	SK24	New Black	700	3318	28	3	34	4
43651/1	PN503	Beige 4	200	736	4	2	15	3
43901/2	SA12	Black 1	1050	5187	18	1	26	2
43902/1	SA12	Champagne 73	350	1729	23	3	32	2
43985/2	PN704	White 0	300	1071	20	1	29	2
44075/1	PN522	Black 1	500	2675	16	1	20	3
44784/1	TD468	White 0	700	5054	28	3	35	1
44825/1	SA12	White 0	1000	4800	12	4	17	3

Note   Fabritex uses week numbers 1 to 52 and day numbers 1 to 5 only.

Exhibit 4 Sample of Pearlwear orders showing promised and actual delivery times

Order #	Quality	Shade	Fabritex promised delivery		Fabritex actual delivery	
			Week #	Day #	Week #	Day #
42322	SK28	Black 1	18	1	20	1
43360	PN523	Beige	39	1	44	3
43600	PN522	White 0	22	3	26	1
43651	PN503	Beige 4	12	3	23	1
43671	PN713	Beige 4	39	2	43	4
43893	PN522	White 0	25	1	29	1
43900	SA12	White 0	18	4	24	2
43904	SK28	Black 1	18	1	20	3
43906	SK28	Champagne 73	29	1	32	2
43924	SA9	White 0	16	2	21	2
43985	PN704	White 0	9	3	21	3
44207	PN522	White 0	38	1	43	1
44212	SA12	Black 1	26	4	25	4
44213	SK24	White 0	32	3	33	4
44214	SK24	Black 1	35	3	35	1
44224	SA9	Black 1	44	2	42	5
44347	SK51	Beige 4	21	3	22	1
44354	SK33	White 0	29	3	33	4
44643	SK51	White 0	22	1	25	1
44649	SK51	White 0	39	1	42	2
44650	SK51	White 0	30	1	29	4
44662	SK33	White 0	22	1	23	4
44663	SK33	White 0	34	4	34	3
44674	SK51	White 0	38	4	41	4
44687	SK51	White 0	23	4	27	2
44754	PN704	White 0	23	1	22	1
44755	PN704	Black 1	28	1	27	1
44784	TD468	White 0	26	1	32	1
44825	SA12	White 0	25	3	28	1
44826	SA9	Champagne 73	34	1	41	3
44827	SA9	Black 1	38	3	37	1
44832	SA12	Black 1	42	2	40	5
44849	SK24	White 0	24	3	24	1
44852	SK28	Champagne 73	37	3	37	4
44935	SA12	Champagne 73	35	3	33	5
44952	SK33	White 0	17	2	22	1
44976	SA12	Champagne 73	42	4	40	3
45060	TD468	Black 1	38	4	38	4
45074	SA9	Champagne 73	23	3	26	2
45075	SK24	Black 1	22	1	28	3
45175	SK24	White 0	40	4	40	2
46096	SK33	White 0	20	2	26	4
2611	SK51	White 0	27	1	29	5
2612	SK51	White 0	19	2	23	2
2613	SK51	White 0	28	2	30	3
2614	SK51	White 0	38	4	40	5
2669	SK33	White 0	25	2	23	1
42302/1	SK24	Black 1	28	1	30	5
43231/1	SK24	New Black	34	1	38	2
43651/1	PN503	Beige 4	15	4	25	1
43901/2	SA12	Black 1	31	3	32	2
43902/1	SA12	Champagne 73	32	2	36	5
43985/2	PN704	White 0	31	1	34	5
44075/1	PN522	Black 1	25	2	31	3
44784/1	TD468	White 0	36	5	35	5
44825/1	SA12	White 0	22	3	23	2

Notes 1 Fabritex uses week numbers 1 to 52 and day numbers 1 to 5 only.
2 The orders above are typical Pearlwear orders over a sample period.

Exhibit 5 Fabritex share of Pearlwear spend by fabric[1]

Specification	Estimated share of Pearlwear spend (per cent total)	Specification	Estimated share of Pearlwear spend (per cent total)
PN503	100[2]	SA42	0
PN522	21	SA45	0
PN523	100	SK24	42
PN640	0	SK28	29
PN704	100	SK33	100
PN713	100	SK51	100
SA12	100	TD680	0
SA9	100	TD468	32

Notes 1 The table shows the sales and marketing director's estimates of Fabritex's share of the Pearlwear spend on a selection of fabrics.
2 100 per cent of the total means Fabritex is the sole supplier and 0 per cent of the total means Fabritex does not supply the fabric.

Exhibit 6 Regularity of Pearlwear orders

Fabrics ordered on an irregular basis	Fabrics ordered on a regular basis
PN503	SK51
PN523	PN522
SA9	PN704
SK28	PN713
SK33	SA12
	SK24
	SK51
	TD468

Note The classification of Pearlwear fabrics was made by the Fabritex operations planner and will change over time.

Questions

1 Evaluate the marketing strategy to grow future sales revenue.

2 What are the order-winners and qualifiers for the Pearlwear business?

3 How well does operations fulfil its strategic role re the Pearlwear business?

4 What advice would you offer the company?

Future Investments Group

Sarah Durran manages the Bristol Office of the Future Investments Group (FIG), serving customers in southwest England and London. She was travelling home from the head office in Leeds after having been to a presentation about the Group's new pension scheme. The new scheme targets the small business market segment and had been piloted earlier this year in Scotland and is due to be launched next month in London. All the signs were that it would be well received by customers and sales projections are very good.

Sarah reflected:

It's good news that sales of our new pension scheme are doing so well, but how to cope with the increased workload from the demand for this new pension policy when our staff are already working flat out is difficult to envisage. Meeting customers' requirements is a key factor in our business, but keeping costs down is also crucial. Just allocating more staff is not always the solution, particularly as demand seems to be constantly changing.

The team

Sarah manages 8 part-time and 10 full-time members of staff, most of whom also work some overtime (see Exhibit 1). Between them, they process five types of work associated with setting up and managing a range of pension products:

- **New policies** – involves setting up new pension policies for either corporate or individual clients. Corporate customers tend to be small and medium-sized companies, with typically 10–15 people in the pension scheme, whereas individual customers are typically self-employed, sole traders or part of small partnerships.

Exhibit 1 Typical working hours per week for each team member

| Team member | # hours worked | | | | | Typical overtime per week (# hours) | Total # hours including overtime |
	Mon	Tue	Wed	Thu	Fri		
Dave	7	7	7	7	7	10	45
Kathy	7	7	7	7	7	1	36
Julie	7	7	7	7	7	5	40
James	7	7	7	7	7	5	40
Rob	7	7	7	7	7	5	40
Karl	7	7	7	7	7	5	40
Sue	7	7	7	7	7	5	40
Steve	7	7	7	7	7	5	40
Charles	7	7	7	7	7	5	40
Jim	7	7	7	7	7	5	40
Tina	7	7	7	7	–	–	28
Nicky	–	7	7	7	7	–	28
Jill	7	7	4	–	–	–	18
Jenny	–	–	4	7	7	2	20
Rosy	–	4	4	4	4	2	18
Vicki	4	4	4	4	–	2	18
Melanie	–	4	4	4	4	2	18
Pam	4	4	4	4	–	2	18
Total	92	107	108	107	92	61	567

This case study was written by Terry Hill (University of Oxford) and Alex Hill (University of Kingston). It is intended as the basis for class discussion and not as an example of good or bad management. © AMD Publishing.

- **Servicing existing policies** – concerns dealing with queries about existing policies, providing current pension holding statements on request, issuing automatic policy updates twice a year and arranging the administrative tasks for managing pensions from contributions to pension payments at the end of the period.
- **Policy revisions** – when customers wish to alter aspects of a pension, such as contribution levels, these are handled under this aspect of the overall task.
- **Outstanding payments** – if an individual has stopped paying into a pension scheme at the agreed level, then the reasons behind this failure to make the agreed contributions need to be investigated and arrangements made to accommodate the new position.
- **Suspended policies** – where individuals fail to pay into their pension scheme at the agreed level on three consecutive occasions, the pension policy is suspended. The reason for failing to pay into the scheme then needs to be established, subsequent action determined and agreed and the new pension assessed and explained.

During a typical working week, time is spent not only on processing work but also on other activities such as training and rework (see Exhibit 2). Developing people is a key issue within the business and this involves a significant amount of training, where more experienced staff spend time with team members as they process different types of work. In fact, Melanie and Pam, who have been with the business since it started, spend almost 30 per cent of their time training colleagues.

The level of complexity varies across the five types of work. The extent of each team member's ability to process each of these tasks also differs, and is linked to their experience and the amount of training received in their time at FIG. Exhibit 3 shows Sarah's recent skill review of her team which assessed each member's level of experience and ability to process the different types of work.

Using a scale of 0 to 5, Sarah estimated the length of time it would take each team member to process a certain type of work. The skill levels she allocated are as follows:

0 no knowledge
1 initial training received
2 can process basic work with help
3 can process basic work without help
4 can process difficult work with help
5 can process difficult work without help and can train others to complete this category of product.

Although Sarah realized that this was only an approximation, she found it a useful tool to prioritize the training needs within the team.

The skills

Processing the different types of work associated with pensions requires different levels of experience and varying types of skills. The core activities of the team are setting up 'new policies' and 'servicing existing policies'. When

Exhibit 2 Time spent in a typical working week by each team member

Team member	Time spent on each activity during a typical working week (# hours)					
	Processing work	Other				Total
		Training[1]	Rework	Miscellaneous		
				Tasks[2]	Management	
Dave	26	4	2	6	7	45
Kathy	29	4	1	2	–	36
Julie	24	2	1	6	7	40
James	34	2	1	3	–	40
Rob	34	2	1	3	–	40
Karl	31	2	1	6	–	40
Sue	32	5	1	2	–	40
Steve	32	5	1	2	–	40
Charles	31	2	1	6	–	40
Jim	34	2	1	3	–	40
Tina	24	2	–	2	–	28
Nicky	24	2	–	2	–	28
Jill	14	2	1	1	–	18
Jenny	14	3	2	1	–	20
Rosy	15	–	2	1	–	18
Vicki	13	2	2	1	–	18
Melanie	10	5	2	1	–	18
Pam	10	5	2	1	–	18
Total	**431**	**51**	**22**	**49**	**14**	**567**

Notes 1 Covers all training including being trained, for example on new skills and products, and training other staff including help, support and questions on the job.
2 Includes meetings and groups to discuss work-related issues, problems and improvements.

someone joins the business they tend to start in one of these two areas, as this provides the basic knowledge required for processing the other types of work. Although not an absolute prerequisite, it makes sense for a team member to spend time on the 'new policies' and 'servicing existing policies' tasks before being trained on the other types of work.

After an in-depth study, Sarah was able to summarize the training time and relevant experience level associated with each type of work (see Exhibit 4). This list is typical for someone with relatively little experience in pensions or in a related investment business environment. The times also reflect the fact that the training would not be undertaken on a full-time basis:

- **'New policies' and 'servicing existing policies'** – have no prerequisites in terms of other skills and take about 6 and 12 months respectively to achieve ability level 4.

- **'Policy revisions'** – before team members can be trained on 'policy revisions' it is best if they have a skill level 4 in both 'new policies' and 'servicing existing policies'. Training in this task to ability level 4 takes about 12 months.

- **'Outstanding payments'** – training here is best undertaken when a team member has a skill level 4 in 'servicing existing policies'. Once started, it would take a typical team member 9 months to reach ability level 4 in this type of work.

- **'Suspended policies'** – finally, to begin training on 'suspended policies', it is best if a team member has a skill level 2 for 'new policies' and skill level 3 for 'servicing existing policies' (see Note 2 on Exhibit 2). Training here would take 6–12 months to achieve ability level 4.

Furthermore, not only is there a variance in the level of difficulty between the types of work, but also within a single activity

Exhibit 3 Level of experience and ability of each team member

Team member	Experience (# years)	Ability by job type (rating 1 low to 5 high)[1]				
		New policies	Servicing existing policies	Policy revisions	Outstanding payments	Suspended policies
Dave	5.0	5	5	3	5	5
Kathy	1.5	5	4	5	2	2
Julie	2.0	5	4	4	3	2
James	1.0	2	1	3	0	1
Rob	0.5	3	1	0	0	0
Karl	2.0	1	3	0	3	2
Sue	2.0	1	2	0	3	2
Steve	0.5	3	1	0	0	0
Charles	2.0	1	3	0	3	2
Jim	1.0	2	1	3	0	1
Tina	1.0	3	1	0	0	0
Nicky	1.0	3	1	0	0	0
Jill	3.5	5	5	4	3	3
Jenny	5.0	5	5	5	4	4
Rosy	7.0	5	5	5	4	4
Vicki	8.0	5	5	5	5	5
Melanie	10.0	5	5	5	5	5
Pam	10.0	5	5	5	5	5

Notes 1 Sarah's assessment of the skill ability of her team members is as follows:
   0 no knowledge
   1 training received
   2 can process basic work with help
   3 can process basic work without help
   4 can process difficult work with help
   5 can process difficult work without help and can teach others

   2 As you will see, there is a link between a team member's experience (column 2) and the ability rating given for each job type.

Exhibit 4 Prerequisites to start training and typical length of time to be trained up to ability level 4 for each job type

Job type	Ability level required within other job type before starting		Typical training time (# months)[1]
	New policies	Servicing existing policies	
New policies	–	–	6
Servicing existing policies	–	–	9
Policy revisions	4	4	4
Outstanding payment	–	2	3
Suspended policies	2	3	3–6[2]

Notes 1 The typical time above reflects the fact that training would not be undertaken on a full-time basis.
   2 The typical training time for 'suspended policies' varies between 3 and 6 months. The actual time would reflect the ability level of the member of staff. The higher the ability level on 'new policies' and 'servicing existing policies' the person had before starting to learn how to handle 'suspended policies', the shorter the training time required.

itself. For example, in 'servicing existing policies' 30 per cent of the jobs received tend to be easy and 70 per cent hard. This has an impact on the length of time it typically takes to process them, with hard jobs taking longer than easy jobs. The split between easy and hard jobs for other types of work is provided in Exhibit 5.

In addition to working within a team, FIG regularly sets up project groups that are drawn from a number of teams and departments from the regional offices. One of Sarah's roles is to put forward team members to be considered as possible participants in these groups. To help her think about the non-technical skills needed for such groups, Sarah again put her views onto paper, making an assessment of the non-technical skills her team members currently held (see Exhibit 6).

Exhibit 5 Typical mix of jobs received and times to process them

Job type	Work mix (% jobs)[1]		Typical processing time (# hours)[2]	
	Easy	Hard	Easy	Hard
New policies	80	20	0.75	1.00
Servicing existing policies	40	60	0.40	0.50
Policy revisions	50	50	2.50	3.00
Outstanding payment	80	20	0.50	1.00
Suspended policies	80	20	1.00	2.00

Notes 1 Team members with an ability of 1, 2 or 3 can process easy jobs. Hard jobs require an ability of 4 or 5.
        2 Processing times include time for rest and relaxation.

Exhibit 6 Sarah's assessment of 'business competencies' for each team member

Team member	Business competency (1 = basic and 3 = high level)				
	Teamwork[1]	Motivation[2]	Business awareness[3]	People development[4]	Process improvement[5]
Dave	1	3	3	1	3
Kathy	3	3	2	3	3
Julie	2	1	2	2	2
James	2	2	1	2	1
Rob	3	2	1	3	2
Karl	3	3	2	3	3
Sue	2	2	1	2	1
Steve	3	2	1	3	2
Charles	3	3	2	3	3
Jim	2	2	1	2	1
Tina	1	2	1	2	1
Nicky	1	2	1	2	1
Jill	2	2	2	2	2
Jenny	3	2	2	2	2
Rosy	1	1	2	2	2
Vicki	1	1	2	2	2
Melanie	3	1	2	3	2
Pam	3	1	2	3	2

Notes 1 The ability to work in a team/team skills
        2 Level of ability to get a job done (action-oriented dimension)
        3 How well team members know the overall business, including outside their own section
        4 How oriented a person is to develop other people
        5 The ability to identify, seek out and implement improvements on an ongoing basis

Exhibit 7 Demand profile by job type for the last six weeks

Job type	Demand by week (# customer requests received)					
	0	−1	−2	−3	−4	−5
New policies	270	285	310	300	315	292
Servicing existing policies	241	270	230	240	225	247
Policy revisions	13	13	12	11	11	10
Outstanding payment	45	40	39	34	30	27
Suspended policies	35	30	27	22	31	25

Note   Week 0 = current week, week −1 = last week.
The average for the last six weeks is considered sufficiently accurate to use
as a forecast of future demand levels.

Exhibit 8 Backlog profile by job type for the last six weeks

Job type	Backlog by week (# customer requests waiting to be processed)					
	0	−1	−2	−3	−4	−5
New policies	260	276	290	315	325	337
Servicing existing policies	242	269	288	330	360	382
Policy revisions	10	9	10	6	6	4
Outstanding payment	60	52	37	30	33	30
Suspended policies	63	52	40	30	30	40

Note   Week 0 = current week, week −1 = last week.

The load

For the final part of managing the demand/capacity task, Sarah needed to assess the demand that the team needs to handle. Exhibit 7 shows the typical mix of work received in the regional office. The other aspect of volumes (and, more importantly, a key performance measure) is the number of outstanding customer requests waiting to be handled. Exhibit 8 shows the profile of the backlog of work at the beginning of the current week and for the previous five weeks. Sarah's overall assessment of the last six weeks was that they have been typical and over the whole period would represent an average weekly level of demand by job type.

Reflections

Sarah reflected:

Over the last few weeks I have placed additional emphasis on reducing the backlog of customer requests particularly in the 'new policies' and 'servicing existing policies' work categories. As these are the main activities for us to handle, then much

attention is given to keeping them at acceptable levels. My aim is to reduce the backlog to the equivalent of about one week's demand. With the new scheme about to be launched next month in my region, it is essential that I have an understanding of what the current picture is like. Fortunately I have several staff with extensive experience and these I will use as the core team to handle the new product demand. In this way, queries and approaches will be managed so that we are best able to take on this new product and its uncertainties.

The advantages of putting my thoughts down on paper are that I can see all the different aspects at a glance. This will make it easier for me to manage my team both in terms of what we're able to do (capacity) and the demand volumes we can expect to receive. What I need to do now is find out what insights these analyses provide.

Question

1   Assess the demand/capacity in Sarah's team and comment.

Georgian Frames

Georgian Frames is a small company engaged in making and installing new Georgian-style, premeasured windows to replace existing windows in the homes of its customers. Exhibit 1 details the activities required to complete the task of removing the old and installing a new window. Although occasionally more than one window will be installed at a site, at present about 75 per cent of all jobs involve the installation of a single window. The critical path diagram representing this set of activities is shown in Exhibit 2.

The recent company sales growth has necessitated allocating more men to window installation on a full-time basis. However, increasingly, there are days when it is necessary to install a window on two separate sites. While Georgian Frames wishes to maintain sales growth, it needs to keep capital invest-

ment to a minimum. Therefore, it does not wish to purchase a second vehicle (necessary to transport men, tools and windows to the customer's premises) unless it is essential. In addition, it also needs to keep labour costs to a minimum in order to stay competitive, while maintaining acceptable profit levels.

Question

1   Faced with a growth in demand for the installation of new, Georgian-style windows, yet wishing to keep capital investment as low as possible, advise the company on how best to handle the installation of windows at two separate sites, no more than half an hour's drive from one another.

Exhibit 1 Principal activities involved in replacing a window on site

Activity	Time units (½ hour) to do the task, depending upon the # men available			Minimum # men required to do the job
	1 man	2 men	3 men	
Load vehicle at yard and prepare	2	1	1	1
To site	2	2	2	1
Unload and check the window size	1	½	½	1
Prepare site	2	1½	1	1
Remove old frame	2	1½	1	1
Offer new frame to the opening	–	1	1	2
Load old frame onto vehicle	1	½	(note 7)	1
Finish installation	4	3	2	1
Load tools and so on onto vehicle	1	½	(note 7)	1
Return to yard	2	2	2	1
Load old frame and tools onto vehicle	2	1	½	(note 7)

Notes   1   Where two windows and other items are loaded onto a vehicle with three men, the time taken will be the same as that for one window and other items with two men.
2   It is customary for the vehicle driver to participate in the window installation activities.
3   The activity times given are the average for these tasks and take account of allowances for fatigue, rest, mid-morning and mid-afternoon breaks.
4   In the network diagram (Exhibit 2) the work throughout is carried out by two men. The men, on returning to the yard, do other work such as priming and sanding window frames.
5   The time to travel from one site to another would take ½ hour.
6   Activity 'remove old window frame' is not dependent upon 'prepare site'.
7   For three men, the activities 'load old window frame onto vehicle' and 'load tools and so on onto vehicle' are combined into the one activity 'load old frame and tools onto vehicle' which takes ½ of one time unit.

Exhibit 2 Network diagram for the activities given in Exhibit 1 with a two-man team

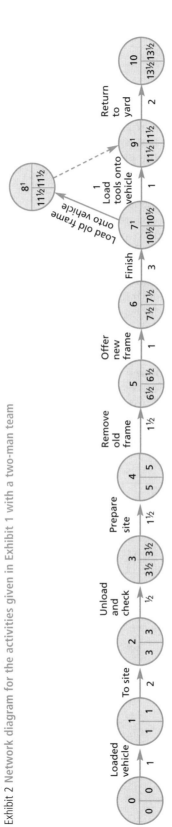

Note 1 Activities 7, 8 and 9 are shown to run in parallel. If it were decided to run these activities in sequence, the overall time taken would be the same.

Ghent Fireworks

In March, last year, Ghent Fireworks (GF) celebrated 100 years in the fireworks business. It had, in its time, experienced most of the growth problems of a typical manufacturing company, but was now an established name in the UK market for its firework products.

Perhaps the most significant change in direction for the company occurred five or six years ago when, based upon its traditional business and reputation as a fireworks manufacturer, GF applied and gained registration on the UK's Ministry of Defence (MoD) list of assessed contractors, having met the requirements as laid down in relevant Defence Standards. This successful application now opened up home and export markets for all types of pyrotechnic products. Typical of these would be smoke generators in a range of colours, hand-held, ground, grenade and trip-wire flares, small arms simulators (single and multi-shot), explosion, flame and smoke simulators, thunderflashes and rocket motors.

Sales

While sales for fireworks showed a steady growth, pyrotechnic sales had increased noticeably in the past three years, to the point where sales last year for the first time exceeded those of fireworks; current sales are anticipated to be higher still (see Exhibits 1 and 2).

Fireworks

By far the biggest proportion of firework sales (value and units) was to the general public, and the trend in recent years had been to sell them in boxes through wholesale and retail outlets. GF sells boxes of fireworks in seven sizes with current retail prices up to £150. Other firework sales were for large orders from organizations of different types. These orders would typically comprise fireworks at the top end of the price range sold to the general public, or more normally from their wide range of

Exhibit 1 **Actual and forecast sales**

Sales (£m)	Current year minus							Current year[1]
	7	6	5	4	3	2	1	
Fireworks	4.2	4.5	5.5	5.9	6.1	6.5	6.7	7.0
Pyrotechnics[2]	–	0.2	1.5	2.5	3.2	5.9	7.0	7.9
Total	4.2	4.7	7.0	8.4	9.3	12.4	13.7	14.9

Notes   1   Current year figures are forecasts.
        2   Exports for pyrotechnic products were 70 per cent last year and are expected to increase to 75 per cent this year.

Exhibit 2 **Firework types, current catalogue**

Firework category	# sizes in each category
Lights	14
Showers	18
Fountains	42
Rockets	25
Catherine wheels	8
Roman candles	22
Volcanoes	16
Shells	60
Mines	7

designs in the product categories of displays, set pieces and daylight fireworks. To fulfil these orders (which comprised some 10 per cent of the total value of firework sales), the top end of the price range and daylight fireworks were usually taken from existing finished goods stock and the specials (that is, displays and set pieces), which comprise four-fifths of these orders, were made to a customer's specification. The range of fireworks sold currently is shown in Exhibit 2.

About 85–90 per cent of all GF's fireworks

This case study was written by Terry Hill (University of Oxford). It is intended as the basis for class discussion and not as an example of good or bad management. © AMD Publishing.

sales are for displays on bonfire night on 5 November each year. (Bonfire night is celebrated in the UK to mark the failed attempt by a group of Catholics to blow up the Houses of Parliament in 1605. The incident is known as the 'Gunpowder Plot'.) Orders are taken at the spring toy fairs at Brighton and Harrogate, or by direct order. Delivery of all these orders is made from August onwards and customers normally settle their invoices in November or December each year.

Pyrotechnics

Sales for pyrotechnic contracts have increased significantly in the last three years and are forecast to be £7.9 million for this year (see Exhibit 1). The size of contracts awarded so far has varied from £60,000 to £3.0 million. The latter contract was in fact awarded last month – the previous largest contract had been for £1.9 million. Contracts currently in manufacture or recently finished had values ranging from £52,000 to £850,000. Each contract received is always for one product only, such is the nature of the business. Thus, if a customer wanted a number of products, it would be required to place a contract to cover each product, even if two or more contracts were placed with the same supplier. The

Exhibit 3 **Chance of GF receiving a pyrotechnic contract for a previously made product**

# years after receiving the first contract	Chance of receiving an order with the same product specification[1] (per cent)
1	Nil
2	10
3	15
4	15
5 and over	20

Note 1 The low chances of receiving a repeat order are attributable to the fact that the range of products required by GF's customers is very wide, and although many of these products' specifications may not be changed, the tendency is for customers to order several years' requirements at a time. Combine this with the fact that GF may not be asked to tender or may not get the order, then the chances of receiving a contract for the same product are small.

chances of GF receiving a contract for a product which it had made before are given in Exhibit 3.

Pyrotechnic sales are the responsibility of the CEO, Ray Livingstone, although the preparation of quotations and the control of the commercial side of the contracts is handled by the quotations and contracts department which reports to the commercial director, as shown in Exhibit 4. Ray considers that this segment of GF's sales is the growth area within the company:

> Now that we are becoming established in this market, the opportunity to maintain current sales

Exhibit 4 **Ghent Fireworks organization chart**

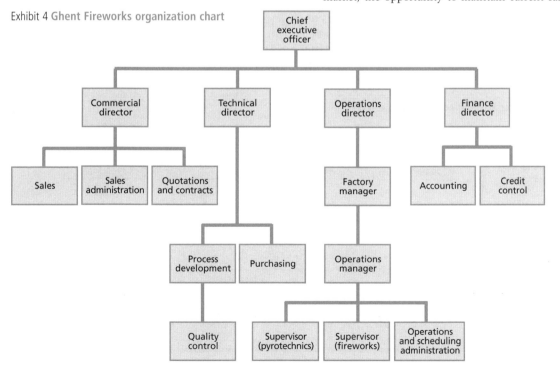

growth should be achievable. However, sales are not as predictable as on the fireworks side of our business for two important reasons. The first is that we are not certain which contracts, if any, we shall secure. This leads to the problem, therefore, of deciding how many and for which contracts to tender. Too few or too many orders won will bring its own set of operations problems – a case in point is the £3.0 million contract we have just received. Furthermore, as we are not well established in pyrotechnics, it would be ill-advised to turn down the opportunity to tender if asked. Many of our orders are for export contracts and dealing with different cultures has its own set of problems. The second reason is that not being well established also means that we are less certain about our customers and the nature of the repeat business from them, even though this would be for different products.

Operations

In the mid-1950s GF moved to its present site on the outskirts of Dundee – an arrangement of about 30 small production units which have been added to over the years. The limitations on the amount of explosives which can be held in a given area forces this organizational configuration onto GF and any other manufacturing company in this line of business.

GF has a total of 143 employees, of whom 104 are direct workers. Manufacturing usually works on a single shift basis from 7.30 am to 4.00 pm except in times of high throughput. At these times extra people have been employed on a part-time basis, spanning a wide range of 2.5–5-hour daytime shift

combinations. Recently though, when a large contract has been going through manufacturing, the company has worked two 12-hour shifts based on the full-time workforce and supplemented by part-timers and a few temporary full-timers who also worked the 12-hour shift pattern.

Fireworks

The manufacturing process for fireworks comprises four main stages, as shown in Exhibit 5. Each of these stages (except stage 3 which takes place after stage 2) is completed in a separate building because of the ruling on explosives described earlier.

All fireworks are packed into boxes or against a specific customer order. However, completion of this stage will always depend upon the appropriate mix of fireworks being available. Thus Box 17 comprises 17 different types of firework from within the categories given in Exhibit 2, all of which have to be available before packing can commence.

Whereas the mixing and filling activities are confined to small areas, packing takes place in a larger factory area which has been designated solely to firework packing. Fireworks after stage 3 in the process are now ready for packing. On completing stage 3 they are stacked into containers and transported to the packing area.

Pyrotechnics

The manufacturing process to complete pyrotechnic products is similar from one product to the next, as outlined in Exhibit 6. Working to the quality

Exhibit 5 **Manufacturing process for fireworks**

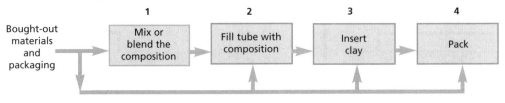

Exhibit 6 **Manufacturing process for pyrotechnic products**

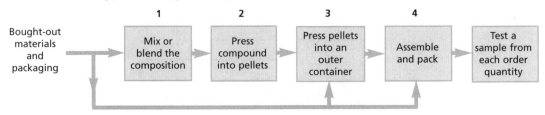

Exhibit 7 Operations stages to produce a flare

Stage

1 Mix compound to product specification provided by customer and specified by process development.

2 Press compound into pellets – a simple press is used.

3 Assemble or press pellets into the required outer containers – again, a simple press is used.

4 Assemble ignitor and any other components (for example a spike) onto the container. Paint, stencil, silk screen, heat shrink the required identification onto the container. The identification is specified by the appropriate Defence Standard and the customer. Process development specifies the process to be used to make the required identification.

5 Cap, tape flares together, pack in outer container and label.

6 Test product samples out of each order quantity processed.

requirements of relevant Defence Standards (for either UK or export sales – in fact, being an MoD reg-

istered company is almost a prerequisite to win export contracts for pyrotechnic products), the specification against which GF quoted goes first to process development. This function then specifies the appropriate way in which the product should be manufactured. Once these process specifications have been established they are handed over to production who can then schedule them into manufacturing once the required components and packaging are available. A more detailed summary of the processes through which a typical pyrotechnic product goes is given in Exhibit 7.

Operations planning and scheduling

The operations planning and scheduling tasks are provided by the operations and scheduling administration department (see Exhibit 4) which reports to the operations manager. The procedures are outlined in Exhibit 8.

Exhibit 8 Operations planning and scheduling procedures

Fireworks

Operations planning and scheduling is based primarily on forecast sales in the first few months of each financial year (that is, 1 December onwards) and later (after the spring toy fairs and receipt of direct orders) on the basis of sales orders. Placing purchase orders with appropriate suppliers is based on a monthly schedule, which is two months firm (that is, a committed schedule) and two months tentative. Operations schedules are laid down against these material, component and packaging deliveries, with daily adjustments made according to the combinations of materials/components/packaging that are in stock and to minimize manufacturing disruptions. To achieve this, the operations and scheduling administration department works closely with the relevant supervisor.

Pyrotechnics

The procedure involved in pyrotechnic contracts is as follows:

1 Tender. A tender is made by the quotations and contracts department, based upon an assessment of past contracts of a similar nature and a working knowledge of the operations involved to complete the work. However, there is no formal feedback of information from operations to quotations and contracts of actual production achievement (for example actual throughput times) nor is this information systematically collated by operations for this purpose.

2 Order received. Where a tender is successful and an order is received, the specified delivery date of the tender is triggered off

on the basis of order receipt. Hence, a tender will specify that the delivery required is, say, four months from receipt of the order.

3 Parts are ordered. These usually take one month. However, if parts have a longer lead time, this is taken into account when setting the specified delivery time.

4 Process development is completed on the basis of an advanced batch for some 50 sets of materials, components and packaging. These are completed in the process development department but do not normally involve operations in these procedures. This department produces a process specification to be followed by manufacturing.[1] However, the specification does not normally include a synopsis for operations of the problems, difficulties and 'things to watch for' as experienced by the process development department. It will include a proofing procedure which details the tests to be made and sample size to be taken from each manufacturing order quantity.

5 Operations converts the process specification into a set of working instructions:
   - tasks involved
   - safety precautions to be taken (for example footwear and protective clothing)
   - explosive limits to be adhered to.

6 Materials are issued in line with the relevant Defence Standard and a record of which material was used and the supplier is kept with the order quantity of products. This is to allow all materials and so on to be traced in case of problems later in the process or when the product is being used by the customer.

7 Each order quantity is then proofed (see Exhibit 9).

Note 1 As the process equipment and conditions of working are very different (for example laboratory as against high volume manufacturing), the failure of process development to develop the suggested process specification in line with the conditions in which manufacturing will work leads to many of the initial 'proofing' failures.

Fireworks

Following the peak sales in November each year, fireworks are manufactured initially in line with sales forecasts and then later in line with the firm sales orders received from spring onwards. Individual orders that do not relate to 5 November sales are met as and when they are required. To keep operations volumes steady, the aim each month is to produce one-twelfth of the forecast annual sales. The procedure used is to order materials and other requirements in line with these sales forecasts and then make the same quantity of the high volume fireworks each month, and to make two months of some of the lower volume fireworks one month, and then two months of the other lower volume fireworks the next month and so on. Phil Mills, operations director, explained:

> If we are to meet our August-onward deliveries, it is essential that we make about £560,000 of fireworks each month. If we fail to do this we will find it very difficult to meet our deliveries later in the year. Based on the trade-offs and associated costs, it has been decided to adopt this method rather than any alternative.

Operations schedules are established in line with inventory levels and anticipated deliveries of the required materials, components and packaging. However, because the process is fairly flexible and some fireworks are already in work-in-progress, the packing programme can be adjusted in line with what is available to pack and the packaging in stock. The manufacturing process before packing can also be adjusted from the laid-down schedules, again in line with the materials and packaging available in inventory.

Pyrotechnics

A pyrotechnic contract typically has to be delivered within four months of GF receiving the order. Although delivery times do relate, to some extent, to the size of the contracts, the bigger the quantity involved, the longer the delivery lead time, and vice versa. The procedure used to schedule this into operations is given in Exhibit 8. The first step is for process development to determine the best way to manufacture the particular product. Using laboratory process facilities, process development will select from a limited number of different ways of making the product in order to meet the agreed specification. The increase in work in this department means that on average it takes one month to issue a process specification. The quality control department is responsible for testing the samples taken from the manufacturing order quantities which comprise a contract, and Exhibit 9 provides an analysis of the number of sample failures generally experienced.

The other activity that delays the start of manufacturing is the procurement of production quantities of materials, components and packaging. To meet the MoD standards, all suppliers must be on the MoD register. This restricts the number of suppliers from which companies such as GF may choose. It has taken up to six weeks to procure production quantities of some items (quantities suffi-

---

Exhibit 9 **Sample failures for pyrotechnic contracts and their source**

In order to complete a pyrotechnic contract, operations manufactures a number of order quantities which typically equate to two shifts of work (this size of order quantity is considered sensible in terms of the explosive limits and the volume it represents going through the different processes). Each order quantity has to be 'proofed' (that is, inspected) by the quality control department (QCD). For example (and in line with the customer specification), these will comprise vibration testing, ignition burn length and damp test. The size of sample taken from an order quantity reduces over the production runs to meet the whole contract quantity and in line with the failure rates observed. To complete the test procedures on the first sample takes at least two days and sometimes five or more. Tests on later samples take less time.

If a sample fails the proofing, manufacturing will be stopped until the problem has been checked out. This may result in an internal manufacturing process change or a rejection of a particular component(s) and discussion with the supplier(s) involved.

Order quantity	Samples taken that fail proofing by QCD (percentage)
1st	25
2nd	10
3rd	Occasional
4th	Rare
5th onwards	None
Source of failure	*Percentage of total failure*
Production process	95
Component supply	5

cient for some 50 products can normally be obtained in a week by process development) but usually it takes up to three to four weeks from receipt of an order to production quantities being received.

When the first order quantity is completed, a sample is taken for 'proofing', as explained in Exhibit 9. However, operations, under pressure to meet the delivery promise on a contract, invariably has no option but to continue to manufacture without waiting for the results of the proofing phase. If changes subsequently have to be made, the rework involved is completed by production as soon as possible.

Inventory

The results of an inventory check at the end of February, earlier this year (the first quarter of the current financial year), are shown in Exhibit 10. The inventory check showed a 10 per cent loss on the evaluation of fireworks (that is, the value of work-in-progress (WIP) for fireworks was 10 per cent less than expected, based upon the materials issued). This, however, was not considered unusual and is accounted for by the material losses in the manufacturing process, especially at the 'fill tube with composition' stage. However, this same check on WIP for pyrotechnics is computed at the end of each contract and normally there is little need to adjust the WIP value.

Exhibit 10 **Inventory value by category and operations type (£000s) at 1 March, current year**

Product category	Raw materials/ components	Work-in-progress	Finished goods[1]	Total
Fireworks	290	245	1378	1913
Pyrotechnics	168	490	–	658
Total	458	735	1378	2571

Note 1 The opening finished good inventory for fireworks on 1 December last year was £0.37m (which is normal for this time of year) and nil for pyrotechnics. The other categories of inventory have remained steady throughout these three months.

The future

Ray Livingstone concluded:

The increase in pyrotechnic sales in recent years has been important on two counts. Firstly, it has given us an important boost in overall sales revenue. Secondly, it has provided us with an alternative product range in itself which also provides a balance in activities to being solely in fireworks, with the added cash flow advantages. Fortunately, we have such a flexible workforce that we can move them from fireworks to pyrotechnics and vice versa without much disruption. Similarly, we can increase our capacity temporarily with part-time and full-time employees. In fact, winning the recent pyrotechnic contract for £3.0 million has meant that we have now decided that to meet all our sales commitments in fireworks and pyrotechnics we shall have to run a second shift as we did once before with a large contract. Our permanent employees will be divided into two groups so as to form the basis for each shift. We are now recruiting temporary staff to bring the shift members up to the required level. Achieving delivery on the contracts is not only important in itself but also has significant consequences in terms of cash flow.

Questions

1 What advice would you offer the company in terms of:

(a) how best to meet the manufacturing requirements of the products involved

(b) any improvements to existing operations planning and control procedures, with supporting reasons?

2 Comment in detail on any other operations management issues that you consider pertinent to Ghent Fireworks.

Case study 10

Holmgren Engineering

Thanks for detailing your findings, Peter. As we've all had copies of your report for some time, I now suggest we open up the discussion on your proposals.

John Svensson, CEO of Holmgren Engineering (HE), was addressing the management team following Peter Wiklund's presentation on his proposed changes to the layout and process for the future manufacture of the Hetvatten range of products.

Background

Holmgren Engineering (HE) was established almost 40 years ago. Initially it was a small heating engineering firm started by Benny Holmgren offering a range of related services.

It grew and later expanded into manufacturing its own products. It continued as a family business until it was taken over some 10 years ago by Karlsson Invest, a conglomerate with a range of businesses involved in building and construction-related activities. The last few years have seen a continued increase in sales although there has been a slight fall-off in profits (see Exhibit 1).

Based in Halmstad, HE is in the industrial conurbation centred on Gothenburg in southwest Sweden (see Exhibit 2). Although initially an installer of equipment and provider of support services, HE is now only involved in the manufacture and selling of water storage systems. In fact, since it was taken over by Karlsson Invest it has moved even more into

Exhibit 1   Sales revenue, EBIT[1] and inventory data – current and past two years

	Current year –2	Current year –1	Current year
Sales revenue (index)	100.0	111.5	125.6
EBIT (% sales revenue)	10.3	8.6	7.4
Inventory (SKr000)[2]			
• raw material and components	3,144	5,052	5,352
• work-in-progress[3]	180	144	168
• finished goods	720	924	1,680
Total	4,044	6,120	7,200

Notes   1   EBIT = earnings before interest and tax.
2   SKr = Swedish krona.
3   Work-in-progress includes issued materials and part-made products.

Exhibit 2   Outline map of Northern Europe

Key   A = Austria
B = Belgium
CH = Switzerland
CZ = Czech Republic
DK = Denmark
NL = The Netherlands
SL = Slovak Republic
UK = United Kingdom

This case study was written by Terry Hill (University of Oxford) and Pär Åhlström (Chalmers University of Technology, Gothenburg). It is intended as the basis for class discussion and not as an example of good or bad management. © AMD Publishing.

developing and manufacturing water storage products which include mains pressure heating systems.

Products

HE manufactures a range of products on its Halmstad site. The part of its range addressed by Peter Wiklund's report is sold under the Hetvatten Plus trademark. This comprises a family of products which vary by size of heating coil and storage capacity (see Exhibit 3). These products are sold throughout Sweden and parts of Europe. Normally, the delivery lead time is three to four weeks, but shorter deliveries can usually be met where necessary.

Operations

The Hetvatten Plus product range is basically made to a standard design and configuration. Larger houses and growing demand for hot water has led to an increase in the product range over the last decade. However, in operations terms, the current range is not difficult to handle. The principal changes concern the external dimensions of the product and the different sizes of heating coil. But these require few, if any, alterations to the basic design.

The present layout and other related cost information are given in Exhibits 4 and 5. Currently, products are made in order quantities of five. As shown in Exhibit 4, an order quantity moves through the different processes, with the tasks completed on all five products before the total order quantity is moved to the next stage.

Exhibit 3 **Hetvatten Plus product range**

| Model | Storage capacity (litres) | Dwelling types | | | Dimensions height × width (cm) |
		# bedrooms	# baths	# showers	
A	120	2 or 3	1	–	1500 × 500
B	140	2 or 3	1	1	1500 × 550
C	160	2–4	1 or 2	1 or 2	1500 × 600
D	180	3–4	1 or 2	1 or 2	1600 × 600
E	200	3–5	2	1–3	1700 × 600

Exhibit 4 **Present factory layout**

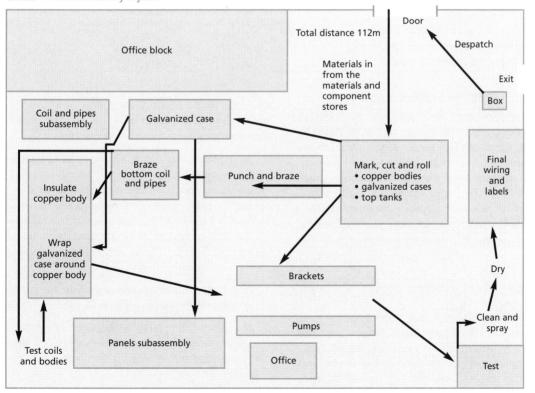

Exhibit 5 Costs (SKr) per unit

Category		Models				
		A	B	C	D	E
Cost per unit	Material	4,200	4,800	6,360	7,068	7,908
	Labour	1,260	1,284	1,320	1,464	1,656
	Overheads	900	900	900	900	900
	Total	6,360	6,984	8,580	9,432	10,464

Note   1   Costs are based on an average weekly production of 100 units.

Operations scheduling

The production programme is agreed weekly. Based on known orders and forecast sales it looks four weeks ahead, with week 1 fixed and weeks 2–4 tentative.

Currently, parts are bulk ordered, with weekly call-offs agreed at the beginning of each month. Most material and components are delivered on the first day of each week, with sufficient parts for the production planned for that week, and held in the material and components stores, which is located on the same site but in a different building from the one outlined in Exhibit 4.

Working on agreed weekly schedules (see Exhibit 6), materials are issued to the production area on a daily basis.

Exhibit 6 Production figures for weeks 11–18 of the current year

Models	Units produced in the following week #							
	11	12	13	14	15	16	17	18
A	10	15	10	10	10	10	10	15
B	15	15	10	10	10	15	10	15
C	40	40	40	30	40	40	40	40
D	30	30	25	20	35	30	30	30
E	5	5	10	10	5	5	10	5
Total	100	105	95	80	100	100	100	105

Notes   1 The above production figures are representative of the mix of models produced in the current year.
2 Issues to the shop floor are in order quantities of five.
3 The number of boilers is based on the planned capacity within a week and the mix of boilers scheduled to be manufactured.
4 Week 14 included a public holiday and, therefore, comprised only four working days.
5 All products are included in figures for the week in which they were completed. Therefore, no part-made boilers are included in the above figures.

Production engineering report

The report presented by production engineering reviewed the current operations procedures used to make the Hetvatten Plus range. Its principal recommendation was to change the layout and the way of manufacturing these products. In essence, products would now be made in order quantities of one compared to the current order quantity of five. Also, products would be transferred by rollers, with staff pushing them from one work station to the next.

Overview of the proposed changes and benefits to be gained

On John Svensson's invitation, Peter Wiklund gave an overview of the proposed changes and also detailed the benefits to be gained. Using an overhead projector, Peter explained the detail and rationale of the proposals and highlighted the ben-

efits that would result. What follows is a summary of Peter's presentation and the key points of clarification requested by those at the meeting:

As you know, a typical boiler comprises four principal subassemblies – copper body, top tank, galvanised casing and the electrical unit. As shown in the current layout [see Exhibit 4], these subassemblies are produced in separate systems and come together, as required, at the assembly stage. You can also see from the layout details that the distance travelled totals 112 metres.

One of the initial tasks was to evaluate the current system and propose changes on whether to:

- make-to-order (MTO) or make-to-stock (MTS)
- make in order quantities (whether five or a different quantity) or make individually (one-piece flow)

● hold stocks of subassemblies or make them as part of the final product assembly stage.

To help in this evaluation, we used Exhibit 7 which also gives the agreed scores on each dimension for the eight options.

My recommendation, in the first instance, is to adopt option 7 [Exhibit 7], as holding subassembly stock will take some pressure off the system. Later, when the revised arrangement is running well, we can eliminate this feature. [Details of the revised layout and other changes are given in Exhibits 8 and 9.]

However, to be able to change successfully to the new way of working will require a number of tasks to be completed. These are listed in the report distributed earlier [see Exhibit 10]. Once the changes have been implemented we expect to gain the following advantages.

Peter then went through the list of advantages listed in Exhibits 11 and 12 and explained each in full.

Given the need to improve our overall performance and the premium we are giving for reducing costs and taking out overheads, I feel that these changes are ones which will, in themselves, lead to noticeable inventory reductions, additional floor space needed to make new products in the future and shorter manufacturing lead times for the Hetvatten Plus product range. For these reasons I wish to implement these proposed changes as quickly as possible.

Questions

1 Examine the current operations process used at Holmgren Engineering. What are the key features of this way of making products?

2 What are the key changes that enable the proposed method of production (one-piece flow) to work?

3 Evaluate the benefits of these proposed changes and highlight the principal gains to be made.

4 What factors would need to be carefully managed to ensure a successful implementation of these proposals?

Exhibit 7 Evaluation of alternative approaches to manufacturing, used as a basis for selecting the changes to be introduced

#	MTO versus MTS[1]	Batch size	Sub-assembly stock yes (✓) or no (✗)	Dimension and score (1 = good; 4 = poor)						Total score
				Efficiency	Inventory	Speed of throughput	Space/ movement	Response/ variability	Quality	
1	MTS	5	✓	1	4	3	4	3	4	19
2	MTS	5	✗	3	3	4	3	3	2	18
3	MTS	1	✓	2	3	1	2	3	2	13
4	MTS	1	✗	4	2	2	1	3	1	13
5	MTO	5	✓	1	3	3	4	1	4	16
6	MTO	5	✗	3	2	4	3	1	2	15
7	MTO	1	✓	2	3	1	2	1	2	11
8	MTO	1	✗	4	1	2	1	1	1	10

Note 1 MTO = make-to-order; MTS = make-to-stock

Exhibit 8 **Proposed factory layout**

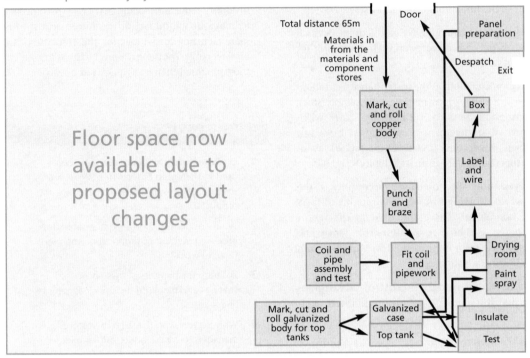

Exhibit 9 **Summary of proposed operations changes for the Hetvatten Plus product range**

The changes proposed and the principal benefits resulting from them have been summarized below:

Current operations

● Currently Hetvatten Plus products are made in order quantities of five.

● All five products go to operation 1 where the work is completed before all five products go to operation 2 and so on through the entire process.

Move to flow production

● Under the 'flow' production system, batches of five will be eliminated and work will be carried out on an order quantity of one.

● The physical structure of manufacturing will be altered to a U-shape production line (Exhibit 8).

● Single boilers will be moved on trolleys around the line.

● Subassembly components will be made off the main line and added to the part-made boiler on the line.

● A JIT process will be set up for raw material suppliers from stores to the line, and a JIT process will operate with component suppliers.

Human resource changes

● Currently operators concentrate their work on one area, but may be required to assist on different sections, or move to the subassembly area if the preceding stage is longer and holds up production flow.

● In the process flow system, there will be less need for operators to move around. They will be assigned specific tasks and will keep to that operation through the day (this may consist of two or three steps). This should improve productivity as there will be less time lost through walking about. However, the new U-shaped flow system enables operators to maintain eye contact and allows each operator to have a better view of the whole process.

Exhibit 10 Tasks to be completed as part of the change to one-piece flow production

Before the move to the one-piece flow production, we need to undertake the following tasks:

1 Remove changeover times (particularly on punches).

2 Estimate the need for any two-man lifting requirements.

3 Develop a U-shaped manufacturing layout to minimize distances between operations.

4 Position tooling and materials close to the relevant operations.

5 Establish standard work methods.

6 Balance the line capacity.

7 Encourage teamworking, particularly through a new payment system, setting consistent performance targets and adopting a different management style.

8 Reduce or eliminate delays in spray painting.

9 Control dust from the rockwool insulation operation.

10 Possibly eliminate the final water test.

Exhibit 11 Advantages of the one-piece flow process

1 The advantages accruing from 'one-piece flow' are that it:
- reduces the floor area required, with the freed-up space being used for the manufacture of a new product
- increases quality
- facilitates teamworking
- reduces the walking distances involved
- increases flexibility
- reduces work-in-progress (WIP) inventory
- leads to higher control of throughputs
- increases focus for the continuous improvement teams
- improves operator's overall vision by means of the U-shaped layout

2 The advantages accruing from making-to-order as opposed to making-to-stock are:
- lower finished goods inventory
- increased flexibility in production planning
- lower raw material inventory
- ability to cope with higher product variety
- materials can be delivered directly to the work stations

3 The advantages relating to the presence of subassembly inventory within the process are that it:
- facilitates labour balancing
- affords the opportunity to make and feed parts to the point of use
- enables faster throughputs
- improves inventory control with the use of *kanban* systems

Exhibit 12 Specific advantages to be gained from the proposed changes in operations

The advantages accruing from the proposed changes in operations include:

1   **Reduction in labour content** – less walking due to the smaller working area under the revised conditions.

2   **Elimination of set-up times** – the purchase of additional equipment (see Exhibit 13) means that set-ups will be eliminated.

3   **Reduced tooling costs** – the elimination of tool changes (see 2 above) means that some SKr 36,000 of tool damages per year would also be eliminated.

4   **Raw material inventory** – it has been agreed to change the call-off arrangements with suppliers. Materials (and particularly the high value items) are to be delivered more frequently. However, it is intended to hold raw material inventory steady even though sales revenue will increase in the next year by 44 per cent. Later it is intended that the supplier delivers some items (particularly the high value items) directly to the line on a daily basis.

5   **Work-in-progress inventory** – with the reduction of batch sizes from five to one, work-in-progress inventory will be reduced to SKr 36,000.

6   **Finished goods inventory** – the orientation of the company from a make-to-stock to a make-to-order approach will result in the finished goods inventory ceiling being reduced from a high of 1750 units (equivalent to SKr 10,500,000) to a maximum of 300 units (equivalent to SKr 1,800,000).

7   **Floor space** – the change in order quantities from five to one will result in a 50 per cent saving in floor space (see Exhibit 8).

8   **Distance travelled by a typical product** – resulting from the floor space gains, the product in future will travel 65 as opposed to 112 metres (see Exhibits 4 and 8).

Exhibit 13 Additional equipment investment

As part of the shop floor changes, the following additional equipment was purchased in order to reduce material movements, the time of operations and the number of set-ups involved

Equipment description		#	Costs (SKr)	
			Per unit	Total
Folding machine		1	30,000	30,000
Roller		1	18,000	18,000
Punches	small	3	7,200	21,600
	large	1	9,600	9,600
Fly presses		2	9,600	19,200
Air test unit		1	18,000	18,000
Jenny		1	1,200	1,200
Lifting table		1	18,000	18,000
Create test area, introduce racking/storage bins and other layout changes		1	12,000	12,000
Total		12	–	147,600

Hunting Swift

Hunting Swift (HS) manufactures a range of pumps and turbines for the petrochemical industry. The current product range consists of 20 basic units offered in a total of 110 sizes (that is, some five sizes per unit) and, on average, each size can be manufactured in up to 10 different materials. All products are manufactured to the very precise standards of the American Petroleum Institute in order for HS to avail itself of world export markets and the rigorous international requirements of the industry.

Typically a unit consists of some 350 parts, of which about 120 require some machining. The other 230 are bought-out components which go into the final assembly. The machining processes within the company comprise 21 work centres such as centre lathes, turners, millers, drills and borers. The machining requirements of the different parts vary greatly from as little as a single operation of three minutes on one work centre to as high as a total of 13 hours on some 8–10 operations spread over seven work centres. About 65 per cent of machined parts are common to more than one type of end-product and in a typical year there are 1000 of these common parts, the cumulative demand for which exceeded 28,000 items (see Exhibit 1). Once all the materials are on site, the majority of the manufacturing process time is taken up in the machine shop.

HS submits tenders to the major oil companies and civil engineering contractors who design and build petrochemical plants. The order quantities are small, with a maximum of four similar units on any one order. Total unit sales in recent years have risen to about 280 for all pumps. A similar quantity is anticipated for the coming year. The delivery time offered to customers for a typical unit is six months, with some suppliers quoting three-month delivery on castings. At the other end of the delivery spectrum, some small items are held in stock or are same-day delivery.

Exhibit 1 Typical demand patterns for common parts

Demand for parts	# parts	# items
0–10	488	1,939
11–20	213	2,912
21–50	168	5,112
51–100	78	5,420
101–200	30	3,894
201–300	11	2,543
301–500	7	2,757
501–1000	5	3,653
Total	1000	28,230

The products supplied by HS have a long life and consequently generate a significant demand for spares. For instance, in the last full year there were 300 orders for spares. These orders were for 1400 different parts with, typically, several different parts on each order. When the order quantities for each part were totalled, they exceeded 12,000 items and accounted for about 50 per cent of the total sales revenue. The typical delivery time for spare parts was also quoted as six months where many machining operations were required. Other parts (for example small components where the quantities required were high but they were either bought-out or require little machining) were quoted two to three months for delivery.

Questions

1 What are the critical operations scheduling features?

2 What is the key operations scheduling task?

3 Outline the development of a suitable scheduling system for the business.

The Ipswich Hospital NHS Trust

The head of pharmacy at the Ipswich Hospital set the scene:

> It all began after attending a one-day course on 'Quality for Hospital Pharmacists' This not only fired me up but also confirmed that the problems we faced and opportunities that we had were not, by any means, unique. But, more importantly, it provided a way forward. It offered an approach which was easy to explain and made sense in practice. Since that time all the staff have attended a similar programme, and continuous improvement teams have been formed. Initial work has started and progress in other areas is under way. We all believe this to be a sustainable initiative as it is core to the tasks and services we provide.

Background

The Ipswich Hospital NHS Trust is a large hospital on the edge of the town with over 800 beds. In a typical 12-month period, the hospital handles more than 100,000 inpatients and new outpatients, with follow-up outpatients (existing outpatients seen a second, third and more times) totalling about a further 150,000 visits. There are currently nine medical directorates for which wards are allocated in line with inpatient demand (see Exhibit 1).

Exhibit 1 General hospital information

Directorates		# wards/specialist units
General	medicine	7
	surgery	6
Elderly services		6
Maternity and gynaecology		6[1]
Trauma and orthopaedics		4
Paediatrics		2
Specialist surgery		1
Oncology and haematology		1
Anaesthetics		1[1]

Note   1   Includes a specialist unit.

The pharmacy department offers a range of core and non-core services to the rest of the hospital (see Exhibit 2). These are typically provided during weekdays between 8.30 am and 5.30 pm, with an additional on-call, out-of-hours service. Increasingly, some of the services are provided on the wards or in other areas within the hospital. This reflects the growing need to give specialist help at the point of provision, the growing range of drugs available, with its attendant diversity, and the subsequent need to recognize and control the side effects of and between different medications.

The continuous improvement initiative

On his return from the one-day course 'Quality for Hospital Pharmacists', the head of pharmacy discussed the potential use of these ideas and approaches with the senior pharmacists in the department. The decision to undertake this initiative was agreed in principle and arrangements for all staff (pharmacists, technicians, assistants and clerical) to attend a similar day's training on quality were concluded. The costs for this training were met by all the major drug companies. To accommodate the need for releasing staff, three one-day courses were arranged, with about one-third of the staff (see Exhibit 3) attending at a time.

The head of pharmacy explained:

> The initiative itself, its department-wide scope and the fact that everyone went through the same one-day programme were a real help in getting everyone on board. In addition, there was one unforeseen advantage. This came from the need for everyone to cooperate in order to cope with the normal workload in the pharmacy department on the days when the programmes were held, as only two-thirds of the staff were here. This, in many ways, increased the level of cooperation so essential for the success of this type of initiative.

Exhibit 2 Pharmacy department information

1 Core services – the following services are provided for all directorates:

	Activities
Supply	● inpatient dispensing ● outpatient dispensing ● discharge prescription dispensing ● distribution ● portering
Procurement	● purchasing ● invoice reconciliation ● clerical ● financial data provision
Clinical	● drug information ● prescription monitoring ● patient counselling ● stock 'top up' ● ward stock control ● therapeutic drug level ● monitoring
Manufacturing	● licensable manufacturing ● prepackaged drugs ● resuscitation box ● provision ● quality control ● extemporaneous dispensing

2 Non-core services – the following services are provided to some but not all the directorates:

● ward round participation
● directorate liaison role
● self-medication scheme
● centralized intravenous additive scheme (CIVAS)
● cytotoxic drug reconstitution
● education and training to nursing and other healthcare staff

Exhibit 3 Pharmacy department staff and SIT members

1 Pharmacy department staff

Grade	# FTEs[1]
Pharmacists	13.5
Technicians	16.0
Assistants	5.0
Clerical	3.5

2 Section improvement team (SIT) members

Clinical services

Pharmacy manager	1
Pharmacists	2
Technicians	1
CIP coordinator	1

Manufacturing

Pharmacists	2
Technicians	3
CIP coordinator	1

Dispensing

Pharmacists	2
Technicians	3
CIP coordinator	1

Stores and distribution

Pharmacy resource Manager	1
Technicians	3
CIP coordinator	1

Note   1 Full-time (staff) equivalents.

The 'away days', as the one-day courses were called, covered many aspects including mission statements, role of continuous improvement initiatives, useful techniques to use (for example brainstorming), procedures to follow and how to go forward. On completing the away days, the continuous improvement programme (CIP) was officially launched, with a steering group and four sectional improvement teams (SITs) to organize the programme, identify priorities and set up additional teams to address selected key areas where required (see Exhibit 4). To provide additional momentum, the pharmacist with specific responsibility for quality assurance was given the role as the CIP coordinator. The steering group comprised one member from each SIT, the head of pharmacy and the CIP coordinator.

The CIP coordinator was a member of each SIT in order to provide coordination across the whole activity. Membership of the SITs is given in Exhibit 3.

The SITs' role was to undertake projects themselves, to identify potential areas for improvement and suggest a team to undertake the task. This would be chosen from all the staff within the department to reflect existing workloads, the CIP itself and the knowledge of and involvement in the issues under review.

Many of the improvements were simple in nature, easy to implement and yet provided a clear sign to all of what could be achieved. An example

Exhibit 4 Steering group and the four SITs

Steering group: pharmacy improvement team

| Clinical services | Dispensing | Manufacturing | Stores and distribution |

from each of the SITs is provided below to illustrate the type of problems reviewed and the improvements undertaken:

- **Clinical services** – the provision of ward visits by pharmacists had developed over several years. This involved prescription monitoring, drug information provision, patient counselling as well as the drug supply function. However, on checking it was clear that the service provided to the wards varied according to the pharmacist involved. The team, therefore, drafted and agreed standards for these clinical pharmacy activities in order to raise standards and allow performance to be audited.

- **Dispensing** – the basic procedure within the dispensary is to dispense drugs for both in-patients and outpatients. The initial dispensing is typically undertaken by dispensing technicians, with the final check completed by a pharmacist.

  As pharmacists working in the dispensary were involved in several tasks (for example giving advice to medical staff, ward staff and outpatients), the benches on which dispensed prescriptions were held awaiting a final check very often became congested. The team suggested plastic trays to separate prescriptions and thereby simplifying checking. These trays were also colour coded to indicate the level of urgency involved and hence enable priorities to be set.

- **Manufacturing** – staff rotate in the manufacturing department on a three-month basis. Some staff may only be seconded to this department

once a year. In order to help refresh and/or update staff on the basic rules of 'good manufacturing practice', a document was compiled containing basic information and highlighting any procedures that have been recently revised.

- **Stores and distribution** – out-of-date stock was analysed in terms of value and cause. As a result, stock levels of individual items were adjusted, a regular review of expensive items was installed and a weekly monitoring of any stock with a short shelf life was initiated.

Reviewing problems

As well as the one-day programmes on quality arranged for all staff, supporting documents were distributed and discussion sessions were held on what to do and the next steps to take. The CIP coordinator explained:

> In the early days it was more necessary to give a lead on translating the ideas into a way of working and helping groups to begin identifying and resolving improvement ideas. Part of the approach was to categorize problems into one of three types [see Exhibit 5].

To help start the programme the section teams chose internal type 1 problems as they were easy to implement. The four examples given earlier were typical of these. However, we have broadened the scope of the problem types to include more complex but, hopefully, more rewarding improvement opportunities. Two of these on which initial information has been gathered are to improve the effectiveness of the portering service, the procedures to handle the return of non-stock drugs to the pharmacy department and also the procedures used to recycle and redistribute them.

The porters' problem

A group was set up to look at the effective use of the porters' time. The team comprised one person from each of the four SITs, the two departmental porters and the CIP coordinator. Requests for items to be dispensed for inpatients are made in one of three ways:

- stock items for wards where orders arrive in a black box via one of the porters
- non-stock items for individual patients
- medication requests for patients who have been discharged and will go back to their own home.

Exhibit 5 Categories of problems

Problem type		Description
Internal	1	Concerning only one section in the pharmacy department
	2	Concerning two or more sections in the pharmacy department
External		Involves one or more departments outside the pharmacy department

The latter two types of request come directly from a ward, via a ward pharmacist or in a ward's red bag via one of the porters.

Drugs and other items that wards require are distributed as follows. Requirements for these items are either requested by a ward or listed by pharmacists on their ward rounds:

- *Bulk fluid items* (for example one litre bags of dextrose and sodium chloride) are taken by two technical assistants who go round from ward to ward in line with stated needs.

- *Black boxes* are used to transport stock items to wards and departments. These orders are given out in bulk form (that is, not broken down into quantities for individual patients). These boxes are also used by a ward as a means of returning unused drugs to the pharmacy department.

- *Red bags* are used to transport non-stock orders and dispensed medication to and from wards. Several deliveries of red bags are made in a single day from the dispensary.

Requests for urgently needed drugs were often telephoned through and nursing staff would then bring down the relevant prescription and collect the drugs. Most prescriptions, however, were collected by the pharmacy department porters using the red bag system and distributed either later that day or the next day. As a general rule, 15 per cent of all requests for 'urgent drugs' were required immediately, 80 per cent for delivery that day and 5 per cent the following day.

The principal role of the porters was to collect boxes/bags containing drug requests from the various wards and clinics, return these to the pharmacy department and distribute the boxes/bags later that day with the dispensed drugs inside. Pharmacy staff (including the porters) believed that a more efficient use could be made of the porters' working day 'to improve the service given to internal customers (within the department) and external customers (within the hospital)'. Over a period of several months, data were collected on the work undertaken and service provided by the porters, details of which are given in Exhibit 6. In addition, a fishbone analysis was prepared showing where porters' time was not efficiently used, a copy of which is provided as Exhibit 7, with accompanying notes provided as Exhibit 8.

As explained earlier, in addition to the collection and delivery service provided by the portering staff, wards, theatres and other units need drugs and other medicines on a more urgent basis and, therefore, cannot wait for the next scheduled delivery by the porters. In these instances, nursing staff telephone the department with the request and later collect the items personally or they are delivered by other pharmacy staff as needs be. This happened throughout the day and Exhibit 9 shows the aver-

---

Exhibit 6 Tasks undertaken and service provided by pharmacy department porters

General information

The pharmacy department employs two porters whose prime task is to collect the empty boxes and bags used to distribute drugs around the hospital and deliver these back to the wards, theatres and special units when the required drugs have been dispensed. Controlled drugs (for example pethidine and morphine) and other drugs are handled in the same way except that controlled drugs have to be signed for on receipt by one of the nursing staff on the relevant ward. The two porters share the wards. The split reflects the distances involved and size of the wards in terms of average number of patients and range of illnesses (for example intensive care units vis-à-vis an orthopaedic ward). All wards have one red bag and one black box which are marked with the name of the ward.

The daily routine

1 Boxes and bags are collected between 08.00 and 09.30 each day. The pharmacy staff then dispense requests from each ward.

2 At around 10.45 one set of boxes is delivered. The remaining wards' boxes are delivered from 11.30.

3 Any controlled drug requests are delivered in the morning rounds, with additional requirements being met in the afternoon.

4 Between 13.45 and 14.30, the porters again collect the bags from the wards and the morning procedure is replicated, with the afternoon deliveries (which are typically fewer) taking place between 16.00 and 17.00.

5 In between the collecting and delivering parts of their task, the two porters undertake general work around the department and also make journeys to deliver the one-off requests for drugs and other medicines when available.

Exhibit 7   Fishbone analysis completed on 'why the porters' time is not used effectively'

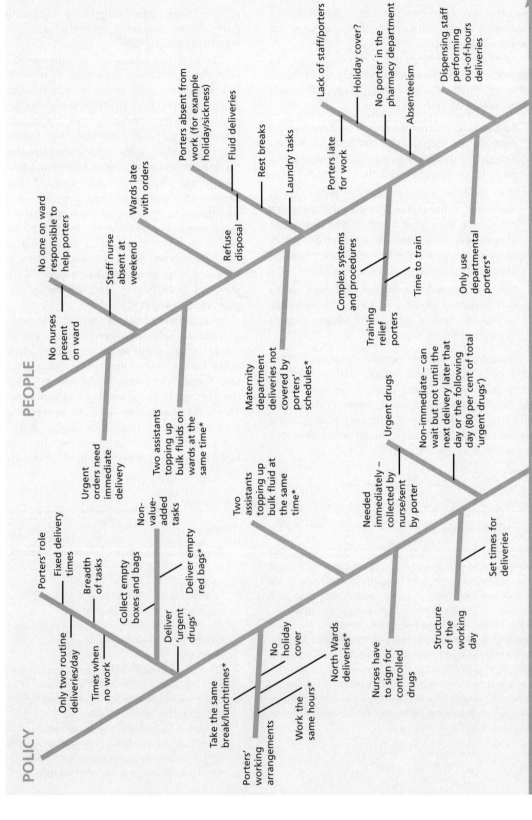

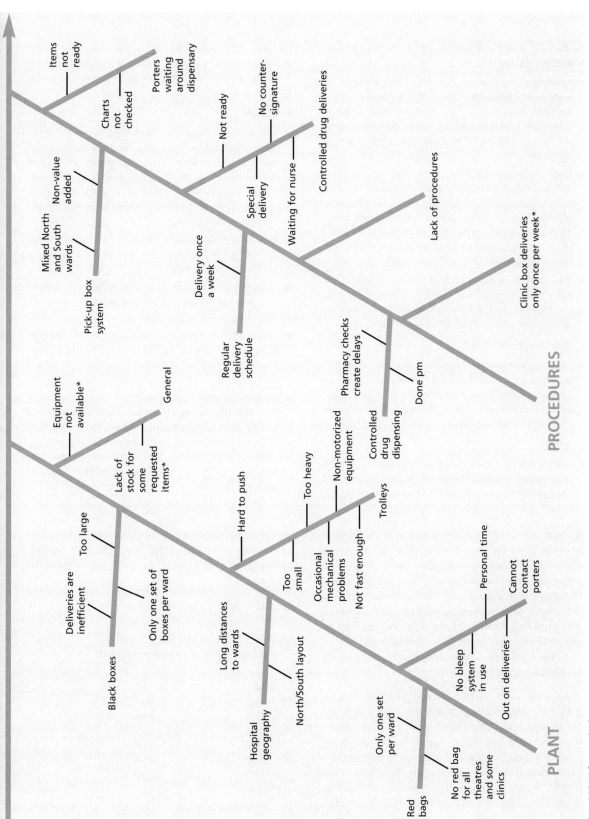

PLANT

PROCEDURES

Items not ready

Porters waiting around dispensary

Charts not checked

No counter-signature

Not ready

Controlled drug deliveries

Non-value added

Mixed North and South wards

Special delivery

Waiting for nurse

Lack of procedures

Pick-up box system

Delivery once a week

Clinic box deliveries only once per week*

Equipment not available*

General

Regular delivery schedule

Pharmacy checks create delays

Done pm

Lack of stock for some requested items*

Hard to push

Too heavy

Non-motorized equipment

Controlled drug dispensing

Too large

Too small

Occasional mechanical problems

Not fast enough

Trolleys

Deliveries are inefficient

Only one set of boxes per ward

Long distances to wards

Personal time

Cannot contact porters

Black boxes

Hospital geography

North/South layout

No bleep system in use

Out on deliveries

Only one set per ward

Red bags

No red bag for all theatres and some clinics

*See Exhibit 8 for more details

Exhibit 8 Notes on Exhibit 7

1 PEOPLE ISSUES

● **Maternity department deliveries not covered by porters' schedules** – the porters do not deliver or collect from this department as part of their normal schedule. Consequently, the pharmacy department does not schedule the timing of deliveries or collections to the maternity department.

● **Only use department porters** – the current policy is to use only pharmacy department porters to undertake the distribution and collection service described in the case study narrative. Previously, when short, porters from other departments or those with general hospital duties were used but, due to a lack of knowledge and experience of the tasks, this alternative is no longer used.

● **Two assistants topping up bulk fluids on wards at the same time** – currently, two assistants visit the wards to top up or replenish the bulk fluid stocks. It is considered that only one assistant is necessary to undertake this task.

2 PROCEDURES

● **Clinic box delivered only once per week** – certain deliveries are made just once a week, whereas all others are completed every day. The once-a-week deliveries present planning difficulties because of the existing tight schedules to complete all the daily tasks.

3 PLANT

● **Lack of stock for some requested items** – relates to the pharmacy department not having sufficient inventory so that it can meet ward and other requests on an 'on-demand' basis.

● **Equipment not available** – on review it was found that the equipment (for example boxes) was only checked at the time of use.

4 POLICY

● **Two assistants topping up bulk fluids on wards at the same time** – the pharmacy department provides a 'top-up' service for bulk fluid items (for example one-litre bags of dextrose and sodium chloride) which does not require technical know-how to complete. Also, this task was noted under section 1 of this exhibit, entitled 'People Issues', but presenting a different dimension.

● **Take the same break/lunchtimes** – the porters' work schedule includes starting at the same time and taking the same break and lunchtimes.

● **Work the same hours** – as mentioned above, the porters' work schedules include starting and finishing at the same time.

● **Deliver empty red bags** – porters occasionally have to deliver empty red bags to a ward so that the ward can put its waste into a bag for collection by a porter. There is only one red bag per ward.

● **North Ward deliveries** – deliveries to the North Ward are made first. However, as clinical pharmacists visit these words later in the day, many of the dispensed items required by these wards were not known or completed in time for the porters' delivery. This then necessitated a second delivery, as the drugs would fall under the 'non-immediate' category of 'urgent drugs'.

---

age number of calls that led to a delivery/collection by other than the two porters. The figures given here are based on a representative four-week period.

Certain drugs in general use (for example paracetamol, aspirin and some antibiotics) were kept on each ward. The dispensing of these was handled and controlled by the nursing staff and requests to 'top up' levels were made on a regular basis.

As the lead person of the improvement team on this review explained:

> Although most requests are adequately dealt with by the current arrangements, the nature of medicine and hospital service is that there are many requests and the demand from wards and other units is, understandably, ongoing through the day [the data given in Exhibit 9 show the extent of the calls]. What we also discovered when analysing this 'other' demand was that as many as 60 per cent of

the requirements are not needed immediately but cannot wait until the next porters' round. However, if we could increase the number of

Exhibit 9 Number of calls by nursing staff for urgently needed drugs and other medicines that were collected by nursing staff or delivered by pharmacy department staff when a porter was not available

Time of day	# calls by nursing staff
0830–0930	3.1
0930–1030	6.9
1030–1130	10.0
1130–1230	10.2
1230–1330	29.5
1330–1430	22.0
1430–1530	16.4
1530–1630	6.6
1630–1730	32.4
1730 onwards	26.8

porters' deliveries, the intermittent demand would reduce noticeably.

The lead person of this SIT then explained that although there is much pressure on the dispensing aspect of the department's work, fitting in an additional delivery schedule would not add to the total dispensing workload. 'In fact, the very opposite as "formal" demands would replace the "informal" nature of these requirements and at the same time take away some of the urgency associated with these requests', she reflected.

The problem of non-stock drugs

As explained earlier, frequently used drugs are normally held by a ward as part of its own stock. Drugs with low and irregular demand are classed as non-stock drugs (that is, not part of the ward stock) and are issued as and when required. The non-stock drugs are generally referred to as 'yellow labels' which refers to their distinctive packaging. The procedure for handling yellow label items is now explained. During the daily ward visits, a pharmacist monitors each patient's drugs chart and requests the supply of any drug not routinely stocked by a ward. The number of tablets to be provided is determined on a sliding scale that reflects the nature of the ward. An initial provision is made and, as the 'run out' time approaches, all the non-stock items for a patient are topped up by a further 8 or 15 days according to each situation. When non-stock drugs are no longer required (for whatever reason), the bottles containing the residue stock are returned to pharmacy.

Because of the high cost of drugs, directorates throughout the hospital were actively looking for ways to reduce costs. Recently, for example, the Elderly Services Directorate had approached the pharmacy department to discuss how they may be able to reduce this element of cost.

Until 18 months ago, non-stock drugs returned to pharmacy would, where possible and where appropriate, be checked, recycled and reissued and the directorate in question credited with the full savings. Loosely packed tablets (that is, those not individually blister packed but dispensed in a bottle) would, for reasons of patient safety, invariably be incinerated, whereas those in blister packs would invariably be recycled and reissued. However, since that time, growing workloads and staff reductions had meant that all non-stock drugs (whether loosely packed or in a blister pack) returned were now incinerated.

To find out the size of the yellow label returns, in terms of drug costs and the time involved for a pharmacy technician to check and restock the returns, an analysis of all non-stock returns was made over a four-week period. This also involved reintroducing the practice of checking and, where possible, recycling the drugs in question. Details of this study are given in Exhibit 10 (over the page), and these data provide a representative sample of the returns made. Based on the yellow labels returned from five of the wards in the Elderly Services Directorate and whether or not they could be recycled, the annual value of all non-stock tablets returned for the whole hospital was estimated at about £45,000.

To reduce the cost of yellow label returns, the team recognized the need to address both causes and symptoms. The reasons were identified by the elderly care standards group working with the pharmacy continuous improvement team selected to address this problem. They identified the following reasons why yellow labels were returned:

- patient discharged
- drugs discontinued
- patient's death
- duplicate supply on the ward
- patients transferred to another ward, but the drugs were not sent with them.

In order to identify the causes, the nursing staff recorded the reason why any yellow label tablets were returned. The results are shown in Exhibit 11.

The analysis also examined the issues behind each of these reasons, the results of which are given in Exhibit 12.

Exhibit 11 Reasons for yellow label returns

Reasons		Per cent of total
Discontinued use of drug		39
Patient	discharged	41
	died	9
	transferred	6
Duplicate supply		1
Other		4
Total		100

Exhibit 10 An analysis of a representative sample of all yellow label returns from five elderly care wards during a typical four-week period

The following details are for a representative sample of all yellow label returns received from five elderly care wards during a typical four-week period – a total of 20 days.

1 The time involved by pharmacy technician staff includes a 15 per cent uplift to cover starting and finishing the procedure and normal rest allowance.

2 The total value of the drugs recycled in this period was 68 per cent of all the drugs returned. The other 32 per cent were considered not suitable for reuse and were incinerated for reasons of safety.

3 On several days in this four week period there were no returns recorded. The sample opposite was chosen to reflect typical recycled yellow label values and the time needed to recycle these items by a pharmacy technician.

| Day # in the four-week period | Yellow labels | | | Pharmacy technician time to recycle the item (minutes) |
| | Total # returned | Recycled items only | | |
		#	Total value (£s)	
1	13	11	66.49	12
	7	7	25.03	14
	9	5	21.04	18
	10	10	15.16	12
5	20	8	44.04	13
	7	5	9.52	10
	18	14	50.64	15
8	7	4	7.97	6
	14	13	24.74	18
	4	1	0.49	4
	15	14	33.40	35
	2	2	6.19	12
10	12	6	48.65	9
	7	1	0.63	15
	2	0	–	2
11	6	5	18.18	14
	5	3	7.64	5
	8	7	43.79	7
16	26	9	17.19	40
	8	2	2.17	6
	9	3	1.37	16
	6	1	0.10	8
20	38	26	125.25	55
	22	13	47.25	50
	17	10	12.40	15
	31	28	187.56	65

Exhibit 12 Reasons why yellow labels are returned

Discussion around the reasons why yellow labels are returned provided the following information:

1 **Drugs discontinued** – this was always the result of a doctor's decision to change a patient's drugs for medical reasons.

2 **Patient discharged** – when patients were discharged, the non-stock drugs that they were taking would always be returned to the pharmacy department. The hospital specialist responsible for a patient would then prescribe the same or some of the same items to take home. The reason for this procedure was to ensure control and avoid patients taking medicines which may have been appropriate during their hospital stay, but not in the post-hospital phase of their treatment. It was considered that, because of the risks, the associated need to control drug prescription could not and should not be changed.

3 **Patient transferred** – this is where a patient was transferred from one ward/unit to another inside the hospital.

4 **Duplicate supply** – drugs already held on the ward, but their availability had not been identified.

5 **The sliding scale** – the normal procedure was to issue a further 8 or 15 days' supply of a non-stock drug two days before the current supply would be used up. The choice of 8 or 15 days was based on a one- and two-week timescale.

The CIP review

The head of pharmacy explained:

Although it is not many months since this programme started, the results are very encouraging. Staff involvement is high and we have attempted to keep a 'sensible' level of activity to maintain interest and yet create a manageable load. The porters and yellow label analyses are an important departure as it is spreading the initiative across the department and the hospital at the same time. This not only presents an opportunity for larger savings but also helps to further integrate the pharmacy department's activities into the hospital as a whole and link us more firmly with our external customers and their needs. Here's hoping that the latest two initiatives will yield sizeable and realizable results. That would be a big boost for us all.

www.ipswichhospital.org.uk

Questions

1 Examine the approach used to introduce the continuous improvement programme within the pharmacy department at the Ipswich Hospital and comment.

2 Review the 'porters' problem' and that of 'non-stock drugs' detailed in the case study. What advice would you offer?

Lloyds TSB

In the early 1980s, the UK bank Lloyds TSB was struggling to meet its financial targets and the promises that it had made to its shareholders. It was a difficult situation needing radical change. As Brian Pitman (the CEO at the time) explains:

> The turning point came in 1986, when we decided to sell our retail banking operation in California. Our bank acquisition there in 1974 had been hailed as healthy diversification away from our UK home market, and many of our executives still viewed Lloyds Bank California as a crucial foothold in a state with one of the world's largest, most affluent and fast-growing economies. The problem was that, however appealing the market, we had absolutely no competitive advantage there. Our market share was negligible and we were in no position to compete with giants like the Bank of America.

This was the first of a number of activities over the next couple of decades that resulted in turning the business around, increasing its market capitalization fortyfold and delivering an average annual shareholder return of 26 per cent, a rate that not only outpaced its UK banking rivals but also put it in a league with market stars such as Coca-Cola, GE and Gillette.

To many people the decision to sell off the California operation may have implied weak management. But the reality was that it was not earning back its cost of equity and thus not contributing to the overall value of the business. In fact, as the outcome showed, it was a sound decision. A Japanese bank paid over the odds for it and the Lloyds TSB share price rose overnight. For Pitman and his team, this experience was a defining one. It showed them that managing a business involves making some difficult and often testing decisions. But at the same time it also revealed the benefit of setting a course and sticking to it, a belief that grew stronger over the following years as they changed the business direction from sales growth to profitability. As Pitman now reflects:

> We couldn't believe how well this decision went for us. It proved that we were starting off down the right track. However, we soon realized that creating change in a business is not simply about putting in place some new performance metric or a new accounting method. We had to work hard to get people to change their beliefs and put in the appropriate infrastructure and delivery systems necessary to change. Only then would we have created a significant and sustainable improvement.

Setting the objective of the business

When Pitman arrived at Lloyds in 1983, his initial task was to get the whole company to agree on what constituted success. Initially, consensus had to be reached by the board members of the organization and then later with the management team that would create the transformation and implement the change. Only when the objectives of the business were understood could appropriate strategies be determined and actions put in place.

As Pitman reflects:

> I want to emphasize that I didn't have a hidden agenda here; I didn't know myself what the right answer was. But I did want to be sure we came up with a single definition of success and a single means of measuring it. Without this clarity, I feared that we would muddle along, with our efforts diluted by the pursuit of multiple goals.

The objective of the discussions with other board members was to create a single, well-defined performance measure that would replace the existing array of implicit objectives currently being used to manage the business. The continual belief was that with a single objective, you are much more likely to get coordinated and concentrated action.

This case study was written by Alex Hill (University of Kingston). It is intended as the basis for class discussion and not as an example of good or bad management. © AMD Publishing.

They were finding that the current, woolly goals in the business were getting them nowhere as they weren't specific enough to have an effect on people's performance.

The board set about this task during two long, hard meetings. Finally, and somewhat reluctantly, they agreed on a single governing objective of improving shareholder value with return on equity (ROE) as a means of measuring this. The decision to use return on equity as their key measure reflected the fact that not only is this a key indicator of profitability, but it is also one that investors rely on as a measure of how well a company is using its money. The target for this measure was that each business in the group must deliver an ROE that exceeds the cost of equity, which at the time was about 17–19 per cent.

To ensure that the corporate objective of improving shareholder value was consistent throughout the organization, it was linked into how executives were measured and rewarded. Previously, managers' salary increases had been linked to inflation, now they were linked to the ROE of their part of the business and the business as a whole. Before long, the cry 'improve ROE' could be heard all around the organization.

However, it wasn't just top executives who benefited from this change in policy. High performance standards were set for people throughout the organization and they were rewarded when these standards were met. As Brian Pitman comments:

> The metrics varied of course. We didn't tell someone in cheque processing to improve his operation's return on equity. We measured him on something over which he had control, like productivity and accuracy. But, whatever the measure, we made sure it represented at least a small part of the shareholder value puzzle.

And, on top of this, nearly everyone in the company had stock options in Lloyds, not only at senior management level but also throughout the business. Through stock incentive plans, people were able to accumulate a level of capital that would have been impossible through their own savings.

Selecting the right markets

Once people started to accept that profitability was more important than growth within the business, Pitman and his team were able to undertake a major analysis to determine which markets were creating value and which were not. They were astonished to find that only a small proportion of the total business was generating most of the value, while more than half the business was earning less than the cost of capital.

It was this analysis that led them to exit the Californian market, which at 8 per cent ROE was less than half the cost of capital. The decision to move out of the merchant banking business came next, with the realization that it couldn't compete effectively against the big US investment banks, even in their home markets. Closing down the merchant banking operation, although a highly unpopular decision in the business, resulted in a significant improvement in overall company results.

However, not everyone in the business saw the light so quickly! At one point Pitman got so exasperated that he said to people:

> I want you to start your business plan for this year with a list of the businesses we're going to get out of. I don't want you to tell me what we're going to get into. If we don't get out of underperforming businesses, we won't have the resources to invest in the things that will guarantee us a profitable future.

But, slowly, the change started to come and the decision was made to focus the business more on the UK financial services market that consisted of retail banking, mortgages, insurance and investments. Although the traditional retail banking activities that Lloyds had in place at the time were not that profitable, they were seen to provide both a distribution channel and existing customer relationships that would allow it to move into the more lucrative mortgage, insurance and investment segments.

The initial starting point was selling insurance products purely as a broker. However, this proved so successful that the decision was made to acquire Abbey Life. Shortly after this, the acquisition was made of Cheltenham & Gloucester, a building society specializing in home mortgages. In both cases, the companies retained their brands but sold their products through the existing Lloyds branch network. And the merger with TSB later on in 1995 further expanded its distribution capabilities, to the point at which Lloyds TSB now has over 2,000 branches across the UK.

As the marketing director reflects:

> Once the decision had been made to concentrate on UK financial services, we then completed extensive customer research to help us understand what their

drivers are and what they want from a bank. We realized that trust in our brand name and our existing relationships with customers meant we could sell more products in this market. Part of our strategy has, therefore, been to acquire and retain higher value customers by expanding our customer relationship management capabilities and developing tailored offerings for key segments. We introduced a number of new products and services such as the Createcard and the Premier credit card and the Lloyds TSB branded gas, electricity and home telephone products. Another success has been our wealth management facility that provides a tailored service to our most affluent customers. Given the increasingly competitive nature of the UK financial services market, it is important that we continue to find new and innovative products that add value for our customers.

An outline of the products that the bank sells into each of its markets is shown in Exhibit 1.

Creating the right culture

At the heart of all the improvements made is the change in culture within the business. As Pitman reflects:

For people to become truly committed to a strategy, they have to believe in it. In our case, they had to believe that profitability was more important than sales growth. They also had to believe in the importance of concentrating on those businesses with profit potential and selling the others. If they adopt such convictions, and don't simply pay lip service to them, it will change the way the business operates.

However, the reshaping didn't occur without huge resistance. Individuals' beliefs are hard to change and the adoption of a management philosophy imposes a tough discipline on the whole business. People had to accept that it was right for the company to get smaller, stay closer to home and concentrate on unglamorous products like mortgages and insurance, while exiting more prestigious services such as investment banking and currency trading. This proved difficult. There was great resistance to shedding unprofitable customers and products, getting out of unprofitable markets and closing unprofitable facilities.

As Pitman concludes:

In getting people to focus on anything, you can't impose a mind-set. It emerges from a learning

process in which they become persuaded that an objective is worthwhile and then apply their talents to realizing it. The process often involves heated debate; indeed, I find that disagreement is the key to getting agreement. Without disagreement, people simply fall into line with no real commitment to the change programme. What's important is getting people to arrive at a meeting of minds around a small number of central beliefs, which will determine their behaviour and ultimately the company's performance. And you don't do this by being a dictator. You do this by leading people on a journey of learning that will reveal to everyone new insights about how to create value for your shareholders.

Making the change

Once the direction of the business had been set, the markets selected and the product portfolio defined, the next stage was to make the change happen. The first step was to convince people that the change was right, but then the operations changes in the business had to be made. As the operations director comments:

We knew that we wanted to concentrate on the UK financial services and increase the number of services that we sold into this market. But the answers to the questions of how to deliver these services and how to structure the operations of the business were still unknown. Based on the customer research conducted, it was clear that while our branch network gave us a significant advantage over many of our competitors, we also needed to develop other systems for delivering services to our customers. The first step was to set up telephone banking and our internet banking service followed shortly after. They both proved to be highly successful. In fact, last year the usage of our telephony channel increased by a further 29 per cent, some 260 million transactions were processed over the internet and direct sales through these channels represented nearly 40 per cent of the total for the year.

As well as setting up the new delivery systems, significant changes had to be made to the infrastructure of the business. As the operations director explains:

The sale of the business in California meant that certain facilities and operations had to be closed down. At the same time, significant work was done developing new areas, such as the call centres for telephone and internet banking, and merging the

Exhibit 1 Lloyds TSB services and products within its different markets

Services and products in UK retail banking and mortgages

Services and products	Detail
Current accounts, savings and investment accounts, and consumer lending	The retail branches of Lloyds TSB bank offer a broad range of branded products and C&G provides retail investments through its branch network and a postal investment centre
Card services	The bank provides a range of card-based products and services, including credit and debit cards and card transaction processing services for retailers. The Group is a member of both the VISA and Master-Card payment systems and is the third largest credit card issuer in the UK
Cash machines	The Group has one of the largest cash machine networks of any leading banking group in the UK and personal customers of Lloyds TSB Bank are able to withdraw cash, check balances and obtain mini statements through 4,210 cashpoint machines at branches and external locations around the country. In addition, it has access to a further 37,000 cash machines via LINK in the UK and to cash machines worldwide through the VISA and MasterCard networks
Telephone banking	Telephone banking continues to grow and the Group provides one of the largest telephony services in Europe. At the end of 2002, 3.2 million customers had registered to use the services of PhoneBank and the automated voice response service PhoneBank Express
Internet banking	Internet banking provides online banking facilities for personal and business customers and enables them to conduct their financial affairs without using the branch network. Over 1.9 million customers have registered to use the Group's internet banking services
Business banking	Small businesses are served by dedicated business managers based in some 450 locations throughout the UK. Customers have access to a wide range of tailored business services from traditional banking products through factoring, insurance and investments to non-financial solutions to their business problems, for example the debtor management service, providing legal support to help customers recover debts, and prospect finder, providing customers with a tailored list of potential customers for their business. Lloyds TSB is one of the leading banks for new business start-ups, with around one in five opening accounts with the Group
UK wealth management	Private banking provides a range of tailor-made wealth management services and products to individuals from 40 offices throughout the UK. In addition to asset management, these include tax and estate planning, executor and trustee services, deposit taking and lending, insurance, and personal equity plan and ISA products. At the end of 2002, client funds under management totalled some £10 billion
Lloyds TSB Stockbrokers	Lloyds TSB Stockbrokers undertakes retail stockbroking through its Sharedeal Direct telephone service
Cheltenham & Gloucester	Cheltenham & Gloucester is the Group's specialist residential mortgage provider, selling its mortgages through branches of C&G and Lloyds TSB bank in England and Wales, as well as through the telephone, internet and postal service, C&G TeleDirect. The Group is the third largest residential market lender in the UK, with a market share of 9.3 per cent, loans outstanding at the end of 2002 of £62.5 billion and over 980,000 borrowers

Services and products in insurance and investment

Services and products	Detail
Scottish Widows	Scottish Widows is the Group's specialist provider of life assurance, pensions and investment products, which are distributed through the Lloyds TSB branch network, through independent financial advisors and directly to the consumer via the telephone, internet and face to face
General insurance	Lloyds TSB General Insurance provides general insurance and broking services through the retail branches of Lloyds TSB and C&G, and through a direct telephone operation and the internet. The business is the market leader in the distribution of household insurance in the UK
Scottish Widows Investment Partnership	Scottish Widows Investment Partnership manages funds for the Group's retail life, pensions and investment products. Clients also include corporate pension schemes, local authorities and other institutions in the UK and overseas. At the end of 2002 funds under management totalled some £70 billion

continued

Exhibit 1 (continued)

Services and products within wholesale markets

Services and products	Detail
Treasury	Treasury is a leading participant in the sterling money market. It is active in currency money markets, foreign exchange markets and also in certain derivatives markets to meet the needs of customers, and as part of the Group's trading activities, including liquidity management
Corporate	Corporate provides a wide range of banking and related services, including electronic banking, large value lease finance, share registration, venture capital, correspondent banking and capital markets services to major UK and multinational companies, financial institutions and, through a network of dedicated offices, to medium-sized businesses in the UK
Asset finance	Through the Lloyds TSB commercial finance, Alex Lawrie and autolease brands Lloyds is a market leader in invoice discounting, factoring and contract hire. The Black Horse branded point of sale finance operation has leading positions in the motor, motorbike and caravan markets. Specialist personal lending, store credit, small/medium ticket leasing and the recently acquired Dutton-Forshaw motor dealership complete this group of businesses

Services and products within international banking

Services and products	Detail
The Americas	The Group has operated in the Americas for over 130 years and has offices in Argentina, Colombia and six other countries. In addition there are private banking and investment operations in the United States
New Zealand	The National Bank of New Zealand is the country's second largest bank and provides a full range of banking services through some 160 outlets
Europe	The Group has private banking operations for wealthy individuals outside their country of residence. The business is conducted through Switzerland and four other countries overseas. There are additional corporate and private banking operations in Belgium, Netherlands, France and Spain
Offshore banking	Offshore banking comprises all the Group's offices in the Channel Islands and Isle of Man providing a full range of retail banking, private banking, trust and financial services to overseas residents and islanders, together with deposit services offshore for UK residents
Middle East and Asia	There are banking operations in Hong Kong, Singapore, Tokyo, Malaysia and Dubai

business with the activities gained through the acquisition of Abbey Life and C&G. However, these are not just one-off actions. We are continually looking to further improve the efficiency of the business. As a result, we have recently decided to establish an operational centre in India, and are continually exploring the scope of outsourcing and moving more processes offshore.

The future

Brian Pitman has now retired, but the values he created are still present in the business's objectives and strategic direction for the future. As his successor Maarten van den Bergh states:

The business environment in which we operate is characterized by increasing levels of competition, volatile equity markets and increasing government intervention in, and regulation of, the financial services industry. Against this backdrop, we continue to concentrate on our long-standing principles of prudent and sustainable revenue growth from the creation of value for customers, tight management of our cost base and strong credit risk management. Growing our sales revenue is key to sustaining profits over the next few years and we will be investing heavily in our core markets of wealth management, long-term savings and investments, business banking, our core retail franchise and in new technology.

Central to the continued implementation of this strategy is a policy of acquisition and divestment. Only recently Lloyds TSB has acquired Goldfish to further improve its credit card and personal loans portfolio, whilst at the same time selling off its branches in Guatemala, Honduras and Panama to Corporacion UBC International S.A. This is a continuation of its decision to concentrate on the UK financial market, which is now the most significant part of its business, both in terms of sales and profit (see Exhibit 2).   **www.lloydstsb.com**

Exhibit 2 Lloyds TSB financial performance 1988–2002

Summary of financial performance

Measure	Annual financial performance				
	1998	1999	2000	2001	2002
Total income (£m)	7,442	8,318	8,776	8,889	8,878
Operating expenses (£m)	3,876	3,884	4,279	4,776	4,915
Trading surplus (£m)[1]	3,566	4,434	4,497	4,113	3,963
Other costs (£m)[2]	618	905	712	952	1,356
Profit before tax (£m)[3]	2,948	3,529	3,785	3,161	2,607
Dividends per share	22.2	26.6	30.6	33.7	34.2

Notes 1 Trading surplus = Total income – Operating expenses
2 Other costs include aspects such as general insurance claims, bad debt provisions and amounts written off fixed asset investments.
3 Profit before tax = Trading surplus – Other costs

Income by main business 1998–2002

Main business	Income (£m)				
	1998	1999	2000	2001	2002
UK retail banking and mortgages[1]	3,606	4,033	4,105	4,115	4,232
Insurance and investments[2]	1,371	1,736	2,011	1,964	1,766
Wholesale markets	1,379	1,437	1,521	1,837	1,949
International banking	1,086	1,112	1,139	972	931
Total	7,442	8,318	8,776	8,889	8,878

Notes 1 UK retail banking and mortgages consists of the Group's UK retail businesses, providing banking and financial services to personal and small business customers; mortgages; private banking and stockbroking.
2 UK financial services consists of UK retail banking and mortgages and insurance and investments.

Profit by main business 1998–2002

Main business	Profit before tax (£m)				
	1998	1999	2000	2001	2002
UK retail banking and mortgages[1]	1,424	1,657	1,682	1,205	1,172
Insurance and investments[2]	948	873	1,447	1,421	1,231
Wholesale markets	729	728	749	852	626
International banking	434	444	501	357	379
Other items[3]	−587	−173	−594	−674	−801
Total	2,948	3,529	3,785	3,161	2,607

Notes 1 UK retail banking and mortgages consists of the Group's UK retail businesses, providing banking and financial services to personal and small business customers; mortgages; private banking and stockbroking.
2 UK financial services consists of UK retail banking and mortgages and insurance and investments.
3 Other items includes aspects such as: central group items, pension provision, (loss) profit on sale and closure of businesses, write-down of finance leases and restructuring provision.

Number of employees (full-time equivalent) by main business 1998–2002

Main business	# employees (000s)				
	1998	1999	2000	2001	2002
UK retail banking and mortgages[1]	50	49	49	52	48
Insurance and investments[2]	7	7	6	6	6
Wholesale markets	8	8	8	9	11
International banking	14	13	13	12	12
Other	1	1	1	2	2
Total	80	78	77	81	79

Notes 1 UK retail banking and mortgages consists of the Group's UK retail businesses, providing banking and financial services to personal and small business customers; mortgages; private banking and stockbroking.
2 UK financial services consists of UK retail banking and mortgages and insurance and investments.

Questions

1 What are Lloyds TSB's corporate and marketing strategies?

2 What is the operations strategy of the company?

McDonald's Corporation

It is a cold Thursday afternoon in early December in Eastborough, a small town in southern England. Some of the hardy shoppers are busily making day-to-day purchases, with others getting organized for Christmas. The main shopping area is pedestrianized and at the end of the street, shining through the gloomy light, is a bright yellow M indicating the site of one of the town's two McDonald's restaurants.

Through the main entrance the interior is warm and well lit, with a hubbub of activity around the counter area. It is a medium-sized restaurant with seating for 193 people, divided between two floors. The restaurant is open seven days a week, from 7am to midnight.

Asking a few customers why they use McDonald's produces few surprises. An energetic six-year-old nudges his younger sister and declares 'we like the chicken nuggets'. As their mother explains:

> It's convenient at the end of our shopping, right in the town centre. It's not too expensive and the children like the food.

It is not only the food that appeals to the younger generation. The two youngsters dash over to select from a tree laden with balloons and flags to add to the toy they received earlier. The restaurant encourages this idea of the 'McDonald's Experience', with a strong focus on what appeals to children. Children's parties for special occasions, such as birthdays, are regularly catered for and special events, like face painting, are frequently organized. On the previous Mother's Day, daffodils were available for children to give to their mother. On Father's Day phone cards were distributed, so that children could ring the lucky parent.

But the age range using the Eastborough restaurant is wide. As an older couple explain:

> The service is quick and you know what to expect. The quality of the food on this visit will be as good as when we came in last week and the week before.

The themes of knowing what to expect in terms of product quality and speed of service at a reasonable price, in clean and bright surroundings, are reiterated by other customers. Richard and Maurice McDonald laid down the original philosophy shortly after World War II as:

> Everything prepared in advance, everything uniform. All geared to heavy volume in a short amount of time.

The success of the McDonald's approach led to dramatic growth. In 1954 the McDonald brothers first appointed Ray Kroc, the driving force in the expansion of the McDonald's chain, as a franchisee in San Bernadino, California. In 1961 Kroc bought all rights to the McDonald's concept for $63 million. By 1963 the 500th restaurant had opened in the USA and in 1967 the first restaurants were opened in Canada and Puerto Rica. In 1968, the Big Mac was introduced and the 1000th restaurant opened. By 1996 McDonald's had 21,000 restaurants in 101 countries. Sales exceeded $30 billion. In the UK, the first restaurant was opened in 1974 in southeast London. The number in the UK has now risen to 750 outlets employing over 40,000 people, with sales of £1 billion.

Restaurant layout

The Eastborough restaurant layout comprises a seating area, spread across two floors, and a working area (see Exhibit 1). In quiet periods, sections of seating are closed off for cleaning. The seating area is patrolled by dining area hosts/hostesses, whose primary role is to keep the area clean and tidy.

The main sections in the working area (see Exhibit 2), are the

- *Counter* – this restaurant has ten stations for tills
- *Production area* – here food is prepared and held in bins prior to serving to customers

This case study was written by Terry Hill (University of Oxford) Alex Hill (University of Kingston) and R. Lily. It is intended as the basis for class discussion and not as an example of good or bad management. © AMD Publishing.

Exhibit 1 Overall layout of Eastborough restaurant

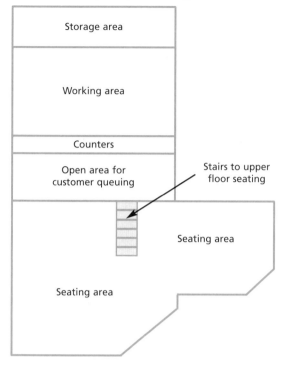

- *Grill area* – where the meat products are grilled
- *Chicken station* – where chicken and fish are cooked.

Serving customers

As a result of competition in the fast-food industry and increasing consumer preference for healthier food, McDonald's has steadily expanded the range of food and drinks provided from the original offering of burgers, drinks and fries (see Exhibit 3) to include breakfast, sandwiches and salads (see Exhibits 4 and 5). In addition to being sold as individual items, many of the products are packaged into special offers, listed as Extra Value Meals. For example, the Big Mac Meal consists of a Big Mac, a drink and a portion of fries. One panel exhorts customers to 'make it large – have large fries and a large soft drink with your Extra Value Meal'. Special promotional items are also added from time to time such as ribs or Mexican chicken.

Customers entering the restaurant typically divide into those who know exactly what they want, and immediately join the shortest queue, and those who stand and study the menu panels for a short period. When the customer reaches the front of the

queue and asks for his food, the counter person employs two selling techniques. The first is known as 'selling up', which involves augmenting the order, by either suggesting a larger portion or an additional item, such as a drink. For example when a customer requests 'hamburger and fries', the counter person responds 'Would you like large fries'?

The other technique is called 'suggestive selling'. Here an order for a 'Big Mac and medium fries' would be greeted by suggesting to a customer the nearest Extra Value Meal alternative (for example a Big Mac Meal) that would cost a little more than the original order but give better overall value. Suggestive selling aims to increase sales as the alternative offered includes additional items, such as drinks or fries.

The counter person punches the order into the till. For the standard items listed below, the food would be available in the bins in the production area:

- Big Mac
- Filet-O-Fish
- Chicken nuggets
- Cheeseburger
- Quarter pounder with cheese
- Hamburger
- Vegetable Deluxe
- Quorn premiere
- Grilled chicken sandwich.

The counter person then picks the food in a set sequence:

- Cold drinks
- Hot drinks
- Fries
- Boxed burgers/sandwiches
- Wrapped burgers/sandwiches.

The drinks machines have a selection of buttons, corresponding to the drink sizes on offer, to dispense the appropriate amount. Different sized serving containers are used for portions of regular, medium and large fries. The sequence for a typical order for a Big Mac, coffee and fries, to eat in the restaurant, is as follows:

- Punch order into the till, as the customer details the items
- Place tray on counter
- Pour coffee and place on tray
- Walk over to fries and fill container
- On way back to counter, take Big Mac from bin
- Place items on tray
- Take the money.

Exhibit 2 Eastborough restaurant working area

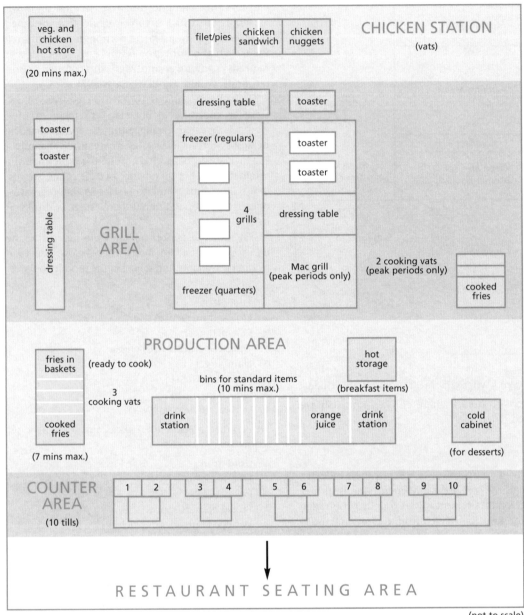

(not to scale)

If an item of food is not available in the production area, the counter person calls the order to the production person who calls the food order to the grill area. The item is then prepared as a priority. In slack periods, certain standard items with low demand are only cooked to order. In the Eastborough restaurant, Filet-O-Fish, Vegetable Deluxe, Chicken Caesar salad, Chicken ranch salad and Garden side salad all fall into this category.

When an order is not immediately available, the counter person takes the money for the order (a till can only deal with one order at a time), asks the customer to stand aside and wait, and starts to deal with the next person in the line. At the server's discretion, the customer is requested to take a seat and the order is brought over by the staff. This might apply to an elderly customer or a parent struggling with several children.

Exhibit 3 Original menu

MAIN MENU

Hamburger – beef patty, regular bun, tomato ketchup, mustard, dehydrated onions, dill pickle slices

Cheeseburger – beef patty, regular bun, cheddar cheese slice (processed), tomato ketchup, mustard, dehydrated onions, dill pickle slices

Double Cheeseburger – beef patty x 2, regular bun, cheddar cheese slice (processed) x 2, tomato ketchup, mustard, dehydrated onions, dill pickle slices

Bacon McDouble with cheese – beef patties x 2, streaky bacon, quarter bun, cheddar cheese slice (processed), tomato ketchup, mustard, dehydrated onions, dill pickle slices

Big Mac – beef patties x 2, Big Mac bun, Big Mac sauce, cheddar cheese slice (processed), lettuce, dehydrated onions, dill pickle slices

Big Tasty – beef patty, Big Tasty bun, Big Tasty sauce, tomato slice, a cheese slice made with Emmental, lettuce

Quarter Pounder with cheese – beef patty, quarter bun, cheddar cheese slice (processed), tomato ketchup, mustard, fresh onions, dill pickle slices

McChicken Premiere – coated chicken patty, focaccia bun, salsa sauce, sour cream and chive sauce, lettuce

McChicken Sandwich – coated chicken patty, McChicken Sandwich bun, sandwich sauce and lettuce

Chicken McNuggets – coated Chicken McNuggets

Chicken Selects – Chicken Selects with either barbeque dip, sweet curry dip, sweet and sour dip or tomato ketchup dip

Filet-O-Fish – fillet portion, regular bun, cheddar cheese slice (processed), tartare sauce

Fish fingers – cod fish fingers

DESSERTS

Apple pie – crispy pie filled with hot apple chunks and apple sauce

DRINKS

- Milkshakes – banana, chocolate, strawberry or vanilla
- Coca-cola – regular and diet
- Fanta orange ▪ Sprite

Exhibit 4 Breakfast menu, extended desserts menu and extended drinks menu

BREAKFAST MENU

English muffin and preserve – English muffin, butter and strawberry jam

Egg McMuffin – egg, butter and cheddar cheese slice in an English muffin

Sausage and Egg McMuffin – pork sausage patty, egg, butter and cheddar cheese slice in an English muffin

Double Sausage and Egg McMuffin – pork sausage patty x 2, egg, butter and cheddar cheese slice in an English muffin

Bacon and Egg McMuffin – streaky bacon, egg, butter and cheddar cheese slice in an English muffin

Double Bacon and Egg McMuffin – streaky bacon x 2, egg, butter and cheddar cheese slice in an English muffin

McBacon Roll – streaky bacon, brown sauce and butter in a roll

Big Breakfast – scrambled eggs, pork sausage patty, hash brown, butter and English muffin

Big Breakfast Bun – scrambled eggs, pork sausage patty, big breakfast bun, cheddar cheese slice, brown sauce

Pancakes with sausage – pancakes, pork sausage patty, butter and pancakes syrup

Hash brown

DESSERTS

Cadbury Chocolate Donut – topped with Cadbury milk chocolate

Yoghurt Burst – strawberry pasteurized low fat yoghurt

McFlurry + Rolo – delicious soft dairy ice cream swirled with pieces of chocolate Rolo and a smooth caramel sauce

McFlurry – soft dairy ice cream whirled with pieces of Nestlé Smarties, Cadbury Crunchie or Cadbury Dairy Milk

McMini – three mini treats: Cadbury Choc Chip Brownie, Cadbury Byte and mini donut topped with Cadbury chocolate

Fruit & Yogurt – Danone yogurt layered with strawberries and topped with blueberries

Fruit Bag – slices of fresh apple and grapes, washed and ready to eat

Ice Cream Cone – Fresh soft dairy vanilla ice cream served in a crunchy cone with a Cadbury 99 Flake

Apples – natural whole apples

DRINKS

- Coffee – cappuccino, latte and ground ▪ Tea
- Hot chocolate ▪ Organic milk (semi-skimmed)
- Pure orange juice

Exhibit 5 Salad plus menu

MAIN MENU – Salad plus

Quorn Premiere – Quorn fillet, foccacia bun, sweet chilli sauce, Hellmann's extra light mayonnaise, sliced tomato and square cut lettuce

Grilled Chicken Sandwich – grilled chicken patty, tomato and olive bun, basil grilled chicken sauce, mozzarella cheese rectangle, sliced tomato, rocket, slivered onion

Chicken Caesar Salad – grilled chicken patty, premiere chicken patty, salad leaf, cherry tomatoes, Italian cheese, dressing for Caesar salad

Chicken Ranch Salad – grilled chicken patty, premiere chicken patty, salad leaf, cherry tomatoes, ranch cheese, Edam cheese, coloured cheddar cheese, salad bacon bits, dressing for ranch salad

Garden Side Salad – salad leaf, balsamic dressing

DESSERTS

Yoghurt Burst – strawberry pasteurised low fat yoghurt

Fruit & Yogurt – Danone yogurt layered with strawberries and topped with blueberries

Fruit Bag – slices of fresh apple and grapes, washed and ready to eat

Apples – natural whole apples

DRINKS

Mineral water
Robinsons fruit shoot

If a customer requests a non-standard item, for example, a Big Mac with no cheese, the counter person identifies the non-standard item when punching the order into the till. This causes a 'grill slip' to be printed at a terminal in the grill area. When the item of food is prepared, the grill slip travels with it to the production area. The production person then calls the counter person to indicate that the order is available.

The restaurant aims not to exceed a maximum time for the customer waiting in line of two minutes and a maximum waiting time of one minute from the order being placed. Periodically, actual performance on waiting times is checked with a stopwatch.

At the Eastborough restaurant, customers eating the food in the restaurant account for 64 per cent of sales. The balance is for takeaways.

Production planning

Production planning is guided by a computer package. The schedule manager, who can be either the restaurant manager or the first assistant manager, prepares a daily chart of projected sales by hour throughout the day. The previous three weeks' sales and the sales for the same period last year are used as inputs to the schedule manager's prediction. From the sales forecast, the computer package generates proposed bin levels by product for the production area. The resulting chart is displayed on the wall. In practice, the production person, who controls the bin levels, uses the chart as a guide but can often spot more precisely a surge or fall in demand, for example when schoolchildren call in at the restaurant before catching their buses out of town.

The computer also helps in planning manning levels. From a weekly sales forecast, a package generates the required crewing levels for the different areas of the restaurant. The crewing levels are affected by both volume and product mix. The level of demand varies substantially. For the Eastborough restaurant, the periods of high demand are lunchtimes, Friday evening after 5pm, and all day on Saturdays and Sundays. Some typical manning levels are given as Exhibit 6.

The Eastborough restaurant employs a total of 100 staff, of whom only 12 are full time. The age profile reflects the UK average, with 70 per cent of employees being 16–20 years old. Pitching the number of staff at the right level throughout the week is key to the smooth operation of the restaurant. If the staffing level proves to be out of line with actual demand, then the options are limited. If there is excess staff, the manager will ask if anyone wishes to go home. If demand is unexpectedly high, staff not scheduled

Exhibit 6 Examples of manning levels for the Eastborough restaurant

Type of period	Example	# staff within each area of the restaurant				
		Supervision	Dining area	Counter area	Grill area	Total
Quiet	Weekday afternoon	1	1	2	3	7
Medium activity	Monday to Thursday lunchtime	1	2	4	5	12
Busy	Saturday lunchtime	3	8	13	24	48

to work are contacted, but there is no guarantee that they will be available and willing to come in to work at short notice. In periods where staff loads fall short of actual demand, everybody has to operate that much more 'slickly'. To facilitate this the manager ensures that all employees are allocated to those jobs in which they perform most efficiently, known as 'aces in their places'. All managers, including the restaurant manager, carry out routine food preparation if required by the level of customer demand.

Production control

To handle the high volumes and meet the fast service required, there is a defined McDonald's approach to each aspect of preparing and serving the food and drinks on offer. At the start of the day, the production person runs the bins in the production area up to the required levels by requesting sufficient products from the grill area and chicken station. In periods of high demand, there is a person allocated to the job of 'the bin'. The task involves managing the flow of products, calling for production as needed, keeping the bin stock organized and fresh, thereby acting as the interface between the staff preparing food and the counter staff who serve the customers. During slow periods, counter staff would normally call orders from the back as needed to maintain minimum inventory levels. To guarantee that customers were only served with hot and fresh products, food was held for no longer than 10 minutes after wrapping before being either sold or discarded.

The production person liaises closely with the food preparation areas and roles change slightly as different areas come under pressure. Normally, the production person will fetch the food, when ready, from the grill area. Food from the chicken station and quarter pounders from the grill area are normally boxed at the station and taken to the production person.

As explained earlier, food is held for a maximum of 10 minutes in bins in the production area, checked with the aid of a purpose-designed clock. The outer rim of the clock has a series of numbers in different colours. These are repeated but offset on the inner rim. When the clock hand reaches a new number on the outer rim, a corresponding plastic tag is placed in the bin. If food before that tag is still in the bin when the number is reached on the inner rim of the clock, then that food is removed and discarded.

Sue Kemp, who often runs the bin during busy times on her shift, described her job:

> Having worked here for some time, I have a good sense of when our peaks occur and how demand levels vary. But, there will still be times when I am caught out. I'll build up the bin before the peak starts and then try to run production as smoothly as possible through the busy times. Placing variable demand on the system typically causes problems and at busy times can increase staff pressure to the point of causing some tension. There are charts telling us how much stock to hold at different volume levels, but I need to watch what is selling, gauge customer flows and take into account how experienced the production staff are to judge how much to have in each bin. I'd rather have too much than keep a customer waiting.

Preparing products

The main products use several common ingredients as illustrated by Exhibit 7. All food preparation is carried out according to carefully detailed rules. For example, fries must be left for a minimum of 45 minutes to defrost, before cooking. This is to minimize the amount of water reaching the fry vat. When cooking fries, a duty timer sounds after 30 seconds, indicating that the fry basket must be lifted from the shortening and shaken. This separates the fries and prevents air mixing with the shortening. Fries must be cooked for three minutes, plus or minus five seconds. The maximum holding time for fries is seven minutes, after which the fries must be discarded. During busy periods an operator works full time on cooking fries, while in slack periods counter staff cover this task.

To ensure that employees are familiar with these rules, an Observation Check List (OCL) is prepared for each product. The OCL is also used to assess an employee's level of proficiency. A typical sequence for preparing food is as follows:

- A call comes the production person 'Four Big Macs, please'.

- The bun for the Big Mac is in three sections, designated the heel, the club and the crown. The operator on the dressing table loads the four heels and clubs of the buns into a toaster. After 35 seconds a timer sounds and the operator transfers the heels and clubs onto the dressing table.

Exhibit 7 **Main ingredients for a selection of products**

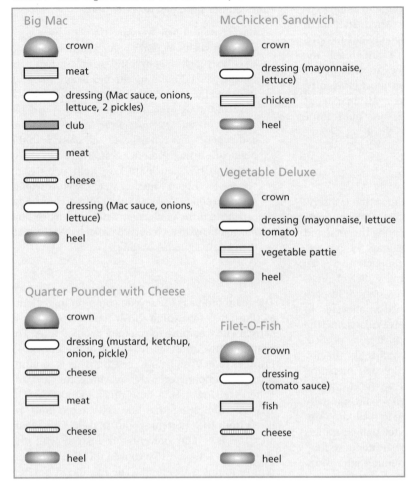

Big Mac

- crown
- meat
- dressing (Mac sauce, onions, lettuce, 2 pickles)
- club
- meat
- cheese
- dressing (Mac sauce, onions, lettuce)
- heel

Quarter Pounder with Cheese

- crown
- dressing (mustard, ketchup, onion, pickle)
- cheese
- meat
- cheese
- heel

McChicken Sandwich

- crown
- dressing (mayonnaise, lettuce)
- chicken
- heel

Vegetable Deluxe

- crown
- dressing (mayonnaise, lettuce tomato)
- vegetable pattie
- heel

Filet-O-Fish

- crown
- dressing (tomato sauce)
- fish
- cheese
- heel

- The operator loads the crowns into the toaster.
- At the same time, the grill operator, prompted by the timer alarm, lays eight pieces of meat onto the grill. The grill takes exactly 42 seconds to grill both sides of the meat.

- During this time the operator at the dressing table puts the Mac sauce, onions, lettuce and cheese onto the heels and clubs. Sauces are delivered in preset amounts from a dispenser.
- Two pickled gherkins, which, according to the relevant OCL, must not be touching, are placed on the club.
- The grill operator puts a piece of meat onto each dressed heel and club.
- The dressing table operator assembles the buns, adds the now toasted crowns, stacks the buns and gives them to the production person at his station.
- The product is then wrapped and placed in the rack, with the appropriate time card. The whole process, shown in Exhibit 8, takes about two minutes.

Staff training

Good teamwork and familiarity with the set routines for dealing with customers, storing the food and preparing the meals are essential to the successful operation of a McDonald's restaurant. After joining McDonald's, staff are expected to reach a set level of expertise, designated 5-star, within five months, or ten months if a part-timer. An employee's performance is assessed against a given task using the appropriate OCL. Each OCL details precisely the steps to prepare a product. To gain 5-star status, employees must undertake two satisfactory OCLs for each area of operation. The restaurant manager

Exhibit 8 **Preparing the Big Mac**

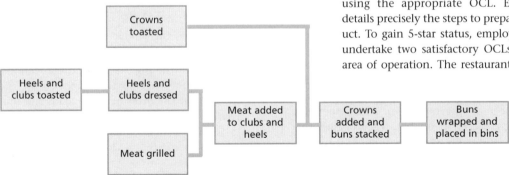

Crowns toasted

Heels and clubs toasted → Heels and clubs dressed

Meat grilled

Meat added to clubs and heels → Crowns added and buns stacked → Buns wrapped and placed in bins

and each area leader carry out one OCL each day. Because of the high number of staff, this is a major activity for the restaurant manager.

It is customary to work alongside the employee being assessed for a period on a particular task and then mark up the OCL. All 5-star employees are qualified to carry out OCL assessments. The pass on an OCL is 90 per cent on each of the two sections on the checklist. The first section covers food preparation and the second general issues, such as neatness and cleanliness of uniform. All OCLs are filed.

Each quarter an external audit is carried out, usually by the manager of another McDonald's restaurant. Fifteen employee files are selected and the restaurant is graded, based on the OCL scores achieved. Annually, the restaurant is subjected to a more intensive audit, known as 'Full field'. A group of supervisors from other restaurants complete OCLs on all operations during one dayshift and one nightshift. In this and other ways, the corporate tradition of managing all outlets under the motto QSC&V (Quality, Service, Cleanliness and Value) is reinforced.

Recent pressures

When the first McDonald's restaurant opened it represented a breath of fresh air for the American population. Surprisingly it took until 1969 for the company to spread this fever through its international division, which has now reached 119 countries on six continents. But, with high-profile international presence comes the perpetual challenge of remaining relevant in the eyes of ever more demanding consumers. One result is the recent pressure from a variety of sources such as health groups, an obesity court case in the US, competition from alternative outlets and changing consumer tastes.

The outcome is that, after a sustained spell of seemingly relentless international growth and financial success, the business is starting to struggle for the first time in its history. Stock prices have fallen, restaurants are being closed and competitors are fighting back to challenge McDonald's reign as the world's number one fast-food chain. Analysts are now beginning to ask questions such as:

- Has the McDdonald's way failed to adapt quickly enough to match changing patterns of consumer taste?

- Is the company lacking in strategic direction and focus?

- As sales slump, restaurants close and customers vote with their feet, what does Mcdonald's plan to do to stop the rot?

Recent changes

While Mcdonald's can be accused of many failings during this troubled time, sitting on its laurels is not one of them. As Alex Hardy (retail analyst) comments:

> In its attempts to turn the tide, one of the more straightforward strategies has been to revamp the menu to include items such as chicken, pancakes, sandwiches and salads [see Exhibits 4 and 5]. Activity on the acquisition front has also been lively, with the purchase of Donatos Pizza, Boston Market and a chain of Mexican restaurants. But restoring the glory days is going to take much more than a new menu and some additions to the portfolio.

An example of a more fundamental development was the introduction of the 'made for you' service delivery system. Originally launched in 1998, it was the centrepiece of a $400 million investment to increase sales at its 12,700 US restaurants by improving product quality in the face of stiffening competition from Burger King and Wendy's, who many believed offered hotter and tastier food. The new thinking was to do away with those precooked slabs of meat and prepare sandwiches to order, with freshly toasted buns too. In order to make this happen, each store installed an array of equipment: Pentium III computers to coordinate the orders, 'rapid toasters', and temperature-controlled 'launching zones' to replace the old heat lamps and holding bins. It represented somewhat of a stepped change, but in reality the chain was simply playing catch up with the competition.

While McDonald's claims that the quality of its products has indeed improved, waiting times in the restaurants have doubled to an average of 2–3 minutes per order, slow-lane performance in the cutthroat fast-food business. But this is just an average figure, and 15-minute waits are not unusual. As one McDonald's franchisee comments:

> When the factory across the street blows the whistle and 100 people walk in, you've got to have some food ready. 'Made for you' doesn't allow you to cope with that.

Other initiatives introduced recently include:

- *McDonald's experience* – it continues to explore the theme of McDonald's as an experience by developing a high-profile partnership with Disney, targeting families with Happy Meals, introducing play areas for children, and even inviting senior citizens to some restaurants to play bingo

- *Core offering* – as well as the more straightforward menu changes, other regional developments have taken place. In France, McDonald's has taken the brave step of modelling its restaurants on contemporary architecture. In the UK, there is an ongoing attempt to create menus more suited to local tastes. In the US, the plan is for a $400 million investment programme to renovate every restaurant older than 15 years and this has meant that some have been created with a 'Diner inside' to provide two different experiences in a single store

- *Reputation* – as a reaction to the recent pressures from health groups, the company is also trying to improve its image and reputation through involvement and sustained investment in projects such as 'sports coaching' and its commitment to social responsibility.

Alex Hardy reflects:

McDonald's has started the process of changing the direction of its business, but this is only the beginning. Its success to date and rapid expansion have been achieved through its broad franchise network, which will also be key to its future. However, its current relationship with franchisees has suffered from arguments about covering the costs of installation of the new 'made for you' delivery system which ended up being much higher than expected and was not wanted by many of the franchisees. McDonald's needs to regain their support without which it will not be able to turn things around.

www.mcdonalds.com

Questions

1 Review the service delivery system. How does this meet the needs of the business?

2 Review the recent changes in the business. What has been their impact?

Northmore Finance Direct

Sam Boston, operations director at Northmore Finance Direct, explained:

> The next phase is to determine how to broaden our product range in the 'direct' market so as to enable us to build a business that can sustain adequate growth and provide a broader sales revenue platform in the future. The initial steps of testing and proving this product strategy are now successfully completed and arrangements are now in hand to develop the case for an investment of some £12 million to be made during the next 12–18 months in order to deliver the systems and procedures that will need to be in place to handle these new products.

Background

Retail credit facilities had been developed in the 1950s to meet the growing demands of customers. The white and electrical goods sectors were some of the first where this facility was successfully introduced. In the early 1960s, Northmore Bank bought out Axia Loans, a personal loan company, with the aim of developing the opportunities to sell different forms of loan finance to existing and new customers.

Part of this growth was initiated by Northmore Bank writing to its customers to advise direct finance opportunities. The success that followed and the opportunity for future growth of personal loan products led to the decision five years ago to separate Northmore Finance Direct (NFD) from Northmore Bank, with the former's task to concentrate on developing the personal loans market. At that time some 75 staff were transferred to an office block across from an existing Northmore site in Guildford, together with existing IT systems. Within a few months agreement was reached to take an exact copy of the account management IT system, delete the data entries and use the program for the new loan business. This program was supplied and managed by Software Data Systems, a third-party supplier. Within three years, the growth and opportunities in the personal loans market were further signalled when NFD moved into the phase of TV advertising.

Northmore Finance Direct – the concept

The increasing use of the telephone as a medium for marketing and selling within a range of financial services has gathered pace since first introduced in the late 1980s. The NFD vision coupled a recognition of the opportunity and growing importance of this selling channel to:

- using different media opportunities from doorstep drops to press and TV advertising as ways of stimulating awareness within the general public to the availability of personal loans

- create a service that would meet the changing needs and expectations of customers in terms of its user-friendly, quick response and flexible nature

- build on the strength of the bank.

The decision to separate NFD clearly reinforced the intent by Northmore Bank to develop the personal finance loan market using direct channels. In those early days, the need to maintain and accelerate sales revenue growth was one of the newly fledged company's principal tasks. The drive to grow sales was appropriately high on the corporate agenda and the results are provided in Exhibit 1.

Expanding its customer base was the key factor in achieving this. In the early days, the customer list of Axia Loans was an essential input into the company's sales activities. As advertising grew so did the company's own customer base. The need to expand also led to the company looking for 'affinity' partners as a new source of potential customers. These arrangements enabled NFD to have access to a partner's customer list under an agreed commercial arrangement. Currently, the number

This case study was written by Terry Hill (University of Oxford). It is intended as the basis for class discussion and not as an example of good or bad management. © AMD Publishing.

Exhibit 1 Trends within NFD for the last six years

Aspect		Current year minus					Current year
		5	4	3	2[1]	1	
New business volumes (£s) (percentage of total)	traditional[2]	100	100	100	82	63	33
	direct[3]	–	–	–	181	37	67
	total	100	100	100	100	100	100
Customer accounts (percentage of total)	traditional	n/a	n/a	100	91	71	61
	direct	–	–	–	9	29	39
	total	n/a	n/a	100	100	100	100
Average monthly applications (indexed)[4]	traditional	100	150	367	300	317	167
	direct	–	–	–	100	600	1150
	total[5]	100	150	367	300	717	933
# staff (FTEs) indexed[6]		100	134	439	536	1182	1512

Notes
1 The current year minus 2 figure for new business volumes for the direct channel is based on a part year only.
2 The figures for traditional business includes both 'original' and 'affinity'.
3 The figures for direct business include:
   ● TV and press advertising   ● newspaper inserts
   ● mailshots to NFD customers   ● doorstep drops
4 Two years ago 70 per cent of all applications were received by post and 30 per cent by telephone. So far this year, 7 per cent have come by post and 93 per cent by telephone.
5 These figures relate to total applications, not the sum of the individual figures for 'traditional' and 'direct'.
6 FTEs = full-time equivalents.

of listings totals 15 and Exhibit 2 gives details of some of the contracts.

● **Traditional** – comprises applications that result from mailings to the customer lists that were part of the Axia Loans purchase plus any repeat business from these customers. The rate of loan interest offered at the time of a mailing is at a fixed level.

● **Affinity** – comprises applications that result from mailings to the customer lists belonging to other corporations. Again, the rate of loan interest is at a fixed level.

● **Direct** – applications in this segment are a direct result of NFD's activities. They comprise 'repeat' business that involves non-TV-based advertising channels, as well as TV advertising. Additionally, interest rates are not fixed but vary in line with the principle of 'rate for risk'. In this way, the loan rate offered reflects an applicant's personal circumstances concerning the degree of risk involved in making a personal loan. Whereas traditional and affinity businesses are based on a fixed rate included as part of the advertisement, 'rate for risk' allows the rate to be varied as explained earlier and hence increases the catchment area and eventually the number of agreements made.

Northmore Finance Direct – the origins

In the early years, the 'traditional' activity enabled NFD to get off the ground, while 'affinity' arrangements helped to fuel the required volume growth. The decision to use TV advertising as a medium for accessing a broader applicant base coupled with the 'rate for risk' principle of assessing and agreeing applications changed the profile of NFD.

Exhibit 2 Details of past and current affinity partnerships

Size of mailing list (000s)		# partnerships		
		Total	Terminated	Ongoing
10–50		4	–	4
50–100		2	2	–
100–200		5	2	3
200–500		6	1	5
500–1000		2	–	2
1000–2000		1	–	1
2000+		1	1	–
Total	partnerships (#)	21	6	15
	mailing list (000s)	8721	3970	4751

Note   Total numbers on the mailing list are the actual numbers involved.

Having taken the strategic view that the core of its personal loan business needed to be centred on a direct, telephony-based product, where to locate operations to meet these new dimensions was a key step that could affect the quality of the support required. The strategy was to build a brand that would stand on its own. If successful, it was estimated that after five years some 80 per cent of its business would be self-generated by customers. The first five years investment in advertising (the annual TV advertising budget alone is about £14 million) and other brand-building activities needed to be made in order to get to a position where future investments would be lower and made primarily to reinforce brand recognition rather than stimulate new business. Thus, most applications in the future would not be made as a direct result of advertising, but due to existing customers initiating calls based on the strength of the brand and the association of NFD's name with personal loan opportunities. During the first five years, however, the advertisement-led demand resulted in customer calls characterized by high peaks with different timescales depending on the medium used. Some of these patterns, which are now used as part of the call centre model, are included as Exhibit 3.

Whereas the initial NFD activity had been suitably accommodated near to Northmore Bank's existing facilities so the transfer of staff did not affect the setting up of the required operation, the increase in volumes in the last two to three years and the change in orientation and accelerated growth anticipated with TV advertising resulted in the need for more office space and the opportunity to consider where best to locate the operations activities to support direct business activities.

The alternatives narrowed down to Guildford and Leicester and, as a telephony-based facility is not location-dependent, the choice concerned issues other than geography. The final decision to develop NFD in Leicester was principally made in recognition of the dynamic nature of TV advertisements and the need for operations to be able to effectively support the short-term response patterns involved (see Exhibit 3). Locating in Leicester would thus avoid bringing existing contracted agreements, work patterns and cultures from the past into a facility where the demands on operations were markedly different. A fresh start seemed to make a lot of sense.

Operations

The corporate decision to create NFD as a stand-alone facility signalled the real development of the direct personal loan business. Direct marketing had been initiated with some press advertising and mail shots to NFD customers and within two years over one million letters were being sent monthly to prospective customers. However, in the early days the need to increase volumes and meet sales targets was the overriding corporate priority. New ideas and alternatives to existing approaches were part of the experimental environment that drove the company forward.

As sales grew so did operational requirements. However, in these early times operations was absorbed in keeping pace with growth, coping with the changing patterns of demand and meeting the day-to-day tasks as they occurred. One outcome was that operations gave too little time to learning about the different demands resulting from the array of marketing plans and initiatives. In part, operations got caught up with the general groundswell in activity and did not keep pace with the essential developments called for by the learning curve associated with high growth.

Relying on inherited IT systems that were bespoke and not well-suited to personal loan products, operations found itself with too little insight into what it was being asked to do. Even the performance measures in place were insufficiently robust to provide operations with the input into corporate discussion about growth and what constituted necessary support from operations.

Although marketing and operations discussed major initiatives, the result was too often a compliant response from operations, more by default than design. Commitments were asked for and duly given. The outcome was far from satisfactory.

Two years ago, NFD appointed Sam Boston to the position of operations director. One of his first tasks was to evaluate the current position and decide on the best way of improving it. Sam explained:

Getting the basics right became a priority task. The business had an excellent 'can do' culture and a very strong and necessary entrepreneurial spirit. But, operations developments had not kept pace. Staff efforts to get around systems constraints were unstinting, but the solutions were largely paper-based and 'band aid' in nature. Systems needed to become more robust, match the needs of the

Exhibit 3 **Examples of the impact of different types of media on operations**

Below are three examples of the response patterns which result from different types of media, both in terms of the shape and timescales involved

Telephone response pattern for a newspaper advertisement

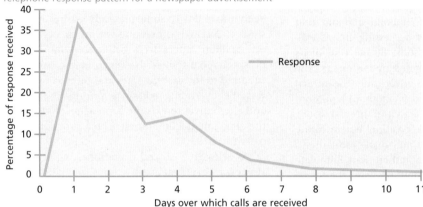

Telephone response pattern for a mailshot

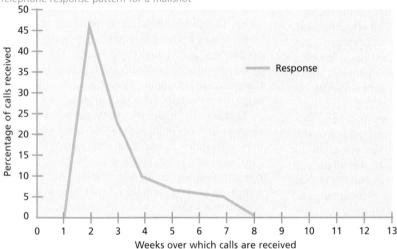

Telephone response pattern for a TV advertisement

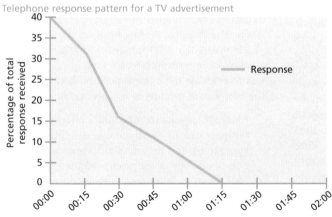

expanding business and more automated in order to free up staff time for doing what they do best – talking to customers.

Operations management skills had also not kept pace. Performance measures, analyses and an understanding of the core processes needed to be in place as the basis for improving key operations activities.

The other big step was a planning tool, a way of modelling the impact of different forms of advertising on capacity [see Exhibit 4]. Without this, we would still be in the times of feast and famine that were a hallmark of the early years. In fact, this development was an essential prelude to our successful move into TV advertising that is characterized by higher peaks of activity over shorter timescales. Also, the models help marketing and operations to have a shared understanding of the issues affecting both sides. They provide a common language to help ensure that we both work together to improve overall business performance.

Since those early days we have now set realistic performance targets [see Exhibit 5 for some key ones] and use data to help us understand market developments and take an increasingly proactive role in developing products, customers and market support [see Exhibit 6]. Also, as we expand our business we know that we are moving away from the 'safer' customer profiles into those which carry more risk [see Exhibit 7]. We need to develop operations to meet these and similar characteristics if we are to maintain our past success into the future.

Exhibit 4 **Media options: direct and indirect characteristics**

DIRECT CHARACTERISTICS

1 TV advertising – direct response (DRTV) and brand response (BRTV):

- overall annual spend equates to some 35,000 spots
- DRTV   – generates immediate response and call volumes
          – 'shelf life' about one hour
- BRTV   – builds brand awareness at different times of the day
          – stimulates calls over a longer time period than DRTV
- the number of calls generated varies depending on the slot purchased. For example:
          – '11.00 coffee time' – low response but considered to be quite cost-effective
          – between the two halves of major soaps – very high brand awareness and call responses, but too extreme to manage effectively the resulting call handling capacity requirement
- spot costs reflect viewing levels
- TV companies hold the right to allocate and/or reallocate slot times. Gazumping is not uncommon and up to 25 per cent of all slots can be reallocated at short notice

2 Press advertisements:

- media spend totals 500 press advertisements
- many press advertisements are booked over a month in advance to aid planning
- 'distress' space (that is, short, usually 24 hours, notice placements) is offered occasionally at low prices

- trend to generate more calls at the weekend

3 Door drops:
- comprises the distribution of 25 million leaflets
- very cost-effective
- uncertain lead times re delivery – part of the low-cost dimension
- run size usually 5 million leaflets

4 Inserts:
- media spend equates to 1.4 million packs
- cost-effective medium
- mailed using Sort 3 (that is, third-class post) as part of the cost-effective delivery
- delivery lead times can vary up to 14 days

INDIRECT CHARACTERISTICS

Response patterns are also influenced (sometimes quite markedly) by the following:

- **Geography and TV channels** – different regions and TV channels produce varying response levels
- **Source** – affinity partners have different consumer characteristics. Freemans, for example, produce a very high proportion of postal rather than telephone applications
- **Seasonality** – it is too early yet to understand the effects of seasonality. So far, Northmore Direct has only experienced one Christmas period and two Easter periods
- **The weather and competitor activity**
- **Telephone familiarity** – the acceptance of the direct channel to market appears generally to be growing in popularity. Consumer behaviour is changing dynamically on different days of the week

Exhibit 5 **Service levels – current standards**

Aspect of service		Standard
Answering calls	average speed	10 seconds
	# to be answered within 15 seconds	80 per cent
	maximum # calls to voicemail or abandoned	2 per cent
All post to be acknowledged within		24 hours
Data input accuracy		98 per cent
Referred applications turnaround		80 per cent in 4 hours

Exhibit 6 Operations data monitoring market responses over time

Exhibit 7 **Operations data monitoring the levels of potential fraudulent applications in Northmore Bank**

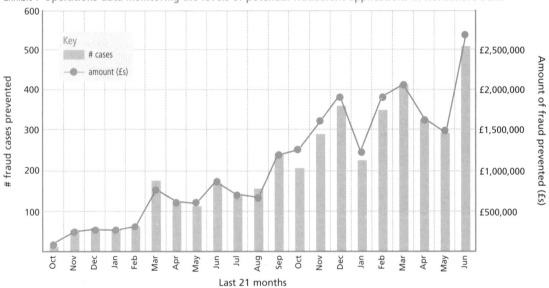

Leicester call centre

The use of TV as an advertising medium for personal loans was, at the time, new not only to NFD but also to the market in general. Given the pioneering nature of the project, the first phase was to test the market in three regions within the UK. Operationally, this was a major initiative, especially given the decision to open every hour of every day throughout the year. To minimize the overall risks during this test phase, it was decided to subcontract the telephony tasks to an outside supplier. During the first months the third-party telephony unit undertook the prime tasks of handling calls and the other duties of the personal loan advisers. However, if the market test proved a success, the intention was always to bring this function in-house, so a dedicated team under separate management was set up.

The Leicester site was designated and the facilities were refurbished and equipped, key appointments, such as the call centre manager, made and staff recruited and trained in line with a planned start-up.

With the success of the test phase, a full national 'rollout' was launched. To help the transition in operations, the third-party support and Leicester call centre ran in parallel for the first six months, gradually moving over this time from an 80/20 to a 20/80 responsibility for call handling. After that, the call centre was on its own.

The need to plan and collaborate key activities was a major factor in the functions of the business coming together. Arranging capacity in line with anticipated volumes in particular was recognized as a core activity. At the beginning this was particularly difficult, with no historic market data to go on. Over the period that followed, improvements became the priority task in operations. As Pam Whitely (the call centre manager) explained:

> From the beginning it was apparent that operations needed to become involved in discussions on markets. Anticipating the volume of calls and the capacity which needed to be available to support and maintain required service levels was an essential task. The operations and marketing functions have worked together to gain a comprehensive understanding of the dynamics which drive these issues and have jointly developed a number of predictive volumes and resources models. The media agency used to promote NFD also participates in this process on a quarterly basis in order to optimize the use of capacity and minimize costs in line with the amount of business written. How we achieve this is directly affected as much by the level of capacity and capability in the call centre as by the marketing and advertising plans that stimulate initial demand.

She went on to explain that the broad statements of demand were translated into capacity statements first covering each month, then each week and finally planning call centre capacity on a half-hourly basis, with service levels measured every 15 minutes. In the same way, marketing's predictions covering the number of calls are forecast half-hourly as is the number of calls delivered. Pam concluded:

> It is essential that all involved become better at providing relevant inputs into this dynamic service equation. The better the inputs, the better the

outputs. Creating then meeting demand makes for a better business.

She then outlined other features within the centre:

- Marketing plans, as explained earlier, are translated into the number of calls first at a monthly level for aggregate planning purposes and then to a weekly and finally a daily basis. In capacity terms this needs to be translated into the number of personal loan advisers (PLAs) at the level of each half-hour of the day.

- Telephony support is available every hour of every day in the year. The capacity allocations reflect the anticipated daily demands and these, together with other key factors, are monitored on a half-hourly basis each day. Exhibit 8 provides an example of the detail recorded in this control document.

- The procedure followed by a PLA is as follows:
  - customer telephones in
  - PLA asks a series of set questions
  - the information given by a customer is fed into the system which advises the rate to be offered – the 'rate for risk' principle
  - printed confirmation of the offer is generated by the system and mailed to the prospective customer
  - customer signs the agreement
  - cheque is mailed on receipt of the signed agreement
  - the loan is then managed.

For some 80 per cent of applications, a PLA is able to tell a customer immediately whether or not the loan is agreed and the interest rate to be applied. Of this 80 per cent, 7 per cent are declined. The 20 per cent that are referred go to the credit department at Guildford where each case is reviewed by underwriters on a first-in, first-out basis. Referred customers can telephone later using a different number to find out if their loan has been approved.

- To enable a PLA to advise a decision, the data files need to be available in terms of access. The current system is supplied, maintained and managed by an outside agency. Currently, the 'system is up' (that is, the data are available for a PLA to advise a decision) at the following times:

Mon to Fri	0700–2200
Sat	0700–2100
Sun	0700–1700

Exhibit 8 Call centre – daily measurement

Monday

Service level

100%
90%
80%
70%
60%
50%
40%
30%
20%
10%
0%

Number of calls

400
350
300
250
200
150
100
50
0

Time

00:00
01:00
02:00
03:00
04:00
05:00
06:00
07:00
08:00
09:00
10:00
11:00
12:00
13:00
14:00
15:00
16:00
17:00
18:00
19:00
20:00
21:00
22:00
23:00

3675 direct calls expected by marketing

6041 direct calls received

5079 direct calls answered

84% service level

5083 estimated call centre capacity

Key
Total calls offered
Calls overflowed in
Calls overflowed out
Service level
4-week marketing prediction of calls offered
Call centre capacity

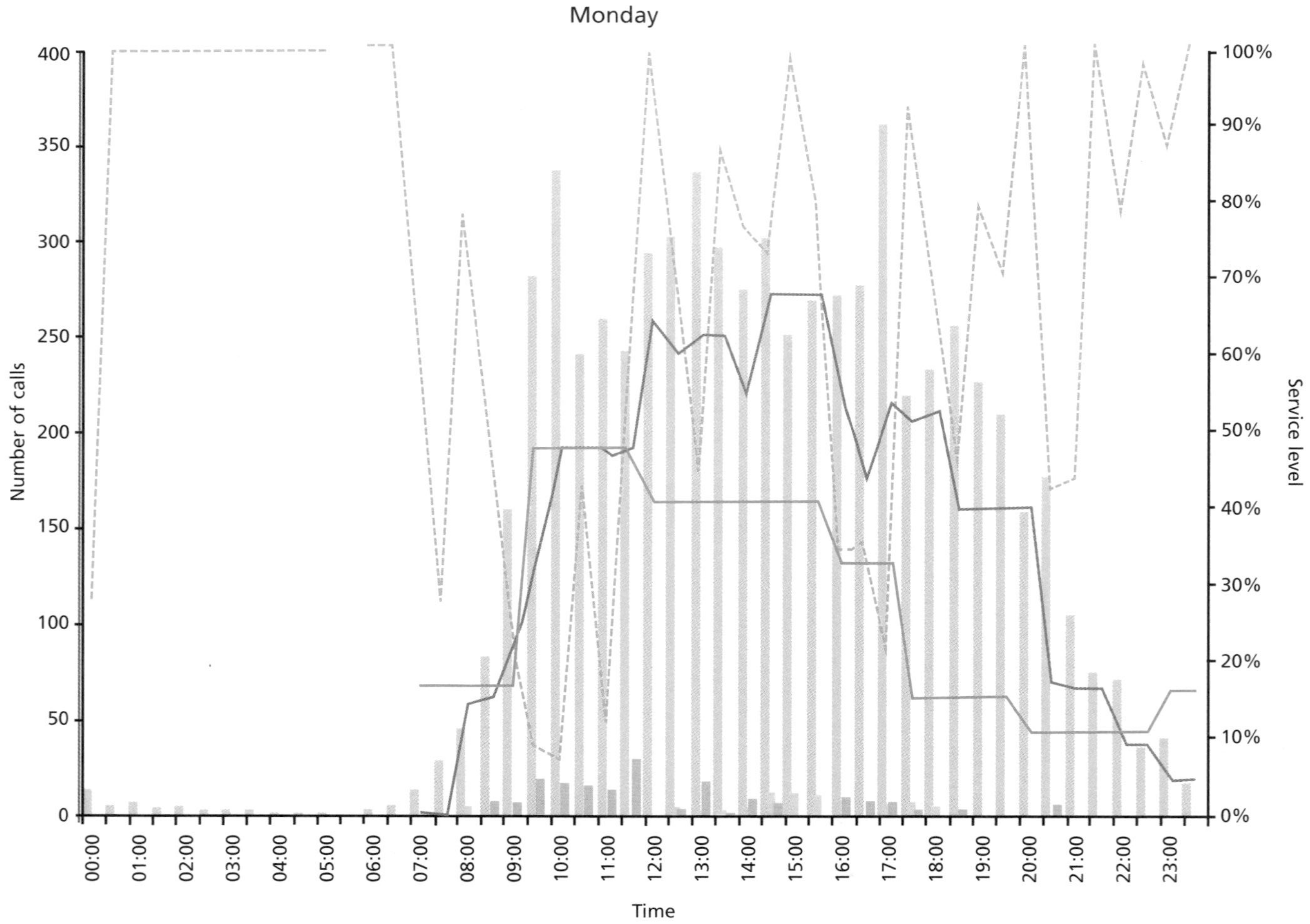

At other times, the system information is being downloaded, which typically takes some two or three hours. When the system is not up, PLAs take handwritten notes of an application and then key this in when the system is next up.

Rate for risk – operations implications

As mentioned earlier, NFD introduced a loan product to be priced on a 'rate for risk' basis. In other words, the rate offered to customers would be based on their own individual circumstances, rather than on the market norm where a standard, uniform rate was offered to all customers.

A clear and detailed understanding of the credit risk issues was critical to this strategy. This involved being able to analyse the risk for each customer accurately, to make the loan decision and set a price accordingly. In the early 'traditional' days, such an understanding was less important as the standard rates were very high (25–35 per cent on occasions) and customer's expectations involved a delay before a decision was given.

Credit scorecard developments to address these issues became a core task. Also, as most calls are from unknown customers, it is vital to continue to update and improve these skills and keep abreast of changes in the market circumstances.

Telemarketing skills are also critical in operations. Starting in new business acquisition, the success of NFD is heavily dependent on optimizing sales opportunities, from chasing accepted customers who have not drawn down their loan through to selling insurance products, all of which have a major influence on income. Finally, telemarketing techniques are fundamental to relationship development with customers in a direct business, starting with initial welcome calls to telephone contact early on.

Reflections

Looking back, NFD has grown significantly over the past few years. The decision to direct mail its customers to advise them of personal loan opportunities has fuelled a business currently growing annually at 50 per cent. The initial step of moving to the current Guildford site, using existing staff and IT systems, minimized investment and other costs in the start-up phase of the new business.

Sam Boston reflected:

The vision of offering an 'open all hours' product seems to fit today's lifestyle and the growth we have seen bears witness to that fact. To meet the needs of the next developments within NFD, the investment discussed in the opening section is essential. The key business drivers underpinning this reflect the developments that must be made to address inherited issues and future requirements. For a direct business, operations needs to become the engine which drives the customer relationship, rather than its classically perceived role of being only responsible for undertaking back-office tasks.

Whereas the advertisement or brand name will stimulate the initial customer call, transacting the business, identifying customer needs, maximizing sales opportunities afforded by a call and fulfilling customer expectations needs to be clearly seen, understood and delivered by operations.

Adding value is the name of the game! With the TV-based products successfully launched, the business is now developing a deeper branded strategy, addressing opportunities to widen our product range and deepen relationships with our customers. The discussions embody a clear recognition of the role that operations, marketing and other key functions need to play together to win in our chosen markets.

Questions

1 Outline the development of the personal loan business described in the case study.

2 With regard to the call centre, how does the service delivery system work?

3 What are the key tasks for operations in supporting the growth of the personal loan business? How well is operations meeting these requirements, what key issues need to be addressed and what changes and developments need to be made?

Platt Green Electronics

Platt Green Electronics (PGE) is a small company that manufactures and assembles a small range of oscilloscopes. There is only one basic product but this is sold in four versions: mains supply, direct current supply, battery pack (including charger) and mains pack. The oscilloscopes are also sold with or without a probe and connector. These latter items are also sold individually.

The operations process involves the following principal phases: purchasing materials and components, metal fabrication, printed circuit boards (PCB) manufacture, PCB test, subassembly, assembly, test pack and dispatch. The policy of the company is to use outworkers to complete parts of these processes, with the others being performed inside the plant. The oscilloscope cases and drilled blanks to take the components are fabricated in the metal shop. From these, subassemblies are made which, together with other parts, are then assembled before test and packing. The component parts and subassemblies for each product are shown in Exhibit 1.

The present workforce comprises three full-time and two part-time staff, employed at the plant, with 12 outworkers who can allocate up to 20 hours per week to PGE's work – see Exhibit 2. Production levels average 20 oscilloscopes per week. Probes and connectors are bought in and require little additional work. The products are sold as standard items to meet a range of different industrial applications.

Exhibit 1 **The number of components and subassemblies by product type**

| Product | # components | | # subassemblies |
	In-house	Bought-out	
Mains	20	85	9
Direct current	32	105	10[1]
Battery pack	26	92	6
Mains pack	30	70	4
Total	108	352	29

Note   1   Eight of these subassemblies are also common to the mains version of this product.

Exhibit 2 **The operations process**

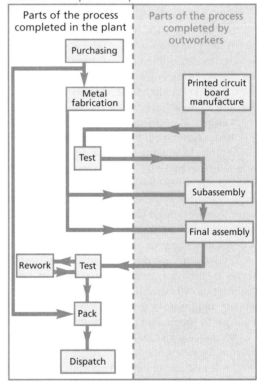

The weekly production levels, although averaging 20 units, can vary from week to week depending upon the number of oscilloscopes requiring rework after final assembly test. The amount of time it takes to correct the faults can vary from 0.5 to 6.0 hours. At the moment, the full-time staff are responsible for the rework activity.

Questions

1   What are the critical operations scheduling features?

2   What is the key operations scheduling task?

3   Outline the development of a suitable scheduling system for the business.

This case study was written by Terry Hill (University of Oxford). It is intended as the basis for class discussion and not as an example of good or bad management. © AMD Publishing.

Pret A Manger

Esther O'Halloran is having problems making an 'All Day Breakfast Sandwich' with egg, bacon and tomato. This is the first time she has worked in a Pret kitchen, despite having been with the company for the past year and a half. Her role as the head of recruitment and retention doesn't normally call upon her sandwich-making skills, but this is part of a Pret initiative to send all managers into an outlet each quarter to familiarize themselves with the daily operation of their stores. The belief is that a good knowledge of how products are made, how customers are served and the interface between customers and Pret's service delivery system will lead to better decisions in all aspects of the business.

O'Halloran reflected:

It really helps you keep your feet on the ground. You get to know your team and find out if there's anything you could be doing better, anything you could change. Head offices often lose sight of what it's like on the shop floor and what their staff are exposed to on a daily basis. It's keeping in close communication with the team that helps motivate them.

And this is just one of the ways in which Pret inspires the 2200 employees who work for it worldwide. Whether they are preparing a sandwich, serving up Pret's famous chocolate brownie or pouring a drink, the important contribution of staff at every level is acknowledged, as illustrated by its 'reward and recognition' programme stretching across its 140 stores, predominantly in the UK, but also in New York, Hong Kong and Tokyo.

Background

Pret A Manger was described by the UK's *Times* newspaper as having 'revolutionised the concept of sandwich making and eating'. Sinclair Beecham and Julian Metcalfe, two college friends, founded Pret in 1986. They saw an opportunity in London to introduce a sleek, healthy fast-food concept designed to offer an alternative to the hamburger–fries–shake menus around at the time and took the name Pret A Manger, French for 'ready to eat', from a restaurant in Hampstead, a London suburb that had tried to keep McDonald's from setting up business in the area.

Since the first store opened, Pret has been hugely successful, expanding rapidly in the UK and more recently abroad. Corporate policy is to own and manage all new shops so as to provide maximum control of the brand and ensure a consistently high standard in all shops. In fact Beecham and Metcalfe believe:

If there's a secret to our success so far, we like to think it's our determination to focus continually on quality. Not just our food, but in every aspect of what we do. Quality fresh food is our passion. We go to extraordinary lengths to avoid the chemicals, additives and preservatives common to so much of the 'prepared' and 'fast' food on the market today.

This factor is reflected in the Passion Facts (see Exhibit 1) found in shops and on packaging, which document their continual search for what they feel are Pret-quality ingredients.

Store environment

One of the things that really make Pret stand out from its competitors is the industrial chic decor within its shops. Each store has a crisp, clean environment comprising reflective brushed aluminium walls and diamond-shaped floors. All equipment has that stainless-steel modern look, from refrigerated cases to cash registers and coffee brewers, with a few touches of colour here and there that add to its overall, distinctive nature; for example the yellow wall and orange ceiling with suspended, exposed pipes and the burgundy Pret star logos found on entrance mats, packaging and menu boards.

This case study was written by Alex Hill (University of Kingston). It is intended as the basis for class discussion and not as an example of good or bad management. © AMD Publishing.

Exhibit 1 **Some examples of Pret A Manger's Passion Facts**

2 New Pret ham comes from Farm Assured farms, which guarantees the pigs are reared on a vegetarian diet. The colour, texture and taste of our ham is a world apart from the skinny, slippery, square stuff commonly found in most sandwiches. All our hams are hand-glazed with cloves and then baked in the oven. As a final touch we now hand trim 95% of the fatty white bit – leaving just enough to provide the perfect flavour.

14 The never-ending development of our Brownie is typical of Pret. We've improved the recipe 33 times over the last few years. Each change is miniscule but detectable. John J Hess said, 'A race horse that runs a mile a few seconds faster is worth twice as much. That little extra proves to be the greatest value.' Same with our Brownie we think.

9 If you agree that our Lemon Cake is fantastic, we've got Alan Miles to thank. Alan is the blacksmith who invented and manufactured the huge metal grid, which drizzles fresh lemon juice on each and every slice we make. Pret cakes really are handmade with superb natural ingredients; they always have been and always will be.

25 Mr Sheepshanks is fanatical about mayo. This is just as well, as he makes ours. He insists on using fresh eggs (never dried or reconstituted), but the real secret to great mayo is the size of the bubbles after mixing. They should be tiny. Sheepshanks uses a microscope to check his.

57 Our unique fruit and onion chutney has something spiritual about it. Mark Lake, a blender of Port and Calvados, discovered the bizarre recipe, which uses balsamic vinegar rather than the cheaper stuff. Bubbling away gently for hours and hours in small chutney pans, this nectar does something to Bramley apples, onions and spices which we think makes our Double Cheddar Sandwich really special. Sorry it took us 12 years to discover Mark. Better late than never.

11 Only Pret's Oat and Fruit Slice is stirred by hand with a four-foot long oar. Strange as it may seem, we've found that mechanical mixers turn the ingredients into a horrid pulp. Hand mixing the ingredients adds a lot of work but greatly improves the flavour. It is partly for this reason that the texture and taste of the product is so good.

24 Our freshly pressed Carrot Juice is part of our range of 100% natural juices. It is packed full of vitamins and nutrients and, unlike so many of today's trendy health drinks, contains no chemicals or additives. Apparently fresh Carrot Juice enjoys a bizarre reputation for helping to fight the effects of jet lag… Something to do with antioxidants? Anyway, we sell it because it tastes good!

12 Our Pecan Pie is covered with pecan halves. Curiously enough this fact speaks volumes about its quality. Pecan halves are juicy and have more flavour than pecan bits. It is this attention to detail that makes Pret food worth coming back for time and again. Pret cakes really are handmade with superb natural ingredients; they always have been and always will be.

41 Of all the ingredients we use, our avocados have to be the most temperamental. Treat them badly and they just don't taste right. That's why they have a huge ripening room all to themselves and why our avocado chap turns each one of them by hand, every day. It makes sure they ripen evenly and that every bite of avo is a perfect one.

38 Basil's a nightmare in sandwiches. It's a delicate herb that bruises easily, so most people use pesto instead. Pesto is OK, but it's just not as good as fresh basil. We like our basil tasty and whole. So we order it in handpicked bunches and have it delivered daily. We add the leaves to sandwiches one-by-one.

Menu

Pret sells a variety of items including sandwiches, baguettes, wraps, sushi, salads, yoghurt pots, cakes, deserts, crisps and a range of bottled beverages, brewed coffees and teas. The breakfast menu differs slightly from the lunch menu, although the majority of the items offered are the same (see Exhibits 2 and 3). Up to 31 types of food are offered in each store. Of the menu items available about 12 repeat, with the rest changing on a daily basis. In fact, nearly 70 new items were introduced last year into each store.

As the operations director explains:

> Our customers want to be able to purchase a variety of different products, so to keep our menu exciting and innovative, we're constantly introducing new products and flavours. Even though probably only one idea in every 20 makes it through our testing process, on average a new product goes on sale in our UK shops every four days. Existing products are continually being improved. For example, the recipe for the chocolate brownie has been improved 33 times over the last few years. Each change is miniscule but detectable.

Exhibit 2 Typical breakfast menu

Bakery

Low Fat Blueberry Muffin
Plain Croissant
Chocolate Croissant
Almond Croissant
Pretzels
Seville Orange Muffin
Mixed Berry Muffin
Breakfast Baguette
Smoked Salmon, Egg & Cress Breakfast Baguette

Cakes and Desserts

Toffee Waffles
Chocolate Cake
Chocolate Goddess Cake
Oat & Fruit Slice
Pret Brownie
Carrot Cake
Banana Cake
Apple Cake
Lemon Cake
Raspberry Carnage
Blueberry Carnage
Chocolate Fudge Cake

Pret Yoghurt Pots

Honey and Granola Pret Pot
Raspberry Pret Pot
Pret Brownie Pret Pot
All Day Breakfast Bowl
Very Berry Breakfast Bowl
Pret Fruit Salads Fruit Salad

Fresh Fruit

Banana
Large Granny Smith Apple
Pink Apple
Seedless Grapes

Drinks and Juices

Pure Pret – Lemon
Pure Pret – Orange (sparkling juice drink)
Pure Pret – Apple
Pure Pret – Ginger Beer
Pure Pret – Iced Tea
Pure Pret – Yoga Bunny Detox
Vitamin Volcano
Mango, Pineapple & Lime Yoghurt Drink
Blood Orange Juice

Large Size Orange Juice
Pret Still Water
Pret Sparkling Water
Coke – 330ml Can
Diet Coke – 330ml Can
Pure Pret – Cranberry
Pure Pret – Grape & Elderflower
Orange Juice
Apple Juice
Carrot Juice
Vanilla Yoghurt Drink
Strawberry Smoothie
Mango Smoothie
Apples & Pears Smoothie

Pret Coffee

Cappuccino
Latte
Mocha
Espresso
Macchiato
Filter or Americano
Hot Chocolate
Tea

Note: A typical meal of something from the Bakery, a Pret Yoghurt Pot and a drink will cost between £3.50 and £5.50.

Service delivery system

The first Pret A Manger shop had its own kitchen where fresh ingredients were delivered early morning and food was prepared throughout the day. Every Pret store since has followed this model. All the sandwiches, wraps, baguettes, deserts and salads are made one by one in every shop each day. A set number of products are assembled at the beginning of the day and stocked in the shop front from where the customers select and pay for their meal (see Exhibit 4). This stock level is then replenished during the day in line with demand. The aim is to continually meet the high quality and freshness standards set. As a result, if any of the products assembled that day have not sold by the time the

Exhibit 3 Typical lunch menu

Sandwiches

More Than Mozzarella
Mature Cheddar & Pret Pickle
Gourmet Prawn
Coronation Chicken
Kippered Salmon & Horseradish Dressing
Three Cheese & Roasted Tomatoes
White Crab & Crayfish
Wheat Free Open Salmon & Egg Mayo
Humous & Oven Roasted Tomatoes
Egg Mayo
Egg and Tomato on Rye
Tuna Mayo Sandwich
Wheat Free Open Avocado & Italian
Cheese
Big BLT
Chicken & Avocado
Chicken Caesar
Ham Cheese & Pickle
All Day Breakfast
Super Club
Ham & Eggs Bloomer
Black Pepper Chicken Bloomer
Smoked Salmon
Crayfish & Rocket

Baguettes and Wraps

Avocado Salad Wrap
Three Cheese 'n' Chutney Baguette
White Crab, Crayfish & Rocket Baguette
Tuna Mayo Baguette
Brie Tomato & Basil Baguette
Ham & Cheese Baguette
Humous Salad Wrap
Tuna Nicoise Salad Wrap
Chicken Salad Wrap

Sushi and Salads

Prawn Cocktail Salad
Basil Pasta & French Dressing
Crayfish & Sweet Chilli Dressing
Tuna Salad
Humous & Pitta Salad

Chicken & Bacon Caesar Salad
Vegetarian Sushi
Deluxe Sushi

Bakery

Low Fat Blueberry Muffin
Seville Orange Muffin
Mixed Berry Muffin

Pret Yoghurt Pots

Honey and Granola Pret Pot
Raspberry Pret Pot
Pret Brownie Pret Pot
All Day Breakfast Bowl
Very Berry Breakfast Bowl

Fresh Fruit and Fruit Salad

Banana
Large Granny Smith Apple
Pink Apple
Seedless Grapes
Fruit Salad

Cakes and Desserts

Caramel Crunch Cheesecake
Lemon Cheesecake
Chocolate Mousse
Pret Shortbread
Toffee Waffles
Chocolate & Orange Baked Cheesecake
Raspberry Carnage
Blueberry Carnage
Chocolate Cake
Chocolate Goddess Cake
Oat & Fruit Slice
Pret Brownie
Pecan Pie
Carrot Cake
Banana Cake
Apple Cake
Chocolate Fudge Cake

Crisps

Organic Popcorn: sea salt flavour

Organic Popcorn: honey flavour
Nut Munch
Hand cooked Pickled Onion Crisps
Hand cooked Lightly Salted crisps
Hand cooked Salt & Vinegar crisps
Hand cooked Sea Salt & Black Pepper crisps
Hand cooked Cheddar & Chive crisps
Pret Vegetable Chips

Drinks and Juices

Pure Pret – Lemon
Pure Pret – Orange (sparkling juice drink)
Pure Pret – Apple
Pure Pret – Ginger Beer
Pure Pret – Iced Tea
Pure Pret – Yoga Bunny Detox
Vitamin Volcano
Mango, Pineapple & Lime Yoghurt Drink
Blood Orange Juice
Large Size Orange Juice
Pret Still Water
Pret Sparkling Water
Coke – 330ml Can
Diet Coke – 330ml Can
Pure Pret – Cranberry
Pure Pret – Grape & Elderflower
Orange Juice
Apple Juice
Carrot Juice
Vanilla Yoghurt Drink
Strawberry Smoothie
Mango Smoothie
Apples & Pears Smoothie

Pret Coffee

Cappuccino
Latte
Mocha
Espresso
Macchiato
Filter or Americano
Hot Chocolate
Tea

Note: A typical meal of something from Sandwiches, Cakes, Crisps and a drink will cost between £3.50 and £7.50.

store closes, they are given to local charities rather than being stored and sold the following day.

Service in the shop is fast and friendly, with members following strict service guidelines, such as serving every customer within 90 seconds. The challenge of providing a fast, efficient and professional service to the customer is exciting and there is a buzz among the staff. To ensure that this happens, store managers tend to spend about 80 per cent of their time on the shop floor and hold team meetings twice a day to help ensure that every member knows what to do.

People

A key element of Pret's success is the way it recruits, motivates, trains and develops its staff. As the gen-

Exhibit 4 Typical Pret service delivery system in the kitchen and the storefront

Kitchen

Fresh ingredients are delivered to each store on a daily basis. Chilled foods are placed into a back-of-house walk-in cooler, while a small amount of frozen goods, including part-baked croissants, baguettes and cookies, are stored in a reach-in freezer. Staff in each outlet begin food assembly at 7 am, and refresh the food supply throughout the day as needed.

In a large outlet, 10 stainless-steel prep tables and refrigerated ingredient display units are arranged so employees can assemble fresh ingredients into sandwiches (on average 1500 are made daily), then wrap and package then in logoed boxes (inscribed with the Pret logo and message 'handmade in Pret today' and listing natural ingredients) for presentation in refrigerated display units located in the store area.

Certain designated sandwiches are made at specific tables. Assembly instructions, along with photographs of how each ingredient is positioned, are available at each station for employees' reference. Deserts and salads are assembled here, as well.

Also in the kitchen are coffee brewers, a bean grinder, a tea brewer and a countertop slicer for cutting meats and vegetables. The only product heated on the premises is soup. These are delivered to each unit in one gallon sealed plastic bags and rethermalized in a 10 gallon electric steam-jacketed kettle before being taken out front and placed in tureens for holding and serving.

Each kitchen is equipped, as well, with sinks for washing the cutting boards, scoops and other utensils, and for sanitizing fruit and vegetables. Overhead steel shelving units are positioned throughout the kitchen, while floors are protected by water-resistant, non-stick vinyl.

After preparation and assembly, all items are taken to the front of house for display. Refrigerated items, including bottled beverages, are placed in one of five floor-to-ceiling refrigerated cases that have been positioned side by side near the entranceway.

A set number of products are assembled at the beginning of the day and stocked in the storefront. This stock level is then replenished during the day in line with demand. The store manager is responsible for connecting the demand and stock levels in the storefront with the work completed in the kitchen. This also includes items such as sushi, drinks, juices or yoghurt pots that are brought in pre-assembled and stored in the kitchen before being moved into the storefront.

Storefront

In the storefront, customers help themselves to the products they want and bring them up to the counter to pay. All products apart from hot drinks and soup are stored in the shop front and replenished from the kitchen in line with demand. When customers come to the counter to pay for their products, they can order hot drinks or soup, which are then either made or served-to-order.

A centrally positioned serving counter is situated perpendicular to the refrigerated cases. During busy periods of the day, eight cashiers are positioned shoulder-to-shoulder to offer a quick and efficient service to their customers. The aim is to serve customers in 90 seconds or less.

Behind the unit from left to right are a reach-in refrigerator used primarily for milk storage, two tea dispensers, a drip coffee dispenser, coffee machines that produce cappuccino, latte, mocha and espresso drinks, two soup tureens and a convection oven for baking croissants and cookies, as well as tomatoes, almonds and pine nuts.

Products made in the oven are placed either into take-out bags or on 12-inch aluminum round trays. Seating is available at larger units with up to 72 stools with aluminum bases and vinyl cushions placed at bar-counters lining the walls and at round tables with marble tops.

Note The above is based on Boss, D. (2002) 'Pret A Manger: Chain profile', *Foodservice Equipment and Supplies*, June, p. 49.

eral manager of one of the London stores in Oxford Street says:

> The interview process was so lengthy I knew it was a good company, they won't take just anybody. We get so many job applications each week and it is important that we select the right people for the business. The company has a reputation for being a great employer and that means that many people want to work here.

In fact Pret takes the recruitment process so seriously that, as part of the second interview stage,

candidates work in a shop for part of a day and the team they have worked with then decide if they get the job. Pret believes this approach is one of the reasons why the organization reduced staff turnover threefold last year, to less than 60 per cent of the industry average. As Esther O'Halloran comments:

> We're incredibly privileged that so many creative, hard working and talented people have chosen to work for us. We're often asked about the secret of our customer service training. There is no secret. In fact, there is no customer service training. Instead,

Exhibit 5 Examples of Pret's reward and recognition training and development programmes

Reward and recognition programmes

The objective of the Pret reward and recognition programmes is to motivate employees to serve good food with a positive attitude. As a result, more than 80 per cent of all Pret workers receive recognition rewards each week.

Examples of these activities include:

- **Buddy system** – Pret's initiative to send all its management into a Pret outlet each quarter as a 'buddy' to better familiarize themselves with the daily operation of their stores. It allows office staff to keep in touch with the shop floor and what their team is exposed to on a daily basis. It also serves to motivate the staff working on the shop floor.

- **'Mystery Shopper' reward** – once a week, one staff member wins a 'Mystery Shopper' reward, a gift card worth £50 in cash. In shops that score nine or more, every team member earns a bonus of 75p per hour for every hour they have worked that week.

- **'Star Team' awards** – once a month a few store managers are awarded with a cash reward to take their team out on the town. During quarterly meetings, the head office picks the top 20 retail locations and gives those employees an extra week's vacation and a party, compliments of Pret.

- **Staff parties** – when the work is done there is still fun to be had. Pret A Manger spends £250,000 on staff parties twice a year and subsidizes Friday night drinks at bars each week.

- **Staff appraisals** – each store manager completes staff appraisals every four months. This is an opportunity to talk to team members about their performance, give praise where appropriate and identify future career and development opportunities. It also helps to foster good relations between managers and their team.

Training and development programmes

There are systematic and extensive training and development programmes for both managers and workers:

- **Managers** – three months' training, starting from the bottom up, with two weeks as a team member, four weeks as a team leader and six weeks management training, including modular courses on health and safety, employment and human resources.

- **Workers** – a 12-week probationary period during which they are first trained as team members. Afterwards, they can move to team leader, trainer or barista if they choose. Once they reach each level, they are given a pay rise and a £50 gift card. They are also given some £50 vouchers which they pass on to colleagues who have helped them attain promotion to encourage team building.

---

we employ people with personality who we think have the potential to give genuinely good service – people who like mixing with other people, who are good humoured and like to enjoy themselves.

This reduction in staff turnover has helped to pave the way for the firm's planned expansion over the next three years, from 118 shops employing 2300 staff to 163 shops employing around 3400 staff. It is these carefully chosen team members who will be responsible for its transformation into a leading sandwich shop chain. In return, it aims to offer its staff a fun and open working environment, reward, recognition, training, development and career opportunities. Exhibit 5 shows some examples of these initiatives. The result has been that over the last few years Pret has won a number of awards including being voted #10 in the *Sunday Times* 50 Best Companies to Work For in the UK in 2001, while in 2002 *Fortune* magazine rated it as one of the top ten places to work in Europe.

The future

With its ambitious plans for expansion over the next few years, Pret continues to refine the formula that has led to its current success. Key to this will be not only the suppliers and outlets it selects, but also, more importantly, the people it recruits. As Esther O'Halloran points out:

> We had over 5000 applicants last year so the training and incentives that we use seem to be working. It is crucial though that we continue to use the right recruitment policies to create a culture in which people will want to stay. Despite the industry's reputation for high staff turnover, we don't currently seem to have a problem and there are some instances where members have remained at the same store since it opened more than three years ago.

As well as expanding its number of sites, Pret is also expanding the range of services it offers its cus-

Exhibit 6 Pret's breakfast and lunch delivery service

Steps involved in the delivery service

As well as coming into the store to select and pay for their food, customers can now also order fresh, handmade breakfast or lunches for their next business meeting. Orders of £20 or more are delivered free of charge within Pret's delivery zone.

The breakfast and lunch menus are the same as those available in the shops, apart from the hot drinks and soup. However, in addition to the normal products on offer, customers can also choose from a range of sandwich platters, as shown below.

Customers wishing to receive either a breakfast or lunch delivery service initially have to open an account with Pret. Once this has been done, they can select what they want from the online menu. As long as they order before 10am, the food can be delivered that day. Alternatively, food can be ordered up to seven days in advance if required.

After the order has been placed, a confirmation is sent by email before one of the Pret team members delivers the food directly to the desired location, ready to serve in smart presentation boxes. If necessary, there is a customer services helpline telephone number to assist with any queries.

Typical delivery service platters

As well as the breakfast and lunch menus available in the shops, customers can also choose from a range of sandwich platters:

Breakfast	Lunch
Croissants Selection Box	Pret Selection Platter
Breakfast Baguette Platter	Pret Variety Platter
Breakfast Sandwich Platter	Veggie Platter
Muffin Platter	Meat Platter
Cake Platter	Fish Platter
Brownie Bag	Pret Baguette Platter
	Muffin Platter
	Cake Platter
	Brownie Bag

Note   Breakfast platters and lunch platters typically cost between £5.00 and £15.00.

tomers. Last year it introduced a delivery service that means as well as coming into the store to order food, customers can also have food delivered direct to them (see Exhibit 6). As the head of marketing explained:

> Our customers tend to be young professionals who want a fast and efficient service with a variety of high quality products. To date, we have been able to offer that to them when they come into one of our stores. However, given that they are often very busy and short for time we felt that a delivery service might often be a more convenient solution for them. The challenge for us is to try to recreate the Pret experience in a different service environment.

www.pretamanger.com

Questions

1 In which market does Pret A Manger compete?

2 Review the service delivery systems used in a Pret outlet.

3 How well do the service delivery systems meet the needs of the market?

4 What is the role of operations in Pret's success both now and in the future?

Redman Company

Redman Company is a wholly owned subsidiary of Bomat Industries. Although all its sales are internal within the group, it is judged under normal commercial rules, of which one is profit performance.

Its task is to take the requirements, discuss them in detail with the 'customer' and then prepare initial drawings to ensure that the product meets requirements. On the basis of this, it agrees a price and delivery schedule and then proceeds to manufacture it. The principal steps involved from that stage onwards are described below and summarized in Exhibit 1.

In order to meet the requirements of its customers, Redman Company, in essence, prepares drawings and cost estimates in line with a customer's stated requirements and then arranges for the whole task to be completed and delivered to the customer's premises.

With regard to manufacturing, the company buys in standard parts from suppliers and also seeks quotations for and organizes the making of any special parts from chosen subcontractors. The company is responsible for issuing materials to both its own manufacturing unit and subcontractors. While much of this material is in inventory, any other material is purchased locally, with guaranteed short deliveries. When the component parts are received from subcontractors, Redman brings these together with the relevant subassemblies made in-house and completes the final assembly prior to delivery.

When placing orders for component parts with local subcontractors, the company has developed a policy of requiring estimates, the acceptance of which coincides with the placement of the order (activity 6 in Exhibit 1).

Internal pressure to reduce costs has led the company to review its current practice. As part of this revision, it has listed the activities involved and determined how long each one currently takes to complete. Furthermore, it has estimated that, for each day the total assembly duration could be reduced, there

Exhibit 1 **Schedule of principal activities in the manufacturing task**

Activity	Place at which the activity would be completed	Normal duration (# days)
1 Assemble component parts and subassemblies to make the final product	Redman	10
2 Prepare final drawings	Redman	5
3 Make subassemblies	Redman	15
4 Make and deliver component parts	Subcontractor	20
5 Obtain estimates for special parts from relevant subcontractors[1]	Redman	20
6 Accept quotation and place an order on the relevant subcontractor[2]	Redman	3
7 Issue appropriate standard components and/or materials:[2]		
Internally	Redman	2
To subcontractors	Redman	5
8 Deliver to customer	Redman	4

Notes   1   Includes the decision on whether or not to subcontract the work.
2   Both activities 6 and 7 can start as soon as activity 5 has been completed.

This case study was written by Terry Hill (University of Oxford). It is intended as the basis for class discussion and not as an example of good or bad management. © AMD Publishing.

would be a saving on each order of £200 per day. These savings, however, cannot be made without some additional costs. Details of these, together with the activities where potential reduction in time is available, are given in Exhibit 2.

1 From the information provided, prepare a network diagram and identify the critical path.

2 As the company wishes to improve its financial performance on each contract undertaken, advise it on the action it should follow so as to maximize profits.

Exhibit 2 Opportunities to reduce total lead times and associated costs

Activity	# days to complete each activity		Cost £s[3]
	Normal #[1]	Shortest #[2]	
1 Assemble component parts and subassemblies to make the final product	10	8	60
2 Prepare final drawings	5	5	–
3 Make subassemblies	15	11	80
4 Make and deliver component parts	20	11	160
5 Obtain estimates for special parts from relevant subcontractors	20	20	–
6 Accept quotation and place an order on the relevant subcontractor	3	3	–
7 Issue appropriate standard components and/or materials:			
Internally	2	2	–
To subcontractors	5	2	40
8 Deliver to customer	4	4	–

Notes 1 The normal number of days required to complete each activity, as given in Exhibit 1.
2 The shortest possible time (days) needed to complete each activity.
3 The increased costs incurred for each day's reduction achieved in completing an activity (that is, reducing the normal time taken to the shortest possible duration).

Richmond Plastics

Richmond Plastics produces a wide range of products that fall into three categories: items that it sells to several customers, items that are designed for one customer who calls off from a blanket order with the required notice, and items made on a subcontract basis.

The first two items are for products that typically have a number of bought-out components added to them and require specific labels and packaging before they can be assembled and packed. While some subcontract items also fall into this category, others comprise products that are bulk-packed into second-hand cartons and require no labels.

The principal manufacturing processes involved are injection moulding and assembly. A typical product has one or more parts that are moulded. These then go direct to assembly or into work-in-progress (WIP) stores prior to assembly. After assembly and packing the products go into the finished goods warehouse. The injection moulding machines are grouped into one of four sizes, with each mould going onto only one size of machine (see Exhibit 1).

As many of the products are bulky and the volumes can total up to 4000 shots (the injection of material into a mould to form a product) per eight-hour shift, it is important to keep WIP inventory to a minimum. A mould can be either single or multi-impression, that is, producing one, two or more products in each shot. The mould shop works on a 24-hour basis for five days per week, with some weekend working on particular orders as necessary. The assembly department rarely works overtime except to meet the peak demands prior to Christmas – the normal working week is 37.5 hours. In addition, Richmond Plastics occasionally subcontracts work to one or two other moulding companies in times of high demand. When this happens, some of the products are returned to Richmond Plastics as WIP for inspection, assembly and packing, while others (usually where quality is less critical) are assembled and packed at the subcontractor's premises and then delivered to Richmond Plastics' finished goods warehouse.

Exhibit 1 **Number of machines by machine group**

Moulding machine group	# machines
1	29
2	14
3	10
4	4
Total	57

Questions

1   What are the critical operations scheduling features?

2   What is the key operations scheduling task?

3   Outline the development of a suitable scheduling system for the business.

This case study was written by Terry Hill (University of Oxford). It is intended as the basis for class discussion and not as an example of good or bad management. © AMD Publishing.

Riviona Bank

Since Riviona Bank was established in the early 1990s, its book value has grown consistently year on year to a point where the current value of outstanding mortgages is €14 billion while the balance in savings accounts is €10 billion (see Exhibit 1). Michael Jones (Riviona chief executive) explained:

Exhibit 1 Riviona Bank book value

Product	Book value €m (current year minus)				
	4	3	2	1	0
Mortgage	n/a[1]	7,052	10,940	10,554	13,888
Savings[2]	3,393	8,183	9,189	9,847	10,192
Balances at year end	3,393	15,235	20,129	20,401	24,080

Notes 1 Mortgage products only introduced 3 years ago.
2 Includes both business and personal savings.

We are proud of our success to date, which is why we feel that although our plan for the next five years is aggressive, it is also achievable. The target is to grow the overall book value to €39 billion, with mortgages at €27 billion and savings at €12 billion (see Exhibit 2). The increasingly competitive nature of these markets means that to maintain our desired margins we need to achieve this projected level of growth with current staff levels. I know that this is a challenge. But, ever since we set up the bank, we have successfully met a number of exacting targets. The key has been the recruitment of some outstanding people, and I strongly believe that we have the right team in place to make these coming years as profitable as the last. The recent changes in customer service will provide the foundation upon which to build our future.

Michael Jones was addressing the executive board of the bank as part of a review of current performance and the future targets set by the company.

Riviona Bank was set up in 1994 as a subsidiary of the Klaus Group AG based in Germany. For many years, Klaus had wanted to expand its portfolio and move into the UK savings and mortgage market and it saw Riviona as a way to do this. To get the bank up and running, the CEO involved in successfully growing one of its major banks in the US was appointed, having the appropriate experience and expertise. In the first few months, sales and profits greatly exceeded forecasts and this initial success has continued to the present day. Since he left the bank, his successor, Michael Jones, has maintained and improved the corporate structures and approaches that he had introduced (see Exhibit 3).

Exhibit 2 Forecasted Riviona Bank book value

Product	Book value €m (current year plus)			
	0	1	2	3
Mortgage[1]	13,888	18,770	23,098	27,368
Savings	10,192	10,288	11,242	11,947
Balances at year end	24,080	29,058	34,340	39,315

Note 1 Includes both business and personal savings.

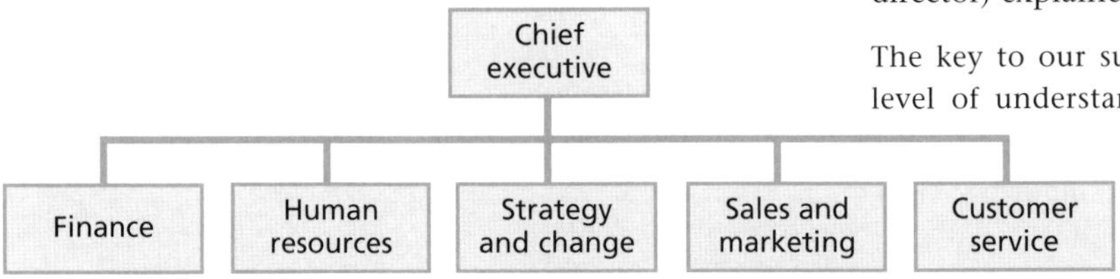

Products and markets

Jim White (sales and marketing director) explained:

The key to our success is the high level of understanding and know-

Exhibit 3 Riviona organizational structure

Chief executive — Finance | Human resources | Strategy and change | Sales and marketing | Customer service

Exhibit 4 Number of savings customers and number of mortgage holders

Product			# customers	# customers with a mortgage product as well	
				Offset mortgage	Other mortgage
Personal	One product only	Direct[1]	240,165	335	7,212
		Notice[2]	46,538	23	687
		Bond[3]	2,106	0	4
		ISA	11,447	24	335
	Two products only	Direct and Notice	32,490	48	812
		Direct and Bond	2,086	1	20
		Direct and ISA	15,272	34	812
		Notice and Bond	951	1	7
		Notice and ISA	2,529	3	50
		Bond and ISA	44	0	0
	Three products only	Direct and Notice and Bond	857	3	9
		Direct and Notice and ISA	4,109	13	155
		Direct and Bond and ISA	244	0	3
		Notice and Bond and ISA	79	0	3
	All four products	Direct and Notice and Bond and ISA	165	0	7
Business	One product only	Direct	37,144	–	–
		Notice	9,547	–	–
		Bond	355	–	–
	Two products only	Direct and Notice	3,084	–	–
		Direct and Bond	458	–	–
		Notice and Bond	412	–	–
	All three products	Direct and Notice and Bond	256	–	–

Notes 1 'Direct' product is a direct access savings account where money can be drawn from the account without giving notice to the bank.
2 'Notice' product is a savings account where a notice period of 30 days must be given to the bank before money can be withdrawn.
3 'Bond' is a savings bond.

ledge that we have of our markets. To continue this trend and meet our future targets over the next few years, we conducted a detailed review and analysis of which segments we should target, the products we need to sell and the sales channels through which we get business.

The business is split into the two major product groups of savings and mortgages. Jim White explained:

The customers choosing our savings products are broken down into personal and business. Within these, there is a small range of product categories. Whereas most personal and business customers have purchased just one product, we are increasing our efforts to cross-sell both within savings products and also across into mortgages. Exhibit 4 gives details of the number of customers we have by personal

and business category and also the level of cross-selling achieved to date. From this you can see that at present we do not offer ISA savings products or mortgages to our business customers. In terms of

Exhibit 5 Total number of mortgage products sold

Lender	Type of product	# products sold last year			
		Jan	Apr	Jul	Oct
UK total	Discount	71,175	62,481	71,630	58,277
	Fixed	38,351	37,376	38,783	45,892
	Tracker	30,460	30,326	30,144	28,232
	Premium	22,420	25,150	22,452	23,778
	Standard	11,234	10,257	10,578	14,174
	Capped	2,447	2,217	1,890	1,436
	Other	41,812	38,180	41,446	46,734
Riviona Bank	Discount	1,775	2,187	2,841	3,668
	Fixed	613	554	537	454
	Other	168	486	53	166

Exhibit 6　Sales volume and value for mortgages and savings

Product type	Sales channel		Sales for a typical month	
			Volume	Value (€000s)
Mortgage	Introduced	independent financial advisor	1,981	215,803
		mortgage intermediary	516	56,642
		estate agent	82	8,416
		other	53	3,980
	Direct		317	450
Savings	Introduced		1,495	2,123
	Direct		1,913	2,716

mortgages, we tend to sell mainly discounted or fixed products, although there is significant scope to develop other offerings, as shown in Exhibit 5.

These products are sold to customers using two different sales channels. 'Direct' sales are those made by Riviona's own staff, whereas 'introduced' sales are made by a third-party organization such as an independent financial advisor. Exhibit 6 gives details of the sales volumes and values for each product by each sales channel for a typical month.

Customer service

The customer service function within the bank is responsible for handling and processing the demand for saving and mortgage products received by mail, telephone and the internet. The task includes pro-cessing customer applications (which may include a part-selling task), clarifying details, completing the application, setting up the product or account and the subse-quent maintenance and servicing. As well as handling inbound tele-phone calls, outbound calls are also made by the mortgage sales contact centre to sell products to existing customers.

As Jane Gillanders (customer service director) explains:

Working in customer services means that you get involved in different aspects of the business, which makes it exciting but also very demanding at the same time. We undertake four key activities in the department: mortgage sales, mortgage new business, mortgage servicing and savings [as described in Exhibit 7]. And there are a variety of challenges involves in managing these [see Exhibit 8]. One of my key tasks is to ensure the interface between sales and marketing and us operates smoothly and effi-ciently. The activities they undertake to stimulate demand need to be carefully coordinated so that we have sufficient capacity in place to meet this. It is also important to understand the form in which this demand will come – by mail, phone or the internet. Managing this mix of work flows is crucial. As well as the ongoing day-to-day requirements, we also under-

Exhibit 7　Key customer service activities

Activity	Description
Mortgage sales	Outbound telephone calls are made to sell mortgage products to new customers and inbound calls are received as a result of advertising activity
Mortgage new business	This comprises the steps to process an application for a mortgage through to releasing funds to the customer. After receiving a mortgage application, an agreement in principle (AIP) is made over the telephone that is then confirmed in writing. A number of checks, such as property valuations, are then conducted by third-party organizations. The customer service staff coordinate these and ensure that everything is complete before sending a formal offer to the customer. Finally, the funds are released to enable the customer to purchase the property. Typically, the whole process takes 35 days, with a formal offer being given after 20 days
Mortgage servicing	Once a mortgage has been set up, there may be a number of servicing activities that subsequently occur during its life. For example, there may need to be a credit re-assessment of the customer. On certain types of mortgage products, the customer is also able to request a 'payment holiday' and defer interest payments for a period of time
Savings	Unlike mortgages, savings new business and servicing occurs in the same area. The main reason for this is that the new business processing for savings is not as complex as the mortgage new business process outlined above. Applications are received for savings products, processed and the relevant account details set up on the computer system. Once savings products have been set up, they are serviced during their life. Customers will tend to make a number of deposits and withdrawals from their accounts (depending on the nature of the product). The activities associated with these transactions are handled by the customer service function

Exhibit 8 Managing the customer service function

Issue	Description
Managing the interface between customer service and sales and marketing	Reflecting priorities within different sales channels while coordinating staff levels in line with the demand created by marketing initiatives. The key here is to explain to sales and marketing the full impact of their activities on customer service
Managing changes in the customer service function	Ensuring that it can capitalize on the recent changes made, the changes planned for the future and then deliver the required results. This also involves managing senior management's expectations about what results are realistic
Matching capacity to demand	Forecasting demand and ensuring that there is sufficient resource to meet this requirement, while keeping a tight hold on costs
Managing the mix of work flows	Much of the work flow within customer service is still paper-based, for example mortgage applications, housing valuation reports, quarterly statements sent out to customers and notifying interest rate changes. The need to update the process technology to enable it to convert from paper to electronic formats is critical. It would, however, involve training and development issues as well as the investments in technology. And, before it chooses to automate its systems, it needs to ensure that the right processes are in place, otherwise it will simply be processing inefficient activities more quickly
Managing staff through the process of change	Ensuring that staff understand why changes are made and what they involve. This is an ongoing process as staff are continually moved from technical to customer-related skills

take a number of projects such as the recent restructure. Staff can find the changes that result from these initiatives quite unsettling, and it is important to keep them constantly informed and up to date on where we are.

Before the restructure

Jane Gillanders explained:

Earlier this year, we restructured customer service to better equip us to meet the demands the business will face over the coming years. Prior to these changes the call centre handled all customer telephone calls. For mortgage products, the call centre handled an application up to the 'agreement in principle' (AIP) stage and then mortgage new business processed it from this stage up to the

'formal offer'. Subsequent servicing would either be completed by the call centre for simple changes or by mortgage new business for more complicated requests. The same breakdown of tasks was also used for savings products. [Exhibit 9 shows the service delivery system for mortgage and savings products prior to the restructure.]

For mortgages, the separation was, in essence, that initial applications and subsequent 'straightforward' servicing were completed by the call centre, while mortgage new business handled setting up a mortgage, the final agreement and any non-straightforward servicing issues. For savings, the servicing phase was typically straightforward, and consequently the call centre usually handled the initial contact with the customer and the subsequent servicing of these products. After the initial contact with the call centre, new products were then set up in the savings new business back-office function. There were a number of advantages of this system. In the front office, fluctuations in the level of savings and mortgage calls could be managed across the whole of the call centre, and demand was easier to forecast as the length of time taken to handle a call centre task was more similar and predictable. In the back office, tasks typically vary much more in terms of the work involved and the amount of processing time required. This arrangement ensured that all our highly skilled, back-office staff was well utilized and working on tasks that are typically more difficult than those handled in the call centre.

However, there were also certain disadvantages in the previous way of working. It was not possible to move individuals between front and back office and some customer requirements were delayed as they were not able to be resolved in a one-stop shop fashion, often leading to high levels of work-in-progress within the system. There were a number of unproductive activities involved in the process, such as the handoffs between front office and back office staff. Also, and more importantly, we were finding that because staff only completed one step in the process and then passed on the job, they were not highly motivated in their work, feeling very little ownership for the tasks they completed and the customers they served. We are hoping that staff will be much more motivated and customer-oriented in the new organizational arrangements and that there will be a higher quality of service.

Exhibit 9 Service delivery systems for mortgage and saving products before restructure

Mortgage customer
written contact

FRONT OFFICE		**BACK OFFICE**

Call centre

Mortgage new business

Mortgage customer telephone call and internet contact

- Answer telephone calls and receive internet contact from mortgage, personal savings and business savings customers
- Process mortgage new business transactions:
  - Verbal applications
  - Verbal agreement in principle
  - Verbal application enquiries
- Process mortgage servicing transactions:
  - Verbal request from general administration

Savings customer telephone call and internet contact

- Process personal and business savings new business transactions:
  - Verbal applications
  - Verbal application enquiries
- Process personal and business savings servicing administration
  - Verbal general administration
  - Verbal deposit
  - Verbal withdrawal

Request for transaction →

- Receive written contact from mortgage customers
- Process new business transactions:
  - Verify customer details
  - Coordinate third-party activities
  - Issue formal offer
  - Release funds
- Process servicing transactions
  - Written request for general administration
  - Credit reassessment
  - Overpayments and payment holidays
  - Securities
  - Offsetting
  - Banking
  - FCR
  - Deeds control
  - Filing

Savings new business

- Receive written contact from personal and business savings customers
- Process new business transactions:
  - Verify customer details
- Process servicing transactions:
  - Written general administration
  - Written deposit
  - Written withdrawal

Request for transaction →

Savings customer written contact

After the restructure

Since the beginning of this year, the arrangements described in the last section have been changed. The front- and back-office structure has been replaced by contact centres, with each of these now involved in all aspects of serving a customer. The current structure comprises teams that handle all the setting-up and servicing tasks of the three product groups: mortgages, personal savings and business savings. Within mortgage new business, personal savings and business savings, there are smaller teams that handle a group of customers by categories of surname (A to F, G to O, P to Z), whereas within the mortgage servicing contact centre, teams are split by function (such as customer accounts, securities and banking deeds). Within each small team, staff can handle all aspects of relevant products. Exhibit 10 provides an overview of the changes in service delivery that this created.

Jane Gillanders explained:

In the process of restructuring, we have moved from a more functional structure, with separate front and back offices, to a more team-based approach where all activities for a set of mortgage or savings customers are conducted. Initially, this involved the physical relocation of most of the staff to ensure that members of each team are sitting together. Now we are starting on the long process of training to create the required level of resource flexibility between front- and back-office tasks within each team. We are hoping that once this training is complete, the teams will be able to self-manage themselves and allocate staff to different activities within varying periods of demand. One of the keys to making this work is to ensure that not only are people cross-skilled, but that they also develop the capability to manage how they allocate time so that there is no increase in the waiting time of incoming telephone calls.

Exhibit 10 **Service delivery systems for mortgage and saving products after restructure**

↓ Mortgage new customer
↑ written contact

MORTGAGE TEAM

Mortgage sales contact centre	Mortgage new business contact centre
• Answer telephone and internet contact from mortgage customers • Process new business transactions: – Verbal applications – Verbal agreement in principle – Verbal application enquiries	• Receive written contact from mortgage customers • Process new business transactions: – Coordinate third-party activities – Issue formal offer – Release funds

← Mortgage new customer telephone call and internet contact →

Request for transaction →

Mortgage servicing contact centre

← Mortgage existing customer telephone, internet and written contact →

• Answer telephone calls, receive internet and written contact from mortgage customers • Process servicing transactions: – Verbal and written requests for general administration – Credit reassessment – Overpayments and payment holidays	• Process servicing transactions: – Securities – Offsetting – Banking – FCR – Deeds control – Filing

SAVINGS TEAM

← Personal savings customer telephone, internet and written contact →

Personal savings contact centre

• Answer telephone calls, receive internet and written contact from personal savings customers • Process new business transactions: – Verbal and internet applications – Verbal and internet application enquiries	• Process servicing transactions: – Verbal and written general administration – Verbal and written deposit – Verbal and written withdrawal

← Business savings customer telephone, internet and written contact →

Business savings contact centre

• Answer telephone calls, receive internet and written contact from business savings customers • Process new business transactions: – Verbal and internet applications – Verbal and internet application enquiries	• Process servicing transactions: – Verbal and written general administration – Verbal and written deposit – Verbal and written withdrawal

Note   The Twilight Contact Centre does a mix of the above activities to cover both mortgage and savings teams between 17:00 and 22:00, Monday to Friday.

Rationale for restructuring

There were a number of reasons why the decision was made to restructure customer service. Jane Gillanders explains:

> The main reason for restructuring was to get the productivity improvements required to meet the bank's five-year plan of increasing the book value from €24 billion to €39 billion with existing staff levels. Given our experience to date and the data we have gathered, I believe that this is achievable. However, this is only one of the benefits that we expect from the new structure [see Exhibit 11]. Others include increased flexibility of resources, improved service levels, easier to identify training requirements and an increased opportunity to cross-sell products. This last point is integral to meeting the targets that the bank has set itself and will require a significant change in the mindset of customer service staff. We believe that being involved in the total process of serving customers will create a greater understanding of customer needs and hence more opportunity to sell other products to customers while serving them.

The way ahead

Michael Jones reflected on the future:

> The way ahead is going to be difficult. Our growth targets are sizeable in their own right, but coupled with the productivity gains we need to make as well as the need to bed in the organizational changes and implement the necessary process developments we have much to do. Our past performance of growing market share is, in part, the result of identifying the products that meet customers' needs and which offer competitive rates in both the savings and mortgage markets. But how well we manage our customers is also central to maintaining and growing share. Marketing has identified the sectors and segments that best fit our business profile. The contribution of customer service in the initial set-up phase as well as the maintenance and post-sale phase will be a key factor in addressing the stretch goals to which we are committed.

Questions

1 What is the marketing strategy to achieve the corporate objectives of the bank over the next four years? Is it realistic and what are the implications for customer service?

2 Analyse the previous and current customer service delivery systems. What was the rationale for the restructuring?

3 What are the advantages and disadvantages of the before and after customer service organizational structures?

Exhibit 11 **Rationale for restructuring customer service**

Aspect	Description
Increased productivity	By combining front- and back-office tasks, there should be reduced idle time, as agents can complete back-office activities during periods of low call volumes. This will also eliminate the double handling that occurred within the previous service delivery system
Increased flexibility of resource	The new delivery system combines both front- and back-office tasks, therefore it can be managed as a single resource of capacity and each contact centre work group can organize itself more easily to meet the changing demand patterns of customer-facing and non-customer-facing tasks
Improved service levels	It provides the resource flexibility to ensure that the target 'grade of service' offered to customers is continually met. There are two main service level targets: ● Speed of answering telephone calls – the target is to pick up 85 per cent of telephone calls within 15 seconds, and less than 3 per cent of telephone calls abandoned ● Mortgage product agreement in principle – the target is to provide a written AIP confirmation within one day (90% of the time) for cases where all the information is immediately available and provide written AIP confirmation within five days (90% of the time) for cases where not all of the information is immediately available
Easier to identify training requirements	It will be easier to identify where training is required and tailor this to the specific needs of individuals
Increased opportunity to cross-sell products	As staff are now involved in the total process of serving a customer, there is a greater understanding of customer needs and hence more opportunity to sell other products to customers while serving them

Selfridges

Five years ago, Selfridges was considered to be the 'dowdy old dame' of the large departmental store sector and unable to compete with rivals such as Harrods, Neiman Marcus and Bloomingdale's. Since then, it has reinvented itself into what has been described by some retail analysts as a 'combination of the variety of an old-fashioned emporium peppered with ultra-cool style'. To quote Nathan Cockrell, an analyst for Credit Suisse First Boston in London:

> What Selfridges has done is to return to what department stores were a century ago. They've been controversial, they've grabbed fashion and they've provided great marketing and great theatre.

A perfect example of this is the annual month-long events held at its stores. Body-Craze is one such event that set out to explore our fascination with the human body. During the promotion the store pushed everything to do with the human form, from more types of mineral water than you knew existed to body piercing and computer-generated images of what shoppers might look like as they aged. To launch the event, supermodel Elle MacPherson stripped off in a window so a cast could be made of her, and 600 members of the public posed naked on the escalators as part of an installation by New York artist Spencer Tunick. The purpose behind this and the store's other events is simply that, in the competitive world of retail, Selfridges needs to make itself a must-visit place and it seems to be working. As Arnold Aronson, a former chief executive at Saks Fifth Avenue, commented:

> Any major department store chief who has not made his way to Selfridges to study its mix and its operation is not doing his job. The Oxford Street store has become the one to watch, if not emulate.

The history of the store

Gordon Selfridge opened the Oxford Street store on 15 March 1909. His ambition was to create a single entity retail store selling a broad range of products where everyone would be welcome. He viewed the store as a theatre in which products and services were the stars. He came to London from the US where he previously worked as a store manager for Marshall Field's and had adopted some of Field's notorious flair and showmanship. Not only did he use the same architect who had designed the famous Field's store in Chicago, but also when Louis Bleriot flew across the English Channel in July 1909, Selfridge bought Bleriot's plane and suspended it above the store's main shopping floor. In the first week alone, 150,000 people came to the store just to see it.

However, the success and momentum of the early years started to slow and by the 1950s the store has acquired a stodgy reputation. It was rejuvenated briefly in the 1960s with the emergence of swinging London and the birth of the Miss Selfridge label, but even this eventually grew old and was sold off. By the early 1990s, things were starting to reach rock bottom and a decision was made to develop and launch a masterplan that would totally transform the store. The first step was to appoint Vittorio Radice, the Italian son of a furniture designer, as chief executive. He quickly realized that he needed to make Selfridges stand out from the pack if he was going to make a difference.

Radice decided that the traditional advertising and marketing used to date was not the way forward, and to use these approaches to achieve the sort of impact that he wanted to make would have been costly, so he changed tack. Selfridges magazine adverts were stopped and Radice introduced in-store events that were more in keeping with Gordon Selfridges original business concept. The first of these was the Tokyo Life promotion, which was

This case study was written by Alex Hill (University of Kingston). It is intended as the basis for class discussion and not as an example of good or bad management. © AMD Publishing.

effectively a grand celebration of Japanese commerce and culture. Selfridges invested £2 million in the month-long event that featured everything from Japanese performance artists, video arcade games, neon installations and a karaoke bar. This was followed by a Bollywood season the next year, inspired by India's vibrant film industry, and Body-Craze the year after.

The purpose behind these events is to make customers feel that the store is a must-visit place. As Peter Williams, Selfridges' current chief executive, comments:

> It's not about selling socks. You can find socks in any mall. You get them in for BodyCraze, and while they're there, they'll buy socks. And while they're here they know they can choose from a wide range of different products. We have a portfolio of over 3,000 brands and, unlike socks, some of these are highly fashionable one-off products that are not readily available elsewhere.

Creating the right retail environment

Of course there was more to Radice's strategy than simply finding a more effective way to spend the marketing budget. In fact, some of the biggest changes he made cannot readily be seen. One key initiative concerned the use of suppliers. While the majority of department stores still buy most of the merchandise they offer, Selfridges has steadily increased the amount of space it rents to suppliers. In fact, more than half the floor space in the Oxford Street store is now rented by outlets who pay anywhere between 15 and 45 per cent of sales revenue for the opportunity to sell their products. Based on experience, the decision was also made to allow suppliers to choose what goes into the space they rent. As Williams explained:

> This has been our policy since one of our store buyers rejected a Fendi purse that their designer said was the latest thing. 'Our customers just wouldn't be interested,' the buyer sniffed. Was she wrong! Fendi's 'baguette' purse went on to sell millions and we couldn't sell the products we had chosen, which had to be marked down at the end of the season. From then on, we decided to let the vendors live or die with what they thought would sell.

Now, not only is each supplier responsible for selecting which products to stock in its area, but it is also encouraged to be creative with the design of the retail space itself. As a result, Lancaster, a cosmetic company, built its version of a yacht, with white leather curved seats and gleaming metal railings, and Speedo, the sportswear company, constructed fitting rooms named after surfing towns, in which when you close the door you hear the surf roar. These spaces are constantly being recreated to reflect the style and ambiance of the ever-changing brand portfolio within them. As Williams explained:

> We have found that simple touches can make a big difference. For example, the new lingerie department in Oxford Street now features changing rooms with intercoms so customers can just call for a different style or size.

All this adds to the eclectic nature of the store, making it a place to visit and creating an atmosphere that encourages customers to spend time there. Since its transformation, Selfridges has been able to capitalize on the fact that for many people the days spent shopping, browsing and spending money have become a leisure pursuit. They have moved on from buying products that they need to things that they want and often these decisions are made on impulse. In fact, recent research has shown that 80 per cent of shoppers are in the store without a set purpose and spend their money on a replacement, an upgrade or simply a treat. The overall result is that by getting people to spend time in your store you can often get them to buy products that they did not previously realize they wanted.

Delivering the service

As well as managing the customer experience in the store, it is also important to ensure that they receive a level of service that is in line with their expectations. As Bob Harris, the Oxford Street store manager, explained:

> Over the last five years, we have transformed the store into the most sensational shopping experience you can imagine. Customers can indulge themselves in everything from exquisite fashion brands, mouth-watering food and drink, and soothing health and beauty treatments to thrilling sound and vision [see Exhibit 1]. In terms of delivering this wide range of products, we employ a broad mix of people from teenagers in dreadlocks in the body-piercing salon to sleek and sophisticated staff in our classy, half-acre cosmetics section. Thus, one of the biggest challenges is continually training and devel-

Exhibit 1 Departments within the London Oxford Street store

Floor	Departments
Lower ground	Cookshop, technology hall, bookshop, leisure, luggage, music, hardware, base bar, Café 400, Sienna café, celebration service, services lounge, key cutting, shoe repair, British Airways travel shop
Ground	Beauty hall, food hall, Jane Packer flowers, men's accessories, women's accessories, Spirit for women, stationery, Venus flowers, balcony wine bar, Brass Rail coffee bar, The Gallery, Iguazu, fresh oyster bar, Yo! Sushi, information desk, car park access, gift wrapping, food order
First	Menswear, men's shoes, sports hall, Spirit for men, espresso bar, Gordon's café, men's salon
Second	Womenswear (contemporary), women's shoes, hats, Lab café, alterations, car park access, women's personal shopping
Third	Kids' zone, intimate apparel, women's eveningwear, Premier restaurant, The Dining Room
Fourth	Furnishings, bedlinen, bathshop, Well-being, Farmacia, The Gallery, Food Garden café, Haagen Dazs café
Fifth	Hair and Beauty Salon, The Spa

oping our staff so that they have a detailed knowledge of the stock being sold and are able to deliver the service expected by our customers. Every working day they have to make our customers feel part of the show by giving them advice and inspiration in equal measure.

To achieve this, Selfridges has introduced a number of initiatives. To train and develop staff, it uses a combination of different programmes. These vary from those at a basic level through to National Vocational Qualifications (NVQ) programmes and a Certificate in Retailing that it was involved in launching, the first specialist qualification in the industry. Staff are also encouraged to take ownership

Exhibit 2 Recent awards received

Year	Awards received
2002	• London Tourism Awards 2002 • *London* magazine voted Selfridges 'Visitor Choice Best Retailer'.
2001	• *Marketing Week*/Chartered Institute of Marketing 'Phoenix Award' • *Drapers Record* 'Best Multiple Department Store Award' • *Time Out* Retail Awards 'Best Department Store'
2000	• *Retail Week* 'Instore Promotion of the Year (Fashion Week 1999)'
1999	• *Drapers Record* 'Multiple Retailer of the Year Best Store Brand Image' • Top Buyer – Debbie Taylor (Women's Contemporary) • *Evening Standard* 'London Fashion Week Window Display' (commended)
1998	• *Design Week* 'Best New Corporate Identity'

in the company and an 'All Employee Share Ownership Plan' and a 'Sharesave Scheme' have been set up. A staff intranet has also been developed to facilitate communication and help to build a sense of team and community. All this has led to Selfridges winning a number of awards recently, including the *Drapers Record* award for Multiple Department Store, Best Retailer from Maxim and In-store Promotion of the Year from *Retail Week* (see Exhibit 2).

But meeting and maintaining the standards that Selfridges has set for itself is not an easy task. Harris explained:

We use a variety of methods to monitor and measure the level of service that our customers receive in the store, from customer surveys and questionnaires to mystery shoppers. We see this as an important part of assessing the standard of service delivered and the output from this is fed back into staff training and development programmes. However, what's also important is managing all the delivery systems that we have outsourced to our suppliers. In the Oxford Street store, over 50 per cent of the 540,000 square feet floor space is rented to suppliers who manage their own areas staffed by their own people. These cover everything from the different retail outlets themselves to the store's various bars, restaurants and cafes that often share a theme with the adjacent selling floor. And all these have to be coordinated with the various promotional and theatrical activities that occur on a daily basis. Only recently, Kylie Minogue came along to the store to launch her new lingerie line that was initially exclusive to Selfridges and created a huge amount of interest on the first day.

Behind the scenes

The activities that occur in the store itself, however, are supported by a number of key initiatives in the business. As Peter Williams explained:

It's no good us attracting customers into the store and encouraging them to spend time there, if the products themselves are not on the shelves. The improved margins seen in the last two years have been largely a result of better stock management. Central costs have been well controlled and we are continuing to put systems in place to ensure that our multi-site expansion programme benefits from every possible synergy. A milestone development for us was the opening of our new distribution centre in November 2001. This provides a vast purpose-designed space, strategically sited at the heart of the UK motorway network, which will meet the needs of our longer term ambitions as we expand the number of stores we have outside London. At present we are also in Manchester and Birmingham, and we've just recently acquired a site in Glasgow.

When setting up our warehousing and distribution centre near Birmingham, we decided to outsource these operations tasks to our specialist partner Exel. Through working with them, we are continually searching for ways to reduce supply chain costs. As a result, we have made substantial investment in systems technology in recent years, now making Selfridges one of the most efficient retailers in the sector. This has included upgrades to our online systems and entering into a new data-sharing partnership with our suppliers that means products are now bar coded at source, arriving ready for sale with minimum effort at our end. This has yielded huge productivity improvements that enable us to rush the newest products and ideas into our stores, and keep our customers at the forefront of fashion. In fact, cutting-edge business-to-business systems have proved to be one of our most powerful means to increasing profits. As a result, we are leading the drive to sign up vendors and other retailers to electronic supply chain systems that will make manual paperwork a thing of the past.

The future

The impact of these changes at Selfridges has meant that it has gone from strength to strength, to the point that it is delivering increased sales, profits and returns to shareholders (see Exhibit 3). The numbers are telling. While sales at department stores such as Harrods and John Lewis have suffered in the last year, Selfridges is still performing well. Its size may be part of its success, but another key factor is that foreign tourists comprise only 20 per cent of its business, compared with 40 per cent at Harrods. The local residents consider it as much a destination to visit as those on holiday. As Marshal Cohen, of the NPD Group market research firm comments, 'Selfridges connects with the customer – they're in touch and they let the consumer feel they're somehow part of the process.' It does this not only through the activities in the store itself but also through its customer account cards and loyalty schemes, with invitations to events such as fashion shows, food and wine tasting and gallery previews.

The key for the next few years is to ensure that it does not dilute its unique quality as it expands. As one retailer comments:

> It's starting to expand so aggressively. Manchester, Birmingham and now it's bought another site in Glasgow, all without sounding out shareholders about the wisdom of the expansion. I just hope it doesn't lose its sense of vibrancy, its sense of theatre. My favourite thing was always a little sign on the way to the tattoo parlour that says: 'Smile. You're On Stage.'
>
> **www.selfridges.com**

Exhibit 3 Selfridges' financial performance

Overall summary

Measure	Annual financial performance				
	1999	2000	2001[1]	2002	2003
Sales (£m)	307.4	360.0	386.2	402.2	444.9
Profit before tax (£m)	13.9	27.6	36.3	37.6	40.7
Dividend per share (pence)	4.8	5.25	6.0	7.0	7.8

Note 2001 was a 52-week year, the others were 53 weeks.

Annual sales by store

Store	Annual sales (£m)				
	1998	1999	2000	2001	2002
London Oxford Street	290.6	320.3	341.4	348.0	369.1
Manchester Trafford Centre[1]	15.4	38.0	42.8	52.6	57.3
Manchester Exchange Square[2]	–	–	–	–	16.9
London Hotel rental income	1.4	1.7	2.0	1.6	1.6
Total	307.4	360.0	386.2	402.2	444.9

Notes 1 Opened in September 1998.
        2 Opened in Oct 2002

Annual contribution by store

Store	Annual contribution (£m)				
	1998	1999	2000	2001	2002
London Oxford Street	47.1	59.0	67.9	67.9	68.0
Manchester Trafford Centre	1.2	2.7	3.5	6.8	7.1
Manchester Exchange Square	–	–	–	–	0.9
Total	48.3	61.7	71.4	74.7	76.0

Annual central and other costs

Annual costs	Annual performance (£m)				
	1998	1999	2000	2001	2002
Central	33.3	33.0	34.1	35.4	33.9
Other	1.0	1.1	1.0	1.7	1.4
Total	34.3	34.1	35.1	37.1	35.3

Questions

1 Why is Selfridges successful?

2 What are the challenges for operations to deliver this success?

Southwest Airlines

Since its foundation in 1967, Southwest Airlines has gone from strength to strength. Slowly expanding from its base in Dallas, the company has built up its operation to the point where it now serves 59 airports, with 381 planes in operation, and continues to expand.

When describing Southwest Airlines, it is difficult to avoid superlatives. The lowest costs, the lowest fares, the highest levels of asset usage, the best labour relations, the highest wages in the industry; Southwest has all these things and a lot more. At first glance, the company seems to have achieved these goals by running counter to industry practice: there are no operations hubs, there is no emphasis on service extras (quite the contrary) and there has been no heavy investment in IT. Southwest seems deliberately to concentrate on markets that other airlines do not regard as important.

So why has it succeeded? It would be easy to portray Southwest Airlines as a maverick organization, and over the years a lot of attention has focused on Herb Kelleher, its president, co-founder and inspirational leader. But, while not denying Kelleher's influence in creating a strong and enduring company culture, it has to be said that there is more to this picture than the presence of a dynamic leader. Southwest Airlines is, and has been from the beginning, an organization founded on a few basic success principles. It is somewhat surprising to find that, behind the dynamic, thrusting exterior and the lively company culture, there is an organization that is innately careful, even cautious, and risk-averse. While embracing change, Southwest also avoids change for its own sake; there are no grand designs, no plans to grow outside its own niche market and, in an age when globalization seems to be the word on everyone's lips, absolutely no desire to go global. Change in Southwest Airlines is always focused on one or both of the company's two goals: cutting costs and increasing numbers of passengers.

Part of this careful approach can probably be traced to Southwest Airlines' origins. This is a company that didn't get off the ground at all, and for years since has fought a campaign of guerrilla warfare against its larger rivals.

Guerrilla warfare

For the first four years of its existence, Southwest Airlines was an airline in name only, fighting for its existence against rivals who wanted to kill it at birth. When Southwest first applied for certification in Texas in 1967, its competitors, especially Braniff and Texas International, opposed the application through the courts, on the grounds that the Texas market was already saturated and could not support another airline. The case dragged on for years and funds began to run low; Herb Kelleher, then working as Southwest Airlines' corporate lawyer, was eventually reduced to providing his services for free.

Finally, after winning their case in the US Supreme Court, Southwest Airlines was allowed to fly, and in 1977 its first aircraft finally left the ground. Kelleher and his colleagues had learned a valuable lesson. Rather than fight their larger, wealthier competitors head on, they would adopt a classic strategy of guerrilla war: be where the enemy is not.

Over the years, Southwest has systematically targeted airports and routes overlooked or badly served by other airlines. Steering clear of the large, overserved and congested 'hub' airports, Southwest's preferred ground has been the mid-sized airports of the mid-west and the Sun Belt, in cities like Little Rock, Las Vegas, Phoenix and Sacramento. Targeting smaller airports in this way means Southwest can hit other airlines where they are vulnerable. Smaller airports tend to be poorly served by the other major airlines, and lack of competition means fares are high. They also tend to have less traffic and are less congested. As a result, Southwest can compete

---

This case study was written by Terry Hill (University of Oxford) and Alex Hill (University of Kingston). It is intended as the basis for class discussion and not as an example of good or bad management. © AMD Publishing.

against its rivals by offering lower prices and faster service. For short-haul commuters (many of Southwest's flights are of less than an hour's duration), these are deciding factors when choosing a service. This strategy has worked. In 75–80 per cent of the airports where it operates, Southwest is the largest carrier in terms of numbers of passenger boardings.

One example shows how Southwest can not only enter a market but build it into a highly profitable one. When the airline first entered the Los Angeles-San Francisco area, rival airlines operating from the two major airports charged $80–$220 for a one-way ticket. Southwest established a route between the two metropolitan centres, not using the major airports but flying from the smaller, less crowded airports of Oakland and Burbank. Its one-way tickets cost $29–$59. The result? At the start of the year, Oakland-Burbank was the 200th busiest airline route in the USA in terms of numbers of passengers. By the end of the year, it had risen to 21st busiest. Elsewhere in the state, Southwest moved to a position of dominance in the airport of Sacramento, the state capital, and it now carries 20–40 per cent of all passengers in and out of Sacramento. In fact, throughout California, Southwest Airlines now carries over 15 per cent of all airline traffic within the state.

The traffic growth on routes served by Southwest illustrates another 'guerrilla war' aspect to Southwest Airlines. Marxists call it the mobilization of the masses; marketeers call it motivating people to take up the offer. Southwest Airlines does not just see itself as being in the airline business: it is in the transportation business. To that extent, it is not just competing with other airlines, but with other forms of transport including trains, buses and private cars. By offering fares at competitive rates and a swift, efficient service, Southwest is encouraging travellers to switch from other forms of commuting. If the traffic figures are anything to go by, it is succeeding.

There is a third 'guerrilla war' aspect to Southwest Airlines' operations: the lack of a central base. Most airlines operate on a 'hub and spoke' principle, flying the bulk of their passengers between major hub airfields and then transferring them to feeder flights going on to smaller airfields closer to their destination. Theoretically, at least, this is the most efficient model of operation for an airline. However, hub operations require considerable concentration of resources, and if a hub operation goes wrong, there can be severe knock-on consequences.

Hubs also represent a point where an airline can be particularly vulnerable to competition; losing market in a hub airport means the associated feeder traffic dries up as well.

Southwest, almost unique among major US airlines, uses a 'point to point' system. Its route diagram looks more like a spider web than the spokes of a wheel. Most of its flights are of short duration. Therefore, there is no defined centre of operations, no point where Southwest can be said to be particularly vulnerable. Anyone attempting to seriously challenge Southwest's dominance of the regional airline market would have to attack it on a number of points at once.

Such is the popularity of Southwest's service that cities all over the southwestern USA frequently invite the company to begin operating services from their airports. Interestingly, few of these offers are taken up. Southwest is not an aggressive company in that it seeks to challenge its rivals at every opportunity. Instead, the company moves only when it can see a clear advantage. Entry into potential new markets is carefully considered. It has to be; Southwest's margins are wafer-thin, and it cannot afford to spend time on loss leaders building up a market. The company's policy is that a new route has to be profitable from day one.

But when Southwest does decide to go into a market, it goes in hard. New routes typically have a broad spread of flights, timed so that flights are never more than about an hour apart. Passengers are invited to turn up and go; with flights as regular as buses (for example Southwest flies 78 times per day between Houston and Dallas), customers can travel at their convenience, not that of the airline. There are also no formalities of ticket reservation and collection; automatic ticket dispensers can process a credit card and dispense a ticket in under 20 seconds.

Within a short time after entry, Southwest Airlines comes to dominate the market, with affordable flights every few minutes acting like a magnet to pull passengers away from competing airlines. Many airlines would see this as suicidal, with large numbers of flights pushing up costs. Southwest looks at things differently; large numbers of flights allow fixed costs to be spread over a larger number of seats, while running costs are kept to the lowest level possible and are compensated for by the high volumes as Southwest becomes the airline of choice. This strategy often works quite dramatically. Five days after beginning flights from Little Rock, Southwest had scooped up 25 per cent of the market.

This strategy works not only as a means of breaking into new markets but as a means of deliberately attacking rivals. Coming down out of the hills, Southwest entered major airports like Phoenix and Chicago, attacking two competitors, America West and Midway, at their hubs. Unable to compete on price or service frequency, insufficiently flexible to switch their centres of operation, both rival airlines were driven into bankruptcy.

Quality without frills

Compared to many of its competitors, Southwest Airlines offers a distinctly no-frills service. There are no connections to other flights, and no baggage transfer. No meals are served. Seats cannot be reserved. The service resembles not so much an airline as a bus service with wings.

What the airline does offer is cheap, reliable, frequent service that gets passengers from A to B as fast as possible and with a minimum of fuss. There is a definition of quality, which suggests that quality is determined by a product or service's fitness for the purpose for which it was designed. On that criterion, Southwest Airlines can be said to be offering a high-quality service.

One of the keys to the success of the service offering is the constant, continuous focus on the market. It has defined its niche with great success. Southwest's passengers are like commuters; they are going somewhere for a purpose and they want to turn up and go without a lot of fuss or distractions. By not using travel agents to sell tickets, Southwest is able to cut out the agents' commissions and thus reduce its costs – and prices – still further. Because there are always plenty of planes flying and plenty of seats, no computerized reservation system is required; another cost saved and another complication for the customer dispensed with. By operating a turn up and go policy, Southwest is able to offer what are on aggregate the cheapest fares of any airline in the USA. And, because it knows its market and knows that low prices and reliability are what that the market wants, Southwest has been continuously profitable since it first began operations. Not many airlines in the USA can say that.

Would this formula work in a different market? Possibly, but possibly not. Southwest knows its own market, and intends to stay there. Real strength, it is said, comes from knowing your own limitations

and working within them. This is yet another area where Southwest Airlines would seem to have a lead over its rivals.

Doing more for less

Over and over again, the statistics show that Southwest wins by simply working harder than its rivals. Planes turn around faster, and operations has fewer staff. The average number of flights from each airport gate each day is 10.5: the industry average is less than half that number. Southwest's planes spend an average of 11 hours a day in the air, compared with an industry average of eight.

Strategy is focused on keeping operations simple, efficient and inexpensive. Staffing levels are kept to the minimum to do the job. The same applies to infrastructure. IT, for example, is kept deliberately simple and functional. There is no elaborate computerized system needing support and maintenance. The ticket machines were designed by some Southwest Airlines staff members one evening in a bar in Denver, and the prototypes were subsequently built by them in their spare time, using off-the-shelf components.

The frequent take-offs and landings use more fuel and mean Southwest must pay more in landing fees, but still Southwest has the lowest cost per seat-mile of any major airline, less than half that of its major rival USAir. By working its assets harder, that is, by keeping its planes in the air for more hours per day, Southwest has been able to reduce its load factor (defined as the number of paying passengers as a proportion of total seats on each flight required to break even) to just 55 per cent; again, lower than the industry average. This, in turn, means that planes can fly with fewer passengers, meaning more flights can be offered, which increases the number of options available to customers ... and so, on it goes.

Speed and flexibility are keys, operationally as well as tactically. Southwest Airlines ground staff can turn an aircraft around in 15 minutes; most airlines take up to an hour. Superbly trained, staff know their roles intimately, and the result, when a plane taxies up to the gate, is an efficient routine that might be envied by the pit crew of a Grand Prix racing team. The technical side is equally efficient. Southwest flies only one type of aircraft, the Boeing 737, and just four versions of that; spares and maintenance routines can thus be standardized, cutting down still further on costs. Southwest also operates new, fuel-efficient aircraft, rather than trying to make do with an ageing fleet as some of its competitors have done.

Leading by example

There is no doubt that Herb Kelleher himself has been one of the critical factors in the success of Southwest Airlines. A brilliant lawyer, he is also a strategist and an inspiring leader of people. Colleagues comment on his personality, his mental brilliance, his sense of humour, his ability to gain the respect and trust of his employees. This is a man who can in the same day chair a board meeting and do an Elvis Presley imitation at a company party.

Kelleher believes in leading by example rather than by direction. If staff work overtime, he turns up in person to thank them. And once a quarter he spends a day in the front line: serving drinks with the cabin crew, working with the baggage handlers, selling tickets, getting to know both passengers and staff.

This is a tactic that can easily backfire; employees are notoriously adept at sniffing out when their bosses are 'slumming' in hope of ingratiating themselves with the staff. But Kelleher's genuine commitment is never doubted. Where his company is concerned, he wears his heart on his sleeve.

Evidence of this is easily come by. When the Gulf War drove fuel prices up, airline staff set up a payroll deduction programme to help offset the increased costs. The programme, set up without Kelleher's knowledge, quickly raised over $130,000. This was a tiny amount in terms of the overall fuel bill. But, in terms of the sacrifice made by staff, and as evidence of their commitment to the firm, this was an enormous gesture. Even the name of the programme, Fuel from the Heart, showed the strength of feeling.

Kelleher is a leader rather than a manager. Within the company, staff at all levels are given wide discretion in carrying out their duties; they know what is expected of them, and are free to work out how to give the best service possible. Kelleher's role is more fundamental; he is the central focus of the company's culture, the pillar around which that culture revolves.

A culture of commitment

Kelleher's commitment to the firm is one of the building blocks of the company's culture. The struggle for survival in the early days, and Kelleher's role in it, have passed into Southwest Airlines legend. Events like Fuel from the Heart have also become part of that legend.

History is important in Southwest Airlines. The walls of the corporate headquarters in Dallas are lined with memorabilia: old advertisements, photographs of employees and corporate events, even mannequins displaying examples of staff uniforms. The effect is something like a cross between someone's family photo album and a museum. But this is not just reverence for the past; it is recognition that the past is something that can be built on.

Contradictions abound. Nearly all staff are union members; yet the company also has the highest rate of employee ownership of any major airline. As a result, Southwest also has one of the best records of any airline in terms of labour relations. The high levels of employee ownership, plus one of the highest pay levels in the industry, make for labour peace. Another superlative: Southwest also has the airline industry's lowest ratio of staff turnover. And when the airline does hire, it can take its pick from applicants; in one year, the company received over 60,000 applications for just 1,400 jobs.

The lowest prices in the industry, the highest pay in the industry: can this be right? Clearly it can. Southwest Airlines gets by with fewer staff, half or less than the usual number of boarding agents and ground staff (and remember that ground staff turn planes around much faster than any other airline). But those staff work hard and are committed to their jobs, their customers and the company. One intriguing facet to the company's recruitment programme is the use of customers, frequent flyers, to join interview panels. By using customer input directly into the recruiting process, the company hopes to recruit staff whose personalities match customers' expectations.

Close personal contact with customers is another feature of the company's culture. In return, customers tend to be extraordinarily loyal. Frequent flyers get to know staff, not only cabin crew but also ground staff, and are often on first-name terms. Customers are encouraged to tell the company about their likes and dislikes, and they respond; about 5,000 letters from customers are received every month, and all are read and answered.

The quiet revolutionaries

The airline industry is notoriously fraught with perils. More than 100 airlines have gone bankrupt in the USA in the last decade, including some giants of the industry. Half the rest are desperately trying to stave off bankruptcy; few are consistently profitable. Against this background, Southwest Airlines stands out. It does almost everything counter to industry logic, and its performance figures are equally contradictory to industry norms. Most compelling of all, the airline's managers have never got cocky. They continue to be fanatical about cutting costs, they continue to be devoted to their niche and to their customers. They continue with a corporate culture that promotes heroes and involves customers and staff alike in constant innovation and improvement. They take nothing for granted.

Southwest Airlines has achieved something of a revolution in the airline industry in its region by not only taking passengers away from rivals but growing markets and increasing passenger traffic overall. Quietly, working within its own self-defined limits, the company has become a major player in the airline industry. This is a company that embraces change. As Herb Kelleher has pointed out, the airline industry is full of change: how can it be passive when its major assets are moving at over 500 miles per hour? But above all, it is a company that knows itself, knows its customers and is intent on doing whatever it takes to provide the best service possible.

www.southwest.com

Question

1   What makes this airline successful?

Spencer Thompson

Spencer Thompson (ST) is a firm of professional accountants that provides both accounting, finance and management consultancy services to its clients. ST has offices throughout the UK, with the largest in central London.

At the central London office, there is a word processing centre and proofreading department that prepares the majority of reports for clients, together with internal documents, statements, reporting procedures and information papers. There is a manager, supervisor, nine processing staff and three proofreaders employed to provide this facility. The documents received for preparation vary in length from a few pages up to 250 pages or more. The estimated size of a document that users of the centre project when booking facilities ahead of time frequently differs greatly from the final version that the centre eventually receives.

The average output of each person on the word processing phase of the service is 600 lines per day including initial processing and corrections. The demand placed upon the processing facility varies as does the lead time required to meet client and consultancy assignment deadlines.

The process to complete a report or other document consists of initial processing, editing if required, proofreading, making corrections and proofreading the corrections. The three proofreaders provide the editing and proofreading capability in the process. However, in some situations the person writing the report may wish to take the initial typed document, edit or revise the text and then put it back into the process. In some cases, the revisions may be extensive.

Each proofreader averages about 90 pages of work a day. This average covers a typical mix of work and includes the checking of corrections.

Questions

1 What are the critical operations scheduling features?

2 What is the key operations scheduling task?

3 Outline the development of a suitable scheduling system for the business.

This case study was written by Terry Hill (University of Oxford) and KHA Negal. It is intended as the basis for class discussion and not as an example of good or bad management. © AMD Publishing.

Tile Products

Tile Products plc is a small company making fire-retardant ceiling tiles. The tiles are plaster mouldings made to any size or pattern, but the standard size is 2 feet square and the company offers a range of 10 patterns. Any customer requiring either a tailor-made size or pattern would be charged the setting-up costs, which entail making a one-off mould from which the tiles would then be produced.

After the initial work by the founder of the company Ben Graham, upon whose ideas the tile is based, sales had begun to increase over the past three to six months. Sales for the first 12 months of business and the first six months of this second year are given in Exhibit 1. Ben Graham is currently solely responsible for sales besides having overall control over operations and the financial aspects of the business.

Operations

Arthur Marshall, the operations supervisor, is responsible for the day-to-day control of oper-

ations. He has been with the business from the early days. As output requirements increased, the company employed two additional moulders, Ian Yates and Maurice Coles , who are now both fully trained. For at least half his time Arthur Marshall does the jobs of moulding and packing besides helping, as do Ian and Maurice, to unload materials and load up dispatches.

The working week is from Monday to Friday, 8.00 am to 4.30 pm with half an hour for lunch. If overtime is worked it is usually in the evening, but occasional Saturday working is arranged depending upon order volumes and delivery requirements.

The layout of the factory is shown in Exhibit 2 and the method of working is described in Exhibit 3. Although some tiles are made-to-stock, production tends to follow sales orders because of the lack of information on sales patterns and volumes. It is anticipated, however, that once sales have reached a higher level, production will be against sales forecasts for each pattern type.

Exhibit 1 Tile sales in the first 18 months of business

| | Year 1 | Year 2 | | | | | |
		Jan	Feb	Mar	Apr	May	Jun
Standard tiles:							
Classic	2,050	–	1,400	–	–	–	–
Georgian	2,850	–	–	600	650	–	400
Victorian	3,800	1,000	–	–	250	1,000	500
Modern	2,400	–	–	800	–	400	100
Simplicity	2,850	–	–	900	–	300	300
Scandinavian	1,600	–	500	–	–	–	900
American[1]	–	–	–	–	–	400	600
Scottish[1]	–	–	–	–	500	700	300
Floral	2,800	700	–	–	–	–	600
Heraldic[2]	750	–	100	–	300	200	300
Customer's own design	1,000	–	–	–	200	400	–
Total	20,100	1,700	2,000	2,300	1,900	3,400	4,000

Notes   1   Not introduced until April of year 2.
        2   Some designs (for example Heraldic) tend to be ordered as part of a ceiling pattern rather than as the main design.

Source Company records.

This case study was written by Terry Hill (University of Oxford). It is intended as the basis for class discussion and not as an example of good or bad management. © AMD Publishing.

Exhibit 2 **Existing shop-floor layout**

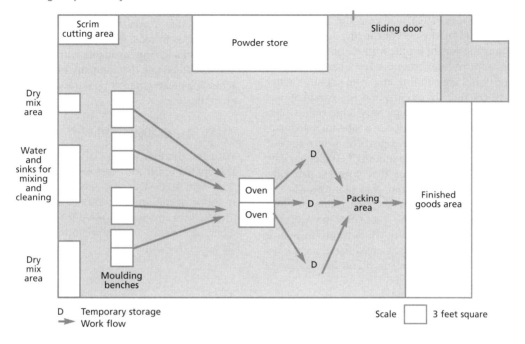

Exhibit 3 **Current methods of working**

Moulding

A moulder mixes the dry materials in the appropriate area, moves to the water sink and completes the mixing stage. He returns to the moulding bench and pours the mixture into the mould. He then goes to the scrim cutting area, cuts scrim (a synthetic gauze to help bond the tile) to the appropriate size and returns to the moulding bench. He places the scrim into the mould and then puts down the lid of the mould. The required pattern is in the mould base and the scrim, therefore, is placed in what will be the back of the tile. At the end of the initial drying cycle, the tile is lifted from the mould, carried to the oven and hung by lugs which form an integral part of the back of the mould. The moulder returns to the mould, cleans off any excess plaster and then repeats the process. The normal practice is to cut two or three pieces of scrim at a time and place them near at hand. This saves a journey to the scrim cutting area.

Typically a moulder works three moulds and very occasionally four. A person working all the time on moulding makes, on average, 60 tiles in an eight-hour day. In addition, the moulders and Arthur Marshall unload and load vehicles besides packing tiles once they have been baked in the ovens.

Drying

The drying process is in two stages. The initial drying or setting takes place in the mould as described above. This takes 15 minutes from pouring the plaster mixture into the mould to the time for lifting. The second drying stage takes place in the ovens. There are currently two fixed-position ovens each of which holds 90 tiles. When the oven has a full load (although

occasionally this part of the process is started with a part-load due to delivery requirements), the heat is brought up to the required temperature of 75 °C and the tile is baked for eight hours.

Packing

When the tile has been oven-dried, it is allowed to cool for a minimum of 30 minutes. Then the ovens are unloaded and the tiles are stacked on edge between the ovens and packing area (see Exhibit 2). When the tiles have accumulated or delivery requirements are pressing, each tile is packed individually and then four tiles are packed into an outer carton. The packed tiles are then stored in the finished goods area, by pattern, and up to three outer cartons high (the cumulative weight restricts storage height).

Dispatch

Sales orders are met from stock (unless it is a special tile and then these are made only to order) and the finished goods are stored in such a way as to facilitate stock rotation and so ensure that the older tiles are dispatched first.

Technical note

The materials used in making fire-retardant ceiling tiles are relatively fast setting which precludes the opportunity to make larger mixes than is the present practice. Consequently, each moulder may only mix sufficient for one moulding cycle which ensures that the required technical specification is achieved.

Company performance

Following a loss in the first year, the position has improved and by the end of the first half of year 2 the company was in profit, with margins of almost 20 per cent of sales revenue. Sales for the second half of year 2 are running at a level slightly higher than in the first six months and the company has submitted tenders for some very large orders. Ben Graham's immediate concern is operations capacity: a good moulder would produce, under current methods of working, a maximum of 60 tiles per day.

Ever since the start of the business, Ben Graham's attention had been directed towards the product. It had been necessary to refine the fire-retardant qualities of the tiles and improve the other aspects of tile quality while trying to reduce the costs of raw materials. Considerable steps have been achieved in this direction and arrangements

are now in progress to get the appropriate certification for the fire-retardant properties of this newly designed tile. Once this has been achieved, Graham's aim is to reduce the price per tile in line with the material savings available with the new design. This would enable the company to increase sales by achieving greater market penetration with the lower price tile.

Study of operations methods

With the increase in sales of existing tiles and the anticipated uplift in orders following a decrease in price as described above, Ben Graham requested a study of operations methods in order to establish the facilities and staff required for these higher volumes. The results of this preliminary investigation are given in Exhibit 4.

Exhibit 4 **Study of existing methods**

Moulding	Standard minutes[1,2]
Load mould (including mix ingredients)	1.30
Cut scrim[3]	0.27
Inital setting of tile in the mould	15.00
Unload tile to oven and hang	1.50
Packing	
Pack four tiles, then to an outer carton and stack	4.70

Notes 1 Standard times include an appropriate allowance for rest.
2 All times include the travel elements involved.
3 Based on cutting three pieces of scrim per journey. The standard time of 0.27 is the average time per piece.

Questions

1 What will be the future capacity requirements of the company?

2 Review the existing layout and suggest improvements.

Too Short the Day

Giles Chamberlain, the production manager of the Playhouse Theatre, set out for work on Monday morning. Over the weekend he had drawn up a priority list of the important longer term tasks he needed to accomplish and now he was mulling them over. Among the important items was the need to find new suppliers for several high-cost materials and those materials used in relatively large quantities in order to reduce the ever-increasing production costs. However, to help achieve this he needed to develop and agree new procedures with the administrator about planning the production of shows. This would not only help to reduce overtime working and the casual labour bill but would also mean that materials could be ordered in advance, enabling lower prices to be secured, rather than the present position where sourcing was usually based on fast delivery. In addition, some months ago he had been asked to draw up plans and expenditure estimates with the stage manager (see Exhibit 1) regarding proposals to provide new facilities on stage,

Exhibit 1 **Organization chart for the production manager's responsibilities at the Playhouse Theatre**

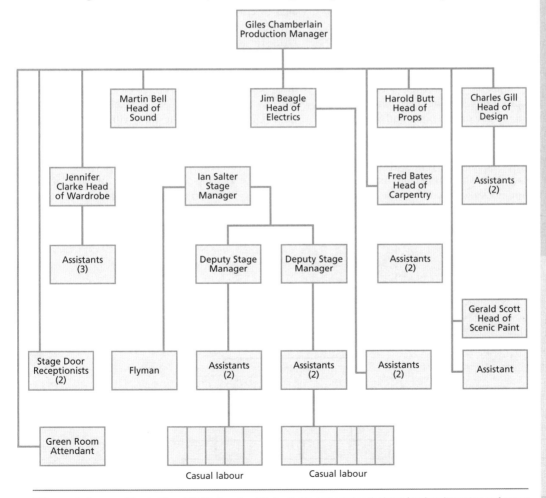

This case study was written by Terry Hill (University of Oxford). It is intended as the basis for class discussion and not as an example of good or bad management. © AMD Publishing.

which would offer more scope to designers and less work to provide the necessary requirements of a typical production. Finally, he had to discuss the increased use of modular stage designs with the head of carpentry in order to reduce the timber costs and construction time to produce a show.

By the time he reached the theatre, he was pleased about the approaching day and anticipated taking steps towards the resolution of these tasks, some of which he had intended getting down to for the past six to nine months. As he entered the building, the stage manager, Ian Salter, called him and explained that he needed more casual labour than planned due to the agreed changes made last Friday to the forthcoming play *Joseph and the Amazing Technicolour Dreamcoat*. They discussed the proposed increases and agreed on the course of action to take. He asked Ian to advise him on the outcome and to let his secretary, Mary Wright, know the costs involved. In the conversation, Ian had also reminded Giles of several items which needed either purchasing or progressing from suppliers.

On entering his office, Giles found on his desk some invoices and also the time sheets for the casual labour employed last week. In order not to keep the pay procedure waiting, Giles checked the wage claims, made one or two notes and authorized for payment those without queries. He then checked the invoices and telephoned the head of electrics (Jim Beagle), the head of carpentry (Fred Bates), the head of sound (Martin Bell) and head of wardrobe (Jennifer Clarke) to confirm the items and

quantities had been received. Neither Jim Beagle nor Jennifer Clarke answered so he made a mental note to ask them later in the day. He then made several telephone calls to outside suppliers in line with his earlier discussion with Ian Salter and asked for information to be put into the post.

Giles then telephoned Mary Wright to ask her to come up to his office. While he waited, he telephoned the local fire officer to check a point of detail that had come up in conversation with the assistant director (see Exhibit 2) late last week. Following the discussion he checked his file containing details of the local fire regulations and marked the appropriate section. Just then, Mary entered. He discussed some points of administrative detail and handed over the signed invoices and authorized casual labour time sheets. Mary handed over the morning mail and explained one or two points.

After a coffee break, Giles went down to the stage area to check on the progress being made on the alterations for the current production *The Sons of Light*. He walked over to Ian Salter to ask how the work was progressing. 'The problem is fitting the rostrum onto the stage', explained Ian. 'Fred (head of carpentry) is working on an idea I have in order both to ensure fit and keep it stable once in position.' Giles discussed the idea with both Ian and Fred and together they came up with another possibility. Giles looked on as first one idea then the other was tried. Further discussion took place until a satisfactory solution was reached. Before leaving the stage area, Giles then checked the casual labour time

Exhibit 2 **Playhouse Theatre organization chart**

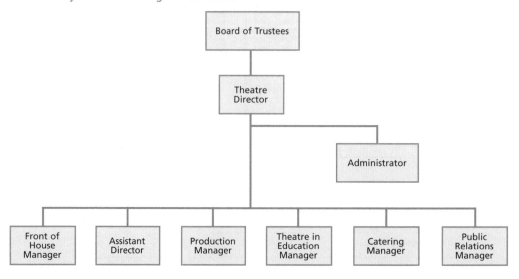

sheet queries with Ian, particularly about the level of overtime that had been worked, asked Ian to get overtime authorized in future, reinforcing the necessity to keep all costs within production budgets.

Giles then set off to see the head of wardrobe, Jennifer Clarke, to discuss the final cost of the current production and tomorrow's proposed trip to London with the head of design, Charles Gill, to buy new costumes for a future production of *The Play What I Wrote*. The discussion addressed costs, costume resale policies and the budget limits for the new costumes. Before he left, Giles also checked out the invoice query he had had that morning. By the time this discussion was over and Giles had walked back to his office, it was lunchtime. He made a few notes on points that had been made in the morning and then went off to lunch.

When he returned, there was a note from the theatre director's secretary advising him that his meeting with the director would have to be put back to 3.30 pm. He then made a telephone call to a supplier of special effects to order a smoke gun for a future production. As he was discussing the request, Mary Wright entered with letters for him to check and sign, together with the second delivery of mail. Having cleared the letters, Mary made one or two points contained in these and then left. Giles checked through both lots of mail in detail, made some notes and prepared his replies. He then telephoned Mary and asked her to come to his office at about 3.00 pm.

As he got up, a telephone call came through from a company enquiring about a shower unit which it had loaned to the theatre for a production which finished earlier in the year. Giles left the office and immediately bumped into Gerald Scott, head of scenic paint. Gerald discussed the need for some particular paints he required and asked if the request could be dealt with urgently. Giles agreed to this and continued into the stage area. He checked with Ian Salter that the earlier problem was now resolved. Ian also took the opportunity to enquire if he could use the theatre's large van to pick up some props for the next production, to which Giles agreed. On seeing Jim Beagle he crossed over and asked him about some queries on invoices concerning the purchase of electrical equipment and consumables. Giles then continued on to the carpentry shop to discuss with Fred Bates the next production in terms of deadlines for props and scenery. Fred also took the opportunity of handing over purchase requisitions for tools and timber, explaining that some of the items were urgent. On returning to his office, the administrator telephoned him about a touring theatre due the month after next. He asked Giles to note in his diary the date of a meeting he had arranged to discuss the detailed requirements with the touring theatre's agent. Just then Mary Wright entered and from then until his scheduled meeting at 3.30 pm he dictated letters, handed over filing and recorded dates in both diaries. Mary also asked him to call in to see the assistant director about an employee later that afternoon.

Meetings with the theatre director took place at least twice weekly and involved discussions on a number of issues. Today included an up-to-date progress report on the current production, rehearsal planning for the next two productions and the forward planning for both in-house and touring shows. Like most meetings, this one lasted about 45 minutes and Giles, on leaving it, had a list of points to check out and to confirm the detailed arrangements made. This information was normally required within 24 or 48 hours, at the latest, and formed part of the next meeting's agenda.

When he left the director's office he called in to see the assistant director and checked through the terms of employment details for a new member of staff due to start next week. He also mentioned the fire regulation query and agreed to let the assistant director have sight of the relevant section. He then went to see Harold Butt, head of props, to ask about the shower unit query. Harold explained that it had been broken after the production had ended and, consequently, was thrown away some weeks ago. Giles asked some questions on detail and then returned to his office, telephoned Martin Bell and Jim Beagle and asked them to come to see him. He then called the company about the shower unit, explained the problem, asked the price involved and agreed for them to send an invoice for the replacement cost. When Martin and Jim arrived, he discussed details of the special effects required for the next two productions, checked the up-to-date position and the lead times involved for those parts which were not yet ready. He noted the points and completion dates discussed in order to report back to the theatre director. He then telephoned Charles Gill, head of design, to ask him to come up to the office. Between Jim and Martin leaving and Charles arriving, Giles telephoned a paint supplier regarding the artistic paints request and also made an appointment to talk to an artist's agent about the requirements for a one-man show booked into the theatre in three weeks' time. By then Charles had arrived. Giles asked for a progress report on the design implications for three future productions: *The Irresistible Rise of Arturo UI*, *The Miser* and *Oliver Twist*. As a result of this discussion, Giles agreed to schedule further discussions with all those involved in these productions as time was now pressing in order to ensure that all aspects of these shows could be scheduled on time. He again made appropriate notes in order to report the details back to the director.

Giles then went back to the stage area as he had arranged to supervise a trial fit-up for the next production. He discussed aspects with the heads of the departments involved, noted the agreements and asked them to assess the deadlines to meet the necessary changes. By the time this was finished, the scheduled stage conversion back to that evening's performance had begun. Just as he was about to leave the stage area, Giles was beckoned by the front of house manager who wanted to discuss the provision of cover for two people (one on holiday and one who was ill) for tomorrow's matinee and

evening performance. Giles agreed to arrange the cover, and went back to his office. He then made a series of notes following the afternoon's discussions and, when he glanced at his watch it was 6.40 pm. Time to go home.

Busy? he asked himself. Too busy he thought. He had, on reflection, covered all the necessary aspects of his job, and put a lot of necessary effort and pressure behind the important tasks to ensure that present and future shows would be successful productions. But he had spent no time at all on the longer term tasks he had set himself that morning. 'I seem to be doing well', he thought, 'and both my superiors and subordinates seem to appreciate the job I do and the role I fulfil. But, what is my job? Earlier today, it all seemed so clear, but now I am not so sure.'

Questions

1 What do you think of Giles Chamberlain's day?

2 Comment on the situation described in the case study and be prepared to propose any changes that you think would be beneficial.

The Turn of an Unfriendly Card

First State Bank (FSB) of California thought it could relocate its centre for producing credit cards and update its technology at the same time, improving efficiency and saving costs. Instead, they ended up with cost overruns, long delays and an even longer list of angry customers. What went wrong?

It started off as a relatively simple cost-cutting measure. FSB's credit card production centre is where cards are encoded and embossed (see Exhibit 1) and then dispatched in line with agreed schedules. The centre was to be relocated from its existing premises in the Los Angeles suburb of Burbank to a less expensive location in Pasadena. At the same time, executives in charge of credit card services decided to introduce new and more efficient card-processing technology. It all seemed quite sensible; combine the move with the new technology and get all the pain over with in one go. But things did not quite work out that way.

First, and unforeseen, a problem of potential credit card fraud arose just as the move was about to start. Measures were at once taken to deal with this. The high-profile nature of credit card fraud and the large and growing size of associated losses meant that additional controls were introduced and tight monitoring of every step in the service delivery system was the order of the day. These actions were essential and fast detection was paramount. But the increased security lengthened the time it took, resulted in increased backlogs and caused delays in issuing cards to customers. Customer complaints streamed in.

Staff and managers at the centre were still trying to pick up the pieces when the move began. Delays caused by the move were compounded by further delays when the new technology developed unexpected glitches.

Senior executives at FSB noted the problem and tried to find out what was going on. Unfortunately, the management information system (MIS) had dried up. The project team to manage the move included two FSB managers, but the head of the team, an outside consultant on a short-term contract, had simply not established formal MIS reporting procedures. Regular project meetings were the key link between the project team and senior management, but, because in the early stages all seemed to be going well, senior managers had stopped attending these. By the time the situation reached critical point, the gap between solution and problem was too wide to bridge by a single span – effective control had been gradually eroded.

Once the project team leader's contract expired and he left the project, FSB managers were able to identify the issues and problems fully, take action and reassert control.

Eventually, the backlog cleared and the centre was able to operate as forecast. In the meantime, 18 months of stress had resulted in unhappy staff and even more unhappy customers. The full cost of FSB's cost-cutting measure is only just beginning to emerge.

Moving forward

'Venerable' and 'trustworthy' are words sometimes considered synonymous with FSB. It is indeed one of California's oldest banks,

Exhibit 1 The tasks of embossing and encoding

Cards in corporate colours and printed with corporate logos and information such as 'valid from', 'expires end' and, on the reverse side, authorized signatory statements are received by the production centre from suppliers in this form. The centre then embosses and encodes the cards in line with its customers'

requirements. The embossed data (the raised printing on a card) cover the account number, relevant start and end dates and the user's name. Inserting data such as the customer's name, account number and other coded details onto the magnetic strip is known as encoding.

This case study was written by Terry Hill (University of Oxford). It is intended as the basis for class discussion and not as an example of good or bad management. © AMD Publishing.

founded during the gold rush days of the nineteenth century; reputedly, its first deposit was a sack of gold dust from diggings in the hills above Sacramento. But FSB has moved with the times. Early this century it set its sights on becoming the leading commercial bank in California and although it has never quite overtaken its rivals, it now has 1100 branches and is the fourth largest deposit-taker in the state.

Some years ago, the company began the process of moving its headquarters from San Francisco to Los Angeles, to be, as bank President Gerry Wilcox put it, 'closer to the centre of the action'. The move was phased over three years, with the transferral of credit card services to a location in Burbank. The process went smoothly – indeed, more smoothly than anticipated. The move complete, FSB was ready, in the words of its president 'to begin competing in the twenty-first century'.

The move was a success, and FSB began closing the gap on its larger rivals. One area where FSB was particularly successful was in the marketing of credit cards. Although the United States already has an enormous number of credit card issuers, FSB started to carve a place for itself by offering lower interest rates and service charges, targeting some previously untouched affinity group markets, and introducing a wide range of personalized cards. Aggressive direct sales campaigns encouraged people to switch from their present card to an FSB Visa or Mastercard, and these too had some success.

However, even though the move had gone more smoothly than anticipated, the costs of the move had been greater than forecast. The top brass at FSB began looking at cutting costs. Among other measures, Wilcox ordered a review of FSB's property portfolio. High up on the list of expensive properties came the credit card production centre's location in Burbank. FSB's vice-president in charge of operations, Juan Antonio Perez, instigated a search for new premises and came up with a suitable site in Pasadena, still in the Los Angeles area and within a reasonable distance of group headquarters. The owners of the Pasadena site were willing to do a straight swap, their building for the Burbank location plus a favourable price adjustment. Within a few months the paperwork was signed and the move scheduled.

Security and efficiency

As it happened, the decision to move came at a time when credit card services was undergoing a number of changes. Several new products were coming on-stream, including two that marketing classed as crucial to its product strategy. Also, and again as a cost-cutting measure, credit card services was planning staff reductions in response to FSB's corporate directive. Operating units were required to make reductions, and the production centre was no exception, having been set a target for reductions from 56 to 37 staff over 18 months.

New, highly automated credit card production technology had also become available, which required only one person to handle all stages of producing a new card. As a consequence, the production centre managers were confident that they could cut staff costs and increase productivity at the same time. The centre produced around 10 million cards annually and was currently running at full capacity, given its existing technology. According to the targets set by the marketing plan, 14 million cards a year would be needed in the near future.

Until 18 months ago, all the centre's customers were internal (that is, within FSB and it subsidiaries). To increase sales revenue, marketing proposed to sell the card preparation capability to other companies outside FSB. Since then, this segment has grown rapidly and been an increasingly important factor in overall sales revenue growth. In many ways the new, non-FSB customers were similar to the centre's traditional customers, wanting fast delivery, the ability to meet the specification of each card and service system security. Although price was a factor, it was more so with non-FSB customers. But even here, it was not a key criterion for gaining and retaining contracts. As Juan Perez put it:

> We're in the credit card age where you can't really survive in modern day America without one. No credit card in this country and you're like a fish out of water. What we aim to offer our customers is security and efficiency. We have to get cards to our customers safely and as quickly as possible.

Juan Perez admits that card services managers were initially unhappy when told of the proposal to relocate the production centre. Card services executives were called in for a meeting with himself and Gerry Wilcox shortly after the Pasadena site had been chosen. At that time the senior card services manager had expressed reservations about the effect the move would have on the new product launch and the downsizing and new technology initiatives. However, they were assured that the move would be phased, there would be a full month to test the new premises before the move would begin and full training in the new technology would be provided. The department would 'barely feel the bump' was the way it was explained. In fact, by introducing the new technology at the same time as the move, the department would be able to get all its transition problems over in one go.

The business case for the move seemed unanswerable. The new building would cost $2.3 million to fit out, and the hardware and software installation for the new card-processing technology would require another $4.2 million. Further costs, particularly for IT investment, were estimated at $100,000 and severance payments to redundant staff would cost around $250,000. The total investment required would be just under $7 million.

Against this, FSB could expect to save in rental, maintenance and staff costs around $9 million in the first three years and not including the benefits of the agreed price adjustments on the buildings. Furthermore, the new premises (which provided better facilities, particularly in terms of security and cabling) and the new technology offered opportunities to develop further income streams, by providing additional services to both internal and external customers. The proposition was presented to card services as 'an answer to their prayers'; they could bring in the new technology, cut staff, develop new products and new customers all at once. All they had to do was move premises.

An agreement was reached over the timing of the move; the first phase would start in July of the following year, and the move would be made over four months on a product-by-product basis. Card services began discussions with the human resources department over laying-off redundant staff, and Perez gave the bank's property services arm the go-ahead to close the deal on exchanging premises.

Bad day in Burbank

A month before the proposed move, Frank Dexter, card services manager, wrote in a memo to Gerry Wilcox:

> We have detected a very large increase in reports of lost cards. There was a slight rise in March and then a more pronounced one in April. Last month we received reports of 345 lost cards, the highest ever recorded. Looking at the dollar value of purchases

made on these cards at the time they are reported stolen, I think we must conclude that we are dealing with a serious case of fraud.

> Subject to your approval, I am contacting the postal service authorities and also the police. I will delay this if it is deemed necessary to give public relations time to prepare a statement.

Gerry Wilcox immediately telephoned Frank and gave permission for the authorities to be contacted. He also set up a special audit team to conduct an investigation inside card services.

In the end, the source of the fraud was never detected. The special audit team, the post office and the police all drew blanks. To be sure, however, the special audit team recommended that double-checking procedures should commence at once throughout the card-issuing process, particularly in the production centre at Burbank. This recommendation was approved just a week before the first phase of the move to Pasadena was due to begin.

The impact on the production centre was immediate. Double-checking meant that two people had to check information at certain key stages of card production. For security purposes (that is, to avoid collusion), they could not always be the same two people at each stage. Carefully designed work flows were interrupted and productivity dropped like a stone. Within three months, delivery time for cards had increased from three to four days to three to four weeks.

Customer complaints mounted. So did complaints from staff. Already concerned about the move, unsure about the new technology and knowing that some of their colleagues were due to be laid off, employees at the production centre found their work patterns severely disrupted. Some felt that the increased security measures reflected on their own honesty. Morale declined and the centre's operations manager reported an increase in sick days taken by staff.

Frank Dexter says now:

> I am convinced that we could have managed the problem caused by the additional security checks. We could even have managed them in conjunction with the move and the introduction of new technology. The problem is, we never knew what was going to happen in time to take preventive action. We were always two steps behind.

The man from Inex

To oversee the move to Pasadena and the introduction of the new systems, FSB had established a three-person management team. Two of the team were FSB managers, Carrie Burnett from card services and Alex Orloff from operations. The team leader, Tom Maxwell, was an outside consultant from the consultancy firm Inex. He had been contracted for a year to plan and oversee the move and its implementation. Inex was an experienced consultancy company that had played an important role in the relocation of FSB's head office from San Francisco to Los Angeles. However, Tom Maxwell had never worked with FSB before.

Progress reports were logged onto the FSB management information system, but there was also a project group set up to oversee these developments. This consisted of the three team members, Frank Dexter and four other senior managers (three from card services and one from IT). This project group had been meeting with the management team on a monthly basis since the management team was first established. Dexter chaired the meetings initially, but Maxwell did most of the talking. He had, as Carrie Burnett later recalled:

> a unique management style, at least in my experience. He was very confident and gave the impression that everything was well under control. He was well-spoken and his manner was always reassuring. He reminded me a bit of a doctor dealing with a patient.

Nine months after the recommendation was approved, the detailed plans for the move were in place. Project meetings were rapidly becoming a formality. The project did not seem particularly difficult to start with and was going smoothly; Maxwell was confident that everything would take place according to plan. Like Burnett, the senior managers took his assurances at face value and stopped showing up for meetings, preferring to pull reports off the MIS. Dexter himself was becoming increasingly preoccupied with the fraud issue and was content to leave the move in the hands of Maxwell and his team.

More delays

The technology supplier for FSB's credit card production centre was – and still is – Amcard International, one of the leading suppliers of this kind of technology. Many of the leading banks used Amcard, and there was a long relationship between the company and FSB. Tom Maxwell, explained Frank Dexter, was not exactly told to use Amcard as the supplier, 'but he was guided in that direction. After all, we already knew about the new technology, and its capabilities. It fitted our plans.'

With existing technology, the different steps in card production were performed at different work stations, each with a particular piece of equipment and a member of staff required to operate it. Amcard's new AM-9, however, combined all these steps into one process carried out by a single machine and operated by a single member of staff. Fewer machines were required, less floor space was need and fewer staff were necessary.

Amcard was contracted to supply 12 of the new AM-9s, and the software required to operate them. The original contract was to have been signed nine months before the move. This would have allowed a period in which the software would be tested. The plan also included time for staff to be trained on the new processes. In this way the new technology could be phased in – as each team was trained, appropriate card production orders would be switched to the new site and existing equipment closed down.

Six months before the planned move, however, the contract had still not been signed. Amcard, anxious that the deal might be about to fall through, contacted Tom Maxwell and was assured that all was well. Early in January he met with Amcard's local managers and signed the contract. Although Amcard agreed to reduce its lead times slightly, the planned delivery was now October, some three months after the relocation would start.

'The first I heard of this', says Frank Dexter, 'was in early July.' It was just after the fraud issue had been reported to the police and Dexter, preoccupied, passed an offhand comment to Burnett during a meeting on a separate issue that he was looking forward to seeing the new machines. Burnett 'looked stunned. She didn't say anything, nothing at all.'

'Of course I didn't say anything', says Burnett. 'What could I say? Tom had reported the delay at the project board meeting, but Frank wasn't there. He'd also logged the report onto the MIS. I assumed Frank had made a mistake.' But in fact, Tom Maxwell had never directly reported the delay to Dexter or any other senior manager. Confident of his own abilities, he had assumed he could manage the delay and still bring the project in on time.

How does this work, again?

By mid-July, part of the plan was rolling out – and part of it was not. Amcard, as per contract, began conducting two-day training sessions on site in Burbank, with a demonstration machine that had been set up for the purpose. Tom Maxwell gave the okay for the training sessions to go ahead, despite the backlog of work that was already building up thanks to the security checks and despite the fact that the staff would not now be using the new machines for real for another three months.

There were also complaints that the training was not detailed enough. Whereas formerly each staff member was only responsible for a part of the production process, now they were required to manage the whole thing. It was not only the technology that was unfamiliar, it was the job itself.

Predictably, by the time staff were settled into their new office in Pasadena, they had forgotten most of what they learned. The old machines had to be moved over from Burbank and crammed in as best was possible in floor space that had been designed to accommodate the AM-9s; then they had to be taken out and the Am-9s installed in a rush. There was no time for any more training; the backlog of card orders had now reached critical proportions, and staff were told they would have to learn 'on the job'. Amcard provided a technical representative on site for the first week, and a telephone helpline after that; but even with this assistance, production was slow for the first month.

Paper chase

One final misunderstanding compounded the situation. The AM-9s, in addition to processing the cards themselves, also processed the paper templates. Marketing had advised that five different templates were needed, and the project team had proceeded on this assumption. They had then turned to the technical specification and looked at the paper required for the templates. Amcard's recommendation was to use paper of 110–120 grams weight. But paper was expensive, and costs were overrunning. Burnett and Orloff agreed with Maxwell's suggestion that they save money by using a lighter weight of paper. They settled on 90 grams – not so much lighter, it was thought, to

make a difference – and ordered one million sheets (about one months' supply) to be ready for the roll-out of the new machines. Then marketing dropped a bombshell. The templates arrived in late September, about two weeks before the delivery of the new machines. Instead of the promised five, there were 17. Staff had just two weeks to learn these and how to use them before putting them into production.

Within the first week of operation with the AM-9s in October, the scale of the error over paper weight became clear. The paper was too light to feed properly through the machines. The form feeds tended to scoop up two or three sheets at a time, which would then slip and jam inside the machines. On the first day of operation, machine downtime averaged 40 per cent. With help from the Amcard technical rep, staff managed to reset the form feeds, but the paper continued to slip and jam. As well as lost time there was high wastage.

By the first of November, the project team gave in. The remainder of the million sheets were scrapped and the costs written off. A further million sheets of 120 gram paper were ordered, with a request for emergency delivery. Another $80,000 had been lost.

Late, late, late

By mid-November, even with proper paper and the machines working as designed, production had dropped to 25,000 cards per day, exactly half that required. Back in the Burbank office, the complaints hotline was receiving over 100 calls a day, from branches and customers, concerning delays to cards. According to the company's complaints procedure, each complaint had to be written out and then faxed to the relevant department. Carrie Burnett recalls seeing the faxes 'like a blizzard' in the Pasadena office, coming in faster than they could be dealt with. Responding to the complaints took much time and contributed to more delays.

However, life started to become easier. The Inex contract with Tom Maxwell expired at the end of November and was not renewed. Carrie Burnett took over as manager of the production centre, and was given full access to whatever resources she needed to get the situation under control. Alex Orloff stayed on as her deputy, and was able to persuade IT to assign them technical staff on a full-time basis until the problems could be sorted out. By working overtime, staff have now managed to clear most of the order backlog, waiting times are down to about 10 days, and production has reached 90 per cent of optimum. Frank Dexter believes the centre will be back on track in another three months, and ready then to carry on with plans for expansion.

But what price has had to be paid? The forecast cost savings from the move have been largely eroded. The potential is there for productivity gains and new product introductions; that part of the plan, at least, was merely put back in time. But the real cost, in disgruntled customers, remains to be counted. In the end, just how badly FSB will be affected will have to be measured by the number of customers who defect to other card issuers or the number who, confronted with one of FSB's slick marketing presentations, hold up their hands and say, 'Thanks, but no thanks!'

www.fsbankcal.com

Question

1   What went wrong in the First State Bank of California's move to upgrade its credit card centre technology?

Weavers Homeopathic Products

As John Mason, CEO of Weavers Homoeo-pathic Products (WHP), explained:

> The use of alternative medicines has continued to increase over the last few decades and sales for our products have reflected this growth. In particular, sales of our creams and ointments have grown year on year and the initial contract with a leading UK retail pharmacy chain has recently been renewed. Furthermore, this new contract not only includes two additional products but also shows a marked increase in volumes for existing ones.

Background

WHP has been a manufacturer of homoeo-pathic products since the early 1920s. These comprise creams, ointments and tablets for a wide range of ailments and conditions. The company is part of Breugen, a French-based conglomerate principally involved in foods and pharmaceuticals. The group has a number of manufacturing sites in the UK and the rest of Europe but WHP is the only one that makes and sells homoeopathic products. The manufacturing unit is located on the outskirts of Winchester in the west of England.

Products

Homoeopathic products use natural ingredients (for example calendula flowers) that, in liquid form, are added to the tablet, ointment or cream to arrive at the end-product. WHP makes a range of products. Although sales of tablets and ointments show some growth, there has been a marked increase in the sales of creams over the last few years. As shown in Exhibit 1, sales are made to four types of outlets. Sales to the multiple retailers have grown significantly since their introduction and now account for almost half the total. Bob Dale (VP marketing) explained:

> This trend is likely to continue, given the new contracts signed last week. Our two bestselling creams have, as we hoped, taken off and schedules from the big two retailers have increased significantly. Whereas last year we sold a total of about 1.7 million tubes of all our creams and ointments [see Exhibit 2], the projections for next year show an increase of more than 35 per cent. Given the two recent contracts with multiple retailers, we are confident of meeting, if not exceeding, these projections.

Most products are sold from stock. The exceptions are the special orders placed by doctors and pharmacists for any product, whether it is a tablet, ointment or cream. These are handled on a one-off basis in the dispensary. But most sales are for standard products that are made against forecasts or known call-offs. Having products in stock to meet delivery requirements is important for all customers but particularly so for the multiple retailers who measure our delivery reliability performance on a weekly basis. Meeting schedules, therefore, is a prerequisite for growing sales particularly in this segment.

Exhibit 1 Current sales information

1 Product split

Product type	Percentage of sales (£s)
Creams and ointments	70
Tablets	30
Total	100

2 Customer types

Customer type	Percentage of total sales	# customers
Multiple retailers	48	2
Small independent retailers	29	310
Wholesalers	22	22
Other	1	X[1]

Note 1 The number of customers in this group totals several hundred. The customers vary over time but always comprise low volume orders.

This case study was written by Terry Hill (University of Oxford). It is intended as the basis for class discussion and not as an example of good or bad management. © AMD Publishing.

Exhibit 2 Detail of last year's sales (units)

Tablets	Annual sales (# bottles or blisters)
Painkillers	158,100
Indigestion	126,400
Arthritis	82,000
Sleeping	61,800
Anxiety	55,300
Diarrhoea	38,100
Anti-nausea	21,400
Migraine	15,600
Relaxation	9,200
Appetite suppressant	4,600
Bronchitis	2,400

Creams and ointments[1]	Annual sales (# tubes)
Skin moisturiser 101	374,600
Sun cream	350,700
Antiseptic cream	163,100
Dry skin cream	129,200
Pain relieving cream	112,800
Hair pomade	105,500
Insect repellant cream	95,400
Acne cream	90,100
Nappy rash ointment	88,700
Healing ointment	61,000
Strain ointment	32,100
Chilblain ointment	25,700
Burn ointment	19,300
Haemorrhoid ointment	4,600

Note 1 The difference between a cream and an ointment is that the latter is oil-based and the former is not. As a non-oil-based product, a cream can be absorbed by the skin.

Sales orders

Orders are received by telephone, online (in the case of the two multiple retailers), post, fax and from sales representatives. The relevant paperwork is then created in the sales office. For small and medium volume orders the invoices are sent to the dispensary where the orders are then picked and packed. Inventory for some low volume demand products is kept in this area. The inventory for the other low volume demand products is kept in the finished goods warehouse. Any specials (low volume demand products not kept in stock) are made up in the dispensary and then handled as other low volume orders. Depending on parcel weight, orders are sent by mail or private carrier. Larger volume orders go to the finished goods warehouse where they are picked and packed before being delivered by the same private carrier service referred to earlier.

Operations

The operations process for each product starts with the production of the 'mother tincture'. The natural ingredients are crushed to a pulp (or fine powder if appropriate) and dissolved in alcohol. The 'mother tincture' is the undiluted version of a product and is used in the manufacture of tablets, creams and ointments. The tinctures are typically produced on a seasonal basis in line with the availability of the actual ingredients. All active ingredients are held in the potency room (see Exhibit 3).

Products for which there is regular demand are kept in stock. Other products are only made on receipt of an order, as explained in the next sections. Currently, manufacturing quantities produced are for a minimum of one working day, with high demand products made for two or occasionally three working days. This is to avoid the set-ups incurred on product changes.

Doctors, pharmacists and retail outlets specializing in homeopathic medicines frequently place orders for low demand products. These are not kept in stock and so are manufactured only on receipt of an order. All those orders for small quantities (one or two tubes of a cream, for instance) are manufactured in the dispensary. Here, on receipt of an invoice, a member of the dispensary staff checks the product formula, collects the ingredients and prepares and packs the product.

Tablets

Standard base tablets are purchased as a raw material and the actual ingredient is added on the packing line. The tablets are then loaded into a feed drum which passes them through the active ingredient dispenser. At this point the tablets are then either routed through to blister pack or bottle machines depending upon the packing requirements. The tableting machine has been designed to switch from blister to bottle pack, but can only feed one pack form at a time. Details of set-up times and throughput speeds are given in Exhibit 4.

Creams and ointments

Creams and ointments go through the same manufacturing procedures. The first step is to make a standard cream or ointment base to which the active ingredient is added. This is then transferred to the feed hopper which, in turn, is linked to the tube-filling machine. Once filled, the tubes are sent on pallets to the cream-packing bay where six tubes

Exhibit 3 Shop floor and dispatch layout

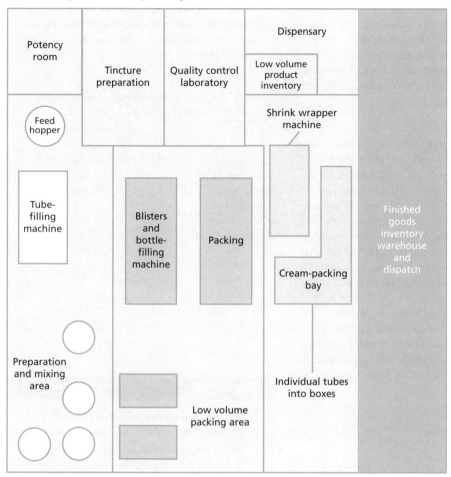

are placed into a box before they are shrink wrapped. All tubes are 27 cm in size. Two operators run the tube-filling machine. One operator is responsible for filling and refilling the hopper with product and keeping the filling machine supplied with empty tubes. The second operator takes the filled tubes, stacks them into a tray and then carries each tray to an area where it is collected and taken to the cream packing bay. The hopper holds sufficient cream/ointment to fill 1000 tubes, and there are 374 empty and 300 filled tubes respectively in a tray. Whenever the hopper is empty or a tray is full/empty, the designated operator stops the filling process to complete the necessary task of getting more empty tubes or taking filled tubes to the designated area. Whereas filling the hopper takes five minutes, removing/collecting a tray of tubes only takes half a minute in each instance.

Both operators can undertake either job on the cream-filling line and typically work half a day on each task. The key is to keep the filling

Exhibit 4 Tablet and cream manufacture

Product	Operation	Set-up time (minutes)[2]	Throughput speed (#/minute)
Tablets[1]	Blister pack	60	60
	Bottle fill	30	70
Creams and ointments	Tube fill	50	36
	Tube pack	–	72

Notes 1 Both blister and bottle packs of tablets are hand-packed in the same area (see Exhibit 3).
      2 To reduce changeover times, manufacturing order quantities are designed to be either one or two working days in length.

machine fully loaded with empty tubes. This requires the full attention of the operator at the front of the machine. At the other end, the task is lighter and only occupies the person about 50 per cent of the time when the machine is running. Filled tubes are discharged onto a small working area where they are collected, several at a time, and placed in a tray.

Working patterns

The 'normal working' day comprises seven hours with one 15-minute period during both the morning and afternoon when all staff take a break. Lunchtime is one hour but does not form part of the working day. The two, shorter, 15-minute breaks, on the other hand, do form part of the rest and relaxation associated with a normal working day. (There is a need for rest to form part of the day. Typically, the 'rest allowance' would be about 15 per cent of a working day. This allowance is often taken, in part, as scheduled breaks (similar to the 15-minute breaks described here) or shorter breaks taken at individually chosen times. Lunchtime is unpaid and does not, therefore, form part of a working day.) During these breaks all equipment is stopped but there are no further delays when the machines are restarted.

The future

John Mason concluded:

> The new contracts and increased schedules for our cream products have confirmed our view that the projected forecast sales growth will be met. Holding finished goods inventory [see Exhibit 5] is essential in the support of our customers and to meet their

lead time and on-time delivery expectations. With future sales showing considerable growth, we are now in the process of checking whether operations can meet these projected volumes. An increase of 35 per cent looks to be a major task.

Exhibit 5 **Finished goods inventory levels for the cream and ointment products**

Product	Current inventory (# tubes)
Skin moisturiser 101	48,386
Dry skin cream	46,056
Healing ointment	34,185
Hair pomade	23,284
Antiseptic cream	16,490
Insect repellant	16,012
Nappy rash ointment	14,506
Sun cream	12,889
Haemorrhoid ointment	10,210
Chilblain ointment	9,024
Acne cream	8,155
Burn ointment	6,810
Pain relieving cream	5,216
Strain ointment	649

Questions

1. What manufacturing processes are used by WHP to make and package its products?

2. Assess the capacity issues within the processes used. Are John Mason's concerns about weekly sales forecasts substantiated?

3. Advise the company on what steps, if any, it should take.

What They Teach You at Disney U(niversity)

Just remember: two Ds, two Ss and three emotions.

Thirty-six pencils record this information in notebooks, ensuring that their owners will know, if asked, the names of the Seven Dwarfs: Doc and Dopey, Sleepy and Sneezy, Happy, Grumpy and Bashful.

The mnemonic for Snow White's friends is an essential element of the curriculum at Disney University at Walt Disney World Resort, whose principal function is to indoctrinate more than 16,000 new employees each year to the unique ways of the Walt Disney Company. The plain office building that serves as a schoolhouse, located on the northern edge of Walt Disney World Resort near Orlando, Florida, swarms with seasonal workers hired for the summer rush. The instructor, identified by his name tag only as Jim, has the blond coiffure, youthful athleticism and breezy confidence of a college fraternity president. The coat of his grey suit hangs as casually from his shoulders as an open beach shirt, and a shock of yellow hair juts straight out over his forehead like a sun visor.

This is an orientation class, but it is not called orientation – nor are the new workers known as employees. They are cast members, and the class is known as traditions. Throughout the day the cast members will learn other Disney terms. Ninety per cent of the labour force, hourly employees from street sweepers to store clerks to ride operators, wear costumes, not uniforms. They are not on duty but on-stage. During breaks they are off-stage. Visitors are guests; cast members are hosts and hostesses.

At the start of the class Jim had said:

Working at Disney is like going to a foreign country. You have to learn a new language and a new culture.

At a time when employees' attitudes, productivity and quality of work are problems throughout corporate America, Disney seems immune to the maladies of the age. America's leading corporations – from General Electric to General Motors – have dispatched executives to Disney University to discover how Disney inspires its staff to meet the company's exacting standards.

No visitor has to spend much time in the park before he begins to wonder whether Disney feeds some magic potion to its employees, perhaps learned from a certain former sorcerer's apprentice. So confident is Disney that cast members will charm guests that it has devised ways to force contact. One example: many of the wares in the park's ubiquitous gift shops bear no price tags, requiring shoppers to ask the cost.

If all this frenzied friendliness makes Walt Disney World Resort sometimes seem a bit like Stepford South, its success is beyond dispute. Sixty per cent of Walt Disney World Resort's visitors are repeaters. Together, Walt Disney World Resort, Disneyland Paris Resort, Paris, Tokyo Disneyland Resort, Japan and their California cousin, Disneyland Resort, accounted for $5.5 billion of the company's almost $23 billion in 1998 revenues. The company's ability to retain workers is rare in the service sector, which nationally suffers from a 40 per cent annual turnover; Disney's is lower by one-third. For office and administrative workers, Disney's attrition rate drops to a mere 6 per cent.

None of this happens by accident. Disney's hiring policies are designed to find workers who will fit the company mould. Disney takes people who are normally gregarious and trains them to be more so. Looks do not matter; attitude and personality do. The casting department puts more weight on interviews than résumés; Disney wants people who look questioners in the eye.

Today the pressure on casting is greater than ever, for this summer alone they were looking to hire 2000. Disney cannot be as selective as it once was; the labour pool in Central Florida has shrunk as a result of the boom Walt Disney World Resort started. At one time Disney had ten job seekers for every hourly position; now the ratio is three to one. (For managerial positions the reverse is true. This year Disney will fill 300 jobs for which it will receive 70,000 résumés.) More and more representatives of Florida's large semi-retired population are showing up on Walt Disney World Resort work lines. Disney recruits hourly workers on 130 college campuses and advertises in major markets for positions in hotels and restaurants.

All new employees must attend traditions classes before starting work, even those hired for a week at spring break. There, in a classroom decorated with posters and pictures depicting great moments in the company's history (for example Mickey Mouse's first cartoon, *Snow White and the Seven Dwarfs*, *Fantasia*, the opening of Disneyland Park) they are inoculated with the Disney corporate culture. Everything in the room has a purpose: the shape of the table (round to instil a sense of teamwork), the method of introductions (each person gives not only his own name but that of the person to his right again to instil a sense of teamwork), the taking of a test on Disneyland Park that involves remembering the names of as many Disney characters as possible in an allotted time period (and each table consults on answers, again to instil a sense of teamwork). In case someone has somehow missed the point, Jim makes it again: if one employee makes a mistake, a guest goes home unhappy. He warns:

> We never say, 'it's not my job'. If someone asks us a question, we know the answer. If we see a piece of trash on the ground, we pick it up.

Like all instructors, Jim is not assigned to the university permanently. Nor is he an executive. He is an hourly employee – intended to be a role model – who conducts the class one day a week for one year. Disney puts a time limit on teaching to ensure that its instructors will be fresh and enthusiastic. Some are still in their first year with the company.

'Disney is a first-name company', Jim tells the class. That is tradition number one. If the policy promotes informality, it is also meant to reduce individuality. So are the company's strict grooming standards. 'Why do we have them?' Jim asks rhetorically. 'To make everyone blend in, to promote the whole show, not individuals.' Men cannot have moustaches, beards, long sideburns or hair touch-

ing the ears or collar. Women may wear one small ring on each hand and earrings no larger than a penny (a recent liberalization from previously mandated posts); they cannot have long or brightly painted fingernails, large hair decorations or long necklaces. Thanks to Walt Disney World Resorts, Orlando must be one of the world's principal markets for plain black shoes. Acceptable styles are displayed in a glass case near the area where cast members pick up their costumes; twice a month a shoemobile makes the 25-mile drive from town.

The morning session ends with a three-minute videotape called 'Making Magic'. It shows employees volunteering to take pictures of guests, so that the whole family can be in the picture, as well as doing other good deeds. At the end, Michael Eisner and President Frank Wells are joined by Mickey and Donald (Disney's first-name policy extends to omitting even their surnames) while the tune of 'When you wish upon a star' swells in the background.

Disney manages to Disneyfy its employees despite an hourly pay scale that begins at $6.25, which company officials describe as competitive for service workers in the Orlando area. There are raises after six months, a year and annually thereafter, but all hourly positions carry a salary cap regardless of longevity. The carrot is that Disney promotes liberally from within.

Disney's low entry level pay but fast advancement system enables the company to retain employees who have the ability to move up without offering rewards to those who do not. Based on performance, hourly workers are promoted and can join the management ranks as salaried workers. On the other hand, image-conscious Disney prefers not to fire anyone, since it views every human being on the planet as a potential customer and does not want to offend a single one. Instead, it tries to find new positions for problem employees, something that is easy enough to do at a park with 1100 job descriptions and steady turnover.

Underlying all this is an unflagging company-wide obsession with excellence. Disney workers paint every trash can to blend with nearby scenery; they steam-clean every piece of pavement and wash every window in the Magic Kingdom and Epcot every day. Disney designers stayed in low-budget hotels around the park and then pencilled in extra soundproofing and double sinks for the Caribbean Beach resort in order to beat the competition. Disney gardeners have trimmed the oaks on Main

Street, USA, in the Magic Kingdom to the identical shape every day since the park opened; they have clipped the shrubbery in heavily travelled areas into shapes of penguins, elephants, swans and camels. The gardeners travel enough miles on lawn mowers each year to circle the earth 14 times. Atop the Italian Pavilion in Epcot is a four-foot angel; although it is too high for visitors to discern, Disney coats it with the most expensive gold paint available – 14-carat gold leaf.

In all this there ought to be lessons for the rest of corporate America. It sounds so simple; take the long-term view, insist on quality, recognize that courtesy pays, offer low-level employees incentives for advancement rather than money, hire by giving more weight to personality than credentials and expand by filling the public's needs rather than your own.

www.disney.com

Question

1 How does Disney maintain the reputation for excellence within its service delivery system?

Wilson Pharmaceuticals

Wilson Pharmaceuticals has been manufacturing and selling its mouth ulcer treatment (Ulcercare) for the last 15 years. At the time of its introduction, there were few products in this area of healthcare. The product consists of a small glass bottle, with a cork and printed label. The bottle is filled with a pink fluid (the chemical formulation for which had been derived by Wilson's own research laboratories), leaving enough room to fit a cotton bud in the neck of the bottle without inducing spillage. Twelve double-ended cotton buds are included in the pack, providing sufficient for 24 individual applications

The treatment is made by dipping one end of a cotton bud into the fluid and then apply-ing it directly to the infected area within the mouth. The package is made from rolled card tube. This tube is in three parts – a single inner and two close-fitting outer tubes, each closed with a card disc which forms the top and bottom of the pack (see Exhibit 1). Inside the inner tube is a small card cup into which the glass bottle fits. This cup is surrounded by corrugated paper sheet which holds it firmly in the inner tube. The cotton buds fit between the glass bottle and the corrugated paper, thus providing additional protection for the bottle. The top and bottom of the outer tube are closed by a label, and the disc of the top tube is covered by a circular label.

Exhibit 1 **The current production design**

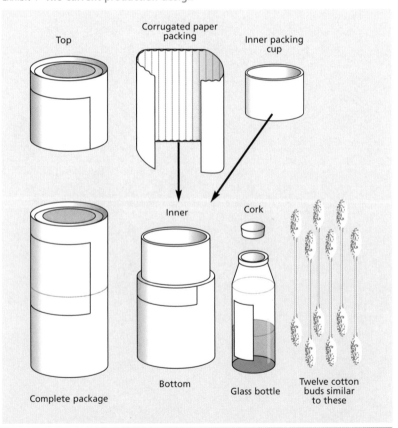

This case study was written by Terry Hill (University of Oxford) and KHA Negal. It is intended as the basis for class discussion and not as an example of good or bad management. © AMD Publishing.

Over the past 18 months, sales for Ulcercare have been declining steadily. Enquiries revealed that two large competitors have introduced their own products in this range, which are lower in price than Ulcercare. The current profit margin enjoyed by Wilson's product, although above average, is not sufficiently high to withstand a price reduction in line with the competitors' products.

As part of their review of the situation, the executives involved turned to the question of product costs, details of which are included as Exhibit 2.

Question

1 What approach should be followed in an investigation to reduce the costs of Ulcercare and what practical design changes would you suggest? In all instances, relate your analyses to the details and cost information provided.

Exhibit 2 **The cost breakdown for Ulcercare**

Cost/100 items	Materials (£)
Ulcer fluid	2.55
Bottle	1.85
Cork	0.95
Bottle label	0.25
Card cup	0.80
Corrugated paper	0.20
12 double-ended cotton buds (total)	1.76
Inner tube	1.05
Top tube	1.33
Bottom tube	1.33
Tube label	0.65
Disc label	0.25
Assembly and packing labour	3.86
Total materials and labour	16.83

Yuppie Products

The Yuppie Products Company produces a line of furnishings for hotels and restaurants. Among the items manufactured is the Yuppie executive water pitcher whose product structure is shown in Exhibit 1. Components A and B are manufactured by the firm's plastic moulding shop and components C, D, E and F are purchased from a supplier. The Yuppie executive water pitcher is completed by the final assembly department located at the firm's plant in Geneva. (A flow diagram indic-

ating the different manufacturing stages in the Geneva plant is shown in Exhibit 2.)

The firm's products are supplied to customers from stock held in the company's distribution centres which are located in Amsterdam and Rome. A distribution requirements planning (DRP) system is used to plan and schedule the replenishment of inventory at the distribution centres and the scheduling of production operations at the Geneva plant. (See Exhibit 3 for sample information used by

Exhibit 1 Product structure

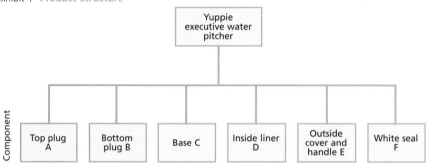

One unit of each component is required to produce one Yuppie executive water pitcher

Exhibit 2 Manufacturing system

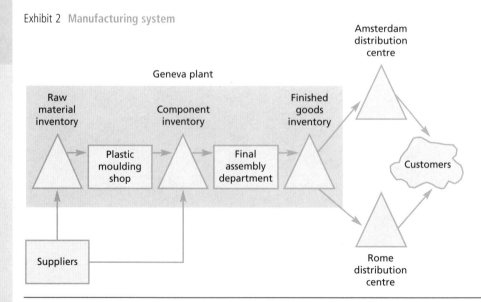

This case was prepared by Professor William Lee Berry as a basis for class discussion rather than to illustrate either effective or ineffective handling of an administrative situation. © IMD International. Reproduced by permission.

Exhibit 3 Distribution requirements planning worksheet

Part A: Distribution centre planning records

Yuppie executive water pitcher
Amsterdam distribution centre

		Week							
		1	2	3	4	5	6	7	8
Forecast[1]		10	10	10	10	10	10	10	10
Scheduled receipts[1]		20	0	0	0	0	0	0	0
Projected available[2]	10	20	10	20	10	20	10	20	10
Planned shipments[1]		20		20		20			
Firm planned shipments									

Order quantity = 20 units
Transportation lead time = 2 weeks
Safety stock = 5 units

Yuppie executive water pitcher
Rome distribution centre

		Week							
		1	2	3	4	5	6	7	8
Forecast[1]		20	20	20	20	20	20	20	20
Scheduled receipts[1]		0	0	0	0	0	0	0	0
Projected available[2]	45	25	5	25	5	25	5	25	5
Planned shipments[1]		40		40		40			
Firm planned shipments									

Order quantity = 40 units
Transportation lead time = 1 week
Safety stock = 5 units

Part B: Master production scheduling (MPS) records

Yuppie executive water pitcher
Geneva central warehouse

		Week							
		1	2	3	4	5	6	7	8
Gross requirements[1]		20	40	20	40	20	40	0	0
Scheduled receipts[1]		0	0	0	0	0	0	0	0
Projected available[2]	40	20	40	20	40	20	40	20	40
MPS[1]		60		60		60	0	0	0

MPS order quantity = 60 units
Production lead time = 1 week
Safety stock = 10 units

A

B

Exhibit 3 cont'd

Part C: Materials requirement planning records

Item A – top plug

		Week							
		1	2	3	4	5	6	7	8
Gross requirements[1]		60	0	60	0	60	0	0	0
Scheduled receipts[1]		60	0	0	0	0	0	0	0
Projected available[2]	65	65	65	5	5	5	5	5	5
Planned orders[1]		0	0	0	60	0	0	0	0

Order quantity = 60 units
Production lead time = 1 week
Safety stock = 5 units

Item B – bottom plug

		Week							
		1	2	3	4	5	6	7	8
Gross requirements[1]		60	0	60	0	60	0	0	0
Scheduled receipts[1]		0	0	90	0	0	0	0	0
Projected available[2]	35	–25	–25	5	5	35	35	35	35
Planned orders[1]		0	90	0	60	0	0	0	0

Order quantity = 90 units
Production lead time = 3 weeks
Safety stock = 5 units

Item C – base

		Week							
	1	2	3	4	5	6	7	8	
Gross requirements[1]		60	0	60	0	60	0	0	0
Scheduled receipts[1]		0	0	120	0	0	0	0	0
Projected available[2]	15	–45	–45	15	15	75	75	75	75
Planned orders[1]		0	120	0	0	0	0	0	0

Order quantity = 120 units
Purchasing lead time = 3 weeks
Safety stock = 10 units

Part D: Shop-floor control reports

Plastic moulding department scheduling report				
Shop order number	Component item	Order quantity	Order due date[1]	Machine time (in days)[3]
10-XXY	A	60	week 1	3
10-XZV	Z	20	week 1	1
10-XXX	G	45	week 2	2
10-XYZ	B	90	week 3	4

Notes 1 As of the beginning of the week.
2 As of the end of the week.
3 The plant works five single-shift days per week.

the DRP system.) This information is updated daily by the company's computer system.

The DRP system

The firm's distribution requirements planning system includes four main elements:

1 Time-phased order point (TPOP) records for each end-product stocked at a distribution centre (Exhibit 3, Part A).

2 Time-phased master production scheduling (MPS) records for each end-product produced by the Geneva plant (Exhibit 3, Part B).

3 Time-phased material planning records for each component part manufactured or purchased by the Geneva plant (Exhibit 3, Part C).

4 Shop-floor control reports used to schedule production in the various plant departments (Exhibit 3, Part D).

A standard format is used for all the time-phased planning records. The first row contains a weekly forecast of demand for the product item. The second row contains the delivery schedule for any orders that have been relayed for shipment to the distribution centres or for production in the plant. The third row provides a projection of the closing inventory each week, and the fourth row indicates planned orders that are scheduled for release so that inventory shortages are not incurred. The schedule for the planned orders takes into account the order quantity, lead time and safety stock information for each item as shown below the item record.

The DRP system coordinates the planning of operations in the distribution centres, the plant and the suppliers (as illustrated by Exhibit 4). For example, the planned order row information in the distribution centre TPOP records is summarized and displayed as the gross requirements row in the records (see arrow A in Exhibit 3). Likewise, the MPS

Exhibit 4 **Distribution requirements planning information system**

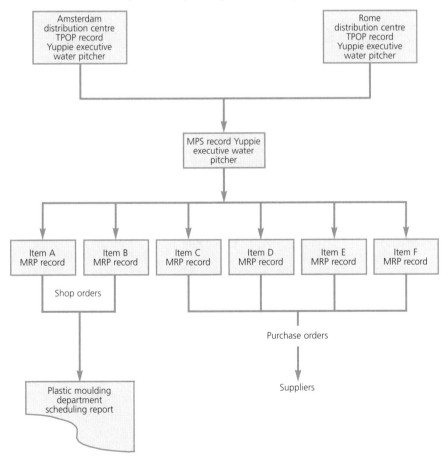

Exhibit 5 Distribution requirements planning worksheet

Part A: Distribution centre planning records

Yuppie executive water pitcher
Amsterdam distribution centre

		Week							
		1	2	3	4	5	6	7	8
Forecast[1]		10	10	10	10	10	10	10	10
Scheduled receipts[1]		20	0	0	0	0	0	0	0
Projected available	10								
Planned shipments[1]									
Firm planned shipments									

Order quantity = 20 units
Transportation lead time = 2 weeks
Safety stock = 5 units

Yuppie executive water pitcher
Rome distribution centre

		Week							
		1	2	3	4	5	6	7	8
Forecast[1]		20	20	20	20	20	20	20	20
Scheduled receipts[1]		0	0	0	0	0	0	0	0
Projected available[2]	45								
Planned shipments[1]	35								
Firm planned shipments									

Order quantity = 40 units
Transportation lead time = 1 week
Safety stock = 5 units

Part B: Master production scheduling (MPS) records

Yuppie executive water pitcher
Geneva central warehouse

		Week							
		1	2	3	4	5	6	7	8
Gross requirements[1]									
Scheduled receipts[1]									
Projected available[2]	40								
MPS[1]									

MPS order quantity = 60 units
Production lead time = 1 week
Safety stock = 10 units
Production lead time = 3 weeks

Exhibit 5 cont'd

Part C: Materials requirement planning records

Item A – top plug

	Week							
	1	2	3	4	5	6	7	8
Gross requirements[1]								
Scheduled receipts[1]	60							
Projected available[2]	65								
Planned orders[1]								

Order quantity = 60 units
Production lead time = 1 week
Safety stock = 5 units

Item B – bottom plug

	Week							
	1	2	3	4	5	6	7	8
Gross requirements[1]								
Scheduled receipts[1]			90					
Projected available[2]	35							
Planned orders[1]								

Order quantity = 90 units
Production lead time = 3 weeks
Safety stock = 5 units

Item C – base

	Week							
	1	2	3	4	5	6	7	8
Gross requirements[1]								
Scheduled receipts[1]			120					
Projected available[2]	15							
Planned orders[1]								

Order quantity = 120 units
Purchasing lead time = 3 weeks
Safety stock = 10 units

Part D: Shop-floor control reports

Plastic moulding department scheduling report

Shop order #	Component item	Order quantity	Order due date[1]	Machine time (in days)[3]
10-XXY	A	60	week 1	3
10-XZV	Z	20	week 1	1
10-XXX	G	45	week 2	2
10-XYZ	B	90	week 3	4

Notes 1 As of the beginning of the week.
       2 As of the end of the week.
       3 The plant works five single-shift days per week.

row information in the MPS records is used to calculate the gross requirements in the material requirements planning (MRP) records for the component items, using bill of material information (see arrow B in Exhibit 3, Part B to Part C).

Finally, information in the MRP records is used to establish priorities for the scheduling of production in the plant. Orders are scheduled in sequence according to their due date. The due dates for open shop orders contained in the scheduled receipts row of the MRP records are shown on the scheduling reports for individual departments in the plant. For example, the due date of week 1 for the order of 60 units for item A is shown both in the MRP record for this item, and on the scheduling report for the plastic moulding department in Exhibit 5, Part D. Currently, two open shop orders for Yuppie executive water pitcher components are waiting to be processed in the plastic moulding department – items A and B. All the orders shown on the plastic moulding department scheduling report are made complete in one operation, and are subsequently ready for the final assembly department.

The MRP record for item C, the base, is shown in Exhibit 5, Part C; this item is produced by a plastic moulding company in Taiwan. Because of lengthy overseas shipment times, the purchasing lead time for this item is a firm three weeks and the current open order of 120 units will not be received until the beginning of week 5.

Questions

1 Given the information in the MRP records in Exhibit 3 of the case study, are the priorities (due dates) valid for the open shop orders for component items a and b on the plastic moulding department scheduling report in Exhibit 3, part D? What changes, if any, would you make to the following: the planned shipments to Rome and Amsterdam distribution centres, the MPS and the due dates for the open shop orders in the plastic moulding department?

2 The on-hand inventory balance for the Yuppie executive water pitcher at the Rome distribution centre has just been found to be incorrect. An inventory adjustment has been entered into the DRP system (at the start of week 1) changing the on-hand inventory to 35 units. What impact will this change have on the DRP system records and the schedules at the Geneva plant? (Please use the work sheets in Exhibit 5 of the case study to answer this question.)

3 The forecast for the Yuppie executive water pitcher demand at the Amsterdam distribution centre has just been increased from 10 to 15 units per week. Likewise, the forecast for the Yuppie executive water pitcher demand at the Rome distribution centre has just been decreased from 20 to 10 units per week. Assuming that the revised forecasts are introduced into the DRP system records at the start of week 1, what impact will this change have on the DRP system records and the schedules at the Geneva plant? Assume that the replenishment order quantity for the Amsterdam distribution centre has been changed from 20 to 30 units, and the replenishment order quantity for the Rome distribution centre has been changed from 40 to 20 units.

The Zara boutique clothing store on Calle Real in the northern Spanish city of La Coruna is buzzing. Customers have made the journey here on a rainy Saturday morning to see what new exciting styles are available this week. The red tank tops and black blazers seem to be a hit, but customers are also asking for these styles in beige and bright purple. Faced with not knowing which styles and colours will be in demand, most fashion companies invest heavily in forecasting ahead of the upcoming season. But not Zara. Store managers are able to spot these trend changes and type them into their hand-held computer on Saturday in the safe knowledge that they will arrive early the next week.

As Rosanna Padine, commercial director, explains:

> There is a very strong link between the store managers and the central design team based at our head office in La Coruna. Each store is electronically linked to head office so we can view and assess sales on a real-time basis. This allows us to make sure that we can adapt quickly to customers' wants and desires. Take last week with our new khaki skirt that we initially just stocked in Spain to see how it would sell. In our Coruna store it was sold out in a couple of hours. After speaking to Barcelona, it was apparent that sales were brisk there too. We decided that we should test it out elsewhere, so overnight we sent out 2,800 skirts to our 500 plus stores worldwide. The results were clear, the skirt was a hit and within the next few days our stores in Europe, Asia, and North and South America had stocks of the khaki skirt.

This mix of intelligence gathering, fashion instinct, technology investment and savoir-faire allows Zara to set in motion something unique in the clothing trade. Being able to translate the latest trends into products in less than 15 days and delivering them to its stores twice a week means that it is able to catch fashion trends while they are hot, thus responding quickly to the fast-changing tastes of young urban consumers. Keith Mortimer, European retail analyst, says:

> Nobody else can get new designs to stores as quickly. Unless you can do that, you won't be in business in ten years. Zara continuously analyses its value chain and seeks to achieve control on as many sections of it as possible. By focusing on reducing time between design and sale, it has developed a production cycle that is entirely different from fashion sector norms. The design team that is working through out the season studies everything from the clothes worn on hit TV series to how clubbers dress. This means there is a continuous stream of new products that ensures customers come back to see what's new. Its clothing has filled an untapped niche: Prada at moderate prices.

Customers seem to love the results of this high-velocity operation. Often they queue in long lines at Zara's stores on designated delivery days, a phenomenon that has been dubbed in the press as 'Zaramania'. And this popularity is generating tangible, bottom-line results as well as admiration from the fashion world (see Exhibit 1). Over the last five years average annual profits have grown at 30 per cent, which is 45 per cent faster than its four industry rivals.

Exhibit 1 Zara net store openings, number of company-managed and franchised stores, selling area, net sales and operating income (2000–2002)

Data	Annual value		
	2000	2001	2002
Net store openings	53	60	65
Company-managed stores	382	435	487
Franchised stores	24	31	44
Selling area (000s sqM)	408	480	562
Net sales (€mn)	2,044	2,435	2,913
Operating income (€mn)	327	440	540

This case study was written by Alex Hill (University of Kingston). It is intended as the basis for class discussion and not as an example of good or bad management. © AMD Publishing.

A global success

Founded in 1963 as a maker of ladies' lingerie, Zara opened its first store in 1975 in the city of La Coruña. By 1989, the company had 98 retail shops and production facilities distributed around Spain. In the same year the company started its international expansion by opening a shop in Lisbon, Portugal. This was the beginning of what has become a huge expansion plan across the world. It is now the largest and most profitable unit of Inditex SA (its parent company), the Spanish clothes manufacturer and distributor, with over 500 stores distributed throughout Europe, Middle East, Asia Pacific and the Americas (see Exhibit 2).

As Jonathon May, retail consultant, comments:

This rapid expansion means that Zara has three characteristics that distinguish it from its competitors. Firstly, it is the fastest-growing retail business not only in Europe but also across the world. Secondly, it has successfully exported its formula internationally at a time when many other clothing companies in the middle and lower-middle market have found international growth difficult. For example, Next is a fantastic company, but has always struggled to export its particular format. And thirdly, it has created a simple, singular message for all its customers. The shopping experience is upscale, while the product offering is very much good quality, but not best quality, at a good price. It might well have sacrificed a little technical quality but it has more then made up for it through design product in terms of fabrics, colours, patterns and styles. If you go into a store these characteristics immediately hit you. Then when you look at a garment, you will see that the price tags are big and colourful, emblazoned with the flags of a dozen countries, each accompanied by a local currency price that is the same for that item around the world, from Madrid to Riyadh to Tokyo.

Challenging the competition

In times when a combination of recession and some merchandising mistakes have forced Gap and comparable European stores like Sweden's H&M to retrench, Zara continues to expand. Much of the success is due to its unusual structure. For decades most clothing retailers have outsourced their manufacturing to developing countries in pursuit of lower costs and greater efficiencies. Zara bucked this

Exhibit 2 Number of Zara stores by region and country[1]

Region	Country	# stores
Europe	Andorra	1
	Austria	4
	Belgium	15
	Cech Republic	1
	Cyprus	3
	Denmark	2
	Finland	1
	France	71
	Germany	21
	Greece	23
	Iceland	1
	Italy	3
	Luxembourg	2
	Malta	1
	Poland	4
	Portugal	35
	Spain	200
	Switzerland	2
	The Netherlands	4
	Turkey	8
	United Kingdom	17
Middle East	Bahrain	1
	Israel	11
	Kuwait	3
	Lebanon	2
	Qatar	1
	Saudi Arabia	8
	United Arab Emirates	4
Asia-Pacific	Japan	6
	Singapore	1
Americas	Argentina	5
	Brazil	10
	Canada	9
	Chile	3
	Dominican Republic	1
	El Salvador	1
	Mexico	29
	United States	8
	Uruguay	2
	Venezuela	7

Note   1 Of these 531 stores, Zara owns 487 and the other 44 are franchises.

trend, taking a different stance. It felt that it would be better off developing a business that was able to respond quickly to shifts in consumer tastes and so made the decision to set up a vertically integrated business model, spanning design, just-in-time production, marketing and sales. As such, it now produces more than half its own clothes at its ultramodern factory in northern Spain rather than relying on a network of disparate and often slow-moving suppliers. H&M, for instance, has 900 suppliers and no factories, whereas Zara makes 40 per cent of its own fabric and produces 60 per cent of its merchandise in-house. 'Vertical integration has gone out of fashion in the consumer economy,' says David Johnston, a retail consultant in London. 'Zara is a spectacular exception to the rule.'

The result is that Zara is more flexible than its rivals in responding to ever-changing fashion trends. It can make a new line from start to finish in three weeks, against an industry average of nine months. It introduces 10,000 new designs into its stores each year, none of which stay there for more than a month. This constant refreshment of the store offering creates a sense of excitement that attracts new shoppers and ensures that old ones return. It is also radically changing the way that people shop. As David Johnston explains:

> If customers see a product that they like in the store, they know that it will only be there for four weeks, not four months, and that they will probably not be able to find it after that. It stimulates customers to buy now and creates a greater velocity of shopping. This is quite a different situation to the high streets of old and more and more retailers are finding it difficult to compete. For example, C&A chose to exit the UK market and the Japanese basics retailer Uniglo has closed all but five of its stores here. Boring, staple clothing is being killed off!

However, its not just the traditional high street chains that have been affected. Even supermarket clothing retailer George at Asda has been inspired to react, by producing a collection called Fast Fashion.

Keeping up with fashions

According to Inditex Chief Executive Jose Maria Castellano:

> Fashion expires, much the same way yogurt does. Being so quick allows us to reduce to a minimum the risk of making a mistake, and we do make mistakes, with our collections.

With this in mind, the designers at Zara work hard to constantly update, mix and match popular styles rather than simply flooding the market with a limited range. As Rosanna Padine, commercial director, explains:

No one wants to dress like everybody else. It is important always to have fresh fashion. We have found that not only does our business model allow us to offer mid-market chic at downmarket prices, it also protects against slip-ups. Whereas most retailers have already committed up to 60 per cent of their production at the start of the season, at Zara the figure is only 15 per cent. This makes it easier to dump a range that turns out to be unpopular and, like everyone else, this can happen.

Although mistakes can happen, Zara tries to minimize them by pushing its designers onto aeroplanes and sending them out in search of new trends. They spend their time looking through stacks of fashion magazines, attending fashion shows and frequenting fashionable cafes, restaurants and bars. Rosanna Padine explains:

> We find that it is particularly good to listen to our customers as they know better than anyone what they want. Our designers are then like sponges soaking up information about fashion trends from all over the world and translating them into new ideas. The constant travel, catwalk shows and even music videos mean that a look seen on MTV can be in the stores within a month. Traditionally fashion collections are designed only four times a year, but on average we will produce over 10,000 different designs each year. While the style and shape of the garments may not vary hugely each time, they are be produced in a wide variety of different fabrics, colours and patterns.

> From the beginning of our international expansion in 1989, we have always focused on developing products for the global market. We felt that it was important to capitalize on and exploit the many benefits of international product and brand uniformity, such as product development and manufacturing costs, logistics and inventory costs, and a consistent product and brand image across all markets. The development of global products is the full responsibility of the design team at our head office in Spain. They consist of three different types of people from fashion, marketing and retail. Drawing on each of their backgrounds and using information gathered through regular field research and computerized store data, the team makes all the decisions regarding developing and launching new products, for example which products, the timing of the launch, the quantity of the production run and how many should be shipped to each country.

The result is that we have an international product line that can be found in all stores, the only difference being the proportion of items in each store.

However, these are not the only centralized decisions taken by the team. It is also responsible for pricing in each country. All garments are displayed in stores with an international tag showing the different prices in the respective countries. Prices are globalized, taking into account the difference in local market conditions, the problems of potential parallel imports, and to make sure we position the product uniformly. Once the team has decided the type of product, the price and quantities to be held in each store, then we are ready to start the production process.

The production and distribution system

For a fashion business, Zara is also unique in the way that it is driven by consumer feedback. As Mike Shearwood, Zara's UK managing director, explains:

Our store managers are the most important people in the Zara business. Selecting from over 10,000 lines a year, they are responsible for placing the orders with the factory and central office in Spain. These orders are placed twice a week and determine the type and quantity of products that will be stocked in their store. We rely on their ability to understand and monitor how well products are selling in order to ensure that we have the right stock at the right time in the right place.

Each store manager receives information via a hand-held computer showing images of the products that can be ordered. Based on sales over the last few days and trends that seem to be emerging, they decide which products and how many to order. In head office, there is a section dedicated to each country and the store manager will usually talk to them once or twice a day and three to five times on order days. The firm's commercial sections then liaise with the designers and factories to make sure that the products meet the needs of the local customers for each store. While there is an initial trend framework set up at the beginning of each season, modifications are continually made in response to the reaction of customers to each range.

As well as operating its own worldwide distribution network out of its facility in Spain, Zara also designs and manufacturers products here too. Lead times for new designs average from four to six weeks, but may be as little as two. Zara achieves this by holding fabric in stock and then cutting and dyeing it at the last minute. With its team of commercials sniffing out new fashions while keeping in constant contact with store managers, the company can spot and react to trends quickly, including taking something stylish off a music video that has just been released. Other retailers, in contrast, need an average of six months to design a new collection and then another three months to manufacture it.

Store managers also send in new ideas. The 200-plus designers decide if it is appealing, and then come up with specifications. The design is scanned into a computer and zapped to production computers in manufacturing, which cut and dye the material that is then assembled into clothes by outside workshops. The in-house manufacturing plant is futuristic, with large cutting machines that are run by a handful of technicians in a laboratory-style computer control centre. The dying part of the process occurs in small units in another part of the factory. By dying products after they have been cut, they are able to minimize the quantities of dye used and so help control costs.

For most garments, the company owns every part of the production process, apart from sewing. Fabrics come from places such as Spain, Southeast Asia, India and Morocco and are cut and coloured at the company's state-of-the-art factory. Using information gathered from stores, production managers decide how many garments to make and which stores will get them. The fabric is sewn together at 400 cooperatives run by local seamstresses before being shipped around the world. This combination of real-time information sharing and internalized production means that Zara can work with almost no stock and still have new designs in the store twice a week, as opposed to the six weeks that it traditionally takes most competitors. The twice weekly deliveries help keep Zara stores seeming fresh, and store clerks heighten the sense of rapid turnover by changing the location of key items.

Retail stores

In keeping with the philosophy of the rest of the business, the stores themselves are designed by an in-house team of architects with a 'white box' style that evolves as it goes along in terms of signage and lighting or, for instance, the introduction of escalators. They are very minimal in design and the way in which clothing is presented. However, the rapid turnover of products and changing location of key items results in keeping customers curious and keen to see the latest styles. It finds that this in itself is sufficient to draw shoppers into the store. Also, and unlike most of its competitors, Zara's approach to advertising is as minimal as its store interiors. It only consists of taking a full-page local newspaper advert twice a year, the night before it has a sale.

As Mike Shearwood comments:

> Our main media are the location of the stores and the shop windows. Our business model lends itself to the fact that our products are ones that customers want to buy, so we do not have to persuade them to buy the products we want to sell. Because of the short production and distribution lead times, there is less need to discount, except at those two sale periods each year. In fact, we do not really have to have a sale at all, but we find that it works well as a promotional tool.

The future

Keith Mortimer, European retail analyst, reflects:

> In terms of the future for Zara, the question now is how far can it go with the concept of design-on-demand retailing, which it runs with almost no advertising outside its biannual store-wide sales. There is nothing wrong with it taking advantage of its rivals' weaknesses to grab market share. But

Zara's still entirely Spanish management team will have to be careful not to indulge in the overexpansion that has floored so many of its rivals. The further the group gets from its heartland, where it has faced only modest competition, the more its model will be stretched. The chain is now well known in South America and Europe, but less so in the US where it has just opened six stores in the New York area. Yet again this year, they will be pursuing a very aggressive expansion plan, claiming that the only restraining factor is the availability of suitable real estate. Given this, it will probably begin using the web to sell clothes as finding new store sites becomes more difficult. This may help to boost its low profile in the US, as consumers there are less reluctant to buy online than in Zara's homeland of Southern Europe.

www.zara.es

Questions

1   What underpins the success of Zara in its chosen markets?

2   Outline the production and distribution systems.

3   How do the production and distribution systems meet the needs of the markets?

Acknowledgements

The author and publishers wish to thank the following for permission to use copyright material:

AMD Publishing, whose cartoons well illustrate many points in this book, for Exhibits 1.8, 1.10, 2.1, 2.11, 2.13, 3.2, 3.11, 3.12, 4.1, 4.2, 4.5, 4.6, 5.18, 6.13, 6.14, 7.1, 7.12, 8.1, 9.1, 9.14, 10.9, 10.15, 11.23, 12.12, 12.17, 13.8, 13.11, 14.3, 14.6, 15.16, 16.5, and 16.14.

AMD Publishing for all Long Case Studies, except cases 28 and 30, in Part 5.

BMW Group for Exhibits 9.6 and 9.8.

Disney Enterprises for permission to reprint Case study 28.

Land Rover for Exhibits 6.6 and 9.9.

McGraw Hill for permission to reprint Exhibits 8.8 and 10.2 adapted from Vollman et al., *Manufacturing Planning and Control Systems for Supply Chain Management* (5th edn) (2004); Exhibits 11.5 and 11.6 adapted from Juran et al., *Quality Planning and Analysis;* and Exhibit 11.7 adapted from Crosby, *Quality is Free* (1979). Copyright © McGraw Hill.

Open University for Exhibits 9.7 and 9.11.

Palgrave Macmillan for permission to reprint Exhibits 6.15 and 6.21 from Terry Hill, *Manufacturing Strategy: Text and Cases* (2nd edn), Palgrave Macmillan (2000).

Pearson Education for permission to reprint Exhibit 1.12 adapted from Bloom et al., *Taxonomy of Educational Objectives,* published by Allyn & Bacon, Boston, MA. Copyright © 1984 by Pearson Education.

Professor William Lee Berry and IMD International for permission to reprint Case study 30.

Remora Electrical Limited, Sheffield UK, for Exhibit 10.19.

Rolls Royce plc for Exhibit 9.5.

Roger Beale, whose cartoons also well illustrate many points in this book, for Exhibits 3.10, 5.12, 9.2, 10.25, 13.18, 13.19 and 13.24.

Every effort has been made to trace all the copyright holders but if any have been inadvertently overlooked the publishers will be pleased to make the necessary arrangements at the first opportunity.

Answers to Self-check Tests

Chapter	1	2	3	4	5	6	7	8	9	10
1 Managing Operations	B	C	A	C	B	C	C	A	C	B
2 Operations Strategy	C	A	B	B	C	B	A	B	B	C
3 Managing People	A	C	C	A	B	A	A	B	B	C
4 Designing and Developing Services and Products	C	A	C	C	A	C	B	A	C	A
5 Designing Service Delivery Systems	C	C	A	B	C	A	A	A	B	B
6 Designing Manufacturing Processes	C	B	C	A	C	B	B	A	B	C
7 Location and Layout	C	C	B	C	A	B	C	C	B	B
8 Managing Capacity	A	A	A	C	C	A	B	B	C	B
9 Technology Developments	C	B	C	C	A	C	C	A	A	A
10 Operations Scheduling and Execution	B	A	A	C	B	A	C	B	A	B
11 Managing Quality	B	B	B	B	C	A	C	A	A	C
12 Managing Inventory	C	A	B	A	C	B	B	B	A	C
13 Managing the Supply Chain	A	C	C	B	B	C	B	C	C	C
14 Process and Delivery System Reliability and Maintenance	C	B	A	A	B	C	C	B	A	C
15 Time and Productivity	B	B	C	C	C	A	A	A	C	C
16 Improving Operations	B	C	A	B	C	C	B	A	C	C

Index